Forensic and Legal Psychology

Psychological Science Applied to Law

SECOND EDITION

▷ **Mark Costanzo**
Claremont McKenna College

▷ **Daniel Krauss**
Claremont McKenna College

WORTH PUBLISHERS
A MACMILLAN EDUCATION COMPANY

Associate Publisher: Jessica Bayne
Senior Acquisitions Editor: Christine Cardone
Assistant Editor: Catherine Michaelsen
Associate Media Editor: Anthony Casciano
Marketing Manager: Lindsay Johnson
Marketing Assistant: Allison Greco
Art Director: Diana Blume
Cover Designer: Blake Logan
Interior Design: Diana Andrews
Illustration Coordinator: Janice Donnola
Photo Editor: Robin Fadool
Photo Researcher: Brenda Harris
Managing Editor: Lisa Kinne
Director of Editing, Design, and Media Production: Tracey Kuehn
Project Editor: Julio Espin
Production Manager: Julia DeRosa
Composition: Northeastern Graphic, Inc.
Printing and Binding: RR Donnelley

Cover art: Diana Moore, *Justice* 1994 Martin Luther King Jr. United States Federal Courthouse, Newark, NJ. Commissioned through the Art and Architecture Program, Fine Arts Collection, U.S. General Services Administration. Photo credit: Blake Logan.

Library of Congress Control Number: 2014947192

ISBN-13: 978-1-4641-3890-4
ISBN-10: 1-4641-3890-7

Printed in the United States of America

First printing

Worth Publishers
41 Madison Avenue
New York, NY 10010
www.worthpublishers.com

For my three magnificent daughters:
Marina, Zoey, & Sophia   –M.C.

To Trina, the boys, and Buff.—D.K.

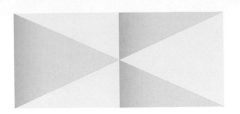

About the Authors

MARK COSTANZO received his Ph.D. in social psychology from the University of California at Santa Cruz. He is a professor of psychology at Claremont McKenna College and a member of the plenary faculty at Claremont Graduate University. He has published research on a variety of law-related topics including police interrogations, false confessions, jury decision-making, sexual harassment, attorney argumentation, alternative dispute resolution, and the death penalty. Professor Costanzo is author of the books *Just Revenge: Costs and Consequences of the Death Penalty* and *Psychology Applied to Law.* He has co-edited four books, including *Expert Psychological Testimony for the Courts* and *Violence and the Law.*

Professor Costanzo has served as a consultant for more than 100 criminal cases and has provided expert testimony in state, federal, military, and juvenile courts. He has received Outstanding Teaching and Mentoring Awards from the American Psychology-Law Society (APLS), the Society for the Psychological Study of Social Issues (SPSSI), the Western Psychological Association (WPA), and the Society for the Teaching of Psychology (STP).

DANIEL KRAUSS completed a joint-degree program in psychology and law at the University of Arizona, receiving his J.D. and then his Ph.D. in clinical psychology and psychology, policy, and law. He is a professor at Claremont McKenna College and is a member of the plenary faculty at Claremont Graduate University. Professor Krauss has published a large number of research articles and book chapters relating to clinical psychological evaluations for the courts, legal and psychological expertise, and jury decision-making. He is the co-editor of *The Law and Public Policy: Psychology and the Social Sciences* book series published by the American Psychological Association (APA) Press.

Professor Krauss is licensed to practice law in Arizona, is a member of the United States Supreme Court bar, and has served as the United States Supreme Court Fellow to the U.S. Sentencing Commission. He is a licensed clinical psychologist in the state of California, and a diplomate in forensic psychology, board certified by the American Board of Professional Psychology. Professor Krauss was a recipient of the Early Career Research Award by the Western Psychological Association.

Brief Contents

Contents

Why We Wrote This Book

Every year, each of us teaches a course in either Forensic Psychology or Psychology and Law. Our combined teaching experience—spanning more than three decades—prompted us to write this book and guided our writing process. Our goal was to produce a student-friendly textbook, a book that is both accessible and rigorous. Drawing on research in social, cognitive, clinical, and developmental psychology, we demonstrate how psychological science can be used to enhance the gathering of evidence, improve legal decision-making, reduce crime, and promote justice.

One aspect of this book that makes it a distinctive alternative to existing textbooks is writing style. Of necessity, all textbooks designed for a particular course must be similar in content. Often, it is how content is presented that makes a book appealing to students and instructors. We've taken great care to write *Forensic and Legal Psychology* in a lively, engaging style. When presenting research findings, we portray the research process as a kind of detective story—an effort to unravel a mystery through systematic data collection. We also make extensive use of real cases and trials to draw students into the material and to illustrate the relevance of research findings. To make sure our writing was clear and engaging, every chapter was reviewed and edited by both students and scholars. Finally, to enhance the visual appeal of the book and to clarify research findings, we use numerous tables, graphs, photos, and figures throughout the text.

Forensic and Legal Psychology is intended to provide a comprehensive introduction to the varied, expanding field of psychology and law. The chapters that follow explore virtually every aspect of legal system psychologists have studied. We emphasize how research and theory can deepen our understanding of key participants (e.g., criminals, police, victims, lawyers, witnesses, judges, and jurors) and basic psychological processes (e.g., decision-making, persuasion, perception, memory, and behavior change) in the legal system. In addition to core chapters on topics such as eyewitness identification, jury decision-making, child custody, and the insanity defense, we include full chapters on a few topics not well covered in most textbooks. For example, our chapter on the psychology of forensic identification (DNA, fingerprints, and physical trace evidence) explores an increasingly important area of psychology and law. Contrary to media depictions, the process of matching trace evidence to a criminal suspect relies heavily on human judgment and is prone to error based on perceptual and cognitive biases. We have also devoted an entire chapter to the rapidly evolving area of workplace law (a topic that includes issues such as sexual harassment, prejudice and discrimination, and work-family conflicts). Full chapters are also devoted to risk assessment (a key consideration in arrest, sentencing, and parole decisions); prisons (an expanding area of research and employment for psychologists); lie detection; and the death penalty.

This is an introductory textbook. We assumed that students taking the course will not yet have a strong foundation in psychology or research methods. Although many students who take forensic or legal psychology are psychology majors, many are not. Because the course has become an attractive breadth requirement for students majoring in criminal justice, pre-law, legal studies, anthropology, sociology, and political science, we wrote this textbook to be accessible to students from a variety of academic disciplines. We hope this book provides a lucid overview of the field and conveys our enthusiasm for the many applications of psychological science to the legal system.

 ## NEW TO THE SECOND EDITION

In this thoroughly revised second edition, we have responded to comments from students and instructors and have added new research and new pedagogical features to enhance the reading experience of students. A few such changes include:

- More than 400 new research citations.
- More than 50 new legal case citations.
- Expanded coverage of the impact of technology in the courtroom.
- New material on the use of neuroscience and brain scan evidence in criminal cases.
- Expanded coverage of research on the death penalty.
- Updates throughout the book to reflect the new DSM-5.
- Added coverage of alternatives to prison.
- New material on the use of large data sets to predict and prevent crime.

New and enhanced pedagogical features include:
Focus on Careers

These new boxes contain brief descriptions of possible careers in psychology and law. The psychologists featured describe the characteristics of their jobs, the training that prepared them for their careers, and what they like (and dislike) about their jobs. Highlighted careers include Police Psychologist (Chapter 3); Trial Consultant (Chapter 6); Social Science Research Analyst (Chapter 11); Violence Risk Expert (Chapter 14); and Correctional Psychologist (Chapter 16).

Scientific American Spotlights

A unique feature of this text is the use of brief articles and excerpts from the pages of *Scientific American Mind*. The boxed articles and excerpts have been judiciously selected to highlight important new research relevant to the study of psychology and law. The *Scientific American* Spotlight boxes explore the following topics: the use and misuse of brain scans in the courtroom (Chapter 1); the questionable effectiveness of the D.A.R.E. program (Chapter 1); the use of group interrogation to reveal lying (Chapter 2); increasing cognitive load to detect lying (Chapter 3); using DNA to create sketches of suspects (Chapter 4); predictive policing (Chapter 5); the long-term effects of recovered memory therapy on mental health (Chapter 11); the use of projective tests in child custody cases (Chapter 12); the relationship between mental illness and violence (Chapter 14); the use of the Implicit Association Test (IAT) to detect subtle racial and age-related biases (Chapter 15); and the use of technology and social media to identify the best employees (Chapter 15).

To reinforce student learning and encourage students to think more deeply about concepts, each chapter ends with a list of Discussion and Critical Thinking Questions. Too often, students become fixated on memorizing without understanding. Questions provided at the end of each chapter help combat that tendency by encouraging students to think about what they have learned and go beyond mere memorization by considering the implications of the ideas the chapter presents. These critical thinking questions help students make connections between research findings and the functioning of the legal system. Finally, a list of Key Terms at the end of each chapter allows students to immediately test their comprehension and retention of information. For quick reference, key terms from every chapter are compiled and clearly defined in an extensive Glossary at the end of the book.

SUPPLEMENTS AND MEDIA

We are pleased to offer an enhanced supplements and media package to accompany this textbook. The package has been crafted by experienced teachers to help instructors teach their course and to give students the tools to develop their skills.

For Instructors

The Instructor's Resource Manual includes extensive chapter summaries, learning objectives, suggestions for in-class presentations, projects, and assignments, as well as tips for integrating multimedia into your course. It also includes a list of suggested readings for each chapter. These readings include books and journal articles and reports of original research as well as scientific reviews.

The Test Bank features approximately 35 multiple-choice and 5 essay questions per chapter. Also included in the Test Bank are chapter-specific Web quizzes (15 questions each) that can be made available to students via your Course Management System.

Diploma Computerized Test Bank (available for Windows and Macintosh on one CD-ROM) allows instructors to add an unlimited number of questions; edit questions; format a test; scramble questions; and include pictures, equations, and multimedia links. With the accompanying gradebook, instructors can record students' grades throughout a course, sort student records, and view detailed analyses of test items, curve tests, generate reports, add weights to grades, and more. Blackboard- and WebCT-formatted versions of the Test Bank are also available on the CD-ROM.

ACKNOWLEDGMENTS

This book has only two authors, but many people reviewed the chapters and offered their insights and criticisms. Reviewers included both scholars and students. Many instructors and researchers generously agreed to read and comment on all or part of the book. The names of these reviewers are listed below. This book is much stronger because of their efforts. We are grateful for their insights and assistance.

We are grateful to the following colleagues who served as expert reviewers for the second edition:

Lynn Barrieau, Mount Wachusett Community College; Marcus T. Boccaccini, Sam Houston State University; Brian Bornstein, University of Nebraska-Lincoln; Elliott Currie, University of California; David DeMatteo, Drexel University; Kathleen Dudemaine, University of the Virgin Islands; Robert W. Dumond, Southern New Hampshire University; Donald Dutton, University of British Columbia; Phoebe C. Ellsworth, University of Michigan; Robert E. Emery, University of Virginia; Russell K. Espinoza, California State University, Fullerton; Jonathan J. Koehler, Northwestern University School of Law; Lindsay Malloy, Florida International University; Diane Mello-Goldner, Pine Manor College; Daniel C. Murrie, University of Virginia School of Medicine; William O'Donohue, University of Nevada; Amy J. Posey, Benedictine College; Nicholas Scurich, University of California at Irvine; Brent Snook, Memorial University; Emily Stark, Minnesota State University, Mankato; Nancy Kay Steblay, Augsburg College.

Because we wrote this book for college students, we sought out advice and feedback from our own students. Over the course of two years, students in *Forensic Psychology* and *Psychology and Law* classes at Claremont McKenna College read drafts of each chapter. Their comments were essential in helping us to improve the clarity and readability of the text. The students listed below read and commented on one or more chapters in this book.

Cristina Acosta
Matthew Armstrong
Lauren Avera
Natalya Belotserkovskaya
Michelle Bieber
Drew Bloomingdale
Stephanie Brockman
Erin Butler
Bree Byrne
Joe Carman
Selena Carsiotis
Alex Castillo
Fabiola Ceballos
Locky Chambers
Shawna-Kay Chambers
Corinne Cho
Natasha Cunningham
LillyBelle Deer
Elizabeth Denison
Jennica Derksen
Tessa Dover
Daniel Fogel
Rebecca Geissler
Jennifer Haime
Moose Halpern

Allison Holmes
Benjamin Hughes
McKenzie Javorka
Annika Jessen
Dayna Kamimura
Tiffany Keith
Kacey Klein
Allison Lewin
Brittany Liu
Marika May
Niclaus Marineau
Keith Mendes
John McCabe
Sarah McFadden
Elizabeth Mora
Shahrzed Nikoo
Matthew O'Brien
Therese Orbea
Jessica Palmer
Krystia Reed
Andrea Riddervold
Emily Rodriguez
Jennifer Rodriguez
Allysa Rueschenberg
Alison Ryan

Nicole Sady-Kennedy

Micah Sadoyama

Debbie Schild

Nisha Shah

Netta Shaked

Tamara Shuff

Sam Slayen

Rochelle Smith

Susan Sparrow

Marilyn Springel

Meg Stiaszny

Alison Strother

Amber Taylor

Ali Taysi

Jamie Terbeest

Christopher Vandover

Katherine Wernet

Ryan Wessels

Other than the two authors, the person most responsible for getting the second edition into print was our editor at Worth Publishers, Christine Cardone. Chris's enthusiasm helped fuel the project from start to finish. She made herself available to us throughout the writing process and her advice was essential in helping us make the right decisions. Chris not only provided insight and guidance, she also provided much-needed support and occasional prodding along the way. Chris's assistant editor, Catherine Michaelsen, was essential in getting the chapters, graphics, and art into production. Cheri Dellelo was indispensable in bringing this book to print. She read every chapter and provided detailed feedback. Her meticulous editing throughout the writing process helped us write a better book. Julio Espin, our project editor, oversaw the mysterious process of transforming our manuscript into a real book. Finally, our photo researcher, Brenda Harris, tracked down the right photos and helped us make key decisions about the illustrations in this text. We are grateful to all the people at Worth for their energy and advice.

—*Mark Costanzo and Daniel Krauss*

Psychology and Law: A Cautious Alliance

▶ **A Brief History of Psychology and Law**
▶ **A Clash of Cultures**
▶ **Roles Played by Psychologists Interested in Law**
▶ **Five Pathways for Influencing the Legal System**
▶ **Has Psychology Influenced the Courts?**

A defendant stands accused of a terrible crime. Lawyers make opening statements, witnesses are called, motives are questioned, secrets are revealed. In their closing arguments, lawyers make impassioned pleas to the men and women of the jury. Jurors struggle to find the truth. In a hushed courtroom, thick with tension, the jury foreperson announces the verdict: "We find the defendant . . . ."

The courtroom trial is a staple of great and trashy literature, of distinguished films and lousy TV shows. This is so because the trial is a compelling psychological drama. There is the question of motivation—was it love, hate, fear, greed, or jealousy that caused the behavior of a criminal? There is persuasion—lawyers and witnesses attempt to influence a judge or jury, and, during deliberations, jurors attempt to influence each other. Perceptual and cognitive processes come into play—eyewitnesses must remember and report what they saw, jurors must sift through evidence to reach conclusions. Finally, there is decision-making: The goal is to reach a decision, a verdict. And, if the verdict is guilty, there is a choice about what punishment the defendant deserves.

The trial is the most visible piece of our justice system. But it is only a small piece. When we look beyond the trial, we find that the legal system is saturated with psychological concerns. Every area of psychology (e.g., developmental, social, clinical, cognitive) is relevant to some aspect of law. Here are a few examples:

Developmental psychology—Following a divorce, which kind of custody arrangement will promote healthy development of the child? Can a child who commits a murder fully appreciate the nature and consequences of his or her crime?

Social psychology—How do police interrogators make use of principles of coercion and persuasion to induce a suspect to confess to a crime? Do the group dynamics of juries influence their verdict decisions?

Clinical psychology—How can we decide whether or not a mentally ill person is competent to stand trial? Is it possible to predict whether a mentally ill person will become violent in the future?

Cognitive psychology—How accurate is the testimony of eyewitnesses? Under what conditions are eyewitnesses able to remember what they saw? Do jurors understand jury instructions in the way that lawyers and judges intend the instructions to be understood?

In the abstract, psychology and law seem like perfect partners. Both focus on human behavior, both strive to reveal the truth, and both attempt to solve human problems and improve the human condition. However, in practice, the relationship between psychology and law has not always been smooth or satisfying. ◀

1

A BRIEF HISTORY OF PSYCHOLOGY AND LAW

Scholarly disciplines seldom have clear starting points. Only in retrospect can we look back and identify the small streams that eventually converge to form a strong intellectual current. What is clear is that a full appreciation of the possible applications of psychology to the legal system began to emerge in the early years of the twentieth century. In 1906, Sigmund Freud gave a speech in which he cautioned Austrian judges that their decisions were influenced by unconscious processes (Freud, 1906/1959). He also noted that insights from his theory could be used to understand criminal behavior and to improve the legal system. However, it was two events in 1908 that triggered a broad recognition among psychologists that their ideas might be used to transform the legal system. The first event was the publication of a book entitled *On the Witness Stand*. The author was an experimental psychologist named Hugo Munsterberg. He had been a student of Wilhelm Wundt (the person generally regarded as the founder of modern psychology), and he left Germany to direct the Psychological Laboratory at Harvard.

Munsterberg wrote *On the Witness Stand* with the purpose of "turning the attention of serious men to an absurdly neglected field which demands the full attention of the social community" (Munsterberg, 1908, p. 12). His book succeeded in getting the attention of the legal community, although it was not the kind of attention he had hoped for. In 1909, a leading legal scholar published a savagely satirical critique of what he considered to be Munsterberg's exaggerated claims for psychology. In the article, Munsterberg was put on trial for libel, cross-examined, and found guilty (Wigmore, 1909). Not only did *On the Witness Stand* receive an icy reception from legal scholars, it also failed to mobilize research psychologists. Despite his achievements, Munsterberg is only begrudgingly acknowledged as the founding father of psychology and law.

A second important event occurred in 1908: In the case of *Muller v. Oregon,* the Supreme Court ruled that the workday of any woman employed in a laundry or factory could be limited to 10 hours. Lawyer Louis Brandeis (who later became a Supreme Court justice) filed his famous **Brandeis Brief** in that case. His basic argument was as follows:

When the health of women has been injured by long hours, not only is the working efficiency of the community impaired, but the deterioration is handed down to succeeding generations. Infant mortality rises, while the children of married working-women, who survive, are injured by inevitable neglect. The overwork of future mothers thus directly attacks the welfare of the nation (Muller v. Oregon, 1908).

Hugo Munsterberg & Karl Llewellyn. (A: *Science Source,* B: *Bettmann/Corbis*)

The *Muller* decision was a major victory for the progressive movement, which sought to reduce work hours, improve wages, and restrict child labor. Most important for psychology, Brandeis's brief opened the door for U.S. courts to use social scientific evidence. Ironically, the "social science"

cited by Brandeis would not be considered valid science by modern standards; it was little more than unsystematic observations and the casual use of medical and labor statistics. But the important point is that, later, far more rigorous research would enter the courthouse through the door pushed open by Brandeis.

During the two decades following the Brandeis Brief, the legal system showed little interest in social science. Then, in the late 1920s and into the 1930s, the **legal realism** movement reenergized the dormant field of social science and law. Legal realists reacted against the established order represented by "natural law." According to proponents of natural law, judicial decisions were thought to reflect principles found in nature. The task of judges was to deduce, through careful logic, the single correct decision in a particular case. In contrast, the realists believed that judges actively constructed the law through their interpretations of evidence and precedent. Further, these constructions of the law served particular social policy goals. In one of the first critiques of classical jurisprudence, Oliver Wendell Holmes wrote that the law,

> . . . cannot be dealt with as if it contained only the axioms and corollaries of a book of mathematics . . . . The very considerations which judges most rarely mention, and always with an apology, are the secret root from which the law draws all the juices of life. I mean, of course, considerations of what is expedient for the community concerned. Every important principle which is developed by litigation is in fact and at bottom the result of more or less definitely understood views of public policy (Holmes, O.W., 1881, p. 2–3).

These were revolutionary ideas at the time. Holmes and other legal scholars argued that law was not merely rules and precedents—it was the means through which policy ends were achieved. The legal realists argued that the social context and social effects of laws were as important as the mechanical application of logic. Realist scholars sought to look beneath "legal fictions" and formalisms to examine the actual behavior of lawyers and judges.

In 1927, the dean of Yale Law School appointed a psychologist to the faculty in an effort to, ". . . make clear the part of the law in the prediction and control of behavior" (Schlegel, 1979, p. 493). Optimism about the potential for a fruitful partnership between psychology and law was widespread in the writings of the time. In 1930, the American Bar Association (ABA) journal proclaimed that, "The time has arrived when the grim hard facts of modern psychological inquiry must be recognized by our lawmakers despite the havoc they may create in the established institutions" (Cantor, 1930, p. 386).

The realist movement was an early example of the influence of psychology on the law. The two towering psychologist–philosophers of the time—William James and John Dewey—had already championed the ideas of pragmatism, induction, and scientific approaches to the study of social issues (Dewey, 1929; James, 1907). Legal realists embraced the idea that the law needed to pragmatically promote the common good and make use of social scientific research. By 1931, Karl Llewellyn, a leader of the realist movement, enumerated several core principles: (1) because society is always in flux faster than the law, laws must be continually reexamined to make sure they serve society well; (2) law is "a means to social ends and not an end in itself," and (3) law must be evaluated in terms of its effects (Llewellyn, 1931, p. 72). Realism's reconceptualization of the law was an enormous success.

African American student escorted to high school by National Guard troops enforcing school integration (*Everett Collection Historical/Alamy*)

Llewellyn's fundamental principles now enjoy almost universal acceptance among the legal community.

Although the realists set in motion a revolution in how people thought about the functions of law, the movement was much less successful in promoting the use of research findings. Curiously, few of the legal realists had collaborated with psychologists or other social scientists. The enthusiasm of the legal realists was based on rather naive assumptions about the nature of psychological science. Following the 1930s, disillusionment about the utility of social science set in. Finding the answers to psychological questions proved to be more complicated and arduous than the realists had supposed. Even worse, the answers provided by social scientists tended to be complex, and predictions about behavior tended to be probabilistic (that is, expressed in terms of the increased likelihood of an event occurring rather than as a certainty). Disenchantment and disengagement seemed to settle in for more than a decade.

In May 1954, in the case of *Brown v. Board of Education,* the U.S. Supreme Court voted unanimously that keeping black and white children segregated in separate schools was a violation of the Fourteenth Amendment's guarantee of "equal protection under the law." That historic decision—widely regarded as one of the most important Supreme Court rulings of the twentieth century—was a milestone in the slowly maturing relationship between social science and the law. The ruling was not only monumental in its impact on American society; it was the first to make explicit use of research provided by social scientists. The legal briefs submitted to the Court included a document entitled, *The Effect of Segregation and the Consequences of Desegregation: A Social Science Statement.* It was signed by 32 prominent social scientists. Many of the sources provided in that statement were cited in footnote 11 of the Court's decision, and a few key passages from *Brown* echo the arguments made in the statement. Chief Justice Earl Warren wrote:

> . . .the policy of separating the races is usually interpreted as denoting the inferiority of the Negro group. A sense of inferiority affects the motivation of a child to learn. Segregation with the sanction of law, therefore, has a tendency to retard the educational and mental development of Negro children and to deprive them of some of the benefits they would receive in a racially integrated school system (Brown v. Board of Education, 1954).

The Court further concluded that separating black children merely because of their race, ". . . generates a feeling of inferiority as to their status in the community that may affect their hearts and minds in a way unlikely to ever be undone" (*Brown v. Board of Education,* 1954, p. 488). Although the true impact of social science in the *Brown* decision has been questioned, there is little doubt that it raised the hopes of social scientists (Hafemeister & Melton, 1987). *Brown* held out the promise that the highest court in the land would be receptive to social scientific research.

The social and intellectual climate of the late 1960s nurtured the fledgling field of psychology and law. In 1966, Harry Kalven (a lawyer) and Hans Zeisel (a sociologist) published an influential book entitled *The American Jury.* This seminal work (discussed more fully in Chapter 13) summarized a multiyear study of how juries and judges reach their decisions. Karl Menninger's book *The Crime of Punishment*, also published in 1966, advocated much greater use of therapeutic methods to rehabilitate criminals. These books gave psychology and law a much-needed boost. There was great enthusiasm about psychology's potential for improving the legal system.

Within the broader psychological community, there was a growing eagerness to find ways of applying theory and research to areas such as law. In his 1969 presidential address to the American Psychological Association (APA), George Miller (a distinguished cognitive psychologist who had spent virtually all of his career conducting basic research in the laboratory) called for "giving psychology away"—that is, for using psychological knowledge to solve pressing social problems (Miller, 1969). In the same year, Donald Campbell called for much more extensive use of the research methods he and other scientists had pioneered. The opening sentence of his 1969 article neatly sums up his approach and conveys the optimism of the time:

> The United States and other modern nations should be ready for an experimental approach to social reform, an approach in which we try out new programs designed to cure specific social problems, in which we learn whether or not these programs are effective, and in which we retain, imitate, modify, or discard them on the basis of apparent effectiveness on the multiple imperfect criteria available (Campbell, 1969, p. 409).

Psychologists interested in the legal system were also feeling optimistic about psychology's possibilities. In 1969, they established the *American Psychology-Law Society (APLS)*, proclaiming that, ". . . there are few interdisciplinary areas with so much potential for improving the human condition" (Grisso, 1991).

The intermittent flirtations between psychology and law did not mature into a steady relationship until the late 1970s (Packer & Borum, 2013). The first issue of the APLS's major journal, *Law and Human Behavior*, appeared in 1977. Since then, several other journals that feature psycholegal research and theory have appeared (e.g., *Behavioral Sciences and the Law*; *Criminal Justice and Behavior*; *Journal of Empirical Legal Studies*; *Law and Society Review*; and *Psychology, Public Policy, and Law*). Scientific organizations other than APLS (e.g., the *Law and Society Association*, the *American Board of Forensic Psychology*, the *Society for Empirical Legal Studies*) have law and social science as their main concern. There are even a handful of "double doctorate" programs that award a Ph.D. in psychology and a J.D. in law, and well over half of all university psychology departments now offer an undergraduate course in psychology and law (Bersoff et al., 1997; Burl, Shah, Filone, Foster & DeMatteo, 2012). The relationship between the two disciplines has expanded and deepened over the past 40 years. This is clearly a boom time for the field. The future is uncertain, but there is reason for optimism.

 ## A CLASH OF CULTURES

Many scholars have found it useful to think of psychology and law as fundamentally different cultures (Bersoff, 1999; Carroll, 1980; Goldberg, 1994). This section explores the nature and consequences of these cultural differences. The concept of **culture** has been defined in a variety of ways. One pioneer in cross-cultural psychology wrote that, "Culture is reflected in shared cognitions, standard operating procedures, and unexamined assumptions" (Triandis, 1996, p. 407). Culture has also been defined as, ". . . the set of attitudes, values, beliefs, and behaviors shared by a group of people, and communicated from one generation to the next" (Matsumoto & Juang, 2007, p. 7). People from a particular culture tend to share basic assumptions about the relative importance of competing goals, how disputes should be resolved, and what procedures to follow in striving for goals.

When anthropologists and psychologists contrast different cultures, they focus on the relative prominence of beliefs and behaviors. Different cultures do not fit neatly into discrete categories; they fall along different points on a continuum. By comparing the cultural tendencies of law and psychology, we can understand why psychology and law have sometimes become frustrated with each other and we can see how the two disciplines might work together more productively. Many of the difficulties in the interactions between psychology and law can be traced to underlying differences in goals, methods, and styles of inquiry.

Goals: Approximate Truth versus Approximate Justice

One basic source of tension between psychology and law is that "psychology is descriptive and law is prescriptive" (Haney, 1981). That is, psychology tells us how people actually behave, and the law tells us how people ought to behave. The primary goal of psychological science is to provide a full and accurate explanation of human behavior. The primary goal of the law is to regulate human behavior. And, if someone behaves in a way that the law forbids, the law provides for punishment. Put somewhat idealistically, psychological science is mainly interested in finding truth, and the legal system is mainly interested in rendering justice. Although neither absolute truth nor perfect justice is fully attainable, scientists must strive for an approximation of truth and courts must strive for an approximation of justice.

In his classic study of cultural differences, Geert Hofstede found that cultures could be usefully differentiated on the dimension of "uncertainty avoidance" (Hofstede, 1991). Cultures high on this dimension develop elaborate rules and rituals in an effort to promote clarity and stability. Legal culture ranks high on uncertainty avoidance. Because people expect the courts to resolve disputes, the legal system must assimilate the ambiguities of a case and render a final, unambiguous decision. Putting an end to a dispute requires a clear, binding ruling. People are found guilty or set free, companies are forced to pay damages, child custody is decided, and criminals are sent to prison. While it is true that an investigation or a courtroom trial can be characterized as a search for the truth, that search is conducted in service of a judgment: guilty or not guilty, liable or not liable. And, if a defendant is found culpable, the judgment becomes one of consequences: How much money should the defendant pay in damages? What kind of probation should the court impose? How long should the prison sentence be? To resolve a conflict, a conclusion must be reached. Because the legal system can never achieve perfect justice, it must settle for approximate justice in the form of conflict resolution. In a democracy, it is crucial to resolve disputes in a way that *appears* fair and promotes social stability. Although citizens may disagree with many specific decisions of the courts, they must have faith in the overall fairness of the system.

In contrast, uncertainty is intrinsic to the scientific process. No single research study is ever conclusive, and no finding is truly definitive. Over time, uncertainty is reduced, but all conclusions can be revised or reversed by contrary data. The scientific process emphasizes the use of testable hypotheses, valid and reliable measures, statistical standards for accepting a conclusion, and replications of findings over time. The ultimate "truth" of a particular explanation of human behavior may be unknowable but, over time and multiple investigations, theories are revised and psychologists are able to construct increasingly useful explanations of human behavior. Judgments made by scientists are not dichotomous (like guilty or not guilty); they are probabilistic. That is, scientific conclusions are stated in terms of probabilities. Indeed, the tendency for scientists to talk in terms of likelihoods and to couch their conclusions in caveats and qualifiers is something the courts (and the general public) find frustrating. In science, no conclusion is final and current understandings are tentative and subject to revision.

Another implication of the differing goals of psychological science and the legal system is that psychology emphasizes the characteristics of groups, while the law emphasizes individual cases (Goldberg, 1994). Psychological scientists conduct research to uncover general principles of human behavior. Because individuals are idiosyncratic, knowing how one person behaves does not necessarily tell us how everyone else behaves in the same situation. The reverse is also true; knowing how people behave in general does not necessarily tell us why a specific defendant behaved in a particular way. This situation often creates problems. If a 10-year-old boy walks into his fourth-grade classroom with a loaded gun and shoots one of his classmates, a psychologist might be called to testify. A developmental psychologist might testify about the cognitive abilities and moral reasoning of 10-year-olds. A social psychologist might summarize the results of research about how children are affected by watching violence on television or in video games. But, in court, the essential questions must be: "Why did *this boy* kill another child?" and "What should happen to reform or punish *this boy*?"

A related point is that, "the law emphasizes the application of abstract principles to specific cases" (Carroll, 1980). Lawyers, plaintiffs, and defendants cannot bring an idea to court and ask the court for a ruling. They must bring a specific case with particular characteristics. A judge's ruling may set an important new precedent, but the immediate goal is to make a decision about a specific case. Consequently, the law evolves one case at a time. The law's emphasis on the individual defendant or plaintiff explains why courts have been more receptive to clinical psychologists than to other types of psychologists. Clinicians examine and draw conclusions about a particular person. Like lawyers, they are oriented toward the individual case.

Methods: Rulings versus Data

The law is based on authority; psychology is based on empiricism (Goldberg, 1994). Whereas law advances through the accumulation of rulings produced by courts, psychology advances through the accumulation of data produced by scientists.

Because cultures differ in the amount of deference and obedience given to people in positions of authority, this dimension (sometimes called "power distance") is often used to differentiate cultures. The legal system is explicitly hierarchical (i.e., it would rank high on power distance). If a court of appeals overrules the decision of a lower court, the lower court must accept the ruling. Higher courts simply have more authority. And if the Supreme Court issues a ruling, the matter is settled—at least until the high court agrees to take up the issue again. (Figure 1.1 shows the hierarchical structure of the U.S. court system.) In comparison, psychology is much more egalitarian. Although there are power relations within scientific communities (e.g., editors of prestigious journals and directors of funding agencies hold considerable power), the structure is far more democratic. Any researcher, even a low-status one, can conduct a study that challenges a prevailing theory of human

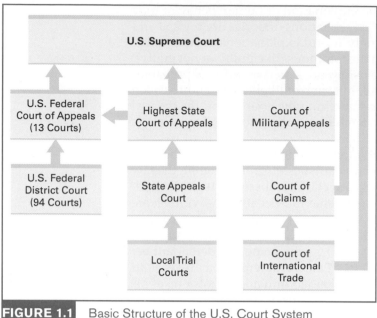

FIGURE 1.1   Basic Structure of the U.S. Court System

behavior. If the data are compelling, the theory must be modified.

Part of the method of law involves deference for past rulings. All cultures are shaped by history, but they differ in how much value they place on history. In some cultures, people make offerings to the spirits of their ancestors and believe that those ancestors actively intervene in the affairs of the living. Although lawyers and judges don't pray to their ancestors for guidance, the past is an active force in their professional lives. As Oliver Wendell Holmes observed, "Law is the government of the living by the dead" (Holmes, 1897, p. 469). Attorneys and judges are obliged to place current facts in the context of past rulings. They must link the present to the past. When lawyers argue in front of judges, they cite **precedents:** past decisions on legal issues in cases that are as similar as possible to the current case. The persuasiveness of a legal argument rests to a substantial extent on whether the argument can be tied to existing precedents. In making their rulings, judges are strongly constrained by the doctrine of *stare decisis* or "let the decision stand." The idea is not to move too far from established precedent. Each precedent is, ". . . a statement simultaneously of how a court *has* held, and how future courts *ought* to hold" (Llewellyn, 1931, p. 72).

In contrast, psychological scientists live in a more future-oriented culture. They believe that our current understanding of human behavior can and should be continually revised in light of new and more extensive data. Scientific theories are made to be broken. New techniques, better measures, and more inclusive sampling of participants continually force psychologists to modify their explanations of human behavior. Progress may be slow at times; but, as long as research continues, it is inevitable.

Style of Inquiry: Advocacy versus Objectivity

In the U.S. legal system, a judge or jury makes the decision of guilt or liability after hearing evidence and arguments. Lawyers acting as adversaries attempt to reveal evidence in the context of the **adversarial system.** A fundamental assumption of the U.S. system is that truth will emerge from a contest between opposing sides. Lawyers advocate for a particular version of events and a particular interpretation of evidence. They actively promote a one-sided view of the facts. Attorneys make opening statements and closing arguments to advance their version of the evidence, they call witnesses who will support that version, they challenge the assertions of witnesses called by the opposing side, they raise objections, and they try to rattle witnesses and undermine their credibility. Lawyers even do a bit of acting at times; for example, they might feign disbelief or outrage at the testimony of a witness who challenges their version of events.

Indeed, attorneys *must* be advocates for their clients. The American Bar Association (ABA) **Code of Professional Responsibility** requires that lawyers "represent their clients zealously within the bounds of the law." Some lawyers put it even more bluntly:

> **Lawyers make claims not because they believe them to be true, but because they believe them to be legally efficacious. If they happen to be true, then all the better; but the lawyer who is concerned primarily with the truth value of the statements he makes on behalf of clients is soon going to find himself unable to fulfill his professional obligation to zealously represent those clients. Another way of putting this is to say that inauthenticity is essential to authentic legal thought (Campos, 1998).**

There are ethical limits on zealousness. Lawyers cannot knowingly permit witnesses to lie under oath (this is called **"suborning perjury"**). But the fact that lawyers are sometimes required to vigorously defend people or corporations that have done terrible things is one reason that lawyers, as a group, are not held in high esteem among members of the general public.

In contrast, scientists must strive for objectivity. Of course, humans are not capable of perfect objectivity. It is not uncommon for researchers to disagree about the correct interpretation of data or to zealously defend a theoretical point of view. In this sense, scientists sometimes behave as advocates. It is also true that values infiltrate the research process—values influence which topics scientists choose to investigate, how they interpret their data, where they publish their findings, and whether they attempt to apply their findings. Science is a human process shaped by human choices. Whenever choices are made, values and biases inevitably come into play. However, even if a particular researcher strays from an objective reading of his or her data, others who view the data will be more dispassionate (or at least biased in a different direction). And, if a researcher collects data using biased methods, the findings are unlikely to be published or taken seriously by others in the scientific community.

Objectivity is an ideal that resides not only in the individual researcher but, more importantly, in the scientific community as a whole. Individual researchers strive for an objective reading of their data. And, although a particular scientist may be too invested in a particular theory to be fully objective, science is an ongoing, public, self-correcting process. Research findings are published as articles or presented at conferences and subjected to criticism by other scientists. Scientists' confidence in the validity of a conclusion rests on the findings of multiple researchers using different research methods. Only over time, through the sustained, collective efforts of many scientists, is the ideal of objectivity achieved.

The Importance of Bridging the Two Cultures

Given the fundamental differences in the cultures of psychology and law, and the difficulty of changing the legal system, why bother trying? After all, many psychologists have the luxury of choosing which topics to investigate. Research questions are often guided by the curiosity of an individual researcher. Other areas of applied research (for example, business and education) are often more welcoming to the insights and techniques of psychologists. So why take on the burden of trying to influence the legal system?

There are good reasons. First, law is important. The law shapes our lives from womb to tomb. It dictates how our births, marriages, and deaths are recorded. It regulates our social interactions at school, work, and home. The legal system has the authority to impose fines, to forbid certain behaviors, to send people to prison, and even to kill people in the execution chamber. It employs millions of people and consumes billions of dollars. Second, many issues confronted by the legal system are inescapably psychological. Questions about what people consider fair, why people commit crimes, and how the behavior of criminals can be changed are all essentially psychological questions. They are also largely empirical questions—questions that can be answered by conducting research and analyzing data. Because the legal system is so pervasive and powerful, many social scientists believe that we are ethically obliged to help ensure that the consequential decisions meted out by the courts are based on the best available scientific knowledge. Although the two cultures of psychology and law continue to clash at times, there are now many examples of fruitful interaction.

 ## ROLES PLAYED BY PSYCHOLOGISTS INTERESTED IN LAW

Given the fundamental differences in the cultures of law and psychology, how should the two interact? If both cultures can be enriched through contact, how might this contact occur? Three broad forms of interaction are possible. Though conceptually distinct, the three roles are complementary rather than exclusive. Each role highlights a different means by which psychological science makes contact with the legal system.

A field of study is perhaps best defined by the activities of people working in that field. Given the three roles described below, our working definition of **forensic psychology** will be, "the use of psychological knowledge or research methods to advise, evaluate, or reform the legal system."

TABLE 1.1

Core Components of Graduate Training in Forensic Psychology

1. *Substantive psychology*—knowledge of basic areas of psychology (e.g., clinical, cognitive, developmental, experimental, social).
2. *Research design/methodology and statistics*—designed to prepare students to conduct research and/or be informed consumers of research.
3. *Conducting research*—performing original empirical research that culminates in a master's thesis or doctoral dissertation (except in PsyD programs).
4. *Legal knowledge*—foundations and sources of law, legal research, relevant civil and criminal case law, legal rules, and professional guidelines relating to expert testimony.
5. *Integrative law–psychology knowledge*—overview courses on forensic psychology and knowledge of research in psycholegal areas (e.g., eyewitness identification, jury decision making, and the treatment of offender populations).
6. *Ethics and professional issues*—relating to general research and practice, and forensic research and practice.
7. *Clinical forensic training* (for those in clinical programs)—forensic mental health assessments, forensically based interventions, and/or forensic consultation.

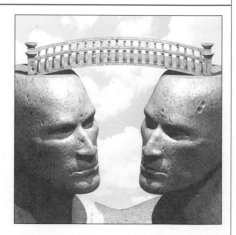

SOURCE: *Adapted from: DeMatteo, D., Marczyk, G., Krauss, D.A., & Burl, J. (2009). Educational and training models in Forensic Psychology.* Training and Education in Professional Psychology, 3, 184–201.

Psychologists as Advisors

Sometimes lawyers and judges welcome the perspectives of psychologists through testimony in court. Lawyers simply hire a psychologist to testify on some aspect of a case. For example, clinical psychologists have testified about whether a particular defendant meets the legal definition of insanity, whether a defendant is competent to stand trial, and whether a defendant is likely to be dangerous in the future. This type of relationship is easy because it requires no major accommodations from the legal system: The nature and boundaries of the relationship are predefined by the legal system. Psychologists simply fill the role they have been asked to fill.

Psychologists acting as **trial consultants** also serve as advisors to the legal system. In this capacity, attorneys hire psychologists to help with jury selection, witness preparation, or trial strategy. In general, trial consultants use psychological knowledge to attempt to shape the trial process in ways that produce favorable outcomes for paying clients. Like psychological experts who are hired to testify at trial, trial consultants are hired to provide expertise in the service of litigants. For example, if a company that manufactures household appliances is being sued for making toaster ovens that tend to explode and cause fires, the company might hire trial consultants to identify jurors who will be sympathetic to the company's case. The effectiveness and ethical implications of trial consulting are covered in Chapter 6.

If a case is appealed to a higher court, it is possible for psychologists to contribute to written arguments (called **briefs**) submitted to the court. Such briefs might summarize the findings and conclusions of research conducted by psychologists. These briefs can be excellent vehicles for major professional organizations, for example, the Association for Psychological Science (APS) or the American Psychological Association (APA) to provide well-considered, data-based conclusions to the courts. As such, they are valuable opportunities for influence. Yet, here as well, the law defines how and on what terms psychological research will be used.

Psychologists as Evaluators

More than a century ago, Oliver Wendell Holmes asked the pointed question: "What have we better than a blind guess to show that the criminal law in its present form does more good than harm? Does punishment deter? Do we deal with criminals on proper principles?" (Holmes, 1897, p. 469).

The basic proposition of **evaluation research** is that the effectiveness of every social program ought to be evaluated. Programs are put in place to achieve goals, and it is only fair (some would say it is ethically necessary) to ask if the programs are achieving those goals. For example, if a community establishes a program where police officers attempt to reduce drug use by talking to elementary school students about the dangers of drugs, it is fair to ask whether students exposed to the program are less likely to use drugs than students who are not exposed to the program (see the *Scientific American Spotlight* box in this section). If we decide to send juvenile offenders to military-style boot camps or to make them work on chain gangs, it is important to ask whether those offenders are less likely to continue a life of crime than juveniles who are placed on probation or sent to a juvenile detention facility. If the instructions given to jurors are intended to help jurors understand and follow the law, it is crucial to determine if jurors understand the instructions as intended. Psychologists and other social scientists have collected and analyzed data to answer such questions. Their research findings will be discussed in the chapters that follow.

Most evaluation research asks questions about a specific legal practice or policy. For example, do executions deter potential murderers? Do drug treatment programs

SCIENTIFIC AMERICAN SPOTLIGHT

Does the D.A.R.E. Program Work?
By Scott O. Lilienfeld and Hal Arkowitz

The most widely publicized teen substance abuse prevention program is Drug Abuse Resistance Education, better known by the acronym D.A.R.E. Created in 1983 by the Los Angeles Police Department, D.A.R.E. asks uniformed police officers to go into schools to warn students about the dangers of drug use and underscore the pluses of a drug-free way of life. In most cases, the officers do so once a week, typically for 45 to 60 minutes, for several months. D.A.R.E. is immensely popular; according to the program Web site, it has been put in place in 75% of U.S. school districts and 43 countries. D.A.R.E. bumper stickers, D.A.R.E. T-shirts, and police cars emblazoned with the word D.A.R.E. are familiar fixtures in many U.S. communities.

(IMAGE SOURCE/AURORA PHOTOS)

Despite this fanfare, data indicate that the program does little or nothing to combat substance use in youth. A meta-analysis (mathematical review) in 2009 of 20 controlled studies by Wei Pan and Haiyan Bai revealed that teens enrolled in the program were just as likely to use drugs as were those who received no intervention.
A few clues to D.A.R.E.'s deficiencies come from Pim Cuijpers of the Netherlands Institute of Mental Health and Addiction. In a review of 30 studies published in 2002, she attempted to pinpoint the common elements of successful programs. Cuijpers reported that the most effective ones involve substantial amounts of interaction between instructors and students. They teach students the social skills they need to refuse drugs and give them opportunities to practice these skills with other students—for example, by asking students to play roles on both sides of a conversation about drugs, while instructors coach them about what to say and do. In addition, programs that work take into account the importance of behavioral norms; they emphasize to students that substance use is not especially common and thereby attempt to counter-

act the misconception that abstaining from drugs makes a person an oddball.
In a 2011 review of various substance abuse prevention programs, Melissa Stigler and her colleagues buttressed these conclusions. They further observed that programs that unfold during many sessions—ideally, over several years—garner especially strong results, probably because they provide students with lessons that are reinforced over time, as children mature and encounter different environments.
D.A.R.E. lacks some of these key elements. It typically lasts only months rather than years. Moreover, it affords students few opportunities to practice how to refuse offers of drugs. Indeed, Cuijpers noted that purely educational programs that involve minimal or no direct social interaction with other students are usually ineffective. Merely telling participants to "just say no" to drugs is unlikely to produce lasting effects because many may lack the needed interpersonal skills. Programs led exclusively by adults, with little or no involvement of students as peer leaders—another common feature of D.A.R.E.—seem relatively unsuccessful, again probably because students get little practice saying no to other kids.
Worse, D.A.R.E. programs might occasionally backfire when it comes to the use of milder substances, such as alcohol and cigarettes. In a 2002 review, Chudley Werch and Deborah Owen reported a slight tendency for teens who went through D.A.R.E. to be more likely to drink and smoke than adolescents not exposed to the program. Small negative effects for D.A.R.E.-like programs on drinking and smoking were also reported in a 2009 study by Zili Sloboda and her colleagues. The reasons for these potential boomerang effects are unclear. Yet by emphasizing the hazards of severe drug abuse, D.A.R.E. may inadvertently convey the impression that alcohol and tobacco are innocuous by comparison.

reduce rates of drug addiction? Usually, the research conducted to answer these types of questions is initiated by social scientists. Although it is essential to ask, "Does it work?" the question is more complex than it first appears. A particular part of the legal system may have multiple goals, and some of these goals may be in conflict. Consider prisons. When we send a criminal to prison, we may have multiple goals: to remove the criminal from civilized society; to punish the criminal for the pain he caused to others; to rehabilitate the criminal so that when he returns to society, he will not revert to a life of crime. While abusive, unpleasant prisons may serve the goal of punishment, they may militate against the goal of rehabilitation and even make criminals more dangerous. Should the goal of punishment or the goal of rehabilitation take priority? Also, as noted earlier, one of the goals of the legal system is to inspire public confidence. This raises another question: What if an ineffective or harmful practice enjoys broad public support? Should that practice be retained or abandoned?

Evaluators distinguish between formative and summative evaluations (Donaldson & Scriven, 2003). Formative evaluations provide ongoing information about a program's effectiveness so adjustments can be made. The information gathered from formative evaluations is used to guide program development and help the program become successful. In contrast, summative evaluations attempt to sum up how well a program has met its goals. Often, summative evaluations judge overall effectiveness and recommend whether a program should be continued or abandoned. In the legal system, the approach is usually formative—the issue is not whether to continue or abandon a practice, but how a practice can be improved or fine-tuned. Hence, evaluation researchers try to discover not only *if* a program works, but also *how* a program works. Making wise decisions about which components of a program need to be modified presupposes a clear understanding of how that program works.

Some researchers take a more expansive view of the legal system and attempt to critically evaluate law as a system embedded within the larger society. This more encompassing perspective allows for the asking of big, fundamental questions: Why are some acts defined as criminal while other injurious behaviors are not? Why are some types of crimes aggressively prosecuted while other types are not? How do legal procedures come to be viewed as legitimate or illegitimate by citizens in a given culture? Whose interests are served by the legal system? Which outcomes are just?

How might research tell us whether parts of the legal system work as intended? (A: *Photos 12/Alamy*, B: *Paul Conklin/ PhotoEdit*, C: *Photodisc/ Image Source/Getty Images*)

There are both disciplinary and methodological reasons why sociologists, criminologists, and anthropologists have been more likely than psychologists to address such questions. First, psychologists generally take the individual or the small group as their level of analysis. They tend not to look at large systems or whole societies. Second, psychology still tends to be a science that places high value on controlled experimentation and careful measurement. Larger questions are often regarded as messier and less amenable to controlled, systematic research.

Psychologists as Reformers

If we use psychological theory and research to find out which aspects of the legal system need to be improved, the next step is to improve them. Evaluation and understanding without any attempt at reform is an empty exercise. Still, many psychologists are uncomfortable playing the role of reformer. Many researchers are trained in a "basic" or "pure" science model. This means that researchers ask questions to satisfy their own curiosity or to test the propositions of a theory. The practical application of whatever knowledge is generated is left to others. To actively promote change in the legal system, the psychologist must step away from the role of objective scientist. And, the farther the scientist moves from that role, the more uncomfortable he or she is likely to become.

There is also the issue of *when* psychologists have sufficient confidence in their findings to advocate a particular change in the legal system. Of course, scientists are fallible, and what we believe is true today might not be regarded as true tomorrow. Still, if we wait for absolute certainty before communicating our findings or arguing for a position, we will wait forever. Even though psychological science can only provide incomplete answers, the procedures and practices of the legal system ought to be based on the best information currently available (Faigman, 2004). We must remember that much legal practice is based on little more than tradition, convenience, and the untested intuition of legislators and judges. The real question is not whether our research findings are final or infallible; it is whether the current state of knowledge based on carefully conducted research can be used to improve current practice in the legal system.

 ## FIVE PATHWAYS FOR INFLUENCING THE LEGAL SYSTEM

Knowledge generated by social scientists enters the law through several routes. The next section describes some pathways social scientists use to make contact with the legal system.

Expert Testimony

Jurors, judges, and legislators cannot be expected to know everything. Therefore, people who have acquired specialized knowledge through education and experience—**experts**—are called upon to testify in courts or in front of legislative bodies. In courts, the process usually works like this: An attorney representing one side or the other in a trial proposes that a particular expert be allowed to testify, and the presiding judge decides whether to allow the testimony. The lawyer believes that the expert will strengthen his or her case. The judge has other concerns. He or she must decide if hearing the expert testify will help juries discover the true facts in a particular case. Juries are the **triers of fact.** That is, in a jury trial, it is the jury that must listen to the evidence and decide on a verdict based on the facts presented at trial. If a judge decides that ordinary jurors already know what the expert has to say, or decides that the proposed testimony would only confuse jurors, or decides that the expert testimony would have too much impact on the jurors, that judge can refuse to allow the testimony. Rule 702 of the *Federal Rules of Evidence* sets the legal standard for permitting expert testimony in federal cases:

> **If scientific, technical, or other specialized knowledge will assist the trier of fact to understand the evidence or to determine a fact in issue, a witness qualified as an expert by knowledge, skill, experience, training, or education may testify thereto in the form of an opinion or otherwise.**

In practice, this standard gives enormous discretion to judges in deciding whether to allow expert testimony.

In the case of *Daubert v. Merrell Dow Pharmaceuticals, Inc.* (1993), the Supreme Court held that judges must serve as **gatekeepers** for scientific testimony. In effect, judges were told to assess the scientific validity of potential testimony before allowing the purportedly scientific evidence to be heard at trial. To assist judges, the Court listed four criteria that should be used when deciding whether to admit scientific testimony: the testability or "falsifiability" of the theory or technique (whether the technique can be proven false through data collection); whether the scientific findings have been subjected to peer review (generally through publication in a peer-reviewed journal); whether there is a known rate of error (how often a test or technique produces incorrect results); and whether the conclusions are generally accepted in the relevant scientific community. Unfortunately, the Court did not provide full and clear explanations of these criteria. Some scholars have noted that, ". . . the Court's treatment of validity was at best generic and superficial, and at worst, specious and uninformed" (McAuliff & Groscup, 2009, p. 29). Further, the criteria leave plenty of room for disagreement and discretion. If two judges are faced with the identical expert testimony, one might decide the testimony is admissible and the other might decide that it does not meet the *Daubert* standard of admissibility.

Along with *Daubert,* two later Supreme Court decisions—*General Electric Co. v. Joiner* (1997) and *Kumho Tire Ltd. v. Carmichael* (1999)—have come to be collectively known as the ***Daubert* trilogy.** This trilogy of decisions expanded the **gatekeeping role** of trial judges. Whereas *Daubert* made judges responsible for evaluating the research methods and statistics that provide the basis for an expert's testimony, *Joiner* held that appellate courts should not second-guess a trial judge's decision to exclude expert testimony. Instead, they should defer to the trial judge's ruling on whether scientific testimony should be admitted into evidence. In *Kumho,* the Court made a further clarification: ". . .that a court's gatekeeping responsibilities extended to all expert opinion, not just the scientific variety" (Faigman & Monahan, 2009, p. 7). In sum, the trial judge has the authority and the responsibility to evaluate the validity and relevance of any proposed expert testimony.

Not everyone agrees that judges are well-equipped to play the role of gatekeeper. As the minority opinion in *Daubert* disapprovingly observed, the decision obliged judges to become "amateur scientists"—a role beyond their training and expertise. Indeed, research demonstrates that judges are not especially skilled at distinguishing between high-quality and low-quality research. For example, in one study, 144 circuit court judges were asked to evaluate psychological evidence in a sexual harassment case (Kovera & McAuliff, 2000). Although the researchers systematically varied the methodological quality of the research presented to judges, methodological quality did not influence the judges' evaluations of quality or their decision to admit the evidence. Both weak and strong research was admitted at the same low rate (17% of judges admitted the research), indicating a lack of scientific sophistication among judges (and perhaps a bias against psychological research). Other research supports this general finding (Dahir et al., 2005). Although a survey of 400 state court judges found that 91% supported the "gatekeeping" role established by *Daubert,* the vast majority could not adequately define *Daubert*'s four guidelines for admissibility (testability, peer review, error rate, and general acceptance). Two of the guidelines were reasonably well understood by judges, and two were poorly understood. Seventy-one percent of the judges understood the scientific peer review process, and 82% also demonstrated a clear understanding of general acceptance. However, only 6% understood the meaning of testability and only 4% clearly understood the concept of "error rate" (Gatowski et al., 2001).

SCIENTIFIC AMERICAN SPOTLIGHT

Neuroscience in the Courtroom
By Michael S. Gazzaniga

Aided by sophisticated imaging techniques, neuroscientists can now peer into the living brain and are beginning to tease out patterns of brain activity that underlie behaviors or ways of thinking. Attorneys already are attempting to use brain scans as evidence in trials, and the courts are grappling with how to decide when such scans should be admissible. Down the road, an ability to link patterns of brain activity with mental states could upend old rules for deciding whether a defendant had control over his or her actions and gauging to what extent that defendant should be punished. No one yet has a clear idea of how to guide the changes, but the legal system, the public, and neuroscientists need to understand the issues to ensure that our society remains a just one, even as new insights rock old ideas of human nature.

Unacceptable Evidence (for Now)

With the growing availability of images that can describe the state of someone's brain, attorneys are increasingly asking judges to admit these scans into evidence, to demonstrate, say, that a defendant is not guilty by reason of insanity or that a witness is telling the truth. Judges might approve the request if they think the jury will consider the scans as one piece of data supporting an attorney's or a witness's assertion or if they think that seeing the images will give jurors a better understanding of some relevant issue. But judges will reject the request if they conclude that the scans will be too persuasive for the wrong reasons or will be given too much weight simply because they look so impressively scientific. In legal terms, judges need to decide whether the use of the scans will be "probative" (tending to support a proposition) or, alternatively, "prejudicial" (tending to favor preconceived ideas) and likely to confuse or mislead the jury. So far, judges—in agreement with the conventional wisdom of most neuroscientists and legal scholars—have usually decided that brain scans will unfairly prejudice juries and provide little or no probative value.

Judges also routinely exclude brain scans on the grounds that the science does not support their use as evidence of any condition other than physical brain injury. Criminal defense attorneys may wish to introduce the scans to establish that defendants have a particular cognitive or emotional disorder (such as flawed judgment, morality, or impulse control), but—for now at least—most judges and researchers agree that science is not yet advanced enough to allow those uses.

Functional magnetic resonance imaging (fMRI) offers an example of a process that can provide good scientific information, of which fairly little is legally admissible. This technology is a favorite of researchers who explore which parts of the brain are active during different processes, such as reading, speaking, or daydreaming. It does not, however, measure the firing of brain cells directly; it measures blood flow, which is thought to correlate to some extent with neuronal activity. Further, to define the imaging signal associated with a particular pattern of brain activity, researchers must usually average many scans from a group of test subjects, whose individual brain patterns may diverge widely. A defendant's fMRI scan may appear to differ greatly from an average value presented in court, but could still be within the statistical boundaries of the data set that defined that average. Moreover, scientists simply

Judges' limited understanding of scientific methods is troubling. Clearly, if judges are to serve as effective gatekeepers, they need to assume responsibility for learning about scientific methods.

The *Daubert* trilogy has had a clear impact on trial courts. Lawyers now file more motions to limit or exclude the expert testimony proposed by lawyers on the other side of the case (Dixon & Gill, 2002). In addition, judges are now more likely to exclude expert testimony, even if based on valid science (Vickers, 2005). Interestingly, instead of relying on the specific criteria mentioned in *Daubert*, judges appear to be basing their admissibility decisions on characteristics of the expert, such as education, experience, skill, and knowledge of the subject matter (Faigman, 2013; Merlino, Murray, & Richardson, 2008).

Ideally, expert witnesses educate the jury—they summarize research findings in a clear, impartial manner. One of the ethical dilemmas posed by expert testimony is that psychologists can occasionally be swept into the currents of the adversary system. It is important for experts to remember that, in contrast to the role of objective do not always know the prevalence of normal variations in brain anatomy and activity in the population (or groups within it). Showing a defendant's brain scan without data from an appropriate comparison group might profoundly mislead a jury.

Neuroscience and Criminal Defenses

How one defines a defendant's *mens rea*, or mental state, in a given context has a major effect on how much responsibility to ascribe to him or her. In ongoing fMRI-based research, Read Montague of Baylor College of Medicine and Gideon Yaffe, a law professor at the University of Southern California, study whether certain addicted individuals suffer from a subtle form of "risk blindness." Reasonable people learn not to rob stores by realizing that committing the crime would jeopardize their ability to enjoy a life with friends and family, pursue rewarding careers, and so on. Montague and Yaffe see indications, however, that at least some addicts cannot think through the benefits of those alternative courses of action. Potentially their findings could justify modifying the "reasonable person" standard in criminal law so ad-

Before a brain scan of a defendant can be presented as evidence in court, the judge must rule that it is admissible. (*Michael Gazzaniga/Scientific American April 2011/Brown Bird Design*)

dicts could be judged against what a reasonable addict, rather than a reasonable nonaddict, would have done in a given situation; such a finding might then lead to acquittal or reduction in punishment for an addicted defendant.

When the foregoing examples are taken together, profound questions emerge about how our culture and the courts will manage antisocial behavior. As neuroscientist William T. Newsome of Stanford University has asked, will each of us have a personalized "responsibility" ranking that may be called on should we break the law? If we soon all carry our personal medical histories on a memory stick for reference, as some experts predict, will we also perhaps include a profile derived from knowledge of our brain and behavior that captures our reasonableness and irresponsibility? Would this development be good for society and advance justice, or would it be counterproductive? Would it erode notions of free will and personal responsibility more broadly if all antisocial decisions could seemingly be attributed to some kind of neurological deviations?

expert witness, lawyers ". . . are expected (indeed, professionally and ethically obligated) to conduct a biased search for facts. Their job is to build the best case they can for their client, not to find facts helpful to the other side" (Saks & Lanyon, 2007, p. 280). This basic truth is crucial because experts are not supplied to lawyers; they are almost always chosen by lawyers representing a particular side in a specific case. Naturally, in their role as adversaries, lawyers often "shop around" to find an expert who will support their side. They turn to experts who have done well for them in prior cases, they e-mail other lawyers and ask for the names of experts who might provide favorable testimony, and they may have telephone conversations with a few potential experts to get a sense of who might provide the strongest testimony.

Once a suitable expert is found, he or she may be "prepared" for trial. During this preparation, insufficiently cautious experts may be seduced into thinking of themselves as part of an adversarial team. It is in the interest of lawyers to create this mindset. Sometimes subtly and sometimes bluntly, lawyers may let their experts know that they are working on behalf of a just cause and that the opposing team is misguided or untrustworthy. Once an expert is hired, lawyers often try to find the strongest form of testimony the expert is willing to give. Because lawyers act as advocates for their client's interests, they tend to prefer experts who will make unambiguous statements and reach clear conclusions in support of their side of the case.

In a seminal article on expert witnesses, Michael J. Saks described three roles that expert witnesses might assume.

The *conduit-educator* strives to present a full and accurate picture of the current state of psychological knowledge. He or she realizes that, "To do this may be to be a mere technocrat, rather than a human being concerned with the moral implications of what I say and with the greater good of society. The central difficulty of this role is whether it is all right for me to contribute hard-won knowledge to causes I would just as soon see lose" (Saks, 1990, p. 295). In this role, the expert faithfully represents a field of knowledge.

In the second type of role, the *philosopher-advocate,* the expert makes concessions to the adversarial climate of the courtroom and allows personal values to shape testimony. He or she might say, "There is a greater good at stake in this case, and that is (fill in the blank: desegregating schools, seeing to it that this child goes to the right home, keeping people from being executed, seeing to it that people are executed, etc.). I must advocate for those outcomes, and that obviously means giving testimony that involves clever editing, selecting, shading, exaggerating, or glossing over" (p. 296).

In the final role, that of *hired gun,* the expert essentially "sells out" and capitulates to the adversarial demands of the courtroom. A hired gun intentionally shapes his or her testimony to help the side of the hiring attorney.

Many commentators have excoriated experts who are willing to assume the role of hired gun (Edens et al., 2012). Margaret Hagen, an experimental psychologist, wrote a scorching indictment of biased mental health professionals who have testified in court as experts. In her book (provocatively titled, *Whores of the Court*), she cites several cases in which psychotherapists, social workers, and psychiatrists have made unequivocal statements that have no research support (e.g., it is possible to tell if a particular young child is lying, or if a particular memory is accurate). She argues that these "self-styled psychoexperts" are often motivated by the money they receive for their testimony or by a missionary-like zeal to promote a particular cause (Hagen, 1997).

It is rare for an expert witness who shades or misrepresents research findings to be prosecuted for misconduct. Perjury requires lying about verifiable facts. Experts are called to offer expert opinions. And because opinions are neither true nor false, even highly unusual opinions cannot be described as lies. An expert may be biased, ignorant about relevant research, or even incompetent, but that is not the same as being a liar. As one state supreme court put it, "It is virtually impossible to prosecute an expert witness for perjury" (*Sears v. Rutishauser,* 1984, p. 212).

While it is true that unscrupulous "experts" have sometimes testified in court, the ethical guidelines established by psychologists conform rather closely to the *conduit-educator* role. Here are a few quotes from the guidelines (American Psychological Association, 2013):

> **Psychologists must, ". . . recognize the adversarial nature of the legal system and strive to treat all participants and weigh all data, opinions, and rival hypotheses impartially" (p. 9).**

> **Psychologists must not, ". . . participate in partisan attempts to avoid, deny, or subvert the presentation of evidence contrary to their own position or opinion" (p. 16).**

When "... their own cultures, attitudes, values, beliefs opinions or biases
... diminish their ability to practice in a competent and impartial manner,
forensic practitioners may take steps to correct or limit such effects, decline participation in the matter, or limit their participation" (p. 10).

Clearly, psychologists' primary loyalty must be to their discipline. They must strive
to report the current state of scientific knowledge accurately (Brodsky, 2013).

Cross-Disciplinary Training

One way to increase the use of social science by the legal system is through education. It is during postgraduate training (graduate school or law school) that students fully dedicate themselves to careers in psychology or law (see Table 1.2 for

TABLE 1.2	
Graduate Training Programs in Legal and Forensic Psychology	
Nonclinical Doctoral Programs	
Alliant University	Ph.D. in Forensic Psychology
Arizona State University	Law and Psychology J.D./Ph.D. program
Cornell University	Ph.D. or Dual Degree (Ph.D./J.D.) program in Law, Psychology, and Human Development)
Florida International University	Ph.D. with emphasis in Legal Psychology
Georgetown University	Ph.D. in Psychology with concentration in Human Development and Public Policy
John Jay College of Criminal Justice	Ph.D. in Psychology
North Carolina State University	Ph.D. In Psychology and the Public Interest
Simon Fraser University	Ph.D. in Psychology with a Psychology and Law or Clinical-Forensic concentration
University of Arizona	Ph.D. and/or J.D.
University of California-Irvine	Ph.D. in Criminology, Law and Society or in Psychology and Social Behavior
University of Florida	Ph.D. in Criminology and Law; and joint J.D./M.A. program
University of Illinois at Chicago	Ph.D. with concentration in Psychology and Law
University of Minnesota	Ph.D. in Social Psychology with a research concentration in Social Psychology and Law; joint J.D./Ph.D. can be customized
University of Nebraska	Joint J.D./ Ph.D. program
University of Nevada—Reno	Ph.D. in Social Psychology with concentration in Psychology and Law
University of Texas at El Paso	Ph.D. in Applied Psychology with the Legal Psychology Group
University of Wyoming	Social or Developmental Ph.D. with concentration in Psychology and Law
Clinically Oriented Doctoral Programs	
Alliant International University	Ph.D. or Psy.D. in Forensic Psychology
Argosy University—Chicago	Psy.D. with concentration in Forensic Psychology
Arizona State University	Law and Psychology J.D./Ph.D. Program
Carlos Albizu University in Miami	Psy.D. with concentration in Forensic Psychology
Chicago School of Professional Psychology	Psy.D. with concentration in Forensic Psychology
Drexel University	J.D./Ph.D. or Ph.D. with concentration in Forensic Psychology
Fairleigh Dickinson University	Ph.D. with Forensic Specialization
Fielding Graduate University	Ph.D. with concentration in Forensic Psychology
Forest Institute of Professional Psychology	Psy.D. with concentration in Forensic Psychology

continued on next page

Fordham University	Ph.D. with concentration in Forensic Psychology
John Jay College of Criminal Justice	Ph.D. with emphasis in Forensic Psychology
Massachusetts School of Professional Psychology	Psy.D. with concentration in Forensic Psychology
Nova Southeastern University	Psy.D. with concentration in Forensic Psychology
Pacific University	Psy.D. with emphasis in Forensic Psychology
Palo Alto University	Ph.D. with Forensic emphasis, Ph.D./J.D. with Golden Gate University School of Law
Sam Houston State University	Ph.D. with emphasis in Forensic Psychology
Simon Fraser University	Ph.D. in Clinical-Forensic Psychology
Spalding University	Psy.D. with concentration in Forensic Psychology
Texas A&M University	Ph.D. with emphasis in Forensic Psychology
Texas Tech University	Ph.D. with emphasis in Forensic Psychology
University of Alabama	Ph.D. with concentration in Psychology and Law
University of Arizona	Ph.D. with emphasis in Forensic Psychology
University of Illinois at Chicago	Ph.D. with minor in Psychology and Law
University of Nebraska	J.D. / Ph.D. joint degree
West Virginia University	Ph.D. with emphasis in Forensic Psychology
Widener University	J.D./Psy.D. joint degree

Master's Programs

Adler School of Professional Psychology	M.A. in Counseling, Specialization in Forensic Psychology
Argosy University	M.A. in Forensic Psychology
American International College	M.S. in Forensic Psychology
California State University, Los Angeles	M.S. in Forensic Psychology
Chicago School of Professional Psychology	M.A. in Forensic Psychology or M.A. in Forensic Psychology: Applied Forensic Services
College of Saint Elizabeth	M.A. in Forensic and Counseling
Fairleigh Dickinson University	M.A. in Forensic Psychology
George Washington University	M.A. in Forensic Psychology
Holy Names University	M.A. in Forensic Psychology; dual M.A. in Forensic and Counseling Psychology
John Jay College of Criminal Justice-CUNY	M.A. in Forensic Psychology
Marymount University	M.A. in Forensic Psychology
Massachusetts School of Professional Psychology	M.A. in Forensic and Counseling
New York Law School	M.A. and Certificate in Mental Disability Law
Palo Alto University	M.A. in Forensic and Correctional Psychology
Roger Williams University	M.A. in Forensic Psychology
The Sage Colleges	M.S. in Forensic Mental Health
Tiffin University	M.A. in Criminal Justice with concentration in Forensic Psychology
University of Colorado at Colorado Springs	M.A. in Clinical or Experimental with concentration in Psychology and Law
University of Denver	M.A. in Forensic Psychology
University of Florida	M.A. or joint J.D., M.A. in Criminology, Law, and Society
University of Houston-Victoria	M.A. in Forensic Psychology
University of Leicester	M.Sc. in Forensic Psychology
University of Nebraska	Joint J.D./M.A. in Clinical or Social Psychology or Masters of Legal Studies
University of North Dakota	M.S. or M.A. in Forensic Psychology
Valparaiso University	Joint J.D., M.A. in Counseling

Data from: *American Psychology-Law Society (2013) / Hall, T. A., Cook, N. E., & Berman, G. L. (2010). Navigating the expanding field of law and psychology: A comprehensive guide to graduate education. Journal of Forensic Psychology Practice, 10, 69–90.*

a list of graduate training programs in legal and forensic psychology). The impact of a solid introduction to the law (for graduate students in psychology) or a solid introduction to social science (for law students) may be felt long after school has ended. Exposure to psychological science is likely to make lawyers and judges more receptive to strong scientific testimony. It is also likely to make judges and lawyers appropriately less receptive to testimony based on shoddy science or testimony lacking a solid scientific foundation. Conversely, exposing psychologists to legal training is also likely to have beneficial effects. Psychologists with a sophisticated understanding of law are better equipped to ask questions and seek answers that are useful to the legal system. They may also be more likely to communicate their findings to legal professionals.

The best arrangement for obtaining dual training in the disciplines of psychology and law is a matter of some controversy. Some have argued for double doctorate programs that lead to both a J.D. in law and a Ph.D. in psychology. Unfortunately, such programs generally require about seven years of graduate study. Also, to earn a J.D., students must take a full complement of law classes, some of which (e.g., Corporations, Tax, Wills and Trusts, Property) have limited relevance to the study of psychology and law. One former director of a double doctorate program reached the conclusion that, "Having both degrees is unnecessary for making a contribution to psycholegal studies. Indeed, expertise in one discipline with a basic knowledge in the other is probably sufficient" (Melton, 1987, p. 492). Ph.D. programs that offer specialization in psychology and law often include substantial training in areas of criminal and civil law that are of interest to psychologists.

A final training model involves encouraging psychologists who already have their Ph.D. to earn a master's degree in legal studies in only one year. Unfortunately, few law schools offer such programs. In contrast, lawyers with an interest in enhancing their knowledge of psychology can select from scores of master's programs in psychology offered at universities across the country. However, because many lawyers lack the requisite background in statistics and research methods, significant remedial work may be necessary. An understanding of the social scientific approach to generating valid knowledge is critical for applying psychology to the legal system.

There is now some assistance for judges who want to develop their scientific judgment. In response to the Supreme Court's ruling in *Daubert*, the Federal Judicial Center (the research arm of the federal courts) established several training programs to help judges responsibly fill their expanded role as gatekeepers. Some states and a few universities (e.g., the National Judicial College in Reno, Nevada, and the Adjudication Center at Duke University) offer judges workshops on scientific evidence. These workshops are designed to teach judges how to evaluate the validity of the science behind various types of expert testimony. Judges without the time or inclination to attend classes can turn to a reference book—*Modern Scientific Evidence*—that strives to make scientific testimony accessible to judges (Sanders et al., 2013).

***Amicus Curiae* Briefs.** The *amicus curiae* ("friend of the court") **brief** has proven to be a useful tool for educating judges about relevant psychological research. The "friends" are interested and knowledgeable parties who do not have direct involvement in the case. The goal of such briefs is to summarize the relevant body of research and to clarify the overall meaning of a set of findings. The American Psychological Association, through its Committee on Legal Issues (COLI), has filed *amicus* briefs in a wide range of cases dealing with issues as diverse as jury size, the death penalty, gay rights, abortion, the prediction of dangerousness, rights of mentally ill patients, the effects of employment discrimination, sexual behavior, and the courtroom testimony of child witnesses. The contents of several of these briefs will be discussed later in this book.

The involvement of scientists in *amicus* briefs can be controversial. Here, as in other areas, some believe that scientists too easily slip into becoming advocates when presenting research via *amicus* briefs. Some scholars describe briefs as ranging along a continuum with "science translation" at one pole and "advocacy" at the other. That is, we can either dispassionately report and clarify the meaning of relevant research findings (translation), or we can take a strong position based on the available psychological knowledge (advocacy) (Melton & Saks, 1990). But, even a science translation brief might advocate a position because the accumulated research often supports a particular judicial decision. A group of psychologists who have extensive experience in developing *amicus* briefs offered the following guidance:

> **It is possible to be scientific without being neutral, to be objective yet form an opinion about the implications of the research. If the data warrant a particular conclusion, then it may be reasonable for brief writers to advocate for a legal decision that would reflect the knowledge gained from the research (Roesch, Golding, Hans, & Reppucci, 1991, p. 12).**

An interesting example of an *amicus* brief was submitted to the Supreme Court in the 1999 case of *Kumho Tire Co. Ltd. v. Carmichael* mentioned earlier in this chapter. The case involved eight members of the Carmichael family who were riding in their minivan. When a tire blew out, the minivan crashed, killing one member of the Carmichael family and injuring seven others. In support of their case against Kumho Tires, the Carmichaels had hoped to have the testimony of a "tire failure expert" admitted at trial. The trial judge excluded that testimony. In a unanimous decision, the Supreme Court ruled in favor of the tire company, holding that federal court judges have broad discretion in exercising their responsibilities as gatekeepers for expert scientific testimony.

The *amicus* brief had nothing to do with minivans or tire failure. It addressed the issue of how juries respond to expert testimony. Tire company attorneys had submitted documents asserting that juries ". . . give great (and sometimes undue) deference to expert testimony," that ". . . an expert frequently ends up confusing jurors and effectively takes the jury's place if they believe him," and that ". . . jurors often abdicate their fact-finding obligation and simply adopt the expert's opinion" (Vidmar et al., 2000, p. 385). The *amicus* brief submitted by a group of 18 social scientists reviewed the evidence on jury decision-making and reached a contrary conclusion: "The great weight of evidence challenges the view that jurors abdicate their responsibilities as fact finders when faced with expert evidence or that they are pro-plaintiff, anti-defendant, or anti-business. . . . the data tend to indicate that jurors are often skeptical of plaintiff claims. . ." and that jurors do not, "suspend critical reasoning skills whenever experts testify at trial" (p. 388).

Briefs offer some advantages over expert testimony: They are typically written by a team of researchers, they are often reviewed by a professional organization (although this review may be rushed), and the research studies that form the basis for the brief are listed in a reference section. Sometimes scholars must point out that research findings are inconclusive or that definitive answers are not yet available.

Other times, a body of research allows clear conclusions and recommendations. However, even when the research supports a strong position, an *amicus* brief is only one small factor influencing a judicial decision.

Broad Dissemination of Research Findings

Much of the impact of social science may come through an indirect route. If research findings are widely disseminated through the popular media, those findings eventually influence the thinking of legal professionals. Judges, lawyers, and jurors do not live in caves set off from the larger world. They are part of the larger culture and receive most of their information about social science informally, through Web sites, newspapers, magazines, and television. Indeed, studies show that judges are far more likely to read *Psychology Today* than law or social science journals. As one researcher put it, "... the mention of findings of a particular study or group of studies in *Time* magazine may have a substantially greater impact on the law than publication in a prestigious social science journal will" (Melton, 1987, p. 492).

Face-to-face dissemination is also possible through "continuing education" (CE) programs. Each year, judges and lawyers are required to complete several CE courses as a way to stay up-to-date with new developments in the law. Many scholars have urged psychologists to participate in CE programs. For example:

> Psychologists should become involved as presenters in federal and state continuing education meetings for judges and lawyers. Their presentations offer the potential to educate the judiciary and the lawyers who practice before them about what constitutes science and what are accepted methods and data analytic techniques in science, as well as provide broad surveys of the current state of knowledge in various substantive areas of psychology and the limitations of that knowledge (Sales & Shuman, 2007, p. 28).

Many psychological scientists actively disseminate the results of research to decision-makers in the legal system with the realistic recognition that the impact of their efforts is seldom swift or certain. Of course, efforts to communicate research findings should not only be directed at lawyers and judges. In a democratic society, it is ultimately the public that must place its trust in the legal system. If scientists want the public to understand psychological knowledge, we must also intensify our efforts to make scientific findings accessible to the public.

Influencing Legislatures and Public Policy

Much of the effort to bring psychology to the legal system has focused on the courts. However, legislatures also make law. Sometimes, psychologists try to influence the thinking of legislators on a specific issue. For example, over the past 30 years, hundreds of studies have explored the conditions under which eyewitnesses are likely to provide accurate reports about crimes they have observed (see Chapter 7). Many psychologists serving as expert witnesses have summarized these findings for judges and juries in individual cases. Such testimony is an effective means of educating jurors and judges about factors influencing the accuracy of eyewitness identifications. However, expert testimony comes after someone has already made an identification. Research findings would have a greater impact on the legal system if they were taken into account as identifications were being made. In 1998, a team of psychologists translated the voluminous research on eyewitness testimony into a series of recommendations for use by police, lawyers, and judges (Wells et al., 1998). Working with the *National Institute of Justice,* the psychologists formulated several specific, research-based procedures for gathering eyewitness evidence. Use of these procedures dramatically improves the accuracy of identifications by eyewitnesses, and there has been considerable progress in persuading police departments to adopt the guidelines (Kolata & Peterson, 2001).

Finally, psychologists and other social scientists make direct attempts to influence legislatures through the lobbying efforts of their professional associations (e.g., the American Psychological Association and the Association for Psychological Science). These lobbying efforts are generally aimed at obtaining better funding for initiatives of special interest to psychologists—for example, graduate training and basic research, promotion of mental health, prevention and treatment of violent behavior, improvement of childhood education and services for children, or the development of fair and effective testing practices in school and work settings. In addition to lobbying for particular funding priorities, psychologists frequently testify before the U.S. Congress and sometimes advise senators and representatives while serving on legislative staffs.

HAS PSYCHOLOGY INFLUENCED THE LEGAL SYSTEM?

Psychology's attempts to influence the legal system have produced mixed results. In some cases, it appears that there has been a substantial impact. For example, an examination of the impact of *amicus* briefs submitted by the APA found that the Supreme Court's opinion often mirrored the reasoning and language of the briefs (Tremper, 1987). Other times, however, it seems that judges have made use of social scientific evidence only when it was supportive of the ruling a judge wanted to make anyway. And, sometimes, the courts have ignored, dismissed, or misrepresented the findings of social scientific research.

On balance, it appears that the presentation of social science evidence raises the consciousness of judges and forces them to take research evidence seriously. One common perspective is that presenting research evidence to the courts "keeps judges honest" by forcing them to articulate clearly the basis for their decisions, even when they rule in a way that contradicts that evidence. Some scholars have argued that,

> Psychology's input may compel judges to act like judges, stating clearly the fundamental values and normative premises on which their decisions are grounded, rather than hiding behind empirical errors or uncertainties. In this sense, we can regard psychology's recent efforts as successes (Grisso & Saks, 1991, p. 396).

Judges may be reluctant to embrace the findings of social scientific research for both intellectual and personal reasons (Faigman, 2004). Intellectually, judges know little about empirical research and are unable (or perhaps unwilling) to make sense of it. Indeed, as noted earlier, legal and social scientific views of the world are often in conflict. But the resistance is not only intellectual. There are also personal reasons behind the reluctance of judges. Judges tend to be self-confident, politically conservative, and protective of their prestige and power. When confronted with empirical research, they are likely to feel that they do not need help from social scientists; they are likely to suspect that social scientists are politically liberal, and they may view social science as undermining their power (Tanford, 1990). Efforts to increase the receptivity of courts may need to target both intellectual and personal forms of resistance.

▶ IN CONCLUSION

This opening chapter was an attempt to present the big picture—a sort of aerial view of the field. Each chapter that follows will focus on a specific region of the legal landscape. However, not all areas of the legal system have received equal attention from social scientists. Some areas (e.g., eyewitness identification) have received intense scientific scrutiny, while other areas (e.g., antitrust law, product liability) have been largely ignored. This should not be surprising. Just as film and literature tend to focus on the most dramatic aspects of the law—for example, police investigations or the courtroom trial—psychologists tend to focus on topics that are psychologically rich and interesting. Our map of psychological processes in the legal system is incomplete. Some territories have been well mapped by researchers, some areas have barely been explored, and some territories are still uncharted.

▶ DISCUSSION AND CRITICAL THINKING QUESTIONS

1. Are judges qualified to evaluate scientific evidence? Can you think of alternatives to using judges as gatekeepers?

2. Could the legal system be improved by taking psychological methods and principles into account? How?

3. What obstacles prevent an easy interplay between psychology and law?

4. Under what conditions should expert psychological testimony be considered relevant? When should it be excluded?

5. What are the distinctions among advising, evaluating, and reforming?

6. What new guidelines were created by the *Daubert* trilogy, and what effects have these cases had on lawyers and judges?

▶ KEY TERMS

adversarial system (p. 8)
amicus curiae brief (p. 21)
Brandeis Brief (p. 2)
brief (p. 11)
Code of Professional
   Responsibility (p. 8)

culture (p. 5)
Daubert trilogy (p. 15)
evaluation research (p. 11)
experts (p. 14)
forensic psychology
   (p. 10)

gatekeepers (p. 15)
gatekeeping role of judges
   (p. 15)
legal realism (p. 3)
precedent (p. 8)
stare decisis (p. 8)

suborning perjury (p. 9)
trial consultants (p. 11)
trier of fact (p. 14)

2 Interrogations and Confessions

- ▶ The Power of a Confession
- ▶ The Evolution of Interrogation Techniques
- ▶ Inside the Modern Interrogation Room
- ▶ The Problem of False Confessions
- ▶ Should Interrogators Be Allowed to Lie?
- ▶ Potential Solutions to the Problem of False Confessions

On a spring evening in 1989, Trisha Meili was jogging in New York City's Central Park when she was pulled from the jogging path into a nearby ravine. She was raped and brutally beaten. She was found unconscious, having lost more than 70% of the blood in her body. Miraculously, she survived. And, mercifully, she has no memory of the attack. Because of the savage assault she endured more than 20 years ago, she still suffers from balance, hearing, vision, and memory problems (Meili, 2003).

In the hours and days following the attack, police quickly focused their investigation on a group of boys—aged 14 to16—who had harassed several other people in the park earlier that evening. Six boys were interrogated over the course of a day and half, and five of them finally confessed to the rape and beating of the jogger. Although a hair found on one of the boys appeared to match the hair of the victim, the main incriminating evidence was the confessions. In those confessions, the rape was described in detail and the boys accepted responsibility for their crimes. Here are a few excerpts from the confession of one of the boys (Kharey Wise) convicted in the case.

- "Raymond jumped on top of her . . . . He was wild. When they dragged her down, that's when Steven stripped off her clothes with the knife. He hit her in the face with a rock and that's what knocked her out."
- "If you're with them, you have to show a little effort around there too, so I had to get into it too . . . . They were on top of her, raping her completely. I was playing with her legs. I was going up and down her legs. I wasn't doing as much as they was doing."
- "Steven was gonna kill her, they were gonna kill her so she don't identify us. Yusef said, "Don't kill her man, don't kill her. Bad enough you raping her. Don't kill her man."
- "This is my first rape. I never did this before and this is gonna be my last time doing it. I've never, this is my first experience. We went to the park for trouble and we got trouble, a lot of trouble. That's what they wanted and I guess that's what I wanted . . . I can't apologize. I think it's too late. Now what we gotta do is pay up for what we did."

All five of the boys who confessed were convicted. Their sentences ranged from 5 to 15 years in prison (Sullivan, 1992).

For more than a decade, the case appeared to be solved. The perpetrators of a brutal crime had been caught, tried, convicted, and imprisoned. Then, in 2002, a prison inmate

named Matias Reyes underwent a religious conversion, contacted authorities and informed them that he alone had raped the Central Park jogger. He was already serving time for four rapes and a murder committed in the summer of 1989. A DNA sample from Reyes was compared to DNA from a semen stain on the jogger's sock. It was a match. The five boys were eventually exonerated. All five confessions had been false.

How is it that an innocent person is persuaded to falsely confess to a horrible crime? And how is it that a false confession can appear to be authentic? The answers to these questions can be found in the process of police interrogation. Police have several psychological tools at their disposal during an interrogation of a suspect. These powerful tools sometimes enable police to persuade guilty suspects to confess their crimes. At other times, these same tools lead innocent suspects to confess to crimes they did not commit.

This chapter explores the specific techniques used by police in the interrogation room and the psychological effects of those techniques on criminal suspects. However, it is important to note at the outset that interrogation is a particular example of basic processes studied by psychological scientists. These processes include compliance, persuasion, obedience to authority, and decision making under stressful conditions (Kassin, 2008; Leo, 2008). ◀

Trisha Meili, Matias Reyes, and Kharey Wise. (A: *AP Photo/Ed Reinke*, B: *NY Daily News Archive via Getty Images*, C: *NY Daily News Archive via Getty Images*)

▶ THE POWER OF A CONFESSION

The job of the police is to find criminals and gather evidence sufficient to secure convictions. Careful analysis of a crime scene might turn up important physical evidence, but it is the leads and evidence uncovered through the questioning of witnesses and suspects that often produce a conviction. If the police believe someone is responsible for a crime—that is, if the person is a suspect—the goal of the questioning is to elicit a confession. A handful of studies have examined how frequently interrogations culminate in confessions. Somewhere between 39% and 48% of suspects make full confessions when interrogated by police, and an additional 13% to 16% of suspects make damaging statements or partial admissions (Moston, Stephenson, & Williamson, 1992; Softley, 1980). Police officers estimate that they are able to elicit self-incriminating statements from 68% of the suspects they interrogate (Kassin et al., 2007).

For good reasons, police prefer confessions to other types of evidence. First, confessions save time. Trials can be avoided because suspects who confess usually plead guilty. The slow, tedious process of gathering and analyzing evidence, and of finding and questioning witnesses, can be streamlined or even circumvented. Because guilty suspects who confess often tell interrogators where crucial evidence can be found (e.g., where a gun or money or a body is hidden), additional evidence becomes less critical. Second, and most important, a confession may be the closest prosecutors can get to a guaranteed conviction. Understandably, juries almost always convict defendants who have confessed to committing a crime. In effect, a confession puts the suspect on the fast track to conviction (Leo, 2008).

Many legal scholars have noted the surpassing power of confessions. In the case of *Colorado v. Connelly,* Supreme Court Justice William Brennan wrote that:

> Triers of fact accord confession such heavy weight in their determinations that the introduction of a confession makes the other aspects of a trial in court superfluous, and the real trial, for all practical purposes, occurs when the confession is obtained. (*Colorado v. Connelly,* 1986, p. 173)

There is much research to suggest that Brennan's observation is correct. In a study of the impact of a confession, researchers had mock jurors read summaries of four types of criminal trials: theft, assault, rape, or murder (Kassin & Neumann, 1997). Each trial contained weak circumstantial evidence plus either a confession, an eyewitness identification, or character witness testimony. Confessions led to a conviction rate of 73%, significantly higher than the 59% conviction rate produced by the next most powerful type of evidence (eyewitness testimony). In two follow-up studies, confessions were rated as significantly more incriminating than any other form of evidence, and were also rated as the piece of evidence that most powerfully influenced verdicts. Another study (Kassin & Sukel, 1997) examined whether people are able to discount coerced confessions. Mock jurors read transcripts involving no confession, a low-pressure confession, or a high-pressure confession. In the low-pressure versions of the transcript, the suspect confessed right after police started questioning him. In the high-pressure version, the suspect was said to be in pain, his hands cuffed behind his back, and one of the police officers waved his gun in a menacing manner. Mock jurors had no problem recognizing that the high-pressure confession was coerced, and they reported that they disregarded the involuntary confession. But their verdicts indicated otherwise: In the low-pressure condition, 62% of the jurors found the defendant guilty, in the high pressure condition, 50% of the jurors voted "guilty," and in the no confession condition only 19% voted for conviction (see Figure 2.1). Put differently, even a clearly coerced confession boosted the rate of conviction by 31%.

The findings from these experiments are consistent with other research on the power of confessions. In an important study of actual false confessions, Steven Drizin and Richard Leo (2004) examined 125 proven false confessions (e.g., cases in which DNA evidence proves the person who confessed did not commit the crime). In this large sample of actual cases, when suspects falsely confessed, then pled *not guilty* and proceeded to trial, they were convicted 81% of the time. That is, even though the confessions were false, jurors were not able to recognize them as false. In sum, the available evidence indicates that a confession is extremely difficult for jurors to discount or ignore, even if that confession is false, even if it is coerced, and even when there is little corroborating evidence.

These findings can be partly explained by the **fundamental attribution error**—the tendency to attribute other

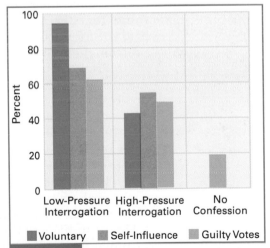

FIGURE 2.1 The existence of a confession—true or false—predisposes juries toward reaching a guilty verdict. Mock jurors were asked whether they judged the confession to be voluntary, whether it influenced their verdict, and whether they would vote to convict. *(KASSIN & SUKEL, 1997).*

people's behavior to dispositional causes (traits, personality) and to dismiss the situational pressures acting on the person. There is a large body of research in social psychology demonstrating that when analyzing another person's behavior, we tend to underestimate the power of situational forces (Nisbett & Ross, 1991). In the case of confession evidence, we tend to discount the pressures of the interrogation process as a cause of a suspect's confession.

When a defendant has confessed, defense attorneys will sometimes argue that a confession was coerced by police and should therefore not be admitted at trial. The judge will then be asked to rule on the admissibility of the confession. The judge may rule that a confession was coerced and therefore inadmissible. But such rulings are rare (Leo, 2008). If, instead, the judge rules that the confession is admissible, it is presented to the jury with other evidence. In some states, jurors are instructed to judge for themselves whether the confession was voluntary, and to disregard any statements they believe were coerced (Fulero, 2004). But although jurors often recognize that many standard interrogation tactics are coercive, they also believe that such tactics will not induce innocent suspects to falsely confess (Blandon-Gitlin, et al., 2011). Further, if there is other compelling evidence that a suspect is guilty (e.g., DNA or fingerprints) jurors are highly tolerant of coercive interrogation tactics (Shaked-Schroer, Costanzo, and Berger, 2013).

THE EVOLUTION OF INTERROGATION TECHNIQUES

For obvious reasons, guilty suspects usually resist confessing their crimes. Police try to break down this resistance through the process of interrogation. Police interrogation techniques have evolved over more than a century. The arsenal of techniques has been thinned by laws governing police use of force, and refined by decades of experience. Interrogation techniques have become increasingly sophisticated, moving from direct physical violence (what was traditionally called "the third degree"), to covert physical torture that leaves no trace, to purely psychological means of coercion (Leo, 2008).

Prior to 1930, police frequently used beatings and brutality to extract confessions. Varieties of physical abuse included beating suspects with fists, gun grips, rubber hoses, and blackjacks; burning the skin with cigarettes; use of electric shocks; twisting a man's testicles; and dragging or lifting female subjects by their hair. But, in 1931, a government commission produced a report that became a major catalyst for reform. The *Report on Lawlessness in Law Enforcement* documented widespread abuses by police and focused attention on the treatment of suspects in police custody.

The publicity and legislation generated by the report led to a shift from overt physical abuse of suspects to covert forms of abuse that did not leave a physical trace. These covert forms of brutality included pushing a suspect's head into a toilet almost to the point of drowning, or holding an uncooperative suspect by the feet so that they hung upside down out of a high window or in a tall stairwell. Phone books could be stacked on the head of a suspect so that when the books were hit with a nightstick it would produce excruciating pain but leave no bruises. Suspects might also be forced to stand upright for hours at a stretch or have their faces pressed against a dead body in the morgue (Leo, 1992). Physical abuse could be combined with deprivation, isolation, and intimidation. Sleep deprivation is an especially effective means of lowering the resistance of suspects, and withholding food, water, and toilet privileges can also make a suspect more willing to talk (Ratcliff & Van Dongen, 2009). Isolation in a cold, dark cell could also be used to persuade the suspect to tell the police what they wanted to hear.

A series of legal decisions pushed police away from covert physical brutality toward more psychological forms of coercion. Since 1961, confessions have generally been ruled as inadmissible if judged to be the result of physical force, sleep or food deprivation, prolonged isolation, explicit threats of violence, clear promises of lenient sentences, or explicit promises of immunity from prosecution (*Culombe v. Connecticut,* 1961; *Davis v. North Carolina,* 1966; *Reck v. Pate,* 1961; *Townsend v. Swain,* 1963). Since the *Miranda v. Arizona* decision of 1966, all suspects must be informed of their constitutional rights to remain silent and to have an attorney present during questioning. If you have spent any time watching police dramas on television, the process of reading suspects their **Miranda rights** is probably familiar to you. There are four parts: (1) You have the right to remain silent. Anything you say can be used against you in a court of law; (2) You have the right to have an attorney present during questioning; (3) If you cannot afford an attorney, you have the right to have an attorney appointed to you prior to questioning; and (4) Do you understand these rights as I have explained them to you? If the suspect in police custody has not been "Mirandized," any subsequent confession can be excluded at trial.

Surprisingly, only about 20% of suspects in police custody choose to exercise their Miranda rights. The remaining 80% waive their rights and submit to a full interrogation without an attorney present (Leo, 1996). It is not entirely clear why so many people waive their Miranda rights, but it is clear that we are accustomed to waiving our rights. We do it often—we sign waivers when we open bank accounts, we sign waivers when we change physicians or dentists, and we routinely click on the "agree" button without reading the long, legalistic privacy agreements on web sites. Police detectives who want suspects to answer their questions have developed ways of de-emphasizing Miranda warnings to improve the probability of a waiver. For example, an analysis of actual recorded interrogations found that police officers speak significantly faster when delivering the Miranda warnings, rushing through without checking for understanding (Domanico, Cicchini, & White, 2012). One researcher summed up the problem this way, " . . . police routinely deliver the Miranda warnings in a perfunctory tone of voice and ritualistic manner, effectively conveying that these warnings are little more than a bureaucratic triviality" (Leo, 1992, p. 44). Truly innocent suspects may waive their rights because they feel they have nothing to hide (see Figure 2.2), and guilty suspects may not want to appear uncooperative. Finally, most suspects are probably neither calm nor clear-thinking when they are being taken into custody. They may not fully realize they are waiving their rights.

The rulings cited above may give the impression that only a fully voluntary confession can be used against a defendant. This is true only if we use an expansive definition of "voluntary." To evaluate "voluntariness," the Supreme Court has held that trial judges must look at the **totality of circumstances** surrounding the confession (*Culombe v. Connecticut,* 1961). In a series of rulings

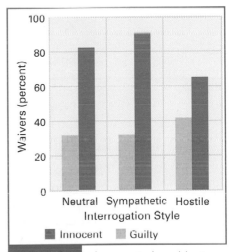

FIGURE 2.2   In one study, subjects who were guilty or innocent of a mock crime (stealing $100) were confronted by a neutral, sympathetic, or hostile "Detective McCarthy" who asked if they would waive their rights and talk. Only 36 % of guilty subjects agreed, but 81% of innocents waived these rights, saying later they had nothing to hide or fear (Kassin & Norwick, 2004). Innocents are especially at risk for waiving rights to counsel and silence that were established by the U.S. Supreme Court in Miranda, believing they have nothing to hide. Yet longer exposure to questioning leaves them at greater risk for a false confession.

over the past 30 years, the courts have permitted police to use a variety of creative lies and theatrical tricks to persuade suspects to confess. Police have been permitted to: assemble a phony lineup and tell the suspect that a fictional eyewitness identified him (*People v. McRae,* 1978), tell a suspect in a murder case that the victim had "pulled through" and identified him as the attacker (*Collins v. Brierly,* 1974), have a police informer pose as a prison inmate and promise his cellmate (the suspect) that he would provide protection from violent prisoners in exchange for a confession (*Arizona v. Fulminante,* 1991), and hold a suspect in a cell without visitors or phone calls for 16 days (*Davis v. North Carolina,* 1966).[1]

While all courts might agree that confessions obtained by physical brutality are illegal, what constitutes psychological coercion is far more ambiguous. And whether or not coercion occurred is seldom entirely clear based on the information provided to judges. If a defendant claims that police threatened or intimidated him, and the police deny his allegations, it is difficult for the judge to take the word of the defendant. Lawyers refer to such disputes as "swearing contests" (police swear there was no coercion and the defendant swears there was). Police usually win such contests, and most confessions are admitted at trial (Drizin & Reich, 2004).

 ## INSIDE THE MODERN INTERROGATION ROOM

Although it is still possible to find instances of physical mistreatment of suspects in police custody, it is far more common for police to rely on purely psychological techniques for extracting confessions. For example, in the time-tested **good cop–bad cop approach,** two interrogators work as a team. The "bad" cop (typically the larger, more intimidating member of the pair) through words and nonverbal behavior shows his anger with the lying suspect and expresses his belief that the suspect should receive the most severe punishment possible. In contrast, the officer playing the good-cop role will show the suspect sympathy and understanding (although the good cop may eventually express disappointment that the suspect is continuing to lie). The bad cop may even scold the good cop for wasting time talking with the lying suspect. Frequently, the angry display of the bad cop and the apparent interest of the good cop in helping the suspect will induce the suspect to confess to the good cop when the bad cop leaves the room (Cialdini, 2008; Skolnick & Fyfe, 1993).

Police officers read manuals on effective interrogation techniques and receive training about how to extract confessions from uncooperative suspects. In the most widely used guide for police officers, Fred Inbau, John Reid, Joseph Buckley, and Brian Jayne (2013) offer detailed advice on every aspect of the interrogation process including how to set up the interrogation room, what questions to ask, appropriate nonverbal behavior for the interrogator, how to respond to questions or denials by a suspect, and how to handle passive or defiant suspects. Even peripheral details such as the type of chairs in the interrogation room receive serious attention: "Straight-back chairs should be used for the suspect as well as the interrogator. Other types of chairs induce slouching or leaning back, and such positions are psychologically undesirable" (p. 30).

At the heart of what is often referred to as the **Reid technique** are "the nine steps of interrogation" (Figure 2.3). While this step-by-step procedure captures the general flow of many interrogations, several psychologically powerful aspects of the process deserve deeper examination. Underlying the nine steps are four basic influence strategies. These foundational strategies include: (1) loss of control, (2) social isolation,

First, in step 1, interrogators accuse the suspect of having committed the crime (citing real or fabricated evidence). ➡ In step 2, the interrogator offers the suspect some possible excuses for the crime. ➡ Next, in step 3, interrogators persistently cut off attempts by the suspect to deny involvement in the crime. ➡ Step 4 involves overcoming the explanations offered by the suspect to support the denials (e.g., someone accused of an armed robbery might claim that he does not own a gun, or that he did not need money, or that his strong religious upbringing would prevent him from committing such a crime). ➡ Step 5 is an effort to hold the attention of the suspect who may have become withdrawn after an extended and intense period of questioning. At this stage, the officer must appear sincere and understanding. He or she may move closer to the suspect and use touching such as " . . . a pat on the shoulder, or in the case of a female, a gentle holding of the suspect's hand." ➡ By the time the process reaches step 6, suspects are usually showing visible signs of "giving up" and the interrogator is directed to maintain eye contact and to move the suspect toward an admission of guilt. ➡ Step 7 involves reframing the issue as a choice between having committed the crime for a good reason, or having committed the crime for a bad reason. ➡ The final two steps involve eliciting a full confession (step 8) ➡ and writing out the confession (step 9) so that it can be signed by the suspect.

ESSENTIALS OF THE REID TECHNIQUE

CRIMINAL INTERROGATION AND CONFESSIONS

SECOND EDITION

Fred E. Inbau
John E. Reid
Joseph P. Buckley
Brian C. Jayne

FIGURE 2.3   The nine steps of interrogation described by the Reid technique.
(Jones & Bartlett Learning)

(3) certainty of guilt, and (4) exculpatory scenarios (Costanzo & Leo, 2007). The first two strategies focus on the conditions created to facilitate the interrogation process, and the second two involve the content and style of communication.

The process of interrogation is built on **loss of control.** Suspects are interrogated in a small, sparse room, where every aspect of the situation—including the physical environment, the direction and pacing of the conversation, and the length of the interrogation—are controlled by the interrogator. A key goal is to remove the psychological comfort of familiar surroundings, and to communicate—in blunt and subtle ways—that the suspect has lost control of the situation. As noted above, interrogation training includes recommendations on even the smallest aspects of the interrogation environment (size of room, lighting, furniture type and arrangement) as well as behavioral scripts (when to stand and when to sit, when to move closer, key phrases to use). In short, the interrogation is a tightly controlled, psychologically disorienting situation in which the normal rules of social interaction no longer apply. This loss of control leads the suspect to feel vulnerable, anxious, and off-balance (Leo et al., 2009).

A second, related strategy of interrogation is **social isolation.** Suspects are almost always interrogated alone. This is done to deprive the suspect of emotional support and to minimize contradictory information. The presence of a friend or ally might bolster the suspect's resistance to persuasion and might lead to additional challenges to the interrogator's version of events. The combination of loss of control and social isolation frees up interrogators to create the social reality of the situation. Police—who are presumably experts in the inner workings of the criminal justice system—can make a variety of claims about the strength of the suspect's case and how that case will be seen by others. Alone in a carefully constructed, somewhat surreal environment, it is impossible for a suspect to independently assess the interrogator's claims about the crime and the evidence.

The third strategy is **certainty of guilt.** Indeed, many interrogations begin with a direct accusation that the suspect committed the crime (step 1 of the Reid technique).

SCIENTIFIC AMERICAN SPOTLIGHT

Group Interrogation may help to Reveal Liars
By Rachel Kaufman

Interrogate suspects separately and get them to incriminate one another—that's how cops do it. New research suggests that a better way to catch colluding criminals might be to interview them together. In a recent experiment in the *Journal of Applied Research in Memory and Cognition* with more than 40 pairs of subjects, half were told to steal £10 and then convince an interviewer of their innocence. The other pairs were told the money had gone missing. The truth tellers interrupted one another four times as often and were much more likely to add to or correct their friend's account. The liars said less and hardly interrupted.

(*John Lund/Sam Diephuis/Getty Images/Blend Images*)

The deceivers were not simply more taciturn, however. "It's a myth to think suspects are reluctant to talk," says social psychologist Aldert Vrij of the University of Portsmouth in England. "Mainly U.S. police manuals promote this myth." Further, in the antiterrorism situations for which Vrij's research is designed, a "no comment" could lead a person to be taken off a plane or denied entry to a country. Because liars must talk in such situations, an interviewer who paid attention to a pair's interruptions and contradictions might better tell truth from fiction than one seeking only suspicious silent types.

A simple, straightforward narrative only hints at falsehoods when suspects share a cover story, Vrij says. One truth teller and one liar in a pair will act differently from either two liars or two truth tellers. Because many terrorist acts are planned by groups, this finding suggests group interviews can be a useful tool for law enforcement and border patrols. As Vrij explains, "truth tellers' interaction with one another comes naturally and is not natural for liars."

An innocent suspect will respond to this accusation with denials, but interrogators are trained to challenge, cut off, and dismiss all denials. If interrogators believe a suspect is guilty, everything about their demeanor conveys a simple message: "You did it, we know you did it, it is futile to deny your guilt, and any jury or judge that sees the evidence will convict you" (Leo et al., 2009).

To impress the suspect with the strength of the case against him, and to bolster the claim that denial is futile, police may use a variety of **evidence ploys.** That is, they will cite real or fabricated evidence that clearly establishes guilt. Sometimes there is actual evidence that implicates the suspect (e.g., an eyewitness who places the suspect at the scene). If no real evidence exists, police may lie about its existence. They may claim to have an eyewitness, or fingerprints, or hair samples, or tire tracks that link the suspect to the crime. Police can be highly creative in their efforts to convince suspects that the evidence against them is overwhelming. A careful analysis of actual interrogations revealed some of these creative false evidence ploys (Ofshe & Leo, 1997). The researchers noted that " . . . an investigator is constrained only by the limits of his imagination and his ability to lie convincingly" (p. 1033). For example, one interrogator claimed to have satellite photos showing a defendant leaving the house where the crime had been committed. Another interrogator scraped the trigger finger of a young man accused of shooting two people, then told the young man that by testing his skin cells using a "neutron-proton-negligence-intelligence test," police could detect whether the suspect fired the gun. A third interrogator told a murder suspect that the last image seen by the murder victim is forever imprinted on the retina of the victim. That image—which would likely show the suspect—was now being developed like a photographic negative. These seemingly scientific claims are very difficult for suspects to refute. A suspect might be sure that he was not seen by anyone near the scene of the crime, but he cannot be sure he was not seen by a satellite floating in the stratosphere.

The fourth influence strategy involves constructing **exculpatory scenarios.** To clear the path for an admission of guilt, interrogators offer face-saving justifications or excuses for the crime. For example, it might be suggested to a murder suspect that he killed the victim by accident or in self-defense. By suggesting minimizing or exculpatory reasons for committing a crime, police imply (but avoid saying explicitly) that anyone making a judgment about the act (e.g., a judge, jury, or employer) will be likely to recommend lenient treatment. In interrogation manuals, this technique is known as using "themes" (Inbau, et al., 2013; Senese, 2005).

Exculpatory scenarios work by shifting blame from the suspect to someone else (e.g., the victim or an accomplice), or to the circumstances surrounding the act, or by redefining the act itself. Such scenarios suggest alternative, morally justifiable motives for committing a crime. For example, someone suspected of committing an armed robbery might be asked questions that suggest honorable explanations for the crime, "Did you plan this, or did it just happen on the spur of the moment?" or "Was this your own idea or did someone talk you into it?" or "I'm sure this money was for your family, for some bills at home. It was for your family's sake wasn't it?" (Inbau et al., 2013, p. 167). Even with repugnant crimes such as rape and child molestation, the interrogator is taught to sympathize with the suspect, for example, by suggesting that anyone, under similar circumstances, might have acted in the same way as the criminal did. For the crime of rape, Inbau and his associates urge interrogators to make comments such as:

> **We humans are accustomed to thinking of ourselves as far removed from animals, but we're only kidding ourselves. In matters of sex, we're very close to most animals, so don't think you're the only human being—or that you're one of very few—who ever did anything like this. There are plenty of others, and these things happen every day (p. 99).**
>
> **Joe, this girl was having a lot of fun for herself by letting you kiss her and feel her breast. For her, that would have been sufficient. But men aren't built the same way. There's a limit to the teasing and excitement they can take; then something's got to give. A female ought to realize this, and if she's not willing to go all the way, she ought to stop way short of what this gal did to you (p. 109).**

Such scenarios justify the crime and make it seem almost mundane (e.g., "these things happen every day") and deflect blame from the criminal to the victim or others (e.g., "what this gal did to you"). The implication is that the criminal's actions were reasonable and that, therefore, the consequences may not be that serious. Suspects are offered a limited choice, " . . . a choice between an inexcusable or repulsive motivation for committing the crime and one that is attributable to error or the frailty of human nature" (p. 165). So, a child molester is asked to choose between being viewed as someone who has made a mistake, or being viewed as a vicious sexual predator who will continue to threaten the community. Similarly, a suspect in a homicide case is asked to decide whether he impulsively shot someone in self-defense, or whether he is a cold-blooded, remorseless killer. Of course, choosing either of these rigged alternatives involves admitting to committing the crime. Delivered against the backdrop of the techniques that have preceded them (loss of control, social isolation, accusations of guilt, attacks on denials, evidence ploys), exculpatory scenarios are intended

CORE PRINCIPLES OF SOCIAL INFLUENCE

The influential, best-selling book *Influence: Science and Practice,* 5th edition (Allyn & Bacon, 2008), was written by social psychologist Robert Cialdini. Drawing on hundreds of research studies of conformity, compliance, and persuasion, Cialdini distilled the research findings down to six core principles that underlie the most effective efforts to influence others. Are any of these principles used by police to elicit incriminating admissions from suspects? If so, how?

1. Authority—We are more likely to comply with the requests of people who hold positions of power and people that we believe have expert knowledge in the relevant area.
2. Reciprocity—We feel obligated to return favors. If you do someone a favor or give them some type of "gift," they will be more likely to comply with a later request from you.
3. Liking—We tend to say "yes" to people we feel positive toward. That "liking" can be the result of physical attractiveness, perceived similarity, or special treatment.
4. Scarcity—We place greater value on things that are in short supply. An object or offer may be perceived as scarce because it is available only for a limited time or because there are only a few more available.
5. Social Proof—When we are uncertain about what action to take, we tend to look to people around us to guide our choices and behaviors. We attempt to

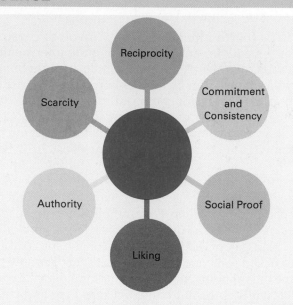

gather information about how other people behave in the situation.

6. Commitment and Consistency—Once we make a commitment—especially a public commitment—we increase the likelihood that we will honor that commitment. A verbal or written pledge or promise motivates us to act in a way that is consistent with that pledge.

to persuade the suspect that the only way to improve his bleak, hopeless situation is to accept a scenario that minimizes his moral and legal culpability.

The strategies of certainty of guilt and exculpatory scenarios avoid direct threats of punishment ("If you don't admit you did it, the judge is going to lock you up and throw away the key") and direct promises of leniency ("The judge will go easy on you if you just admit you did it"). Instead, certainty of guilt *implies* a threat of severe punishment and the use of exculpatory scenarios *implies* a promise of leniency. In combination, the four psychologically powerful tactics described above are designed to cause a guilty suspect, "to recognize that the game is over and that he is caught" (Ofshe & Leo, 1997, p. 1010). Unfortunately, this unreal, hopeless situation occasionally convinces innocent suspects that their only option is to acquiesce and falsely admit guilt.

THE PROBLEM OF FALSE CONFESSIONS

It is extremely difficult for most of us to imagine confessing to a crime we did not commit. To understand how false confessions can happen, it is instructive to look at the case of Thomas Sawyer.

Thomas Sawyer was a golf course groundskeeper whose neighbor was raped and then strangled to death. Sawyer suffered from severe social anxiety, and when police questioned him he blushed, fidgeted, avoided eye contact, and began to sweat profusely. This behavior made police suspicious. They had learned that Mr. Sawyer was an avid fan of TV police shows and they invited him to come to the police station to "assist" with the investigation. He was happy to help. The investigating officers asked Sawyer to help them imagine different scenarios of how the murder might have been committed. Only then did the interrogators accuse him of being the murderer. At first, Sawyer vigorously denied having committed the crime. But, over the course of a 16-hour interrogation, he came to believe that he was the killer.

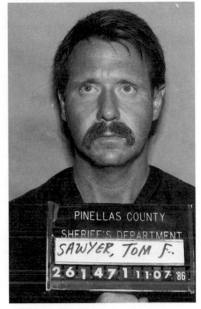

To prove his innocence, Sawyer submitted to a polygraph examination (a lie-detector test) and provided hair and fingerprint samples to the police. It shook his confidence badly when the police lied to him and told him that he had flunked the polygraph test. Still, he could not remember raping and killing the woman next door. During the time that Sawyer was "helping" the police, he had confided that he was an alcoholic. Knowing this, police suggested that he might have experienced an "alcoholic blackout" during the murder. That would account for his memory loss. A final lie from the interrogators led to a full confession—his hair sample matched hairs found on the victim's

Thomas Sawyer. (*Courtesy of Pinellas County Sheriffs Department*)

body. Confronted with this information, Sawyer became reluctantly convinced of his own guilt: "I guess all the evidence is in," he said, "I guess I must have done it." During the final phase of the long interrogation, police shaped and reshaped Sawyer's memory of the murder by providing him with details and urging Sawyer to incorporate those details in his account of the murder (Ofshe, 1989).

We do not know—and it may be impossible to know—how many false confessions occur each year or what percent of the total number of confessions are false. Many defendants are convicted solely on the basis of their confession. Some claim during and after trial that their confessions were actually false—the result of intimidation, deception, fatigue, or abuse. Occasionally, these confessions are later exposed as false when other evidence (usually DNA) identifies the actual perpetrator of the crime. But far more often, the conviction stands. As many researchers have noted, *proven* false confessions are only the "tip of a much larger iceberg." That is, the false confessions we know about are only the tiny, visible piece of a much larger whole that is hidden from view. This is true because the kind of DNA evidence that is usually necessary to prove that the wrong person confessed is only available in a small minority of criminal cases. Also, some cases involving false confessions do not become public because they are dismissed by prosecutors prior to trial, or because they are kept secret to protect the privacy of juvenile suspects (Drizin & Leo, 2004).

What we do know is that approximately 25% of known wrongful convictions involve false confessions (www.innocenceproject.org, 2013). Also, the analysis of proven false confessions mentioned earlier in this chapter found that 80% of proven false confessions occurred in murder cases, another 9% involved rape, and 3% involved arson (Drizin & Leo, 2004). This surprising overrepresentation of very serious crimes is partly because the biological evidence (e.g., blood, semen, skin cells) necessary for DNA exoneration is much more likely to be available in cases of murder or rape. It might also be a result of the strong pressure on police to swiftly solve cases involving violent crimes (Gross, 1996; Warden, 2003).

We also know that many documented false confessions are the result of vulnerable people being subjected to the powerful influence tactics deployed in the interrogation room. Suspects can be vulnerable in a variety of ways. They may be young, inexperienced, naive, easily dominated, under the influence of drugs, submissive to authority, of low intelligence, mentally ill, sleep deprived, or simply terrified (Leo et al., 2009; Redlich, 2004). Gisli Gudjonsson, a psychological researcher who used to be a police officer, has developed questionnaires to assess suggestibility and compliance and has shown that people known to have falsely confessed typically score significantly higher on such traits than people who do not falsely confess (Gudjonsson, 2003). Of course, police do not screen suspects for vulnerability and then treat highly suggestive suspects more gently. As illustrated in the case of Thomas Sawyer, if someone is suspected of committing a crime, his or her vulnerabilities will be sought out and fully exploited.

Of all the individual vulnerabilities that have been identified by researchers, perhaps the most dangerous vulnerability is youth. For example, 32% of proven false confessions have been given by suspects under the age of 18 (Drizin & Leo, 2004). This is a surprisingly high false confession rate because only 8% of suspects arrested for murder and only 16% of suspects arrested for rape are under the age of 18 (as noted above, nearly all—89%—of proven false confessions were for murder or rape) (Snyder, 2006). The problem is that being young is associated with psychological traits such as greater suggestibility, impulsiveness, emotional arousability, and a tendency to focus on the present rather than the future (Redlich, 2010; Redlich & Meissner, 2009). Indeed, brain-imaging research has revealed that key brain structures such as the limbic system (an area that plays a large role in emotional regulation) and the prefrontal cortex (an area associated with long-term planning and rational decision making) are not fully developed until the early 20s (Steinberg, 2007). The psychological tendencies of youthful suspects significantly raise the risk of false confessions. Fortunately, there seems to be some recognition among potential jurors that juveniles are more suggestible and more easily manipulated in the interrogation room (Najdowski & Bottoms, 2012). However, even though police as well as jurors may realize that juvenile suspects are more easily influenced, police interrogators still rely on the same interrogation tactics that they use with adult suspects (Reppucci, Meyer, & Kostelnik, 2009).

Although suspect vulnerabilities (e.g., suggestibility, mental illness, cognitive impairment, and being a juvenile) clearly raise the risk of false confession, the process of police interrogation appears to be the primary cause of most false confessions (Leo, 2008). The powerful psychological pressures applied to suspects in the interrogation room sometimes induce innocent suspects to make false admissions. These pressures lead to what Deborah Davis and Richard Leo (2012) have called "interrogation-related regulatory decline." That is, the process of interrogation results in a breakdown of self-regulation—the ability to control our thoughts, emotions, and behaviors in pursuit of our goals. Interrogation techniques are designed to deplete our ability to self-regulate and to impair our ability to think rationally. To avoid making a false admission, a suspect must usually withstand a host of stressors including physical discomfort, isolation, severe fatigue, extreme emotional distress, as well as the deceptive and confrontational questioning techniques described earlier. All the effort expended to withstand this onslaught weakens the suspect's will power and mental focus. One critical challenge for the suspect is to maintain focus on his long-term interest of denying any involvement in a crime. A growing body of research shows that the process of interrogation leads to "short-sightedness"—a tendency to give priority to the short-term goals of escaping the interrogation room and appeasing the interrogators (Madon, Guyll, Scherr, Greathouse, & Wells, 2012; Madon, Yang, Smalarz, Guyll, & Scherr, 2013). Over the course of an interrogation, the immediate goal of relief from the pressures of interrogation is likely to become more important than the more distant goal of avoiding possible prosecution sometime in the future.

Finally, the mindset of innocent suspects may put them at special risk of false admissions. Because innocents tend to believe that their innocence will be obvious to jurors, judges, and lawyers, they may be less concerned about making an admission. Innocents may believe that any false admission they make during the interrogation will be easily recognized as bogus once they escape the interrogation room (Davis & Leo, 2010; Kassin, 2012).

Types of False Confessions

Several classification schemes have been proposed to differentiate between types of false confessions (see Kassin & Gudjonsson, 2004; Ofshe & Leo 1997). For our purposes, it is useful to distinguish between four types of *false* confessions by looking across two dimensions: *instrumental or authentic* and *voluntary or coerced*. Instrumental confessions are those offered as a means to an end, to achieve some goal. Often, the goal is simply to bring an end to a highly aversive interrogation. In contrast, authentic false confessions are the result of a confessor's genuine but false belief that he or she may have actually committed the crime. Coerced false confessions are produced by intense psychological pressures (and occasionally physical pressure) from interrogators, while voluntary false confessions are given freely by the confessor (Costanzo & Leo, 2007). As shown in Table 2.1, crossing the two dimensions yields four basic types of false confessions.

There have been actual cases involving all four types of confessions. **Instrumental–coerced false confessions** occur when, as a result of a long or intense interrogation, suspects confess to crimes they know they did not commit. This is the most commonly identified type of false confession in criminal cases (Drizin & Leo, 2004). In this type, suspects become convinced that the only way to end the interrogation or to receive more lenient treatment is to agree that they committed the crime in question. Sometimes, suspects come to believe that (even though they are innocent) the apparently compelling evidence against them will lead others to conclude that they are guilty. They are likely to conclude that accepting the exculpatory scenario suggested by interrogators is the best option for avoiding severe punishment. Other times, innocent suspects come to believe that if they simply agree to the scenario offered by the interrogators, they will be released and will then be able to "straighten everything out later" and prove their innocence. The five confessions in the Central Park jogger case described at the beginning of this chapter are examples of instrumental–coerced false confessions.

Instrumental–voluntary false confessions occur when suspects knowingly implicate themselves in crimes they did not commit in an effort to achieve some goal. For example, a member of a criminal gang or

TABLE 2.1		
Four Types of False Confessions		
	Coerced	*Voluntary*
Instrumental	End interrogation by acquiescence	Protect someone else Gain notoriety
Authentic	Confessor becomes persuaded that he or she is guilty	Confessor is delusional or mentally ill

organization may voluntarily falsely confess to a crime to protect someone higher up in the organization. Or, a parent may intentionally offer a false confession to protect his or her child from being convicted of a crime (Gudjonsson, Sigurdsson, & Einarsson, 2004). The goal might even be to become famous. After he was captured, the serial killer Henry Lee Lucas falsely confessed to scores of unsolved murders in an apparent attempt to gain notoriety as the most prolific serial murderer in history. People have voluntarily confessed for a variety of peculiar reasons—to impress a girlfriend, to provide an alibi for one's whereabouts while having an affair, to get revenge on police by making them look incompetent (Gudjonsson, 2003).

An **authentic–coerced false confession** occurs when, as a product of a long or intense interrogation, a suspect becomes convinced—at least temporarily—that he or she may have actually committed the crime. This was the type of confession offered by Thomas Sawyer, whose case was described earlier in this chapter. In most such

HOT TOPIC

The Use of Torture in Interrogations

In the years following the terrorist attacks of 9/11/ 2001, the U.S. government began to use torture as a means of extracting information from terrorism suspects. In 2003, details of CIA interrogation tactics became public. Perhaps the most notorious abusive interrogation method (called "waterboarding") involved binding a suspect and forcibly submerging his head underwater or pouring water into his nose and mouth without allowing him to breathe.

Using this technique, a struggling suspect is forced to experience the terrifying sensation of drowning and imminent death. Porter Goss, former director of the CIA, defended waterboarding as a "professional interrogation technique" (Human Rights Watch, 2005), and some members of Congress continue to defend the use of torture when interrogating suspected terrorists (Mazetti, 2013).

There is no doubt that such practices violate ethical codes of conduct as well as international and national treaties and laws (e.g., Universal Declaration of Human Rights, 1948; the Geneva Convention, 1949; the United States Congress Joint Resolution Opposing Torture, 1984; the United Nations Convention against Torture and other Cruel, Inhuman or Degrading Treatment, 1984, 1987). In addition to ethical and moral questions about the use of torture, there are also important questions about the effectiveness of torture as a tool for gathering information.

Because torture-based interrogations are conducted in secret, there is no direct research on the effectiveness of torture as an interrogation device. However, as described

(MARK EVANS/GETTY IMAGES)

in this chapter, there is irrefutable evidence from the criminal justice system that techniques far less coercive than torture have produced verifiably false confessions in a surprising number of cases. Indeed, a summary finding from decades of research on criminal interrogations is that coercion increases the probability of false confessions (Kassin et al., 2010). In the civilian justice system, a confession might be viewed as coerced if there were clear promises of leniency, direct threats of punishment, sleep or food deprivation, or if the interrogation was excessively long. In contrast, it is precisely such tactics, as well as deliberate physical and psychological cruelty, that are routinely used in torture-based interrogations. Such tactics increase the probability of gathering false information (Costanzo & Gerrity, 2009).

There is no evidence that torture is an effective means of gathering reliable information. Many survivors of torture report that they would have said anything to "make the torture stop," and people who claim that "torture works" offer as evidence only unverifiable anecdotal accounts (McCoy, 2005). Even if there are cases where torture may have preceded the disclosure of useful information, it is impossible to know whether less coercive forms of interrogation might have yielded the same or even better results (Costanzo & Gerrity, 2009). It is also impossible to know the ratio of accurate to inaccurate information gained through torture. Finally, when military action is based on false information extracted through torture, the lives of soldiers and civilians are put in jeopardy.

confessions, the confessor does not develop false memories but, instead, comes to believe that he may have committed the crime despite having no memory of doing so (Ofshe & Leo, 1997b). He may accept the suggestion of the interrogators the he "blacked out" during the crimes or "repressed" his traumatic memories of committing the crime. In some cases, interrogators have suggested (and innocent suspects have come to believe) that the suspect suffers from multiple personality disorder and that a separate, submerged personality—unrecognized by the confessor—temporarily emerged to commit the crime. In a few exceptional cases, intensely coercive interrogations have caused innocent suspects to create false but vivid memories of crimes they did not commit (Wright, 1994; see Chapter 11 for an account of the Paul Ingram case).

Finally, an **authentic–voluntary false confession** occurs when someone suffering from delusions confesses to a crime with little or no pressure from interrogators. In high-profile, well-publicized cases, police investigators sometimes receive multiple unsolicited confessions from mentally disturbed people who appear to believe they committed the crime. For example, in the sensational 1947 murder and mutilation of a young actress (dubbed the "Black Dahlia" by the press), more than 50 people came forward to confess to killing her. More recently, dozens of people have falsely confessed to the 1996 murder of Jon Benet Ramsey (Karlinsky & Burke, 2006).

SHOULD INTERROGATORS BE ALLOWED TO LIE?

Police in the United States are legally permitted to use false evidence ploys to induce a suspect to confess. They are permitted to say that they found a suspect's DNA or fingerprints at the crime scene or that witnesses have identified the suspect. Sometimes, lies told by an interrogator induce a truthful confession to a horrible crime. But even when lying works, should it be permitted? Would most suspects eventually confess even if the interrogators do not deceive them? Several lies told to innocent suspects have led to proven false confessions. Would there be fewer false confessions if police were not permitted to tell lies in the interrogation room? And would banning the use of lies result in large numbers of guilty criminals avoiding conviction?

The answers to these questions are not entirely clear, although there is some relevant research from outside the United States. England and Wales restrict police behavior during interrogations far more than does the United States. In 1986, enactment of the **Police and Criminal Evidence Act (PACE)** made it illegal to trick suspects or lie about evidence as a means of inducing suspects to confess. All interviews with suspects conducted at police stations must be audio-recorded so that they can be evaluated by lawyers (called "solicitors" in England), judges, and jurors. Bullying, threats, and intimidation are not permitted, and police are required to call in an "appropriate adult" to witness the interview of any suspect who is deemed "vulnerable" (usually because of youth or low intelligence).

These reforms were set in motion by a few sensational cases involving false confessions. One such case came to be known as the "Guildford Four." In the fall of 1974, members of the Irish Republican Army exploded bombs in two pubs in the city of Guildford. Five people were killed and 57 were injured. Just over a month later, the police interviewed an Irishman named Paul Hill. He signed a written confession and implicated his friend Gerry Conlon. Mr. Conlon confessed and implicated several other people including two (Carole Richardson and Paddy Armstrong) who made partial admissions while in police custody. Despite the lack of any physical evidence or any eyewitness linking these four defendants to the bombings, all four were convicted and sentenced to life imprisonment. All four ended up being released from prison after serving 15 years. The long investigation that led to the eventual release of the Guildford Four found that fear of the police, intimidation by interrogators, lies told by the police, isolation of the suspects during interrogations, and police fabrication of key evidence caused the four false confessions.

It is not entirely clear whether the reforms established by the PACE Act have helped or hurt the ability of the police to elicit *true* confessions. Some researchers have found that although pressure tactics, intimidation, and trickery have declined substantially, the number of admissions of guilt during police interviews is not lower than it was before the PACE reforms (Bull & Soukara, 2010; Irving & McKenzie, 1989). However, one study found that prohibited tactics such as the use of threats, lies, and promises have merely moved outside the interrogation room. That is, before the audiotaped interview begins, police are likely to have "off the record" conversations outside the police station (McConville, 1992). These conversations may incorporate many of the old-style pressure tactics previously used by police.

Back in the United States, courts have given the police permission to lie during interrogations. And police interrogators clearly believe that the ability to lie is a potent weapon in their arsenal. However, looking beyond the interrogation room, some observers worry that lying by police may undermine public confidence in the police and reduce the willingness of citizens to cooperate with law enforcement (Slobogin, 2003). Another concern is that approval of lying during interrogations may remove inhibitions against lying in other important contexts, such as testifying in court. If it is justifiable to lie to a suspect for the purpose of securing a confession, it may not be that large a step to believe that it is justifiable to bend the truth during courtroom testimony for the purpose of securing a conviction.

POTENTIAL SOLUTIONS TO THE PROBLEM OF FALSE CONFESSIONS

In books and films depicting police work in the future, interrogation has become unnecessary. Crimes are easily solved through the use of technology—omnipresent video recorders, devices that tap directly into the suspect's memory, improved collection of DNA, or infallible lie-detection devices. However, for the foreseeable future, police will continue to rely on interrogation. Especially for serious crimes such as homicide, police rely disproportionately on confession evidence to clear criminal cases (Gross, 1996). Interrogation remains an essential investigative tool. The challenge is to find ways of reducing the risk of false confessions, and to find ways of detecting false confessions after they occur. But how might this be accomplished? Although no single reform is sufficient to solve the problem of false confessions, several partially effective reforms have been proposed. These reforms follow directly from the research summarized above.

Video Recording of Interrogations

One way to help jurors decide how much coercion occurred during an interrogation is to let them watch a video recording of the process. Voluntary video recording of interrogations is now spreading to police agencies across the United States (Sullivan, 2004). Over the last decade, numerous scholars have called for the mandatory electronic recording of interrogations (Kassin et al., 2010; Westling, 2001). According to national surveys of police practices, more than a third of large police departments make video recordings of *some* interrogations (Sullivan, 2006). The practice is more common in serious cases, for example, those involving assault, rape, or murder.

Electronic recording has many potential benefits—instead of hearing testimony about what happened in the interrogation room, judges and jurors can see and hear for themselves what happened. The broad range of suspect and interrogator behavior—subtleties of what was said as well as how it was said (verbal and vocal cues), and the rich variety of visual cues (facial expressions, gestures, posture, touch, personal space, and gaze)—can be captured on camera. Much of the emotional meaning of an interaction is carried by nonverbal cues, and intimidation, fear, disorientation, and exhaustion are easier to see than to hear (Archer, Costanzo, & Akert, 2001; Knapp & Hall, 2007). If interrogators were abusive or threatening or intimidating, it should be apparent in the recording.

Electronic recording creates a permanent, objective, reviewable record of the interrogation that can later be evaluated by judges, lawyers, jurors, and experts. In cases where there is reason to believe a confession might be false, we can review the recording and carefully compare the known facts of the crime with information actually provided by the suspect to see if there are inconsistencies or contradictions. Although several states require police to record interrogations in their entirety in some or all criminal cases, most police departments (as well as the F.B.I.) still do not record interrogations or only selectively record the admission, not the interrogation that produced it (Drizin & Reich, 2004).

An important psychological issue concerns the impact of recorded confessions on the people who view them. One problem is that jurors often do not see recordings of interrogations in their entirety. Sometimes a relatively brief (e.g., half-hour) segment of the video is shown at trial. This brief "recap" may misrepresent what actually happened during a multihour interrogation. The video recap shown to jurors typically contains the clearest admission of guilt the police were able to obtain, and that admission is likely to weigh heavily in the decision-making of jurors or judges (Kassin & Gudjonsson, 2004). In many cases, interrogators do not even turn on the video camera until after the suspect has confessed and his confession is clear and well rehearsed. Consequently, what a jury might see is the end product of a long, grueling process of interrogation. The coercive process that culminated in a confession may not be salient to jurors and, by the time a confession is made, the suspect is likely to look exhausted and defeated. This exhaustion and lack of expressiveness may convey to jurors the impression that the defendant is a cold, remorseless criminal (Costanzo & Leo, 2007).

A specific psychological bias arises from the camera's point of view. If the camera is aimed only at the suspect, viewers of the video cannot focus their attention on the interrogators. Psychological research has shown that people who are more visually salient are viewed as more influential (Fiske & Taylor, 2008). In a series of experiments, Daniel Lassiter and his colleagues had people evaluate a confession that had been recorded from three camera angles: One showed only the suspect, another showed only the interrogator, and a third showed both the detective and the suspect. They found that those who saw the "suspect-only" video rated the confession as much less coerced than those who viewed the other versions (e.g., Lassiter, 2010; Lassiter & Geers, 2004). Research shows that judges are also susceptible to this perspective bias (Lassiter, Diamond, Schmidt, & Elek, 2007). It appears that a suspect-only camera focus causes observers to discount the situational pressures of the interrogation (e.g., fatigue or intimidation by police officers). In contrast, the more neutral **equal-focus camera perspective** showing both the suspect and the

(*upper*) Suspect-only camera perspective; (*lower*) equal-focus camera perspective. What is significant about each of these views of an interrogation? (*UPPER: DANIEL LASSITER, LOWER: REPRINTED WITH PERMISSION OF DANIEL LASSITER*)

interrogator best enables jurors to assess the voluntariness of the confession and the coerciveness of the interrogation.

Although some police have initially resisted the use of video recording, most interrogators embrace this reform after trying it out. In a survey of 238 police departments in 38 states, Sullivan (2004) found strong support for recording interrogations. Police support video recording because it reduces the necessity for note-taking, frees up the interrogators to focus on the suspect, enables officers to replay portions of the interrogation to check information, reduces the number of defense claims of coercion, and reduces the amount of time interrogators spend in court defending their interrogation practices. It has also been noted that the use of video cameras in the interrogation room has civilizing effects on the behavior of interrogators. That is, police who are being recorded might be more careful to avoid questionable behavior or aggressive forms of coercion (Drizin & Reich, 2004; Sullivan, 2004).

Finally, routine recording would create a large data archive that would allow researchers to determine with much greater precision how interrogations go wrong to produce false confessions. Such an archive would greatly enhance our ability to specify the best interrogation practices (Leo et al. 2009).

Time Limits on Interrogations

Courts and legislatures should specify objective time limits for interrogations. Lengthy interrogations are not only inherently unfair; they are far more common in false confession cases. On average, routine interrogations last about two hours (Cassell & Hayman, 1996; Leo, 1996). Interrogations leading to false confessions often last longer than six hours (Drizin & Leo, 2004). Longer interrogations appear to increase the risk of false confessions by fatiguing suspects and thus impairing their ability and motivation to resist pressure. As researchers have explained:

> . . . sleep deprivation and exhaustion may lead to greater interrogative suggestibility via deficits in speed of thinking, concentration, motivation, confidence, ability to control attention, and ability to ignore irrelevant or misleading information. (Davis & O'Donahue, 2003, p. 957)

Imposing a time limit on interrogations should reduce the risk of false confessions without undermining the ability of police to elicit true confessions from the guilty (Costanzo & Leo, 2007). As Inbau and his colleagues (2013) point out, "rarely will a competent interrogator require more than approximately four hours to obtain a confession from an offender, even in cases of a very serious nature. . . . Most cases require considerably fewer than four hours" (p. 597).

The "Appropriate Adult" Safeguard for Vulnerable Suspects

Youth is a particularly important risk factor for false confessions (Drizin & Leo, 2004). For this reason, many scholars have recommended that juveniles should be provided with an "appropriate adult" during questioning. This adult might be a lawyer or other person (independent of police) who is specially trained to fill this role. Mentally impaired suspects should also receive special treatment by interrogators.

Some jurisdictions have already moved toward adopting such practices. In the wake of several false confession cases involving children and teenagers in Chicago, the state of Illinois enacted a law requiring that all children under age 13 be provided with an attorney before their interrogation in murder and sex-offense cases. Similarly, after eliciting false confessions from vulnerable suspects in several high-profile cases, the Broward County Sheriff's Office in Florida began to require detectives to make a reasonable effort to have an appropriate adult present before questioning a developmentally disabled suspect (Drizin & Leo, 2004). Although a minor's parent may be the appropriate adult in some cases, research on false confessions has uncovered an unanticipated problem with this approach: Parents may work against the interests of their children. For example, in the Central Park jogger case described at the beginning of this chapter, some of the parents present during the interrogations functioned as allies of the police, urging their children to confess. In some cases, parents may falsely believe their child is guilty, and in other cases parents may come to believe that offering a confession is the only way to improve their child's situation.

Expert Testimony on Interrogations and Confessions

If a disputed confession is introduced at trial, the jury will naturally want to know how an innocent person could possibly have been made to confess falsely, especially if to a heinous crime. As the Supreme Court held in *Crane v. Kentucky* (1986),

> . . . a defendant's case may stand or fall on his ability to convince the jury that the manner in which the confession was obtained casts doubt on its credibility. . . . Stripped of the power to describe to the jury the circumstances that prompted his confession, the defendant is effectively disabled from answering the one question every rational juror needs answered: If the defendant is innocent, why did he previously admit his guilt?

The use of scientific expert testimony in cases involving a disputed interrogation or confession has become increasingly common (Kassin, 2008; White, 2003). There is now a substantial and well-accepted body of scientific research on this topic, and case law supports the admissibility of such expert testimony. Although there have been some cases in which courts have not permitted expert testimony, such cases are exceptional; social psychologists have testified in hundreds of criminal and civil trials (Fulero, 2004). Indeed, survey research has found that roughly three-quarters of jurors believe that it would be helpful to hear an expert witness testify about police interrogation techniques, and about the reasons why innocent suspects sometimes falsely confess to crimes (Costanzo, Shaked-Schroer, & Vinson, 2010). When such testimony is presented, it appears to have a modest but appropriate effect in educating jurors about the likely impact of interrogation tactics on suspects (Blandon-Gitlin, Sperry, & Leo, 2011).

The purpose of expert testimony at trial is to provide an overview of research and to assist the jury in making a fully informed decision about what weight to place on the defendant's confession. Specifically, expert witnesses can assist the jury by discussing research documenting the phenomenon of police-induced false confessions by explaining how particular interrogation methods can raise the risk of a false confession, and (if a recording of the interrogation is available) by talking about the tactics used in a particular case and the nature of the admissions (Costanzo & Leo, 2007; Kassin, 2008). By educating the jury about the existence of, the psychology behind, and the risk factors for false confessions, expert testimony should reduce the number of confession-based wrongful convictions.

► IN CONCLUSION

Interrogation is an essential investigative tool. However, because it involves the deployment of powerful influence techniques, it needs to be monitored and scrutinized carefully. Social scientists have documented the reality of false confessions, identified many of their causes, and have proposed reforms that would reduce the frequency of false confessions. Although we want police interrogators to have the tools necessary to find the truth, we do not want them to coerce false admissions from innocent suspects. The interrogation room is one of many domains where the rights of an individual (who is presumed innocent) must be balanced against the powers of the state. Police and ordinary citizens have a common interest: to find ethical and effective ways of maximizing the number of true confessions while simultaneously minimizing the number of false confessions.

► DISCUSSION AND CRITICAL THINKING QUESTIONS

1. Why do innocent suspects sometimes confess to crimes they did not commit?

2. Should police be allowed to lie to suspects during interrogations in the interest of solving crimes? Should interrogators be permitted to tell suspects that their fingerprints were found at the crime scene if this is not true? Are some types of lies acceptable but other types not acceptable?

3. Which changes—if any—should the legal system be required to make to reduce the incidence of false confessions? What can be done to make it easier to detect false confessions?

4. How do the four types of false confessions differ? Which type do you think is most common or most rare? Why?

5. If we could prove that the "third degree" or outright torture was effective in extracting true confessions from criminal suspects, would you be in favor of using such techniques? If such tactics worked, should they be permitted in our legal system?

6. Which of the four foundational strategies of the Reid technique do you believe is most likely to lead to a false confession? Why?

7. Are there ways to help jurors recognize a false confession as false?

► KEY TERMS

authentic–coerced false confessions (p. 40)
authentic–voluntary false confessions (p. 41)
certainty of guilt (p. 33)
equal-focus camera perspective (p. 43)

evidence ploys (p. 34)
exculpatory scenarios (p. 35)
fundamental attribution error (p. 29)
good cop–bad cop approach (p. 32)

instrumental–coerced false confessions (p. 39)
instrumental–voluntary false confessions (p. 39)
loss of control (p. 33)
Miranda rights (p. 31)

Police and Criminal Evidence Act (PACE) (p. 41)
Reid technique (p. 32)
social isolation (p. 33)
totality of circumstances standard (p. 31)

3 Lie Detection

Even the earliest legal systems had techniques for detecting lies. For example, in an ancient form of **trial by ordeal,** a suspect who denied committing a crime was required to plunge his arm into a pot of boiling water and pull out a stone. The arm was then bandaged. If, after three days, the burns were not infected, the person was judged to be telling the truth (Hans & Vidmar, 1986). The theory was that God would intervene on behalf of an innocent person and reveal the truth by preventing infection. The legal system no longer relies on divine intervention to reveal liars. However, people working on behalf of the legal system (i.e., investigators, lawyers, jurors, judges) often rely on their own eyes, ears, and intuitions to catch liars. Sometimes investigators resort to machine-assisted lie detection, such as the polygraph. Because uncovering the truth is a central goal of the legal system, this chapter looks at our ability to tell lies and our ability to tell when other people are lying. ◀

THE COMPLEXITY AND PERVASIVENESS OF DECEPTION

The world is full of lies. Deception is an essential lubricant of social interaction. If you think about the novels you have read or the movies you have seen, chances are that one of the key plot elements is a lie told by one of the main characters. Even college students lie. In one study, pairs of college students were asked to get to know each other while being secretly videotaped. One member of the pair then reviewed the videotape and indicated the points at which they had deceived their interaction partner. In this brief encounter (about 10 minutes), students admitted to telling, on average, 2.9 lies. Some of the lies were complete fabrications, but most were little lies—for example, exaggerations aimed at making oneself appear more impressive, or the use of misleading behaviors to make the interaction partner feel good (e.g., feigning interest in a boring topic) (Feldman, Forrest, & Happ, 2002).

From an evolutionary perspective, lying is adaptive. That is, it serves a useful function that promotes survival. One great evolutionary advantage that we humans have over many other species is our ability to work and hunt together in cooperative, coordinated groups. It has been argued that our facility at bending, reshaping, spinning, and shading the truth is what enables relatively harmonious group interaction. There is even a model of human intelligence—called the "Machiavellian intelligence hypothesis"—which holds that a great leap forward in human intelligence was triggered by the need for humans to develop the essential social skills of manipulation, pretense, and deception (Dunbar & Shultz, 2007). Our capacity to deceive is a fundamental part of human nature, and it makes the detection of lies less straightforward than is commonly supposed.

Lying is not only ubiquitous, it is also multifaceted. The varied words for deception convey something about its complexity. We can lie, mislead, misinform, trick, fake, betray, fool, cheat, con, confabulate, delude, dupe, dissemble, deceive, distort, fabricate, exaggerate, prevaricate, pretend, distort, feign, falsify, or misrepresent. We can be inauthentic, disingenuous, or downright mendacious. Each of these words conveys a slightly different shade of meaning, though all imply a bending or violation of the truth. In addition, there are lies of commission (saying something that is not true) and lies of omission (leaving out crucial details that might reveal the truth). There are well-rehearsed lies and spontaneous lies. There are lies told to help others and lies told to hurt others, or to help ourselves at the expense of others. We may lie about our past experiences or our future plans. There are lies we feel justified in telling and those we feel guilty about telling. Sometimes we unintentionally give a false account of events because we were not paying full attention to what happened or because our memories of events are sketchy or wrong. Bella DePaulo, a well-known expert on lying and lie-detection, puts it this way: "Lying is just so ordinary, so much a part of our everyday lives and everyday conversations that we hardly notice it. And, in many cases, it would be more difficult, challenging, and stressful for people to tell the truth than to lie" (Henig, 2006, p. 11).

CAN WE TELL WHEN OTHERS ARE LYING?

When a case goes to trial, it is jurors who must decide whether a particular witness is lying or being truthful. Courts in the United States have expressed great confidence in the ability of jurors to detect lies by carefully observing each witness' "manner of testifying" and "demeanor on the witness stand" (Fisher, 1997; Judicial Committee on Model Jury Instructions, 2013). Further, as discussed in Chapter 2, part of a police interrogator's job is to act as a sort of human lie detector—to scrutinize the suspect's nonverbal behavior, to look for inconsistencies in the suspect's story, and to decide whether the suspect is telling the truth.

Is the legal system's faith in the lie-detection abilities of jurors and interrogators misplaced? Psychological research has examined human lie-detection abilities in hundreds of studies. In most of these studies, participants view videotapes of people telling either the truth or a verifiable lie. Judges typically view a large number of such videos and classify them as either truthful or deceptive. Because there are only two choices—lie or truth—the chance rate of accuracy is 50%. Put differently, you could get a score of 50% correct by simply flipping a coin and using a rule such as "heads, it's a lie; tails, it's the truth." In 2006, Charles Bond and Bella DePaulo statistically synthesized the results from 384 research studies that tested lie-detecting powers of more than 24,000 people. Their findings were as follows: People can do better than chance in distinguishing truth from lies, but not by much. The overall rate of accuracy was 54% percent. When the liars had time to plan out and rehearse their lies (as is almost always the case in legal settings), their lies were slightly harder to detect, and if observers were able to compare the same person lying and telling the truth, they were slightly better able to recognize the lie. However, such advantageous and disadvantageous conditions move accuracy rates up or down only by about 2%. As Bond and DePaulo note, "Despite decades of research effort to maximize the accuracy of deception judgments, detection rates barely budge" (p. 231). This extensive research should shake our faith in the ability of jurors and judges to tell whether a witness is lying. Clearly, there is no "Pinocchio response," no dead giveaway, no obvious visible signal that someone is telling a lie.

Perhaps police officers are much better at seeing lies that the rest of us miss. After all, police officers have extensive experience with criminals who lie about their involvement in crimes. Maybe this experience gives them an edge at lie detection. There is some direct evidence on this point. In one study, prison inmates gave true and false videotaped confessions to crimes they did or did not commit. Next, police detectives and college students judged the truthfulness of each statement. Although college students performed slightly better than chance at distinguishing true from false confessions, police detectives did not. Another interesting difference between the two groups was that detectives were significantly more *confident* about the accuracy of their judgments. That is, even though detectives were wrong more often than students, detectives were more confident that they were right. Detectives also showed a bias toward judging false confessions as true. And, the tendency of police detectives to infer guilt increased with job experience and interrogation training (Kassin, Meissner, & Norwick, 2005).

A serious problem is that interrogators are trained to "read" verbal and nonverbal behavior as a means of determining whether a suspect is lying. This training may wrongly increase confidence in lie-detection skills, even though it does not increase the ability to differentiate truth from deception. Unfortunately, the behavioral cues interrogators are taught to focus on (crossing legs, shifting and fidgeting, grooming gestures, avoiding eye contact) are flawed indicators of deception (DePaulo et al., 2003). Indeed, these cues are consistent with a prevalent but mistaken **liar's stereotype.** In a survey of more than 2,500 people in 63 countries, about 70% of respondents believed that when lying, people tend to avert their gaze, squirm, touch themselves more, and stutter (Bond & DePaulo, 2008).

In experiments using actual interrogation-training videos, training does not improve the ability to detect lies. It does, however, make people more confident about their judgments and cause them to list more reasons for their judgments (Kassin & Fong, 1999; Vrij, Mann, & Fisher, 2006). In studies where police officers watch video clips of real-life police interrogations and make judgments about deception, they do worse when they rely on the verbal and nonverbal cues emphasized in police training (Mann, Vrij, & Bull, 2004). Given their training, it may not be surprising that police investigators estimated that they can detect lies with an accuracy of 77%—an estimate that exceeds their actual accuracy rates by about 25 percentage points (Kassin et al., 2007). This overconfidence is consequential because interrogators sometimes wrongly but fervently believe a suspect is guilty merely because of his or her "suspicious" nonverbal behavior during their initial interaction. Because interrogators falsely assume that the suspect is behaving in ways that indicate guilt, they may subject an innocent suspect to a high-pressure, psychologically coercive interrogation. Then, if that suspect confesses, interrogators may view the confession as confirming their initial presumption of guilt and as justifying the use of questionable interrogation tactics (Leo et al., 2009).

Flawed interpretation of a suspect's verbal and nonverbal behavior is likely to fuel a phenomenon psychologists call **confirmation bias** (Meissner & Kassin, 2004). Scores of research studies demonstrate that once we form a strong belief about someone, we tend to both seek out information that confirms that belief and to dismiss information that contradicts that belief. If an interrogator believes a suspect is guilty, the confirmation bias may be triggered. He or she will be prone to interpreting the suspect's behavior (particularly ambiguous behavior such as nervous fidgeting, gaze, and anxious facial expressions) as further evidence of deception and guilt. As research on wrongful convictions indicates, police sometimes misperceive an innocent suspect as guilty because the suspect did not behave the "right way" when questioned (Costanzo & Leo, 2007; Davis & Leo, 2006; also see Chapter 2). In light of the research, interrogators need to be taught that they cannot reliably intuit whether a suspect is innocent or guilty based on their hunches about the meaning of a suspect's "suspicious" demeanor. When faulty cues to deception are combined with the confirmation bias, police officers may put enormous pressure on innocent suspects. Some will falsely confess.

▶ THE DEVELOPMENT OF THE POLYGRAPH

The hope for an infallible device that can reveal if someone is lying is understandable. Such a device could revolutionize crime investigation, plea bargaining, and trials. The police could simply hook suspects up to a lie-detector machine and ask questions such as, "Did you kill him?" or "Did you rape her?" or "Did you rob the convenience store?" Because the job of jurors in most trials is to decide if a defendant committed the crime in question, most trials might be streamlined or even eliminated. The machine could do the difficult job of deciding who is telling the truth, and much of our current legal system would be rendered superfluous. Of course, the hope for such a magical device is far from being realized.

Lie-detection devices monitor physiological changes. People hooked up to a **polygraph** (from the Greek *poly* meaning "many" and *grapho* meaning "write") usually have a blood pressure cuff around the upper arm, a pneumatic tube stretched across the chest, and electrodes on the fingers of one hand. Older machines tracked changes in physiological reactions with multiple pens that wrote on a moving strip of graph paper. Now bodily changes are displayed on a computer screen. The polygraph reveals physiological responses to questions asked by an examiner. The theory of the polygraph test is simple: Lying causes physiological arousal. Specifically, the theory holds that the act of lying causes a rise in blood pressure, an increase in skin moisture, and changes in heart rate and breathing patterns.

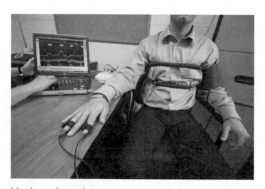

Under what circumstances should the legal system trust the results of a polygraph exam? (*Guy Bell/Alamy*)

The person generally credited with developing the modern lie detector is William M. Marston, a flamboyant lawyer and psychologist who believed that measurable changes in blood pressure could reveal whether someone was lying. The optimistic Dr. Marston declared that his discovery of physiological reactions correlated with lying signaled ". . . the end of man's long, futile striving for a means of distinguishing truth-telling from deception" (1938, p. 45). In his spare time, Marston created the comic book character Wonder Woman. Like other superheroes, Wonder Woman wore a cape and fought crime. She also carried a magic lasso that served as a lie detector—any criminal cinched up in her lasso was compelled to tell the truth.

During the 1960s, 1970s, and much of the 1980s, polygraph use was a lucrative business. Independent polygraph contractors offered employers a quick and seemingly scientific method for deciding who to hire and who to fire. People who were being considered for a job could be asked to submit to a lie-detector test before they were hired. Once job candidates were strapped into the lie detector, they might be asked about whether they had ever used illegal drugs, whether they had ever lied to a former boss, whether they had told the truth on every question on the job application, or whether they had stolen money or office supplies from a previous employer. People "caught" lying were unlikely to receive a job offer. Pre-employment screening using the polygraph was often supplemented by postemployment polygraph testing. Especially when employers were losing money because of employee pilfering, a polygrapher could be called in to test the suspected workers and find the thief. To meet the surging demand for lie detectors, training schools were established across the United States. Most offered short programs (a few weeks to a couple months) that granted student's certification in polygraphing. During this period, more than two million people per year submitted to polygraph testing (Lykken, 1998). Entrepreneurs had created a multimillion-dollar industry.

The use of the lie detector as a method of deciding who gets a job and who keeps a job was nearly abolished by the federal Polygraph Protection Act of 1988. That Act prohibited *most private employers* from using polygraphs to make decisions about who gets or keeps a job. However, public employers are exempt. Police departments, the Central Intelligence Agency (CIA), the Federal Bureau of Investigation (FBI), the National Security Administration (NSA), the Drug Enforcement Administration (DEA), and the Secret Service still routinely use lie detectors for employment screening (see Figure 3.1). There are also exemptions for some commercial businesses. For example, businesses that supply security personnel to facilities that affect public safety (e.g., nuclear power plants or public water supplies) are usually exempt. Following the terrorist attacks of September 11, 2001, the polygraph has been widely used for national security purposes. Sometimes, it is also used in the criminal justice system.

Polygraph Examiner

Polygraph Examiner

Work Schedule:	Full Time
Salary:	$53,350 - $115,742*
Location:	Washington, DC metropolitan area

The CIA's Office of Security is actively seeking individuals who currently are, or are interested in becoming federally certified Polygraph Examiners. Polygraph Examiners are being hired to successfully complete a five-year Polygraph Examiner tour. Upon successful completion of the five-year tour, Polygraph Examiners will be re-evaluated to determine if mission needs will allow the examiner to become a full time staff employee within the Office of Security.

Polygraph Examiners screen and vet individuals in support of the CIA's mission and protect this nation's classified information.

There are multiple entry-level through full performance Polygraph Examiner openings.

*Upon successful completion of the federal Polygraph Examiner certification training program the officer will receive Polygraph Premium Pay.

FIGURE 3.1   *(CIA Polygraph Examiner Job Description)*

ℱOCUS ON ℭAREERS

Police Psychologist
Gregory DeClue, Ph.D., ABPP
(forensic)
Police and Forensic Psychologist

(GREGORY DECLUE)

Police psychologists consult with, and provide services for, law-enforcement agencies. The client is the law-enforcement agency. The police psychologist must adhere to the Ethical Principles of Psychologists and Code of Conduct, and must be respectful of individuals' rights. However, their recommendations are made in terms of what is best for the law-enforcement agency.

The most frequent task of many police psychologists is pre-employment psychological assessment. The psychologist reviews records, conducts a semi-structured interview, and administers, scores, and interprets objective psychological tests that have been shown to be job-relevant. The results of such evaluations typically include a recommendation to the law-enforcement agency about whether to hire a particular applicant. A less frequent activity, but just as important and challenging, is fitness-for-duty evaluations. The law-enforcement agency may request an evaluation and professional opinion about whether a law-enforcement officer is psychologically fit to continue to perform his

or her duties. These are high-stakes and sometimes complex evaluations. The psychologist must be prepared to respond to administrative or judicial challenges to his or her results and recommendations.

In more than 20 years of work as a police psychologist, I have conducted more than 1,500 evaluations. Additional, less-frequent tasks have included active consultation during crisis negotiations, post-shooting interviews, post-incident stress debriefing, psychological counseling, case management, and participation in the development of a new law-enforcement agency.

Throughout my time as a police psychologist, I have continued to work

as a forensic psychologist in independent practice, primarily dealing with criminal cases. Working with cops and robbers, the jailers and the jailed, has been comfortable for me. It has always been my job to do professional work, gather objective data, form sound decisions, and tell the truth. Occasionally, there have been forensic cases that have caught the attention of a law-enforcement agency. For example, I remember a small courtroom filled with uniformed police officers when I took the stand to testify about the sanity of a man who had been charged with assaulting a police officer in the police station. Eventually, as my forensic caseload has included more cases involving interrogations and disputed confessions, my work has focused more on preventing wrongful convictions than on supporting law-enforcement agencies.

This is important and challenging work. For those interested in pursuing a career in police psychology, I recommend a strong education in clinical, counseling, or organizational psychology, followed by direct work experience supervised by a well-established police psychologist.

REPRINTED BY PERMISSION OF GREGORY DECLUE, PH.D., ABPP.

The resurgence in use of the polygraph has re-energized the conflict between two important groups: people who rely on the polygraph for their livelihood, and people who seek an objective assessment of the device. There is a continuing split between practitioners who have great faith in the polygraph and scientists who are interested in a dispassionate evaluation of its validity. Practitioners tend to have confidence in the validity of the polygraph and in their own ability to tell when someone is lying. A lack of clear feedback allows examiners to preserve their confidence. If a suspect labeled as "deceptive" later confesses or is found guilty, the examiner's suspicions are confirmed. But, if a suspect who was been labeled as "deceptive" fails to confess or is acquitted, a polygraph examiner can conclude that the suspect merely beat the rap. Further, if a guilty person passes the polygraph exam, the error is seldom revealed—guilty people generally do not brag to the examiner that they beat the test.

THE PROCESS OF POLYGRAPHING

To be used as a lie detector, the polygraph machine must be combined with systematic questioning procedures. The measured physiological reactions are reactions to specific questions asked by the examiner conducting the polygraph test. The three most widely used procedures are described below.

John A. Larson of the Berkeley, California, police department developed the first systematic questioning procedure for use with the polygraph machine. The **relevant–irrelevant test (RIT)** made use of nonarousing questions that are not relevant to the behavior being investigated (e.g., "Is today Thursday?" or "Are we in the city of Minnesota?") and relevant questions that should be especially arousing for the person who actually committed the crime ("Did you kill Joe Doe?" or "Did you steal the money?"). The examiner is especially interested in the *difference* in the strength of the physiological responses when the suspect answers the two types of questions. If a guilty suspect denies involvement in the crime, his or her reactions to the relevant questions should be stronger than reactions to the irrelevant questions. Such a response pattern would be classified as deceptive. Only a few research studies have evaluated the RIT. Those studies show a disturbingly high rate of a particular type of error: **false positives.** That is, innocent people are very likely to be misclassified as guilty (Horowitz, Kircher, Honts, & Raskin, 1997)

A second questioning procedure—the **comparison question test (CQT; formerly called the "control question test")**—was designed to correct some of the problems associated with the older RIT. Variations of CQT are by far the most frequently used techniques for polygraphing. Like the RIT, the CQT relies on the measurement of *relative arousal*. That is, it is assumed that physiological reactions while lying will be elevated as compared to physiological reactions while telling the truth. The name CQT highlights the importance of **comparison questions.** These questions involve behaviors that are uncomfortable for suspects but are not directly related to the crime under investigation. For example, a suspect might be asked, "During the first 20 years of your life, did you ever take something that did not belong to you?" or "Before age 21, did you ever do something dishonest or illegal?" or "Have you ever lied to get out of trouble or to cause a problem for someone else?" These questions are deliberately broad so that anyone who answers "no" is assumed to be lying. Indeed, comparison questions are sometimes referred to as "known lie" questions. Reactions to comparison questions are compared to reactions to "relevant" questions about the specific crime being investigated. The basic proposition of the CQT is that innocent suspects will react more strongly to the comparison questions and guilty suspects will respond more strongly to the relevant questions about the crime. Examiners who use the CQT want suspects to answer "no" to the comparison questions, but they also want the examinee to feel uncomfortable about their denials. Because of the importance of comparison questions, the CQT relies on the examiner's skill and stage-managing ability. The examiner must persuade the suspect that the polygraph can detect lies so that the suspect will be nervous about lying.

Scoring of the polygraph charts is done numerically. One commonly used scale runs from −3 to +3. No difference between a particular comparison question and the relevant question with which it is paired is coded as "0." Noticeable differences are coded as "1," strong differences are coded as "2," and dramatic differences are coded as "3." If reactions to a relevant question are stronger than reactions to a comparison question, a negative number is assigned. The opposite pattern leads to a positive number. Negative scores are thought to indicate deception, while more positive scores indicate truthfulness. If three relevant questions are compared to three comparison questions, a total score of −6 or lower would lead the polygrapher to conclude that the suspect was deceptive (Lykken, 1998, Iacono, 2008).

Although the CQT is an improvement over the older RIT, it places a heavy burden on the skills of examiners. Examiners must be able to formulate a delicately calibrated series of comparison questions that elicit stronger reactions than relevant questions if the suspect is innocent, but weaker reactions than relevant questions if the suspect is guilty. An alternative form of the CQT, called the positive comparison test (PCT), uses the relevant question as its own comparison. That is, the relevant question (e.g., in a rape case, "Did you use physical force to make her have sex with you?") is asked twice. The alleged rapist is instructed to tell the truth once and to tell a lie once. This method allows for a direct comparison of responses to the same question (Iacono & Patrick, 1999).

Weaknesses in the Process

There are several general problems with any approach to lie detection using the polygraph. One set of problems concerns the person being tested. First, some people are so controlled or emotionally nonreactive that lying produces little physiological response. Second, there is no guarantee that innocent people will not react strongly to questions about whether they committed a crime. Indeed, a jaded criminal may be less likely to react to lying than an innocent person being accused of a terrible crime. Third, if the person being tested does not have faith in the validity of the polygraph, he or she may not respond in the way examiners suppose. Guilty people who have no faith in the test may not be concerned about lying because they have no fear of detection. Innocent people who have no faith in the test may be especially anxious while answering relevant questions because they fear being falsely accused of a crime they did not commit (Iacono, 2008).

The polygrapher must typically convince the suspect that the tube and electrodes recording his or her reactions are nearly flawless detectors of deception. Indeed, "A CQT is preceded by a lengthy interview that serves to convince the suspect that the polygraph can determine to an extremely high degree of accuracy whether the suspect is lying or not" (Meijer & Verschuere, 2010, p.326). To convince the person being tested that the test is virtually infallible, examiners sometimes resort to trickery. One technique is to use known facts about the person being examined to demonstrate the sensitivity of the lie detector. Polygraphers generally have considerable background information at their disposal. Factual information about an employee or job applicant can be gleaned from personnel files. Information about a suspect in a criminal investigation can be pulled from police case files. The person being examined can be asked to lie in response to a series of direct questions about his or her background (Were you born in Madison, Wisconsin? Have you ever been convicted of burglary? Are you 25 years old?). The examiner will then tell the suspect exactly which answers were lies. This bogus demonstration is often enough to convince the examinee that the machine can expose the truth.

Another problem is lack of standardization. The content of questions, the number of questions, the demeanor of the examiner, and the scoring all vary from one polygraph test to another. Relevant questions must vary depending on the nature of the crime being investigated, and even comparison questions can vary. It is extremely difficult to standardize the behavior of all polygraphers. Some examiners—because of their appearance or demeanor—induce great anxiety in the person being tested.

Some examiners let their suspicions about a suspect's guilt influence their interpretation of the polygraph charts. Moreover, there is considerable subjectivity in the scoring. There is no precise point at which the differences between comparison responses and relevant responses cross over from "noticeable" to "strong" or from "strong" to "dramatic." The polygrapher must make a judgment call. Although technology can now measure extremely small differences in arousal, and make scoring more precise, the final judgment is a dichotomous one: Was the suspect lying or telling the truth?

Finally, suspects may attempt to fool the polygraph through a variety of "self-stimulation" strategies. Lie detection depends on the measurement of relative arousal—a comparison between the amount of arousal following relevant questions and the amount of arousal following irrelevant or comparison questions. There are two ways to reduce the discrepancy between the two levels of arousal: elevate arousal during comparison questions, or suppress arousal during relevant questions. In one experiment, researchers trained guilty subjects who had committed a minor theft to augment their physiological responses to the comparison questions by either biting their tongues or pressing their toes to the floor. These techniques for thwarting the polygraph—called **countermeasures**—reduced the detection of guilty suspects by 50%. Moreover, examiners were not able to tell that the suspects were manipulating their own arousal (Honts, Raskin, & Kircher, 1994). Mental countermeasures (e.g., counting backward from 200 by increments of 7) are especially unlikely to be detected by examiners, although they appear to be somewhat less effective in fooling the polygraph (Elaad, & Ben-Shakhar, 2009).

 ## RESEARCH ON THE POLYGRAPH

It is not unusual for professional polygraph examiners to claim impressively high accuracy rates ranging from 90% to 99%. But these rates may not be as impressive as they first seem. Suppose a local branch of a bank employs 100 people. Over the course of a few months, two of those employees, working together, steal several thousand dollars from the bank. Every employee is given a polygraph test to find out who stole the money. Results indicate that two employees (Sandy and Sam) are the thieves. However, the real thieves are actually Mandy and Max. The results of the polygraph have cleared two guilty people and caused two innocent people to be falsely accused. But even though the results of the polygraph were terribly wrong, the polygrapher can still claim an accuracy rate of 96%. All but four people were correctly classified.

Empirical studies attempting to test the accuracy of the polygraph fall into two categories: laboratory studies and field studies. Laboratory studies make use of **mock crimes.** People participating in such studies are randomly assigned to be either guilty suspects or innocent suspects. Guilty suspects are instructed to commit a pre-arranged crime, for example, stealing an object from a store or an office. All suspects are told to deny any involvement in the crime. Both innocent suspects and guilty suspects then submit to a polygraph test. The great advantage of laboratory studies is that because we know for certain who is telling the truth and who is lying, we know for certain if polygraphers were right or wrong in their judgments. Field studies use situations in which people are actual suspects in a real crime. Some field studies have used employees being tested in cases of suspected theft, and other studies have used polygraphs administered during police investigations of serious felonies (e.g., rape, murder). The great advantage of field studies is realism. The consequences of failing the test are very serious—suspects might lose a job or be charged with a serious crime. Because the stakes are so high, the emotional arousal measured by the polygraph is likely to be quite high. Unfortunately, in field studies, we often cannot be certain who is really lying: Sometimes polygraphers misclassify innocent suspects as guilty or misclassify guilty suspects as innocent. No matter what we use as the criterion of accuracy—confessions, convictions, or judgments by panels of experts—field studies have some error built into their judgments of accuracy.

There have been several major reviews of research on the accuracy of polygraph testing. These reviews include a total of 109 studies using the comparison question technique (Ben-Shakhar & Furedy, 1990; Ekman, 1985; Honts, 1995; Kircher, Horowitz, & Raskin, 1988; National Research Council, 2003; Van Iddekinge, Roth, Raymark, & Odle-Dusseau, 2012). Reviewers included only the best studies—those that used careful, valid research designs. Figure 3.2 shows a breakdown of the overall accuracy rates averaging across all studies.

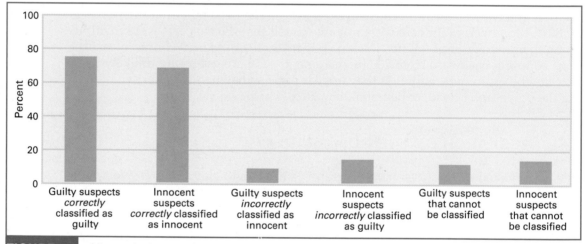

FIGURE 3.2   Hits and misses using the polygraph

As most of the reviewers noted, these accuracy rates are likely to be somewhat inflated for several reasons. One reason is that, in the great majority of studies, the consequences for lying were very low. In the laboratory studies, subjects caught in a lie were not arrested, put on trial, or sent to prison. Put differently, subjects had little motivation to tell successful lies. Some researchers have attempted to increase motivation by offering subjects a $20 reward for fooling the polygrapher into thinking that they are telling the truth when they are lying. While this may be a useful experimental manipulation, it is very far from the motivation felt by real criminals. A second reason is that subjects in these studies typically have no experience or training in countermeasures that would decrease the polygrapher's ability to detect arousal on key questions. Finally, the types of simple lies that tend to be told in controlled studies may be unrealistic representations of lies about real crimes. Some prominent deception researchers summarized the larger problem in this way: "Lying can be a complex, situation-dependent activity, with a variety of degrees and levels of prevarication, and the ability to detect simple deceptions in laboratory settings may not translate into a usable technology in less controlled situations" (Wolpe et al., 2005). (Read more about research on lying in the Scientific American Spotlight box in this section.)

SCIENTIFIC AMERICAN SPOTLIGHT

The Burden of Lying
By Wray Herbert

Detecting lies and liars is essential to effective policing and prosecution of criminals, but it is maddeningly difficult. Most of us can correctly spot barely more than half of all lies and truths through listening and observation—meaning we are wrong almost as often as we are right. But scientists are still working to improve on that result, and among them is social psychologist Aldert Vrij of the University of Portsmouth in England. Vrij has been using a key insight from his field to improve interrogation methods: The human mind, despite its impressive abilities, has limited capacity for how much thinking it can handle at any one time. Therefore, piling on demands for additional, simultaneous thought—or cognitive "load"—compromises normal information processing. Because lying is more cognitively demanding than telling the truth, these compromised abilities should be revealed in detectable behavioral clues.

Why is lying more demanding? To start, you need to invent a story, and you also have to monitor that tale constantly so it is plausible and consistent with the known facts. That task takes a lot of mental effort that innocent truth tellers do not have to spend. You also need to actively remember the details of the story you've fabricated so that you don't contradict yourself at any point. Remembering a fiction is much more demanding than remembering something that actually occurred. Because you're worried about your credibility, you're most likely trying to control your demeanor, and "looking honest" also saps mental energy. And you're not just monitoring yourself; you're also scanning your interrogator's face for signs that he might be seeing through your lie. That's not all. Like an actor, you have the mental demands of staying in character. And, finally, you have to suppress the truth so that you don't let some damning fact slip out—another drain on your mind's limited supply of fuel. In short, the truth is automatic and effortless, and lying is the opposite of that. It is intentional, deliberate, and exhausting.

Here are a few strategies that Vrij and his colleagues have been testing in the laboratory, which they describe in a recent article, "Outsmarting the Liars: Toward a Cognitive Lie Detection Approach" (Vrij, Granhag, Mann, & Leal, 2011). One intriguing strategy is to demand that suspects tell their stories in reverse. Narrating backward increases cognitive load because it runs counter to the natural forward sequencing of events. Because liars already have depleted cognitive resources, they should find this unfamiliar mental exercise more taxing than truth tellers do—which should increase the likelihood that they will somehow betray themselves. In fact, that is just what happens in the lab: Vrij ran an experiment in which half the liars and truth tellers were instructed to recall their stories in reverse order. When observers later looked at videotapes of the complete interviews, they correctly spotted only 42% of the lies people told when recounting their stories without fabrication—below average, which means they were hard to spot—but a remarkable 60% when the liars were compromised by the reverse storytelling.

Another tactic for increasing liars' cognitive burden is to insist that suspects maintain eye contact with their questioner. When people have to concentrate on telling their story accurately—which liars must, more than truth tellers do—they typically look away to some motionless point, rather than directly at the conversation partner. Keeping eye contact is distracting, and it makes narration more difficult. Vrij also tested this strategy in the lab, and again, observers spotted lies more easily when the liars were required to look the interrogator in the eye.

(*Darrin Klimek/Getty Images*)

A third strategy that could be surprisingly effective is to ask suspects to draw a picture. Putting pencil to paper forces people to give spatial information—something that most liars have not prepared for as part of planning their lies and that, therefore, overtaxes their mental resources. When Vrij and his colleagues asked volunteers what their offices looked like, after instructing half to tell the truth about their occupations and half to lie, both truth tellers and liars gave the same amount of detail in their verbal responses. But when Vrij asked them to draw their offices, the liars' drawings were much less detailed than those of the truth tellers. In another of the experiments, volunteers were questioned about a lunch date that only some subjects had actually attended. The liars' verbal descriptions of the restaurant did not match up as well with their drawings as did the truth tellers'—and the inconsistencies exposed the lies.

Still, we can say that under carefully controlled conditions (some would say, "under highly unrealistic conditions"), polygraphers appear to be able to catch about 74% of guilty suspects and exculpate about 68% of innocent suspects. They fail to catch about 21% of guilty suspects, and they falsely accuse about 16% of innocent suspects. These rates of accuracy are clearly better than chance, but are they strong enough to have practical utility for the legal system? Probably not. First, most polygraph tests given in the course of actual criminal investigations are not done under carefully controlled conditions. For example, there is usually no blind review of polygraph charts. Second, although we can point to an overall accuracy rate of more than 70% for identifying guilty suspects, we cannot say whether a particular suspect who flunks a polygraph test belongs in the true positive category or the false positive category. If that suspect becomes a defendant in a criminal trial, is it fair to let a jury hear that he or she flunked the test? Again, probably not. Our legal system is based, in part, on the idea that it is better to let 10 guilty people go free than to convict one innocent person.

The use of the polygraph as an employment-screening device is even more problematic than its use in the criminal justice system. Since the terrorist attacks of September 11, 2001, the use of polygraphing by the U.S. government has expanded dramatically. Applicants for jobs at the CIA or the FBI or other agencies connected with national security are now routinely polygraphed. An official at the FBI has estimated that about 25% of applicants fail their polygraph exam (Eggen & Vedantam, 2006). For many thousands of applicants (the exact number is uncertain), such failures have the personally devastating consequence of stopping a promising career in its tracks. The science clearly suggests that employment screening using the polygraph has an unacceptably high rate of error. In a landmark review of the evidence in 2003, the National Academy of Science concluded that if a polygraph test were given to 10,000 job applicants, and the applicant pool contained 10 spies, two of the spies would pass the test and about 1,600 innocent nonspies would fail (National Research Council, 2003). Even if we set aside issues of ethics and fairness, the gain of screening out eight spies would need to be balanced against the lost talents of the 1,600 who erroneously "failed" the test. Further, nonpolygraph employment screening might produce better results.

LEGAL STATUS OF THE POLYGRAPH

Although most Americans seem to believe that the results of polygraph tests are strictly inadmissible as evidence in court, the truth is more complicated. Twenty-three states have banned the use of polygraph evidence in court, but many states allow for the use of polygraph evidence under special circumstances. Only one state—New Mexico—routinely permits the results of polygraph tests to be presented at trial (*State v. Dorsey*, 1975). The 1993 U.S. Supreme Court decision in *Daubert v. Merrell Dow Pharmaceuticals* (described in Chapter 1) did not specifically address the admissibility of polygraph evidence, but it did rule that the admissibility of scientific evidence could be determined on a case-by-case basis. Evidentiary hearings can now be held to decide whether the results of lie-detector tests meet standards of scientific validity. In the 1998 case of *United States v. Scheffer*, Justice Clarence Thomas clearly expressed the legal system's two major concerns about polygraphing. First, he noted the lack of consensus about scientific validity:

". . . the scientific community remains extremely polarized about the reliability of polygraph evidence" (p. 1264). Second, he expressed the concern that allowing lie-detector evidence into the courtroom would usurp the role of the jury: "A fundamental premise of our criminal trial system is that the jury is the lie detector" (p. 1266).

In 1995, just two years after the *Daubert* decision, polygraph evidence was admitted in a case involving an insurance claim (*Ulmer v. State Farm*). After their house burned to the ground, Robert Savoie and Jessie Ulmer submitted a claim to the State Farm insurance company. State Farm initially denied the claim, alleging that the homeowners (or someone they hired) had intentionally set the fire for the purpose of collecting insurance money. As part of his investigation into the alleged arson, the state fire marshal asked Robert and Jessie to take polygraph tests. They agreed. Results indicated that they had not set the fire and had not hired anyone else to do it. State Farm was not convinced and sought to suppress the polygraph evidence, arguing that it is not scientifically reliable. However, the judge decided to allow the polygraph evidence at trial. He based his decision on several factors: that polygraphs had been the subject of numerous scientific studies published in peer-reviewed journals, that many scientists believe the results are more accurate than chance, and that the polygraph evidence was essential to Robert and Jessie's claim of innocence.

Results of a lie-detector test may be especially crucial *before* trial: Tests may be used to decide whether a case is pursued or used to help the police extract a confession. In cases in which physical evidence is inconclusive or too weak to justify a trial, the decision about whether to devote resources to a case or charge a suspect with a crime may hinge on the results of a polygraph test. If prosecutors have a weak case, they have little to lose if the suspect passes, and they gain considerable leverage if the suspect fails. For example, in a case of date rape (where a man says that sexual intercourse following a date was consensual and a woman says it was the result of physical force), police may ask one or both parties to submit to a lie-detector test before any further investigation is pursued or abandoned. In a case of sexual harassment in the workplace, where the accounts of an alleged victim and alleged harasser diverge wildly, attorneys may suggest lie-detector tests, with each side stipulating in advance that the results will be admissible in court. In such instances, the polygraph is being used (or misused) to establish the credibility of a potential witness.

AN ALTERNATIVE POLYGRAPH-BASED TECHNIQUE: THE GUILTY KNOWLEDGE TEST

A final technique that makes use of polygraph equipment does not attempt to detect lies. Instead, the **guilty knowledge test (GKT)** is intended to detect whether someone knows facts only a criminal would know. The logic is that a guilty person will recognize scenes and events from the crime that an innocent person will not recognize. This recognition will be reflected in elevated physiological arousal. For example, two suspects in a murder case could be shown 10 photographs, one of which is a photograph of the murder victim. Only the actual killer should react strongly to the photo of the victim. This fundamentally different approach to identifying guilty suspects was developed by David Lykken.

Lykken describes how a GKT might have been created to detect whether O. J. Simpson killed his ex-wife. In the most sensational trial of the past few decades, Simpson was tried for the murders of his former wife Nicole Brown and her friend Ronald Goldman. On a June night in 1994, Nicole Brown was brutally murdered just inside the front gate of her Brentwood condominium. Her throat was slashed. The wound was so deep that her head was nearly severed from her body. Mr. Goldman was killed in the same entryway, stabbed more than 30 times. Ms. Brown was wearing a black halter sundress. A bloody glove was found at the scene. Here are four questions from a 10-question hypothetical GKT devised by Professor Lykken (1998):

1. You know that Nicole has been found murdered, Mr. Simpson. How was she killed? Was she drowned? Was she hit on the head with something? Was she shot? Was she beaten to death? Was she stabbed? Was she strangled?
2. Where did we find her body? Was it: In the living room? In the driveway? By the front gate? In the kitchen? In the bedroom? By the pool?
3. I'm going to show you six pictures of Nicole's body. One of them shows her just as we found her. In the other five pictures her body has been transposed to other locations, places where we might have found her but did not. Which one of these pictures show Nicole where we found her? Is it: This one? This one? This one? . . . , etc. [Note: The body is not actually moved; computer-altered photographs are used.]
4. Nicole was dressed in one main color when we found her. What color was she dressed in? Was it: White? Black? Pink? Blue? Green? Tan?

Notice that each question has six multiple-choice answer options. For each question, physiological responses to the first answer option are thrown out. Responses to this **unscored buffer** question are discarded because people tend to react more strongly to the first item in a series. In a well-constructed GKT, each question should be followed by at least five good alternative answers. That is, all five options will seem equally plausible to an innocent suspect, and an innocent suspect will have a one-in-five chance of reacting most strongly to the correct option. In the simplest version of scoring, anyone with a stronger physiological response to 6 of the 10 correct options is classified as having guilty knowledge of the crime (see Figure 3.3 for a sample chart from a GKT).

Experimental findings on the validity of the GKT are quite promising. Most of the research on the GKT has been conducted in the laboratory, using mock crimes. For example, in one study, people committed a mock theft. They waited

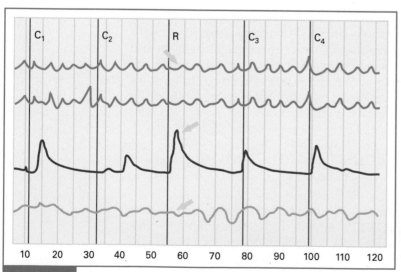

FIGURE 3.3 The profile above suggests that the person being tested is reacting to a question about the crime (the column labeled "R"). When a crime detail is mentioned, her breathing slows (*top arrow*); she sweats more, indicated by increased skin conductivity (*middle arrow*); and her heart rate momentarily drops (*bottom arrow*).

until a particular office was unoccupied, snuck into that office, rifled through a few drawers, and stole something of value (they were told what to steal). The stolen object was then hidden in an empty locker in a nearby hallway. Both innocent and guilty subjects were then interrogated using the GKT technique. Looking across eight such studies, Lykken (1998) found an impressive hit rate: 96.7% of innocent subjects were correctly classified as innocent, and 88.2% of guilty subjects were correctly classified as guilty. In a study using a GKT in actual criminal investigations in Israel, Eitan Elaad and his colleagues (1992, 2009) found that they could correctly identify 97% of innocent subjects and 76% of guilty subjects. Clearly, the GKT seems to be highly accurate in correctly identifying innocent suspects and thereby avoiding false positive errors (Ben-Shakhar, Bar-Hillel, & Kremnitzer, 2002).

Although the GKT is the most promising polygraph-based technique to be studied, there are clear limits to its usefulness. First, a sufficient number of crime facts from a well-preserved crime scene must be available so that valid GKT questions can be constructed. Second, these facts (e.g., where a body was found) must not be widely publicized until after suspects have been questioned, so that only the perpetrator will know the crime scene facts. Police, interrogators, and the media must keep the critical information secret. Third, the guilty person must remember details surrounding the crime. While it is probably reasonable to assume that a murderer will remember whether he stabbed or shot his victim, he may not remember the color of the victim's clothes. While he is likely to know that he killed someone in the woods, he may not know that he left behind a bloody glove. Memory is not always reliable under the best of circumstances. Murderers and other criminals are likely to be rushed, and their capacity to perceive and remember may be clouded by fear or rage. Criminals frequently commit their crimes while under the influence of alcohol or drugs. In short, what criminals don't know can't hurt them on the GKT.

While promising, the GKT may not be applicable to a large number of crimes. If a husband comes home to find his wife dead on the kitchen floor, he knows much of what the murderer knows. Both he and the murderer will have guilty knowledge. If a man and his accomplice rape and kill a woman, both know the details of the crime but only one may be guilty of murder. A man accused of rape may admit to having sex with a woman but will often claim that the sex was consensual. In each of these cases, it may not be possible to construct a reliable GKT. One study examined the files of 61 FBI criminal cases in which the CQT polygraph test had been used. The researchers concluded that the GKT could have been used effectively in only 13% to 18% of these cases (Podlesny, 2003).

A final limitation has nothing to do with the GKT itself, but with the resistance of professional polygraphers. Currently, polygraphers are often granted considerable latitude in devising questions, conducting interviews, and interpreting polygraph charts. Part of the skill of examiners lies in convincing suspects that the machine is infallible and in intuiting which suspects are trying to hide something. Routine use of the GKT would reduce polygraphers to "mere technicians." Ideally, the person who hooks up suspects to the lie detector would simply read questions (or show pictures of the crime scene), but not have any knowledge of which answers are correct. The activities and prestige of the polygrapher would be greatly reduced. Understandably, polygraphers are reluctant to lower their status. (To read about a lie-detection technique that does not make use of a polygraph machine, read the Hot Topic box in this section.)

HOT TOPIC

Lower-Tech Lie Detection: Words and Wizards

Most efforts to detect lying have deployed new technologies for the purpose of exposing lies. But a few techniques that do not require elaborate hardware have also been tried. One such technique—**criteria-based content analysis (CBCA)**—uses systematic analysis of written statements to assess the truthfulness of a description of an event. The technique originated in Western Europe as a method of assessing the credibility of statements made by child witnesses in sexual assault cases. It has been admitted as evidence in criminal cases in Germany, Sweden, and the Netherlands (Vrij, 2004). Carefully trained coders examine transcribed statements made by witnesses and rate the strength of 19 types of statements. For example, statements are rated on logical structure, amount of detail, and context (space and time). Despite its relatively high acceptance in European courts, the validity of CBCA is still in question. One significant problem is that the CBCA does not appear to discriminate between whether a child is familiar with a behavior and whether that child actually performed the behavior (Blandon-Gitlin, Pezdek, Rogers, & Brodie, 2005). A second approach that relies on written accounts of alleged crimes is called "reality monitoring" (RM). RM

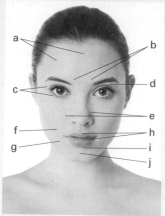

Paul Ekman and Wallace Friedman, in the 1970s, set up a classification system for human facial expression, part of which is lettered in this photo. The Facial Action Coding System identifies 43 sets of muscles, which often work in tandem to facially express emotion. For instance, the contractions of the muscles labeled (e)—superioris aleque nasi—usually indicate disgust. When the orbicular eye muscles (c) contract, a true smile results. Wizards may notice these muscular changes in faces better than the rest of us do. (KONSTANTIN SUTYAGIN/SHUTTERSTOCK)

involves an analysis of written account characteristics such as clarity, realism, and emotionality of description, as well as spatial and temporal information. Research using the RM coding technique has found that truth and lies can be correctly classified at a rate of about 63% (Nahari, Vrij, & Fisher, 2012).

A different approach has looked for people who can detect lies using only their own powers of observation. As part of a program of research spanning more than 30 years, Maureen O'Sullivan and Paul Ekman have tested the lie-detection abilities of more than 12,000 people. Their tests involve watching videotapes of people telling the truth or lying about opinions, emotions, or whether they have stolen money. So far, 42 lie-detection **wizards** have been identified. These wizards are able to tell when someone is lying more than 80% of the time (O'Sullivan, 2007). The wizard group includes people from several professions, including arbitrators, secret service agents, and psychotherapists. These expert lie detectors seem to notice more—and more subtle—verbal and nonverbal cues. They may also think about these cues differently than the rest of us do. It is not yet clear precisely what strategies the wizards use or whether those of us who are average lie detectors can be trained to become wizards (Bond, 2009).

THE POLYGRAPH AS COERCION DEVICE

Toward the end of his career, John A. Larson—developer of the RIT questioning technique—became disillusioned with the widespread misuse of the lie detector. He complained that, "the lie detector, as used in many places, is nothing more than a psychological third degree aimed at extorting confessions as much as the old physical beatings were" (Skolnick, 1961, p. 703). Even today, polygraphs are frequently used as a means of inducing suspects to confess. If you are being interrogated as a suspect in a criminal investigation, police officers may suggest that you take a polygraph test. This offer is usually presented as an opportunity to "prove your innocence." According to police interrogation manuals, whether you agree to take the test or resist taking the test is diagnostic of guilt:

> "If he [the suspect] agrees and seems willing to take the test as soon as possible, this usually is an indication of possible innocence. . . . A guilty person to whom a proposal has been made for a polygraph test will usually seek to avoid or at least delay submission to the test. . . . [attempts to avoid or delay] are usually strong indications that the suspect is guilty."
> (Inbau et al., 2013, p. 151)

But even if you agree to take the test and tell the whole truth, interrogators may inform you that the machine indicates that you are being deceptive.

Indeed, sometimes the polygraph plays a key role in eliciting a false confession. Eighteen-year-old Peter Reilly returned home one night to find his mother beaten, bloodied, and near death, collapsed on her bedroom floor. He phoned 9-1-1 for help, but by the time the ambulance arrived, his mother had died. He was asked to sit outside in a squad car while police looked for clues to solve the murder. He was later taken to the police station where he was interrogated and took a lie detector test. The police told him he had "failed" the test and that he must have beaten and killed his mother. Here is an excerpt from the portion of the tape-recorded interrogation in which Reilly was confronted with the results of the polygraph:

Peter Reilly: The [polygraph] test is giving me doubts right now. Disregarding the test, I still don't think I hurt my mother.

Police Sergeant: You're so damned ashamed of last night that you're trying to just block it out of your mind.

Peter Reilly: I'm not purposely denying it. If I did it, I wish I knew I'd done it. I'd be more happy to admit it if I knew it. If I could remember it. But I don't remember it . . . . Have you ever been proven totally wrong? A person, just from nervousness responds that way?

Police Sergeant: No, the polygraph can never be wrong, because it's only a recording instrument, recording from you.

Peter Reilly: But if I did it, and I didn't realize it, there's got to be some clue in the house.

Police Sergeant: I've got this clue here [the polygraph charts]. This is a recording of your mind.

Peter Reilly: Would it definitely be me? Could it be someone else?

Police Sergeant: No way. Not from these reactions. (Barthel, 1976, pp. 38–39)

In many cases, a polygraph is used as just one more tactic for pressuring suspects to confess. In their research on false confessions, Richard Ofshe and Richard Leo found that, "while the nominal purpose of a lie detection test is to diagnose the subject as truthful or deceptive, the primary function of any lie detector test administered during an interrogation is to induce a confession" (1997a, p. 1036). Rather than simply saying "I don't believe you" and accusing the suspect of lying, the polygraph enables an interrogator to say that the machine "indicates that your answer was deceptive" or that "you're holding something back" or "you're not telling us the whole truth." It is no longer just the interrogator who is accusing the suspect of lying. Now, a seemingly objective piece of technology is calling the suspect a liar. The polygraph can sometimes re-energize a stalled interrogation. Even in cases in which there is no strong incriminating evidence, the polygraph enables interrogators—through technological sleight-of-hand—to point to seemingly scientific evidence that the suspect is guilty.

HOW JURORS RESPOND TO POLYGRAPH EVIDENCE

When juries are permitted to hear about the results of polygraph tests, it appears they generally find the results persuasive. Consider the case of Buzz Fay. Fay was released from prison after serving two years of a life sentence. He was sent to prison for aggravated murder, convicted of shooting Fred Ery during the robbery of a liquor store. After being shot, Mr. Ery was rushed to a hospital, given pain medication, and, while still conscious, asked about who shot him. While suffering from loss of blood and dying in a hospital room, Mr. Ery first replied, "It looked like Buzz, but it couldn't have been." But later, just before death, he said, "Buzz did it." The police realized their case was weak—there was no physical evidence implicating Fay, only the contradictory testimony of a dying, sedated man. So they made Fay's attorney an offer: They would drop all charges if Fay passed a lie-detector test. Of course, everyone would need to agree in advance that the results would be admissible in court. Because Fay was innocent, the offer seemed like a quick way to put the matter to rest. But Fay failed the test. Then he failed a second test. Fay was convicted by a jury and sent to prison primarily on the results of his polygraph test (Cimerman, 1981).

This is not the only case in which the results of the lie detector appear to have changed the outcome of a criminal trial. Although there is little systematic research on how much weight jurors attach to polygraph evidence, the few studies available suggest that jurors take such evidence seriously. For example, in one study, mock jurors were presented with the case of a mentally disturbed defendant who had a history of confessing to crimes he did not commit. Even though testimony by psychiatrists indicated that the defendant was prone to false confessions, 52% of mock jurors voted to convict him of murder. However, when testimony about the results of a lie-detector test showed that the defendant had lied about committing the crime, only 28% voted to convict. When the researchers added a statement by the judge, that the polygraph was "only 80% accurate," 40% voted not guilty (Cavoukian, 1979). In another study, 20 law students who reviewed the relevant evidence found a defendant "not guilty." They were later given an opportunity to change their verdict when provided with information that the polygraph is 99.5% accurate and that the defendant had failed the test. Given this additional information, 85% of the mock jurors changed their minds and voted guilty (Lykken, 1998). Finally, survey research shows that experts in psychophysiology who are knowledgeable about polygraphing are far more skeptical about the results of polygraph testing than are members of the general public (see Figure 3.4).

Research on this topic is quite limited and more research is clearly needed. What is clear is that several

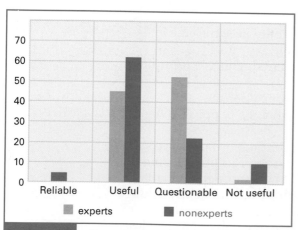

FIGURE 3.4   Percentages of experts' and nonexperts' opinions about the usefulness of polygraph test results as an indicator of subject's truthfulness (*Myers, B., Latter, R., & Abdollahi-Arena, M.K. (2006). The court of public opinion: Lay perceptions of polygraph testing. Law and Human Behavior, 30, 509–523.*).

people have been sent to prison because of polygraph results and that mock jurors can be influenced by the results of a lie detector test. Whether jurors are swayed by polygraph evidence is likely to depend on several factors: how persuasive the examiner is when testifying in court, the amount and persuasiveness of rebuttal testimony, the strength of other evidence, the sophistication of jurors, and the judge's instructions to the jury.

 ## LOOKING FOR LIES IN THE BRAIN

The polygraph is a stress-based system of lie detection. Because it monitors physiological signs of arousal, it can be fooled by an emotionless liar or an anxious truth-teller. In an attempt to move beyond the polygraph, several researchers have adapted technologies for studying the brain for the purpose of detecting lies. These newer methods look at brain activity during truthful and deceptive responses.

fMRI

In 2000, Daniel Langleben and his colleagues began a program of research using **functional magnetic resonance imaging (fMRI)** of the human brain to understand lying. The fMRI yields a video image of the brain in action. The "action" of the brain is captured by taking a photographic image of how much oxygen is being used in every part of the brain at a given point in time. Using current technology, these measurements can be taken about every 2 seconds. These spaced photos of the brain are then strung together to form a moving image of brain activity. This procedure allows scientists to see which regions and structures in the brain are most active when performing different kinds of tasks.

Participants in an fMRI study of lie detection must lie flat on their back in a machine that is about the size of a compact car. They are strapped in so that their heads and bodies are perfectly still. In one study (Langleben, 2008), subjects were told to lie about whether they had a particular playing card (the five of clubs) in their pocket. Photos of playing cards flashed on a screen above the faces of the subjects, and the subjects pressed a button indicating "no" when they did not have the card. Even when the five of clubs flashed on the screen, subjects were instructed to press the "no" button. In variations of this basic experimental procedure, sometimes subjects were given two cards to hold, and given the choice of whether to lie or tell the truth about the cards they were holding. The basic research question was, "Do lying and truth-telling produce differences in brain activity that are detectable by the fMRI?" The answer seemed to be "yes." A few regions of the brain, for example, the prefrontal cortex (the area right behind the forehead) and the parietal cortex (near the rear of the brain) were, on average, more activated when subjects were lying. These findings raise some intriguing possibilities. Perhaps because the prefrontal cortex is associated with higher forms of reasoning, its

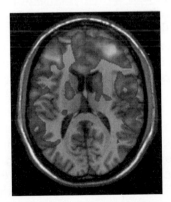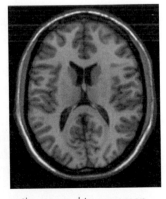

Did you steal the watch? The question, posed to a woman who stole a watch as part of an experiment, produced the MRI image on the left. The image on the right was taken when she was asked about stealing a ring (she did not steal a ring). (A: COURTESY STEVEN J. LAKEN, PH.D. IMAGE BY ANDREW KOZEL AND MARK GEORGE MEDICAL UNIVERSITY OF SOUTH CAROLINA. B: COURTESY STEVEN J. LAKEN, PH.D. IMAGE BY ANDREW KOZEL AND MARK GEORGE MEDICAL UNIVERSITY OF SOUTH CAROLINA)

activation during lying reflects the greater cognitive work necessary to tell a lie; and perhaps because the parietal cortex is associated with physiological arousal, its activation during lying reflects the increased anxiety produced by telling a lie.

In an interesting extension of these fMRI lie-detection studies, Giorgio Ganis and his colleagues had 10 subjects tell either a spontaneous lie or a rehearsed lie. The subjects were interviewed about a notable experience at work or on vacation. For some experiences, they were given a chance to rehearse a false, alternative version of their experience. Next, strapped into an fMRI scanner, they answered questions deceptively, sometimes with spontaneously produced lies and sometimes with previously memorized lies. Their results confirmed that the two types of lies produced very different patterns of activation in the brain. For example, whereas spontaneous lies were associated with brain regions implicated in visual imagery, rehearsed lies activated areas associated with the retrieval of episodic memories (Ganis, Kosslyn, Stose, Thompson, & Yurgelun-Todd, 2003). That is, different types of lying seem to produce different patterns of brain excitation. Even when we peer into the brain—the starting point of physiological reactions—we find that lying is not just one simple thing.

Although it is tempting to focus on the lie-detection potential of dazzling new technologies, the limitations of research findings need to be fully acknowledged. First, although the fMRI is an exciting technological advance, it is far from perfect. It is not portable, it is expensive, and it requires a motionless subject who must remain silent. At present, it is only able to take snapshots of the brain no more rapidly than every 2 seconds. Given the speed of neural transmissions, that is a long way from a real-time readout of the brain in action. In addition, the studies themselves have limitations. Pushing "yes" or "no" buttons in response to relatively trivial questions is quite different from high-consequence lying about a serious crime in an effort to avoid prison. Because the experimental procedure is cumbersome and expensive, nearly all fMRI studies have examined only 10 to 20 people. Although average lie–truth differences in brain activity were observed in the study group as a whole, findings are far too varied and weak to isolate deception at the individual level (Kozel, Padget, & George, 2004; Langleben, Willard, & Moriarty, 2012). Put differently, there is large variation in the areas and combination of areas activated by lies in individual subjects, and no one subject showed a strong, consistent activation pattern while lying (Spence et al., 2004).

Although scientists and legal scholars have consistently argued that fMRi lie detection should not yet be admitted in court (Langleben & Moriarty, 2013), several for-profit companies have been pressing to enter the courtroom. In 2010, a federal court in Tennessee excluded fMRI expert testimony about a defendant's veracity (*United States v. Semrau*, 2010). The defense had sought to introduce the testimony of Dr. Steven Laken, CEO of *Cephos*, a private company that uses fMRI for "lie detection and truth verification." Dr. Laken was going to testify at trial that an fMRI test had revealed the defendant was truthful when he denied committing Medicare fraud. *Cephos* describes itself as "the world-class leader in providing fMRI lie detection" and claims, "over 97% accuracy in blind clinical testing." Other companies now offer similar lie-detection services. *No Lie MRI, Inc.* claims that their technology "represents the first and only direct measure of truth verification and lie detection in human history!"

EEG

Another approach to seeing lies in the brain relies on the decades-old technology of the **electroencephalogram (EEG).** Despite its age, it has an important advantage over the fMRI: Instead of taking a reading every 2 seconds, the EEG is able to read neural impulses continuously in milliseconds. Although the fMRI is better able to locate *where* the activity of lying might occur in the brain, the EEG is better able to tell precisely *when* a change in activity occurs. The EEG monitors brain activity by means of electrodes pressed to the scalp. In experimental research, brain waves of the subject are typically measured using a stretchy netted cap embedded with more than 100 dime-sized electrodes. Readings are taken of event-related potentials (ERPs)—electrical patterns that arise in response to an event or stimulus. Of particular interest is the P-300 wave, a wave pattern that indicates electrical activity in the brain about 300 milliseconds after a stimulus is shown to a person being tested for deception.

In a study by Jennifer Vendemia and her colleagues, student volunteers put on the electrode-studded cap and watched a computer screen that flashed obviously true or false statements (e.g., "Grass is green" or "Mickey Mouse shot Abraham Lincoln" or "A snake has 13 legs"). The volunteers were instructed to respond with either "true" or "false," depending on the color of the letters in which the statement was written (Vendemia, Buzan, Green & Schillaci, 2006). The researchers were able to detect a change in the brain waves between 250 to 600 milliseconds after the volunteers were presented with a statement that required them to lie. Researchers speculate that this fluctuation in brain waves represents the intent to suppress a truthful response and replace it with a lie.

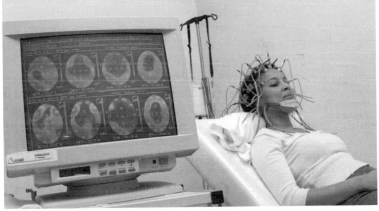

Person wearing electrode cap for EEG recording
(AJ Photo/Science Source)

Based on the EEG research, a psychologist named Lawrence Farwell is now marketing a lie-detection technique he has dubbed "brain fingerprinting" (see www.brainwavescience.com). This technique is essentially the guilty knowledge test described earlier in this chapter. But instead of using a polygraph, Farwell uses P-300 waves to judge whether a subject is lying. This technique has received enormous media attention and more than a million dollars in support from the CIA. *Time* magazine even included Dr. Farwell in its list of the "next wave of 100 Innovators who may be the Picassos or Einsteins of the 21st century." The "brain fingerprinting" method shares the limitations of the guilty knowledge test described earlier in this chapter. In addition, Farwell's claims of accuracy have not been confirmed by other scientists (Rosenfeld, 2011; Wolpe, Foster, & Langleben, 2005). The statistical method used to analyze the EEG data is kept secret, so other researchers cannot independently evaluate its validity. Here, as with the polygraph, there is a tension between those who want to exploit new technologies quickly for financial profit and those who want open, scientific evaluations of accuracy.

 ## TELLING LIES FROM THE EYES

We are less likely to trust someone with "shifty eyes," and facial flushing or blushing is likely to make us suspicious. One of the newer lie-detection methods tracks the tiny, subtle heat changes in the skin near the eyes. These shifts in temperature are caused by increased blood flow to capillaries in the skin of the face. A team of researchers from the Mayo Clinic and Honeywell Laboratories have developed a system that uses **high-definition infrared thermal imaging** to monitor minis-cule shifts in the heat of the human face. The changes are displayed on a computer screen, with the hot zones shown in red. Like the polygraph, the theory underlying this method is that lying will produce arousal and this arousal will cause a nearly instantaneous physiological change—in this case, warming around the eyes. In a small-scale test of this technique, 20 volunteers were randomly assigned to one of two groups. Eight subjects were instructed to stab a mannequin, steal $20 from it, and then deny having committed the mock crime. The thermal-imaging system cor-rectly identified 6 of the 8 subjects who were lying, and 11 of the 12 subjects who were telling the truth. These same subjects were also polygraphed. That test correctly identified 6 of the 8 mock criminals, but correctly identified only 8 of the 12 innocent subjects (Levine, Pavlidis, & Everhardt, 2002). Unfortunately, more recent research indicates that thermal imaging misclassifies too many truthful airline passengers as liars because of anxiety not caused by lying (Warmelink et al., 2011).

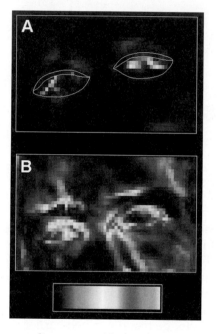

High-resolution thermal images of the face of a "guilty" subject. Images were obtained before lying (top image) and after lying (lower image) in response to the question, "Did you steal the $20?" White oval lines indicate eye contours. (COURTESY OF IOANNIS PAVLIDIS, ECKHARD-PFEIFFER PROFESSOR, COMPUTATIONAL PHYSIOLOGY LAB, UNIVERSITY OF HOUSTON)

Still other forms of lie detection and **credibility assessment** (the new catch phrase for lie detection) are being developed, often in collaboration with the National Center for Credibility Assessment (NCCA) located at Fort Jackson Army base in South Carolina. Substantial U.S. government funds have been allocated to the development of new lie-detection methods and technologies the government hopes will eventually prove useful in criminal or terrorist investigations. For example, **eye movement memory assessment** tracks visual attention to a scene based on eye move-ment, scanning path, pupil dilation, and gaze fix-ation to help assess guilty knowledge (Cook et al., 2012). Another technique under development—**laser Doppler vibrometry**—might eventually be capable of monitoring physiological stress (e.g., changes in respiration, heart rate, muscle trem-ors) through means of a near-infrared light beam aimed at the neck of a subject a few hundred feet away. Of course, any new device that can be used at a distance, without the awareness of the person being investigated, opens up new uses (e.g., security screening at airports and public events), as well as new invasions of privacy.

▶ IN CONCLUSION

As brain- and body-monitoring technology advances in the coming decades, it will create significant challenges for the law. Faced with such technologies, we will need to define the boundaries of **cognitive privacy**. When, for example, would we be able to refuse to be hooked up to a machine that might peer into our brains and see our lies? What level of reasonable suspicion or probable cause would be deemed suffi-cient to compel us to submit to such a machine? Would the use of such devices vio-late our constitutional right against self-incrimination? Should our thoughts—even our deceptive ones—be beyond the reach of the law? And, under what conditions and to what extent should the evidence revealed by such machines be admissible in court?

Use of the polygraph has been controversial for decades, and newer technologies have generated new controversies. What is not controversial is that small, subtle physiological changes can be detected and recorded by sophisticated measuring equipment. Each year, advances in technology make such measurements more precise and more numerous. Blood pressure was the first measure to be touted as a means of detecting deception, and heart rate, respiration, and skin moisture were later added to the list. Technological advances now make it possible to monitor modulations in the voice, dilation of the pupils, tension in the facial muscles, and neural activity in the brain. It is conceivable that more sensitive physiological measures will eventually permit us to tell when someone is lying. However, the enduring problem is that there appears to be no distinctive set of physiological responses exclusively associated with lying. There is no unique tone of voice, no distinctive rhythm to the heartbeat, no precise change in blood pressure, and no signature pattern of neural excitation in the brain. Although the technology of physiological monitoring is likely to become more accurate and impressive, if there is no clear signal to detect, these advances cannot produce a fully trustworthy method of detecting lies. It may turn out to be impossible for technology to uncover "the truth, the whole truth, and nothing but the truth."

► DISCUSSION AND CRITICAL THINKING QUESTIONS

1. How much does the subjective judgment of the polygraph examiner influence the interpretation of the polygraph test? Could you design a system to eliminate or reduce the amount of subjectivity in interpreting polygraph results?

2. Should employers be allowed to polygraph potential employees to decide whom to hire? Should employers be allowed to use the polygraph to help find out who is responsible for employee theft?

3. Can you tell when someone is lying to you? How? Do you think police interrogators are better than most people at detecting lies? What are the consequences if police interrogators are not especially good at lie detection?

4. Is it more important to reduce false positive or false negative errors in lie detection? What are the consequences of each type of error?

5. Should the results of polygraph exams or other lie-detection tests be admissible in court? Would it be possible for jurors to give proper weight to such testimony if experts who support and oppose the use of such evidence were allowed to testify?

► KEY TERMS

cognitive privacy (p. 68)
confirmation bias
  (p. 50)
comparison question
  (p. 53)
comparison question test
  (CQT) (p. 53)
countermeasures
  (p. 55)

credibility assessment
  (p. 68)
criteria-based content
  analysis (CBCA) (p. 62)
electroencephalogram
  (EEG) (p. 66)
eye movement memory
  assessment (p. 68)
false positive (p. 53)

functional magnetic
  resonance imaging
  (fMRI) (p. 65)
guilty knowledge test
  (GKT) (p. 59)
high-definition infrared
  thermal imaging (p. 68)
laser Doppler vibrometry
  (p. 68)

liar's stereotype (p. 49)
mock crimes (p. 55)
polygraph (p. 50)
relevant–irrelevant test
  (RIT) (p. 53)
trial by ordeal (p. 47)
unscored buffer (p. 60)
wizards (p. 62)

4

The Psychology of Forensic Identification: DNA, Fingerprints, and Physical Trace Evidence

On March 11, 2004, a series of bombs exploded in Madrid's subway system. One-hundred-ninety-one people were killed and 1460 were injured. In the hours following the attack, police discovered a blue plastic bag filled with detonators inside a van. That van was parked near a subway station where the bombs seem to have been planted. Spanish police managed to lift a few fingerprints from the blue bag, and digital images of these prints were sent to the FBI crime lab in the United States. Using its "integrated, automated, fingerprint identification system" (IAFIS), the FBI compared the prints from the bag to those in its computerized database of more than 200 million prints. The computer identified 20 possible matching prints. The fourth closest match belonged to the left index finger of Brandon Mayfield, an attorney living in Beaverton, Oregon. His fingerprints were in the database because he had served in the Army. A senior FBI fingerprint examiner looked at the prints and declared that Mayfield's print and the print from the Madrid bombing were, "a 100% match." That examiner then asked two other FBI examiners to look at the prints. Both agreed that the prints were a clear match.

Mayfield was put under covert surveillance, his phone was tapped, and his office was secretly searched. They learned that he was married to an Egyptian woman, that he had recently converted to Islam, that he regularly attended a mosque, and that he had served as the lawyer for a man who had been convicted of trying to join the Taliban. These facts strengthened the FBI's conviction that Mayfield had been involved in the bombing. Like a jigsaw puzzle, all the pieces seemed to fit together. But 10 days after Mayfield's prints were transmitted to the forensic division of the Spanish national police, the Spanish informed the FBI of their conclusion: The fingerprints did not match and were "conclusively negative." This dissenting opinion from the Spanish police did little to weaken the FBI's confidence. Certain that they had the right man, FBI agents went to Mayfield's office, handcuffed him, and escorted him to jail. During pretrial hearings, the fingerprints were examined by an independent expert who agreed with the FBI: There was a "100% certainty" that the fingerprints matched. Later, on the same day that the expert confirmed the FBI's conclusion, Spanish police announced that they had identified the fingerprint on the blue detonator bag as belonging to Ouhnane Daoud, an Algerian man living in Spain. Four days later, the case against Brandon Mayfield was dismissed.

How was it that the premier law enforcement agency in the country—the FBI—using its much vaunted, state-of-the-art computerized fingerprint system came to such a mistaken conclusion in such a high-profile case? And why was this error not swiftly discovered and reversed, except by a police department in Spain? What role did Mayfield's religious affiliation play in the accusations against him? Why did three experienced FBI examiners and one independent examiner not express any doubt about the identification? Although the answers to these questions are not entirely clear, it is clear that many forms of physical identification—including fingerprints—are not immune to the biases that shape the psychological processes of perception, judgment, and decision making. In this chapter, we explore how biases in cognition and research methods can lead to identification errors and we explore how such errors might be avoided. ◀

TRACE EVIDENCE IN CONTEXT

Forensic science is typically defined as the collection, analysis, and interpretation of physical evidence. **Forensic identification** is the process of linking a piece of physical trace evidence to an individual, usually a criminal suspect.

It may be impossible to commit a crime without leaving behind some kind of physical trace. Even an illegal transfer of funds leaves behind an electronic trail. People who commit burglary, rape, or murder are likely to deposit some form of physical evidence at the crime scene—tire prints from a car, sole prints from a shoe, fabric from clothes, marks from a tool used to break into a home, fingerprints left on surfaces at the crime scene, perhaps even bite marks on a slice of pizza or the skin of the victim. There might also be biological evidence—blood, saliva, semen, skin cells—that allow for the possibility of DNA identification. Traces are not only left behind, tiny bits of trace evidence may also be carried away when the criminal leaves the scene. Decades ago, Paul Kirk expressed the enthusiasm many investigators felt about the importance of trace evidence:

> Wherever he steps, whatever he touches, whatever he leaves, even unconsciously, will serve as silent witness against him. Not only his fingerprints or his footprints, but his hair, the fibers from his clothing, the glass he breaks, the tool mark he leaves, the paint he scratches, the blood or semen he deposits or collects . . . . This is evidence that does not forget. It is not confused by the excitement of the moment. It is not absent because human witnesses are, it is factual evidence. Physical evidence cannot be wrong, it cannot perjure itself; it cannot be wholly absent, only its interpretation can err. (Kirk, 1953)

But how can we know that a piece of trace evidence came from one specific defendant? We must be able to find some measurable quality that is unique for every person. This search for a foolproof means of distinguishing one human from all other humans began more than a century ago. The first identification technique hailed as scientific was called **anthropometry.** It was devised by Alphonse Bertillon, a French police investigator, in 1883. Anthropometry required taking 11 measurements including left foot length, cranium size, height, length of the arm, and length of the middle finger (see Figure 4.1). His system was used for more than two decades until it was abandoned in favor of fingerprints. This shift occurred in 1903, when a new prisoner in Fort Leavenworth prison was found to have nearly identical measurements to an inmate already in that prison. Although the two prisoners could not be distinguished on the basis of their 11 Bertillon measurements, their fingerprints were discernibly different (Saferstein, 2010).

Bertillon was a pioneer in the field of **biometrics**—the identification of an individual person based on measurable anatomical traits. Modern biometric systems attempt to identify people based on recognition of distinctive patterns in a person's fingerprints, iris, retina, or face. (See Table 4.1 to learn more about the properties of modern biometric traits.)

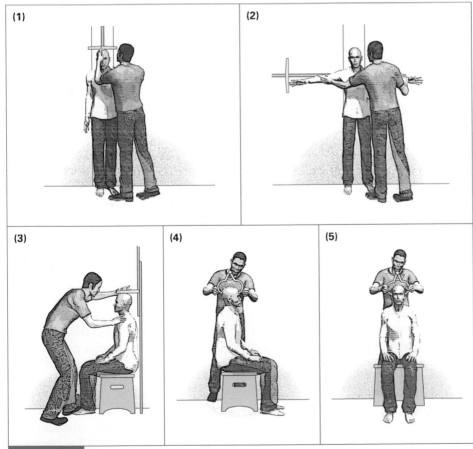

FIGURE 4.1   Chart illustrating five of the Bertillon measurements

MEASURES AND MEANING IN FORENSIC IDENTIFICATION

First, some basic terms and procedures. Forensic identification usually rests on a comparison between two samples. The first sample may include **trace evidence** *left at* the scene of the crime (e.g., fingerprints, hair, skin cells, fibers from clothes), or trace evidence *transported from* the scene of the crime (e.g., carpet fibers, hair or blood from a victim). Samples of the trace evidence are then compared to samples taken from a suspect or a tool used by the suspect. If that comparison reveals that the features of the two samples are substantially similar and that there are no substantial, unexplainable differences, the two samples are said to come from a "common source" and the forensic scientist is said to have made a **source attribution** (Houck & Siegel, 2010). A scientist might then report that the samples are a "match." An even stronger term, **individualization,** is sometimes used to express the conclusion that a trace found at the crime scene came from this source to the exclusion of all other sources in the world (e.g., that a fingerprint came from the left index finger of the defendant). If the analyses reveal substantial inconsistent features between the samples, a scientist might report that the suspect or defendant is **excluded** as the source (e.g., that a fingerprint came from someone else). Finally, if the trace evidence is incomplete, or contaminated, or impossible to analyze with precision, an analyst will conclude that the comparison is **inconclusive.**

Scientists who examine physical traces distinguish between class characteristics and individual characteristics. *Class characteristics* are features that are common to a general class or category of objects (e.g., a pattern of tread shared by a particular style of women's Nike running shoes). *Individual characteristics* are features presumably unique to a single object (e.g., the specific scrapes, scars, and wear patterns on a suspect's running shoe). It is these distinctive characteristics that have the potential to establish uniqueness. While it may be helpful to know that a defendant in a burglary case owns a style of running shoes that left a print at scene of the crime, it is far more helpful to know that the prints of the shoe found at the crime scene perfectly match the marks and scrapes on the soles of the defendant's shoes. Consequently, the goal of the forensic scientist is to find trace evidence that could have come from one and only one person.

 ## WHEN DOES A TRACE "MATCH" A SOURCE?

Many forms of forensic evidence have been used widely in the courts for decades only to be later abandoned when their accuracy has been found to be lacking. For example, it was not until 2004 that the use of bullet matching evidence fell out of favor with the courts. The technique had been used in thousands of trials, nearly always on behalf of the prosecution. For more than 30 years, the FBI and other law enforcement agencies had offered testimony that bullets recovered from a crime scene could be matched to other bullets found in possession of a suspect or defendant. This matching was accomplished by means of chemical analysis of the composition of the bullets (i.e., the relative proportion of tin, silver, arsenic, copper, bismuth, and zinc). The assumption—and it was little more than an assumption—was that only bullets from the same box would be extremely similar in their trace elements, and that bullets from different boxes would be quite dissimilar. However, a study by the National Research Council (2004) found that not only could bullets from different boxes have nearly identical chemical profiles, but that the chemical composition of bullets from

MODERN BIOMETRICS

Terrorism threats and technological advancements have spurred rapid development in the field of biometrics. Many of your physical characteristics can be scanned and analyzed to verify that you are really you. Some biometrics (e.g., the geometry and distinctive characteristics of your face, and your distinctive way of walking) can be recorded from a distance using a high resolution camera. For instance, this can allow police to identify you in a crowd in a public place. Other biometrics, such as fingerprints and iris scans must be taken at close range. Some strengths and weaknesses of four common biometric identifiers are summarized in the table below.

TABLE 4.1

Biometric Traits

Property	Fingerprint	Face	Iris	Voice
Distinctive	High	Low	High	Low
Permanence	High	Medium	High	Low
How well trait can be sensed	Medium	High	Medium	Medium
Speed and cost efficiency	High	Low	High	Low
Willingness of people to have trait used	Medium	High	Medium	High
Difficulty of spoofing the trait	High	Low	High	Low

Source: *Adapted from "How The Metrics Measure Up" in "Beyond Fingerprinting," by Anil K. Jain and Sharath Pankanti, Scientific American Inc., Sept. 2008.*

the same box could have significantly different chemical profiles. Further, because as many as 35 million bullets can be manufactured at a time, chemically similar bullets might be found in boxes spread throughout the world.

Sometimes, the courts have allowed pseudoscience to enter the courtroom under the cover of science. For example, handwriting analysis has occasionally been presented as evidence. Analyses of the size, slant, and shape of letters have led handwriting experts to conclude that a handwritten note—such as "this is a robbery, put all your money in the briefcase" or "we have your child, we will contact you with our demands"—was written by a particular person. Unfortunately, there is no compelling evidence that such experts can decode handwriting with a high degree of accuracy. Rates of error for handwriting vary from 40% to 97% (Mnookin et. al., 2011; Risinger, 2002). A big part of the problem is that, unlike biological or chemical traces, handwriting is dynamic. A particular finger will leave the same print in March as it leaves in May, but handwriting may vary dramatically over that time period. In addition, suspects might try to disguise their writing, a sprain or injury to any one of several muscles or bones in the hand may cause writing to change, and the use of alcohol or drugs can influence the appearance of writing. While signatures may be written so frequently that they are written in a distinctive, habitual style, most criminals do not sign their notes. And many of us do not hand write much except our signatures. Instead, we type—into laptops, desktops, and handheld devices.

A final complication in matching a trace to a source is that many cases require conclusions about rare events and unusual materials. For example, the footprint of a murderer may be obscured because he stepped in maple syrup that oozed across a kitchen floor, or spackle that was on the floor of a construction site. Because there is little research on how syrup or spackle might distort footprints, a forensic scientist would need to mount a minor research program to generate evidence that would enable her to make an accurate identification.

COMMUNICATING THE SIMILARITY OF A TRACE AND A SOURCE

Based on laboratory analysis of a physical trace found at the crime scene, forensic scientists must reach a conclusion about whether that trace matches a particular criminal suspect or defendant on trial. Usually, the scientist must then describe the nature and certainty of that match to a jury and a judge. William Thompson and Simon Cole (2007) have described four ways in which forensic identification experts communicate their findings to jurors and other relevant audiences. The first three types of testimony express matches between class characteristics, while the fourth type expresses a match between a trace and a specific, individual source.

Perhaps the simplest approach is a nonstatistical **qualitative statement** of the strength of a match. This is a relatively subjective statement that a match is weak or moderate or strong. For example, the organization that studies the analysis of bite marks as a way of identifying criminals (the American Board of Forensic Odontology, ABFO) recommended that testimony be offered in "six degrees of certainty" about whether a suspect is the source of the bite mark: (1) inconclusive, (2) suspect is not the source, (3) improbable that the suspect is the source, (4) possible that the bite mark came from the suspect, (5) probable that the bite mark came from the suspect, and (6) source attribution to a reasonable medical certainty. Although the keywords in this formulation—"inconclusive" and "probable" and "medical certainty"—lend an air of scientific legitimacy to bite mark testimony, there are no precise standards for deciding when a match moves up or down a degree on the six-point scale. The decision about the degree of match is subjective and the distinctions between degrees are rhetorical rather than mathematical (Page, Taylor, & Blenkin, 2011). Further, there is no compelling evidence that two experts looking at the same evidence would reach the same conclusion about which qualitative statement should be used (Page, Taylor, & Blenkin, 2013).

A second approach—**simple match**—also does not make use of statistical statements. The expert merely says that the trace and the source share certain class characteristics. For example, a tiny shard of glass found in the defendant's car might be said to "match" or be "consistent with" the glass from a broken bedroom window in the victim's home. Such simple match statements are not accompanied by the types of probability statements that would be needed to discern the certainty of the match. It would be useful to know, for example, that the type of glass is used in 90% of bedroom windows, or that the type of glass was not used in residential windows until 2006. Such statements would help jurors to estimate how likely it is that the glass fragment in the car came from the particular broken window in the victim's home. Unfortunately, for many types of evidence, this type of statistical data has never been compiled and is not part of expert testimony.

The more detailed **match plus statistics** statement incorporates statistics that place the match in context. Typically, such statistics give information about how rare or common a particular matching characteristic is in the relevant population. If the characteristics shared by the trace and the defendant are statistically rare, they are more informative. Because red hair is rare and black hair is common, a red hair found at the crime scene carries more weight to incriminate a red-haired defendant than a black hair does for a black-haired defendant. Similarly, a crime scene print from a size-9 men's shoe is less informative and incriminating than a print from a size-14 shoe. In addition, the population of interest must be taken into account—a red hair at a crime scene in Tokyo will be more damning to the red-haired defendant than the same red hair found at a crime scene in Dublin. Unfortunately, statistical data on the frequency of source characteristics are usually limited or imprecise.

The fourth and final way of expressing a match is called "individualization." Individualization requires that scientists are able to say that the match is so detailed and perfect that the trace could have only come from one person. In some areas, experts routinely assert claims of individualization. When testifying about tool mark impressions, experts have been advised by their professional association (the Association of Firearms and Tool Mark Examiners) to phrase their findings as fitting into one of four categories: (1) trace is unsuitable for microscopic comparison; (2) trace characteristics eliminate the tool as a source; (3) some agreement between the trace and the source; and (4) identification—the high level of agreement between trace and source indicates that the mark was produced by a specific tool.

Surprisingly, professional guidelines require that fingerprint examiners limit their testimony to only one of three conclusions: inconclusive, suspect excluded as source of the print, and individualization (Scientific Working Group on Friction Ridge Analysis, Study and Technology, 2012, 2013). Indeed, the International Association for Identification (IAI)—the primary professional organization for latent print examiners—warns that any examiner who offers testimony about, "possible, probable, or likely friction ridge identification shall be deemed to be engaged in conduct unbecoming" (International Association for Identification, 2004). While this policy may have been intended to restrain experts from providing testimony unless a match is certain, it has also had the regrettable unintended consequence of creating the false perception that fingerprint evidence is absolute and nonprobabalistic (Koehler & Saks, 2010). In addition, the policy may also seduce examiners into exaggerating the certainty of their conclusions, so that they claim 100% certainty of a match even when the actual certainty is significantly lower (Champod & Evett, 2001). In response to a series of scientific critiques of the use of the term "individualization" by fingerprint examiners, the IAI recently made a minor concession to the scientific community by modifying its official definition of the term. Although they still use the term, they changed its definition:

> SWGFAST recognizes that individualization has been used within the latent print community to mean "to the exclusion of all others." The ability of a latent print examiner to individualize a single latent impression, with the implication that they have definitely excluded all other humans in the world, is not supported by research and was removed from SWGFAST's definition of individualization. (Document #103, Individualization/Identification, swgfast.org, 2013).

Many scholars have argued that one of the most useful bits of statistical information would be the error rate of the particular type of evidence match. Put differently, it would be very helpful for jurors to know the answer to the following question: How often are forensic scientists wrong when they decide there is a match? Especially relevant is the *false positive rate*—the probability that an expert will conclude that a match exists when, in fact, there is no match (see Chapters 3 and 14 for a fuller discussion of types of error). A false positive is critically important for the legal system because it might lead to the wrongful conviction of an innocent defendant. Unfortunately, because researchers have not been granted access to the appropriate data, the false positive rate is very difficult to calculate for most types of trace evidence. Part of the problem is that forensic examiners are reluctant to participate in studies that might enable researchers to calculate false positive rates. Those examiners have little to gain and much to lose by participating in research on rates of error. Making an error on a test, or exposing a high error rate might harm a professional's career prospects or damage the reputation of the field of forensic identification.

Some judges have excluded data on false positives on the grounds that such data are not useful because they do not have direct relevance to a particular defendant (National Research Council, Committee on Identifying the Needs of the Forensic Science Community, 2009). That is, judges have argued that knowing that a certain type of matching technique for a particular type of trace evidence results in a false positive match __% of the time is not helpful in deciding whether a false positive match occurred in the particular case at hand (Saks, 2010). A related problem is that judges often allow professional experience to substitute for a solid scientific foundation. Experience becomes the foundation of courtroom testimony (see Chapter 1). Therefore, instead of summarizing research findings that support a statement, experts might rely on statements such as, "The basis of my opinion is my 20 years of experience as a forensic examiner." The usefulness of that experience is impossible for jurors to assess in a meaningful way.

Finally, many scholars have criticized the very use of the word "match" as misleading and prejudicial. In common parlance, use of this word implies a nearly perfect correspondence between two objects or patterns. When describing the degree of similarity between a trace and a source, it may be more objective to use terms such as "consistent with" or "similar to" instead of "match."

MEASUREMENT RELIABILITY AND VALIDITY

How do we decide whether we should place our confidence in a particular measure? Whether we are discussing a psychometric test that attempts to measure intelligence or a biometric test that attempts to differentiate fingerprints, the same basic quality standards apply. To be considered scientifically meaningful, a measure must possess both reliability and validity.

Reliability refers to the consistency or repeatability of a measure or observation. Two forms of reliability are especially relevant to the analysis of trace evidence: Test–retest reliability and inter-rater reliability. **Test–retest reliability** (sometimes referred to as temporal consistency) is high if a measure yields the same results over time. For example, if we measure the height of a barefoot 30-year-old female every month for a year, we would expect that our measurement instrument (a tape measure) would yield the same height estimate month after month. **Inter-rater reliability** (sometimes referred to as "inter-observer agreement") is the degree to which two or more observers or analysts independently arrive at the same measurement. If two people who have no contact with one another measure the height of our hypothetical barefoot 30-year-old, they should both come up with the same number. If one says the woman is 64 inches tall and the other says the woman is 68 inches tall, something is wrong with one or both of the tape measures, or one or both of the measurers. These same standards apply to forensic identification. If asked to determine whether two fingerprints match, an examiner should reach the same conclusion this month as she reached last month (test–retest reliability). And, if we ask an examiner in another state to tell us whether those same two fingerprints match, he should reach the same conclusion as the first examiner (inter-rater reliability).

Measurement validity refers to whether or not a technique measures what it is supposed to measure. A measurement technique may be reliable without being valid (e.g., if the lines on my measuring tape are too close together, it will reliably, time after time, yield a height estimate that is 2 inches too tall). However, a technique cannot be valid without being reliable. Validity is not an either-or, present-or-absent quality. Measures can be more or less valid, and no measure is perfectly valid. In forensic identification it is crucial to ask whether a technique like hair or fingerprint analysis truly measures whether one hair or one print matches another. Put differently, are the identification measures and procedures accurate enough to differentiate a particular print from the prints of other people? Reliability and validity are pillars of scientific measurement. A lack of objectively valid and reliable measures allows subjectivity and inaccuracy to seep into the identification process.

THE SCIENTIFIC FOUNDATION OF FORENSIC IDENTIFICATION: DNA AND FINGERPRINTS

There is enormous variability in the strength of the science buttressing each form of forensic identification. For some identification techniques, there is substantial research demonstrating validity. For other techniques, there is little research supporting their validity. Without a solid scientific foundation, we cannot have confidence in the procedures used to determine the value of a match for identifying a criminal (Saks & Koehler, 2005). Forensic identification procedures can be arrayed along a continuum ranging from entirely subjective to entirely objective. We begin with a description of DNA identification because it is the most objective (though not perfectly objective) form of identification evidence. It can therefore serve as a sort of standard to which other less reliable forms of forensic identification can aspire.

DNA

In 1953, James Watson and Francis Crick published a paper that presented one of the great scientific breakthroughs of the twentieth century: the molecular structure of **DNA (deoxyribonucleic acid).** It is now widely understood that miniscule, tightly coiled strands of DNA carry the genetic instructions for all living cells. The burgeoning field of biotechnology is built on this foundational insight. However, it took more than 30 years for scientists to recognize the forensic potential of DNA. In the late 1980s, Alec Jeffreys and his colleagues discovered that some segments of DNA are unique to individuals, and that, ". . . these hypervariable DNA patterns offer the promise of a truly individual-specific identification system" (Jeffreys, 1993). In 1988, DNA was introduced as evidence in U.S. courts (*People v. Wesley,* 1988). The largest, most frequently used DNA database in the world is the Combined DNA Index System (CODIS) maintained by the FBI.

When biological evidence in the form of blood, saliva, semen, or skin cells is available, DNA can be extracted and then analyzed using computerized measuring instruments. These instruments detect genetic profiles that are visually displayed as genetic characteristics or **alleles** at several locations or **loci** on the DNA strand (Thompson, Ford, Doom, Raymer, & Krane, 2003). Every person has two alleles at each genetic locus—the first is inherited from the maternal side and the second is inherited from

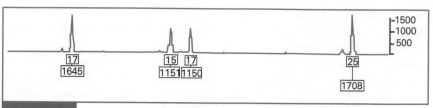

FIGURE 4.2 An example of an electropherogram showing a defendant's DNA profile at three loci. The boxes just below the peaks indicate the alleles, and the lower boxes indicate height of peak.

the paternal portion of the chromosome. The output from DNA tests are typically displayed as a graph (called an electropherogram, see Figure 4.2) showing the height of peaks at specific locations on the human genome. Because testing examines locations where there tend to be substantial variations across individuals, analysts can distinguish between the DNA of different people. (See the Scientific American box in this section to learn more about what can be done with DNA evidence.)

If DNA from the crime scene corresponds perfectly to a suspect's DNA sample, there is clearly a match. If every allele matches, the finding is clear and straightforward. However, sometimes DNA tests yield ambiguous results. A DNA profile from the suspect may match perfectly at several alleles but may not match at other alleles. These anomalies might be due to the poor quality of the DNA collected at the crime scene or contamination of the sample during handling and analysis. When such anomalies are present, the judgment of whether there is a match depends to a large extent on the interpretation of a human analyst (Dror & Hampikian, 2012; Risinger, Saks, Thompson, & Rosenthal, 2002). DNA analyses are almost always contextualized with probability statements. Therefore, when a DNA analyst concludes that two profiles match, he or she will estimate the probability that such a match could have occurred by chance alone. To make this estimate, analysts consult massive computerized databases that show the frequency of each allele in an appropriate reference population. The calculated estimates are referred to as **random match probabilities,** or **RMPs.** These RMPs are presented to a judge or jury when a case is tried. In court, an expert might testify that the probability that the DNA sample found at the crime scene is not from the defendant is 1 in 12 billion. However, some laboratories (including the FBI lab) will state that two profiles match to a "scientific certainty" if the probability that the sample did not come from the defendant is extremely low.

In the case of an imperfect DNA match, we must rely upon the subjective judgment of an analyst. This judgment raises the risk of error. However, in DNA testing, the use of subjective judgment is quite limited, and therefore the risk of error is quite low. DNA evidence stands in sharp contrast to several other forms of trace evidence where analyses rest on a mushy foundation of subjective human judgment. In several areas of forensic evidence, the standards used to define a "match" are vague and open to interpretation. In contrast, because DNA identification was an outgrowth of basic science, it rests on a foundation far more solid than other types of forensic evidence. In addition, because DNA identification was a relatively late arrival in the world of forensic identification, it was subjected to far more scrutiny from the courts than were other, more established forms of identification (e.g., fingerprints, handwriting, bullet characteristics). Unlike these other "time-tested" and "court-tested" methods of identification, proponents of DNA identification were required to prove its scientific validity and its relevance for criminal investigation (Koehler & Saks, 2010; Saks & Koehler, 2005).

SCIENTIFIC AMERICAN SPOTLIGHT

Can DNA Analysis Yield Police-style Sketches of Suspects?
By Christine Soars

Male, short and stout, with dark skin, brown eyes, shovel-shaped teeth, type A+ blood and coarse, dark brown hair giving way to pattern baldness. He would have a high tolerance for alcohol and a higher-than-average risk of nicotine dependence—fortunately, he lived thousands of years before humans discovered smoking. The description of a Stone Age Greenland resident published in February paints an extraordinary portrait of a man who vanished more than 4000 years ago, drawn almost solely from his DNA remains (see drawing below).

The analysis, led by Danish scientists, not only marks the first full sequencing of an ancient human genome but also offers a startling example of how much modern-day detectives can discern just from a suspect's genetic code. Far beyond using DNA to link an individual to a crime scene, forensic profiling is edging toward the capability to create a police-artist-style sketch of an unknown person by reading traits inscribed in the genome. "The body interprets the DNA

DNA sequence viewed through a magnifying glass on a light board. (*Peter Dazeley/Getty Images*)

Sketch of man from 4000 years ago constructed using DNA information (*National News/ZumaPress/Newscom*)

to determine the appearance of the face," says anthropologist Mark Shriver of Morehouse College, who hopes to duplicate that ability within a decade.

The scientists reconstructing the ancient Greenlander had only a few tufts of hair, preserved in permafrost, from which they extracted DNA. The hair itself is dark and thick and contains chemical traces indicating mainly a seafood diet. From the man's genes, the researchers resolved a long-standing debate about the origins of Greenland's paleo-Eskimos by showing he had a pattern of DNA variations most common in Siberian population groups. Having established his ancestral origins in northern Asia, the team could then interpret variations called single-nucleotide polymorphisms (SNPs) in four genes linked to brown eye color in modern Asians. The same method revealed SNPs associated with shovel-shaped front teeth and a dry type of earwax, both traits common in modern Asians and Native Americans. Four more SNPs suggest that he probably had dark skin. Another set of variations typical of populations adapted to cold climates indicates he had a compact body and ample body fat.

Together those traits might not make the ancient Greenlander stand out in a lineup, but they could dra-

matically narrow the search for suspects. A handful of high-profile criminal cases have already demonstrated the utility of even basic prospective information. In 2007, Christopher Phillips and his colleagues at the University of Santiago de Compostela in Spain used markers in a DNA sample obtained from a toothbrush to identify a suspect in the 2004 Madrid train bombing as being of North African descent. Police later confirmed that the terrorist was Algerian.

In an infamous Louisiana serial killer investigation, witness testimony had indicated a Caucasian culprit, but DNA evidence pointed to someone of significant African-American and Native American descent. Police widened their search and eventually caught the killer.

Having more to go on than ancestry, a generally poor indicator of appearance, is the goal of programs such as the DNA Initiative of the National Institute of Justice, which funds research into alternative genetic markers for forensic use. Daniele Podini of George Washington University is developing a forensic kit to determine, by analyzing 50 to 100 genetic markers, a suspect's eye and hair color, sex, and probable ancestry. "The idea is just to provide another investigational tool," he says, "one that can help corroborate the testimony of a witness or reduce the number of suspects. . . ."

Getting more specific gets significantly more difficult, Podini adds. DNA alone offers few clues to age, for instance. With whole cells, researchers could examine telomeres, the chromosomal end caps that wear away with time, but individual health and other factors can influence their shrinkage. One recent study showed that dedicated athletes in their 50s might have the telomeres of a 25-year-old. Another important feature in profiling, height, has hereditary roots but also depends on environmental factors, such as nutrition during childhood.

Practical considerations may be what delays deployment of any but the simplest forensic kits, though. "The forensic field is very, very conservative," Podini says, "so before you actually apply something to casework, it has to be proven beyond a reasonable doubt as something that works well, is reliable and is accepted by the scientific community."

Fingerprints

Sir Francis Galton was an early pioneer in the field of **psychometrics**—the measurement of psychological characteristics. At the 1883 World's Fair in Chicago and the 1884 Health Exhibition in London, thousands of people took a series of tests devised by Galton to assess their intelligence. These crude tests included measures of cranium size, hand strength, reaction time, and making fine distinctions between sounds, weights, and lights. Although his tests are no longer used to assess intelligence, Galton was one of the first to advocate the idea that individual abilities and psychological traits can be objectively measured and the results of these measures can be quantified (assigned numerical values) to distinguish between people. For more than a century, psychologists have labored to develop increasingly refined measures of psychological traits and cognitive abilities. Personality tests, intelligence tests, vocational aptitude tests, and college admissions exams are all attempts to capture some important aspect of character or mental functioning.

By 1892, Galton had applied his interest in measurement to physical traits. In his seminal book—*Finger Prints*—Galton described the patterning of fingerprints (using terms such as "loops, whorls, and arches") and argued that fingerprints are unchanged across the lifespan and that every print is unique (see Figure 4.3). He pioneered the procedure of counting points of similarity as a means of matching two fingerprints to establish identity. Galton used his influence to persuade the British government to adopt fingerprints as a method of identification. By the turn of the century, others (e.g., Juan Vucetich in Argentina) had developed detailed classifications for fingerprints. Variations of these systems are still used today (Cole, 2001). By 1901, a criminal defendant had been convicted on the basis of fingerprint evidence.

The tiny swirling lines on your fingertips and your palms are called **friction ridges.** And, from an evolutionary standpoint, they probably developed to create friction and allow humans to better grasp objects like tree limbs, weapons, and tools. When these prints are found on a surface at the scene of a crime, they are referred to as **latent prints,** and the features of the prints are referred to as **minutiae.** Because they are difficult to see with the naked eye, their visibility is enhanced using powders, special lights, and magnification. In television shows and movies, the process

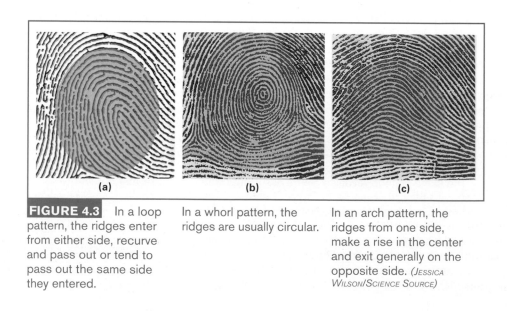

(a)　　　　(b)　　　　(c)

FIGURE 4.3 In a loop pattern, the ridges enter from either side, recurve and pass out or tend to pass out the same side they entered. In a whorl pattern, the ridges are usually circular. In an arch pattern, the ridges from one side, make a rise in the center and exit generally on the opposite side. (*Jessica Wilson/Science Source*)

of fingerprint matching seems swift and precise: A print lifted from the crime scene is fed into a computer and after a few seconds of comparing the print to those in the database, the word "match" flashes on the screen and the perpetrator is identified. In real life, however, computers can only narrow down the number of potential match candidates. It is a human examiner who sorts through these potential matches and makes the final judgment. Further, most fingerprints are not in the computerized database. If the actual criminal's fingerprints are not in the database, there is no way to match a print from the crime scene to a print in the database.

We all learn some dubious facts as we grow up. For example, the 9-year-old daughter of one of your authors already "knows" that no two snowflakes and no two fingerprints are exactly alike. The evidence for these widely shared beliefs is less than compelling. It turns out that some snowflakes are so similar in appearance that they are indistinguishable (Thornton, 2003), and that we do not really know whether "no two fingerprints are identical." Indeed, in the legal system, the critical issue is not whether every fingerprint is unique. The critical issue is the probability of error. That is, "What is the likelihood that a fingerprint will be wrongly identified as matching the defendant (*false positive error*)?" and, "What is the likelihood that a print will be wrongly excluded as coming from the defendant (*false negative error*)?"

One source of error is print quality. Research suggests that when the quality of a latent print is high, fingerprint examiners can make basic judgments of similarity and dissimilarity with a very high rate of accuracy (Tangen, Thompson, & McCarthy, 2011). But the clarity of prints left at crime scenes varies dramatically. A print may be distorted or smudged because it was made with too much or too little pressure. If the surface touched is rough and porous rather than smooth, the print might be unreadable or incomplete. Even prints from the same finger may look very different depending on the position of the finger, the pressure exerted, and the surface that was touched (Cole, 2006; Saferstein, 2010).

Fingerprint matching is accomplished by comparing ridge characteristics. Among the characteristics considered by examiners are bifurcations (when a single ridge splits into two), ends (where a ridge stops), crossovers (two ridges joined by a bridging ridge), and independence (short ridges with clear end points). Many examiners also take into account characteristics such as pores, ridge shape, ridge thickness, and the relative locations of all characteristics (see Figure 4.4). The process of comparing a latent print to that of a suspect involves a series of micro-decisions about whether particular ridge characteristics are dissimilar enough to exclude the suspect as the source of the print. And if there are no dissimilarities that are deemed significant by the examiner, he or she must then decide whether the observed ridge types and locations are so similar that the latent print and the suspect's print are a "match."

So, when does mere similarity cross the critical threshold and become described as a match? In many countries (including the United States), the threshold is intuitive, that is to say, it exists in the mind of the individual examiner. We are asked to trust the professional judgment of the examiner who has been "trained to competency" (swgfast.org, 2013). One group of examiners, sometimes referred to as **ridge-ologists** uses a holistic approach to compare prints.

FIGURE 4.4 Ridge Characteristics (SCIENCE SOURCE)

They look at the "totality" of the print, including all available detail—for example, the size, shape, spacing, and orientation of ridges, as well as the number and location of pores. There have been few attempts to look inside the head of the examiner to discern how such crucially important decisions are made. We do not know how much similarity of ridge type or ridge detail triggers a judgment of individualization. It is troubling that the research that does exist shows substantial variability in *how* examiners analyze the same print (Evett & Williams, 1996; Haber & Haber, 2008). This ambiguity of standards led the Interpol European Expert Group on Fingerprint identification to suggest that, faced with the unfathomably large population of fingerprints, examiners may be tempted to fall back on a crude and flawed heuristic: "Do I *think* it's him or not?"

In continental Europe, examiners must use a more quantitative approach. Each country has specified a minimum number of matching ridge characteristics that must be found in order to conclude that a print came from the suspect. That number ranges from 7 to 16. And, although more points are probably better than fewer points, there is no empirical basis for saying that 7 or 16 or 20 or 50 points is the number necessary for deciding with certainty that two prints match. Even with the highest 16-point matches, errors have been made (Cole, 2005). In the Mayfield case, described at the opening of this chapter, the FBI located 15 points of similarity and even the Spanish authorities found 8 points of similarity (Mnookin, 2004).

Many fingerprint analysts deal with such complications by invoking the **one dissimilarity doctrine**—the idea that no identification will be made if a single unexplained dissimilarity in two prints is discovered. However, in practice, this principle is routinely violated and, "whenever a fingerprint analyst encounters a fingerprint with a dozen or so matching characteristics and one dissimilarity, he will invariably rationalize the dissimilarity somehow, even if the rationalization is contrived" (Thornton & Peterson, 2013, p. 40).

An important issue usually not addressed in testimony about fingerprint identification is the commonness or rarity of a specific ridge characteristic. To conclude that two prints "match," it is important to know what percentage of the population shares that characteristic. If 80% of known fingerprints display a particular ridge bifurcation at the same location on the fingerprint, a match at that point tells us very little. If the characteristic is shared by only 20% of the population, a match at that point would be far more incriminating. Unfortunately, the probability of a particular ridge characteristic and the probability of particular combinations of such characteristics are simply unknown (Zabell, 2005). Instead of discussing the RMPs—as is always done when describing DNA comparisons—some experts simply proclaim, without the benefit of quantitative data, that the latent print could only have come from the defendant and therefore not from any other person in the whole wide world. If there are roughly 6.9 billion people on planet Earth with 10 fingers each, the population of fingers is in the neighborhood of 69 billion.

Psychological Biases in Fingerprint Identification? To the extent that the interpretation of forensic identification evidence is subjective, it can be influenced by cognitive biases. Although there has been little empirical research on this topic, the research that does exist should be distressing to people who value fairness.

A consistent problem in conducting systematic research on fingerprints is that it is difficult to get the cooperation of actual examiners. Studies using nonprofessional examiners have pointed to the possibility of bias. In one study, if untrained subjects were first exposed to emotionally arousing stimuli such as graphic crime scene photos, they were more likely to see two prints as matching (Dror, Peron, Hind, &

Charlton, 2006). In another study, professional latent print examiners were presented with fingerprints they had examined approximately 5 years earlier during the normal course of their jobs. In all cases, those prints had been identified as a clear and definite match. When re-presented to the very same examiners 5 years later, the examiners were given the following misleading contextural information: that the prints were the ones that had led to the mistaken identification of the Madrid bomber. Examiners were then asked to decide if the prints were a "match" or a "nonmatch" or whether there was not enough information to make a clear decision. Using the techniques and procedures they normally use, they came to very different conclusions than they had reached previously. Three out of five examiners changed their earlier "clear and definite" match judgments to "nonmatch" judgments, one stuck to his earlier "match" judgment, and one changed his opinion to "insufficient information to make a definite decision" (Dror, Charlton, & Peron, 2006). In a third study, Dror and Charlton (2006) had fingerprint examiners judge eight pairs of fingerprints they had judged years earlier. All the examiners had been certified and proficiency tested, and all were rated highly by their supervisors. Half of the eight print pairs had been previously rated as matches, and half had been previously rated as nonmatches. Half of the prints were easy to judge (i.e., they were clear and complete) and the other half were difficult to judge (i.e., indistinct and partial). Results indicated that only one-third of the examiners were perfectly consistent in their judgments of a match. Changes in judgments were most likely when the prints were difficult to judge, and when biasing information was given (e.g., "the defendant has confessed to the crime").

There are two important points to make about these findings. First, fingerprint examiners do not appear to be immune to **contextual bias**—the tendency for extraneous influences (emotions, expectations, and motivations) in the immediate environment to taint our judgments. Being shown gory crime scene photos or being told that the suspect has already confessed shapes the decisions of fingerprint examiners. This is important because, in actual practice, fingerprint examiners are not insulated from biasing information such as whether police investigators believe the crime scene print came from the defendant. Second, because the analysis of even very clear prints can be influenced by extraneous information, the analysis of smudged or fuzzy or partial prints may be especially prone to error. Here as in other areas, information such as being told the suspect has already confessed may trigger the cognitive tendency known as **confirmation bias**—an inclination to search out evidence that confirms our beliefs and to ignore evidence that contradicts our beliefs. While there is considerable research demonstrating confirmation bias in a variety of domains (Fiske & Taylor, 2008), there is little direct research on how this bias affects forensic identifications. However, based on experience, some forensic scientists have noted the problem:

> A danger exists that, once the examiner has become satisfied that a match does exist between the evidence and the exemplar, any differences will be dismissed as trivial and insignificant. A different, more forgiving set of criteria may be employed to rationalize away the differences than that originally employed in establishing the match. (Thornton & Peterson, 2013, p. 10).

The use of forensic science in the justice system rests on the claim that prints found at the crime scene can be examined to reveal the identity of a criminal. After more than a century of use in the courtroom, and after tens of thousands of defendants have been convicted based of fingerprint evidence, the research in support of this claim is still exceedingly weak. In a case in which a defendant challenged his conviction based on the unreliability of fingerprint evidence (*State v. Quintana*, 2004), a Utah Court of Appeals upheld the conviction but acknowledged the scientific weakness of fingerprint evidence:

> . . .fingerprint evidence is often all that is needed to convict a defendant, even in the absence of any other evidence of guilt. Unfortunately, our societal acceptance of the infallibility of examiners' opinions appears to be misplaced. Such fallibility, in light of society's trust in forensic certainty, opens our courts to a great risk of misidentification. (p. 8)

It should be possible to devise a more precise fingerprint classification system. Indeed, researchers have begun to apply sophisticated mathematical models to the problem of fingerprint recognition and differentiation (e.g., Neumann, 2012). A mathematically sophisticated system would incorporate pattern recognition software in a way that allows for rapid computerized analysis of latent prints. However, until such a system is devised and refined through systematic research, we will not even be able to verify the frequently repeated claim that "every fingerprint is unique." More to the point, without a better classification system, we will not be able to specify the probability of false positive and false negative errors.

HOT TOPIC

Is There Really a "CSI Effect"?

In recent years, much media attention has been devoted to the so-called **CSI Effect,** named after the popular television show *CSI: Crime Scene Investigation.* In this and other television crime dramas, good-looking people with ample time conduct careful analyses in spacious, gleaming laboratories of glass and steel. Every crime seems to leave trace evidence that can be readily recovered or retrieved through extraordinary means (e.g., in one episode of *CSI*, DNA was recovered from the digestive system of an alligator that ate the murder victim). Thanks to forensic identification, justice is swift and certain.

There is no question that these TV dramas are unrealistic. In real life, crime labs tend to be underfunded and backlogged. Analyses are slow, results can be ambiguous, and there is always the possibility of error. The specific complaint leveled by prosecutors is that *CSI* has led jurors to expect conclusive forensic evidence in every case and that this unrealistic expectation leads to fewer convictions. As one prosecutor put it, such shows "project the image that

(Matthew Rolston/CBS Photo Archive via Getty Images)

all cases are solvable by highly technical science, and if you offer less than that, it is viewed as reasonable doubt. The burden it places on us is overwhelming" (Roane, 2007). In most mass media accounts, the evidence offered in support of such claims is anecdotal—a story or two about juries run amok. The few studies that have been conducted suggest that there is no such effect. Four studies of potential jurors have found no link between *CSI* viewing and expectations about forensic evidence or verdict choice (Kim, Barak, & Shelton, 2009; Mancini, 2012; Schweitzer & Saks, 2007; Shelton, Kim, & Barak, 2007). One study found some evidence of a *CSI* effect (Baskin & Sommers, 2010), but another found a pro-prosecution effect, in that jurors placed too much weight on faulty forensic identification evidence when it was available (Podlas, 2006). In our adversarial legal system, it is not surprising that prosecutors believe that jurors demand too much proof to convict, or that defense attorneys believe that jurors do not demand enough proof. The easiest way for attorneys to explain an unfavorable outcome is to blame the jury.

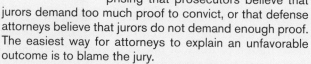

TECHNIQUES OF WEAK OR UNKNOWN VALIDITY

Although DNA evidence is very strong, and fingerprint evidence is moderately strong, there are several types of identification evidence that are not strong at all.

In some criminal cases, a key issue is whether the bullet that wounded or killed or missed a victim came from a gun owned or used by a defendant. To make this determination, analysts compare highly magnified images of the two bullets. Based on their experience and training, these analysts reach a decision about whether the markings, or **striations,** on the two bullets match. Surprisingly, there are no widely accepted standards about how many, or how large, or what types of striations must be present before an analyst can declare a "match" (Schwartz, 2005). If there are discrepancies between striations on the two bullets, the analyst, using mysterious intuitive standards, must assess whether these discrepancies are "significant." To accept that a stated pattern of similarities or discrepancies is meaningful in identifying the bullet, we must simply place our faith in the expertise of the examiner.

Other types of unproven forensic identification involve tools and teeth. If a screwdriver or crowbar or knife is used to pry open the window of a home or business in order to commit a burglary, the window frame will be damaged. An attempt might be made to analyze the markings on the window to see if they match a particular prying tool in the possession of the suspect. The idea is that each tool might leave behind a signature pattern (e.g., scrapes, scratches, dents) that can be distinguished from patterns that might be left behind by other tools. Similarly, if a criminal bites a sandwich or a slice of pizza, or even a victim at the crime scene, the bite mark might be matched to the teeth of a defendant. There is no persuasive research validating tool mark analysis, and one study of practicing forensic dentists found a very high false positive rate—dentists falsely identified an innocent person as the source of a bite 63% of the time (Bowers, 2002).

The advent of DNA as an identification technique has sometimes been used to discredit other established forms of identification. For example, when researchers compared the results of microscopic hair analysis with the results of DNA testing of the same hair samples, the two techniques yielded very different results (Houck & Budowle, 2002). Other than gross differentiations such as short or long, black or blond, there is no strong evidence that hair can be reliably linked to a particular suspect using microscopic comparisons.

Might it be possible to develop and refine bullet striation or tool mark or hair or bite mark matching so that they produce valid and reliable evidence? Perhaps.

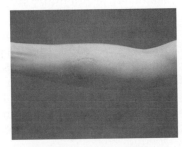

Bite marks and magnified striation pattern on bullets.
(A: FSTOP/FSTOP; B: JOHN NIXON, ATHENA RESEARCH & CONSULTING)

But given the lack of scientific foundation, at least for now, it is appropriate to view these techniques with skepticism.

In the *Daubert* decision (described more fully in Chapter 1), trial court judges were anointed as the gatekeepers for keeping unreliable expert testimony out of the courtroom. *Daubert* opened the door for challenges to long-established techniques (such as handwriting analysis) that had achieved the status of legitimate science not because of established validity and reliability, but only because they had been routinely admitted into evidence at trial (Hartfield, 2002). These challenges have not always been successful, in part because judges lack the training and knowledge to assess the scientific merit of forensic identification techniques (Fradella, O'Neill, & Fogarty, 2004; Kovera & McAuliff, 2000).

The development of DNA identification should serve as a model for other forms of forensic identification. It is both the most modern and most accurate form of identification evidence. Because it was not widely introduced into the courtroom until the late 1980s and early 1990s, it did not carry the mantle of legal legitimacy enjoyed by less reliable but more established techniques such as handwriting, bite mark, or fingerprint identification. Because it was a latecomer, the courts held DNA identification to a much higher scientific standard, demanding the kind of validation that has never been required of older techniques. Rulings that excluded DNA helped to generate needed research and forced scientists to lay a stronger foundation for DNA evidence (Saks, 2010).

 ## REDUCING ERROR AND BIAS

When examiners claim to find a "match" between a crime scene trace and a defendant, there is always an alternative explanation: error. So far, we have focused on scientific foundation. A solid scientific foundation demonstrating the validity of an identification technique is a precondition for trustworthy analysis—a flawed technique does not tell us much even if the laboratory analysis is done well. But even when a technique is reliable and valid, there are other conditions that raise the risk of error. Trace evidence can be improperly collected, or contaminated at some point between collection and final analysis. The examiner can make a mistake in interpreting the sample, or situational pressures can bias the judgment of the examiner.

Valid identification presumes trace evidence that is adequate for testing—the fingerprint must be clear enough to allow for comparison, the murder weapon must be found, the DNA sample must be uncontaminated. A huge potential source of error is the handling of trace evidence. Samples can be mislabeled, accidentally switched, or contaminated by inadvertent mixing with other samples. Fortunately, most laboratories have a variety of procedural safeguards in place to minimize the possibility of laboratory error. Laboratory accreditation, like that offered by the nonprofit American Society of Crime Laboratory Directors, attempts to ensure that labs meet strict standards for the handling and analysis of evidence. A step not taken often enough is *routine retesting* of traces to resolve any ambiguity about findings. If two independent tests of a sample yield the same findings, we can have much greater confidence in the identification (National Research Council Committee on Identifying the Needs of the Forensic Science Community, 2009).

Beyond the quality and handling of evidence are the potential errors that originate in the minds of the examiners. Sometimes, mistakes occur because examiners are inexperienced, poorly trained, rushed, or too eager to find the results that their supervisors seem to favor (Haber & Haber, 2013). To minimize such errors, forensic scientists have turned to proficiency testing and certification of forensic analysts. For example, the FBI issued guidelines calling for analysts to take two proficiency exams each year. A proficiency test involves giving an analyst a sample to examine (e.g., a hair, a latent print, a sandwich with a bite mark on it) using the equipment and procedures he or she usually employs. The test should be **blind** in the sense that the examiner is given no indication of the correct results before or during testing. Even better, the test can be **double blind** in the sense that the analyst does not even know he or she is being tested. That is, the sample should arrive during the course of his or her normal work with no indication that it is part of a proficiency test. In such tests, the true source of the sample is known. Because the hair or fingerprint or bite mark was plucked, pressed, or bitten by a known person, we are able to say with certainty whether or not the analyst reached the correct identification.

Our adversarial legal system adds another layer of potential bias to the analysis of identification evidence. Ideally, physical evidence should be viewed as the property of the legal system, not the property of the either the defense or the prosecution. Unfortunately, trace evidence is almost always tested in laboratories inside of, or closely affiliated with, law enforcement. These laboratories generally act in the service of the prosecution—trace evidence is submitted by police investigators in an effort to help build a case for prosecutors. Typically, it is only later, if trace evidence implicates a particular suspect, that the defense is able to review that evidence (Thornton & Peterson, 2013). The ability of the defense to challenge the validity of a match is heavily dependent on having enough resources to identify and hire independent experts to examine the evidence. What the prosecutor and defender have in common is that both look at trace evidence through the distorted lens of the adversarial system. That is, they ask the simple, partisan question: "How will this evidence help or hurt my case?"

SCIENCE AS THE SOLUTION TO THE PROBLEM OF IDENTIFICATION BIAS

Science is a carefully cultivated, systematic way of seeking answers. Using rigorous methods of data collection and sophisticated statistical analyses, it attempts to filter out normal human biases and selective perceptions. Extensive training is a crucial means for creating a scientific sensibility. Scientists generally receive four or more years of highly specialized graduate education in pursuit of a Ph.D. During this extended training, they are immersed in the procedures and values of modern science. They are taught to gather data using carefully calibrated methods that minimize bias, to be cautious about overgeneralizing their findings, to trust the data, and to share data with other researchers. Most practitioners of forensic science have no such extended training—96% hold only a bachelor's degree (Almirall & Furton, 2003). Without elaborate graduate training, nonscientific values—such as pleasing one's superiors—are likely to take priority over scientific integrity.

The organizational culture and incentive system in forensic sciences are often at odds with the culture of science. Along with advanced training in the philosophy and procedures of science, peer review is a pillar of scientific progress. Peer review serves as a check on the personal biases of an individual scientist. If others examine the procedures used by a particular analyst and reach the same conclusion, we can have much more confidence in that conclusion. Unlike the world of science where several scientists review and critique research studies, the "reviewers" of forensic science—juries and judges—usually lack the scientific sophistication necessary to assess the validity of laboratory findings fully. Also, unlike the open environment of science, where data are shared and research is produced and scrutinized by people with different interests and perspectives, forensic science has been marked by secrecy and fear of negative findings. As Risinger and Saks (2003) note, "Various strategies appear to have been adopted to ensure that positive results will be exaggerated and negative results will be glossed over, if not withheld" (p. 3). For example, a persistent problem has been the failure to use strong research designs, which might generate clear results that reveal the true accuracy of identification techniques.

A related source of potential bias is financial interest. The laboratories and professional organizations that conduct most of the research on identification techniques have a financial and professional stake in demonstrating the validity of identification techniques. This is an obvious conflict of interest. As one scholar put it, forensic identification testing, ". . . is not an independent area of academic science; it is a technical field in which procedures are designed, shaped, and performed specifically to play a role in litigation" (Thompson, 1997, p. 408). Independent, government-funded labs that are not beholden to law enforcement, and boards of oversight comprised of both scientists and practitioners may be our best hope for eliminating bias.

 ## HOW JURORS THINK ABOUT TRACE EVIDENCE

In evaluating trace evidence, jurors must take into account detailed technical information as well as statistical statements about probabilities. They must then combine this complex testimony with other evidence presented at trial and assign appropriate weight to identification evidence in their verdict decision. This task is especially difficult for jurors with low levels of education and little background in math and science (Hans, Kaye, Dann, Farley, & Albertson, 2011).

In several studies, researchers have examined whether and how jurors revise their evaluations of guilt when presented with RMP statistics on DNA samples. One finding is that when researchers compare how much jurors actually adjust their assessments of guilt based on RMPs to how much they "should" adjust their assessments based on statistical models of probability, jurors are too conservative in their adjustments. Put more succinctly, jurors tend to place too little weight on probabilities (Koehler, 2001; Schklar & Diamond, 1999). A second general finding from these studies is that jurors have great difficulty making sense of statistical statements. Faced with probability statements, jurors in several studies make a variety of incorrect inferences about the guilt of a defendant. For example, when told that a defendant matches the perpetrator of a crime on a characteristic found in only 4% of the population, some jurors will conclude that there is a 96% chance that the defendant is guilty (Thompson & Schumann, 1997). Other jurors will interpret the same statement to mean that since 4% of the population could be equal to millions of people, we cannot really infer anything about the defendant's guilt. Still others conclude that there was only a 4% chance that the defendant was actually the perpetrator (Nance & Morris, 2002).

Statistical models and human intuition are often at odds. From a scientific perspective, the statistical information attending DNA analysis is highly desirable. It offers a precision unavailable for other types of trace evidence. However, testimony about probabilities appears to be extremely difficult for jurors to understand. Clearly, we must find better ways of presenting complex information to jurors—ways that preserve mathematical accuracy while simultaneously helping jurors understand the meaning of the data. Some researchers have attempted to frame statistical information in different ways to gauge its effect on jurors. For example, Jonathan Koehler and Laura Macchi (2004) presented mock jurors with a murder case in which DNA recovered from blood at the crime scene matched the DNA of the defendant. A critical defense argument in the case (and in nearly all such cases) was that the DNA match was merely coincidental. The probability of a coincidental match was expressed in several ways. Here are two:

1. The chance that *the suspect* would match the blood drops if he were not their source is *0.001%.*
2. *1 in 100,000 people* who are not the source would nonetheless match the blood drops.

Which statement do you think is stronger? In fact, the two statements are statistically equivalent—they express the same probability of a coincidental match. However, jurors interpreted the two statements quite differently. The first statement was more "prosecution-friendly" in the sense that jurors rated the DNA match as stronger and were more likely to render a verdict of "guilty." The second statement was more "defense-friendly," leading to greater doubt about the match and significantly more verdicts of "not guilty." If simple changes in the form of the match statements can significantly shift perceptions of guilt, it is imperative to clarify the meaning of probability statements for jurors and judges. The outcome of a trial should not hinge on the ability of jurors to understand probability theory. Perhaps the simplest way of defeating this cognitive bias is by presenting statistical evidence to jurors in multiple forms so that they will not be swayed by a particular expression of the same statistical fact.

In the case of fingerprint evidence, juror understanding is both better and worse. Better in the sense that it is much easier to understand an expert witness's assertion of absolute certainty that a latent print matches the defendant's print than it is to understand a complex probability statement. When a fingerprint expert is 100% certain, there is little room for confusion. Juror understanding is worse because jurors are unaware of the limited scientific foundation for fingerprint identification and they are unaware of the weaknesses in the matching process (Reardon, Danielsen, & Meissner, 2005).

▶ IN CONCLUSION

Some forms of error in forensic identification may eventually be minimized or even eliminated by technological advances. For example, fingerprint matching may eventually be done by sophisticated optical scanners and computer programs that compare samples on characteristics too minute to be detectable by the human eye. However, even if technological fixes are eventually found, at least three fundamental problems will remain: (1) weak scientific foundation for many forms of trace evidence; (2) risk of contamination or misinterpretation of the trace evidence; and (3) how the strength of a "match" or near match is communicated to a jury or judge. Interestingly, professional associations have tended to focus on the second problem, establishing consistent procedures for collecting, handling, testing, and documenting trace evidence (see *American Society of Crime Laboratory Directors—Laboratory Accreditation Board*). Uniform and cautious procedures are clearly an essential element of forensic identification. But—with the exception of DNA evidence—the more fundamental issue of scientific grounding has been strangely neglected. This is true even for fingerprint evidence, which has been admissible in court for well over a century.

The courts are the great consumers of forensic identification evidence. If they refuse to allow all but the most reliable evidence, we are likely to see far more effort to evaluate the validity of forensic techniques. We may find that some techniques accepted by the courts for decades need to be discarded as unreliable. Other techniques may prove to be highly reliable, and some techniques for determining a match may need to be refined and made more precise. Scientific evaluation of identification techniques would greatly enhance our ability to free the truly innocent and to convict the truly guilty.

▶ DISCUSSION AND CRITICAL THINKING QUESTIONS

1. Is DNA a better form of forensic identification evidence than fingerprints? Why or why not?

2. Fingerprint evidence is admissible in court. Should it be?

3. How can we make forensic identification evidence more useful to the jurors who must evaluate it?

4. Why was the fingerprint of Brandon Mayfield mistakenly identified as the fingerprint of the Madrid bomber? How might this mistaken identification have been avoided or detected earlier?

5. What is meant by the "scientific foundation" of trace evidence?

▶ KEY TERMS

alleles (p. 79)
anthropometry (p. 72)
biometrics (p. 73)
blind (p. 89)
contextual bias (p. 85)
confirmation bias (p. 85)
CSI effect (p. 86)
DNA (deoxyribonucleic acid) (p. 79)
double blind (p. 89)
excluded (p. 74)

forensic identification (p. 72)
friction ridges (p. 82)
inconclusive (p. 74)
individualization (p. 74)
inter-rater reliability (p. 78)
latent prints (p. 82)
loci (p. 79)
match plus statistics (p. 76)

measurement validity (p. 79)
minutiae (p. 82)
one dissimilarity doctrine (p. 84)
psychometrics (p. 82)
qualitative statement (p. 76)
random match probabilities (RMPs) (p. 80)

reliability (p. 78)
ridgeologists (p. 83)
simple match (p. 76)
source attribution (p. 74)
striations (p. 87)
test–retest reliability (p. 78)
trace evidence (p. 73)

5 Criminal Profiling and Psychological Autopsies

Much of the public was introduced to the practice of criminal profiling by the Academy Award–winning film, *The Silence of the Lambs.* In that film, a young FBI agent, named Starling, and her boss are on the trail of a serial killer who murders young white women and cuts away large pieces of their skin. In one scene, Starling's skills are tested when her boss asks her to look at photographs of the victims and speculate about the killer's identity:

Boss: Look at these [photographs], Starling. Tell me what you see.
Starling: Well, he's a white male; serial killers tend to hunt within their own ethnic groups. He's not a drifter; he's got his own house somewhere, not an apartment.
Boss: Why?
Starling: What he does with them takes privacy. He's in his thirties or forties. He's got real physical strength, combined with an older man's self-control. He's cautious, precise. He's never impulsive; he'll never stop.
Boss: Why not?
Starling: He's got a real taste for it now; he's getting better at his work.
Boss: Not bad, Starling.

Starling's impromptu profile of the killer turns out to be dead on. But, of course, she's a fictional character, and *The Silence of the Lambs* is only a movie. Is it really possible to make valid inferences about a criminal's age, race, gender, living circumstances, and personality based only on information from a crime scene? ◄

 THE PROCESS OF PROFILING

Profiling is the process of drawing inferences about a criminal's personality, behavior, motivation, and demographic characteristics based on crime scenes and other evidence. The techniques of criminal profiling were pioneered by the FBI's Behavioral Science Unit (BSU), and have been used in the United States, Canada, the United Kingdom, Sweden, Finland, Germany, and the Netherlands (Hicks & Sales, 2006).

Profiling techniques (also known as "retroclassifications" or "criminal investigative analyses") have been most famously applied to cases involving **serial killers**—murderers who kill three or more people in separate events with a cooling-off period between murders. Since developing these profiling techniques, the FBI has trained thousands of law enforcement officers.

To create a tentative description—or "profile"—of the criminal, profilers analyze the crime scenes, gather information about the victims, and study both police and autopsy reports. Profiles provide leads for police and help focus the efforts of investigators. For example, officers might be told to look for a white male in his twenties who works nights and lives in a particular part of a city. A profile might also be used to set a trap for the criminal. For example, if police are looking for a serial killer who preys on young prostitutes with long dark hair, an officer with long dark hair may pose as a prostitute in an effort to attract and entrap the killer. In effect, a profile instructs investigators to look for a particular type of person and to ignore other types of people. When questioning suspects, a profile may suggest questions to ask and topics to explore.

Profilers emphasize the importance of the "signature aspect of the crime." This **signature** is the distinctive, personal aspect of the crime (e.g., a particular form of torture used or a particular sexual activity) that presumably reveals the killer's personality. According to John Douglas, one of the agents who developed the FBI's system, the methods used to abduct, transport, or dispose of victims may change, but the signature will remain relatively constant because it is ". . . *why* he does it: the thing that fulfills him emotionally . . . the emotional reason he's committing the crime in the first place" (Douglas & Olshaker, 1997, p. 26).

Although the profiling of serial killers has captured the imagination of Hollywood and the general public, it remains a largely unvalidated technique. The process requires a series of inferential leaps that can be succinctly summarized as moving from "What?" to "Why?" to "Who?" (Pinizzotto & Finkel, 1990). That is, by closely examining of the crime and the victims, the profiler is presumably able to reach conclusions about why the killer committed the crime. An understanding of *why* then leads to inferences about the perpetrator's characteristics and identity. Unfortunately, how profilers move from raw data about a crime to a useful profile of the criminal is neither systematic nor clearly articulated. According to Douglas:

> **The key attribute necessary to be a good profiler is judgment—a judgment based not primarily on the analysis of facts and figures, but on instinct. . . . and ultimately, it comes down to the individual analyst's judgment rather than any objective scale or test. (Douglas & Olshaker, 1997, p. 15)**

He further explains that

> **it's very important to get into the mind of not only the killer, but into the mind of the victim at the time the crime occurred. That's the only way you're going to be able to understand the dynamics of the crime—what was going on between the victim and the offender. (p. 17)**

Indeed, much of the mystique of the profiling process is that it appears to rely on the skilled intuition of a particular profiler. In movie and television depictions of the technique, profilers seem to be as much psychics as investigators. They often enter a trancelike state that allows them to inhabit the mind of a serial killer, to imagine what the killer saw and felt at the time of the killing. As Douglas writes:

> What I try to do is to take in all the evidence I have to work with . . . then put myself mentally and emotionally in the head of the offender. I try to think as he does. Exactly how this happens, I'm not sure. . . . If there's a psychic component to this, I won't run from it. (Douglas & Olshaker, 1997, p. 147)

In literary and media portrayals, the profiler-hero arrives at the scene of a stalled murder investigation, immerses him- or herself in the details of gruesome crimes, and uses mysterious psychological methods to infiltrate the mind and motivations of the killer. Empowered by the profiler's special insights, investigators capture the killer (Gregoriou, 2011). Many first-person accounts of profiling written by former FBI agents also follow a formula: a narrative of the case to be solved, a description of the profile developed by the FBI to assist investigators, a comparison of the characteristics of the actual killer with the profile, and a claim of astonishing accuracy (Risinger & Loop, 2002). But stories and case studies do not constitute real evidence of effectiveness. Systematic research is required to demonstrate the usefulness of profiling or any other technique. This chapter describes several actual criminal profiles and summarizes research on the effectiveness of profiling.

THREE FAMOUS PROFILES

Jack the Ripper

In 1888, Dr. Thomas Bond formulated what might be considered the first criminal profile (Rumbelow, 1975). In that year, "Jack the Ripper" terrorized the East End of London, strangling and slitting the throats of at least five prostitutes (the exact number is a matter of some controversy). The murders were daring and gruesome: The women were attacked and killed on public streets; their bodies were mutilated, and, in some cases, internal organs were removed and taken from the crime scene. The still-warm, mutilated corpses were discovered lying in the streets soon after the ripper had fled the scene. Dr. Bond performed autopsies on two of the victims. Here are his speculations about the physical and psychological characteristics of the ripper based on the characteristics of the crimes (we have added the likely bases for these speculations in parentheses):

- "A man of great physical strength." (*He managed to swiftly subdue his victims; none were able to escape or successfully call out for help.*)
- "A man of great coolness and daring." (*His savage crimes were committed efficiently and in public spaces where they could have been witnessed by passersby.*)
- "The murderer in external appearance is quite likely to be a quiet, inoffensive looking man probably middle-aged and neatly and respectably dressed." (*He managed to enter and exit the crime scene without detection, so he apparently blended in and did not call attention to himself.*)
- "He must be in the habit of wearing a cloak or overcoat." (*It would have been impossible to kill and mutilate his victims swiftly without getting blood on his hands and clothes, and a large cloak or coat would hide the blood.*)
- ". . . solitary and eccentric in his habits, also he is most likely to be a man without regular occupation" (*Someone capable of such depravity would have difficulty interacting with others without raising suspicion or discomfort*).

Unfortunately, Jack the Ripper was never caught, so we cannot assess the accuracy of Bond's pioneering "profile." However, it appears to be the first systematic profile offered to assist police in a criminal investigation.

The Olympic Bomber

Although profiling has been most famously applied to cases involving serial killers, profiling techniques have been used—with varying levels of success—in the investigation of many other types of crimes, including rape, arson, skyjacking, and bombing. One notorious profile was produced in response to a bomb explosion during the 1996 Summer Olympics in Atlanta, Georgia. Based on evidence uncovered at the scene of the bombing and on their database of past bombings at public events, the FBI instructed police to search for a single, white, middle-class male with an intense interest in police work and law enforcement (the kind of person investigators sometimes call a "police buff" or "cop wannabe"). Within days, the police focused their attention on Richard Jewell, a security guard at the Olympic Park who fit the profile in every respect. Mr. Jewell became the target of intense investigation. Because of the need to reassure people that the Olympic venues were safe, Jewell's name and photograph appeared in newspapers across the country and his face was shown on television news programs in several countries. It appeared that the bomber had been caught.

Only after three months—long after the Olympics had ended—did the FBI admit that investigators had uncovered no evidence linking Jewell to the bombing. Of course, the damage to Mr. Jewell's life and reputation could not be easily undone. In 1998, after much additional investigation, the FBI finally charged another man—Eric Rudolph—with the Olympic bombing. Rudolph was an antiabortion activist who was wanted in connection with the bombing of abortion clinics in two states (Sack, 1998). He evaded police for several years, but was finally captured and convicted of the bombing in 2005.

The Mad Bomber

One of the most famous profiles ever produced was also one of the most detailed. It was used to help solve the "Mad Bomber" case in 1957. In 1940, an unexploded bomb was found on a windowsill of the building occupied by the Consolidated Edison

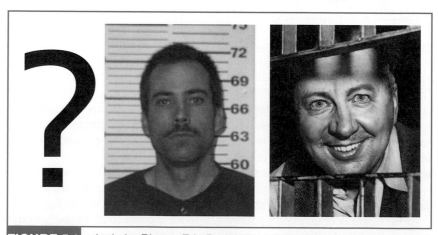

FIGURE 5.1   Jack the Ripper, Eric Rudolph, and the "Mad Bomber" *(B: AP Photo/Cherokee County Sheriff's Dept. C: NY Daily News via Getty Images)*

Company. The note attached to the bomb explained: "Con Edison crooks, this is for you." The perpetrator, who became known as the Mad Bomber, managed to terrorize the public by successfully planting (and sometimes detonating) bombs in locations dispersed across New York City (Ramsland, 2013). He sent several letters and placed a few phone calls to the New York City Police Department and *The New York Times.* Just after the United States entered World War II in 1941, the mad bomber sent a letter to the police declaring that because of his "patriotic feelings" he would, ". . . make no more bomb units for the duration of the war" (Brussel, 1968, p. 21). He was true to his word. No more bombs were found until 1950. But, in the same letter that informed police that his patriotism had inspired him to suspend bombings, he also declared that he would later return to "bring Con Edison to justice" and make them "pay for their dastardly deeds" (Brussel, 1968, p. 23).

Police were baffled. In 1956, they consulted a prominent local psychiatrist named James Brussel in a desperate attempt to generate new leads. Dr. Brussel reviewed the bomber's letters, as well as all the other information the police had collected. Brussel directed the police to look for a man who was between 40 and 50, Roman Catholic, foreign-born, single, and living with a brother or sister. He would be suffering from progressive paranoia and would be a "present or former Consolidated Edison worker." In an especially precise but odd detail, Brussel told police that, "When you find him, chances are he'll be wearing a double-breasted suit. Buttoned" (Brussel, 1968, p. 47). The man the police eventually arrested—George Metesky—was a single, unemployed, 54-year-old former employee of Con Ed who was living with two older sisters. When the police took him into custody, he was allowed to go into his room and change from his bathrobe. He emerged from his room wearing a double-breasted blue suit—buttoned.

Metesky was convicted. The profile of the Mad Bomber turned out to be eerily accurate and entered the folklore of profiling. However, in addition to the accurate details that may have been helpful to police, the elaborate profile constructed by Dr. Brussel also contained inaccurate details and wild psychoanalytic speculations. For example, noting that the Mad Bomber had cut open the underside of theater seats to stuff his bombs into the cushion, Brussel (1968) offered the following analysis: "Could the seat symbolize the pelvic region of the human body? In plunging a knife upward into it, had the bomber been symbolically penetrating a woman? Or castrating a man? . . . . In this act he gave expression to a submerged wish to penetrate his mother or castrate his father. Thereby rendering the father powerless. . . " (p. 63). Brussel also noted that the handwritten *W*s in the bomber's letters "resembled a pair of female breasts as seen from the front and could also pass for a scrotum," and that the bomber's yearning for what he called "justice" was truly a belief that people were ". . . trying to deprive him of something that was rightfully his . . . the love of his mother" (p. 39).

It is important to note that it was not his preference for double-breasted suits that helped investigators locate George Metesky. Police did not stake out men's haberdasheries. The crucial information in Brussel's famous profile was that the bomber was a resentful employee or former employee at Con Edison. It was a search of employee records that led to the identification of Metesky, a worker who had been injured by a boiler at Con Edison. His disability claim (he believed that the accident had given him tuberculosis) was denied, and he was eventually fired from his job. It appears that Brussel's profile merely prompted the police to do what they should have done in 1940 when the first bomb was discovered: search the employee records of Con Edison to try to identify someone who may have felt wronged by the company. Indeed, if modern-day police officers found a bomb with a note about "Con Edison crooks," they would almost certainly examine employee records to generate a list of disgruntled former employees. Of course, that task is far simpler today than it was in 1957, because employment records are now preserved as computer files. The critical information that led to Metesky's arrest was found in letters he wrote to a local newspaper. In those letters, he revealed the following details: he was injured on a job at a Consolidated Edison plant, and the injury occurred on September 5, 1931. These specific details enabled police to focus their search of the employee records (Ewing & McCann, 2006).

CHARACTERISTICS OF SERIAL KILLERS

Because profiling techniques have been most notably used to find serial killers, it is useful to briefly review research on people who commit these rare but horrifying crimes.

No list of characteristics describes every serial killer. However, research has revealed some recurring patterns. Many suffer from some form of brain injury that impairs rational thinking. Most have also experienced some combination of physical, sexual, and/or psychological abuse during childhood. Maladjustment during their childhood sometimes expresses itself in cruelty toward animals (Hickey & Harris, 2013). Nearly all serial killers are white males and are typically of average intelligence. Most seek to dominate their victims before killing them. They tend not to kill using guns, preferring more intimate methods such as strangulation, stabbing, or even torture. Before killing, they often drink alcohol or use other drugs, perhaps to desensitize themselves and lower inhibitions. They tend to select victims of a particular type, for example, only light-skinned adolescent boys. Serial killers often show an obsessive interest in violent pornography, and serial killing is often a highly sexualized crime. A killer's violent sexual fantasies may serve as rehearsals for his crimes, and many serial killers replay past killings in their minds as a means of sexual self-stimulation. Some have even made videotapes of their killings so that they could watch them repeatedly. To feed their fantasy life, a few keep souvenirs from their victims (e.g., a lock of hair) and collect newspaper clippings describing their crimes (Fox & Levin, 2011).

Profilers sometimes distinguish between organized and disorganized murderers (Ressler, Burgess, & Douglas, 1988). **Organized killers** are described as carefully selecting and stalking their victims and planning what they will do to their victims. They show patience and self-control by waiting for the right opportunity and then cleaning up evidence after the murder. They also tend to use more elaborate rituals involving torturing the victim and dismembering the corpse. In contrast, **disorganized killers** tend to be impulsive, picking their victims at random, acting on sudden rage, or following commands to kill from voices in their heads. Disorganized killers are more likely to use any weapon that happens to be available, leave the weapon at the crime scene, and use the dead body for sexual purposes (Ressler, Burgess, Douglas, Hartman, & D'Agostino, 1986). Table 5.1 summarizes the hypothesized differences between organized and disorganized killers. The upper half of the table contrasts crime-scene differences, and the lower portion of the table summarizes the inferred personal characteristics of the two types of serial killers.

TABLE 5.1	
Organized Crime Scene	*Disorganized Crime Scene*
Planned crime	Spontaneous crime
Controlled conversation	Minimal conversation with victim
Scene reflects control	Scene is random / sloppy
Demands submissive victim	Sudden violence to victim
Restraints used	Minimal use of restraints
Aggressive prior to death	Sex after death
Body hidden	Body left in view
Weapon/evidence absent	Weapon / evidence present
Transports victim	Body left at scene
Hypothesized Characteristics of Organized Murderers	*Hypothesized Characteristics of Disorganized Murderers*
At least average in intelligence	Below average in intelligence
Interpersonally competent	Interpersonally incompetent
Skilled work preferred	Prefers unskilled work
Sexually competent	Sexually incompetent
Inconsistent childhood discipline	Harsh childhood discipline
Controlled mood during crime	Anxious mood during crime
Precipitating situational stress	Minimal situational stress
Follows media accounts of his crime	Minimal interest in media accounts of crime
High geographic mobility	Lives/works near crime scene

In the profiling approach developed by the FBI, the organized–disorganized crime-scene taxonomy led directly to inferences about the killer's personality and circumstances. As some prominent profilers explained, "the crime scene is presumed to reflect the murderer's behavior and personality in much the same way as furnishings reveal the homeowner's character" (Douglas, Burgess, Burgess, and Ressler, 1992, p. 21). This simplistic, two-part taxonomy with its long inferential leaps from crime scenes to personality traits became an enormously influential tool for creating profiles. As some early investigators at the BSU put it, ". . . the organized versus disorganized distinction became the great divide, a fundamental way of separating two quite different types of personalities who commit multiple murders" (Ressler & Shachtman, 1992, p. 129).

A more differentiated classification scheme was later proposed by Ronald Holmes and Stephan Holmes (Holmes & Holmes, 2010). The Holmes team examined the characteristics of known serial killers and found that most killers could be grouped into one of four types: visionary, mission-oriented, hedonistic, and power-oriented. According to this scheme, **visionary types** are usually psychotic. They have visions or believe they hear voices from God or spirits instructing them to kill certain types of people. **Mission-oriented types** are less likely to be psychotic and are motivated by a desire to kill people they regard as evil or unworthy (e.g., one set out to kill all physicians who performed abortions). **Hedonistic types** kill for thrills and take sadistic sexual pleasure in the torture of their victims. The fourth type— **power-oriented types**—get satisfaction from capturing and controlling the victim before killing. Although this scheme offers some insight into the varied motives behind these hideous crimes, sophisticated statistical analyses of the co-occurrence of

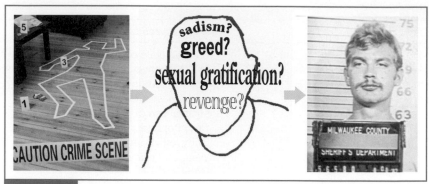

FIGURE 5.2   The process of profiling: Characteristics of the crime lead to inferences about the criminal's motives, which lead to inferences about the identity of the criminal. (*A: Masterfile, C: Ralf-Finn Hestoft/Corbis*)

traits indicate that most serial killers do not fall neatly into one of these somewhat overlapping categories (Bennell, Bloomfield, Emeno, & Musolino, 2013; Taylor, Lambeth, Green, Bone, & Cahiilane, 2012).

 ## RESEARCH ON PROFILING

Despite surging interest in profiling and well-publicized anecdotal evidence suggesting that profiling is effective, systematic research has been slow to develop. An early study conducted in England questioned 184 police detectives who had used a profiler to develop leads about the identity of a criminal (Copson, 1995). Although most detectives reported that they found the process "helpful," profiling led to the identification of a perpetrator in only 2.7% of the cases. When researchers examined the actual profiles created for the police, they found that most profiles were "riddled with inaccuracies and inconsistencies." Although this study has been criticized as limited because it relied on the potentially biased self-reports of detectives, other research methods have also been used to probe the process of profiling.

An early experimental study was conducted by Anthony Pinizzotto and Norman Finkel in 1990. That study compared the accuracy of profiles produced by four different groups: undergraduate college students, clinical psychologists with no profiling experience, police detectives without training in profiling techniques, and police detectives who had completed an FBI profiling training program. All groups evaluated two actual cases—a homicide and a sex offense. The crimes had already been solved, so the true characteristics of the offenders were known. All groups evaluated the same evidence: crime-scene photographs, information about the victim, autopsy reports, and reports written by officers on the scene and detectives investigating the case. Analyses did reveal differences among the groups. The biggest differences were between the trained profiler group and all other groups. The trained profilers studied the materials more closely, spent more time writing their reports, wrote longer reports, and made more specific inferences about the offender's characteristics. Nevertheless, their profiles were significantly more accurate only for the sex offender case. For the sex offense case, the profiles constructed by the profilers were twice as accurate as the profiles constructed by the police detectives, and several times more accurate than the profiles created by college students. Although these findings are intriguing, they are not conclusive. Unfortunately, there were only six people in each of the groups that evaluated the crimes, and the profilers were probably more strongly motivated than the other groups to offer a detailed and accurate profile.

Richard Kocsis and his colleagues followed up with a series of experiments comparing profilers to other groups (Kocsis, Irwin, Hayes, & Nunn, 2000; Kocsis et al., 2002; Kocsis, 2004; Kocsis, 2005). In these experiments, trained profilers, psychologists, detectives, science students, and professed psychics were compared on their ability to provide accurate information about the likely killer in a murder case (Kocsis, 2013). All groups were given a packet of information consisting of crime scene photos, crime reports, and other information investigators typically have at their disposal. After reviewing the evidence, all five groups filled out a questionnaire about the likely characteristics of the murderer (e.g., gender, age, ethnicity, marital status). Because the murderer had already been identified and convicted, researchers already knew the correct answers to the questions. Here is a summary of the findings across all of the studies: The profilers were slightly better at guessing the murderer's physical attributes, but were less accurate than the other groups at inferring murderers' thought processes, social habits, and personal histories. However, even when profilers performed better than other groups, profilers' accuracy rates were fairly low, generally less than 50% (Bennell, Jones, Taylor, & Snook, 2006).

Although these are useful findings, one criticism of these studies is that the number of participants in the profiler group was quite small (a total of 19 profilers when the studies are aggregated, with one study containing only three and another containing only five). These studies have several other methodological problems. They used multiple-choice questionnaires instead of giving participants a chance to generate a profile from scratch. Also, only a small number of the profilers who were asked to participate actually agreed to be a part of a study—this self-selection bias raises the possibility that only the most confident or most motivated profilers volunteered. Finally, the profiler group completed the study away from the supervision of researchers. Perhaps the profiler group took more time to consider the evidence, or perhaps profilers asked colleagues for input into their decisions (Snook, Eastwood, Gendreau, Goggin, & Cullen, 2007).

Other researchers have attempted to determine if there is sufficient stability and patterning in serial crimes to allow profilers to make valid inferences. Andreas Mokros and Laurence Alison (2002) conducted a careful analysis of the characteristics of 100 actual stranger rapes and the rapists who committed them. They coded each crime for the presence of 28 rapist behaviors, including the following: wears disguise; steals personal property; extends time with victim after assault; compliments, apologizes to, or demeans victim; uses surprise attack; blindfolds victim; binds victim; and uses weapon. The researchers then coded police records to learn the rapist's actual characteristics, including age, race, education, marital status, living alone or with others, criminal history, and employment situation. They analyzed their data to answer the question at the heart of the profiling process: "Are similar crimes committed by similar people?" The answer was a resounding "no." No correlation at all. There was no discernible demographic resemblance between the criminals who committed very similar crimes. This stunning lack of correspondence suggests (at least for serial rape) that trying to deduce the attributes of a rapist based on his crime scene behavior may be worse than worthless—it may cause investigators to look for the wrong type of person.

The credibility generally afforded to profiling as an investigative tool appears to be more a function of favorable portrayals in movies and television shows than a function of solid science that demonstrates its effectiveness. A review of the research highlighted this point. Reviewers found that only 27% of published articles on profiling described research studies, and that only 5% of articles focused on theoretical issues. The remaining articles were discussions of profiling, informal summaries of the literature, or descriptions of how a single profile was developed and used in an individual case (Dowden, Bennell, & Bloomfield, 2007). This lack of dispassionate research is critical. We cannot rely on the confident claims of practitioners of profiling because those practitioners have a strong personal and professional stake in promoting the perception that profiling is effective.

 ## PROBLEMS AND PROMISE

Assumptions

Some basic assumptions that undergird criminal profiling have not yet been fully tested or validated. When the assumptions have been tested, they have been discredited by data. First, crime scene characteristics do not seem to fit into neatly bound categories such as "organized" or "disorganized." Instead, they may fall along a continuum, with a few extreme examples being entirely organized or entirely disorganized, but most displaying a combination of types. Second, particular crime scene characteristics do not appear to be reliably associated with particular criminal personality types. The data simply do not allow us to conclude that if a crime scene has a particular characteristic, the perpetrator must therefore be a particular type of person. Third, referring to vague abilities such as "instinct" or "intuition" or "experience" should not be mistaken for clear explanations of the inference process. We do not know how the inference process of profilers works or how it should work.

Cross-Situational Consistency

Another issue concerns how consistent the behavior of an individual criminal is across crimes (Alison, 2005). More generally, although considerable research indicates that aspects of our basic personalities remain stable over time, our behavior is also powerfully determined by the situation (Funder, 2004; Sommers, 2011). For example, if we were trying to develop a profile of you based only on your behavior in a college library, that profile would be very different from the one we would create if we looked only at your behavior at parties, and that profile would be still different from the one we would create if we looked only at your behavior during family gatherings. Context matters. In murder cases, the victim's characteristics (e.g., weak or strong, compliant or defiant), the setting (e.g., secluded or populated), and the killer's emotional state (e.g., agitated or calm) can change. If changing situations lead to changes in the crime scenes, then the resulting profiles would change. Indeed, sometimes investigators erroneously conclude that two crimes are so similar that the same person must have committed them, or they erroneously conclude that two crimes scenes are so different that two different people must be involved. The process of determining whether the same person committed two or more crimes is called **case linkage** (Bennell, et al., 2012; Woodhams, Grant, & Price, 2007).

The Utility of Inferences

Many profiles include speculations that are interesting but of little use to investigators (Alison, McLean, & Almond, 2007; Devery, 2010). For example, consider these speculations about the interpersonal traits of serial killers drawn from profiles:

"unsure of himself," "has problems with women," "poor heterosocial skills." Do you know any males who are not occasionally "unsure of themselves" and that do not have "problems with women" at times? Do such speculations really help us narrow down the population of suspects? In an analysis of 21 American and European profiles created over several years, researchers found that more than 80% of the statements made by profilers were unsupported—that is, the rationales for the statements were not articulated. Further, nearly half of the statements could not be verified even after conviction (e.g., "the killer has a rich fantasy life"), and more than a quarter of the statements were ambiguous and open to interpretation (e.g., "he will have poor social skills") (Alison, Smith, Eastman, & Rainbow, 2003).

In 2005, the self-named BTK killer (a nickname that stands for "bind, torture, and kill") was sentenced to life in prison with no possibility of parole. He had killed at least 10 women. His killing spree began in 1974 and spanned more than 30 years. He had written several letters taunting police and local media in Wichita, Kansas. In their desperate hunt for the BTK killer, local officials sought the expertise of three top FBI profilers who offered their ideas about the killer's identity. Here is the list of statements the profilers offered to guide the Wichita detectives:

- A lone wolf type of personality
- Immature sexual history.
- Heavily into masturbation.
- Women he's been with are either many years younger, very naïve, or much older and depend on him as their meal ticket.
- He drives a decent automobile, but it will be nondescript.
- Lower-middle class, probably living in a rental.
- Middle-class and articulate.
- People might say they remember him but don't really know much about him.
- In his mid to late thirties.
- Might be married, but probably divorced.
- I.Q. at least 105, less than 145.
- This guy isn't mental, but he's crazy like a fox.
- Maybe connected with the military.
- A "now" person needing instant gratification.
- Holds a lower-paying white-collar job, as opposed to blue-collar.
- Might wear a uniform for his job.
- He can function in social settings, but only on the surface.
- He may have women friends he can talk to, but he'd feel very inadequate with a peer-group female.
- Women who have had sex with this guy would describe him as aloof and uninvolved. (Douglas & Dodd, 2007; Gladwell, 2007)

Imagine that you were one of the bewildered investigators faced with this muddled portrait of an elusive killer. Start with the sexual conjecture—look for a guy who masturbates a lot, who is sexually immature, who is aloof in bed, and who has been with women who are either much younger or much older than himself. Generally, these characteristics would not be easily observed by an eyewitness and would not be part of any searchable criminal database. Such information might conceivably be useful to know if you were interviewing suspects, but *if and only if* that information is accurate. Inaccurate information could cause investigators to spin their wheels or go down dead ends. In addition, even if these speculations were accurate, there are problems of ambiguity and verifiability (your authors are both psychologists and we are not sure how to determine whether someone is a "lone wolf, not mental, crazy like a fox, now person"). A final problem with this and other profiles is the number of contradictory elements—the BTK killer would be either lower class *or* middle class, married *or* divorced, would like much older *or* much younger women, and would be average *or* way above average in intelligence.

The actual BTK killer turned out to be a family man, married with two children, living in Park City, Kansas. He had spent four years in the air force, was college educated, and held a steady job at a home burglar-alarm company. He had served as president of the Lutheran church he attended for more than 30 years, and he held leadership positions in the Boy Scouts of America. These specific details would have been very helpful in finding the killer, but these are not the sorts of details that profilers are able to provide. The BTK killer was eventually caught when he sent a disk containing a letter to a local television station. Investigators were able to trace the disk to a computer at his church. This case, like most cases, was not solved by a profile, but by painstaking police work and a slip-up by the criminal.

Persistent Problems

Even when a particular suspect fits a profile, police have an obligation not only to investigate evidence that links the suspect to a crime, but also to pursue evidence that may exclude that suspect from consideration. A serious problem that may result from a profile is what is sometimes called **tunnel vision.** For example, if a profile specifies "a white male in his 30s, who drives a large van, lives alone, and has disturbed relationships with women," and investigators rely on that profile, their focus will be diverted from plausible suspects who do not fit the profile. In this way, misleading profiles may enable criminals to evade capture.

The improvement of profiling techniques will only come with enhanced databases for many types of crimes, systematic research that reveals the conditions under which profiles reliably lead to productive use of investigator resources, and the development of standardized procedures for training profilers and creating profiles. Although profiling has been regarded as a promising investigative tool for decades, that promise is unfulfilled. Two blunt assessments of the current status of criminal profiling are given below. The first is from the former president of the Academy of Behavioral Profiling, and the second is from a team of researchers who conducted a comprehensive review of the available scientific literature:

> . . . **There are currently no accepted educational requirements for criminal profilers, no ethical guidelines, no peer review; nor in many quarters are any of these parameters welcome. . . . The reality is that no research or substantial evidence exists to confirm the validity of one type of profiling over another, or one specific educational experience over another . . . the field of criminal profiling has seen little significant advancement"** (McGrath, 2004).

> **Profiling appears to be an extraneous and redundant technique for use in criminal investigations. Criminal profiling will persist as a pseudoscientific technique until such time as empirical and reproducible studies are conducted on the abilities of large groups of active profilers to predict, with more precision and greater magnitude, the characteristics of offenders"** (Snook et al. 2007).

GEOGRAPHIC PROFILING: AN ALTERNATIVE TO INTUITION

It is useful to contrast intuitive psychological profiling with another relatively established technique: **geographic profiling** (sometimes called "criminal spatial mapping"). Whereas intuitive psychological profiling relies heavily on instinct and inference, geographic profiling relies on maps and mathematics. Key locations associated with serial crimes—particularly crime scenes, but also places where bodies have been dumped or where witnesses have spotted suspicious activities—are plotted on a detailed computerized map (Rossmo & Velarde, 2008). Computer programs with catchy names such as "Predator" and "Dragnet" crunch the data to estimate the general vicinity of the criminal's home or place of work, or a potential location of his next crime. Often, investigators assume that a serial offender stays within a geographic comfort zone and that he is likely to be caught in that zone. The spatial map can be quite detailed, including high crime-risk areas such as bars, nightclubs, parking lots, areas around college campuses, rest stops, and jogging paths (see Figure 5.3). As the number of crimes increases, so should the usefulness of the spatial map. Unlike speculations about a killer's personality, a geographic profile has

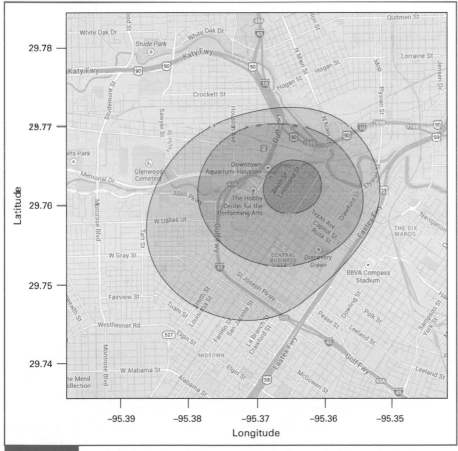

FIGURE 5.3   A Geomap of a criminal's activities: The most distant shaded areas around the periphery are less likely to include an offender's residence, and the shaded areas in the center are more likely to include an offender's residence.

direct implications for investigators; it suggests where to place stakeouts, where to set traps, and where to find potential witnesses who might have seen something suspicious.

Geographic profiling has proven useful in some cases. For example, one such profile helped identify a serial killer who had killed women in several states. His victims were found along major interstate highways. Overlaying the spatial pattern of killings with major trucking routes helped police to find the truck driver responsible for the murders. In a similar case, the so-called "Railway Killer" was identified when investigators developed a geographic profile revealing that all the killings occurred near railway tracks—the killer turned out to be a transient who hopped freight trains to get from one place to another (Hickey & Harris, 2013). Computer programs often look for an **anchor point** from where criminals might launch attacks, and some assume a **buffer zone** around a criminal's home, where he is less likely to commit crimes. Many programs work on the principle of **distance decay,** meaning that the probability of an attack decreases as distance from past crime locations increases (Chainey & Tompson, 2008; Hammond & Youngs, 2011).

Of course, even this more systematic form of profiling has limitations. One such limitation is the quality of the underlying data set and its fit with the case under investigation. Over a 20-day period in the fall of 2002, 10 people were killed by a sniper roaming the Maryland, Virginia, and District of Columbia area. Victims had been shot in public spaces such as malls, gas stations, and bus stops. Not only were the intuitive profiles offered in the case wrong, so was the geographic profile. In the so-called "Beltway Sniper" case, a computer-generated *geoprofile* was constructed based on the sites of the shootings. Extrapolating from those sites, the profile suggested that the killer would likely be living in Montgomery County, Maryland (Horwitz & Ruane, 2003). That speculation turned out to be wrong. The actual killers (a 41-year-old man and his 17-year-old accomplice) were transients who had no real home base. Because the computer program had assumed a home base, it was incapable of supplying useful information. The two killers were eventually apprehended while sleeping in their car at a highway rest stop.

Whereas intuitive profiling relies on the application of human judgment and experience, geoprofiling relies on using statistical techniques to uncover patterns in a criminal's movements and environment. In general, statistical approaches have been found to be superior to intuitive approaches (see Chapter 14). Because geoprofiling is primarily a statistical application that provides concrete information useful in allocating investigative resources, it is more promising than the intuitive personality profiling so often depicted in books, movies, and television shows. But it is not as glamorous or dramatically powerful. Most of us are fascinated with psychological analyses of depravity, but not with statistical analyses of movement patterns.

Particularly in the United Kingdom, the intuitive profiling that gained notoriety during the past few decades is gradually being replaced by what has been called **behavioral investigative advice** (BIA) (Alison & Rainbow, 2011). BIA stresses the role of offering advice to investigators on how to use the media, what questions might be asked during police interviews with suspects, and whether a crime might be part of a series of crimes. Advisors base their advice on the available research and generally make no claims about their ability to penetrate the mind of the serial criminal. Instead of creating a richly detailed psychological portrait of the criminal, the emphasis is on providing useful information to investigators. (To learn more about predictive models for future crimes, see the Scientific American Spotlight box in this section.)

SCIENTIFIC AMERICAN SPOTLIGHT

Predictive Policing: Profiling the Time and Place of Future Crimes
By James Vlahos

Predictive policing techniques combine traditional criminal data with unorthodox information to generate predictions about where crime is likely to happen in the future.

Police computers analyze each crime by time of day, day of the week, and day of the month. Offense locations are parsed by street address, as well as by proximity to places such as ATMs, parks, and bars. The computers are supplied with the paydays of major local employers and the schedules at local concert and sports venues. Everything from the timing of gun shows to the weather and phase of the moon is deemed potentially important.

Evaluating how all these factors might influence future crime requires a partnership between people and machines, with each bringing different strengths to the table. Computers are better at flagging statistical trends, but cops still have to interpret them, says Lt. Col. Howell Starnes. "Until you get that street officer who knows his ward, you won't know what's *causing* the crime," he says. "That's what you've got to look at. Not that you've got a problem—what's causing the problem."

Predictive software does not even need to start with a theory from human overseers, although that can be helpful; the computers can instead troll an ocean of data and devise predictive algorithms automatically, a process known as rule induction. Feed the computer a set of data, and the software will trace combinations of factors that lead to crime, prompting guesses about how novel combinations influence overall future risk. For example, what might happen when there is a gun show scheduled on the same weekend that the weather forecast calls for a heat wave or when there will be a full moon the night of an upcoming payday? The police can essentially throw predictive ideas against the wall, however wacky, and see what sticks. Each time they introduce a new candidate factor, like the schedule of PTA school meetings, they reevaluate the model after the predicted future has happened. How good was the model at foreseeing the crimes that actually wound up happening? "In the end, the model might utilize only a subset of the candidate factors," explains IBM software engineer Bill Hafey, "but it is this subset that constituted the most accurate model."

The factors that lead to crime are multifarious and complex; tracking crime rates back to primary causes remains notoriously difficult. Still, evidence exists that predictive strategies such as Memphis's Blue CRUSH system have helped staunch crime. Since 2006, when Blue CRUSH was instituted, Memphis has shown much sharper drops in the rates of violent and major property crimes than has the rest of the U.S. Violent and major property crimes went down 23 percent.

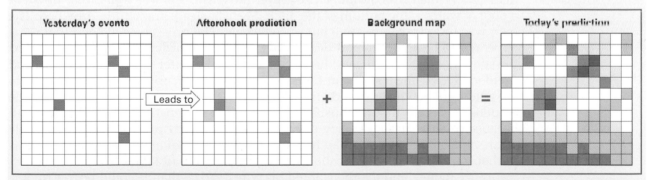

Recent work in criminology has shown that crime shares much in common with earthquakes. Certain areas—be they tough neighborhoods or fault times—are more likely to suffer. And, in the same way that earthquakes spawn aftershocks, a crime will tend to be followed by a temporary uptick in crime rates in nearby areas. Researchers have used this insight to create maps of where crime is likely to happen in the coming days and weeks. They take yesterday's crime reports, build aftershock maps that reflect the increased likelihood of criminal activity in areas close by, and add these aftershock spikes to a background map of typical criminal activity. The police then use the resulting map to dispatch officers to the locations most likely to rumble.

PRECISE PROFILES OR SLOPPY STEREOTYPES?

Examples of loose, subjective profiles can be found in many parts of the legal system. At the extreme, what have been called "profiles" are little more than biased stereotypes. Decisions about who becomes a suspect, who should be interrogated, who should be prosecuted, what evidence is relevant, and who should be convicted are sometimes based on the intuitive profiles held by police officers, attorneys, judges, and jurors. In his classic analysis of police culture and behavior, Jerome Skolnick found that because police officers often find themselves in life-threatening situations, they tend to be alert to ". . . people who may not be engaging in criminal activity, but whose conduct suggests that they might be, or might be the sort of people who would if they could." That is, some people become suspects because they stand out, "as persons whose gestures, language, or attire the police have come to identify as being potentially threatening or dangerous" (Skolnick & Fyfe, 1993, p. 97). In essence, police sometimes rely on intuitive profiles not to solve crimes, but to *predict* criminal behavior. Sometimes these predictions are accurate; sometimes they are not. Too often, people become potential suspects because of easily detected but superficial characteristics like race (see the Hot Topic box for a discussion of racial profiling).

The use of stereotypes or vague profiles can also create problems at trial. In deciding whether to admit testimony at trial, courts must weigh the probative value of the proposed testimony against the potentially prejudicial impact of that testimony. **Probative evidence** provides information that is useful in assessing whether a person committed a crime. Consequently, two questions are crucial: (1) Should information about whether a defendant fits a profile be admissible in court? and (2) Should a defendant's "fit" with a profile be considered evidence?

Deborah Davis and William Follette (2002) describe the case of a man on trial for the murder of his wife. His wife was driving a snowmobile, and he was riding on the back. The woman lost control of the snowmobile and crashed into a ditch. The man and woman were found shortly after the crash. She was found face down in a pool of water at the bottom of the ditch. She was dead, apparently drowned. The man was found face up, alive but unconscious. The prosecutor alleged that what appeared to be an accidental death was actually a murder: The man had caused the snowmobile to crash, held his wife's head underwater until she drowned, and pretended to be unconscious until the rescue. The prosecution was allowed to present evidence that the husband "fit the profile" of a spouse murderer. That "profile evidence" was: (1) that the husband would stand to benefit from his wife's death because of an insurance policy purchased about a year prior to the snowmobile crash, and (2) the husband had had several extramarital affairs during the course of their marriage. The implication was that the man had killed his wife to collect insurance money, and that he wanted his wife dead so that he could be free to pursue other women.

To evaluate the probative value of this evidence statistically, Davis and Follette collected estimates such as the number of men who are unfaithful to their wives (260,000 per million) and the number of men who murder their wives (240 per million). They used this information to calculate the probability that a man who has extramarital affairs is more likely to murder his wife. They concluded that ". . . at maximum, it is .0923% (less than one tenth of one percent) more likely that an unfaithful man will murder his wife at some point in their marriage than it is that a faithful man will murder his wife" (p. 138). Put differently, an inference that a man

HOT TOPIC

Racial Profiling

Racial profiling—using race as an indicator of who might be engaged in criminal activity—has led to several lawsuits. An important early case involved a profile of a serial murderer used by the San Francisco Police Department (Williams, Bazille et al. v. Alioto et al., 1997). In an attempt to catch the killer, the police detained more than 600 black men because they fit a vague profile—a black male, slender to medium build, 5′ 8″ to 6′ tall, 20 to 30 years old, who was traveling either by foot or car between the hours of 8:00 PM and midnight. A court eventually issued an injunction preventing police from stopping black men merely because they fit this broad profile. Another lawsuit arose from the following facts: Although only 17% of drivers on Maryland's highway I-95 were black, 70% of drivers Maryland State Troopers pulled over and searched for drugs were black. At the time, 75% of drivers on the same stretch of highway were white, but only 23% of the drivers who were pulled over and searched were white (Janofsky, 1998).

In 2013, a federal judge ruled that Arizona's Sheriff Joe Arpaio had racially profiled Hispanic drivers and violated their constitutional rights. Police had pulled over hundreds of Hispanic drivers in an effort to crack down on illegal immigration. Sheriff Arpaio had told his officers that one way to tell if someone was in the country legally is whether "they look like they just came from Mexico." The judge held that police could not target illegal immigrants without racially profiling U.S. citizens and legal residents of Hispanic origin.

Easily observed characteristics such as race may be statistically correlated with a particular type of crime. However, focusing on such characteristics as a reason to classify someone as a suspect opens the door to harassment of large groups of innocent people.

National Percentages of Police Traffic Stops and Searches by Race of Driver

	2002 Stopped	2005 Stopped	2002 Searched	2005 Searched
White	8.8	8.9	3.5	3.6
Black/African American	9.2	8.1	11.4	9.5
Hispanic/Latino	8.6	8.9	10.2	8.8

(Vertical axis: Percentage of Drivers Stopped; Horizontal axis: Year)

Used by permission of Project America. Data from U.S. Department of Justice, Bureau of Justice Statistics, National Crime Victimization Survey.

killed his wife *because* he is unfaithful will be wrong more than 99% of the time. The snowmobile case illustrates how inferences drawn from dubious profiles make their way into the courtroom. Judges' decisions about whether to admit or exclude evidence are often partly based on their own subjective profiles about which criminal characteristics are associated with particular crimes. Once judges admit evidence, jurors then may use their own intuitive profiles to help them decide whether the defendant is guilty.

Sometimes the courts take notice of the misuse of unscientific stereotype evidence. In *State of Oregon v. Hansen* (1987), the court overturned the conviction of a high school teacher who had engaged in a sexual affair with one of her students. The appeals court held that it was an error for the trial judge to allow a police detective to testify that Ms. Hansen fit the profile of a child molester:

Detective Robson testified to what might be described as a "profile" of a nonviolent child abuser who is unrelated to the child: physical and psychological "testing" of the child, giving gifts, showing affection, praising, making the child feel comfortable in the abuser's presence, etc. That child abusers use these techniques has no bearing on whether a person who does these things is a child abuser. For example, it is probably accurate to say that the vast majority of persons who abuse children sexually are male. This says little, if anything, however, about whether a particular male defendant has sexually abused a child. . . . The danger of unfair prejudice to the defendant from the unwarranted inference that because the defendant engages in acts that sexual child abusers engage in, she, too, is a sexual child abuser is simply too great (p. 157).

 ## PSYCHOLOGICAL AUTOPSIES

Suppose a man is driving alone on a winding stretch of highway that skirts the edge of a high cliff. His car veers off the road, plunges several hundred feet, crashes into the rocks below, and bursts into flames. The man is killed. This is an example of an **equivocal death.** That is, it is not clear why the car fell from the cliff. One possibility is that the man's death was accidental—Perhaps he was tired and dozed off for a second or two, perhaps he had been drinking, perhaps his attention lapsed while he was trying to find the CD he wanted to play. A second possibility is that the man committed suicide; he knew that the fall was certain to kill him, but he wanted to make it look like an accident so that his wife and children would receive an insurance payout of several hundred thousand dollars (many life insurance policies do not pay survivors if a death was a suicide). A third possibility is that the death was actually a murder disguised to look like an accident—perhaps someone who knew that the man would be driving that stretch of highway tampered with the brakes or steering of his car. In what is called the **NASH system** for death classification, a death can fall into one of four categories: *n*atural, *a*ccidental, *s*uicide, or *h*omicide.

Just as the name implies, a **psychological autopsy** is an effort to dissect and examine the psychological state of a person prior to his or her death. Of course, the analogy between physical and psychological autopsies is not perfect. Injuries on a dead body can be closely examined. A corpse can be cut open, body parts can be weighed, measured, and chemically analyzed. There is no comparable "psychological corpse" to examine. The autopsy-like psychological analysis must rely on less direct sources of evidence. Typically, these sources include any records left behind by the deceased (letters, e-mails, journal entries, cell phone records, audio or video recordings, bank accounts, student or employee records) as well as data about the person gathered from interviews with friends, family members, or co-workers who were in contact with the deceased prior to his or her death. The goal is to reconstruct the dead person's emotional state, personality, thoughts, and lifestyle. Inferences about the deceased person's intentions and emotional state just prior to death are crucial to the analysis (Connor, et al., 2011).

Researchers have developed checklists to assist medical examiners in distinguishing between suicide and accidental death. Most checklists emphasize two basic criteria: whether the death might have been self-inflicted and whether there were clear indications of an intention to die (Botello, Noguchi, Sathyavagiswaran, Weinberger, & Gross , 2013). In many cases, the determination of whether the death could have been self-inflicted is straightforward. It is possible to poison yourself, jump from a tall building, or drive your car off a cliff. It is even possible to drown yourself. But it is quite difficult to beat yourself to death with a baseball bat or shoot yourself from across a room. If investigators conclude that a death was self-inflicted, they must then determine if that death was accidental or intentional. For example, psychologists would be more likely to conclude that the man who drove off a cliff had committed suicide if he had been noticeably depressed, if he had made an effort to "put his affairs in order," if he had been experiencing serious emotional or physical pain, if he had severe financial problems, if he had made previous suicide threats or attempts, if he had made attempts to say goodbye to people close to him, or if he had expressed a desire to die.

Several researchers have proposed lists of questions to ask and issues to consider to help psychologists make the tricky determination of whether someone committed suicide (e.g., Simon, 2006). Below is a 16-issue checklist used to assist psychologists in making the determination.

1. Pathological evidence (autopsy) indicates self-inflicted death.
2. Toxological evidence indicates self-inflicted death.
3. Statements by witnesses indicate self-inflicted death.
4. Investigatory evidence (e.g., police reports, photos from crime scene) indicates self-inflicted death.
5. Psychological evidence (observed behavior, lifestyle, personality).
6. State of the deceased indicates self-inflicted death.
7. Evidence indicates the decedent recognized high potential lethality of means of death.
8. Decedent had suicidal thoughts.
9. Decedent had recent and sudden change in affect (emotions).
10. Decedent had experienced serious depression or mental disorder.
11. Decedent had made an expression of hopelessness.
12. Decedent had made an expression of farewell, indicated desire to die.
13. Decedent had experienced stressful events or significant losses (actual or threatened).
14. Decedent had experienced general instability in immediate family.
15. Decedent had recent interpersonal conflicts.
16. Decedent had history of generally poor physical health.

When information about the dead person and the manner of death is plentiful, such checklists have proven quite useful. In one study, researchers looked at 126 cases in which the cause of death was already known. Coders then attempted to distinguish between suicides and accidental deaths by classifying the deaths on the 16 issues listed above. They were able to distinguish between the two types of death with 92% accuracy (Jobes, Casey, Berman, & Wright, 1991). Of course, there is often inadequate information. Without written records, audio or video recordings, or people in whom the person confided (and who are willing to talk to an investigator), it is difficult to say whether someone took his or her own life.

Often, the findings of a psychological autopsy are equivocal. If the man who drove his car off a cliff had been depressed, we may lean slightly toward a judgment of suicide; but we cannot be sure. Sometimes, the available evidence, though not compelling or conclusive, may be sufficient to settle the legal issue at stake. If the man who drove off a cliff showed no clear signs of being suicidal, his wife and children will probably receive the insurance money.

Legal Status of Psychological Autopsies

Courts have been receptive to expert testimony based on a form of psychological autopsy in some civil cases. When the distribution of assets specified in a will is challenged in court, the conflict usually turns on whether the deceased person was legally competent when the will was written or revised. An investigation or "autopsy" of the state of mind and intentions of a person at the time his or her will was drawn up is critical to a decision about whether the will is legally binding. If medical records and testimony from friends and family members indicate that the deceased was suffering from some form of dementia, the will may be ruled invalid. This limited form of psychological autopsy is routinely allowed in court.

In contrast, in criminal cases, courts have generally been reluctant to allow expert testimony based on psychological autopsies. However, in one criminal case—*Jackson v. State of Florida* (1989)—psychological autopsy testimony was not only admitted, but, on appeal, the trial court's decision to allow the testimony was upheld. The case involved a spectacularly bad mother named Theresa Jackson and her 17-year-old daughter, Tina Mancini. Unemployed and struggling to meet her financial obligations, Ms. Jackson encouraged her underage daughter to take a job as a nude dancer in a nearby strip club. To get around the law, Ms. Jackson changed the birth date on her daughter's birth certificate and forged the signature of a notary. Tina's dancing earned her several hundred dollars a week, but her mother charged Tina more than $300 a week for rent and living expenses. The nude dancing job was a continuing source of conflict between mother and daughter—Theresa Jackson wanted Tina to work more; Tina wanted to quit. Ms. Jackson threatened her daughter and told her that if she did quit, Ms. Jackson would report her to the police for underage dancing. Tina Mancini committed suicide before her 18th birthday.

Following her daughter's death, Theresa Jackson was tried and convicted of forgery, procuring sexual performance by a child, and child abuse. At trial, a psychiatrist concluded that the psychologically abusive relationship between mother and daughter had contributed to Tina Mancini's suicide. Jackson appealed the conviction, claiming that the trial judge should not have permitted psychological autopsy testimony about her daughter. In upholding the lower court's decision, the appellate court found that allowing testimony about the mental state of someone who died of suicide is not qualitatively different from allowing testimony about the sanity of someone accused of murder or allowing testimony about the mental competence of someone who had written a will.

In an inventive attempt to extend the ruling in the *Jackson* case, a defendant argued that an expert should be able to testify in support of his claim of self-defense (*Sysyn v. State*, 2000). The argument was that the defendant shot the victim in the head because she had deliberately attacked and provoked the defendant in an effort to commit suicide. This theory, it was argued, would be strongly supported by the findings of a psychological autopsy showing that the victim was suicidal. The trial court excluded the expert testimony, and an appellate court upheld the conviction.

▶ IN CONCLUSION

At present, we have no good estimates of how often profiles have been useful and how often they have been useless or even counterproductive. We do not know the error rates or the rates of success. Some profiles have led to the arrest of guilty people; some profiles have led to the arrest of innocent people. Some profiles have pointed police in the right direction; others have led police astray and wasted time and resources. And, while police are looking in the wrong direction, the trail of the real criminal can grow cold.

Some variations of profiling techniques—for example, geoprofiling and psychological autopsies—appear to yield useful clues in solving crimes or making sense of an equivocal death. However, the ability of such techniques to generate useful inferences depends on the quality and quantity of available data. Before a geoprofile can be generated, several related crimes must occur. Similarly, if there is little information about the predeath thoughts and behaviors of a now-dead person, a psychological autopsy can only produce equivocal findings. Only continued research will allow us to specify the conditions under which various profiling techniques are useful in moving investigations forward.

► CRITICAL THINKING QUESTIONS

1. When is it reasonable to rely on criminal profiling to solve a crime? When is it counterproductive?

2. Why might people believe that criminal profiling works despite a lack of evidence that it is effective?

3. Under what circumstances is it useful to know that a defendant fits the profile of others who commit the type of crime the defendant is accused of committing? Is it useful to know that a defendant is psychologically similar to other child molesters, rapists, or murderers?

4. Is it ever reasonable to consider race when trying to predict criminal behavior? Is it ever reasonable to consider gender?

5. Do you believe there is sufficient research evidence to demonstrate the usefulness of criminal profiling in cases involving serial killers? Why or why not?

6. Should the findings of psychological autopsies be admissible in court? If so, under what conditions?

► KEY TERMS

anchor point (p. 106)
behavioral investigative
    advice (BIA) (p. 106)
buffer zone (p. 106)
case linkage (p. 101)
disorganized killers (p. 98)
distance decay (p. 106)

equivocal death (p. 110)
geographic profiling
    (p. 105)
hedonistic types (p. 99)
mission-oriented types
    (p. 99)
NASH system (p. 110)

organized killers (p. 98)
power-oriented types
    (p. 99)
probative evidence (p. 108)
profiling (p. 93)
psychological autopsy
    (p. 110)

racial profiling (p. 109)
serial killers (p. 94)
signature aspect of the
    crime (p. 94)
tunnel vision (p. 104)
visionary types (p. 99)

6 Jury Selection

▶ Assembling a Jury: Pools, Venires, and *Voir Dire*
▶ Using Stereotypes and Science to Select Jurors
▶ Juror Characteristics and Attitudes as Predictors of Verdict
▶ Pretrial Publicity as a Source of Bias
▶ An Overview of Trial Procedure

Imagine that you have been selected as a juror. You are plucked from your normal routine and asked to listen for days, weeks, or months to lawyers, witnesses, and a judge. You may hear about specialized but slippery legal concepts—burden of proof, preponderance of evidence, proximate cause, reasonable doubt, mitigation, aggravation, negligence. You may hear about hideous crimes or terrible tragedies. Perhaps someone has been raped or murdered, perhaps faulty construction has caused a building to collapse, perhaps a shoddy medical procedure has resulted in brain damage or death. You may see photographs of dead bodies; you may hear heart-wrenching testimony from surviving victims or the loved ones of dead victims. You will almost certainly hear from competing expert witnesses who view the evidence in very different ways. Your job will be to make sense of it all, to interpret the law, to decide what is fair and just.

Before a jury trial can begin, a jury must be selected. It is often argued that picking a jury is one of the most consequential steps in the trial process. This chapter describes the multistep process of jury selection and reviews research on how jury selection influences verdicts. In preparation for the chapters that follow, this chapter ends with a brief overview of trial procedure. ◀

ASSEMBLING A JURY: POOLS, VENIRES, AND *VOIR DIRE*

Early juries were not designed to be neutral and unbiased. They were comprised of a defendant's neighbors and acquaintances. The logic was that previous dealings with the defendant and prior knowledge of his or her reputation would be useful in assessing the defendant's credibility. An understanding of the defendant would help jurors reach a just verdict. In contrast, modern juries are intended to be impartial. The Sixth Amendment guarantees the right to a trial by an "impartial" jury in criminal cases, and the Seventh Amendment guarantees the right to a trial by jury in most civil cases. Ideally, the jury is an impartial group that represents community values.

But how can we achieve an impartial jury? According to the **Jury Selection and Service Act of 1968** and the U.S. Supreme Court in *Taylor v. Louisiana* (1975), federal and state courts must assemble juries that constitute a "fair cross-section of the community." Some reformers have suggested that the ideal way to assemble juries would simply be to require every adult citizen to register for jury service. Then, for each jury trial, 12 people could be selected randomly from a master list and be required to serve. For a variety of reasons, the actual selection procedure is far more complicated. We depart from this inclusive, perfectly random procedure for reasons of necessity and in an effort to seat a fair, impartial jury. What is usually referred to as jury selection is actually a process of *de*selection. At every step in the long process of assembling a jury, some potential jurors are dismissed or excluded. Every jury consists of the people who remain at the end of this long process of deselection.

From Jury Pool to Venire

To set the process in motion, a local jury commissioner needs a list of the names and addresses of citizens in a particular geographical area who speak English, are over the age of 18, are mentally competent, and who have never been convicted of a felony. Unfortunately, no such list exists. Even if such a list did exist it would need to be updated continually as people died, moved away from or into the area, turned 18 years of age, became mentally incompetent, or became convicted felons. So, jury commissioners must use the best information at their disposal. And, according to the Jury Selection and Service Act of 1968, the "primary source" for identifying eligible jurors is voter registration lists. Many states add lists of licensed drivers and telephone directories to the juror pool. Some states add other government lists, for example, tax rolls and people receiving unemployment benefits or food stamps. But the laws in most states do not require that officials go beyond voter lists. The inability (compounded by a lack of effort in some states) to obtain a full accounting of eligible potential jurors introduces the first layer of bias. The list used by jury commissioners often underrepresents poor people, African Americans, Hispanics, people who move frequently, and people who recently turned 18 (Abramson, 1995; Rose, 2009).

Next, a random sample of jurors is drawn from the jury pool, and everyone in this sample of potential jurors is sent a summons to appear in a particular courthouse at an assigned date and time. The group of prospective jurors that shows up is called the **venire** (from the Latin meaning "cause to come" or "come when called"). Unfortunately, approximately 20% of the people summoned for jury duty simply fail to show up (Mize, Hannaford-Agor, & Waters, 2007). In many places, these no-shows are not aggressively pursued as long as enough people do show up. There are large variations in the size of the venire (also called a panel) depending on where the case is being tried, the rulings of the presiding judge, and the characteristics of the case. For a relatively routine case with a strict judge in a small town, lawyers may begin with a 30-person venire. In a serious, high-profile case that has received a lot of pretrial publicity, the venire may consist of more than 100 people.

No-shows shrink the size of the venire a bit; exemptions and exclusions shrink the venire even further. People who are summoned are asked to indicate on a questionnaire whether they fit into a category that may be legally exempt from jury service (e.g., non-English speakers, people who are legally blind, police officers). Some jurors are lost at this stage, although in recent years the number of automatic exemptions has been reduced and continues to be reduced even further. More potential jurors are lost because of special pleas that jury service would cause them "undue hardship or extreme inconvenience." This vague category can be used to accommodate a vast number of excuses for avoiding jury service. One potential juror may have primary responsibility for the care of a young child, another might suffer from a serious medical condition, and another might have nonrefundable plane tickets to Bali. A juror might also be excused because jury service would cause hardship to the local community—he or she might be the only physician or mortician in a small rural town. To reduce the number of hardship exemptions and make jury service less burdensome, the **one day or one trial** system has been widely adopted. Under this system, potential jurors make themselves available for one day. If they are selected to serve on a jury, they are done when that trial is over. If they are not selected (most people who show up are not selected), they are done with jury duty at the end of the day. Although some trials go on for months, most trials only last about a week. (See Figure 6.1 for a breakdown of the steps of jury selection.)

Voir Dire

The final stage in the process is *voir dire* (French for "to see and tell" or "to speak the truth"). During this stage, attorneys and the judge ask potential jurors a series of questions to determine who will serve on the jury (an unusual aspect of federal courts is that judges tend to conduct *voir dire* and the scope of questioning is much more limited). *Voir dire* is a sort of pretrial interview, usually held in open court. It is during *voir dire* that lawyers (sometimes assisted by consultants) get their chance to remove or "challenge" potential jurors. Lawyers have two types of challenges at their disposal: **challenges for cause** and peremptory challenges. When a lawyer challenges a would-be juror for cause, he or she is claiming that, because of bias or prejudice, it is unlikely that the juror will be able to render an impartial verdict based only on evidence and law. For example, a plaintiff's attorney may not want a physician serving on a medical malpractice case, and a defense attorney may not want a retired police officer on a drug possession trial. A juror can also be challenged if he or she is unable to be fair and impartial or is unable to follow the law (e.g., a juror might say that she would hold it against a defendant if he chose not to testify on his own behalf). In theory, there is no limit to the number of challenges for cause, although the judge must agree to dismiss the juror and the patience of judges is limited.

If a judge refuses to dismiss a potential juror for cause, the lawyer must decide whether or not to use a **peremptory challenge.** Using this more powerful type of challenge, an attorney can dismiss a juror without giving a reason and without approval from the judge. Each attorney is allotted a small number of peremptory challenges—the number varies depending on where the trial is held and on the type and seriousness of the charge against the defendant. In a routine civil trial, each side may be given as few as 3, but in a capital murder trial, each side may get as many as 25. In federal felony cases, the prosecution usually gets 6 peremptory challenges, while the defense usually gets 10. Defense attorneys usually get more peremptory challenges because their clients have more at stake—there is almost always the possibility that a criminal defendant will be sent to prison or that a civil defendant will be ordered to pay damages.

Many critics of the jury system have argued that lawyers use their challenges to "stack" juries. This is true in the sense that lawyers are hoping to remove jurors who might be unsympathetic to their client's case. In an adversarial system, lawyers do not want neutral jurors, they want jurors who will favor their side of the case. However, the underlying purpose of *voir dire* is to create a fair and impartial jury by allowing both sides to eliminate people who—because of their job, life experiences, or attitudes—might be unable to reach an unbiased verdict. *Voir dire* is also used to educate jurors about issues relevant to the upcoming trial, and to get jurors to make commitments about how they will evaluate the evidence. For example, a defense attorney might ask if a juror supports the rule that allows criminal defendants not to testify at their own trial. This line of questioning allows the attorney to emphasize

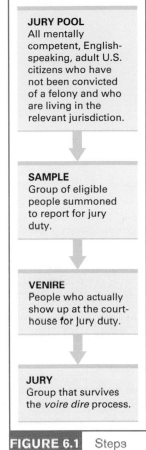

JURY POOL
All mentally competent, English-speaking, adult U.S. citizens who have not been convicted of a felony and who are living in the relevant jurisdiction.

SAMPLE
Group of eligible people summoned to report for jury duty.

VENIRE
People who actually show up at the courthouse for jury duty.

JURY
Group that survives the *voire dire* process.

FIGURE 6.1 Steps in the process of jury selection

to all potential jurors that they cannot hold it against the defendant if she decides not to testify on her own behalf.

In sum, jury selection is a long winnowing process. Some people are excluded because their names do not appear on available lists, more people are excluded because they do not show up when summoned, a few people are legally exempt, some manage to get out of jury service because of real or claimed hardship, and some are dismissed by the prosecution or defense during *voir dire.* It is the people who remain that comprise a particular jury.

Cognizable Groups

In addition to limits on the number of challenges, there are a few other broad restraints on the ability of lawyers to remove people from the jury panel. Because the goal is to empanel an unbiased, representative jury, the law forbids the intentional exclusion of jurors on the basis of race or gender. Members of certain groups are **cognizable** in the sense that they are recognized as sharing a characteristic or attitude that distinguishes them from other potential jurors. Lawyers are prohibited from using their peremptory challenges to eliminate members of some specific cognizable groups. In *Batson v. Kentucky* (1986), the Supreme Court ruled that James Batson—a black man convicted of burglary by an all-white jury—had been denied his Fourteenth Amendment right to equal protection. Prosecutors had used their peremptory challenges to exclude every potential black juror in the venire. The protection provided by *Batson* was extended to the category of gender in 1994 (*J.E.B. v. Ala. ex rel.,* 1994). That is, women or men cannot be excluded during *voir dire* because of their gender.

Do you think jurors might view a case differently because of differences in their age, race, or gender? (*Image Source/Getty Images*)

In practice, if a lawyer uses a peremptory challenge against a black juror, the judge may ask the lawyer for an explanation. That lawyer will then offer a race-neutral explanation for the challenge (e.g., the juror is married to a probation officer). That explanation needs to be seen as credible by the judge. Often, such race-neutral justifications are accepted by the judge and the juror is excused (Sommers, 2008). Since 1995, courts have been asked to prevent the exclusion of potential jurors who are short or obese or Italian American or Irish American. Most such requests have been denied, but courts have extended protection beyond race and gender to include religion. However, although lawyers are not permitted to strike a potential juror because of his or her religious affiliation (e.g., Catholic, Protestant, Jewish, or Muslim), lawyers are allowed to strike a potential juror because of a particular religiously based belief (e.g., a reluctance to sit in judgment of others, a belief that the death penalty is morally wrong; *United States v. DeJesus,* 2003).

Two final points about the meaning of representativeness. First, from a statistical perspective, it is unrealistic to imagine that any group of 12 jurors (or fewer) can be fully *representative* of a much larger community. The sample size is simply too small. Second, while a particular jury may include a diverse assortment of people, no one person is expected to represent the views of a particular constituency. A 25-year-old white female is not expected to try to represent the views of all other white females in their 20s, and a 42-year-old Asian male is not expected to try to represent the views of all other Asian males in their 40s. The best we can hope for is diversity in age, ethnicity, experience, and opinion. Such diversity is likely to reduce the expression of various forms of prejudice (e.g., racism or sexism), promote fuller discussion, and lead to better fact-finding (Crano & Seyranian, 2009). Also, as discussed in Chapter 1, the legal system must have legitimacy in the eyes of the public. If juries systematically exclude women, or particular racial groups, it damages the perceived (as well as the actual) legitimacy of the legal system.

► USING STEREOTYPES AND SCIENCE TO SELECT JURORS

Lawyers preparing to try a case before a jury must attempt to figure out which potential jurors will be least favorable to their side of the case. They do not have much to go on. Some juror characteristics are easy to see—female or male, old or young, thin or heavy, tall or short. Perhaps some of the men have beards. Perhaps some of the women wear a lot of make-up. Maybe some of the potential jurors wear expensive jewelry or have visible tattoos or body piercings. In addition, there may be information from a written questionnaire asking a broad range of questions about likes and dislikes, religious and political attitudes, hobbies and interests. In some cases, the prosecution or defense team will conduct a **social media analysis.** That is, they will scour the Internet—focusing on Facebook, Google, Twitter, and public records websites—to gather personal information and create a fuller profile of each potential juror's attitudes, interests, and experiences (Broda-Bahm, 2011). Finally, there are the answers to the questions attorneys ask jurors during *voir dire* and behavior during *voir dire*. Do potential jurors seem honest or deceptive? Are they well-spoken or fumbling? Do they seem arrogant or humble? Do they seem interested in what the attorneys, the judge, and the other potential jurors have to say? Does a juror seem like she might become the group leader during deliberations?

The problem is that no matter what attorneys are able to find out by looking and listening, they cannot possibly know in advance how a particular juror will respond to the evidence in the case about to be tried, and they cannot know how that juror will influence and be influenced by other jurors in the deliberation room. This uncertainty coupled with the high-stakes consequences of the trial has led many attorneys to search out any information that might give them and their clients an advantage in trying to evaluate jurors. At one extreme are anxious lawyers who, in a misguided attempt to know the unknowable, have paid for the services of handwriting analysts, astrologers, and physiognomists (consultants who make inferences about personality based on facial features such as a high forehead, a strong chin, or thin lips). At the other extreme are a few attorneys who forego *voir dire* and declare that they will accept the first group of jurors called. Usually, this bold declaration is accompanied by a statement that the lawyer believes that every person called is fair, thoughtful, and honest, and that the facts of the case will lead each of them to the correct verdict. Of course, this strategy is intended to convey to jurors that the lawyer is highly confident about the merits of the case and to depict opposing counsel as overly concerned with trying to select a favorable jury. (To see an outline of variations in *voir dire* procedures, see Table 6.1.)

To guide their decision making, some lawyers have developed crude shortcuts for selecting jurors. Manuals for trial attorneys are full of advice on how to pick

TABLE 6.1	
Variations in *Voir Dire* Procedures	
Traditional, Limited Voir Dire	*Expansive Voir Dire*
No pretrial juror questionnaire	Pretrial questionnaire
No social media analysis	Social media analysis
Limited number of questions	Larger number of questions
Closed-ended questions that permit only "yes" or "no" answers	Combination of closed-ended and open-ended questions
Group questioning of prospective jurors	Individual, sequestered *voir dire*
Judge alone conducts *voir dire*	Judge and lawyers both participate

(Adapted from: Hans, V.P. & Jehle, A. (2003). The jury in practice: Avoid bald men and people with green socks? Other ways to improve the voir dire process in jury selection. Chicago-Kent Law Review, 78, 1179–1201.)

jurors. Some of this advice relies on simplistic stereotypes about ethnic and occupational groups. Here is a sampling:

> Women are more punitive than men by a score of about five to one. There's a reason for that: Women always had to toe the line. Women are splendid jurors for the prosecution in rape cases, baby cases . . . . Yuppies are the worst jurors: They fear crime, love property, and haven't suffered enough to be sympathetic. (Spence, cited in Adler, 1994, p. 55).

> The rule of thumb here: artists, writers, musicians, actors and public figures generally make good plaintiff jurors on the civil side, and good defendant's jurors in the criminal case. As plaintiff's counsel and a criminal defendant's lawyer, I love this type of juror. (Belli, cited in Monahan & Walker, 2014, p. 170)

Though there may be a kernel of truth in a few of these stereotypes, they are obviously exaggerated and superficial. But are there any personal characteristics that make a juror more or less likely to convict?

Scientific Jury Selection

Famed defense attorney Clarence Darrow said, "Never forget, almost every case has been won or lost when the jury is sworn" (Kressel & Kressel, 2002, p. 8). Darrow seems to have overstated the case for the importance of jury selection, but there is no doubt that the process of picking jurors can have important effects.

Are lawyers effective in getting rid of jurors who will be unsympathetic to their side of the case? A few researchers have attempted to answer this question. An elegant early study (Zeisel & Diamond, 1978) of this issue examined juror votes in 12 criminal trials. To find out if jurors who were dismissed through peremptory challenges were any more or less likely to convict than jurors who were not challenged, the researchers persuaded the stricken jurors to stay in the courtroom and listen to the case. The votes of this shadow jury were then compared with the votes of the actual jury. Making use of interviews with the shadow jurors and posttrial interviews with the real jurors, the researchers were able to reconstruct how the jury would have decided the case if there had been no peremptory challenges. Did the attorneys' use of challenges tilt the balance in favor of their clients? Not much, if at all. On a scale where 0 means that an attorney made as many good challenges as bad challenges and 100 means that an attorney managed to bump every juror who would have sided against her, prosecutors' average score was near zero (0.5). Defenders did better, but not by much—their average score was 17. This is not to say that all attorneys were ineffective. Despite these unimpressive average performances, there were some attorneys who did very well in specific cases (the highest score was 62). This means that if a skilled attorney is matched against one who is unskilled, the impact of *voir dire* on jury composition could be decisive for the case. Effective use of peremptory challenges appeared to influence verdicts in 3 of the 12 cases studied.

In a later study, the jury selection strategies of seasoned lawyers were compared with those of college students and law school students (Olczak, Kaplan, & Penrod, 1991). The lawyers were no better than the students at judging the personalities of mock jurors or at picking favorable jurors. When lawyers were asked to watch a videotaped *voir dire* and then indicate who they might strike, they were unable to perform better than chance in detecting bias. Also, in a study of four criminal trials, the juries eventually selected were, on average, no better for the prosecution or the defense than the first 12 jurors who were questioned or a randomly selected group of prospective jurors (Johnson & Haney, 1994).

If the average performance of lawyers is underwhelming, maybe selection could be improved through the systematic application of social scientific expertise. That is, maybe psychologists and other social scientists can do better than lawyers. Whereas lawyers rely on their experience and intuition, social scientists rely on data collection.

The first attempt at so-called **"scientific jury selection"** occurred in 1972 during the "Harrisburg Seven" case in Pennsylvania. In that case, a team of social scientists worked to help attorneys defend seven Catholic anti-Vietnam war activists who were accused of pouring blood on draft records, conspiring to blow up underground electrical systems in Washington, DC, and plotting to kidnap the secretary of state. The researchers interviewed more than 800 residents of Harrisburg, gathered demographic information (e.g., race, gender, age, education, income, political orientation, religious affiliation), and measured attitudes relevant to the trial (e.g., attitudes toward the war in Vietnam, the rights of political dissenters, trust in the federal government). Next, researchers examined the correlations between the measured characteristics and attitudes toward the defendants. These correlations were then used to construct profiles of jurors who were likely to be pro-defense or pro-prosecution. The data indicated that the ideal prosecution juror would be a Republican businessman who identified himself as a Presbyterian, Methodist, or fundamentalist Christian, and who belonged to a local civic organization. The ideal defense juror was identified as "a female Democrat with no religious preference and a white-collar or skilled blue-collar job" (Schulman, Shaver, Colman, Emrick, & Christie, 1973). Jury selection by the defense team was guided by these data-based profiles. During *voir dire*, researchers rated every one of the 46 potential jurors on a 5-point scale ranging from "very undesirable for the defense" to "very good for the defense."

Did these techniques work? We cannot say for sure, but the trial ended in a hung jury—10 jurors voted to acquit, and 2 voted to convict. A mistrial was declared and the government chose not to retry the case. Given prevailing public opinion and the strong evidence against the defendants, the outcome was widely regarded as a triumph of scientific jury selection.

Another high-profile case that has been regarded as a triumph of jury selection was the 1995 murder trial of O. J. Simpson. Mr. Simpson—a famous football

Do you think the verdict in the Simpson trial would have been different if the jury had been different? (Bill Robles)

player, a minor celebrity, and occasional actor—stood trial for the brutal stabbing murders of his ex-wife and her friend. The defense team hired a jury consultant who was involved in every stage of the case from pre-trial planning to verdict. In contrast, the prosecutors dismissed their jury consultant on the second day of jury selection and disregarded his advice, preferring to rely on their own intuition (Posey & Wrightsman, 2005). The prosecutor did not even use all of her peremptory challenges.

Jury consultants on both sides of the Simpson case looked closely at data from individual and group interviews. They concluded that African American women would be the group least likely to convict Simpson. Indeed, black women were more than three times as likely as black men to believe that Simpson was innocent (Kressel & Kressel, 2002). This finding was in direct conflict with the prosecutor's intuition that because of Simpson's history of wife battering, women would be much more likely to convict. Interviews with prospective jurors conducted by the jury consultants uncovered other important findings: According to the research, black females were much more likely to excuse and forgive Simpson's physical abuse of his ex-wife and were likely to view the lead prosecutor in the case as a pushy "castrating bitch" (Bugliosi, 1996). In addition, both male and female black jurors were found to be much more receptive to a key theme in the defense case—that corrupt, racist police officers planted evidence to frame O. J. Simpson. Finally, pretrial research showed that well-educated jurors were much more inclined to trust the key incriminating evidence for the prosecution—DNA evidence. The jury that eventually heard the case included eight black women, two white women, one black man, and one Latino man. Only two of the jurors were college graduates and five had reported that they had personally had negative experiences with police officers (Toobin, 1996). Jurors found the DNA evidence unconvincing. In a posttrial interview one of the jurors put it this way, "I didn't understand the DNA stuff at all. To me, it was just a waste of time. It was way out there and carried absolutely no weight with me" (Bugliosi, 1996, p. 68). After listening to evidence and testimony for 8 months, it took the jury less than 4 hours to reach a verdict of "not guilty" on all charges.

Do these two high-profile cases mean that jury consultants can "rig" or "stack" juries? Probably not. An alternative explanation for the outcomes in these cases is that the lawyers in these cases were especially skilled. In general, it may be that attorneys who seek out trial consultants are also more conscientious in preparing their cases, more thorough in questioning witnesses, and more effective in presenting their cases. This conscientiousness and effectiveness may be what leads to success. A second alternative explanation is that, although scientific jury selection does not make a big difference in most trials, it may make a difference in a subset of cases in which juror characteristics strongly influence the interpretation of ambiguous evidence. The two trials described above may have been part of that subset.

The Use of Trial Consultants

Trial consultants are usually hired by companies that are being sued for large sums of money (e.g., a trial might involve an allegedly defective product that caused severe injuries or even death). Sometimes, wealthy defendants hire trial consultants in criminal cases. (See the Hot Topic box in this section on jury consulting and the role of money at trial.) These consultants often employ a data-driven approach both before and during trial. First, a large group (typically 20 to 50) of eligible jurors from the community where the case will be tried are recruited and asked to fill out an extensive questionnaire about their attitudes, habits, and personal characteristics. This group serves as a mock jury. The mock jurors then hear a condensed version of the trial and are questioned about their reactions to the case. Sometimes, the mock juries deliberate as the consultant watches via video or a two-way mirror. The reactions and interpretations of the mock jurors are analyzed to provide insight into both jurors and arguments. One goal is to discover consistent relationships between juror characteristics and responses to the evidence in a particular case. The resulting profiles of favorable or unfavorable jurors then guide the use of peremptory challenges. If a case goes to trial, consultants often design and analyze **supplemental juror questionnaires** that prospective jurors fill out before *voir dire* (these questionnaires are submitted by attorneys and approved by the judge). Questions might include information about personal experiences (Have you ever been misdiagnosed by a physician?), beliefs (Would you describe yourself as a religious person?), and affiliations (Do you donate time or money to any groups, clubs, or organizations?).

Second, and probably more important, by asking mock jurors about their reactions, consultants get a clearer sense of the strengths and weaknesses of a case. Based on such analyses, litigants may decide to settle instead of going to trial, or they may be able to abandon their weak arguments and focus only on their strong arguments. Most consultants have expanded beyond jury selection to the development

HOT TOPIC

Jury Consulting and the Role of Money at Trial

Perhaps the most important question about trial consulting is ethical rather than scientific: Does it promote justice or prevent justice? Just because we can use scientific methods to help select jurors or fine-tune the presentations of attorneys, should we? Jury consultants emphasize that they are merely using more systematic, sophisticated techniques to do what attorneys have always done—to get rid of jurors who might be unsympathetic to their case, and to identify the most powerful arguments to use at trial. It could be argued that when consultants help a weak attorney do a better job of representing a client, they may be improving the adversarial system and serving the interests of justice. But the most basic problem is that consultants usually work for wealthy business interests that are willing and able to pay the fees of consultants. This means that the scales of justice are further tilted in favor of the rich. Because wealthy defendants usually have the advantage of being able to hire the best lawyers, jury consultants often amplify the advantages of rich clients. While it is true that some trial consultants (like some law firms) provide **pro bono** (free of charge) services to clients who cannot afford to pay, these services are only a tiny fraction of the cases taken on by consultants. Of course, the fact that wealthy defendants can afford more justice cannot be blamed on trial consultants. Ideally, in an adversarial system, lawyers representing the two sides of a case should be equally matched. Unfortunately, there is often a mismatch, and the advantage usually goes to the wealthy.

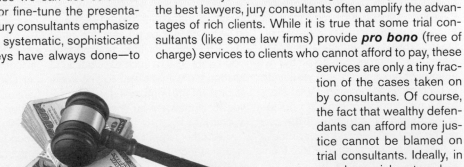

(*spxChrome/Getty Images*)

of trial presentation and strategy. They assist attorneys in crafting arguments that will be optimally persuasive. In high-stakes trials, consultants sometimes assemble a **shadow jury**—a group of 10 to 12 people who are selected to match the demographics of the actual jury. The shadow jury may sit in the courtroom during trial, or hear a condensed version of the testimony presented in court each day, or even watch a videotape of courtroom proceedings if one is available. Because the shadow jury hears the same evidence and testimony as the actual jury, they can be questioned throughout the trial about their reactions to the evidence. Feedback from the surrogate jury can then be used by attorneys to make adjustments in strategy during trial. (See the Focus on Careers Box in this section to learn more about what it is like to be a trial consultant.)

But does trial consulting work? It is difficult to say whether or not trial consultants are effective in helping lawyers select more favorable jurors (Lieberman & Sales, 2007; Posey & Wrightsman, 2005). As noted above, one complication is that

*F*OCUS ON *C*AREERS

Trial Consultant

Jill Huntley Taylor, Ph.D.
Trial Consultant, Director, Dispute
Dynamics, Inc.

As a trial consultant, my goal is to look at each case from a juror's perspective. Using my training in social psychology, I work with trial lawyers to best position their case for a jury. As part of that work, we conduct simulated trials at market research firms in front of panels of "mock jurors" drawn from the community where the case is being tried. Attorneys present the case from both sides and then the mock jurors answer questions and ultimately deliberate the case as if they were the real jurors. Based on the reactions of mock jurors, we work with the attorneys to develop a trial story that jurors should find most persuasive in light of the totality of the evidence they will see and hear at trial.

We also work with the trial team in preparing witnesses for trial. We participate in practice question-and-answer sessions alongside the attorneys. During these sessions, we provide feedback to the witnesses. This work focuses on identifying and reducing distracting behaviors and

(*Courtesy of Jill Huntley-Taylor*)

teaching the witness to be selective in word choice or phrasing to maximize the value of their testimony in court. The goal of such sessions is to assess the witness and to find ways to present the witness in the most favorable light when he or she appears in court.

Another aspect of trial consulting is assistance in jury selection. This work ranges from developing juror profiles based on mock trial data, to writing juror questionnaires, as well as rating and de-selecting jurors. Our recommendations about which jurors to "strike" are based on a constellation of attitudes and experiences that

we have learned make a juror least receptive to the story of our case.

My favorite part of being a trial consultant is the application of social psychology to a dynamic real-world setting. One of the most important areas of research that I apply nearly every day in my work is the story model of juror decision-making (see Chapter 13). Jurors construct a story to explain and understand the evidence and arguments presented at trial. We have learned from social psychology that developing and telling a story that resonates with the jury is critical to success in legal cases.

If you are considering a career as a trial consultant, I would strongly recommend a Ph.D. in social, legal, or cognitive psychology. While there are many successful consultants from different backgrounds and disciplines, training in psychology provides a solid foundation in research, theory, attitude measurement, and statistics. Finally, you must understand that trial consultants work on high-stakes cases in a fast-paced, high-pressure environment. There can be a lot of travel and many late nights spent working. It is an exciting field for anyone with an interest in psychology and the law.

attorneys differ dramatically in their ability to select jurors who will be favorable to their case. If an attorney is doing a good job already, there may be little a trial consultant can do to help. But if an attorney is doing a lousy job, a skilled consultant might be able to improve the attorney's performance significantly. Also, in a close case, where the evidence does not clearly favor one side or the other, careful jury selection might tilt the case in one direction. Although, on balance, evidence of the effectiveness of trial consulting is equivocal, there is some support for the proposition that jury selection can be modestly improved by measuring case-specific attitudes (Brodsky, 2009; Lieberman, 2011).

JUROR CHARACTERISTICS AND ATTITUDES AS PREDICTORS OF VERDICT

Overall, the persuasiveness of the evidence presented at trial is the best predictor of whether a defendant is convicted or acquitted (Devine, Buddenbaum, Houp, Studebaker, & Stolle, 2009; Saks & Kidd, 1986; Taylor & Hosch, 2004; Visher, 1987). That is how it should be. However, if evidence alone were the only factor that determined verdict, we might expect every jury to begin deliberations in complete agreement. This seldom happens. Although every person on a given jury has been exposed to the same evidence and arguments, jurors evaluate and interpret that evidence differently. These differences in how evidence is weighed and understood must be due to differences in jurors' experience, values, and personalities. But the search for juror characteristics that predict verdict has not yielded much. Standard demographic characteristics such as age, education, and income do not provide many clues about what verdict a person will favor (Lieberman, 2011). In an effort to understand the relationship between juror characteristics and verdicts, Steven Penrod (1990) examined 21 juror attitudes and characteristics as predictors in four types of simulated trials—murder, rape, robbery, and civil negligence. The study made use of **multiple regression**—a technique that statistically combines a large group of variables to predict an outcome variable (verdict, in this study). Taken together, the 21 predictor variables accounted for only 5% to 14% of the variance in verdicts, depending on the type of case.

In general, the relationships between juror characteristics and verdict are modest or unreliable. Take gender. Some studies have found that, compared to males, female jurors are slightly more likely to treat accused rapists and child molesters more harshly. But this finding is not consistent. Also, women tend to be more sympathetic to plaintiffs alleging sexual harassment (see Chapters 13 and 15). Here the difference is consistent but not large (Greathouse, Levett, & Kovera, 2009). A more consistent gender difference has to do with jury process rather than outcome—men talk more than women during deliberation. A related finding is that men are more likely to be elected as "foreperson." This seems to happen because men are more likely to be of high occupational status, are more likely to sit at the head of the table (the natural spot for group leaders), and are more likely to speak first (Strodtbeck & Lipinski, 1985).

General Personality Tendencies

A few broad personality tendencies do seem to be associated with jury verdicts. Three traits—locus of control, belief in a just world, and authoritarianism—have been shown to have a modest effect on how jurors interpret evidence and decide on a verdict. Such traits appear to exert an influence on juror decisions only in cases in which the evidence in favor of conviction is ambiguous or less than compelling.

Locus of control refers to how people tend to explain what happens to them. Do you believe that what you get in life (both your misfortunes and your rewards) is usually the result of your own behavior? Or, do you believe that what you get in life is largely due to forces outside your control? People with an **internal locus of control** tend to see their outcomes in life as due to their own abilities or effort. People with an **external locus of control** tend to see their outcomes as due to forces outside them, such as luck or other people with more power. There is some evidence that people's perspective on evidence presented at trial is influenced by their locus of control (Alicke, 2000; Phares, 1976). Consider a sexual harassment case involving a romantic relationship between an upper-level, male manager and a female in a middle-management position. The relationship turns sour and the female breaks it off. Later, she sues the company for sexual harassment. An "internal" juror might be more likely to blame the woman for her difficulties and be less likely to convict. An "external" juror may be more likely to hold the company responsible and decide in favor of the woman.

A separate but related personality characteristic—**belief in a just world**—seems to bear a logical relationship to verdicts and sentencing. People differ in how strongly they believe that "people get what they deserve and deserve what they get" in life. That is, by how strongly they believe that the world is just. Those people who believe in a just world have a tendency to derogate victims—to believe, for example, that women who have been raped may have done something to "bring it on themselves" (Lerner, 1980; Nudelman, 2013). The underlying psychological mechanism seems to be that if we can find a valid (or even an invalid) reason why someone became a victim, we can reduce our own anxiety about becoming a victim. If she had not been out alone at night, or had not drank too much, or had dressed differently, or had stayed away from the bad part of town, maybe she would not have been raped. And, therefore, if we avoid those behaviors, we and the people we love will be safe from harm (Pahlavan, 2013; Hafer, 2000). It is simply too psychologically threatening for some people to believe that sometimes terrible things happen to people for no good reason.

A third personality trait—**authoritarianism**—may also come into play when jurors are deciding cases. People with "authoritarian personalities" have the following characteristics: They tend to have conventional values, their beliefs tend to be rigid, they are intolerant of weakness, they tend to identify with and submit to authority figures, and they are suspicious of and punitive toward people who violate established norms and rules. For example, one of the items on the F-scale (the test designed to measure authoritarianism) is, "Sex crimes such as rape and attacks on children deserve more than mere imprisonment; such criminals ought to be publicly whipped or worse" (Perry, Sibley, & Duckitt, 2013). Those who score high on authoritarianism are more likely to convict and to hand down longer prison sentences. However, if the defendant is a police officer (an authority figure) accused of excessive use of force, authoritarians are much less likely to convict (Narby, Cutler, & Moran, 1993).

Attitudes about the Legal System

Some researchers have argued that it is unrealistic to expect general attitudes or personality tendencies to predict verdicts, but that case-specific attitudes may be moderately predictive of verdicts. There is some evidence to support this view (Webb & Sheeran, 2006). A few scales have been specifically developed to assess attitudes that might be related to verdicts in criminal trials. For example, the **Revised Legal Attitudes Questionnaire** (RLAQ) consists of 30 statements such as the following:

- Too many obviously guilty persons escape punishment because of legal technicalities.
- Evidence illegally obtained should be admissible in court if such evidence is the only way of obtaining a conviction.
- In the long run, liberty is more important than order.
- There is just about no such thing as an honest cop (Butler, 2010; Kravitz, Cutler, & Brock, 1993).

People filling out the questionnaire indicate their level of agreement on a multipoint scale ranging from "strongly disagree" to "strongly agree" (called a **Likert scale**). The points on the scale typically range from "1 to 7" or from "1 to 10."

A second scale designed for use with jurors is called the **Juror Bias Scale** (JBS). It also uses a Likert format and contains statements such as the following:

- Too many innocent people are wrongfully imprisoned.
- Too often jurors hesitate to convict someone who is guilty out of pure sympathy.

These and the other 15 items in the scale attempt to isolate jurors' beliefs about how likely it is that someone who is on trial for a crime actually committed that crime, and how certain a juror needs to be before convicting a defendant (i.e., how they define "reasonable doubt"). The scale also seems to measure general cynicism about the legal system (Brodsky, 2009; Myers & Lecci, 2002).

A third scale, the **Pretrial Juror Attitude Questionnaire (PJAQ),** builds on the items in the Juror Bias Scale. Like the other scales described above, the PJAQ uses a Likert format. It consists of 29 items divided into six subscales (Lecci & Myers, 2008; 2009). Here are the names of the subscales along with a sample item from each subscale: 1) *conviction proneness* ("Criminals should be caught and convicted by any means necessary"); 2) *system confidence* ("When it is the suspect's word against the police officer's, I believe the police"); 3) *cynicism toward the defense* ("Defense lawyers are too willing to defend individuals they know are guilty"); 4) *social justice* ("Rich individuals are almost never convicted of their crimes"); 5) *racial bias* ("Minority suspects are likely to be guilty, more often than not"); and 6) *innate criminality* ("Once a criminal, always a criminal"). In mock jury studies, these more specialized questionnaires slightly improve predictions about how a juror will eventually vote.

A few scales have been specifically developed for use in civil trials. In **civil trials,** a plaintiff sues a defendant for an alleged harm. If the defendant is found liable (responsible for the alleged harm), monetary damages are typically awarded. That is, the defendant is usually ordered to pay the plaintiff for the harm. In addition to **compensatory damages** (meant to compensate the plaintiff for losses), there may also be **punitive damages** (meant to punish the defendant for irresponsible or malicious conduct and to discourage others from behaving similarly). Among the attitudes that appear to be related to verdicts in civil trials include the belief that there is a "litigation crisis" fueled by people filing frivolous lawsuits in an attempt to make money. The opposite belief is that corporations often engage in dangerous or irresponsible behavior that endangers consumers and that such corporations need to be held accountable for that misconduct. The **Civil Trial Bias Scale** consists of 16 items designed to measure attitudes about the appropriate role of government in regulating businesses, appropriate standards for workplace safety and product safety, and whether or not most civil suits are justified (Hans & Lofquist, 1994). Researchers have found modest relationships between "litigation crisis" attitudes and damage awards. Specifically, people who believe that there are too many frivolous lawsuits and people who favor tort reform (placing caps on the size of damage awards) also tend to minimize the blameworthiness of civil defendants and to favor low damage awards (Vidmar & Hans, 2008).

Defendant–Juror Similarity

Sometimes the characteristics of the defendant and the characteristics of jurors interact in ways that influence verdicts. The **similarity–leniency hypothesis** predicts that jurors who are similar to the defendant will empathize and identify with the defendant. Consequently, they will be less likely to convict. This hypothesis is widely held by attorneys and has great intuitive appeal. The hypothesis also seems plausible from a research perspective because there is considerable research showing that similarity promotes interpersonal attraction (Montoya & Horton, 2013). Still, many questions remain: If similarity makes a juror better able to empathize with a defendant, does that empathy then translate into leniency? Do all types of similarity (e.g., race or religion, occupation, or gender) lead to leniency? Can similarity sometimes cause jurors to be more harsh instead of less harsh?

Norbert Kerr and his colleagues conducted two studies to investigate the similarity–leniency hypothesis (Kerr, Hymes, Anderson, & Weathers, 1995). They varied racial similarity between the defendant and jurors as well as the strength of the evidence against the defendant. Black and white mock jurors judged both black and white defendants. When the evidence against the defendant was weak or only moderately convincing, jurors who were racially similar to the defendant were more likely to reach a "not guilty" verdict. It seems that when evidence is inconclusive, we tend to give similar defendants the benefit of the doubt. But sometimes, there was a boomerang effect—similar jurors were occasionally harsher on defendants than dissimilar jurors. For example, if the evidence against an African American defendant was strong, *and* African American jurors were in the minority on the jury, those jurors judged the defendant as guiltier than did European American jurors. The same relationships held for European Americans. If the evidence was strong, *and* whites were in the minority on the jury, they were harsher with white defendants. It seems that, if jurors are outnumbered by members of another racial group, they may feel compelled to treat a racially similar (but probably guilty) defendant more harshly. By doing so, they emphasize their condemnation of the defendant, they disassociate and distance themselves from the defendant, and they are able to maintain a favorable view of their own group.

In other research relevant to this hypothesis, six-person all-white juries and six-person juries that were racially diverse (containing two black members) watched a video of a sexual assault trial with a black defendant. Prior to deliberation, both black and white members of the diverse juries were less likely to vote for conviction. There were also differences in the deliberation process. Diverse juries deliberated longer, discussed more of the evidence presented at trial, and made fewer inaccurate statements about the facts of the case (Sommers, 2006). Put differently, it was not simply that people went easy on members of their own racial group; instead, the presence of black jurors caused white jurors to process the trial evidence more thoroughly.

Similarly, in research looking at cases in which a man is accused of sexually harassing a woman, it was not gender *per se* that was predictive of verdicts. Instead, it was receptiveness to elements of a plaintiff-oriented account of events (e.g., the sexual attention was unwelcome, management tolerated the harassment) or a defense-oriented account (e.g., the woman encouraged the harassment, she is suing the company to retaliate for being fired) (Huntley & Costanzo, 2003). Females are more likely to be receptive to a plaintiff-oriented account of events, but gender alone does not determine verdict.

Given the paucity of research on the similarity–leniency hypothesis, the conclusions presented above are still somewhat tentative. However, it does appear that sometimes similarity does increase leniency, probably because jurors similar to the defendant are more likely to accept the defense account of events. The effect seems to depend on how strong the evidence is and how many "similar" people are members of the jury. It appears that similarity produces leniency only when the evidence against the defendant is inconclusive and when similar jurors outnumber dissimilar jurors. Sometimes, similarity causes jurors to be more, rather than less, harsh in their judgments of a defendant. Further, only race and gender similarity have been investigated. We do not yet know if other types of similarity influence verdicts. The lesson here is the same as in most other areas of psychology and law: Simple explanations are appealing but often wrong. Relationships are complex and variables often combine and interact in ways that produce unexpected effects.

PRETRIAL PUBLICITY AS A SOURCE OF BIAS

In the highly publicized 2013 murder trial of George Zimmerman, the defense attorney decided to open his case by telling jurors the following joke:

> Knock-knock.
> Who's there?
> George Zimmerman.
> George Zimmerman who?
> Alright, good. You're on the jury!

The joke bombed. It turns out that the courtroom is not the best forum for comedy. But the joke illustrates an important point—prior knowledge about a defendant, usually gathered from the mass media, can influence potential jurors against a defendant. Ideally, a juror should arrive at the courthouse knowing nothing about the case that he or she is about to hear. However, for cases that have captured a lot of media attention, it is often difficult to find potential jurors whose impartiality has not been compromised by pretrial publicity.

As discussed throughout this chapter, jurors do not magically shed their prejudices and preconceptions when they walk through the courthouse door. **Pretrial publicity** is sometimes a potential source of prejudice. In a high-profile case (e.g., the murder of a famous person), there is likely to be coverage of the case on TV, websites, and local newspapers before the trial even begins. There tends to be a pro-prosecution slant to this coverage. News reports are typically based on information received from the police department and the district attorney's office. These reports tend to focus on details of the crime, police investigation of the crime, effects of the crime on victims or their families, and incriminating evidence against the defendant. Pretrial publicity often contains information that is not admissible as evidence during trial. Several studies show that people exposed to more news coverage of a crime are significantly more likely to presume that the defendant is guilty (Kovera, 2002; Otto, Penrod, & Dexter, 1994), and some studies have shown that information presented only through pretrial publicity is misremembered by jurors as having been presented at trial (Ruva & LeVasseur, 2012; Ruva, McEvoy, & Bryant, 2007). Further, when researchers statistically combined the results of 44 studies using more than 5500 subjects, they found that people exposed to negative pretrial publicity were significantly more likely to judge the defendant guilty than people who were not exposed (Steblay, Besirevic, Fulero, & Jimenez-Lorente, 1999). Unfortunately, reviews of studies testing the effectiveness of judge's instructions to disregard pretrial publicity have found that such instructions have no remedial effect (Lieberman, Arndt, & Vess, 2009). The biasing effect of pretrial publicity is especially strong when news coverage is emotionally arousing (e.g., focusing on the brutal nature of a murder) and when television (as opposed to print media) is the source of the information (Ogloff & Vidmar, 1994).

In a careful study conducted by Geoffrey Kramer and his associates, 791 mock jurors were exposed to either factual publicity that described a crime but did not incriminate the defendant or emotional publicity intended to arouse negative feelings (e.g., information about a 7-year-old girl who had been the victim of a hit-and-run accident and a plea for help from her big sister). The defendant was then tried in a mock trial. A brief, 12-day delay between exposure to news reports and the mock trial *did* eliminate the bias created by factual publicity but *did not* eliminate the bias created by emotional publicity (Kramer, Kerr, & Carroll, 1990). In addition, the pro-prosecution bias created by pretrial publicity was actually magnified by the process of deliberation—mock jurors were more inclined to convict after deliberation. Postponing a trial may be an effective remedy to some of the problems created by pretrial publicity. However the most effective remedy appears to be a **change of venue:** moving the trial to a community that has not been exposed to pretrial publicity and its biasing effects.

AN OVERVIEW OF TRIAL PROCEDURE

After a jury is selected, the trial can begin. To set the stage for the chapters that follow, it is useful to review the typical sequence of events in a criminal trial. (It may also help to envision the courtroom when you think about the different participants and their roles in courtroom proceedings. See Figure 6.2 to see one of the most common courtroom layouts.) Trials begin with **opening statements** by the opposing attorneys. These statements are not considered evidence. Instead, they are meant to highlight the issues at stake and to provide jurors with an overview of evidence that will be heard. In criminal trials, the prosecution usually goes first and in civil trials (in which one party sues another), the plaintiff goes first. Although the defense usually makes an opening statement right after the prosecutor or plaintiff's attorney, defense lawyers have the option of postponing their statement until it is their turn to present evidence. Defendants are presumed innocent until proven guilty. The reason prosecutors and plaintiffs go first is that they are claiming that the defendant broke the law and, therefore, they must bear the **burden of proof.** In criminal cases, a defendant must be judged guilty **beyond a reasonable doubt,** while in civil cases, the standard of proof for being held liable (responsible for causing the alleged harm) is usually **preponderance of the evidence.** These burden-of-proof standards are difficult for jurors to understand and, unfortunately, the law does not supply unambiguous definitions. However, it is clear that beyond a reasonable doubt is the higher standard. Sometimes, preponderance of the evidence is interpreted as meaning more

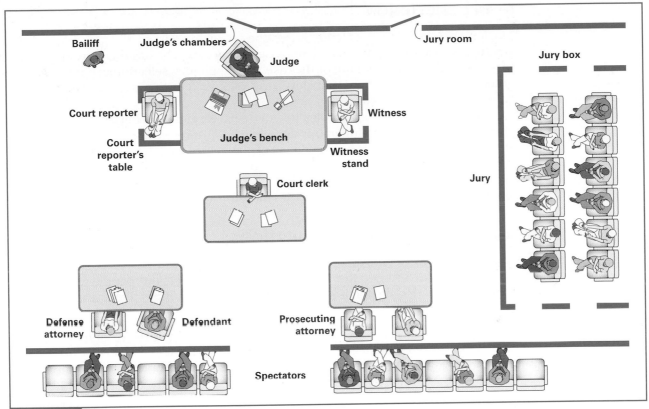

FIGURE 6.2   One of the most common courtroom layouts.

than 50% of the evidence favors one side, and sometimes beyond a reasonable doubt is interpreted as meaning that jurors must be more than 90% certain that the defendant is guilty. Reasonable doubt also is sometimes defined as a doubt for which someone can give a reason (presumably a good reason).

Following opening statements, the prosecutor or plaintiff's attorney calls witnesses to testify. After a witness has been questioned by the prosecutor or plaintiff's attorney (when a lawyer questions a witness she has called to testify, it is called **direct examination**), the defense lawyer may then **cross-examine** (that is, ask questions of) that witness. Next, the attorney who called the witness has an opportunity to question the witness yet again in a process called **redirect** examination. The last opportunity for questioning the witness is given to the defense attorney in **recross** examination. The procedure switches when the defense presents its case: The defense lawyer questions the witness first, followed by cross-examination by the prosecutor or plaintiff's lawyer, followed by redirect and recross. In this way, the two attorneys take turns questioning each witness until both sides have finished presenting their case. After all the evidence has been presented, each attorney makes a **closing argument** (also referred to as a "summation"). Like opening statements, closing arguments are not evidence. They are attempts to persuade jurors that one interpretation of the evidence is the correct one. The prosecution or plaintiff goes first, then the defense, then the prosecution or plaintiff has an opportunity to give a rebuttal. Therefore, the prosecutor or plaintiff's lawyer has both the first and last word at trial.

▶ IN CONCLUSION

The long process of jury selection is designed to yield an impartial jury. Impartiality is difficult to achieve, particularly because lawyers and consultants strive to pick jurors who will favor their side of the case. Although jury selection can influence the outcome of the case, the relationship between jury selection and verdict is neither simple nor straightforward.

Although many Americans try to avoid jury service, serving on a jury is an important way of participating in our democracy. Citizens who serve as jurors receive an education about the inner workings of the justice system. In addition, the jury system restrains the power of government by putting decisions directly in the hands of the people. Quite simply, juries are the most direct means of making the legal system reflect the views and values of the community.

▶ DISCUSSION AND CRITICAL THINKING QUESTIONS

1. How would you change the selection of jury venires? Can you think of ways to improve the representativeness of the pool of people that is summoned and the group who shows up for jury service?

2. Should we eliminate peremptory challenges? If not, how many should be allowed per lawyer per trial?

3. If you were a judge presiding over a trial for drug possession, would you allow the prosecuting attorney to use a challenge for cause against a juror who admits to being a regular user of marijuana? What would you consider a reasonable challenge for cause?

4. Should obese people be considered a cognizable group? How about people with incomes below the poverty line? How about wealthy people?

5. In pretrial questionnaires of potential jurors, how far should lawyers and consultants be permitted to go? Should they be allowed to administer personality tests? Should they be able to ask questions about political views? Religious views? Sexual behavior?

6. Should the use of trial consultants be outlawed? Should the state provide a trial consultant for one side of the case if the other side has hired their own consultant?

▶ KEY TERMS

authoritarianism (p. 126)
belief in a just world (p. 126)
beyond a reasonable doubt (p. 130)
burden of proof (p. 130)
challenge for cause (p. 117)
change of venue (p. 130)
civil trial (p. 127)
Civil Trial Bias Scale (p. 127)
closing argument (p. 131)
cognizable groups (p. 118)

compensatory damages (p. 127)
cross-examine (p. 131)
direct examination (p. 131)
external locus of control (p. 126)
internal locus of control (p. 126)
Juror Bias Scale (p. 127)
Jury Selection and Service Act of 1968 (p. 115)
Likert scale (p. 127)
locus of control (p. 126)
multiple regression (p. 125)

one day or one trial system (p. 116)
opening statement (p. 130)
peremptory challenge (p. 117)
preponderance of the evidence (p. 130)
Pretrial Juror Attitude Questionnaire (p. 127)
pretrial publicity (p. 129)
pro bono (p. 123)
punitive damages (p. 127)
recross (p. 131)
redirect (p. 131)

Revised Legal Attitudes Questionnaire (RLAQ) (p. 127)
scientific jury selection (p. 121)
shadow jury (p. 124)
similarity-leniency hypothesis (p. 128)
social media analysis (p. 119)
supplemental juror questionnaires (p. 123)
venire (p. 116)
voir dire (p. 117)

7 Eyewitness Identification and Testimony

▶ Eyewitness Testimony and the Legal System
▶ The Construction and Reconstruction of Eyewitness Memories
▶ Using Research Findings to Improve Eyewitness Accuracy
▶ Techniques for Refreshing the Memories of Witnesses

Jennifer Thompson was a 22-year-old college student living in North Carolina. At about 3:00 AM one morning, a man broke into her apartment, held a knife to her throat, and raped her. During her long ordeal, the rapist allowed her to get up. When she went to the bathroom, she turned on the light and used the opportunity to get a good look at her attacker. She also managed to briefly turn on a lamp in the bedroom and get another good look at him before he turned off the lamp. When the rapist turned on the stereo, his face was illuminated by the faint light from the stereo equipment. Despite her terror, Jennifer forced herself to study his face. She told the rapist that she was thirsty, and he let her to go to the kitchen to get a drink. The kitchen door—where the rapist had broken into her apartment— was still open. She ran from her apartment to a neighbor's house. The rapist did not follow. But, later that night, less than a mile from Jennifer's apartment, he broke into another apartment and raped another woman.

At the police station, Jennifer looked through sketches of different types of noses, different types of eyes, different mouths. With Jennifer's direction, a police sketch artist created a composite drawing of the rapist. He was an African-American man, in his twenties or thirties, with short hair and a thin mustache. The composite drawing was widely circulated, and the police received several calls from people claiming to recognize the suspect. Based on those calls, police put together a photo lineup of six pictures. Jennifer looked at the photo spread for a few minutes and identified Ronald Cotton, a man who worked at a local seafood restaurant. The detective seemed relieved when she made her identification. "We thought this might be the one," he told her.

When Ronald Cotton heard the police were looking for him, he knew they had made a mistake, so he went to the police station to "straighten the whole thing out." He was arrested for both rapes and placed in a lineup with six other men. Jennifer had little difficulty identifying him. But the victim of the second rape identified a different man, one who the police knew to be innocent. Ronald Cotton was put on trial for the rape of Jennifer Thompson.

No solid physical evidence was presented at trial—no fingerprints, no hairs from the rapist, nothing conclusive from the semen analysis. At the crime scene, police found a tiny piece of foam that might have come from the type of athletic shoe Ronald Cotton owned. There was evidence that Cotton owned a flashlight similar to the one used by the rapist. And, there was a compelling eyewitness identification. As the prosecutor said after the trial, Jennifer Thompson was a "terrific witness." She had made an effort to memorize the face of her rapist, and she had identified him twice—once in the photo spread and later in the lineup. During the trial, she pointed out Ronald Cotton as her assailant and told the jurors she was certain he was the man who had raped her. The jurors were convinced, and Cotton was sentenced to life in prison.

Bobby Poole (top) and Ronald Cotton (middle) at the time of the crime, and a composite sketch of the rapist (bottom). *(TOP: AP Photo/Burlington Police Department, middle: AP Photo / Burlington Police Department, bottom: Courtesy Burlington Police Department)*

Two years into his prison sentence, Cotton was told by another inmate that a third inmate—a man named Bobby Poole—had said that he knew Cotton was innocent. Bobby Poole said he knew this because he was the one who had raped the two women more than two years earlier. Cotton was eventually granted a second trial. At the second trial, Poole testified, but he denied any involvement in the two rapes. There was another witness who had not testified at the first trial: the second rape victim. Although she had identified the wrong man in a lineup two years earlier, she testified that she was now certain that Ronald Cotton was the man who had raped her. At the second trial, Cotton was convicted of both rapes and sent back to prison.

For eight more years, Cotton spent most of his time in prison writing letters to anyone who might be able to help overturn his convictions. He probably would have died in prison if he had not been able to convince a law professor named Richard Rosen to look more closely at his case. Rosen did some investigation and found that the biological evidence in Cotton's case (a semen sample) was still well preserved in a police storage facility. In the 10 years that had passed since the first trial, DNA testing had developed to the point that it could positively identify any offender who left behind biological evidence. The semen sample was subjected to DNA analysis and Cotton was excluded. The sample was then compared to a blood sample from Bobby Poole. It was a match. Ronald Cotton was released from prison, and Bobby Poole was charged with both rapes (Thompson-Cannino, Cotton, & Torneo, 2009).

Several tragedies are associated with the Cotton case. There is the rape and its aftermath—Thompson still has nightmares and still feels afraid when she opens her door at night. There is the tragedy of Ronald Cotton, who spent 11 agonizing years in prison for a crime he did not commit. And, there is the tragedy of several more rapes that could have been prevented if Bobby Poole had been captured and convicted after the rape of Jennifer Thompson. This case illustrates some of the problems with eyewitness identification and some of the tragic consequences of mistaken identification.

When eyewitnesses describe a criminal or pick a suspect out of a lineup, they are relying on memory. So, to understand the process of eyewitness identification, it is essential to understand the basics of how memory works. Psychologists who study memory have found it useful to distinguish between three component processes—encoding, storage, and retrieval. **Encoding** involves gathering information and putting it in a form that can be held in memory, **storage** refers to holding the encoded information in the brain over time, and **retrieval** refers to accessing and pulling out the stored information at a later time (Atkinson & Shiffrin, 1968; Foster, 2008). It is tempting to think of these memory processes as similar to a video recording. Encoding might seem like recording an event with a video camera. Storage is like putting the DVD aside for later use, and retrieval is like popping the DVD into a player and pressing the play button. Unfortunately, this appealing metaphor vastly understates the subtlety and complexity of human memory. (See Chapter 11 for further discussion of memory.)

Errors in memory can occur at each stage of the process. First, information might not be well encoded. Information streams by us each day, and we attend to and encode only a small fraction of that information. Even when we do make an effort to pay attention, our attention sometimes lapses, and crucial information does not get stored. Encoding is imperfect. What we do store in memory is a selective, inexact replica of what we actually heard or saw. Second, there are imperfections in the process of storage. Our **memory trace**—the biochemical representation of our experience in the brain—appears to deteriorate with time. Not only do we tend to forget as time passes, but our memories become more vulnerable to revision and corruption (Flin, Boone, Knox, & Bull, 1992). Finally, even if the memory trace is perfectly preserved in the brain, distortion can occur during the process of retrieval. We may not have the necessary cues to locate and reinstate the stored memory (Surprenant & Neath, 2009). In sum, when we encode an event, we select some aspects and ignore others. The images and sounds we store may decay over time, and the process of retrieval includes some reconstruction. ◀

 ## EYEWITNESS TESTIMONY AND THE LEGAL SYSTEM

As the case of Ronald Cotton shows, in many cases, the testimony of an eyewitness makes the difference between conviction and acquittal. Such testimony is crucial to the criminal justice system because it is often the most compelling evidence presented in court. One study examined 347 cases in which the only evidence was eyewitness testimony. In 74% of these cases, the defendant was convicted. In 49% of the cases in which the defendant was convicted, there was only one eyewitness (Loftus, 1984).

The persuasiveness of eyewitness testimony is only a problem if the witness is mistaken. Unfortunately, research suggests that eyewitnesses are far more fallible than is commonly supposed. Indeed, research on people who have been convicted of crimes but are later proven innocent has revealed that mistaken eyewitness identification leads to more wrongful convictions than any other type of evidence (Innocence Project, 2013). In fact, mistaken identifications played a role in 76% of cases where wrongly convicted persons were released from prison because DNA testing later proved their innocence (Wells, 2006). Figure 7.1 depicts some of the major causes of wrongful convictions.

The *Manson* Criteria

In two key cases—*Neil v. Biggers* (1972) and *Manson v. Braithwaite* (1977)—the courts have emphasized five factors that

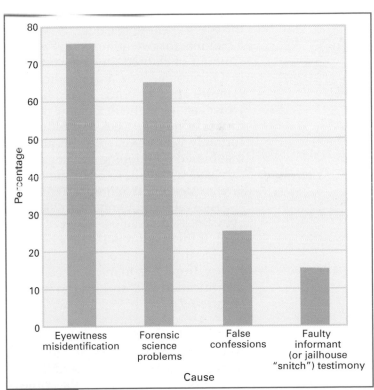

FIGURE 7.1   The four major causes of wrongful convictions. The incidence of other causes—especially law-enforcement misconduct, prosecutorial misconduct, and bad defense lawyering—are difficult to calculate. Percentages add up to more than 100% because many cases involve more than one cause. (Data source: www.innocence project.com)

should be taken into account when evaluating the accuracy of an eyewitness's identification: (1) the witness's opportunity to view the perpetrator, (2) the witness's level of attention, (3) the accuracy of the witness's previous description of the offender, (4) the witness's degree of certainty, and (5) the amount of time between witnessing the crime and making the identification. Although these so-called *Manson* **criteria** seem logical, most are difficult to apply to actual crimes, and one (degree of certainty) is contrary to research findings.

With a few exceptions (e.g., a hostage situation that lasts for hours), it is difficult to evaluate a witness's opportunity to view the perpetrator and it is difficult to evaluate his or her level of attention. Usually, we must rely on witnesses to tell us what kind of opportunity they had to observe and whether they paid close attention to the crime. And, of course, there is no precise measure of attention. Was the witness "mildly attentive," "moderately attentive," or "intensely attentive"?

There is also the issue of time—how long was the witness able to look at the culprit? As you might expect, the evidence suggests that accuracy improves if witnesses look at the face of the criminal longer. But, in most cases, we cannot know how long the witness was able to study the face of the perpetrator. People consistently overestimate the duration of a brief event, especially if the event is stressful. Consequently, time moves slowly for a frightened eyewitness. Estimates of time during a stressful event are generally three to four times the actual time length of the event (Penrod & Cutler, 1999). This means that a witness who estimates seeing a criminal for two minutes may actually have seen the criminal for only 30 seconds. Amount of elapsed time between witnessing a crime and identifying the criminal in a lineup may be a useful indicator of accuracy at the extremes—an identification minutes after the crime should be more reliable than one that occurs a month later. However, it is difficult to know the effects of the passage of time in the intermediate ranges of days or weeks. In addition, as discussed later in this chapter, eyewitness certainty is an unreliable indicator of accuracy. Especially troubling is the finding that biased questioning and lineup procedures can inflate a witnesses certainty and can lead witnesses to overestimate how clear a view they had of the perpetrator (Wells, Memon, & Penrod, 2006).

As Wells and Quinlivan (2009) point out, we must rely on the self-reports of eyewitnesses to evaluate three of the five *Manson* criteria (certainty, view, and attention). If these self-reports have been corrupted by the use of suggestive questioning and identification procedures, they will be misleading indicators of eyewitness accuracy. Ironically, in many cases, the same biased procedures that led to a mistaken identification will also lead to inflated estimates of attention, view, and certainty (Figure 7.2).

How the Legal System Attempts to Expose Eyewitness Bias

At every stage in the process that begins with seeing a crime and ends with testimony in court, there are possibilities for error. First, there is the ability of the witness to observe. Clearly, if the crime occurs at night, or if lighting is poor, or if the witness sees the crime from a distance, the ability to identify the criminal may be impaired. Perhaps the witness's eyesight was poor, maybe the perpetrator was looking away from the witness, or was only briefly in view. Luckily, any good defense attorney will expose such obvious weaknesses during cross-examination. It may even be possible to check some aspects of the witness's description—an investigator with the right equipment could measure the level of ambient light

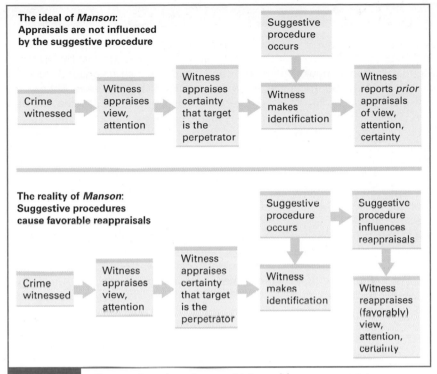

The ideal of *Manson*:
Appraisals are not influenced
by the suggestive procedure

The reality of *Manson*:
Suggestive procedures
cause favorable reappraisals

FIGURE 7.2 Suggestive procedures, which could cause a mistaken identification, also cause inflated standing on *Manson* criteria (from Wells & Quinlivan, 2009).

at a specific time of night, and a tape measure could be used to assess distance between where the witness stood and where the crime occurred. However, we almost always have to rely on the word of the witness about some aspects of what he or she saw.

The legal system has a few time-honored techniques for revealing truth. These techniques include *voir dire* (the questioning of potential jurors during jury selection), cross-examination, and jury deliberation. But these techniques are not terribly effective tools for exposing mistaken identifications (Cutler, 2013). *Voir dire* is intended to expose potentially biased jurors so that attorneys can dismiss them. But there is no set of questions that will reveal whether potential jurors will view eyewitness testimony with appropriate skepticism. Even cross-examination, a very useful tool for bringing out weakness and deceptions in testimony, is quite limited as a means of exposing mistaken eyewitness identifications. It is impossible to expose mistaken eyewitnesses as liars because they are not lying: They sincerely believe what they are saying, but they are wrong. A final safeguard, jury deliberation, places fact-finding in the hands of a group of citizens. Unfortunately, research shows that jurors place undue faith in the reliability of eyewitnesses, place too much weight on eyewitness confidence, and are not very skilled at distinguishing between accurate and inaccurate eyewitnesses (Brewer, 2006; Krug, 2007). (To learn more about court decisions on eyewitness identification post-Manson, see the Legal Update box in this section.)

LEGAL UPDATE

Post-Manson Court Decisions on Eyewitness Identification

Thirty-five years after establishing the *Manson* framework for evaluating eyewitness evidence, the U.S. Supreme court revisited the issue of eyewitness evidence in the case of *Perry v. New Hampshire* (2012). However, the Court declined to use the case to update the *Manson* criteria for evaluating eyewitness evidence. Despite its failure to reform *Manson,* the Court did recognize "the importance and the fallibility of eyewitness identifications" and noted that, "In appropriate cases, some States may also permit defendants to present expert testimony on the hazards of eyewitness identification evidence."

Although the Supreme Court seems to have missed an opportunity to modernize *Manson* in light of several decades of scientific research, several states have been willing to adopt new standards. For example, in *State v. Henderson* (2011), the New Jersey Supreme Court concluded that the *Manson* rule "does not adequately meet its stated goals: it does not provide a sufficient measure for reliability, it does not deter, and it overstates the jury's innate ability to evaluate eyewitness testimony." When there is evidence that suggestive identification procedures were used, the New Jersey framework al-

lows for pretrial hearings about whether eyewitness testimony should be admitted at trial. The framework also calls for enhanced jury instructions that focus attention on the vulnerabilities of eyewitnesses. Those instructions ask jurors to consider relevant factors such as stress, weapons focus, confidence as an "unreliable indicator of accuracy," and cross-racial effects (for the full instructions see, www.judiciary.state.nj.us/pressrel/2012/jury_instruction.pdf).

Oregon has also adjusted its standard. In the case of *State v. Lawson* (2012), the Oregon Supreme Court held that "When there are facts demonstrating that a witness could have relied on something other than his or her own perceptions to identify the defendant," the prosecution must "establish by a preponderance of the evidence that the identification was based on a permissible basis rather than an impermissible one, such as suggestive police procedures." In addition, Oregon established a role for expert testimony for the purpose of enabling "judges and jurors to evaluate eyewitness identification testimony according to relevant and meaningful criteria." Until the U.S. Supreme Court revisits the issue of eyewitness evidence, several states will continue to reconsider the outdated criteria established in *Manson.*

THE CONSTRUCTION AND RECONSTRUCTION OF EYEWITNESS MEMORIES

Memory is not perfect under the best of circumstances, and most crimes do not happen under the best of circumstances. Crimes often happen at night, and the perpetrators are usually in a hurry. Criminals may try to alter their appearance—they wear hats, sunglasses, or even masks. They often wait until no witnesses are around. Witnesses to crimes and victims of crimes are often terrified and more concerned with their own safety than with getting a good look at the criminal. Beyond these general concerns, researchers have discovered several specific biases that influence eyewitness memories.

Cross-Racial Identifications

Emilio Meza was arrested for robbing Sung Woo at gunpoint in the parking lot of a Los Angeles supermarket. Mr. Woo had identified Mr. Meza first in a photo spread and later in a real lineup. At trial, when questioned by the defense attorney, Mr. Woo said, "Sometimes if a Hispanic wears a mustache, it's very tough for me to tell . . . there are too many look-alikes." The defense attorney probed deeper: "There's a saying, sometimes said in jest, 'they all look alike to me'; is that what you're saying?" "Yes sir," Mr. Woo replied (Hubler, 1998).

Mr. Meza, who turned out to be innocent, was eventually released. Although Mr. Woo may have been unusually candid about his limitations as an eyewitness, research shows that he is not alone in having difficulty identifying people from racial groups other than his own (Marcon, Meissner, Frueh, Susa, & MacLin, 2010). Although there is no evidence suggesting that members of any one racial group are any more accurate as eyewitnesses than members of any other racial group, there is an interaction between the race of the witness and the race of the person being identified: Cross-race accuracy is worse than within-race accuracy. That is, it is harder for people to recognize the faces of people outside their racial group than it is for people to recognize the faces of people within their racial group. This tendency is usually referred to as the **cross-race effect** (sometimes called the "own-race bias"). The bias appears to be present in babies as young as nine months old (Kelly et al., 2007) and is consistent in strength for kindergartners, young children, and adults (Pezdek, Blandon-Gitlin, & Moore, 2003).

Race may have played a role in the case of Ronald Cotton—he was black, and Jennifer Thompson was white. A **meta-analysis** (a statistical procedure that compiles the overall findings from a large group of related research studies) of 39 studies found that own-race identifications were significantly more likely to be correct than cross-race identifications, and that the number of misidentifications (false alarms) was significantly higher among cross-racial identifications (Meissner & Brigham, 2001). The own-race bias is not large (misidentification is 1.56 times more likely when the suspect is of a different race than the witness), but it is consequential for the legal system. Many eyewitness identifications involve witnesses of one race trying to identify suspects of another race.

The reasons for the cross-race effect are not clear. Some researchers have suggested that when we observe someone of our own race, we tend to classify their facial features in greater detail. In contrast, we may encode the features of people from other races more superficially, paying less attention to facial characteristics such as shape of face, skin tone, size of features, and hair texture (Fiske & Taylor, 2013). A related explanation is that, because most of us have substantial experience with people of our own race (e.g., members of our own family), we develop better rules for making useful distinctions between faces. Those rules may not be as useful when we apply them to members of other racial groups. Some evidence suggests that our ability to recognize faces from other racial groups improves as we gain more contact with members of that group (Meissner & Brigham, 2001).

Do you think you would be better at identifying a suspect who looks more like you?
(*A: Hero Images/Getty, B: PhotoDisc/Getty Images, C: Bloomimage/Corbis*)

Stress and Weapons Focus

Many people believe that heightened arousal enhances memory. Perhaps family members or friends have told you that they have vivid (and presumably accurate) memories of important events in their lives—a graduation, a wedding, the birth of a child, or the death of a loved one. Arousing events may lead to vivid memories, but the details of these memories may be no more accurate than memories of mundane events.

In an unusual and revealing series of studies, Charles Morgan and his colleagues were able to examine the impact of high stress on eyewitness accuracy by studying 509 soldiers during "survival training" (Morgan et al., 2004). Although the precise details of the training are classified, it is meant to simulate the experience of being captured and held as a prisoner of war. The experience is "modeled from the experiences of actual military personnel who have been prisoners of war" and includes "wilderness evasion" and "mock captivity in a prisoner of war camp." A key variable in the study was whether a mock interrogation (which lasted about 40 minutes) was high or low stress. The critical feature of the high-stress

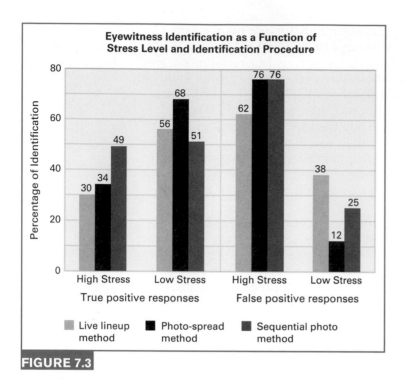

FIGURE 7.3

interrogation was that it included "real physical confrontation."

Figure 7.3 summarizes the findings for participants who were able to identify their interrogator after the training using different types of identification procedures (live lineup, photo spread, or sequential photos—these procedures are described in detail later in this chapter).

Notice that the rate of *correct* identifications was significantly higher for participants in the low-stress condition. Averaging across identification procedures, about 71% of participants in the low-stress condition made a correct identification, compared to about 38% of participants in the high-stress condition. Also, notice that only about 25% of people in the low-stress condition identified the *wrong* person but, in the high-stress condition, 58% identified the wrong person. As the authors note,

Contrary to the popular conception that most people would never forget the face of a clearly seen individual who had physically confronted them and threatened them for more than 30 min., a large number of subjects in this study were unable to correctly identify their perpetrator. These data provide robust evidence that eyewitness memory for persons encountered during events that are personally relevant, highly stressful, and realistic in nature may be subject to substantial error (Morgan et al., 2004, p. 274).

In criminal trials, prosecutors often argue that eyewitnesses who have identified the defendant are surely reliable, because the stress of watching (or being the victim of) the crime would have focused their attention and caused them to remember the event accurately (Pezdek, 2007). These prosecutors are half right: Watching a crime in progress certainly triggers stress. But the effect of this arousal on the encoding of information is generally negative, partly because the arousal frequently includes fear for one's own physical safety. One team of researchers conducted a meta-analysis of 27 studies designed to test the effect of stress on person identification. Their conclusion: high stress impairs memory and consequently reduces the rate of correct identifications (Deffenbacher, Bornstein, Penrod, & McGorty, 2004).

One well-established finding related to stress has been termed the **weapon focus effect.** If eyewitnesses see the perpetrator holding a gun or a knife, their ability to recognize the assailant is impaired. In such situations, witnesses understandably tend to focus their attention on the weapon, partly because it is unexpected in most settings and also because it poses great danger (Steblay, 1992; Pickel, Ross, & Truelove, 2006). Consequently, witnesses pay less attention to other important details of the crime, like the face of the criminal.

Unconscious Transference

When witnesses identify the wrong person, it is usually a meaningful misidentification: Sometimes the person wrongly identified closely resembles the real perpetrator. This is what happened when Jennifer Thompson identified Ronald Cotton as the man who raped her. Ronald Cotton and Bobby Poole were both African-American men in their thirties with mustaches and short hair. Other times, the person wrongly identified is someone seen near the scene of the crime or someone seen as part of the identification process. This situation is called **unconscious transference.** A face that is familiar from one context is transferred to the scene of a crime (Kersten, Earles, & Upshaw, 2013; Ross, Ceci, Dunning, & Toglia, 1994). Robert Buckhout, one of the first psychologists to conduct systematic research on eyewitnesses, staged a series of thefts and assaults in his classroom. Of the students who witnessed the mock crime, 39% showed the unconscious-transference effect. These witnesses incorrectly identified a person who had been in the classroom the day of the crime (Buckhout, 1974). Sometimes, a face seen in a mug shot leads to unconscious transference. This possibility exists whenever an eyewitness sees mug shots before making an identification in a lineup. In a series of studies, prior exposure to mug shots led to a decrease in correct identifications and an increase in mistaken identifications (Deffenbacher, Bornstein, & Penrod, 2006).

In an odd incident that illustrates this effect, a rape victim identified psychologist Donald Thompson as her rapist. The woman gave a vivid, detailed recollection of his face. The only problem was that, at the time of the rape, Thompson was in a television studio giving an interview about the fallibility of memory. The rape victim had seen part of that television interview and unknowingly transferred her memory of Thompson's face onto the rapist (Schacter, 1996).

Leading or Suggestive Comments

In a series of classic experiments, Elizabeth Loftus and her colleagues demonstrated how eyewitness recall could be altered by seemingly trivial changes in the wording of questions (Loftus & Palmer, 1974). Several groups of participants in her experiments viewed films of a car crash. Half the participants were asked to estimate the speed of the car when it "turned right," and the other half were asked to estimate the speed of the car when it "ran the stop sign." Later, when the participants were asked whether they had seen a stop sign, 35% of the first group reported seeing one, while 53% of the second group reported seeing the sign. When a statement about a barn was included in the questioning process, 17% of the participants remembered seeing a barn, even though none appeared in the film. When participants were asked, "Did you see *the* broken headlight?" they were more than twice as likely to recall seeing a broken headlight than participants who were asked, "Did you see *a* broken headlight?" Estimates of the speed of the cars also varied as a function of question wording. Some participants were asked, "About how fast were the two cars going when they *contacted* each other?" In other versions of the question, the words *hit, bumped,* and *smashed* were substituted for *contacted*. Cars *contacting* each other yielded an estimate of 31 miles per hour, while cars *smashing* into each other yielded an estimate of 40.8 miles per hour. Only subtle variations in wording were used, but these tiny variations produced substantial changes in memory.

Recall of a crime scene may also be altered depending on how the eyewitness is initially questioned. In one laboratory study, people looked at slides of a student dorm room that had been burglarized. Experimenters later used selective questioning when asking about details of the crime scene (Koutstaal, Schacter, Johnson, &

Galluccio, 1999). Although there were many textbooks in the picture of the room (apparently thieves are not interested in textbooks), experimenters asked only about particular types of sweatshirts. When questioned later about what they saw, people tended to have good recall of the sweatshirts but poor recall of other objects, such as textbooks. Retrieving memories of sweatshirts made it more difficult to recall aspects of the scene (or event) about which no questions were initially asked. Selectively retrieving only some aspects of a scene "inhibits" recall of other aspects (MacLeod & Saunders, 2008). This phenomenon is called **retrieval inhibition.**

Preexisting Expectations

What we expect to see influences what we actually see and how we remember what we see. One form of expectation is what social scientists call scripts. **Scripts** are widely held beliefs about sequences of actions that typically occur in particular situations. You may have, for example, a script for the first day of a college class. You sit at a desk or table, the professor takes roll, the professor hands out a course syllabus and reviews the course requirements, and so on. We appear to have preexisting scripts for many common situations. Scripts enable us to process information efficiently. Because we know what to expect, we do not have to treat each situation as completely new or unique. But scripts can also lead to error. If information is lacking or insufficiently encoded, we often rely on scripts to fill in gaps in our memory.

Consider the implications for eyewitnesses. In an interesting study of this issue, people were first questioned to determine if there were widely shared scripts for three types of crimes: a convenience store robbery, a bank robbery, and a mugging (Holst & Pezdek, 1992). The researchers were able to uncover widely shared scripts for all three crimes. The convenience store script contained the following sequence of actions—robber cases the store, makes a plan, enters store, looks around, acts like a shopper, waits for an opportunity, goes to cash register, pulls out a gun, demands money, exits store, drives away in a getaway car. In a follow-up study, research participants heard a mock trial of a defendant accused of a convenience store robbery. Most elements of the typical script were included in the evidence presentations. However, key elements of the script (e.g., casing the store, pulling out a gun, and taking the money) were not part of the evidence presented. As predicted, these excluded elements found their way into the mock jurors' memories of the crime. Other research has found that crime details that are not consistent with preexisting scripts are more readily forgotten over time (Garcia-Bajos, Migueles, & Aizpurua, 2012). The lessons from these studies, and many others, is that memory does not begin as a blank DVD. Prior knowledge and beliefs intrude on and get mixed in with observed events.

Witness Confidence

If you were serving on a jury and an eyewitness identified the defendant as the person who committed the crime, how would you know whether that witness was right? Being a reasonable person, you would probably consider viewing conditions: whether the crime scene was well lit, how long the witness had to observe the criminal, how far away the criminal was from where the incident took place, and the witness's eyesight. And, if you are like most other jurors, you would also take into account how certain the witness is. When a witness who has sworn to "tell the truth, the whole truth, and nothing but the truth," points to a defendant in open court and says something like, "I'm sure that's him, I'll never forget that face," jurors and judges tend to be persuaded. And that's a problem. Research indicates that highly confident eyewitnesses tend to persuade jurors (Douglass, Neuschatz, Imrich, & Wilkinson, 2010; Pezdek, 2007). But, although eyewitness confidence is strongly correlated with persuasiveness, it is only weakly correlated with accuracy. A witness's confidence can be a moderately good indicator of accuracy under favorable circumstances (e.g., when viewing conditions are good, lineups are well constructed, and investigators do not ask leading questions), but it may be a meaningless or even misleading indicator of accuracy under less favorable circumstances (Leippe & Eisenstadt, 2007).

One of the reasons confidence is not a good indicator of accuracy is that confidence is likely to increase over time. First, the witness usually gives a verbal description of the suspect to the police. Unless the suspect has bright red hair or a tattoo on his face, it is likely that this description matches thousands of people. Next, the witness may look through a thick book of photographs to see if she can find a photo of the defendant. A vague description has now become a specific face. The witness will have plenty of time to study this face and memorize its features. Police officers may even say that they already suspected that the identified person committed the crime. For example, when Jennifer Thompson somewhat hesitantly identified Ronald Cotton as the man who raped her, the police officer administering the photo lineup said, "We thought this might be the one." Later, the witness may be asked to identify the suspect in a lineup. If the witness has already picked out someone in a photograph, he or she may now simply be picking the person who most resembles the person in that photograph. Finally, the witness may identify the defendant in court. At each stage, the witness gets more specific. Details are filled in, and sketchy memories become more complete. And, at each step, the witness becomes more personally invested in the correctness of the identification. The witness who began by giving a tentative, indefinite description of the criminal may appear on the witness stand as confident and emphatic, free of all doubt.

Gary Wells and Amy Bradfield (1998) conducted a revealing study of how eyewitness confidence can be manipulated. Hundreds of witnesses viewed a security video in which a man entered a Target store. The witnesses were told that just after entering the store, the man pulled out a gun and murdered a security guard. Later, they were asked to identify the gunman from a photo lineup. The 352 witnesses who identified the wrong person were randomly assigned one of three conditions: confirming feedback, contradictory feedback, or no feedback. At the time of their initial identifications, the three groups were equally confident about their identifications. The first group was then told, "Good, you identified the actual suspect in the case"; the second group was told, "Oh, that is not the suspect; the suspect in the case is actually number ___"; and the third group received no feedback. Those who heard confirming feedback later remembered being very certain at the time of the identification, while those receiving disconfirming feedback later recalled being uncertain at the time. Those who were told that they fingered the right man also remembered having a better view of the criminal, having made the identification more easily, and having paid more attention to the crime. Interestingly, witnesses were not aware that they had been swayed by the feedback. This tendency for biased feedback to distort the memory of eyewitnesses is called the **postidentification**

(*Rich Legg/Getty Images*)

feedback effect and has been documented across many studies (Douglass & Steblay, 2006). The source of the feedback does not have to be the investigating police officer. In cases where more than one person witnesses a crime, feedback from a confident co-eyewitness is likely to raise the confidence of the other eyewitness (Goodwin, Kukucka, & Hawks, 2013).

Like memory itself, confidence appears to be malleable. The postidentification boost in confidence might be partly explained by the theory of **cognitive dissonance** (Aronson, 2007). Dissonance theory predicts that once you commit yourself to a particular course of action, you will become motivated to justify that course of action. In the case of eyewitness identification, once you have identified someone as the criminal, that action will be dissonant (inconsistent) with the knowledge that you were uncertain about your identification. That inconsistency will be uncomfortable. It is very difficult to admit that you identified the wrong person, so the most expedient means of reducing dissonance will be to increase your level of certainty. Once you have committed yourself to a particular identification, you become increasingly certain that you picked out the right person.

When the Eyewitness Is a Child

As compared to adults, children provide less information, and somewhat less accurate information, when responding to interview questions about what they witnessed (Melnyk, Crossman, & Scullin, 2009). Children are about as accurate as adults are when presented with lineups or photo spreads, but only if the true perpetrator is present in the lineup (this is called a culprit-present or target-present lineup). If the true perpetrator is absent from the lineup (called a culprit-absent or target-absent lineup), children do worse. Some researchers have noted that this weakness may be attributable to the greater suggestibility of children (Bottoms, Najdowski, & Goodman, 2009). It is possible that simply being asked to look at a lineup implies to children that the adult conducting the lineup wants them to find the criminal among the photos or members of the lineup. Comments from police officers such as "we thought this might be the one" are especially likely to influence children. Indeed, the memories of children seem to be especially negatively impacted by a stress-inducing interview style (Quas & Lench, 2007). The special concerns surrounding child witnesses in cases involving physical and sexual abuse are discussed more fully in Chapter 11.

USING RESEARCH FINDINGS TO IMPROVE EYEWITNESS ACCURACY

At this point, you may be thinking that psychologists are great critics, but they aren't much good at suggesting practical solutions. If eyewitnesses are so fallible, what can be done to reduce the possibility that the wrong person will be convicted? There are several options.

The justice system cannot control who witnesses a crime, how carefully that person observes the crime, or whether the race of the victim is different from the race of the criminal. Such factors, which are outside the control of the legal system, are called **estimator variables.** They are helpful in estimating the accuracy of an identification. However, a leading researcher has argued that social scientists interested in eyewitness identification ought to focus on **system variables**—those factors that are under the control of the justice system (Wells, 1978). For example, the legal system can control how a witness is questioned and how lineups are constructed. Modifications in the type and order of questions asked by police can and should be made if such changes can improve the accuracy of identification.

In 1998, the American Psychology-Law Society (APLS) appointed a committee to review more than a quarter century of research on eyewitness testimony with the goal of developing guidelines for gathering evidence from eyewitnesses. The committee report proposed four simple reforms that dramatically reduce the number of mistaken identifications, with little or no reduction in the number of correct identifications. These modifications concern who administers the lineup or photo spread, the instructions given to witnesses viewing lineups or photo spreads, who appears in the lineup alongside the suspect, and obtaining information about eyewitness confidence (Wells et al., 1998; Wells, 2006). The U.S. Department of Justice used these rules to create guidelines for police and investigators (Department of Justice, 1999). More recent research suggests some additional guidelines. Seven guidelines are summarized below.

1) Blind Lineup Administrators

The first rule is that, "the person who conducts the lineup or photo spread should not be aware of which member of the lineup or photo spread is the suspect" (Wells et al., 1998, p. 627). This recommendation may seem obvious and uncontroversial. However, it is rarely followed. One of the detectives investigating the case nearly always directs the lineup. These detectives often have strong suspicions about who committed the crime, and they may communicate these suspicions (usually unintentionally) to the eyewitness.

A large body of evidence demonstrates how the beliefs and expectations of one person can subtly shape the responses of another person. For example, early studies of teacher-student interactions found that if teachers were told to expect particular children to experience intellectual gains, the teacher conveyed these expectations to students through a variety of subtle cues—encouraging words, positive facial expressions, smiles, tone of voice, and eye contact (Rosenthal & Jacobson, 1968). Similarly, experimenters may unintentionally communicate their expectations to people participating in their experiments. That is why whenever the effectiveness of a new medicine is being tested, the person administering the drug is "blind" to whether the real drug or a placebo is being administered. When we test new drugs, we follow careful procedures and take great care to ensure reliable findings. We do this because the potential consequences of an error—putting an ineffective or dangerous drug on the market—are very serious. We should exercise the same care in gathering eyewitness evidence because the potential consequences of a mistake—accusing and convicting an innocent person—are also very serious. Using a **blind lineup administrator** helps to avoid this error.

2) Bias-Reducing Instructions to Eyewitnesses

The second rule is to tell eyewitnesses that the true criminal "might not be in the lineup or photo spread." This **bias-reducing instruction** removes the presumption that the witness is obliged to choose someone from the available options. In addition, witnesses should be told that, "the person administering the lineup does not know which person is the suspect in the case" (Wells et al., 1998, p. 629). This information discourages the witness from looking to others in the room for clues about who is the "right" person to identify. It forces witnesses to rely solely on their own memory (Quinlivan et al, 2012).

Witnesses tend to assume that the person who committed the crime is included in the lineup. After all, police have gone to the trouble of assembling a lineup and bringing the witness to the police station. They must think they know who committed the crime. In a standard lineup, where the "might not be in the lineup" instructions are absent, witnesses tend to pick whichever person looks the most like the person they remember. The recommended instruction removes the assumption that the real criminal must be in the lineup and lifts the pressure to identify someone.

3) Unbiased Lineups

In an old comedy sketch from the TV show *Saturday Night Live*, police are trying to find a black man who committed a crime. They suspect that Richard Pryor (an African-American comedian) is their man. In the first lineup, Pryor is standing with six white men. But the witness is not sure that Pryor is the culprit. So the police try again. In the next lineup, Pryor is standing with six elderly white women. Still, no identification. In the final lineup, Pryor is standing with six household appliances including a washing machine and a refrigerator. "That's him!" cries the eyewitness pointing to Pryor. This sketch illustrates the reasoning behind the third recommendation: Lineups and photo spreads must be constructed so that the actual suspect does not stand out from the **fillers**—the alternative suspects in the lineup or photo spread (fillers are also called "foils" or "distractors"). That is, all of the people in the photos or in the lineup should resemble each other, and all should match the witness's verbal description of the offender. Nothing about the procedure should draw extra attention to the actual suspect. This requirement may seem obvious, but in many cases, lineups have been rigged to encourage an eyewitness to select the suspect that police believed to be guilty. A meta-analysis of 17 studies found that biased lineups (those with fillers that do not closely resemble the real culprit) led to substantially higher rates of innocent suspect identifications (Fitzgerald, Price, Oriet, & Charman, 2013).

To test whether a lineup is biased, a "mock witness" procedure can be used. Mock witnesses are people who did not see the crime. Each mock witness is given the eyewitness's verbal description of the culprit. For a six-person lineup, if more than 2 out of 12 mock witnesses can pick out the suspect, it is probably not an **unbiased lineup.** If, for example, 5 out of 12 mock witnesses identify the suspect, it means that identification is not a result of true recognition, but of mere similarity to the verbal description (Corey, Malpass, & McQuiston, 1999).

4) Confidence Ratings

To illustrate the importance of Rule 4, here are two quotes, taken several weeks apart, from one eyewitness in a Missouri case:

> **Eyewitness when viewing a four-person lineup to identify her attacker:**
>
> "Oh, my God . . . I don't know . . . It's one of those two . . . but I don't know. . . . Oh, man . . . the guy a little bit taller than number two . . . It's one of those two, but I don't know. . . . I don't know . . . number two?"
>
> **At trial, when asked if she was positive that her attacker was number two in the lineup, if it wasn't a "maybe":**
>
> "There was no maybe about it . . . I was absolutely positive" (Wells & Bradfield, 1998).

Because confidence is likely to change between the time of the lineup and the time of the trial, the fourth recommendation is to obtain a clear statement about how confident the witness is that the person identified is the right person. This statement must be taken immediately after the culprit is identified and *before* any feedback is given to the witness. As noted earlier, confidence tends to increase in the period between the initial identification and testimony in court. Several factors may boost confidence once the person has been identified. The police may tell you that they believe you identified the right person or they may say that other witnesses described the same person. In the quote from the Missouri case above, the lineup administrator simply said "okay" when the eyewitness identified the suspect by saying "number two?"

The confidence boost produced in a witness who has received confirming postidentification feedback (e.g., "we thought he might be the guy who did it") appears to have a direct impact on the perceived credibility of the eyewitness. In studies of this effect, eyewitnesses who received confirming feedback were later judged by others as being more accurate and more confident than witnesses who received no feedback, or witnesses who received disconfirming feedback (Douglass et al., 2010; Jones, Williams, & Brewer, 2008).

5) Video Recording

Although it will never be possible to video record all crimes as they occur, it might be possible to require that all identification procedures be recorded. Ideally, a video recording of the lineup identification would serve as a lasting, objective, audiovisual record of what transpired during the identification process. Attorneys, judges, and juries could see and hear for themselves what instructions were given to witnesses, whether members of the lineup resembled one another, what feedback was given to the witness immediately after identification, how confident the witness appeared during the lineup, what sort of comments were made by police or witnesses, and how long the entire process took (Kassin, 1998). A technological fix may actually be possible in this area. As video recording technology improves (and becomes cheaper), cameras will be able to take in information from a larger area, and recordings will become clearer. Unfortunately, it will never be possible to fully prevent a determined investigator from subverting the intention of video recording by making sure that any biasing behavior takes place outside the view of the video camera.

6) Sequential Lineups

In **sequential lineups,** an eyewitness sees one person (or photograph) at a time, decides whether that person was the perpetrator, and then sees the next person. In contrast, in the more commonly used **simultaneous lineup,** several people are standing side by side (or several facial photographs are laid out next to one another). The underlying logic for using a sequential procedure is to make sure the suspect is not judged only in relation to the fillers. In simultaneous lineups, witnesses tend to compare the people in the lineup with one another and then to identify the person who looks the most like their mental image of the criminal. In other words, eyewitnesses tend to rely on *relative* judgments. Sequential lineups are superior in the sense that they reduce people's ability to compare one candidate with another, making the identification more individualized instead of comparative. Ample evidence suggests that sequential procedures reduce the number of mistaken identifications, and that is why many researchers and legal scholars have advocated for their use (e.g., Douglass & McQuiston-Surrett, 2006).

A large-scale field experiment conducted in collaboration with police departments in four states systematically compared 497 sequential and simultaneous lineups. The sequential procedure resulted in an identification of the suspect in 27.3% of lineups, as compared to 25.5% in the simultaneous lineups (a nonsignificant difference). However, the sequential procedure did produce a significantly lower rate of wrong-person identifications (12.2%) than did the simultaneous procedure (18.1%) (Wells, Steblay, & Dysart, 2012). (See the Hot Topic box in this section to learn more about the obstacles to putting this sort of science into practice.)

7) Expert Testimony

A final safeguard is to have an expert on eyewitness identification testify in court. When testifying in this capacity, psychologists summarize research findings on the conditions that increase or decrease eyewitness accuracy (McAuliff & Kovera, 2007). Although expert testimony on eyewitness identification is now routinely admitted at trial, some judges have been reluctant to admit such experts because they fear

 HOT TOPIC

Translating Science into Practice
The large body of research on eyewitness identification enables us to make clear recommendations to law enforcement personnel. However, whenever research findings are used to modify established practices, some difficulties and complexities usually arise. An initial difficulty is deciding where the threshold lies for making a policy recommendation. That is, at what point do we declare that the research findings are strong and clear enough to justify a specific policy recommendation? For example, although research findings strongly favor sequential lineups, a few researchers argue that those findings may not yet be compelling enough to cross the threshold (Clark, 2012; Ross & Malpass, 2008). As noted in Chapter 1, the practical question is whether recommendations made on the basis of carefully conducted research are an improvement over current practices, many of which are based on little more than convenience or tradition. A second difficulty is resistance to reform among the people responsible for carrying out the reform. For example, Nancy Steblay and Elizabeth Loftus (2008) list some of the objections to reform raised by police and prosecutors who administer lineups: (1) We do not think it is broken, so why try to fix it?; (2) it will cost too much to put the reforms in place; (3) it will slow our investigations and weaken our prosecutions; (4) it is soft on crime; (5) it favors the defense; and (6) we are the professionals, and we know what is best. In addition (as in other areas of psychology and law), there is the fear that if reforms are made, the courts might be flooded with appeals by people who were convicted based on prereform procedures. Finally, even when a police department adopts research-based recommendations for conducting lineups, there is often insufficient training of the police officers who are responsible for putting the reforms into practice (Wise, Safer, & Maro, 2011).

Another difficulty concerns the contingent nature of some research findings. For example, a meta-analysis revealed that the advantage of the sequential procedure depends on whether the actual culprit is present or absent in the lineup. In a culprit-absent lineup, the witness correctly recognizes the culprit is not present 68% of the time when a sequential procedure is used. This recognition occurs only 46% of the time when a simultaneous procedure is used. However, in culprit-present lineups, the culprit is correctly identified 44% of the time using a sequential procedure, but about 52% of the time using a simultaneous procedure (Steblay, Dysart, & Wells, 2011). This increase in correct identifications is likely due to "lucky guesses" in simultaneous lineups. Sequential lineups reduce the incidence of guessing by eyewitnesses who have weak memories (Penrod, 2003). Overall, sequential lineups lead to the benefit of significantly reducing the risk of false identifications but at the cost of some smaller reduction of correct identifications (roughly 8%). Although many prosecutions will go forward and many convictions will be obtained without a positive eyewitness identification, some convictions will be lost.

The process of translating science into best practices is seldom smooth or swift. The people responsible for changing policies and practices are strongly influenced by political and practical considerations. Although scientists may argue that the benefits of a particular reform clearly outweigh the costs, practitioners may come to a different conclusion based on very different weighing of very different considerations. However, despite the challenges of translating science into practice, the science of eyewitness evidence has substantially transformed the procedures for gathering information from eyewitnesses to crimes.

that expert testimony might persuade jurors to dismiss or undervalue all eyewitness identification, even if the identification is accurate.

Brian Cutler, Steven Penrod, and Hedy Dexter (1990) conducted a series of experiments to gauge the impact of being exposed to psychological testimony on the limitations of eyewitnesses. These studies used realistic trial simulations and varied several factors: the conditions under which the eyewitness viewed the crime, whether the identification procedures were impartial or biased, the confidence of the eyewitness, and whether expert testimony about eyewitness identification was present or absent. Experts were subjected to tough cross-examination, just as they would be in a real trial. The expert testimony had the desired effect: It sensitized jurors to the importance of viewing and lineup conditions that compromise or enhance accuracy, and it caused jurors to put less credence in witness confidence as an indicator of accuracy. The mock jurors who did not hear expert testimony overestimated the accuracy of eyewitnesses, did not take into account factors known to reduce accuracy, and placed substantial weight on eyewitness confidence as an indicator of accuracy. It appears that when expert testimony is provided to jurors, they are able to make appropriate use of the information experts provide (Semmler, Brewer, & Douglass, 2012).

What if police departments fail to follow the guidelines described above? As noted by the APLS committee, failure to use unbiased procedures

> . . . invites participation by credible eyewitness experts in the case for the defense, places the prosecutor in the difficult position of having to defend the absence of good procedures, routinely elicits motions to suppress the identification evidence, and risks the jury acquitting the defendant because there is another explanation (the suggestive procedures) as to why the suspect was identified by the eyewitness. (Wells, et al., 1998, p. 638)

Finally, note that the seven guidelines described above are not particularly costly to put into practice. Indeed, improved technology has made the implementation of questioning and lineup reforms easier than it has ever been. The use of laptop computers to present photo lineups can potentially solve several problems and may actually be cheaper than traditional practices. A computer program can select appropriate "fillers" and randomize the order in which the photos are presented. Unbiased instructions can be presented on the computer screen before the session begins, a confidence rating can be recorded just after the witness makes an identification, and a camera on the laptop can record the entire session.

Most important, any financial expense or time cost must be weighed against the considerable human costs of false identifications: Lives of the wrongly identified are disrupted or even shattered, eyewitnesses who later discover their mistakes must live with the knowledge that they were responsible for the prosecution of an innocent person, and the real criminals remain free to commit more crimes.

TECHNIQUES FOR REFRESHING THE MEMORIES OF WITNESSES

Witnesses to crimes sometimes cannot remember critical details of what they saw. Because the memories of witnesses are so crucial, various methods have been tried to "refresh" those memories.

A police hypnotist
demonstrating
her technique
(SHUTTERSTOCK)

Hypnosis

Hypnosis has a long history. Its use began with the French physician Franz Anton Mesmer (the word "mesmerized" is a variant of his name). Mesmer believed that he could induce hypnotic states through the use of "animal magnetism." His ideas were controversial. A scientific committee chaired by Benjamin Franklin investigated his claims and concluded that hypnosis was induced through the power of suggestion (Gauld, 1992). An English physician coined the term **hypnosis** after Hypnos, the Greek god of sleep. Hypnosis has been used during psychotherapy as a technique for improving athletic performance and as a substitute for light anesthesia during medical procedures. In the legal system, its main application has been as a tool for enhancing the memories of crime victims and witnesses to crimes. There is a longstanding debate about whether hypnosis is a unique trancelike state or simply an ability to suspend skeptical thinking and play the role of hypnotized subject. What is clear, however, is that a successfully hypnotized subject enters a relaxed, focused state in which he or she is highly receptive and responsive to suggestions made by a hypnotist (Pintar & Lynn, 2007).

Once hypnotized, eyewitnesses are usually instructed to "rewitness" the event as if they are watching a documentary of the crime on television. They might be asked to "zoom in" on important details (e.g., a getaway car, or license plate, or face) or to "replay" critical parts of the event. People usually recall more information when they are hypnotized than when they are not hypnotized. This phenomenon is called **hypnotic hypermnesia** (the opposite of amnesia). But more information is not necessarily better information. The problem is that memories refreshed through hypnosis may contain a large dose of fantasy and imaginative elaboration. A fragmented eyewitness memory may become fuller and more vivid during hypnosis, not because the true memory has been restored, but because gaps in memory have been filled in with plausible but fictional details. Indeed, research shows that hypnosis does *not* increase the recall of *accurate* information (Eisen, Oustinovskaya, Kistorian, Morgan, & Mickes 2008; Steblay & Bothwell, 1994). A final problem is that once an event is vividly imagined under hypnosis, a witness may become confident that the memory is true (a phenomenon known as "memory hardening").

Skilled hypnotists have occasionally helped to uncover useful information. In 1976, in Chowchilla, California, three masked kidnappers hijacked a school bus carrying 26 children. The children and bus driver were taken to a quarry and buried in a chamber six feet underground. All the captives miraculously escaped, but there were few useful leads until the bus driver was hypnotized. Under hypnosis, he was asked to recount the kidnapping from beginning to end as though he were narrating a documentary film. When asked to describe the vehicle the kidnappers had used, he was able to remember all but one number of the license plate. That license plate number, which the driver did not recall until he was hypnotized, was the clue police needed to find and arrest the kidnappers. The Chowchilla case illustrates an occasionally productive use of hypnosis in the legal system: to uncover or develop information that can facilitate investigation of a crime. When there is little physical evidence to point investigators in the right direction, it may sometimes be useful to hypnotize a witness to see if new information can be uncovered. For example, if a witness recalls a license plate under hypnosis, it may lead to the discovery of more reliable physical evidence (e.g., drops of blood inside a car).

Some advocates of hypnosis note that it may sometimes serve as a useful "face-saving" device. Witnesses who are reluctant or afraid or embarrassed to tell what they know may feel freer to provide information if hypnotized. For example, if a witness who is afraid of reprisal initially says that she cannot remember details of the crime, she may later be reluctant to disclose information because she would have to admit she had been lying earlier. By allowing herself to be hypnotized, she can tell the police what she knows but claim that she only remembered it while hypnotized (Kebbell & Wagstaff, 1998).

The law appears to share psychology's skepticism about hypnosis. Although the law is unsettled about the admissibility of hypnotically enhanced memories, the courts have typically imposed severe restrictions on testimony from hypno-tized witnesses. For example, in 1982 (*People v. Shirley*), the California Supreme Court excluded all testimony about memories that emerged through the use of hypnosis. However, in 1987 (*Rock v. Arkansas*), the U.S. Supreme Court struck down an Arkansas law that banned all hypnotically refreshed testimony. In *Rock*, a woman who had killed her husband remembered under hypnosis that the gun had misfired during a struggle with her husband. Because the trial judge had refused to let jurors hear about what the woman remembered under hypnosis, the woman was granted a new trial. The Supreme Court was careful to note that the basis for its decision was the right of Ms. Rock to testify on her own behalf. Their underly-ing skepticism about the reliability of hypnotically refreshed memories was un-changed. What all this means is that information recalled under hypnosis is not automatically excluded at trial. Whether it is admitted depends on the specific characteristics of the case—for example, whose memory has been refreshed (the defendant, the victim, or an eyewitness), and how carefully the hypnosis sessions were conducted.

The appeal of hypnosis was based on the hope that it would provide access to memories not available during normal consciousness. Unfortunately, memory dis-tortions sometimes created by the process of hypnosis have made the technique much less useful than its proponents had hoped. Hypnosis can elicit false memories, amplify the effects of suggestive questioning, and bolster the confidence of eyewit-nesses (Lynn, Boycheva, Deming, Lillienfeld, & Hallquist, 2009). What is needed is an alternative technique that might boost recall without promoting false or embel-lished recollections.

The Cognitive Interview

One promising alternative has been developed and refined by Ron Fisher and Ed-ward Geiselman (2010). This technique—called the **cognitive interview**—involves a subtle step-by-step procedure designed to relax the witness and mentally reinstate the context surrounding the crime. The goal is to improve the witness's retrieval of accurate information while avoiding the increased suggestibility of hypnosis.

An interviewer using this technique gently guides the witness through several stages. During the first phase, the interviewer attempts to reduce the witness's anxi-ety, to develop rapport and help the witness concentrate. The interviewer asks the witness to report what happened, without interference, thereby avoiding sugges-tive questioning. During the second phase, the witness closes his or her eyes and attempts to reinstate the context of the crime mentally. He or she mentally pictures the setting of the crime and the surrounding sights, sounds, and feelings. The third phase involves probing the images and actions the witness reports. The purpose is to make sure all relevant information is brought out. Then, the witness recalls events in different orders—moving forward in time from beginning to end, then backward from end to beginning. The fourth phase entails taking different perspectives on the crime, such as mentally viewing the event from the perspective of the criminal and the victim. The interviewer records these recollections and reads them back to the witness to uncover errors or omissions. During the fifth and final phase, background information is collected, and the interviewer emphasizes that the witness should call if he or she remembers new information. Overall, the technique involves relaxing the witness, providing multiple opportunities to report everything he or she saw, and avoidance of coercive or leading questions from the interviewer (Fisher & Schreiber, 2007).

Unfortunately, skillful use of the cognitive interview requires police to adopt an interviewing style quite different from their usual style. Police officers are accustomed to interrogating criminal suspects. As described in Chapter 2, they receive extensive training on how to extract incriminating information from these reluctant "interviewees." As Fisher and Geiselman point out, it is difficult for police officers to switch from a coercive, leading, interrogation style when interviewing witnesses instead of suspects. Based on research showing that the cognitive interview improves recall of accurate information without an increase in witness suggestibility, police forces in England and Wales now receive training in the technique (Dando, Wilcock, & Milne, 2009). Police in the United States do not routinely use the cognitive interview.

▶ IN CONCLUSION

Good detectives understand the critical importance of keeping a crime scene uncontaminated. Ideally, if someone has been murdered, investigators photograph the scene from multiple angles. The position of the body, the pattern of spattered blood, and the nature of the wounds are all carefully noted before anything is disturbed. Evidence is preserved and carefully transported so it can be tested for fingerprints or other trace evidence. If blood is found at the scene of the crime, strict testing procedures are followed to prevent contamination of the DNA sample.

In many cases, the crucial evidence is not physical but psychological: It is the memory of a victim or other eyewitness. Like blood and fingerprints, human memory can be easily contaminated and distorted. Psychologists have now revealed the kinds of questioning and investigative procedures that are likely to corrupt existing memories, or even create false ones. If a police laboratory uses sloppy procedures, a DNA analysis can be challenged and discredited. If suggestive or coercive procedures are used to gather information from witnesses, the recollections of witnesses can be challenged and discredited. The reason for handling both physical and psychological evidence carefully is the same: to make sure the right person is arrested and convicted.

▶ DISCUSSION AND CRITICAL THINKING QUESTIONS

1. Why might police departments resist adopting the four rules for conducting eyewitness identifications? Are all four of these rules worth following?

2. If mistaken eyewitness identification has been made, how can it be exposed? What can be done during trial to reduce the impact of the identification?

3. How might hypnosis be misused in the legal system? Does it ever make sense to trust memories uncovered during hypnosis?

4. How does human memory differ from a video recording?

5. What role does confidence play in the process of eyewitness identification? How does it affect eyewitnesses? How does it affect police? How does it affect jurors?

► KEY TERMS

bias-reducing instructions (p. 145)

blind lineup administrator (p. 145)

cognitive dissonance (p. 144)

cognitive interview (p. 151)

cross-race effect (p. 139)

encoding (p. 134)

estimator variables (p. 144)

fillers or foils (p 146)

hypnosis (p. 150)

hypnotic hypermnesia (p. 150)

Manson criteria (p. 136)

memory trace (p. 135)

meta-analysis (p. 139)

postidentification feedback effect (p. 144)

retrieval (p. 134)

retrieval inhibition (p. 142)

scripts (p. 142)

sequential lineups (p. 147)

simultaneous lineups (p. 147)

storage (p. 134)

system variables (p. 144)

unbiased lineups (p. 146)

unconscious transference (p. 141)

weapon focus effect (p. 140)

8 Competency to Stand Trial

On a hot summer afternoon in 1998, Russell Weston, Jr., entered the United States Capitol building through a delivery entrance on its east side. At the official checkpoint, he walked around the metal detector. An officer stationed there—Jacob Chesnut—asked Weston to come back and walk through the x-ray machine. In response, Weston pulled out a .38 caliber handgun and shot Officer Chesnut in the back of the head. Weston exchanged fire with several other Capitol policemen and was shot in the leg. Despite this injury, he turned down a hallway that led to the offices of Senators Tom Delay and Dennis Hastert. He entered Delay's office complex and shot Detective John Gibson, a plain-clothed officer stationed in Delay's outer office. Detective Gibson returned fire and further wounded Weston. Weston was eventually captured. Detective Gibson died of his injuries a short time later.

Soon after the incident, it was discovered that Weston had a long history of mental illness and had been diagnosed with **schizophrenia**—a serious mental illness whose sufferers lose touch with reality. People with schizophrenia exhibit a wide range of psychotic symptoms, including: hearing voices that are not actually there (**auditory hallucinations**); having difficulty thinking and speaking in a coherent manner (**thought disorder** or disorganized thinking); and holding false beliefs (**delusions**) that affect their behavior. Weston told court-appointed mental health professionals that he needed to enter the Capitol building to prevent the United States from being infected by the "Black Heva" disease that he believed was carried by cannibals. He was convinced that cannibalism was caused by a "ruby satellite" locked in a Senate safe. He also expressed the belief that then President Bill Clinton was part of a communist conspiracy that had taken over the government. Two years prior to the Capitol shooting, Weston arrived unannounced at the Central Intelligence Agency headquarters in Langley, Virginia, and told CIA officers that President Clinton was ". . . a Russian clone, brought to the United States for the purposes of a communist insurgency." That same year, Weston had been committed to a state mental hospital against his will for 53 days (for further discussion of involuntary civil commitment see Chapter 14). When questioned by mental health professionals after the Capitol shooting, Weston described himself in heroic terms. He reported that there was nothing wrong with him, and that he alone could save the country from cannibals, communism, and disease.

Weston, or the "Capitol shooter," as he became known, was charged with first-degree murder along with several other crimes, and faced the federal death penalty. More than a decade and a half after the shootings, however, Russell Weston has yet to stand trial for his crimes. He was found incompetent to stand trial, and subsequent psychological treatment

Russell Weston. How severely mentally ill must individuals be before they are judged incompetent to stand trial? *(AP Photo/Montana State Department of Justice)*

RUSSELL EUGENE WESTON JR

has not restored him to competence. In 2004, his charges were suspended but not dismissed.

The legal definition of **competence** refers to whether an individual has sufficient present ability to perform necessary personal or legal functions. There are several different types of legal competencies including: competency to waive Miranda rights, competency to confess, competency to make treatment decisions, competency to execute a will or contract, and competency to take care of oneself or one's finances. This chapter will explore competency as it relates to criminal defendants. We will focus on the most common evaluations performed by forensic psychologists— **competency to stand trial (CST),** which is the ability to participate adequately in criminal proceedings and to aid in one's own defense. Later, we return to Russell Weston's case to explore the intricacies of this issue in more detail. ◀

 THE MEANING OF COMPETENCY TO STAND TRIAL

Defendants have the most to lose during criminal proceedings because their liberty is at stake. Consequently, it is important that they have some idea of what is occurring at every stage in the criminal justice process, from arrest to sentencing. A defendant charged with a serious crime has a right to a trial. But what if the defendant cannot understand what is going on before or during the trial? Perhaps the accused lacks the mental capacity to understand the basics of a legal proceeding. Perhaps he or she is substantially impaired by mental illness. But if we determine some people to be too impaired to stand trial, what should be the definition of "too impaired"? And how can we measure a defendant's level of impairment? Does it matter if the defendant can understand much but not all of what happens in court? These are some of the difficult questions surrounding the legal concept of CST.

There are several reasons to be concerned about CST. If the standard for CST is set too high, many individuals who are simply ignorant about our court system will not face trial. Another set of concerns involves fairness to the defendant. Participation of the defendant in his or her own defense improves the likelihood of a just verdict. In an adversarial system, defendants must be able to provide their lawyers with information about the crime and about the witnesses who testify at trial. Without the assistance of the defendant, the attorney is less able to mount an effective defense. This raises the risk of a mistaken conviction. And, even though a lawyer handles the defense, the defendant remains ultimately responsible for several key trial decisions: whether to plead guilty, whether to waive a trial by jury, whether to testify, and whether to accept a plea bargain offered by the prosecution (Melton et al., 2007).

A final set of concerns has to do with public respect for the criminal justice system. To use the full power of the state to try, convict, and punish defendants who do not understand the nature of the legal proceedings against them undermines the perceived legitimacy of the legal system. It would simply not seem fair. A related but less central concern is that unruly behavior in court by a mentally disturbed defendant could disrupt the dignity of legal proceedings.

The *Dusky* Standard

The legal doctrine of incompetence originated in English common law of the seventeenth century. CST was considered critical because, at the time, defendants usually had to argue their own case. The modern conception of CST was defined by the U.S. Supreme Court in the 1960 case of ***Dusky v. United States.*** Milton Dusky, a 33-year-old mentally ill man, was charged with kidnapping and unlawfully transporting 15-year-old Alison McQuery across state lines. Dusky transported Alison—along with two boys who were friends of his son—from Missouri to Kansas. Alison was acquainted with one of the boys and believed she was receiving a ride to her girlfriend's house. Instead, Dusky drove her to a desolate spot just across the Kansas state line where the two boys raped her. Dusky was eventually arrested and sent for a CST evaluation prior to his trial. The psychologist who evaluated Dusky concluded that he suffered from schizophrenia. The psychologist also testified at a competency hearing that Dusky could not adequately assist in his defense due to his mental illness. The trial court, however, ruled that Dusky was competent to stand trial. He was found guilty at trial and sentenced to 45 years in prison.

Dusky appealed his case to the United States Supreme Court, which agreed with Dusky and his attorneys, holding that the existing trial record did not support his competence to stand trial. The Supreme Court made clear that,

> "... it is not enough to find that 'the defendant [is] oriented to time and place and [has] some recollection of events,' but that the 'test must be whether he has sufficient present ability to consult with his attorney with a reasonable degree of rational understanding—and whether he has a rational as well as factual understanding of the proceedings against him'" (Dusky v. United States, 362, U.S. 402, p. 403).

Notice the word *present* in the CST definition. CST refers to the psychological state of the defendant *at the time of trial*. The defendant's psychological state at the time of the crime is not relevant to a determination of CST (although it is relevant to a determination of insanity, which will be discussed in Chapter 9). Dusky's case was returned or remanded to the trial court for a determination of whether he met the Court's new standard.

The term **adjudicative competence** is often used to capture the various types of abilities needed to participate effectively in all stages of the legal process. In 1993, Richard Bonnie wrote an influential paper arguing that adjudicative competence consists of two underlying components. The first component—foundational competence—involves the capacity to assist counsel and is essential for ensuring the fairness, dignity, and accuracy of the criminal justice system. Foundational competence implies a basic understanding of the trial process as well as the capacity to provide a lawyer with information relevant to the trial. If a defendant is competent to assist counsel, then the second component—decisional competence—comes into play. This component has to do with the capacity to make informed, independent decisions. It is crucial to recognize that an assessment of competence focuses on the defendant's *ability*, not his or her willingness, to perform relevant legal functions. A defendant who is unwilling to talk to his or her attorney is competent unless that unwillingness is based on an irrational belief system. Finally, it is important to note that the threshold for competence is set relatively low for the sake of efficiency—better to have cases decided by the courts than to have them hang in limbo until defendants are restored to competence. For example, a defendant raised in another country who does not understand how our legal system works would be competent to stand trial if he or she has the capacity to be educated about legal proceedings.

Functional Elements of CST

CST is a legal, not a psychological concept. It refers to a defendant's ability to understand and perform a number of discrete court-related functions. These functions include, but are not limited to a defendants' ability to: (1) understand their current legal situation; (2) understand the charges against them; (3) understand the pleas available; (4) understand the possible penalties if they are convicted; (5) understand the roles of the judge, defense counsel, and prosecutor; (6) trust and communicate with defense counsel; (7) help locate witnesses; (8) aid in developing a strategy for cross-examining witnesses; (9) act appropriately during the trial; and (10) make appropriate decisions about trial strategy (Pirelli, Gottdiener, & Zapf, 2011).

Being found CST does not certify robust mental health or even normal mental functioning. Even people suffering from severe mental disorders, psychosis, or developmental disability are often judged CST. In fact, a study of over 8000 competency evaluations found that over two-thirds of individuals suffering from severe disorders were still found competent to stand trial (Warren et al., 2006). Competence merely means that a defendant meets the minimal standard of being able to cooperate with an attorney, and that he or she is aware of the nature and possible consequences of the proceedings against him or her. Indeed, many (if not most) defendants do not fully understand the workings of the legal system.

There is some disagreement about whether CST should be a **flexible standard**—that is, whether a defendant facing very serious charges in a case with complex facts may need to be more competent than someone facing less serious charges and a simpler legal proceeding. Put differently, should the functions that a defendant needs to perform in a trial affect the threshold for competence? In cases involving defendants with amnesia, the courts have suggested that a situation-based assessment of CST may be appropriate. Several courts (e.g., *U.S. v. Wilson*, 1968), have held that, by itself, amnesia for the crime is not sufficient for a ruling of incompetence if other sources of information (e.g., eyewitnesses, police reports, physical evidence) are available. Such information may be sufficient to enable the amnesic defendant and his or her attorney to build an effective defense.

Other decisions by the Supreme Court during the 1990s (*Cooper v. Oklahoma*, 1996; *Medina v. California*, 1992) established a **presumption of CST.** That is, defendants are presumed to be competent unless proven incompetent, and the defense bears the burden of proving that the defendant is incompetent. Furthermore, the **preponderance of the evidence (POE)** standard is used when determining CST. Using this standard, the defense must prove that it is more likely than not that the defendant is incompetent. This is one of several different burdens of proof used by the criminal justice system. The one most students are familiar with—**beyond a reasonable doubt (BRD)**—governs decisions about guilt in criminal cases. Because decisions about criminal guilt involve the greatest deprivation of liberty (imprisonment), a high level of certainty is required. Falling between the high certainty of BRD and the lesser certainty of POE, is the **clear and convincing evidence (CCE)** standard. CCE is used when there is a substantial intrusion on an individuals' liberty short of imprisonment (e.g., involuntary civil commitment, see Chapter 14). Under the POE standard, the judge (or a jury in rare cases) must be more than 51% certain that the defendant is incompetent.

CST VERSUS COMPETENCY TO PLEAD GUILTY AND WAIVE AN ATTORNEY

Issues of competence can arise well before and long after trial. At arraignment, there may be an issue of whether the defendant is competent to decide to plead guilty. In 1938, the Supreme Court held that a guilty plea must be **knowing, voluntary, and intelligent** (*Johnson v. Zerbst*). In part, this means that defendants must understand the charges against them as well as the potential consequences of a conviction (e.g., spending several years in prison). Judges are required to question the defendant to make sure he or she understands that by entering a plea of guilty, important constitutional rights are forfeited: the right to a trial by jury, the right to remain silent, the right to appeal, and the right to confront one's accusers. Later, at the trial stage, a defendant may decide to serve as his or her own attorney. Here again, the issue of competence can be raised. Do such defendants fully understand the consequences of waiving their right to an attorney? You have probably heard the old saying that, "anyone who serves as their own lawyer has a fool for a client." Some lawyers argue that simply asking to represent oneself is evidence of incompetence. The Supreme Court suggested, in *Godinez v. Moran* (1993), that separate psychological evaluations of **competency to waive an attorney** or **competency to plead guilty** are not required once a defendant has been found CST. Some scholars have argued that the Court's decision indicates that the low threshold for CST also applies to competency to waive an attorney or plead guilty. In contrast, others have argued that the inclusion of these separate abilities within the CST decision actually raises the overall threshold for CST (Zapf & Roesch, 2006).

A high-profile case involving a mentally ill man who represented himself may have helped change courts' thinking on the distinction between competency to stand trial and competence to represent oneself. In 1993, Colin Ferguson boarded a Long Island commuter train and calmly opened fire on the passengers, reloading his gun several times. He killed six passengers and injured 19 more before three commuters wrestled him to the ground. Ferguson's attorneys attempted to convince the judge that he was mentally ill, not competent to stand trial, and insane (using a black rage syndrome defense, see Chapter 10 for more details). When the judge found Ferguson competent to stand trial, he fired his attorneys and proceeded to represent himself in a bizarre trial proceeding that was televised on Court TV and spoofed in an episode of *Saturday Night Live.* Clearly suffering from a psychotic illness, Ferguson's examination and cross-examination of witnesses made little sense. He claimed he was charged with 93 counts of criminal conduct because it was the year 1993 and if it was the year 1925 he would be charged with 25 counts. Ferguson also argued that a mysterious stranger named "Mr. Su" stole his gun while he was sleeping on the train and shot everyone. He was eventually found guilty of all six murders and was sentenced to over 300 years in prison. Following Ferguson's strange trial, the courts were ready to reconsider the issue of whether a competent but mentally ill defendant should be able to defend himself without the assistance of counsel.

In 2008, in the case of **Indiana v. Edwards,** the U.S. Supreme Court addressed the issue of competency to waive an

Colin Ferguson was found competent to stand trial and then chose to represent himself. This may have led to changes in the legal standard for a mentally ill people to be able to do this. Should a severely mentally ill person be allowed to represent him or herself if they are found competent to stand trial without any additional assistance or supervision from an attorney? (*Rick Maiman/Sygma/Corbis*)

attorney and its relationship to competency to stand trial. Ahmad Edwards was suffering from schizophrenia when he stole a pair of shoes from an Indiana department store. As he was leaving the store, he was confronted by a security guard. Edwards produced a gun and fired at the guard. The bullet grazed the guard on the leg and then struck an innocent bystander. Edwards was apprehended as he tried to leave the scene and was charged with several felonies. From 2000 to 2005, he underwent a number of CST evaluations. After twice being found incompetent, he was eventually found competent. Before his trial in 2005, the judge denied his request to represent himself. He was subsequently found guilty of attempted murder, battery with a deadly weapon, criminal recklessness, and theft.

The Supreme Court ruled that the judge had been correct in refusing Mr. Edwards's request to represent himself. The Court held that a higher standard of competence than the one announced in *Dusky* could be used to prevent mentally ill defendants from waiving their right to a lawyer and choosing to defend themselves. The Court reasoned that the dignity and fairness of the trial process required the judge to appoint an attorney for a competent but mentally ill defendant, and that the *Dusky* standard presupposed that a criminal defendant had access to counsel because it requires "sufficient present ability *to consult with his attorney*." The Court also alluded to the need for a higher level of competence if a criminal defendant chose to plead guilty. However, the Court failed to specify exactly which skills and abilities a mentally ill defendant needs to proceed without counsel or to plead guilty. Future litigation will hopefully clarify which abilities a mental health professional should assess when performing these types of competence evaluations.

 ## HOW THE CRIMINAL JUSTICE SYSTEM DEALS WITH INCOMPETENT DEFENDANTS

Even if a defendant does not want to raise the question of competence, ethical guidelines require lawyers to tell the presiding judge if they believe that a defendant may be incompetent. Usually, the defense lawyer raises the issue, but prosecutors and judges are also obligated to make sure a defendant is competent. Further, if either attorney raises the issue of the defendant's competence, the presiding judge almost always orders a psychological evaluation. Unlike most other issues decided in court, there tends to be little dispute about providing a competency evaluation when it is requested. Prosecutors seldom object to requests for competency evaluations, and judges rarely deny such requests (Zapf, Roesch, & Pirelli, 2014). Occasionally, lawyers may request competency evaluations for purely strategic reasons to gain some advantage. For example, an evaluation may be requested by either side to delay the trial and give attorneys more time to prepare. Also, prosecutors may request a competency evaluation to prevent the defendant from being released on bail, and either side may seek an evaluation to gain information about the feasibility of an insanity defense (Winick, 2008). Defense attorneys tend to be cautious about ordering a CST evaluation in less serious cases. This is because their clients may end up spending more time incarcerated while waiting for the CST evaluation than they would have if they had been found guilty of the crime with which they were charged. Once the defendant is found competent, information gathered during a competency evaluation cannot be introduced at trial, *unless* the defendant places his or her mental state into evidence, for example, by pleading not guilty by reason of insanity (*Estelle v. Smith*, 1981).

CST EVALUATIONS AND ULTIMATE ISSUE EXPERT TESTIMONY

The issue of CST is typically raised at a pretrial hearing but can be ordered by the judge or attorneys at any time during the trial as long as there is a **bona fide doubt** or a reasonable doubt about the defendant's competency. Bona fide doubt is an even lower standard than the preponderance of evidence standard mentioned earlier in this chapter. At least one, and occasionally more than one, mental health professional—usually a psychiatrist, clinical psychologist, or social worker—is asked to serve as an evaluator. The evaluator will usually interview the defendant, administer psychological tests, review the defendant's history, and write a report. That report will summarize the evaluator's findings and offer a conclusion about the defendant's ability to participate in his or her trial and cooperate with his or her attorney. The evaluation can be done on either an inpatient or an outpatient basis. Inpatient evaluations involve holding a defendant in a mental institution for a period usually ranging from a few weeks to several months. An advantage of evaluations in institutional settings is that they provide multiple opportunities to observe the defendant's behavior over time. They also provide **collateral sources of information** or information from third parties about the defendant's behavior. For example, a prison guard, administrator, nurse, or other mental health professional can provide valuable information about the defendant's abilities to navigate aspects of the institutional environment.

Outpatient evaluations are those that occur outside of mental institutions. They are usually conducted in jails or local clinics and are far more common than inpatient evaluations. These evaluations cost less and intrude less on the rights of the accused because the defendant need not be incarcerated during the evaluation process. Usually, a written report is all that is required by the court. However, it is not uncommon for a judge to ask a psychologist to testify about his or her findings.

In the past, many of these reports focused on the diagnosis of mental illness and/or the wrong legal standard (i.e., insanity). Recent studies suggest that these reports now contain more links between the defendant's mental illness and the resulting trial-related deficits (e.g., the defendant's schizophrenia causes delusions that interfere with the defendant's ability to communicate with his or her attorney; Skeem, Golding, Cohn, & Berge, 1998). However, even today's more focused reports often fail to make explicit connections to many of the defendant's specific competency abilities and deficits. It is not uncommon for evaluators to disagree about the likely effects of psychological disturbance on trial-related abilities. One recent study compared three different independent evaluators across 216 competency cases in Hawaii (Gowensmith, Murrie, & Boccaccini, 2012). The researchers found that all three evaluators agreed on competency or incompetency 71% of the time.

Regardless of the shortcomings of CST reports written by mental health professionals, it is quite rare for a judge to reject the conclusion of an evaluator—especially if the defendant has been found incompetent. Judges have been found to agree with evaluator decisions well over 80% of the time (Zapf et al., 2014; Warren et al., 2006). This makes the final conclusion of a CST report extremely consequential. In the Hawaii CST study, judges agreed with the majority of the three evaluators 92.5% of the time. When judges disagreed with the majority, it was usually in the direction of a finding of incompetency (Gowensmith et al., 2012). In other words, judges were most concerned with avoiding the potential error of allowing an incompetent defendant to proceed to trial. This makes sense because incompetent defendants are given time to be restored to competence, and a conservative judicial approach enables marginally competent defendants to take the time to develop the necessary legal knowledge and skills.

If an evaluator reaches the conclusion that a defendant is incompetent, the report typically contains recommendations for treatments that might restore competence. Indeed, the vast majority of incompetent defendants are eventually restored to competency: Approximately 75% of incompetent defendants are successfully restored and go on to face trial for their crimes within 6 months (Zapf & Roesch, 2011).

Controversy continues to surround how clinical psychologists and other experts participate in CST cases. For the most part, courts allow experts in these proceedings to offer an opinion on whether or not a specific defendant is competent or incompetent to stand trial. This testimony about the appropriate legal decision in a particular case is known as **ultimate issue testimony** because it answers the question at the heart of the proceeding. Many psychologists and legal scholars argue that providing such ultimate issue testimony is inappropriate. They contend that because competency is a legal issue, not a psychological one, it should be decided only by a judge or jury. In other words, they believe the court, not the psychological expert, must determine the precise point at which a defendant's mental deficits rise to the level of legal incompetence. In contrast, others argue that the mental health expert is in the best position to understand whether the defendant lacks important trial capacities due to his or her mental illness (Stafford, 2003). We will return to the question

---

LEGAL SPOTLIGHT

Competency to Be Executed

If criminal defendants are restored to competency, then found guilty and sentenced to death, what level of understanding would they need to have before they could be executed? Although the Supreme Court has ruled that executions do not violate the Eighth Amendment's prohibition against cruel and unusual punishment, it has also held that it would be cruel and unusual to execute an incompetent prisoner who does not understand why he or she is being executed (*Ford v. Wainwright*, 1986). Although similar to CST, this form of competency involves different abilities than CST and an even lower threshold of understanding. The courts are merely trying to prevent the execution of people who do not understand why they are facing the penalty of death. In *Panetti v. Quarterman* (2007), the Supreme Court revisited the issue of competency to be executed and tried to clarify the legal standard introduced in *Ford v. Wainwright*. Scott Panetti held his wife and daughter hostage while he murdered his wife's parents. He was convicted of capital murder and sentenced to death. There was little doubt that Panetti suffered from severe mental illness. He told a psy-

Scott Panetti whose execution was at issue in *Panetti v. Quarterman* (AP PHOTO/TEXAS DEPT OF CRIMINAL JUSTICE)

chiatric evaluator that the government was "in league with the forces of evil," and he was being executed to "prevent him from preaching the gospel." Despite these delusional beliefs, he was found competent to stand trial. Panetti waived his right to an attorney, defended himself in court, and his insanity defense failed. In the Panetti case, the Supreme Court ruled that a criminal defendant needs to have more than a mere factual awareness of the State's justification for execution, and that Panetti's mental illness may have prevented him from understanding the meaning of his punishment. The Court did not, however, explain what would constitute a rational understanding of the State's reason for execution. Future court decisions will be needed before it is clear what level of understanding a severely mentally ill defendant needs before he or she can be put to death. If a defendant is found incompetent to be executed, proceedings are initiated to restore him or her to competency so that he or she can be killed by the state. Mental health professionals might then be enlisted in the ethically troubling process of restoring prisoners to competence for the sole purpose of facilitating an execution (see Chapter 17).

of whether an expert should offer ultimate issue testimony when we discuss other situations in which psychological experts offer testimony to the court (see, for example, Chapter 9). (To learn about competency to be executed see the Legal Spotlight box in this section.)

RESTORATION OF COMPETENCY

It is estimated that over 60,000 criminal defendants are evaluated for CST every year (Bonnie & Grisso, 2000). That is greater than 5% of all felony defendants. According to a recent meta-analysis, approximately 28% of defendants who are referred for a competence evaluation are actually found incompetent (Pirelli et al., 2011).

Research on defendants judged to be incompetent has revealed that such defendants tend to live on the fringes of society. As a group, they are more likely to be unemployed, unmarried, and of lower intelligence than other defendants (Pirelli et al., 2011). They also tend to have a history of treatment for mental illness, show obvious symptoms of current mental illness, have a history of drug abuse, and are charged with a less serious crime (only a small portion are accused of violent crimes; Warren et al., 2006). Further, psychotic illnesses (such as schizophrenia), severe affective disorders (such as bipolar illness), and intellectual disability (i.e., developmentally disabled) are the most common mental health problems diagnosed in defendants found to be incompetent. The presence of a psychotic disorder is the strongest predictive factor of incompetence (Zapf et al., 2014). Yet, none of these factors alone would necessarily cause an individual to be incompetent. The difficulties must directly affect the defendant's abilities to interact with his or her attorney and understand the proceedings. For example, the mere fact that Russell Weston was a paranoid schizophrenic who believed that "Black Heva" disease was causing cannibals to take over the planet did not make him incompetent to stand trial. Rather, his incompetence stemmed from delusional beliefs that interfered with his ability to assist in his own defense: his belief that the judge was part of a governmental conspiracy against him; his belief that the trial was the best means of bringing the communist cannibal conspiracy to light; and his belief that the judge and prosecutor would attempt to place cannibals on the jury.

Prior to the 1972 Supreme Court decision in *Jackson v. Indiana,* defendants judged to be incompetent could be held in mental hospitals for indefinite periods. Indeed, just prior to that decision, researchers found that about half the people found incompetent ended up spending the rest of their lives in mental institutions (McGarry, 1971). Hospital stays often exceeded the amount of time defendants would have served in prison if they had been found guilty of the crime. The *Jackson* decision, however, limited the period of confinement to the time necessary to determine if the defendant could be returned to competence in the **foreseeable future.** As a result of the decision, most states now limit confinement to somewhere between 4 and 18 months. If, after that period, the defendant is still judged to be incompetent, several more extensions can be granted. Significant problems and uncertainties arise if the defendant has still not been restored to competence, even after this extended hospital stay. Sometimes, involuntary civil commitment proceedings are initiated. To commit someone to an institution using involuntary civil commitment laws is difficult, however. The person must either be shown to be **gravely disabled** (unable to care for him/herself or to provide for basic needs like food and shelter) or "imminently dangerous to self or others" (La Fond, 1998; also see Chapter 14). Regardless of the eventual outcome for the individual, the criminal charges against a nonrestorable defendant may be dismissed or suspended. These charges, however, can be reinstated in some circumstances (usually for the most serious crimes) if the individual regains his or her competency-related abilities in the future.

Even if an incompetent defendant is hospitalized, it is not certain that he or she will receive the kind of treatment that will restore competence. The quality of treatment at mental health facilities varies considerably, and sometimes there is little emphasis on restoring legal competence. However, some studies suggest that training specifically designed to explain courtroom rules and procedures can help to restore CST. In one such study, researchers used two groups of defendants who had been judged to be incompetent and who were confined in psychiatric hospitals (Siegel & Elwork, 1990). The treatment group was given information about courtroom rules, personnel, and procedures by means of videotapes, lectures, and discussions. The control group received more standard forms of therapy. By the time the training ended, hospital staff judged 43% of the treatment group to be CST, but only 15% of the control group were judged to be CST. Such programs are likely to be particularly important for adolescents who do not suffer from a mental illness but simply lack the requisite understanding of the criminal justice process. Yet there is little research on which types of programs produce the best results for defendants suffering from different types of problems (Zapf & Roesch, 2011).

Right to Refuse Treatment and CST

Instead of directly educating defendants on legal procedures, **restoration of CST** typically involves treatment with **antipsychotic medication** (Stafford, 2003; Zapf & Roesch, 2011). Antipsychotic medications can reduce the severity and frequency of hallucinations and delusions experienced by severely mentally ill patients. Sometimes, symptoms can even be eliminated. One-quarter of such patients, however, do not improve on these drugs. And, even for patients who do improve, the drugs may produce disturbing physical side effects—muscle tremors, muscle rigidity, and the development of unusual postures. There is also a risk of tardive dyskinesia, a disorder characterized by abnormal involuntary movements of the mouth and face (Oltmanns & Emery, 2011). The likelihood of tardive dyskinesia increases the longer the defendant is medicated, and this side effect often persists even after the medication is discontinued. A new generation of antipsychotics, commonly referred to as atypical antipsychotics, do not produce the same motor side effects as traditional medications. However, these newer drugs are not usually given to mentally ill defendants because they are expensive and difficult to administer involuntarily. Some of these drugs also have potentially lethal side effects if not monitored closely (see Table 8.1 for a summary of pros and cons of the administration of antipsychotic medication).

Sometimes, mentally ill defendants also lack awareness of their illness and see medication as unnecessary. They think that medication is part of a larger plot to hurt or destroy them. Because of the risks and side effects of antipsychotic medication, there is considerable controversy about whether the government should forcibly medicate a defendant in order to restore him or her to competency. One might wonder how defendants deemed incompetent to stand trial could be competent to make decisions about their own treatment. Theoretically, a defendant could hold delusional beliefs about the legal system (e.g., the judge is Satan and she is trying to sentence me to hell), but have a rational reason for avoiding antipsychotic medication (e.g., the side effects associated with the drugs are too severe). In practice, this is unlikely because those defendants who are disturbed enough to meet the definition

TABLE 8.1	
Involuntary Administration of Antipsychotic Medication	
Pros	*Cons*
• Reduce or eliminate hallucinations and delusions experienced by severely mentally ill defendants	• Extrapyramidal side effects (muscle tremors, muscle rigidity, development of unusual postures) • Risk of tardive dyskinesia becoming permanent • Question of violating the defendant's due process rights

of incompetence are also likely to be severely impaired in their ability to reason about treatment choices.

Occasionally, a defense attorney may wish to avoid competency restoration to avoid a trial that might have severe negative consequences for his or her client. For example, in the Capitol shooter case, Weston showed no interest in voluntarily taking antipsychotic medication, and his lawyers likely wished to avoid competency restoration because he potentially faced the death penalty for his crimes. Such cases raise the question: "What must the government prove to justify forcible medication of a defendant for the purpose of restoring competency?" Several Supreme Court decisions bear directly on this issue.

Riggins v. Nevada (1992) dealt with the case of a criminal defendant medicated against his will. While the defendant in the case—David Riggins—was waiting to be tried for robbery and murder, he complained of hearing voices and suffered from severe insomnia. A psychiatrist acting on behalf of the court prescribed a very large dose of an antipsychotic drug (Mellaril) and a relaxant (Dilantin). Riggins had suffered from similar problems in the past and had been treated before using these same medications (although at lower dosages). The drugs were successful in stabilizing Riggins' behavior and he was declared CST. However, because Riggins was relying on an insanity defense, he asked that he not be forced to take Mellaril during his trial. Riggins argued that the drug made him unable to assist his defense lawyer and that the jury should be able to observe him in his non-medicated state—the state he was in when he committed the murder. The judge refused his request and the jury convicted him and sentenced him to death.

However, on appeal, the Supreme Court ruled that forcing Riggins to take these medications deprived him of due process (*Riggins v. Nevada*, 1992). Medical experts at Riggins's subsequent hearings conceded that the very high levels of antipsychotic drugs that Riggins was administered during his original trial were close to toxic levels, and such levels could cause sedation, confusion, and difficulties in concentration. The Court held that involuntary medication was only permissible to achieve essential state interests—such as a fair trial or safety of the defendant or others.

In *Washington v. Harper* (1990), the Supreme Court made clear that a *convicted* criminal should have fewer protections from forcible medication than an individual who is *alleged* to have committed a crime. Harper was a convicted robber who had been in prison for 14 years. He suffered from bipolar disorder, and he had voluntarily taken antipsychotic medication both while in prison and while he was previously on parole. Harper subsequently decided that he no longer wanted to take his antipsychotic medication. The Supreme Court ruled that a court hearing was not necessary to determine whether Harper could be forcibly medicated. It held that a prisoner could be involuntarily medicated if: (1) it was in the prisoner's medical interest as determined by a neutral medical professional, and (2) administration of medication was necessary given the legitimate needs of institutional confinement. In light of these two prior decisions, the question for the courts with regard to defendants deemed incompetent to stand trial was whether they are more similar to a defendant (*Riggins*) or a prisoner (*Harper*).

In *Sell v. United States* (2003), the Supreme Court attempted to clarify what type of proceedings were necessary before an incompetent defendant could be medicated against his will. In this case, Charles Sell, a dentist accused of mail fraud, suffered from psychosis. He believed that communists had contaminated his gold dental fillings, that public officials sought to kill him, and that God had told him to kill FBI agents (Landis, Krauss, & O'Connor, 2003). He was found by the trial court to be incompetent to stand trial, and he subsequently refused to voluntarily take the antipsychotic medication that had helped him in the past. The Supreme Court ruled that a criminal defendant *who was not a danger to himself, herself, or others* could be forcibly medicated if and only if: (1) such treatment was medically appropriate; (2) the treatment was unlikely to have side effects that would undermine the trial fairness; and (3) such treatment was necessary to further a significant government interest, such as the prosecution of a serious crime. Yet, the Court reasoned that such decisions should only occur in rare circumstances, and that other means of imposing medication (e.g., the appointment of a substitute decision-maker because of the defendant's inability to make treatment decisions) should be exhausted first. It is also important to note that the Sell case involved

TABLE 8.2

Important Cases in Competency to Stand Trial

Case	Issue	Holding
Dusky v. United States (1960)	What is the standard for CST?	Sufficient present ability to consult with his attorney with a reasonable degree of rational understanding and whether he has a rational as well as factual understanding of the proceedings against him
Jackson v. Indiana (1972)	How long can an incompetent defendant be held?	The court must make a determination of whether an individual can be restored to competency in the foreseeable future. Usually, this requires determinations every six months or so.
Godinez v. Moran (1993)	Is the *Dusky* standard also used to determine whether a defendant can plead or waive his or her attorney?	Yes, but this decision is later modified by the court in *Indiana v. Edwards* (2008).
U.S v. Sell (2003)	Is a separate judicial hearing required in order to forcibly medicate a nondangerous, incompetent defendant?	Yes, a criminal defendant *who was not a danger to himself, herself, or others* could be forcibly medicated if and only if: (1) such treatment was medically appropriate; (2) the treatment was unlikely to have side effects that would undermine the trial fairness; and (3) such treatment was necessary to further a significant government interest, such as the prosecution of a serious crime.
Indiana v. Edwards (2008)	Can a court require a competent, mentally ill defendant to use an attorney against his or her will?	Yes, there is in fact a higher standard for a competent mentally ill individual to waive counsel than the *Dusky* standard. The standard is knowing, intelligent, and voluntary.

the forcible medication of a defendant deemed not to be a danger to himself or others. If a defendant is a danger to himself or others, courts have allowed forcible medication to restore competency on less strict grounds with fewer procedures.

In the Capitol shooter case, Russell Weston was eventually forcibly medicated based on the criteria outlined in the Sell decision. A series of court decisions ruled that his treatment with antipsychotic medication was medically appropriate (an expert testified that in 70% of cases such medications would substantially decrease psychotic symptoms), the treatment would not affect his trial fairness, and such treatment was necessary to further the significant government interest in prosecuting an alleged murderer (Melton et al., 2007). After several years and the administration of a number of different antipsychotic medications, Weston was ultimately deemed not restorable. He was subsequently civilly committed to the same medical facility he has resided in since his offense—the federal medical complex in Butner, North Carolina. (See Table 8.2 for description of famous cases related to CST.)

ADOLESCENT INCOMPETENCE TO STAND TRIAL

In the 1990s, all 50 states began to allow for juveniles of a certain age to be tried in adult court when charged with serious crimes (Steinberg, 2003; see the Hot Topic box in this section). These so-called "transfers" to adult court have become commonplace, but the competence of this new class of defendants is controversial. Due to their intellectual immaturity, adolescent defendants may lack sufficient

---

 HOT TOPIC

Juvenile Transfer to Adult Court

Although it has always been possible for juveniles to be tried in adult court, the last 25 years have seen a substantial increase in the number of such cases. This increase has been driven by widespread beliefs that adolescents are committing more serious and more repeat crimes, and that such criminals should not be handled within the rehabilitative model of the juvenile justice system (Griffin, Addie, Adams, & Firestine, 2011). In response, legislators adopted new requirements for transfer of such offenders to adult court. For example, many states (38) implemented statutory transfer policies or **statutory exclusions,** which automatically require adolescent defendants who commit certain serious crimes (e.g., murder, manslaughter) and are of a certain age (16- or 17-year-olds in some jurisdictions to as low at 13- or 14-year-olds in others) to be tried in adult court. Additionally, several states have increased the power of prosecutors to ask for transfers from juvenile court.

One of the most controversial examples of these transfer policies in-

Lionel Tate at age 13 *(AP Photo/A. Enrique Valentin, Pool)*

volved Lionel Tate. While his mother took a nap upstairs, 12-year-old Lionel accidentally killed 6-year-old Tiffany Eunick by using professional wrestling moves he had seen on TV. Eunick died of a lacerated liver, fractured skull, broken ribs, and swollen brain. Lionel was tried in adult court. The prosecutor argued that Lionel's acts were not those of child, and sought a first-degree murder conviction. Lionel was convicted of murder and sentenced to life in prison. After serving 3 years of his sentence, his conviction was overturned in 2004 because an appeals court found that his mental competency had not been adequately evaluated before trial. Before a retrial on this issue, Lionel accepted a plea bargain: He pleaded guilty and accepted a sentence of 1 year house arrest and 10 years of probation. Lionel would eventually violate his parole several times and receive a 30-year sentence for possessing a gun while on probation. Current research suggests that transferring juveniles to adult court has little effect on their likelihood of committing future crimes (Griffin, Addie, Adams, & Firestine, 2011).

understanding of the criminal justice system and/or lack the ability to interact effectively with their attorneys (Cox, Goldstein, Dolores, Zelechowski, & Messenheimer, 2012; Viljoen & Wingrove, 2007). Further, beginning in the 1990s, magnetic resonance imaging (MRI) studies, suggested that adolescent brains look and perform differently than adult brains. Adolescent brains lacked fully developed frontal lobes with greater development of neuronal connections or white matter occurring throughout the early twenties. The frontal lobe and these connections are believed to be responsible for impulse control, strategic behavior, and appreciating the risk associated with certain behaviors (Cauffman & Steinberg, 2000). All these functions may have direct bearing on the quality adolescents' decision making during trial.

Some forensic psychologists have argued that competence evaluations should be automatically triggered for juveniles if the defendant is 12 years old or younger; has been previously diagnosed as developmentally disabled or as suffering from mental illness; has a learning disability; is of low or "borderline" intelligence; or if he or she shows significant deficits in attention, memory, or understanding of reality. Researchers have also argued that there should be more intensive CST evaluations for all defendants under the age of 16 (Kruh & Grisso, 2009).

To explore adolescent competence, a team of researchers compared the abilities of nearly 1000 adolescents (ages 11 to 17) in juvenile detention facilities and community settings to approximately 500 young adults (ages 18 to 24) in jails and community settings. Their findings showed that the two groups were significantly different in their functioning on CST-related abilities (Grisso et al., 2003). Youths aged 11 to 13 were found to be less capable in legal judgment, understanding, and decision making than older youths. The younger groups' abilities in these areas appeared to improve until age 16, at which point they did not differ from older individuals. For example, the researchers found that 30% of 11- to 13-year-olds showed impairment in CST-related abilities (see Figure 8.1). In comparison, only 20% of 14- to

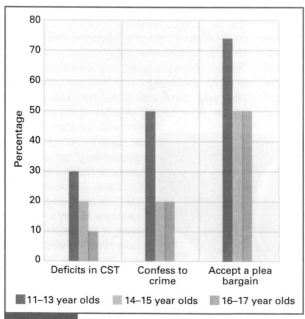

FIGURE 8.1 Research suggests that 11- to 13-year-olds are more likely than older children to have deficits in CST and accept plea bargains.

Lionel Tate at age 18 discussing his plea with his attorney. Tate was once the youngest person sentenced to life in prison in modern U.S. history for killing a young acquaintance, but he received probation after his first conviction and sentence were thrown out. Tate could not stay out of trouble with the law, though. First, he was caught with a knife late at night by police. Then Tate was arrested on charges of robbing a Domino's Pizza delivery man at gunpoint. Do you think Tate looks different to a jury as an 18-year-old than he looked as a 13-year-old? *(AP PHOTO/MIKE STOCKER, POOL)*

15-year-olds, and only 10% of 16- to 17-year-olds showed such deficits. Also, approximately 50% of the 11- to 13-year-old age group would confess to a crime rather than remaining silent during police questioning, as compared to only 20% for young adults. Significant differences were also found in willingness to accept a plea bargain. Three-quarters of 11- to 13-year-olds were willing to accept such an agreement compared to only half of young adults. Given adolescents' deficits in CST abilities, the issue of adolescent competence is likely to generate ongoing debate and continuing research for the foreseeable future.

 ## TESTS AND TECHNIQUES FOR EVALUATING CST

Because CST refers to psychological states and mental capacities, it makes sense to consult clinical psychologists and other mental health professionals when trying to assess the competence of a particular defendant. However, because the law does not prescribe a particular method of evaluation, the specific assessment techniques used by a particular clinician tend to be a function of his or her training, orientation, experience, and sophistication. There is no **gold standard** for deciding CST, no test or combination of tests that reveals with certainty whether a defendant is competent or incompetent. Looking at whether or not a judge agrees with the conclusions of an expert does not tell us much because courts almost always go along with an expert's recommendation on CST. Some have argued that the only true means to test the accuracy of judges' and experts' decisions is to allow a group of defendants who have been found competent as well as a group of defendants who have been found incompetent to proceed to trial. During and after trial, researchers could carefully evaluate the performance of both groups to determine if those found incompetent performed more poorly during the trial process (Zapf & Roesch, 2006). For ethical reasons, such a study has not been performed.

Until the early 1970s, mental health professionals often attempted to measure CST through the use of techniques designed for other purposes. Then, beginning in 1971, researchers began to develop tests specifically designed to evaluate CST. The development of psychological tests specific to legal issues is a growing area in clinical and forensic psychology. Such tests have been dubbed **forensic assessment instruments,** or **FAIs,** to differentiate them from traditional psychological tests not designed specifically to answer legal questions. For example, an IQ test can aid a mental health professional in determining whether a defendant is intellectually disabled, but the IQ score does not answer the legal question of whether the defendant is competent to stand trial. Yet, the most common psychological instruments used in most CST examinations as well as most forensic evaluations are not FAIs but general psychological tests. The **Minnesota Multiphasic Personality Inventory second edition (MMPI-2)** is an example of a widely used psychological test in CST evaluations (Lally, 2003). The MMPI-2 is a general measure of psychopathology based on a participant's responses to 567 true–false questions. While the MMPI-2 offers information on an examinee's psychological distress, symptoms, and possible diagnosis, it does not address the questions at the heart of CST evaluations—the examinee's understanding of the legal system or ability to consult with his or her attorney. In addition to their focus on legally relevant abilities, FAIs hold another advantage over more general psychological tests: They can also be used to compare objectively one defendant's performance with another. That is, using past scores of defendants who have taken the FAI, we can evaluate how a particular defendant performed compared to other defendants who were later found competent or incompetent by the courts.

CST tests were some of the first FAIs ever developed. In 1971, researchers at the Harvard Laboratory of Community Psychiatry introduced the **Competency Screening Test.** People taking this test are asked to complete 22 sentence fragments such as, "When I go to court, the lawyer will _____." and "If the jury finds me guilty, I will _____." Responses are scored as "0" (incompetent), or "1" (uncertain competence), or "2" (competent). One weakness of this early approach is that, because of the wide-open nature of the responses, significant training was required to interpret and score the responses of the person being examined (Lipsitt, Lelos, & McGarry, 1971). A second approach developed by the Harvard group (the Competency Assessment Instrument or CAI) uses a systematic one-hour interview. The CAI was noteworthy for its attention to several components of CST, including:

- the ability to communicate with an attorney
- awareness of defenses that are realistically available
- understanding of the roles played by people in the courtroom
- understanding of the charges and their seriousness
- understanding of the sequence and purpose of trial procedures
- awareness of the likely outcome of the trial and the potential penalties if convicted
- the ability to inform the defense attorney of relevant facts and distortions in the testimony of prosecution witnesses
- the capacity to provide useful testimony on one's own behalf (if necessary)

Since the pioneering work of the Harvard Laboratory in the 1970s, a significant number of tests have been developed to improve the evaluation of competence (See Table 8.3). Based, in part, on Bonnie's distinction between foundational and decisional competency discussed earlier in the chapter, a national network of researchers (funded by the MacArthur Foundation) developed the **MacArthur Structured Assessment of the Competencies of Criminal Defendants (MacSAC-CD).**

TABLE 8.3
Examples of CST Assessment Instruments
Fitness Interview Test-Revised is a structured interview developed by Canadian researchers (Roesch, Zapf, Eaves, & Webster, 1998) to assess the defendant's ability to (1) understand the proceedings, (2) understand possible consequences of the proceedings, and (3) communicate with counsel and participate in defense.
Evaluation of Competency to Stand Trial Instrument-Revised (ECST-R) is an 18-item assessment that uses a semi-structured interview to assess a defendant's factual understanding of the courtroom, rational understanding of courtroom proceedings, and ability to consult with counsel (Rogers, Tillbrook, & Sewell, 2004).
Computer-Assisted Determination of Competence to Proceed (CADCOMP) aims to provide a fuller assessment of a defendant's psychological functioning. A defendant's answers to 272 questions can be scored and distilled into a narrative report by a computer program (Barnard, et. al, 1991).
Competence Assessment for Standing Trial for Defendants with Mental Retardation (CAST-MR) is an instrument designed specifically for the assessment of the developmentally disabled (Everington, 1990). It uses both open-response and multiple-choice questions to assess basic legal requirements, such as the ability to assist defense counsel and to understand how a case moves through the criminal justice system.

An unusual feature of this test is that most of its questions are structured around a hypothetical vignette involving a bar fight:

> Two men, Fred and Reggie, are playing pool at a bar and get into a fight. Fred hits Reggie with a pool stick. Reggie falls and hits his head on the floor so hard that he nearly dies. (Hoge et al., 1997)

CST is assessed by presenting variants of this basic scenario and asking defendants to decide how Fred should respond to questions and assist his lawyer. If a defendant cannot answer a question correctly, he or she is told the correct answer and then asked more open-ended questions to see if the misunderstanding has been corrected. Following the open-ended questions, a few true–false questions are asked to clarify further which areas the defendant may not understand. A small number of additional questions are asked about the examinee's particular legal situation. Three abilities are assessed: understanding of the legal system, reasoning skills, and the defendant's appreciation of his or her own circumstances. Two versions of the "Mac" are available. The 82-item MacSAC-CD takes about two hours to administer and is used primarily for research purposes. The much shorter (22-item) **MacArthur Competence Assessment Tool-Criminal Adjudication (MacCAT-CA)** takes about 30 minutes to administer and is designed to be used by clinicians who are performing competence evaluations for the courts (Hoge et al., 1997).

The **MacArthur Judgment Evaluation (MacJEN)** tool is designed to evaluate immaturity of judgment in adolescents and adolescent decision making in a variety of legal contexts. It currently consists of three vignettes followed by a series of structured interview questions and objective responses. These responses are thought to correspond to three psychosocial risk factors (risk appraisal, future orientation, and resistance to peer pressure), which are believed to change as adolescents age. Poor performance on these measures indicates that the adolescent lacks maturity in his or her decision making and will likely make poorer decisions with regard to important legal issues. This instrument is still under development and no clinical version currently exists.

Modern tests that focus on legal competence have several advantages over more general tests of psychological functioning. The newer, more focused techniques are able to assess understanding of specific legal issues and allow for efficient outpatient assessment of CST. Also, if the test is widely used, it can serve as a common frame of reference for professionals evaluating competence. In using such tests, many forensic psychologists have emphasized the importance of being guided by a **contextual** or **functional approach** when evaluating competence (Zapf et al., 2014). Such an approach requires that evaluators keep in mind the specific demands of the particular legal case. That is, a defendant must not only be severely disturbed, but

> . . . it must be further demonstrated that such severe disturbance in this defendant, facing these charges, in light of existing evidence, anticipating the substantial effort of a particular attorney with a relationship of known characteristics, results in the defendant being unable to rationally assist the attorney or to comprehend the nature of the proceedings and their likely outcome. (Golding & Roesch, 1988, p. 79)

However, the CST instruments that have objective scoring schemes and compare an individual's overall scores to both competent and incompetent defendants (e.g., MacCaT-CA) can make such contextualization of performance somewhat more difficult. These instruments do not offer different cut-off scores for competency based on the complexity of the case. As a result, the evaluator must explain to the court how the same level of objectively scored impairment may lead to a different competency opinion based upon the complexity of a particular defendant's case. Interestingly, although there are many FAIs available, the vast majority of evaluators still do not use FAIs in their actual practice (Gowensmith et al., 2012; Pirelli et al., 2011).

Malingering

Sometimes, psychologists or lawyers suspect that a defendant is faking incompetence to avoid going to trial. In fact, some estimate that as many as 15% of defendants who are evaluated for CST are feigning impairment (Otto, Musick, & Sherrod, 2011). For example, a defendant who is facing a murder trial might claim to be suffering from amnesia. If that defendant really cannot remember anything about the crime, he or she would have a very difficult time assisting an attorney. In response to this problem, some courts have held that because claims of amnesia may be fraudulent, severe memory loss alone does not mean that a defendant should be ruled incompetent (*Morrow v. Maryland*, 1982). The problem of intentional faking mental illness or disability motivated by an external incentive is known as **malingering.** Specifically, malingering is the deliberate feigning or gross exaggeration of physical or psychological symptoms in order to gain a positive outcome (e.g., an insurance payment or compensatory damages) or to avoid a negative outcome (e.g., a long prison sentence). Malingering can be difficult to detect. Some psychological tests contain questions designed to expose malingering, and a few specific tests have been developed to help psychologists detect people who are faking their symptoms (Jackson, Rogers, & Sewell, 2005).

One instrument specifically designed to detect feigning/malingering in the CST context is the **Inventory of Legal Knowledge** (Musick & Otto, 2006). This 61-item true/false test is designed for English-speaking defendants who have some knowledge of the American criminal justice system and are being evaluated for CST (Otto, Mussick, & Sherrod, 2010). It has shown moderate ability to differentiate criminal defendants who are feigning incompetence from those who are not. The **Evaluation of Competency to Stand Trial-Revised (ECST-R)** (Rogers, Tillbrook, & Sewell, 2004) is the only FAI designed for use in CST evaluations that also contains a scale that addresses feigning or malingering.

While it is possible to malinger incompetence to stand trial, the benefits of malingering are not as direct as most people fear. As discussed earlier, being found incompetent does not mean that a defendant is treated as "not guilty." Rather, it simply means that the trial will be postponed while attempts are made to return the defendant to competency. As a result, a criminal defendant who successfully fools a court into thinking he or she is incompetent to stand trial is not likely to gain his or her freedom. The defendant will be hospitalized in a secure facility while attempts are made to return him or her to competency. Once found competent to stand trial, the defendant's trial will resume. If the defendant, like Russell Weston, is found to be not restorable to competency, he or she can be civilly committed if he or she is deemed to be a danger to himself or herself or others (see Chapter 14). If a defendant is not restorable and not dangerous, the defendant's charges will be dismissed, but those charges can be refiled (if they are sufficiently serious) if and when the defendant regains competency-related abilities. If a psychologist suspects that a defendant is malingering, he or she will explain these procedures in detail in the hope that such explanation might make the defendant rethink the production of fake symptoms. In the end, most defendants found incompetent to stand trial are restored to competency.

▶ IN CONCLUSION

CST evaluations are one of the most common evaluations performed by forensic psychologists. The evaluator attempts to determine at the time of the trial whether the defendant has sufficient ability to understand the legal proceedings as well as the ability to assist in his or her own defense. The mere presence of a mental illness is not grounds for a finding of incompetence because the defendant's mental illness must affect the defendant's trial-related abilities. Most individuals who are initially found incompetent are restored to competency by treatment with medication and/or basic training in the workings of the legal system. Of the few individuals who are not restorable to competency, a significant portion will be involuntarily civilly committed to a secure medical facility. In a very small number of cases, however, it may not be possible to restore the defendant to competency and he or she may not meet the standard for civil commitment. In these cases, charges against the defendant must be dropped but these charges can often be reinstated if the individual regains competency.

▶ CRITICAL THINKING QUESTIONS

1. Should CST be one standard or a flexible standard depending on the complexity of the trial (what are the advantages and/or disadvantages of each approach)?

2. What abilities should mentally ill defendants possess before they are allowed to represent themselves?

3. Should there be different standards for adolescent as compared to adult CST and should it matter if they are tried in adult or juvenile court?

4. How should brain developmental differences between adolescents and adults affect CST evaluations?

5. Should forcible medication ever be permitted in CST cases (under what conditions)?

6. What are the strengths and weaknesses of various tests and methods of evaluating CST (is one approach better than the others)?

▶ KEY TERMS

adjudicative competence (p. 157)
antipsychotic medication (p. 164)
auditory hallucinations (p. 155)
beyond a reasonable doubt (BRD) (p. 158)

bona fide doubt (p. 161)
clear and convincing evidence (CCE) (p. 158)
collateral sources of information (p. 161)
competence (p. 156)
competency to stand trial (CST) (p. 156)

Competency Screening Test (p. 170)
competency to plead guilty (p. 159)
competency to waive an attorney (p. 159)
contextual or functional approach (p. 171)
delusions (p. 155)

Dusky v. United States (p. 157)
Evaluation of Competency to Stand Trial Instrument-Revised (ECST-R) (p. 172)
flexible standard (p. 158)

9 The Insanity Defense

On a summer morning in 2001, Andrea Yates filled the bathtub in her home and called her children to the bathroom, one by one. Her three-year-old son Paul was the first child she called. She forced Paul into the bathtub and held his head under water until he stopped breathing. She carried his soaked body to the bedroom, laid him down, and covered him with a sheet. Then, she drowned her sons Luke, age 2, and John, age 5, in the same way. Yates's six-month-old daughter, Mary—who was on the bathroom floor crying while her three brothers were killed—was the next to be held under water. Just as Yates was lifting her daughter's lifeless body from the tub, her oldest child, Noah, age 7, walked in and asked what was wrong with his little sister. When Yates tried to grab Noah, he ran away. She chased him down a hallway, dragged him to the bathroom, and drowned him next to his sister.

After killing all five of her children, Andrea Yates called 9-1-1 and told the operator that she was ill and needed an ambulance. She also called her husband Russell and told him to come home. "It's time," she told him. "I finally did it." Then she hung up. When the police arrived at the scene, they found Noah floating face down in the tub, and his brothers and sister laid out in the same bed. Mary's head was resting on the shoulder of her brother John. His mother had placed his arms around his sister's body. Andrea told police that she had been thinking about killing her children "ever since I realized that I have not been a good mother to them." She said that the children "weren't developing correctly." To the surprise of many, the grieving husband refused to condemn his wife. "I don't blame her a bit," he said. "If she received the medical treatment she deserved, then the kids would be alive and well. And Andrea would be well on her way to recovery" (Springer, 2002). ◀

THE TRIAL OF ANDREA YATES

When Andrea Yates went on trial in 2002, two keys facts were undisputed: She had killed her five children, and she suffered from severe mental illness. Before the trial, a hearing was held to consider whether Yates was competent to stand trial on murder charges. Based on testimony by psychologists who had interviewed Yates and studied her history, she was deemed competent to stand trial. (See Chapter 8 for a full discussion of this issue.) As the trial began, she entered a plea of not guilty by reason

Andrea Yates and her five children. How should the legal system treat a mentally ill mother who kills her children? (A: PHILLIPPE DIEDERICH/GETTY, B: REUTERS/CORBIS)

of insanity. Because Yates had confessed to the murders, and because the physical evidence against her was overwhelming, the trial focused on whether she was legally insane. The question for the experts and the jurors was whether Yates knew the difference between right and wrong.

All the psychologists and psychiatrists involved in the case acknowledged that Yates had false beliefs about Satan, and about what Satan wished her to do. However, prosecution experts declared that these beliefs did not prevent her from knowing that what she did was wrong, while defense experts countered that Yates killed her children to save them from Satan. After listening to week after week of complex expert testimony, a jury of eight women and four men deliberated for less than four hours before finding Andrea Yates guilty. Jurors apparently agreed with the prosecutor in the case, who argued that Yates "made the choice knowing that it was a sin in the eyes of God and a crime in the eyes of the state" (Stack, 2002, p. A18). Her defense attorney reacted bitterly to the verdict: "If this woman doesn't meet the standard for insanity, nobody does. We might as well wipe it off the books" (p. A18). But all the expert testimony about Yates's mental illness may have influenced the sentence she received. When asked to choose between life in prison or the death penalty, jurors took less than an hour to decide to send Andrea Yates to prison.

Andrea Yates unexpectedly received a second trial. During the first trial, one of the prosecution's expert witnesses, Dr. Park Dietz (and the prosecutors themselves following his testimony), had suggested that the facts of the Yates case bore a startling resemblance to an episode of the TV show, *Law & Order*. In that episode, a mother drowned her child in the bathtub and feigned mental illness to escape punishment. It was revealed at trial that Yates was a frequent watcher of the show. As it turned out, Dr. Dietz had a faulty memory of the show—for which he was a frequent consultant—because no such episode existed. Because of Dr. Dietz's faulty testimony and the possible effect it may have had on the jury, a new trial was ordered. During the second trial, the same experts testified for the defense and prosecution, without any reference to the *Law & Order* episode. This time, a jury of six men and six women deliberated for 13 hours over the course of 3 days before eventually finding Yates not guilty by reason of insanity. Yates was subsequently transferred to a secure mental health facility where she will remain until she is deemed no longer a danger to herself or others.

In the trial of Andrea Yates and many other trials, decisions about "insanity" are at the heart of legal proceedings. Insanity remains perhaps the single most controversial area at the intersection of psychology and the law (Zapf, Golding, Roesch, & Pirelli, 2014). Because decisions about insanity require judgments about the psychological functioning of a defendant, **clinical psychologists**—those who study and treat various forms of psychological dysfunction and mental illness—are often crucial to the legal process in such cases. But when clinical psychologists are called upon to evaluate insanity, they must force their psychological diagnoses to fit into the specific categories provided by the law.

Unlike competence, which concerns the defendant's state of mind at the time of the trial (see Chapter 8), the concept of **insanity** refers to the criminal's state of mind *at the time the crime was committed.* Insanity requires that, due to a mental illness, a defendant lacks moral responsibility and culpability for their crime, and therefore should not be punished. The psychological expert must look into the past to determine the defendant's mental state at the time of the crime. Insanity is not a scientific concept used by modern psychologists, but rather a legal judgment that is decided in court. Legal definitions of insanity are crafted by legislators and judges, not by psychologists or psychiatrists. The label of "insanity" does not correspond to any established psychiatric diagnosis, and many mental health professionals are deeply conflicted about being asked to determine whether or not a defendant was legally insane at the time a criminal act was committed.

Even people who clearly suffer from severe mental illness may not qualify as "insane" using the legal definition of insanity. Andrea Yates is a prime example. There was ample evidence that Andrea Yates was psychotic. Following the birth of her first son, Noah, in 1994, Yates began to experience what she called "visions." Then, after the birth of her son Luke in 1999, the visions became stronger and more frequent. She had told psychologists that "there was a voice, then an image of the knife. I had a vision in my mind, get a knife, get a knife . . . I had a vision of this person getting stabbed, and the after-effects" (Springer, 2002). The visions became so disturbing that, in 1999, Yates attempted to kill herself by swallowing more than 40 sleeping pills. On another occasion, she pressed the blade of a steak knife to her neck and threatened to cut her own throat before her husband managed to disarm her.

Yates was diagnosed with postpartum mental illness. That is, she was severely depressed, her depression deepened following the birth of each child, she was plagued by feelings of overwhelming anxiety, and she was sometimes out of touch with reality. She had four stays in a psychiatric hospital because of severe psychological disturbance. Following a suicide attempt, Yates told a psychiatrist that "I had a fear I would hurt somebody. . .I thought it better to end my own life and prevent it" (Springer, 2002). After giving birth to her last child, Yates was given a prescription for Zoloft, a powerful antidepressant, and Haldol, a powerful antipsychotic. She improved, but not for long. She stopped taking the Haldol because of its unpleasant side effects. She began staying in bed all day, developed sores from picking at her nose, scraped lines on her arms and legs with her fingernails, and even attempted to scratch the number "666" (the sign of Satan) into her scalp. She seldom spoke, even to her family, and psychiatrists described her as "mute." She believed that cartoon characters were talking to her from the television programs she watched with her children. As she awaited trial, Andrea Yates could still hear Satan "growling" at her and she could still see satanic images hidden in the walls of her jail cell (Roche, 2006). But, at trial, the crucial question was not whether Andrea Yates was mentally ill. Rather, in accordance with the legal definition of insanity used in many states, the crucial question was whether or not she knew the difference between right and wrong at the time she killed her five children. In the first trial, a Texas jury found that she did know the difference, but in the second trial, a different Texas jury concluded that she did not.

THE EVOLUTION OF INSANITY LAW

The insanity defense is built on the principle that people who commit crimes without full awareness should not be held fully responsible for their actions. This principle can be traced back several centuries and is fundamental to most legal systems. The underlying logic is that it is immoral to convict and punish people who are not responsible for their criminal behavior. In other words, punishing someone who did not know their actions were wrong serves no useful purpose, and does not meet the retributive or deterrence goals of punishment (see Chapters 16 and 17). The **retribution or just deserts** perspective on punishment suggests that the punishment for a crime should be proportionate to the harm committed. It is intended to make the harmed party feel that justice has been served by punishing the perpetrator, and is often referred to by the adage, "an eye for an eye." Yet, retribution requires that the individual who committed the crime exercised free will and understood what he or she was doing. If the offender did not, then the offender is not morally responsible for his or her actions and should not be punished. For example, when a 6-year-old finds his father's gun and shoots and kills a playmate, we recognize that he could not have fully understood the consequences of his actions. Similarly, an insane individual who did not exercise free will in choosing to perpetrate a crime is also not legitimately punishable for retributive reasons.

On the other hand, the **deterrence** perspective on punishment suggests that an individual offender should be punished so that he or she learns that committing a crime leads to punishment (i.e., **specific deterrence**), and so that other similarly situated individuals will vicariously learn that such actions lead to punishment (i.e., **general deterrence**). A severely mentally ill person will usually not be deterred by punishment because his or her reasons for committing the crime are often not rational. As a consequence, such a person cannot evaluate the likely punishment for his or her action before the action occurs. Likewise, punishing one mentally ill defendant will not deter other mentally ill defendants from committing similar violent acts because these individuals will also not be able to evaluate the consequences of their actions rationally.

As early as the Roman Empire, the law dictated that people found to be *non compos mentis*—without mastery of mind—should not be held blameworthy for their crimes. The modern form of "mastery of mind" is *mens rea,* or the "guilty mind" that must accompany wrongful behavior. To be found guilty, it is not enough to commit a criminal act (the *actus reus*); one also must possess a "guilty mind"—an awareness of the wrongfulness of the criminal conduct. Legal proceedings against a criminal defendant begin with the presumption that the defendant was sane and therefore responsible for his or her criminal acts. Sometimes, a defendant's lack of awareness of "wrongfulness" is uncontroversial. But other times—as in the case of Andrea Yates—there may be considerable dispute about the defendant's state of mind at the time the crime was committed.

From the fourteenth through sixteenth centuries in England, a religiously inspired "good from evil" test was used. To be found guilty, the defendant had to understand the difference between good and evil (Platt & Diamond, 1966). In 1724, however, a significant shift took place. In the case of *Rex v. Arnold,* jurors were instructed to acquit the defendant (who had wounded a British Lord in an assassination attempt) if they found him to be "totally deprived of his understanding and memory, and doth not know what he is doing, no more than a brute or a wild beast." This test is sometimes referred to as the **wild beast test** of insanity. This revised instruction meant that insanity had become less a moral failing (failure to recognize good versus evil) and more a cognitive failing—that is, a mental deficiency involving "understanding and memory."

THREE IMPORTANT CASES AND THEIR CONSEQUENCES

The three cases described below sparked important reforms in insanity law. To a much greater extent than other aspects of criminal law, the laws surrounding insanity have been shaped and reshaped by sensational cases and public reaction to those cases. In many instances, changes in insanity law were the direct result of the public's unhappiness with the outcomes of specific cases. Consequently, most attempts to tinker with the insanity defense have occurred in a politically charged atmosphere.

The M'Naghten Case

Daniel M'Naghten (sometimes spelled "McNaughton") was tormented by paranoid delusions. He believed that people in the government were plotting to kill him. In 1843, he set out to kill the prime minister of England (Robert Peel), who he believed was part of a conspiracy against him. By mistake, he shot and killed the prime minister's secretary. At trial, nine medical experts testified that M'Naghten was insane, and the jury found him **not guilty by reason of insanity (NGRI),** even though they were told that he would be sent to a psychiatric hospital instead of prison. He spent the rest of his life in Broadmoor insane asylum.

Queen Victoria was incensed by the sentence given in the M'Naghten case. She demanded that the House of Lords pass new laws to protect the public from "the wrath of madmen who could now kill with impunity" (Eule, 1978). The public was similarly displeased. Fifteen high court judges were directed to establish a new standard of legal insanity. The new rule—which became known as the **M'Naghten rule**—consisted of three components: (1) a presumption that defendants are sane and responsible for their crime; (2) a requirement that, at the moment of the crime, the accused must have been laboring "under a defect of reason" or "from disease of the mind"; and (3) a requirement that the defendant "did not know the nature and quality of the act he was doing, *or* if he did know it, that he did not know what he was doing was wrong." Thus, for a defendant to be found NGRI under the M'Naghten rule, the defendant had to prove that he suffered from a mental illness that affected his ability to understand what he was doing and/or his ability to understand that what he was doing was wrong. The M'Naghten rule was eventually imported from English law into American law. It is sometimes called a **cognitive test** of insanity because it emphasizes knowing and understanding whether one's actions are right or wrong.

But, as many critics noted in the decades following the M'Naghten rule, cognition is only part of "insanity" and maybe not even the most important part. Some states added the term **irresistible impulse** to their definitions of insanity based upon the defendant's **volitional capacity,** or inability to control his or her behavior. Under this revised rule, a defendant could be acquitted if "his reasoning powers were so far dethroned by his diseased mental condition as to deprive him of willpower to resist the insane impulse to perpetrate the deed, though knowing it to be wrong" (*Smith v. United States,* 1954). A mental disorder could produce an uncontrollable impulse to commit the offense, even if the defendant remained able to understand the nature of the offense and its wrongfulness. The "volitional" amendment to the definition of insanity, however, had a short life. The problem was that it was too hard to tell when an impulse was irresistible. That is, how could a jury decide whether the defendant *could not* resist the impulse or simply *did not* resist the impulse? As the American

Psychiatric Association noted in its statement on the insanity defense in 1982, "the difference between an irresistible impulse and an impulse not resisted is probably no sharper than that between twilight and dusk." One attempt to clarify the revised definition was the **policeman at the elbow test.** It was suggested that the impulse had to be so overwhelming that the criminal would have committed the act even if a police officer had stood beside the criminal at the time of the crime.

The Durham Case

The second case to reshape the definition of insanity was not as sensational. It did not involve murder or a famous victim. Monte Durham was released from the U.S. Navy in 1945 because a psychiatric examination found him unfit to continue military service. After a suicide attempt two years later, he was committed to a psychiatric hospital where he remained for two months. His already disordered mental condition appeared to deteriorate even further during a prison sentence he served for car theft and writing bad checks. In 1951, he was arrested for breaking and entering an apartment. Despite having been diagnosed several times as mentally ill, the trial judge refused to let Durham plead insanity. Durham was found guilty at trial, but in 1954, the U.S. Court of Appeals for the District of Columbia overturned his conviction.

Durham's initial conviction generated little controversy, but his appeal prompted a prominent judge to reexamine the M'Naghten rule. Judge David Bazelon reviewed previous court decisions, as well as the opinions of scientific experts. He concluded that the prevailing standard of legal insanity was obsolete and misguided. Judge Bazelon threw out Durham's conviction and ordered a new trial in which a new standard of insanity would be used. According to this new rule—called the **Durham standard or the product test**—"an accused is not criminally responsible if his unlawful act was the product of mental disease or mental defect" (*Durham v. United States,* 1954). Use of the term "mental disease or defect" was a means of modernizing the insanity test by allowing mental health professionals to determine if the criminal behavior was caused by mental illness. Although most psychologists and psychiatrists welcomed the new standard, most courts responded with suspicion or even hostility. Lawyers and judges feared that it shifted the balance too far—that it might lead jurors to attach too much weight to the testimony of mental health professionals. Verdicts might turn solely on expert testimony about whether or not the defendant suffered from a "mental disease." Even Judge Bazelon eventually became dissatisfied with the Durham test of insanity. Eighteen years after it was introduced, the test was removed from use in the District of Columbia courts (*United States v. Brawner,* 1972). Interestingly, the Durham test is still used in New Hampshire.

In response to the dissatisfaction with both the M'Naghten and Durham rules, the American Law Institute (ALI; a committee of prominent legal scholars) proposed a revised standard: "A person is not responsible for criminal conduct if at the time of such conduct, as a result of mental disease or defect, he lacks substantial capacity either to appreciate the criminality [wrongfulness] of his conduct *or* to conform his conduct to the requirements of the law" (Model Penal Code, 1985). The **ALI standard** attempted to satisfy everyone—it included a M'Naghten-like cognitive prong (inability to appreciate wrongfulness) and an irresistible impulse-like volitional prong (unable to conform his conduct). Much was made of other subtle changes in wording. The term "substantial capacity" was thought to allow greater flexibility in judging defendants, and "appreciate" was thought to be better than the words "know" or "understand." The ALI standard enjoyed great success, eventually being adopted by 26 states, with a somewhat modified version being adopted by the federal courts.

The Hinckley Case

It was the ALI instruction that was read to the jury in the trial of John Hinckley, the third major case to reshape the insanity defense. John Hinckley, Jr., was a loner. In 1976, he dropped out of Texas Tech and set out for Hollywood in the hope of making it big in the music industry. During his time in California, he became obsessed with the film *Taxi Driver* and one of the movie's stars, Jodie Foster. He traveled to Yale University, where Ms. Foster was a student. In a delusional attempt to reenact a scene from *Taxi Driver* and win the love of Ms. Foster, Hinckley attempted to assassinate then-President Ronald Reagan. Several hours before he shot President Reagan, John Hinckley wrote a letter to Jodie Foster:

Dear Jodie:

There is definitely a possibility that I will be killed in my attempt to get Reagan. It is for this very reason that I'm writing you this letter now.

As you well know by now I love you very much. Over the past seven months I've left you dozens of poems, letters and love messages in the faint hope that you could develop an interest in me. Although we talked on the phone a couple of times I never had the nerve to simply approach you and introduce myself. Besides my shyness, I honestly did not wish to bother you with my constant presence. I know the many messages that I left at your door and in your mailbox were a nuisance, but I felt that it was the most painless way for me to express my love for you.

I feel very good about the fact that you at least know my name and how I feel about you. And by hanging around your dormitory, I've come to realize that I'm the topic of more than a little conversation, however full of ridicule it may be. At least you know that I'll always love you. Jodie, I would abandon the idea of getting Reagan in a second if I could only win your heart and live out the rest of my life with you, whether it be in total obscurity or whatever.

I will admit to you that the reason I'm going ahead with this attempt now is because I just cannot wait any longer to impress you. I've got to do something now to make you understand, in no uncertain terms that I am doing all of this for your sake! By sacrificing my freedom and possibly my life, I hope to change your mind about me. This letter is being written only an hour before I leave for the Hilton Hotel. Jodie, I'm asking you to please look into your heart and at least give me the chance, with this historical deed, to gain your respect and love.

Another note John Hinckley wrote to Jodie Foster before his attempted assassination of President Reagan. *(Bettmann/Corbis)*

Hinckley shot and wounded four people, including the president. A videotape of the shootings was played and replayed on national television just after the assassination attempt and during Hinckley's 1982 trial. In court, four psychological experts testified that Hinckley suffered from severe psychological disturbance, most likely paranoid schizophrenia. One of these psychiatric experts even introduced one of the first examples of **neurolaw** expert testimony—testimony intending to show a link between brain abnormalities and an individual's illegal behavior. (For more on the use of neurolaw, see the "Hot Topic Box: Brain Scans as Evidence.") The jury found Hinckley "not guilty by reason of insanity."

Several days after the Hinckley verdict, an ABC news poll found that 76% of Americans believed Hinckley should have been convicted (Lilienfeld & Arkowitz, 2011). For many Americans, the NGRI verdict in the Hinckley case seemed to epitomize all that was wrong with the insanity defense: Here was an obviously guilty (albeit disturbed) man whose crime was recorded on videotape. He had the presence of mind to stalk the president, purchase a handgun, and plan the murder attempt.

TABLE 9.1

Important Insanity Standards through History

Popular Name	Important Case	Year	Explicit Language	Key Issue(s)	Still Used?
Wild Beast Test	*Rex v. Arnold*	1774	The offender is not culpable if he is "totally deprived of his understanding and memory, and doth not know what he is doing, no more than a brute or a wild beast."	Cognitive difficulties 1. Does the defendant have memory and understanding?	No
M'Naghten Rule	*M'Naghten's Case*	1843	"It must be clearly proved that, at the time of the committing of the act, the party accused was laboring under such a defect of reason, from disease of the mind, as not to know the nature and quality of the act he was doing; or, if he did know it, that he did not know what he was doing was wrong."	Cognitive difficulties 1. Does the defendant understand what he or she is doing? OR 2. Does the defendant know what he or she is doing is wrong?	Many jurisdictions still use.
Irresistible impulse test OR Policeman at the Elbow	*Smith v. United States*	1954	The person is insane if the defendant's ". . . reasoning powers control his or were so far dethroned by his diseased mental condition as to deprive him of willpower to resist the insane impulse to perpetrate the deed, though knowing it to be wrong."	Volitional difficulties 1. Can the defendant control his or her actions?	No

Yet he was able to avoid being held accountable for his actions because his wealthy parents bought him the services of a high-priced lawyer and several psychological experts to testify on his behalf. At least, that seems to be how the public saw it at the time. Of course, the real story was a bit more complicated. Even the prosecution experts had testified that Hinckley was plagued by a mental disorder of some kind. The most important factor in Hinckley's acquittal was probably the burden of proof in the case. Instead of requiring the *defense* to prove that the defendant was insane at the time of the crime, the **burden of proof** was placed on the *prosecution* to prove (beyond a reasonable doubt) that the defendant was sane. This shift in the burden of proof probably had more to do with the NGRI verdict than the skill of Hinckley's lawyers or experts (Caplan, 1984). A summary of the different legal insanity standards throughout history is displayed in Table 9.1.

TABLE 9.1

Important Insanity Standards through History

Popular Name	Important Case	Year	Explicit Language	Key Issue(s)	Still Used?
Durham Rule	*Durham v. United States*	1954	"An accused is not criminally responsible if his unlawful act was the product of mental disease or mental defect."	Broadest Test 1. Are the defendant's actions caused by mental illness?	Overturned in federal courts by *United States v. Brawner, 1972* Still used in New Hampshire
American Law Institute Test		1962	"A person is not responsible for criminal conduct if at the time of such conduct, as a result of mental disease or defect, he lacks substantial capacity either to appreciate the criminality [wrongfulness] of his conduct or to conform his conduct to the requirements of the law."	Volitional or cognitive difficulties 1. Introduced the concept of "lacks substantial capacity" rather than a complete inability. 2. Can the defendant control his or her actions? OR 3. Does the defendant understand his or her actions are wrong?	By 1982 adopted by the federal courts and majority of states' courts. It is no longer used in federal courts because of *The Insanity Defense Reform Act* adopted in 1984. A minority of states still use the ALI standard.
The Insanity Defense Reform Act	*United States v. Hinckley*	1984	"At the time of the commission of the acts constituting the offense, the defendant, as a result of a severe mental disease or defect, was unable to appreciate the nature and quality or the wrongfulness of his acts. Mental disease or defect does not otherwise constitute a defense."	Cognitive difficulties 1. Is the defendant unable to appreciate what he or she is doing? OR 2. Is the defendant unable to appreciate what he or she is doing is wrong?	Adopted following public outrage after the *Hinckley* decision. Still in use in the federal system and the majority of states.

HOT TOPIC

Brain Scans as Evidence

When John Hinckley went on trial in 1982 for shooting President Ronald Reagan and three others, an expert witnesses called by the defense offered testimony about a brain scan showing that Hinckley possessed "widened sulci" in his brain. The defense proffered this evidence in an effort to show that Hinckley suffered from schizophrenia (widened sulci had been linked to schizophrenia in a number of early studies) and to bolster his insanity defense (*U.S. v. Hinckley*, 1982). It is not clear whether this expert testimony and the brain scan images helped the jury to find Hinckley "not guilty by reason of insanity."

Since the Hinckley trial, a proliferation of neuroscience expert testimony and brain images has been presented at trials. The growing acceptance of cognitive neuroscience in the courtroom has helped to create a new interdisciplinary field of study dubbed "**neurolaw.**" Neurolaw explores the intersection of neuroscience and issues of culpability, responsibility, and punishment in the law. In fact, one recent review tracking neurolaw evidence in the courtroom since 2004 found more than 2,000 cases in which neuroscience evidence has been offered, with more than 600 instances occurring in 2011 alone (Davis, 2012). Some scholars suggest that neuroscience offers a deterministic view of human behavior that is at odds with the law's assumptions of free will (e.g., Blume & Paalova, 2011). Perhaps, its gravest critic—Stephen Morse—contends that specific brain abnormalities are not sufficiently linked to criminal behavior to answer legal questions of culpability, responsibility, and volitional control. Morse argues that "brains do not kill people, people kill people" and that ". . neuroscience has added virtually nothing really relevant to criminal law" (Davis, 2012 p. 4).

Although there is little doubt that the presentation of such evidence is rapidly increasing, little is known about its effects on juror decision-making. Will jurors be unfairly persuaded by dazzling color-enhanced images of brains that seem to link criminal behavior to brain abnormalities? Further, even when group-level studies show that deficits in certain regions of the brain (e.g., the frontal lobe) affect impulsivity, that does not necessarily mean that a particular defendant is less culpable for his or her actions because of deficits in that region of the brain, or that brain impairments led to the commission of a crime. And, although a defendant with a specific brain abnormality may have committed a crime, how many individuals with that same abnormality have not committed crimes? These and other questions will need to be answered as the law continues to grapple with neurolaw evidence and its effects on legal decision-makers.

COMMON MISCONCEPTIONS ABOUT THE INSANITY DEFENSE

Debate about the insanity defense often occurs in the overheated atmosphere created by lurid trials like those of M'Naghten or Hinckley. Following such trials, politicians have denounced the insanity defense in colorful terms. It has been called "a rich man's defense" that "pampers criminals" and a means of providing a "safe harbor for criminals who bamboozle a jury." Further, it has been claimed that trials involving the insanity defense are often "protracted testimonial extravaganzas pitting high-priced prosecution experts against equally high-priced defense experts" (Perlin, 1994, p. 16). A former attorney general has said that "there must be an end to the doctrine that allows so many persons to commit crimes of violence, to use confusing procedures to their own advantage, and then have the door opened for them to return to the society they victimized" (Perlin, 1994, p. 18). The gist of these declarations by politicians is clear: Unscrupulous lawyers are frequently using the insanity defense as a convenient loophole to help violent criminals escape their rightful punishment. Furthermore, gullible, unsophisticated juries can be easily convinced to find a defendant NGRI by "hired gun" psychologists. Many of these beliefs are shared by the public at large. For example, one study found that although about 74% of participants believed that mental illness affects one's capacity to make rational decisions and form criminal intent, 66% believed that insanity should not be allowed as a defense (Zapf, Golding, & Roesch, 2006).

Scholars have noted that much of what the public believes about the use of the insanity defense is simply mistaken. Among the misconceptions surrounding the insanity defense is that it is overused. In fact, the best available data suggest that it is used in less than 1% of all felony cases. When it is used, it fails about 75% of the time (Zapf, Zottoli, & Pirelli, 2009). Further, in 70% of cases in which the insanity defense is successful, both the prosecution and defense have agreed before trial that its use is appropriate. Although surveys indicate that the public believes that NGRI is most commonly used in murder cases, less than a third of insanity pleas involve the death of a victim. Moreover, an insanity defense is no more likely to be successful in a murder case than in any other kind of criminal case.

Contrary to prevailing views, insanity is not a low-risk strategy defendants can easily employ to avoid guilt and gain a lighter sentence. Indeed, when defendants are found NGRI, they end up spending a slightly longer amount of time in custody than do defendants who do not use an insanity defense and who are convicted of similar crimes (Daftary-Kapur, Groscup, O'Connor, Coffaro, & Galietta, 2011). The difference is that for defendants found NGRI, the time is usually served locked in a psychiatric hospital instead of a prison. Strangely, jurors in cases in which insanity is contested are not told that the defendant will not be released because of a NGRI verdict. Failure to provide this information has important implications for verdicts. One study found that giving jurors information about what happens to a defendant found NGRI leads to more NGRI verdicts (Wheatmann & Shaffer, 2001).

 ## POST-HINCKLEY DEVELOPMENTS IN INSANITY LAW

The widely held misconceptions described above and the public outrage in the wake of the Hinckley verdict quickly translated into legislative action. The **Insanity Defense Reform Act (IDRA)** of 1984 turned back the clock on the insanity defense. The ALI standard was largely abandoned in response to changes in the law made in the aftermath of the Hinckley case. The IDRA required that there be a presumption of sanity and that defendants prove "by clear and convincing evidence" that they were insane at the time of the crime. (When a defendant bears the burden of proof for a defense at trial, such as insanity, it is referred to as an **affirmative defense**.) In addition, the volitional prong was dropped from the definition of insanity, and experts were barred from giving ultimate issue testimony (also called ultimate-opinion testimony) about sanity. That is, although experts were still permitted to testify about a defendant's mental state, they would not be permitted to state their opinion explicitly about whether a defendant was sane at the time of the crime. The question of whether a defendant was legally insane at the time of the crime would be left to juries. After months of hearings and tinkering by lawmakers, the insanity law that survived was little more than a slightly retooled version of the 140-year-old M'Naghten rule.

The matter of "ultimate issue" expert testimony remains controversial. Attempts to prevent psychological experts from offering such testimony may not be entirely practical. Several scholars have pointed out that, to be useful, experts must provide opinions that are relevant to the legal definition of insanity (Ogloff, Roberts, & Roesch, 1993). While the expert might be forbidden from using the words "sane" or "insane," lawyers will ask the expert questions about the defendant's understanding of his or her crimes. Although the expert might avoid saying the forbidden words, any meaningful expert testimony is almost certain to reveal the expert's opinion on the issue of insanity. Indeed, in an experiment examining this issue, researchers found that even when experts avoided offering a conclusion about whether the defendant was insane, mock jurors mistakenly remembered that a conclusion had been offered (Fulero & Finkel, 1991). A potential solution to this dilemma, which has been adopted in some states, is to permit experts to offer ultimate-issue testimony, but to instruct jurors clearly that they may give such testimony as much weight or as little weight as they deem appropriate. This instruction makes explicit the role of jurors as the triers of fact.

Following the Hinckley trial, most states moved back toward the more restrictive M'Naghten standard, although 22 states still include some form of the volitional prong in their insanity formulations (*Clark v. Arizona*, 2006). Four states (Montana, Utah, Kansas, and Idaho) have entirely abolished the insanity defense (see Legal Spotlights box), and a majority of the states that still allow it place the burden of proof on the defense, usually by a "preponderance of the evidence" standard. The federal system and Arizona require that the defense prove insanity using the more demanding "clear and convincing evidence" standard of proof (Melton et al., 2007).

Guilty but Mentally Ill

There have been other attempts to "fix" the insanity defense by giving jurors alternatives to the NGRI verdict. The **guilty but mentally ill (GBMI)** verdict is an attempt to bypass the definitional morass of insanity. The GBMI verdict is permitted in 20 states; it is usually an additional alternative verdict to the three more standard options of guilty,

 LEGAL SPOTLIGHT

Is an Insanity Test Constitutionally Required? (*Delling v. Idaho*, 2013)

In 2007, 21-year-old John Joseph Delling went on a month-long 6,500-mile road trip across the western part of the United States. During the trip, he killed at least two of his former high school classmates. Delling had created a list of seven classmates who he believed—even though he had not seen them in years—were stealing his "energy" and "power" in a manner that would eventually kill him. Delling's unsuccessful attempt to kill one of his former classmates helped lead to his apprehension. (He shot this classmate several times, but the classmate survived to pick Delling out of a photo line-up.) Delling's lawyers wished to enter an insanity defense based on his substantial history of mental illness and his delusional belief that he was acting in self-defense by killing the classmates who were "killing him by stealing his energy." Unfortunately for Delling, the crimes he was charged with occurred in Idaho, which had outlawed the insanity defense shortly after the Hinckley trial. At trial, Delling was prohibited from offering a defense based on evidence that, due to mental illness, he did not know that what he did was wrong. While Delling clearly intended to kill his victims (*mens rea*), he wished

to show that his delusions prevented him from knowing that his conduct was wrong. Without this evidence, Delling was convicted of murdering his two former classmates and sentenced to life in prison.

Delling's lawyers appealed his case to the United States Supreme Court, arguing that the Eighth Amendment's "cruel and unusual punishment" clause and the Fourteenth Amendment's due process clause required states to allow an insanity defense. Nevada's Supreme Court had previously overturned state legislation that barred the insanity defense on these grounds and had subsequently reinstated it. However, Idaho's Supreme Court had found its own insanity prohibition constitutional. The United States Supreme Court denied *cert* in the case leaving Idaho's prohibition against the insanity defense in effect. Three Supreme Court justices, however, dissented from the *cert* denial, with Justice Breyer stating "the law has long recognized that criminal punishment is not appropriate for those who, by reason of insanity, cannot tell right from wrong" (*Delling v. Idaho*, 2013). It remains to be seen whether the Supreme Court will eventually decide the issue of whether a state must provide an insanity defense for criminal defendants under the Constitution.

not guilty, and NGRI. Only Utah has adopted a GBMI verdict without also having an NGRI statute (Zapf, Golding et al., 2014). People who are found to be GBMI are found guilty of their crime and sentenced to prison for a period consistent with that verdict. GBMI defendants are supposed to receive treatment for their mental health issues while in prison or be transferred to a secure psychiatric facility. However, a verdict of GBMI offers no guarantee that offenders will receive effective treatment for their mental disorders, leading many scholars to question its usefulness (Zapf, et al., 2006).

Mens Rea Defenses

A substantial number of states allow a defendant to plead **diminished capacity** if he or she lacks the capacity or the *mens rea* for certain crimes. Unlike insanity, a ***mens rea* defense** is only available for particular crimes that require the defendant possess a specific mental state. For example, in many jurisdictions, **first-degree murder** requires that the perpetrator engaged knowingly and in a premeditated manner in the killing of another human being. In such a jurisdiction, a mental health professional could testify that the defendant, due to a mental illness, lacked the capacity to form the **specific intent** to kill another person. This situation might occur, for example, if the defendant believed the victim was a space alien and not a human being. Unlike an insanity defense, the prosecution must prove *mens rea* beyond a reasonable doubt, and the defendant found to lack this element of the crime would simply be found "not guilty" rather than NGRI. However, other, lesser crimes do not include the high level of *mens rea* many specific-intent crimes require. So, returning to our first-degree murder example, the defendant could still be convicted of **second-degree murder or involuntary manslaughter** because these crimes require the defendant to possess a lesser level of intent. Some form of the *mens rea* or diminished capacity defense exists in all the jurisdictions that have abolished the insanity defense, and most jurisdictions allow for both a *mens rea* and an insanity defense.

Like the insanity defense, the diminished-capacity defense has been shaped by sensational trials. In 1978, Dan White, a former police officer and city supervisor, loaded his handgun and climbed through a window at San Francisco City Hall. He shot Mayor George Moscone several times, reloaded, and then killed Harvey Milk, his former colleague on the board of supervisors. Part of White's defense at trial was that his mental state was badly impaired by a deep depression exacerbated by his heavy intake of junk food. The media dubbed this legal strategy the **Twinkie defense.** The jury accepted White's diminished-capacity defense and found him guilty of manslaughter instead of murder. White spent fewer than five years in prison, but killed himself in 1985.

More recently, the Arizona legislature prohibited expert testimony on the *mens rea* component of criminal responsibility for a mentally ill defendant, and the United States Supreme Court upheld this action as constitutional (*Clark v. Arizona* 2006). Eric Michael Clark, a paranoid schizophrenic, had shot and killed an

How did White's famous "Twinkie defense" affect law as it pertains to diminished capacity? (A: *John Storey/San Francisco Chronicle/Corbis*, B: *Evan Skiar/ Photolibrary*)

Arizona police officer. Early one summer morning, Clark took his brother's green Toyota pick-up and began driving around his parents' neighborhood with the radio blasting. A neighbor called the police after Clark's eighteenth lap around the neighborhood. Flagstaff police officer Jeffrey Moritz responded to the call, pulled Clark over, and approached the pick-up. Clark pulled out a gun, shot, and killed Officer Moritz. Clark was found to be actively psychotic and not competent to stand trial. He was eventually restored to competence so his trial could proceed. (See Chapter 8 for further discussion of competence to stand trial and restorability to competence.)

At trial, in addition to providing expert testimony on his insanity (Clark was found sane by the trial court), the defense tried to introduce expert testimony that Clark's paranoid delusions caused him to believe that he was not shooting a police officer (a requirement for a first-degree murder charge). Instead, Clark believed that he had shot an alien inhabiting the body of a human. The Arizona trial court prohibited expert testimony on how Clark's mental illness affected his *mens rea,* and the United States Supreme Court ruled it was not unconstitutional for a state to do this. What remains open following the Clark decision is whether one of the jurisdictions that have already abolished the insanity defense (Utah, Idaho, Kansas, or

TABLE 9.2

Post-Hinckley Changes

Name of Change	Definition	How is this different?	Number of states that use it
Insanity Defense Reform Act of 1984	The presumption of sanity and the burden rests on the defendant to prove "by clear and convincing evidence" that they were insane at the time of the crime.	Institutes an affirmative defense (the defense bears the burden of proof); volitional component is no longer included in the definition of insanity; ultimate issue testimony is barred from being given in court; similar to the M'Naghten test.	Most use the M'Naghten test; 22 states still use some form of the volitional prong in defining insanity; most adhere to the preponderance of evidence standard (federal court & Arizona: clear and convincing evidence standard); four states have abolished the insanity defense.
Alternative to the NGRI Verdict			
Guilty but mentally ill (GBMI). Most states have GBMI in addition to NGRI.	Defendant is found guilty and sentenced to prison for a period consistent with that verdict.	Defendant receives treatment for mental health issues while in prison or is transferred to a secure psychiatric facility.	20 states
Mens Rea **Defense**	Plead diminished capacity; prosecution bears the burden of proof and the defense argues the defendant lacked the capacity to form the specific intent.	Applicable only to crimes that require a specific mental state on the part of the defendant; the defendant can be found "not guilty" but found guilty for crimes with a lesser *mens rea* standard.	Allowed in almost all jurisdictions. Although the *Clark* decision may suggest a change in this.
Mens Rea **& Insanity Defense**	Can be argued together.		

Montana) could also abolish expert testimony on mental illness affecting *mens rea*. A summary of post-Hinckley changes to the insanity defense in various jurisdictions is contained in Table 9.2.

HOW JURORS DEFINE INSANITY

In attempting to craft a definition of insanity, legal scholars and legislators have agonized over whether it is better to use the word "know" or "understand" or "appreciate." They have argued long and vigorously about whether insanity should be defined as an irresistible impulse or as the inability to distinguish between right and wrong. The important question, however, is how actual juries interpret definitions of insanity when reaching a verdict. We can look at each new (and presumably improved) definition of insanity as a loose hypothesis. When lawyers and legislators attempt to craft new definitions of insanity, they are predicting that changing a few words or a key phrase will cause jurors to consider different factors and reach "better" decisions. Although these hypotheses are seldom tested, they are testable. As described above, most revisions in the definitions of insanity were intended to reduce the number of NGRI verdicts.

Rita Simon was one of the first researchers to investigate how jurors interpret different definitions of insanity. Using the same case, she had 10 juries deliberate using the M'Naghten instructions and another 10 juries deliberate using the Durham instructions. Her findings were straightforward: The two instructions produced no significant difference in verdicts. But why? Simon's main conclusion, based on her analysis of the audio recordings of deliberations, was that jurors took the formal language presented in the insanity instructions and translated that language into concepts and meanings that were consistent with their own understanding of insanity and its effects. One of the jurors in the study explained the defendant's behavior this way:

> He knew what he was doing in the sense that he knew how to get into the house, where to find the bedroom, what articles he wanted to take, but he still didn't know the full significance of what he was doing (Simon, 1967, p. 118).

Norman Finkel and his colleagues presented groups of mock jurors with the full range of insanity instructions: the M'Naghten test, the irresistible-impulse test, the Durham test, the ALI test, and no test at all. (Jurors were instructed simply to use their own best judgment.) Their findings echoed earlier findings—the content of insanity instructions did not seem to matter. The researchers reached the following conclusion:

> Tests with markedly different criteria failed to produce discriminably different verdicts, and failed to produce verdicts discriminably different from those produced by a no-test condition . . . jurors do not ignore instructions but they construe instructions, employing their constructs of "sane" or "insane" to determine their verdict, despite the wording of the legal test given to them. (Finkel, 1995, p. 282)

In explaining the ineffectiveness of insanity instructions as a means of guiding jury verdicts, Finkel does not lay the blame on jurors. It is not that jurors are too dense to understand legal subtleties, or that they are careless, or that they are intent on ignoring instructions. Indeed, in his studies, jurors made many distinctions. They made distinctions about the types of affliction from which the defendant was suffering (e.g., epilepsy or stress disorder or schizophrenia), about issues of negligence (e.g., whether a defendant should be held accountable for deciding to stop taking the medication that reduced her paranoia), and about the sort of punishment that a defendant should receive (i.e., hospitalization or prison). Jurors simply failed to respond in the ways that judges and legislators had predicted that they would respond.

Instead of interpreting different instructions differently, Finkel (2007) argues that jurors use their preexisting commonsense notions of insanity to inform and interpret their judgments of a defendant's responsibility and intentions. Consequently, their reasoning about the defendant's mental condition is not constrained by the narrow bounds of legal definitions. Their reasoning is more complex and contextual than the reasoning embodied in the insanity instructions. Jurors look beyond limited notions such as "irresistible impulse" or the capacity to "distinguish right from wrong" to:

> "... an essence that lies in the defendant's capacity to make responsible choices. They also consider and weigh a dimension akin to negligence or recklessness that has been notably absent or conflated in insanity law: culpability for bringing about one's disability of mind." (Finkel, 1995, p. 297)

In another study, Finkel developed and tested an alternative test of insanity that considers how jurors actually make decisions. This alternative test requires juries to answer a series of questions about behavior, state of mind, and culpability. First, jurors are asked to decide whether the defendant's actions caused the harm. Next, they must determine whether the defendant was, "at the moment of the act, suffering from a disability of mind that played a significant role in the defendant's criminal behavior." If the defendant's mental disability is judged to have played a significant role, jurors are then asked to decide if the disability was partial or total, and whether the defendant was "culpable to some degree for bringing about the disability." Using this more systematic scheme, a NGRI verdict is only possible if the defendant is judged to have a total disability of mind and is not culpable for creating that disability (Finkel, 1995).

 ## CLINICAL EVALUATIONS OF INSANITY

It is often asserted that experts cannot agree on whether a particular defendant qualifies as insane. Unfortunately, there has been little research on this issue. Two early studies conducted in Alaska and Hawaii found forensic evaluator agreement rates between 76% (Alaska) and 92% (Hawaii). However, the Hawaii rate may be inflated because the forensic evaluators communicated with each other and did not render truly independent decisions (Gowensmith, Murrie, & Boccaccini, 2013). A recent study has reexamined forensic evaluators in Hawaii, corrected for the problems associated with the previous study, and found substantially lower rates of agreement. From 2007 to 2008, these researchers examined 483 insanity evaluation reports on 165 criminal defendants who were required to complete an insanity evaluation. In Hawaii, three independent evaluators must complete a report for each referred defendant. The three evaluators unanimously agreed in only 55% of the cases, agreeing most often when the defendant had been diagnosed with a psychotic disorder and had been psychiatrically hospitalized shortly before the crime. The forensic evaluators disagreed most frequently when the defendant had been under the influence of drugs or alcohol when he or she committed the crime.

Interestingly, Hawaiian judges followed the recommendation of the majority of the evaluators (two or three evaluators agreeing) in 91% of the cases, and they were most likely to deviate from their recommendation to find the defendant "sane." In other words, contrary to the findings of competency studies described in Chapter 8, judges showed a less conservative approach with regard to insanity. They seemed more concerned about an error in the direction of finding a possibly "sane" person insane than they were about finding a possibly "insane" person sane.

Other research has examined defendants judged to be NGRI and found they share a number of characteristics. Most often, they are males who have not committed a violent crime, have no prior history of criminal offenses, and have a history of hospitalizations for severe mental illness. The psychiatric illnesses most commonly associated with successful insanity pleas are psychosis, mood disorders, and intellectual disability (Zapf, Golding et al., 2014). An analysis of more than 5,000 criminal defendants who were determined to be NGRI found that having a prior criminal history was inversely related to a successful insanity plea. Consistent with previous research, this study also found that defendants with a diagnosis of a personality disorder, or those who were being tried for drug-related charges, and those who were intoxicated at the time of offense, were likely to be unsuccessful in their insanity defense (Warren, Murrie, Chauhan, Dietz, & Morris, 2004).

 ## TESTS AND TECHNIQUES FOR ASSESSING INSANITY

Several specialized tests have been developed to help clinicians assess whether offenders were aware of, and responsible for, their crimes. Much like competency to stand trial instruments, test development in the insanity arena is limited by the lack of a gold standard for determining whether someone is insane. Because judges often defer to the opinions of experts on insanity (note the 91% rate in the Hawaii sample), agreement between judges and an instrument or an expert tells us little about whether someone is truly insane.

Insanity evaluations and the development of instruments to aid psychologists in making them present a number of unique problems, and these problems may explain why existing instruments are seldom used. First, unlike competency to stand trial, insanity involves a retrospective evaluation of the individual's mental state at the time of the crime. This means that the evaluator must attempt to figure out how the defendant was functioning in the past (sometimes years in the past). A lot may have changed since the time of the crime. By the time of the insanity assessment, the defendant may have been treated with medication or therapy (to restore competence or improve his or her mental health), and the effects of substances that may have been present at the time of the crime (i.e., drugs or alcohol) may have worn off. Any instrument designed to evaluate factors relevant to insanity must assess past thinking and behavior based on how a person is currently functioning. Information from collateral sources or third parties (e.g., medical records, school records, police reports, and interviews with family, friends, or police officers) may be useful in revealing the defendant's mental state at the time of the crime. However, records may be sparse or unhelpful, and data from interviews are susceptible to many of the problems associated with retrieved memories. (See Chapters 7 and 11 for further discussion of memory.)

Second, the legal elements of insanity are more nebulous than the components of competency to stand trial. Terms such as "lacks substantial capacity," "unable to appreciate," or "product of a mental illness" are more difficult to quantify than whether an individual has the ability to understand courtroom procedures and communicate with an attorney. Further, it is easier to design psychological tests that examine whether someone has basic knowledge of the criminal justice system than it is to design psychological tests to assess whether someone has the ability to control his or her actions or knows the difference between right and wrong.

Finally, while almost all jurisdictions have adopted the Dusky standard for competency to stand trial, considerable variations exist in states' insanity standards. As a result, a psychological test designed to assess the ALI-based definition of insanity would not be appropriate to use in a M'Naghten jurisdiction. And, even for states that use M'Naghten, there are variations in the terminology each state uses and variations in how case law defines key terms in each jurisdiction. All these factors make it exceptionally difficult to design a psychological instrument to assess insanity.

These problems, though, have not stopped some researchers from trying. One test, the **Mental State at the Time of Offense Screening Evaluation (MSE),** attempts to screen out defendants whose crimes were not influenced by a significant mental disorder (Slobogin, Melton, & Showalter, 1984). If the MSE detects the presence of a mental abnormality that *may* have contributed to the crime, the defendant is referred for a full evaluation. The MSE requires that examiners gather and evaluate information about the defendant's history of mental disorders, the offense itself, and the defendant's current mental state. While the MSE forces the examiner to focus on issues that are relevant to an insanity or diminished capacity defense, it has been criticized for lacking a clear scoring system and strict procedures for administering the test (Nicholson, 1999).

A more-often employed, but still infrequently used, alternative is called the **Rogers Criminal Responsibility Assessment Scales (R-CRAS).** The R-CRAS attempts to translate the legal standards of insanity into components such as the ability to control one's thoughts and the ability to control one's behavior. A total of 25 items are each rated on a numerical scale. For example, one item directs the examiner to indicate whether the defendant was suffering from "delusions at the time of the alleged crime." The five possible responses are: (0) no information; (1) delusions absent; (2) suspected delusions (e.g., no available third-party collateral source); (3) definite delusions that contributed to, but were not the predominant force in, the commission of the alleged crime; and (4) definite controlling delusions, on the basis of which the alleged crime was committed (Rogers & Ewing, 1992). Judgments on each of the 25 items are based on an in-depth interview with the defendant, as well as a review of relevant documents, such as mental health records and police reports. These 25 items are further quantified into five different scales: (1) malingering, (2) organicity (significant brain disorder), (3) major psychiatric disorder, (4) loss of cognitive control, and (5) loss of behavioral control. Although the R-CRAS was originally designed for use with the ALI standard (encompassing both a volitional and cognitive prong), it can be modified for use with either the M'Naghten or GBMI standards.

A clear advantage of the R-CRAS is that it guides and organizes clinical judgments about whether a defendant is criminally responsible for his or her crimes. It forces evaluators to make their judgments explicit and to attend to several aspects of the defendant's behavior before making a global decision. The R-CRAS has demonstrated high reliability in its scoring, and it has been found to be highly consistent with eventual court decisions (more than 95% agreement for mental health professionals' sanity determinations when they use the instrument and more than 70% agreement with insanity decisions by the court) (Zapf et al., 2006). It should be noted that in these studies, the examiners used the R-CRAS to form their eventual opinion, and these numbers are not significantly different from what has been found for examiner insanity opinions not based on the R-CRAS.

The R-CRAS has been criticized on several grounds. Some have argued that the R-CRAS quantifies factors that are inherently qualitative, and as a result, implies scientific precision in insanity ratings that mostly derive from the examiner's subjective opinions (Melton et al., 2007). In other words, it has been criticized for masking examiner judgment in the guise of ratings scales and numbers. The developers of R-CRAS respond that the tool at least offers a structured means to guide the evaluator in assessing important factors that should go into determining a defendant's sanity or insanity. Further research on the use of this and other scales is clearly needed.

Malingering

Just as it may be possible to fake or exaggerate psychological symptoms that might lead to a finding of incompetence to stand trial, it is also possible to fake or exaggerate psychological problems so that the trier of fact might find a defendant insane. One of the most extreme examples of malingering ever recorded involved a serial killer named Kenneth Bianchi. Over a period of five months in 1977 and 1978, Bianchi (who was dubbed the "Hillside Strangler") raped and strangled several young women and left their bodies on the hillsides above Los Angeles. When apprehended, Bianchi denied any involvement in the murders. However, while under hypnosis, his evil alter ego "Steve" surfaced and confessed to the murders. Two psychiatrists who examined Bianchi became convinced that he suffered from multiple-personality disorder and that "Ken" was not aware of, or responsible for, "Steve's" horrible crimes. Eventually, Bianchi exhibited five separate personalities, and his lawyers filed an insanity plea. It took an expert on hypnosis (Martin Orne) to discover that Bianchi was pretending to be hypnotized and consciously inventing multiple personalities (O'Brien, 1985). Bianchi changed his plea to guilty and was convicted of several murders in California and Washington. Note, however, that successful malingering of insanity does not lead to the defendant's release. Compared to defendants who are sent to prison, defendants found NGRI end up spending, on average, an equal or greater amount of time in a secure mental health hospital.

Would knowing whether their verdict would send a defendant to prison or to a psychiatric hospital affect jurors' decisions? (A: *George Steinmetz/Corbis*, B: *Lisa Poole/AP*)

▶ IN CONCLUSION

Jurors who must decide insanity cases and psychological experts who testify in such cases are asked to make an all-or-nothing, black-or-white judgment: Was the defendant legally insane or not? But jurors, like experts, want to make broader, more differentiated judgments about a defendant's mental condition and to think about levels of impairment and degrees of responsibility. In the trial of Andrea Yates, jurors were asked to reach their verdict based on a narrow cognitive-prong-only definition of insanity. The only question was whether Yates knew the difference between right and wrong at the time she murdered her children. The prosecutor argued that, "She knew this was an illegal thing. . . . It was a sin. She knew it was wrong" (Associated Press, 2002). A psychiatrist testifying for the defense said that Mrs. Yates did not know the difference between right and wrong and that she felt she was helping her children by killing them. He testified that Yates believed she was possessed by Satan and that "she believed that, by killing her children, she not only sent them to heaven, but saved them from an eternity in the fires of hell" (CNN, 2002).

The Yates trial highlights three issues that continue to animate the debate over the insanity defense. The first is the conflict between the legal system's use of the old-fashioned term "insanity," with its pinched meaning, and scientific psychology's use of the modern term "mental illness," with its more capacious meaning. The narrow definition of insanity favored by the legal system survives, in part, because it reduces the possibility of a "not guilty" verdict. A second issue concerns public uncertainty about what happens to insane defendants after trial. In the mind of the public, a central problem with use of the insanity defense is what to do with a defendant who is found NGRI. Until the myth that people found NGRI will go free or "get off easy" is dispelled, it may be difficult to move too far beyond the 170-year-old M'Naghten standard. Third, continuing tension between the desire to provide treatment for people who are mentally disturbed and the desire to punish those same people when they commit terrible crimes will continue to shape debate about the insanity defense.

▶ CRITICAL THINKING QUESTIONS

1. Should there be an insanity defense, and, if so, what should be its criteria?

2. Which of the various insanity standards is best? Most just? Most efficient? Easiest to assess?

3. What role should neurolaw evidence play in insanity decisions?

4. Should courts and/or legislatures be allowed to abolish mental illness completely as a defense?

5. How should research on jury decisions in insanity cases affect the standards the courts employ?

6. What factors make evaluating insanity so difficult?

▶ KEY TERMS

actus reus (p. 178)
affirmative defense (p. 185)
ALI standard (p. 180)
burden of proof (p. 183)
clinical psychologist (p. 176)
cognitive test (p. 179)
deterrence (p. 178)
diminished capacity (p. 187)
Durham standard (p. 180)
first-degree murder (p. 187)

general deterrence (p. 178)
guilty but mentally ill (GBMI) (p. 186)
Hinckley case (p. 181)
insanity (p. 176)
Insanity Defense Reform Act (IDRA) (p. 185)
involuntary manslaughter (p. 187)
irresistible impulse (p. 179)
M'Naghten rule (p. 179)
mens rea (p. 178)

mens rea defense (p. 187)
Mental State at the Time of Offense Screening Evaluation (MSE) (p. 192)
neurolaw (p. 182)
not guilty by reason of insanity (NGRI) (p. 179)
policeman at the elbow test (p. 180)
retribution (p. 178)
Rogers Criminal Responsibility

Assessmant Scales (R-CRAS) (p. 192)
second-degree murder (p. 187)
specific deterrence (p. 178)
specific intent crime (p. 187)
Twinkie defense (p. 187)
volitional capacity (p. 179)
wild beast test (p. 178)

10 Battered Woman Syndrome, Rape Trauma Syndrome, and Posttraumatic Stress Disorder

▶ The Ibn-Tamas Trial
▶ Syndromes in Court
▶ Battered Woman Syndrome (BWS)
▶ BWS and the Legal System
▶ The Scientific Validity of BWS
▶ Rape Trauma Syndrome (RTS)
▶ RTS and the Legal System
▶ Posttraumatic Stress Disorder (PTSD)

Beverly Ibn-Tamas married her husband in 1972. From the beginning, their marriage was marked by frequent violent episodes followed by relatively brief periods of calm. During one argument, Dr. Ibn-Tamas pushed his wife onto a cement floor and placed his knee on her neck, causing her to lose consciousness. In other episodes, he beat his wife with his fist and a shoe, and yanked his 6-month-old daughter off a bed.

One morning in 1976, Dr. Ibn-Tamas and his wife argued at breakfast. Although she was pregnant and he had promised not to hit her anymore, Dr. Ibn-Tamas hit her in the head repeatedly with his fists and a rolled-up magazine. He then dragged her upstairs, pulled out her suitcase, and demanded she leave the house. When she refused, he beat her with his fists and a hairbrush. He grabbed a revolver, pointed it at her, and yelled, "You are going to get out of here this morning one way or the other!" The remaining facts were disputed at trial, but according to Mrs. Ibn-Tamas, her husband attacked her again when she begged him to let her stay. She then grabbed the gun he had threatened her with and fired at the door so that he would leave her alone. When he left the room, Mrs. Ibn-Tamas claims she took her now 2-year-old daughter and headed down the stairs toward the front door. Dr. Ibn-Tamas, she alleged, was in front of her yelling "I'm going to kill you, you dirty bitch!" She shot at him several times as he backed down the stairs, striking him in the stomach. He staggered into his office by the front door. Mrs. Ibn-Tamas reported that she raced down the stairs with her daughter. When they reached the bottom of the stairs, her daughter jumped in front of her and screamed "Daddy!" Mrs. Ibn-Tamas testified that she saw her husband crouching in the open doorway of his office with what she said was a gun in his hand. Mrs. Ibn-Tamas fired once more, killing Dr. Ibn-Tamas with a bullet to the head. ◀

 THE IBN-TAMAS TRIAL

In the trial, the prosecution argued that Mrs. Ibn-Tamas's testimony was fabricated and that she intentionally shot her husband. They relied on the testimony of Ms. Mc-Collom, a nurse who had entered the house shortly before the first shots were fired. Ms. McCollom stated that Dr. Ibn-Tamas let her into the downstairs medical office

195

Should battered woman syndrome be allowed as a defense? (*Peter Dazeley/Getty*)

as he was returning to go back upstairs. While Ms. McCollom did not see what occurred between Dr. and Mrs. Ibn-Tamas, she testified that she heard a shot, heard a noise like someone falling down the stairs, heard Dr. Ibn-Tamas say, "Don't shoot me anymore," then another shot. Finally, she heard Mrs. Ibn-Tamas say, "I am not going to leave you, I mean it," and then a final shot (adapted from *Ibn-Tamas v. United States*, 1979).

Mrs. Ibn-Tamas was convicted of second-degree murder. At trial, she was not permitted to have an expert testify about the effects of battering or about an associated syndrome: battered woman syndrome (BWS). The judge ruled that the information that would be provided by such expert testimony was not beyond the ordinary knowledge of the jury, would not assist the jury in reaching a verdict, and was not generally accepted in the field of psychology. Mrs. Ibn-Tamas's conviction was appealed, but a second judge also prohibited expert testimony on BWS because he believed that it was not generally accepted in the field of psychology (see discussion of expert testimony admissibility in Chapter 1). However, before this ruling, the judge was obliged to hear the expert's proposed testimony (out of the earshot of the jury), and this testimony may have affected his eventual sentencing decision. After the second jury again found Mrs. Ibn-Tamas guilty of second-degree murder, the judge sentenced her to only 2 years in prison (Walker & Shapiro, 2003). The Ibn-Tamas trial represents one of the first cases in which BWS expert testimony was offered, and the case raises important questions concerning its use in legal proceedings.

 SYNDROMES IN COURT

Syndromes, like criminal profiles (see Chapter 5), are patterns of behaviors or traits that tend to describe groups of similar people. The term **syndrome** is often used by medical and psychiatric professionals to describe a cluster of related symptoms that lead to a significant dysfunction in the performance of normal activities. In psychology, such concepts help therapists understand and treat people with specific mental and emotional problems. A mental disorder can be defined as

> . . . a **syndrome characterized by clinically significant disturbance in an individual's cognition, emotional regulation, or behavior that reflects a dysfunction in the psychological, biological, or developmental processes underlying mental functioning. (APA, 2013, p. 20)**

The word "syndrome" has also been used to describe a particular set of psychological and emotional reactions to a specific event.

Sometimes, syndromes have been used to explain the actions of people involved in legal disputes. Two of the most controversial and prominent of these "legal" syndromes are BWS and rape trauma syndrome (RTS). BWS has been used to explain the behaviors of women like Mrs. Ibn-Tamas who have been physically abused by their husbands or partners and subsequently injure or kill their abusers. Similarly, RTS has been used to describe how women respond to the trauma of sexual assault. Individuals who suffer from these syndromes may meet the criteria for a common mental disorder, posttraumatic stress disorder (PTSD). PTSD is listed in the *Diagnostic and Statistical Manual of Mental Disorders*, published by the American Psychiatric Association (APA), currently in its fifth edition (DSM-5) (APA, 2013). The DSM is the most commonly used and accepted tool for diagnosing mental disorders. Neither RTS nor BWS are contained or described in the *DSM-5*. One of the notable changes to the *DSM-5*, however, is the explicit inclusion of sexual violence as constituting a traumatic event (a requirement for a diagnosis of PTSD).[1]

 ## BATTERED WOMAN SYNDROME

Until the second half of the nineteenth century, wife battering was treated much less seriously than most other forms of violence. Prior to that time, laws regulating domestic violence were strongly influenced by the concepts of property and privacy. Wives, like children, were treated as property. What a man did with his wife was largely a private matter, and if he thought it necessary to "discipline" her with a "moderate" beating, the law did not interfere. There were other broad limits, however: for example, a beating that led to disfigurement or death was usually prosecuted.

Because physical abuse between spouses or other couples usually occurs in private and is often kept secret, it is difficult to know how often it occurs. Some experts estimate that some form of physical violence occurs quite commonly in intimate couple relationships (Catalano, 2012), but research from the Bureau of Justice Statistics based on a national sample of respondents in the National Crime Victimization Survey, suggests that intimate partner violence has been decreasing substantially (see Figure 10.1).

Although men in intimate relationships are sometimes physically beaten by their female or male partners, *serious* violence against women by their male partners is far more frequent. According to some estimates, about 1 in 5 adult women will experience a significant physical assault by an intimate partner at some point in their lifetime, while only 1 out of every 14 men is likely to suffer such abuse (Tjaden & Thoennes, 2000). Similarly, a recent survey found that, over their lifetime, approximately 3 out of 10 women and 1 out of 10 men will face stalking, physical violence, and/or rape at the hands of

How should laws control violence in intimate relationships? *(AP PHOTO/ MARY ANN CHASTAIN)*

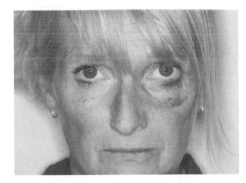

What role should culture play in the development of these laws? *(STEVE PREZANT/CORBIS)*

---

[1]It is important to note that although there is continuing research on women-initiated violence against men and same-sex violence, the vast majority of studies have studied male abuse against female partners. As a consequence, for both historical and research reasons, we have decided to use the term *battered woman syndrome* to describe the battering phenomena, and we have focused largely on male abusers of female victims while recognizing that this behavior is not limited exclusively to this group.

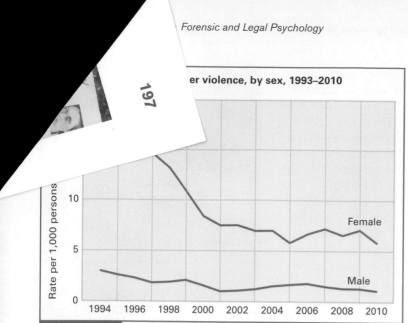

r violence, by sex, 1993–2010

FIGURE 10.1 Note: Estimates based on two-year rolling averages beginning in 1993. Includes rape or sexual assault, robbery, aggravated assault, and simple assault committed by current or former spouses, boyfriends, or girlfriends. Due to methodological changes, use caution when comparing 2006 NCVS criminal victimization estimates to other years. See *Criminal Victimization, 2007*, NCJ224390, BJS Web site, December 2008, for more information. (BUREAU OF JUSTICE STATISTICS, NATIONAL CRIME VICTIMIZATION SURVEY, *1993–2010*)

an intimate partner (e.g., current spouse, former spouse, boyfriend, or girlfriend) (Black et al., 2011). Men are more likely to seriously injure or kill their female partners, and it is male-against-female violence that is most likely to lead to contact with the legal system. Female victims of spousal violence are more likely to report the incident to the police than are male victims (23 percent vs. 7 percent; Brennan, 2011), and spousal homicide rates for female victims, especially young women, "has consistently been about three to four times higher than that for males" (Taylor-Butts & Porter, 2011, p. 33).

The Development of BWS

In her 1979 book, *The Battered Woman*, Lenore Walker first proposed that women who have been victims of long-term abuse suffer from an identifiable cluster of symptoms called **battered woman syndrome (BWS).** Dr. Walker was the expert whose testimony was excluded in the Ibn-Tamas case. Walker based her conclusions on interviews of 400 battered women. She argued that the typical violent relationship moves through a recurring three-phase **cycle of abuse:** (1) **tension-building,** (2) **acute battering,** and (3) **contrition.** An illustration of Walker's cycle of violence can be seen in Figure 10.2.

During the first phase, there is an accumulation of emotional tension and some relatively minor incidents of abuse. Although the woman tries to placate her abuser, these smaller incidents eventually erupt in a serious incident of abuse. This begins the second, acute battering phase. During this phase, multiple incidents of violent battering occur. In the third phase, the batterer may be overcome with remorse. He treats his victim with kindness, expresses his regret for hurting her, and promises never to hurt her again. Especially during the early stages in the relationship, the woman may be successful in temporarily placating her abuser, and there may be long periods of time when the man does not beat her. Although this temporary success may lead her to hope that she can change his behavior, the cycle of abuse eventually resumes and the beatings become more severe and more frequent. According to Walker, women caught in such relationships experience **learned helplessness** and become submissive. That is, over time, women who endure long-term abuse become resigned to their suffering and fail to resist or leave their abuser, even when they may be able to do so. The learned-helplessness component of BWS is one of the syndrome's most controversial aspects, and Martin Seligman, the originator of the concept of learned helplessness, flatly stated that Walker misapplied the concept to domestic violence (Peterson, Maier, & Seligman, 1993).

In a revision of her book in 2000, L. E. A. Walker clarified that her "original intended meaning" of learned helplessness was not that of being "helpless," but rather

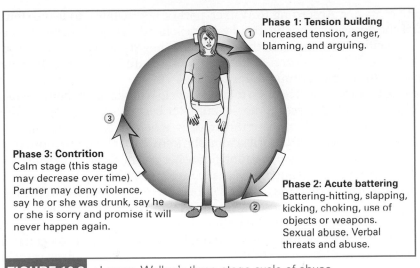

Phase 1: Tension building
① Increased tension, anger, blaming, and arguing.

Phase 3: Contrition
Calm stage (this stage may decrease over time). Partner may deny violence, say he or she was drunk, say he or she is sorry and promise it will never happen again.

Phase 2: Acute battering
Battering-hitting, slapping, kicking, choking, use of objects or weapons. Sexual abuse. Verbal threats and abuse.

FIGURE 10.2 Lenore Walker's three-stage cycle of abuse.

of "having lost the ability to predict that what you do will make a particular outcome occur" (p. 88). Battered women learn that resistance is futile, and use "survival techniques" instead of "escape skills." As one battered woman explained:

> I focused on how to endure his violence with the least amount of damage. I spent a lot of time figuring out how I could feel less pain. For example . . . I would relax my muscles when he grabbed me. In this way, I would not get hurt as much when he dragged me across the room. When he reached for a kitchen knife, I would purposively go near because if I tried to run away, he would throw it. (Yoshihama, 2002, p. 389)

Characteristics of Battered Women

Walker also identified a set of traits she thought were shared by most battered women. These traits include traditional sex role attitudes (such as the belief that women should be submissive to their husbands), poor self-image, and a tendency to accept responsibility for the abuse. Because the battered woman is likely to believe that she brought the abuse on herself, she often feels shame and attempts to conceal the abuse from others. Consequently, over time, she is likely to become socially isolated and increasingly dependent on her abuser. She will see few alternatives to staying with him and will become less able to extricate herself from the relationship (Dutton, 2008). A summary of psychological symptoms associated with battered woman syndrome can be found in Table 10.1.

In part, BWS is an attempt to explain why a woman fails to leave a man who

TABLE 10.1
Symptoms of the battered woman syndrome
Intrusive recollections of the trauma event(s)
Hyperarousal and high levels of anxiety
Avoidance behavior and emotional numbing (usually expressed as depression, dissociation, minimization, repression, and denial)
Disrupted interpersonal relationships from batterer's power and control measures
Body image distortion and/or somatic or physical complaints
Sexual intimacy issues

Adapted from Walker, L. E., The Battered Woman Syndrome. 2009.

frequently beats her. According to Walker, part of her inability to leave stems from a fear that if she does leave, her husband will track her down and kill her. Indeed, many abusers explicitly threaten to kill their victims if they try to escape, and research has found that a significant portion of battered women are killed by their abusers after they have left the home (Plumm & Terrance, 2009).

Also, because the violence often follows a cycle wherein a husband beats his wife, then apologizes and expresses remorse, but later becomes violent again, the abused woman may perceive an imminent threat, even when he is not abusing her. That is, although he may appear temporarily calm, she knows that he will eventually erupt in anger. The battered woman learns to anticipate her partner's violent behavior by carefully attending to his verbal and nonverbal cues for signs of impending violence. This heightened attentiveness to the abuser's subtle behaviors is called **hypervigilance.**

There are often other reasons for a battered woman to feel trapped in an abusive relationship. She may not have the financial resources to survive on her own. She may fear that the police or the courts will not be able to help or protect her. This fear has some basis in reality. Several studies have found that the police are reluctant to arrest batterers, and that restraining orders against violent boyfriends and husbands are frequently violated (Miller, 2004). Fortunately, this has been changing, with many states requiring the police to make an arrest if they have reason to believe that physical violence has occurred between intimate partners, and other states encouraging but not requiring an arrest. Still, even if the batterer is arrested, he will eventually be released. The abused woman may fear that he will return home even angrier than he was before the arrest (Lee, Park, & Lightfoot, 2010).

Characteristics of Batterers

Although there is no diagnosis of "battering man syndrome," there have been attempts to describe the traits and behaviors of men who abuse their partners. Donald Dutton (2007) has distinguished among some basic types of abusers, and Holtzworth-Munroe & Stuart (1994) have found empirical support for a similar typology. Some batterers tend to be extremely jealous and fearful of abandonment. These feelings lead the batterer to be suspicious of his partner's friends and family. Fear and jealousy also motivate him to exert strict control over her contacts and to restrict her outside activities. Dutton has argued that many batterers can be classified as suffering from **borderline personality disorder,** a serious mental disorder characterized by unstable relationships, dramatic mood swings, manipulativeness, intense fear of abandonment, and impulsive outbursts. A man suffering from this disorder may appear superficially normal, but his jealousy and volatility will surface in intimate relationships. This type of batterer is less likely than other types to raise the suspicions of friends and co-workers. Approximately one-quarter of male batterers' fall into this category (Huss & Ralston, 2008).

Another type of batterer—the **generally violent antisocial batterer (GVA)**—is less selectively violent. Instead, this type is generally predisposed to violent behavior toward the people around him. He tends to be antisocial, prone to impulsive behavior, and dependent on alcohol or other drugs. This type of batterer shows the highest recidivism rate (Huss & Ralston, 2008). Such batterers often engage in denial, as expressed in the following quote:

> She just has a knack for bringin' out the worst in me, and as I said, I felt bad after every time afterward. Then again, I guess I had some sort of consolation in the fact that she may have called my mom a fat bitch, you

know . . . I mean, I tried to take some sort of consolation out of what I did. And not place total blame on myself. (Goodrum, Umberson, & Anderson, 2001, p. 228)

A third type of batterer is the **relationship/family-only (FO) batterer.** This type is the most common (estimated to be about 50 percent of batterers) and is characterized by limited marital violence, almost no violence outside the family, lack of a personality disorder, and relatively low rates of alcohol/drug abuse and depression (Holtzworth-Munroe, Meehan, Herron, Rehman, & Stuart, 2000).

Why might it be useful to have profiles or typologies that accurately describe batterers? If clear profiles exist, men who are more likely to engage in battering behavior could be targeted specifically for interventions that could prevent future abusive behaviors. It might also be the case that different types of interventions might work for some types of batterers but not for others. Unfortunately, at this point, there is little research to suggest that the typologies of batterers have led to better prevention or treatment of intimate partner violence. It remains to be seen whether: (1) these types are the only or most useful ones to describe all batterers; (2) these battering types generalize beyond male batterers; (3) the types accurately predict partner abuse over long time periods; and (4) batterer-specific treatment interventions can be devised (Ross, 2011).

BWS AND THE LEGAL SYSTEM

If a woman who has been repeatedly abused by her husband manages to kill him *while* he is violently attacking her, she can argue **self-defense** at trial. However, to plead self-defense, a defendant generally needs to show that: (1) he or she was in danger of **imminent bodily harm** (severe harm in the immediate future); (2) the force used to repel the attack was **reasonable and proportional to the danger that existed** (not excessive in response to the harm faced); and in some jurisdictions, (3) that **no reasonable avenue of escape existed** (there was no easy way to avoid the confrontation or leave the situation). Most battered women who kill their abuser do so during a direct physical confrontation with their batterer (Plumm & Terrance, 2009). Realistically, however, a woman who is smaller and weaker than her partner may have a difficult time fighting him off during an attack. Some battered women kill when their abusers are most vulnerable—for example, when he is asleep or in a drunken daze. Proving self-defense in such a case is difficult because the killing occurred when there was no imminent threat of harm. Here is a description of such a case:

> Rita Felton's 23-year marriage ended when she shot and killed her sleeping husband using his own rifle. Prior to the murder, her husband had beaten and sexually abused her over the course of two decades. He once punched her so hard in the face that her dentures broke. He beat her while she was pregnant, held her down and threatened her with a blowtorch, and forced her to engage in painful and degrading sex acts. He also beat their children and, on several occasions, he threatened to kill her. Although Mrs. Felton had sought help from her community—she called the police to her home several times and she confided in her minister—little help was provided. The police were unable to stop the beatings and her minister advised her to "try to be a better wife." She once separated from her husband for a period of 10 months, but because of financial problems

and her belief that the children would be better off if they were living with their father, she reunited with her husband. The beatings resumed. Three weeks before she killed her husband, Rita Felton unsuccessfully attempted to kill herself. On the day she shot her husband, Mr. Felton had beaten both her and their 15-year-old daughter. Rita Felton waited for her husband to fall asleep before she shot him. At trial, she was convicted of second-degree murder. (State v. Felton, 1983)

If a woman who kills a vulnerable partner stands trial for the murder, her attorneys will typically argue either self-defense or insanity. In such cases, BWS testimony attempts to illuminate a woman's state of mind at the time of the killing and helps jurors understand why the woman may have believed she was in imminent danger, even though she was not actually under direct attack when she killed her abuser. Still, jurors are likely to be skeptical (Hodell, Dunlap, Wasarhaley, & Golding, 2012). If the woman and her attorney decide to use the insanity defense, it must be shown that the battered woman was unable to distinguish between right and wrong at the time of the murder (or, in some jurisdictions, that she could not control her actions). The insanity defense is seldom used in cases in which a battered woman kills her partner because the insanity defense is seldom successful (see Chapter 9).

In cases where a woman who killed her abuser is on trial, it is natural for jurors to ask the question, "Why didn't she just leave him?" At trial, prosecutors are also likely to raise this issue and to challenge the truthfulness of the defendant's account. Here is a quote from the closing argument of a prosecutor at trial:

> I wish Joe [the murdered husband] were here to tell us his side of the story. I don't portray Joe as being a perfect individual, but I question if he was as bad as the picture that has been painted of him. . . . Ask yourself this question: If Joe was all that bad, if he did all those things, why didn't the defendant divorce him? Why didn't she leave him? If she was truly afraid for her life, why didn't she to go Idaho Falls, and visit with her family there? . . . her father said, "I love my daughter. The home is always open to her." (Ewing, 1987, p. 111)

Expert testimony on BWS is intended to provide jurors with a framework for making sense of the battered woman's behavior (Monahan & Walker, 2009). By explaining how the woman perceived her desperate situation, her failure to leave and her decision to resort to violence become easier to understand.

Jurors and BWS

Jurors tend not to go easy on battered women who kill their abusers. Two studies examined the outcomes of 141 actual cases in which battered women were charged with homicide. Some cases didn't make it to trial. The charges were dropped in 3 percent of the cases, and in 9 percent of the cases the women pled guilty. For those cases that went to trial, 76 percent of the women were convicted. Sentences ranged from 4 years to life in prison, with an average sentence of about 26 years (Browne, 1987; Ewing, 1987). A chart depicting the results of this study can be seen in Figure 10.3.

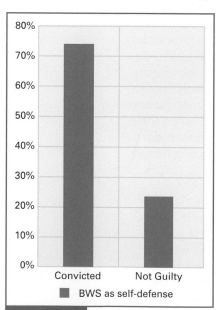

FIGURE 10.3 Legal outcomes for a sample of battered women who were charged with murder. (Based on research from Browne, 1987, and Ewing, 1987.)

According to the available research, expert testimony on BWS does not appear to have a powerful effect on verdicts. For example, a series of experimental studies found that including expert testimony on BWS in simulated trials produced only a modest shift in verdict choice—away from murder and toward manslaughter (a lesser charge that suggests no premeditation on the part of abuser and leads to a shorter sentence). But this shift in verdict only occurred when the expert testimony was accompanied by an opinion that the woman on trial fit the syndrome. In addition to looking at verdicts, the researchers recorded the deliberations of mock jurors. Analyses of these recorded deliberations revealed a slight shift in tone: Mock jurors who heard an expert testify that the woman fit the syndrome made more statements sympathetic to the perspective and actions of the defendant (Schuller, 1994; Schuller, Smith, & Olson, 1994). Other simulation studies have found similarly weak effects or limited support for the impact of BWS on verdicts (Kennedy, 2009).

Another study found that expert testimony on BWS can affect jury verdicts when it is coupled with a **judicial nullification instruction** (Schuller & Rzepa, 2002). A nullification instruction informs jurors that they can disregard a strict interpretation of the law if such an interpretation would result in an unjust verdict (see Chapter 13). Such an instruction lets jurors know that they can decide not to follow the letter of law (i.e., to nullify). Instead, they can impose a punishment based on their commonsense view of justice. Two hundred mock jurors were presented with a simulated case in which a battered woman had killed her abuser. The jurors who heard expert testimony on BWS *and* who were also given a nullification instruction by the judge were the most lenient in their sentencing.

 ## THE SCIENTIFIC VALIDITY OF BWS

Although many mental health professionals accept BWS as a legitimate syndrome, many researchers, clinicians, and legal scholars have criticized the scientific validity and usefulness of the syndrome. One set of criticisms revolves around the original research responsible for the creation of the syndrome (Dutton, 2008; Faigman, 1999; McMahon, 1999). Not all, or even a majority, of the women originally sampled had experienced all three stages (tension-building, acute battering, and contrition) of the hypothesized cycle of abuse. For instance, in her original data set, Walker found that only 65 percent of the cases involved a tension-building stage prior to the battering, and only 58 percent of the cases included a period of loving contrition after the battering episode. Clearly, the data show the limits of trying to explain the behavior of all battered women using a fixed "cycle of abuse" model.

Walker's original study also suffered from faulty data collection. The experimenters who collected the data were aware of the hypotheses of the study, leading to the possibility that they may have intentionally or unintentionally influenced the responses of the participants. This phenomenon—usually referred to as **experimenter bias**—raises the possibility that the researchers compiled biased results that confirmed their hypotheses. Unfortunately, follow-up research on BWS has failed to fix the problems associated with the original study. Most of the subsequent research supporting the existence of BWS has been based exclusively on interviews and self-report of women in shelters. It is likely that many of the battered women living in shelters received information about BWS from therapists and through conversations with other women living at the shelter. When such women report experiencing all of the symptoms associated with BWS, one cannot be sure whether they have re-interpreted their experiences and symptoms in light of their knowledge about the syndrome.

Moreover, there has been no systematic comparison of the symptoms exhibited by battered women, non-battered women, and women who suffer other forms of trauma. Such a comparison would help us determine if the proposed symptoms associated with BWS are specific to battered women, whether they might be also caused by other trauma or mental illnesses, or how common BWS symptoms are in the general population. Without this information it is impossible to know how accurately BWS describes only women who have been battered. Further, even if the BWS cycle of violence explanation is accurate, its learned helplessness component fails to explain the behavior of most interest to the legal system. That is, BWS does not explain why the abuse victim would suddenly become violent. In Seligman's original experiments on animals, the animals that exhibited learned helplessness became depressed and unable to act. While an inability to act may explain why women fail to leave the abuser, it does not explain why a victim might become violent and harm the abuser. (See Figure 10.4 for an overview of learned helplessness experiments.)

Critiques of the scientific validity and legal utility of BWS have pointed out that BWS also does not accurately or fully capture the experience of women who suffer from violent abuse (Meyer, Wagner, & Dutton, 2010). First, there is considerable variability among the psychological and behavioral symptoms displayed by battered women. How a woman reacts is likely to depend on the woman's age,

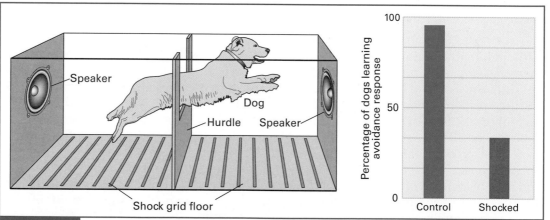

FIGURE 10.4 Martin Seligman, who was searching for an animal model of depression, coined the term *learned helplessness* to describe the behavior of animals in several of his experiments. He restrained two groups of dogs in a harness and administered shocks to these dogs. Dogs in one group were able to stop the shocks by pressing a lever with their nose (control condition).

Dogs in the second group could not escape the shocks (inescapable shock condition). These dogs were later placed in a shuttle-box, where they could avoid shock by jumping over a barrier. Most of the dogs in the previous inescapable shock condition failed to learn to avoid shock, and simply lay down, whined, and accepted the shocks. Dogs in the other condition were more likely to learn to avoid the shock by jumping to the other side of the box.

Seligman argued that prior exposure to inescapable shock interfered with the ability of the dogs to learn in this new situation where escape was possible (SELIGMAN & MAIER, 1967).

resources, experiences, the nature and frequency of the abuse, and whether or not there are children in the home. Second, BWS lacks a standard definition. There are no well-established measures for deciding whether or not a woman should be diagnosed as suffering from BWS. Indeed, labeling a woman as suffering from BWS may not be the best way to help judges and jurors understand what happened. The focus on BWS may narrow the analysis and exclude consideration of other important concerns. In fact, it may be more important to understand the dynamics of the violence, what the woman did to "resist, avoid, escape, or stop" the violence, and the effect of the woman's efforts over time. A variety of situational factors also need to be taken into account—the woman's economic dependence on her abuser, her prior experience with abuse, and the amount of social support she received from friends, family, the police, and medical professionals (Schuller & Jenkins, 2007).

A final criticism of BWS is that it locates the problem in the mind of the battered woman. By focusing on the internal "disease" of the woman, blame for the violence is directed away from the man who batters and away from the failures of the legal system to deal effectively with domestic violence. As one scholar put it, using the term BWS "may inadvertently communicate to the jury or judge the misguided notion of an 'abuse excuse' and perpetuate stereotypic images of battered women" (Dutton, 2000, p. 2). It may also pathologize a justifiable reaction to an extremely difficult situation. Is it sometimes reasonable to harm or even kill a person who has repeatedly abused you or your children and who you are unable to leave? Maybe, instead of creating a syndrome to explain the behavior of women who kill their abuser, the legal definition of self-defense needs to be modified so that it is more consistent with the realities of violent abuse.

To combat the problems associated with BWS, several researchers have proposed an alternative form of expert testimony for the actions of battered women who harm their abuser. Some have suggested that the "syndrome terminology" should be dropped and that reference should be made to expert testimony regarding "battering and its effects" on a woman, rather than BWS *per se* (Dutton, 2008). The scope of the testimony would focus more on the social reality of the woman's situation (e.g., lack of effective community alternatives, inadequacy of police response, risks of leaving) as opposed to her psychological reactions. Schuller and Hastings (1996) assessed the usefulness of such a form of expert testimony, labeled **social agency framework (SAF)** testimony (Plumm & Terrance, 2009), by comparing its effectiveness to traditional BWS testimony. They found that, compared with a no-expert condition, either BWS or SAF testimony, resulted in greater verdict leniency and more favorable evaluations of the woman's claim of self-defense. The only difference between the two forms of testimony involved rating of the defendant's mental stability, suggesting that SAF may be more appropriate for a self-defense case because it does not suggest the victim suffered from a mental illness. Instead, it attempts to offer a detailed explanation of the victim's behavior.

Despite its serious scientific limitations, the concept of BWS has had a significant impact on the legal system. Legal scholars who have been highly critical of the scientific validity of BWS have also noted that the use of BWS has had several positive effects. It has raised awareness of the frequency of domestic violence, it has spurred research on the interpersonal dynamics of violence in intimate relationships, and it has been instrumental in exposing the limitations of the traditional, somewhat sexist legal doctrine of self-defense (Sheehy, Stubbs, & Tolmie, 2012). That doctrine rests on the ideas that violence is justifiable only in response to imminent harm, and that the amount of force used to prevent imminent harm should be proportional to the threat. However, if a woman has been repeatedly abused over a long period by a man who is physically larger and stronger than she is, it becomes difficult to apply the notions of "imminent harm" and "proportional force."

Expert testimony on battering and its effects appears to be admissible for some legal purposes in all jurisdictions in the United States. Yet, a significant portion of state jurisdictions have excluded expert testimony on BWS in some cases. The reasons for excluding such testimony have included rulings by judges that understanding of battering and its effects is already part of the common knowledge of jurors, the questionable scientific validity of BWS, and a concern that expert testimony unfairly bolsters the credibility of the alleged victim (Faigman, 2004). The use of BWS continues to be controversial in the courts and may be waning.

 ## RAPE TRAUMA SYNDROME (RTS)

The debate surrounding another type of commonly used syndrome in the legal system—rape trauma syndrome—is even more heated than the controversy associated with BWS. In 1974, Ann Burgess and Lynda Holmstrom published a research study describing how victims respond to the trauma of being raped. Burgess and Holmstrom interviewed 92 rape victims who had been admitted to a hospital for treatment. Each victim was interviewed within an hour of admission and then interviewed again about a month later. To describe the cluster of symptoms shared by the women in their sample, the label **rape trauma syndrome (RTS)** was coined. In their original conceptualization, Burgess and Holmstrom described recovery from rape as a two-stage process, moving through an acute crisis phase to a longer-term reorganization phase. They believed the **acute crisis phase** typically lasted a few weeks and included severe physical symptoms (e.g., sleeplessness, loss of appetite, trembling, numbness, or pain) as well as severe emotional disturbance manifested in symptoms such as extreme fear, shame, persistent nightmares, depression, or even suicide attempts. In the days and weeks following the rape, the victim's intellectual functioning is also likely to be impaired (Burgess & Holstrom, 1979). The victim may seem dazed, confused, out of touch with her immediate environment, or "in shock." The psychological aftermath of rape is captured in the following quote from a college student's description of her reactions to being raped by the resident advisor in her dormitory:

> I felt as if my whole world had been kicked out from under me and I had been left to drift all alone in the darkness. I had horrible nightmares in which I relived the rape and others which were even worse. I was terrified of being with people and terrified of being alone. I couldn't concentrate on anything and began failing several classes. Deciding what to wear in the morning was enough to make me panic and cry uncontrollably. I was convinced I was going crazy. (Allison & Wrightsman, 1993, p. 153)

The length of the first phase varies, but eventually the rape victim moves into the second phase. Whereas the first phase is an intense reaction to the trauma of being raped, the **reorganization phase** involves the long process of recovery from rape. Rape victims often respond by blaming themselves for not having been able to prevent or stop the rape. They might castigate themselves for walking through a bad area of town, for leaving a window open or a door unlocked. They might blame themselves for not having been able to fight off or run away from the attacker. One survivor wrote that:

> People tell me I shouldn't feel like that, it wasn't my fault, but still I feel like it was. Perhaps I should just have fought harder and not been afraid. Perhaps I shouldn't have let him do this to me. (Divaa, n.d.)

Recovery from Rape and Characteristics of RTS

Sexual assault has an enduring impact on victims. Women who have been the victims of sexual assault are at greater risk of becoming unemployed and divorced. In their original research, Burgess and Holmstrom (1979) found that, although 74 percent of rape victims reported that they had returned to normal functioning about 5 years after the rape, the other 26 percent reported that they had not yet recovered. Although there is recovery, it is important to emphasize that recovery is not a process of "getting over" the sexual assault. Instead, it involves finding ways to integrate the experience of rape into one's life to minimize negative after effects. One rape survivor described 12 years later the impact of rape on her life:

> It becomes part of your person as anything, any type of huge change in your life . . . I am a different person than I was 12 years ago. And it will never go away. You learn to live around it . . . You try to take it and use it to go in a positive direction but it never goes away. (Thompson, 1999)

Among the symptoms most strongly associated with rape are fear, anxiety, depression, self-blame, disturbed social relationships, and sexual dysfunction. These reactions tend to be especially intense during the 3 or 4 months following the sexual assault (Frazier, 2003). Although these same reactions may be associated with other types of trauma, the symptoms are likely to take a particular form in sexual assault victims. For example, in sexual assault victims, fear and anxiety are likely to be most strongly felt in situations or settings similar to the one in which the rape occurred. Also, sexual assault survivors are especially likely to experience a loss of sexual desire and decreased enjoyment of sex with their partners (Campbell & Wasco, 2005). Like other victims of trauma, sexual assault victims face the long-term challenge of regaining a sense of safety and a sense of control over their environment.

Of course, not every sexual assault survivor experiences the same symptoms with the same intensity. Mary Koss and her colleagues (Koss & Harvey, 1991; Koss & White, 2008) describe four broad classes of variables that modulate the responses of rape survivors: (1) characteristics of the person (e.g., age, maturity, coping capabilities, ability to make use of social support); (2) characteristics of the event itself (e.g., the violence of the rape, the duration of the rape); (3) the victim's environment (e.g., support of friends and family, attitudes of surrounding community, physical and emotional safety); and (4) the therapeutic intervention (if any) used (e.g., timing of the intervention, how effectively the intervention empowers the survivor). These resources—both personal and environmental—strongly influence how effectively victims cope with the psychological effects of rape.

 ## RTS AND THE LEGAL SYSTEM

The concept of RTS (like the concept of BWS) was created to serve as a therapeutic tool—to help victims come to terms with their experience, and to help therapists assist rape victims during therapy. Like BWS, it has been appropriated for use in the courtroom. However, expert testimony on RTS is much less likely to be admitted in court proceedings. United States jurisdictions appear to be split on whether such testimony is admissible at trial, and admissibility often depends on the purpose for which RTS expert testimony is being used.

The role of the expert who testifies about RTS is to educate jurors about the reactions of sexual assault victims. A secondary purpose of expert testimony about RTS may be to disabuse jurors of common misconceptions about sexual assault. These so-called **rape myths** include the following: that when a man initiates sexual activity and the woman says she does not want to have sex, she does not really mean it; that the typical rape is committed by someone unknown to the victim (in fact, most rapists are acquaintances of the victim and only about 15 percent of rapes are committed by strangers); and that it is impossible to rape a woman who is unwilling (Black et al., 2011). Because victims respond to sexual assault in unexpected or counterintuitive ways, rape victims can exhibit puzzling behavior, and psychological experts may use RTS as a way of explaining that behavior.

Sexual assault trials usually turn on the issue of consent. Most defendants do not deny having sex with the alleged victim. Rather, they claim that the sex was consensual. To counter a defendant's claim that the victim consented, prosecutors have imported RTS into the courtroom. Psychological experts testifying for the prosecution will point out that the symptoms being experienced by the alleged victim closely match the emotional and behavioral responses predicted by RTS. Used in this way, expert testimony about RTS is intended to bolster the credibility of the alleged victim and thereby improve the odds of convicting the defendant. Conversely, psychological experts testifying for the defense may point out that the alleged victim's behavior was not consistent with how women typically respond to sexual assault. Any lack of fit between the behaviors displayed by the alleged victim and the behaviors predicted by RTS invites jurors to infer that the woman consented to having sex with the defendant.

As previously mentioned victims respond to rape in unexpected or counterintuitive ways. When an alleged rape victim exhibits puzzling behavior, psychological experts may use RTS as a way of explaining that behavior. For instance, in the case of *People v. Taylor* (1990), a 19-year-old woman reported that she had been raped and sodomized at gunpoint on a secluded beach near her home on Long Island. Around 11:00 PM, she returned home, woke up her mother, and told her about the rape. The mother called the police. Initially, the young woman told her mother she did not know who the attacker was. When questioned by police, she again reported that she did not know who her attacker was. However, just a couple hours later, at about 1:15 AM, she told her mother that she had been raped by John Taylor, a man she had known for several years. Mr. Taylor was arrested and put on trial for rape. In fact, he had two trials. During the first trial, no testimony about RTS was allowed. The jury failed to reach a unanimous verdict. During the second trial, the judge decided to allow testimony about RTS. The prosecution used that testimony to help explain two puzzling aspects of the alleged victim's behavior: her reluctance to identify her rapist for more than two hours after the rape and her apparent calmness in the hours following the rape. At trial, a counselor who had worked with victims of sexual assault testified that, because of fear and shock, rape victims sometimes appear calm or dazed during the first few hours following the attack. The counselor also testified that, during this period, rape victims are sometimes unwilling to identify their attackers. The jury who heard this testimony convicted John Taylor.

Although the concept of RTS has served the important function of drawing attention to the effects of sexual assault, research findings on RTS are inconclusive. Burgess and Holmstrom's initial research was quite limited. Only rape victims who were admitted to a hospital were studied, so the sample was somewhat unrepresentative. The vast majority of sexual assaults—especially those committed by dates or acquaintances—go unreported. Also, because there was no control group (e.g., a comparison group of women who had not experienced a trauma or a comparison group of women who experienced another form of trauma), it was unclear which symptoms were specific to sexual assault victims. Finally, the follow-up interviews did not extend beyond one month. Current research demonstrates that some symptoms are strongly associated with sexual assault victims but that the two-stage recovery process hypothesized by Burgess and Holmstrom is not typical (Kennedy, 2009).

Many questions have been raised about the scientific validity of RTS. At its core, RTS predicts that rape victims will show a distinctive pattern of responses and move through a two-stage process. But, as noted earlier, the responses of sexual assault victims are neither uniform nor universal. Further, whether or not a victim shows symptoms consistent or inconsistent with RTS does not tell us whether or not she was assaulted. Consequently, it is problematic to use RTS as a means of assessing the credibility of a woman who claims to have been sexually assaulted. The closeness of the "match" between an alleged rape victim's symptoms and the symptoms specified by RTS is not a reliable indicator of sexual assault. It is impossible to tell a sexual assault victim from someone who had sex voluntarily merely on the basis of her post-event behavior. As explained earlier in this text (see Chapter 5), this faulty profile-matching method can lead to many problems.

Legal Admissibility Problems for RTS

Judges must make decisions about expert testimony admissibility based on an assessment of the scientific validity of the testimony, the helpfulness of the testimony to the jury, and the possible prejudicial impact of the testimony (Schuller & Jenkins, 2007). Additionally, judges must consider whether RTS is outside the common knowledge of the jurors. If the judge believes that such testimony will not provide the jury with new and relevant information, he or she is not likely to admit it because it would not be helpful. Only information assessed as **beyond the ken** of jurors is admitted. There is some research on common knowledge about sexual assault. A number of surveys have attempted to measure public knowledge of sexual assault victim behavior and general acceptance of rape myths. Researchers have found that individuals who adhere more strongly to rape myths are more likely to attribute responsibility to the victim of a sexual assault rather than to the perpetrator (Anderson & Lyons, 2005), that acceptance of rape myths tend to be more pronounced in males, and that males tend to be more lenient in rape trial verdicts and sentencing (Aosved & Long, 2006; Grubb & Turner, 2012).

A judge might decide that allowing RTS testimony would be prejudicial—that is, it might improperly bias the jury against the defendant. Some judges have refused to admit RTS testimony because they believe it will interfere with the jury's essential role as fact-finder (it will **"invade the province of the jury"** or "usurp the role of the jury," as it is sometimes put). These judges believe that allowing an expert to testify about RTS may be equivalent to allowing a witness to say that the woman was sexually assaulted. Some critics have argued that the very use of the word "rape" in RTS necessarily implies that a sexual assault did occur. In court, saying that a woman suffers from RTS may unfairly bolster her credibility with jurors. One court succinctly summarized the problems with RTS in deciding to prohibit expert testimony on it:

> Permitting a person in the role of an expert to suggest that because the complainant exhibits some of the symptoms of rape trauma syndrome, the claimant was therefore raped, unfairly prejudices the appellant by creating an aura of special reliability and trustworthiness. (State v. Saldana, 1982, p. 231)

If a judge does allow RTS testimony, there is a further complication: RTS testimony may open the door to more extensive questioning of a sexual assault victim at trial (Faigman, 2005). Prior to the 1970s, alleged victims of rape could be subjected to extensive questioning about their past sexual experiences. At that time, the reasoning was that a jury needed to know whether a woman was promiscuous to determine whether sexual intercourse was consensual. During the 1970s, so-called **rape shield laws** were passed to prevent lawyers from delving into the sexual histories of alleged rape victims at trial. An unintended consequence of allowing RTS testimony is that if a prosecution expert testifies that the alleged victim of rape suffers from RTS, it can open the door to an examination of the victim's past. A defense attorney, for example, may be permitted to ask the plaintiff about her sexual history in an effort to prove that what appears to be RTS may in fact be a response to other events in her past (e.g., trauma or sexual abuse that occurred prior to the alleged rape).

▶ POSTTRAUMATIC STRESS DISORDER (PTSD)

The use of BWS and RTS in legal proceedings has been hotly debated, in part because the DSMs did not specifically recognize either disorder. Many researchers have advocated for testimony about **posttraumatic stress disorder (PTSD),** as an alternative to both testimony about BWS in cases in which a victim of battering kills or injures the batterer, and testimony about RTS in cases where sexual assault is alleged. There are, however, limitations to such an approach (Dutton, 2008).

PTSD is a more expansive, better-established mental disorder. The *DSM-5* lists PTSD as the primary diagnosis for people suffering from the aftereffects of extreme trauma. The diagnosis of PTSD is reserved for people who have "exposure to actual or threatened death, serious injury, or sexual violence." (*APA, 2013,* p. 271) (see Table 10.2). A diagnosis of PTSD includes four distinct diagnostic clusters or behaviors: (1) re-experiencing of the event, (2) avoidance of stimuli associated with the event, (3) negative cognitions and mood, and (4) heightened arousal or hypervigilance.

TABLE 10.2
Abbreviated DSM-5 Criteria for Posttraumatic Stress Disorder

(Changes from DSM-IV-TR in bold)
 	
A. The person has been exposed to actual or threatened death, serious injury. or **sexual violation.** The exposure must result from one or more of the following scenarios, in which the individual:
  • directly experiences the traumatic event
  • witnesses the traumatic event in person
  • learns that the traumatic even occurred to a close family member or close friend (with the actual or threatened death being either violent or accidental)
  • **experiences first-hand repeated or extreme exposure to aversive details of the traumatic event (not through media, picture, television or movies unless work-related)**
  Note: Criterion has been deleted requiring the person's response to involve intense fear, helplessness, or horror, as this was not found to predict onset of PTSD.
 	
B. The traumatic event is persistently re-experienced through:
  • spontaneous memories of the traumatic event
  • recurrent dreams related to the event
  • flashbacks
  • other intense or prolonged psychological distress
 	
C. Persistent avoidance of stimuli associated with the trauma, including:
  • distressing memories, thoughts, or feelings
  • external reminders of the event
  Note: Several criteria previously included as avoidance symptoms have been reorganized into the new Negative cognitions and mood category below.
 	
D. **Negative cognitions and mood, including:**
  • persistent and distorted sense of blame of self or others
  • feeling of detachment or estrangement from others
  • markedly diminished interest in activities
  • inability to remember key aspects of the event
 	
E. Persistent symptoms of increased arousal, including:
  • aggressive, reckless, or self-destructive behavior
  • sleep disturbances
  • hypervigilance
 	
F. Duration of the disturbance (symptoms in Criteria B, C, D, and E) is more than one month.
 	
G. The disturbance causes clinically significant distress or impairment in the individual's social interactions, capacity to work or other important areas of functioning.

Note: Distinction eliminated between acute (< 3 months) and chronic (> 3 months) phases of PTSD. Addition of two subtypes: PTSD Preschool Subtype in children younger than 6 years and PTSD Dissociative Subtype in persons with prominent dissociative symptoms.

Although PTSD was originally formulated to describe psychological symptoms experienced by combat veterans returning from the war in Vietnam, it has become commonplace for individuals suffering from repeated abuse (physical or sexual) to be diagnosed with this disorder. In fact, rape victims and victims of severe physical abuse are the individuals most likely to develop PTSD (Oltmanns & Emery, 2011).

HOT TOPIC

Controversial Syndromes

Beyond BWS and RTS, a wide array of syndromes has been offered to excuse irresponsible or criminal behavior. These syndrome explanations have ranged from the strange to the absurd. In one case, a fired school district employee sued his former boss, claiming he was unfairly terminated because he suffered from a psychological condition called **chronic late syndrome.** According to his attorneys, people suffering from this condition are not chronically late to meetings, work, or other activities because of conscious choice; rather, they suffer from a psychological disorder that causes them to be tardy.

Testimony about one of the more dubious and highly publicized syndromes—**black rage syndrome**— never reached the ears of the jury. In 1993, Colin Ferguson boarded a Long Island commuter train and calmly opened fire on the white passengers, reloading his gun several times. He killed 6 passengers and injured 19 more before 3 commuters wrestled him to the ground. Prior to the incident, Ferguson filled a number of diaries with paranoid beliefs and homicidal impulses directed toward whites. Based on the 1968 book *Black Rage* written by two black psychiatrists (William Grier and Price Cobbs), Ferguson's criminal defense attorneys were poised to offer a syndrome-based insanity defense for his actions. They believed that they could convince the jury that living in an oppressive and racially unjust society had turned an already psychiatrically impaired Ferguson into a cold-blooded killer. Further, they claimed the condition caused by the experience of oppression—black rage syndrome—could explain his murderous rampage on the commuter train.

Ferguson's attorneys attempted to convince the judge that he was mentally ill and not competent to stand trial. When the judge found Ferguson competent to stand trial, he fired his attorneys and proceeded to represent himself in a bizarre trial proceeding (see Chapter 8). Clearly suffering from a psychotic illness, Ferguson's examination and cross-examination of witnesses made little sense. He claimed he was charged with 93 counts of criminal conduct because it was the year 1993 and he also argued that a mysterious stranger named Mr. Su picked up his gun while he was sleeping on the train and shot everyone. Ferguson was eventually found guilty of all six murders and was sentenced to over 300 years in prison.

Colin Ferguson, who was charged in the Long Island Rail Road commuter-train shooting rampage, is led into the courtroom. *(AP Photo/ Mike Albans, File)*

PTSD versus BWS

Using PTSD instead of BWS has several advantages: PTSD is an established diagnostic category and there are several tests and structured interviews that can be used to assess PTSD. However, critics claim that failure to leave the situation is not well captured by the more general diagnostic category of PTSD. In addition, some sufferers of PTSD do not continue to stay in situations that are causing them harm. Some also do not act out violently against their abuser. Further, like BWS, a label of PTSD pathologizes a woman's reaction to an abusive relationship, characterizing her as mentally disordered rather than as a rational actor doing her best in a traumatic situation (Dutton, 2008). The use of PTSD also opens the door to prosecutors exploring the defendant's past for other traumatic events that may have caused the defendant's current symptoms. Finally, it is not clear how to handle a situation in which a victim of abuse does not meet criteria for PTSD (a realistic issue given only one-third to one-half of domestic violence sufferers will develop PTSD). Can a lawyer suggest that the woman must not have been abused because she does not show the disorder? Given these problems, it is not clear if the diagnosis of PTSD should replace BWS in the courtroom.

Eventually, it may be possible to create a single, large diagnostic category that manages to encompass typical responses to a variety of traumatic events, as well as more specific reactions to particular types of events such as physical battering. Some psychologists have suggested developing more differentiated subcategories of PTSD, such as a subcategory for people who have experienced chronic interpersonal violence like spousal abuse or incest (Walker & Shapiro, 2003). The *DSM-5* moves a little in this direction by removing PTSD from the category of anxiety disorders and creating a new category of stress and trauma-related disorders (APA, 2013).

PTSD versus RTS

Given the problems with RTS expert testimony, many commentators have suggested that it should also be replaced with PTSD in legal proceedings. In fact, individuals who are sexually assaulted are the most likely group of trauma victims to develop the symptoms of PTSD, and some estimates suggest that nearly 50 percent of women who are sexually assaulted will exhibit all the clinical signs of PTSD. These numbers are even higher for women who have experienced more physical trauma during the sexual assault or who have been sexually assaulted on multiple occasions (Oltmanns & Emery, 2011). Some sexual assault and PTSD researchers have also advocated for a subcategory of PTSD specific to rape (Davidson & Foa, 1991). While sexual assault is now included in the list of triggering events for PTSD, such a distinction has yet to be accepted by the authors of the *DSM*.

Camden, New Jersey, U.S.— Logan Laituri. After serving as a an airborne soldier in the Iraq War he has suffered PTSD symptoms, although his claim for PTSD was denied by the VA. *(Toby Morris/Zuma Press*

Advocates of RTS believe that a diagnosis of PTSD fails to fully explain inconsistent behavior on the part of the sexual assault sufferer (e.g., the failure to report a sexual assault until long after it has occurred, the failure to appear distressed by the sexual assault when reporting it, the failure to identify the perpetrator, or continuing to have a relationship with the perpetrator if the alleged attacker was a friend). Further, they suggest that not all sexual assault victims meet the criteria for PTSD and that some individuals who were not raped do meet the requirements. See Table 10.3 for advantages and disadvantages to using PTSD instead of RTS and BWS.

Yet, it is not clear that these problems are outweighed by the possible prejudicial impact of the name "rape trauma syndrome," and the fact that RTS suffers from some of the same specificity issues as PTSD. One group of prominent scholars reached the following conclusion:

> Although RTS has historical importance, it makes for confusing and potentially unscientific expert testimony and should no longer be used in the courtroom. PTSD, although far from being a perfect diagnosis for rape survivors, looks to be a more reliable and valid diagnosis for expert testimony, especially when accompanied by a description of the additional post rape symptoms absent from the PTSD diagnostic criteria. . . . If used

TABLE 10.3

Advantages and Disadvantages of Using PTSD Instead of BWS or RTS as a Defense

Advantages:

PTSD is an established diagnostic category, with several tests/structured interviews for assessment.

Well-established empirical literature exists on treatment and prognosis of PTSD.

New *DSM-5* criteria specifically detail sexual assault/violation as a potential trigger to PTSD.

New *DSM-5* criteria address BWS and RTS symptoms previously lacking in PTSD symptomology, including depression, guilt, and self-blame.

New *DSM-5* criteria also address the tendency to act out against the abuser and other aggressive or self-destructive behavior often seen in battered women.

The reclassification of PTSD in its own chapter on Trauma- and Stress-or-Related Disorders rather than with the anxiety disorders highlights the importance of trauma as a trigger for onset.

Disadvantages:

PTSD criteria are not specific to RTS or BWS, so many specific symptoms most important to the legal system may fall outside the PTSD criteria (e.g., failure to report assault, continued interaction with perpetrator, failure to leave the situation).

Other traumatic events (not battering or sexual assault) could have caused the victim's symptoms, and PTSD allows investigation into the victim's traumatic past.

Not all sexual violence or battered woman sufferers meet criteria for PTSD, and their lack of a diagnosis may be used to suggest that the traumatic event did not occur.

PTSD pathologizes what might be considered normal behavior to difficult circumstances (attacking a batterer), and suggests that the victim is mentally ill rather than rational.

A PTSD diagnosis may shift the legal focus from the contextual factors that may have led to the victim's behavior (i.e., lack of resources, limited social support, social agency framework (SAF) testimony), which may be both more accurate and effective in increasing jurors' understanding of the pertinent issues.

> cautiously and appropriately, expert testimony on PTSD can help to educate the judge or jury about common reactions to rape. (Boeschen, Sales, & Koss, 1998, p. 428)

As an alternative to RTS testimony, these scholars proposed a **five-level model of expert testimony** that might serve as a guide for when expert testimony on sexual assault victims' behavior should be admitted and what type of testimony should be allowed (Boeschen, et al., 1998). At level 1 of the hierarchy, an expert would simply testify about the inconsistent behaviors that research suggests many sexual assault sufferers might engage in and this would hopefully dispel stereotypes (such as rape myths) held by some jurors. At level 2, the expert would testify to the general diagnostic criteria of RTS or PTSD and about common reactions to sexual assault. This would be done without linking those diagnostic criteria to the specific facts of the case. At level 3, the expert would offer an opinion about the consistency of the victim's behavior with RTS or PTSD. Testimony at this level is clearly more controversial, and judges would be more inclined to exclude it (especially if it involved RTS testimony). At level 4, the expert would explicitly indicate

TABLE 10.4	
Five-Level Model of Expert Testimony	

Level 1: Testimony on victim behaviors described by the defense as "unusual" and would describe myths held by jurors

Level 2: Testimony on common victim reactions and general criteria for PTSD or RTS

Level 3: Testimony that the victim's behavior or symptoms are consistent with PTSD or RTS diagnosis

Level 4: Testimony that the victim suffers from PTSD or RTS

Level 5: Testimony that speaks to the "ultimate issue" (i.e., the victim was sexually assaulted)

Adapted from Boeschen, Sales, & Koss, 1998.

whether the victim suffers from PTSD or RTS (Boeschen et al., are wary of such expert testimony, especially with regard to RTS). Finally, at the fifth level, the expert would affirmatively state that the victim is being honest and was sexual assaulted. The authors argue that "level 5" testimony should never be allowed in a legal proceeding. A summary of Boeschen et al. (1998) levels of expert testimony can be found in Table 10.4.

▶ IN CONCLUSION

Expert testimony on syndromes has been used to describe both the behavior of sexual assault victims (RTS) and the behaviors of individuals who have been battered by their partners or spouses (BWS). Although the syndromes were developed for therapeutic and treatment reasons, both have been appropriated by the legal system. Their use in trials has generated considerable controversy because of difficulties associated with how these syndromes were created and because of the ongoing debate over their acceptance by the scientific community as distinct mental disorders. These problems are especially severe for RTS because the label can suggest that a crime (sexual assault) must have occurred for it to have been diagnosed. Nevertheless, courts have demonstrated a willingness to admit expert testimony on both syndromes, with more courts allowing expert testimony on BWS than RTS. This willingness may be waning, as more scholars highlight the problems of using these syndromes.

As a result of the problems associated with these syndromes, many commentators have advocated for expert testimony on BWS and RTS to be replaced with expert testimony on PTSD. There are both advantages and disadvantages to such a replacement. For RTS, it appears that expert testimony on PTSD might have less prejudicial impact on juror decision making. On the other hand, it is not clear that PTSD offers the specificity necessary to explain the behavior and actions of those who have been battered by their spouse or partner.

▶ CRITICAL THINKING QUESTIONS

1. Should expert testimony on BWS and RTS syndromes be allowed in the courtroom (for what purpose(s))?

2. What additional research needs to be completed on BWS and RTS before it is used by the legal system?

3. Is social agency framework (SAF) a better means to present evidence than BWS?

4. Do other psychological syndromes have a place in the courtroom?

5. What level of expert testimony in the five-level model of expert testimony is the most appropriate and useful for BWS? Should it be different for RTS or PTSD?

▶ KEY TERMS

acute battering phase (p. 198)

acute crisis phase (p. 206)

battered woman syndrome (BWS) (p. 198)

beyond the ken (p. 209)

black rage syndrome (p. 212)

borderline personality disorder) (p. 200)

borderline personality batterer (p. 200)

chronic late syndrome (p. 212)

contrition phase (p. 198)

cycle of abuse (p. 198)

experimenter bias (p. 203)

five-level model of expert testimony (p. 214)

generally violent antisocial (GVA) batterer (p. 200)

hypervigilance (p. 200)

imminent bodily harm (p. 201)

invade the province of the jury (p. 210)

judicial nullification instruction (p. 203)

learned helplessness (p. 198)

no reasonable avenue of escape existed (p. 201)

posttraumatic stress disorder (PTSD) (p. 210)

rape myths (p. 208)

rape shield laws (p. 210)

rape trauma syndrome (RTS) (p. 206)

reasonable and proportional to the danger that existed (p. 201)

relationship/family-only (FO) batterer (p. 201)

reorganization phase (p. 207)

self-defense (p. 201)

social agency framework (SAF) (p. 205)

syndromes (p. 196)

tension-building phase (p. 198)

11 Interviewing Children and Memories of Sexual Abuse

▶ The Reported Memories of Young Children
▶ Effective Interviewing of Children
▶ Testimony by Children at Trial
▶ Recovered Memories of Sexual Abuse
▶ Research on Implanting False Memories

Child sexual abuse is an especially disturbing crime because it victimizes the most innocent and defenseless members of society. It is also a disturbingly underreported crime. Very young victims are not able to talk yet, so they are incapable of reporting the abuse. Young children may not interpret sexual exploitation as abuse, particularly if the abuser is a parent or trusted caregiver. Children of any age may fear retaliation, and sexual abusers may explicitly threaten children with retaliation if they tell anyone about the crime. For all these reasons, most child sexual abuse is hidden from the criminal justice system, and estimates of the prevalence of child sexual abuse are imprecise. Looking across several studies, it appears that about 7 to 16% of boys and 18 to 26% of girls experience some form of child sexual abuse (Pérez-Fuentes, 2013; Stoltenborgh, van Ijzendoorn, Euser & Bakermans-Kranenburg, 2011). Because of the secrecy surrounding abuse, the true prevalence could be significantly higher.

Psychologists have been at the forefront of efforts to prevent child sexual abuse, as well as efforts to develop effective treatments for victims of abuse. Psychologists have also taken the lead in examining the validity of unusual claims of sexual abuse. The late 1980s and much of the 1990s were marked by an extraordinary outbreak of reports of sexual abuse. Scores of young children in day care centers reported bizarre acts of sexual abuse at the hands of their preschool teachers. In addition, some adults began to remember long forgotten episodes of being sexually abused as children. This outbreak of sexual abuse allegations ignited a heated debate among psychologists. Were the children's reports accurate? Were recovered memories of sexual abuse true? Although the debates were divisive, they stimulated important new research on memories of abuse and encouraged the development of new techniques for eliciting accurate reports of abuse. ◀

 ## THE REPORTED MEMORIES OF YOUNG CHILDREN

When one of your author's daughters was about 3 years old, she was abducted by a group of aliens who took her for a ride in their spaceship. She also saw an animal that was half-elephant and half-monkey, and she swam across the ocean to Catalina Island (about 26 miles from the beach near our house). At least that's what she told her dad. Although she was an extraordinary little girl, her dad was pretty sure that none of these events really happened. It's not that she was lying; it's just that her capacity to distinguish between fact and fantasy was not yet fully developed. Indeed, considerable research shows that very young children (especially those under the age of about 5) sometimes have difficulty distinguishing between imagined events and real events (Principe, Ceci, & Bruck, 2011). Because the ability to encode, store, and retrieve information is not fully developed in young children, the problems surrounding memory are significantly amplified when a witness or victim is a child (Goodman & Melinder, 2007; see Chapter 7 for further discussion of eyewitness memory). Furthermore, the risk of eliciting inaccurate reports of what happened is much greater when a young child is interviewed using suggestive or biased questioning.

The Day Care Center Cases

Especially during the late 1980s and into the 1990s, several workers in day care centers across the United States were accused of sexually abusing children in their care. These cases captured the attention of the media and helped to spur a new wave of research on how to investigate accusations of sexual abuse. Here are the allegations in three of the most notorious cases.

- In 1985, Kelly Michaels of the Wee Care Nursery School in New Jersey was accused of sexually abusing 20 3- to-5-year-old children. According to allegations, Michaels played the piano naked, licked peanut butter off children's genitals, forced children to drink her urine and eat her feces, and raped children with knives, forks, spoons, and Lego blocks.
- In 1987, Ray Buckey and Peggy McMartin Buckey of the McMartin Preschool in California were charged with 207 counts of child molestation. The accusations included sodomy, taking pornographic photographs of children engaged in sex acts, tunneling underground to rob graves, hacking up corpses in front of children, and sexually molesting children while flying in a hot air balloon.
- During 1989, seven adults who worked at the Little Rascals Day Care Center in North Carolina were accused of sexually molesting 90 children who attended the center. The allegations were wide-ranging and bizarre—children reported that they had been raped and sodomized; forced to have oral sex while being photographed, tied up, and hung upside down from trees; set on fire; and thrown from a boat into shark-infested waters. Some children accused the adults of murdering babies.

What made these allegations especially shocking was not only the bizarre character of the sexual abuse, but the number of children victimized, and the apparent ability of the abusers to keep their sordid activities secret for long periods of time. Surprisingly, in all these cases, there was no physical or medical evidence to support the claims. Also, no parents of the children or other teachers working at the schools ever noticed anything alarming during the many months the abuse allegedly took place.

The Wee Care case contains elements common to many other cases, so it is useful to examine how the allegations developed. Four days after Kelly Michaels left her job at Wee Care Nursery School, a 4-year-old former student was having his temperature taken rectally at his pediatrician's office. "That's what my teacher does to me at school," he told the nurse. When asked what he meant, he replied, "Her takes my temperature." That afternoon, the child's mother notified New Jersey's child protective services agency. Two days later, the boy was interviewed by a state prosecutor. During the interview, the prosecutor made use of an **anatomically detailed doll.** Such dolls have realistic male or female genitalia. They have sometimes been used (and misused) to help reluctant children show investigators what type of sexual abuse may have been perpetrated against them. As an alternative to dolls, some interviewers have also used anatomically detailed human body diagrams usually presented on a large flip chart. Considerable research indicates that, for children under the age of 6, such dolls and diagrams increase the number of false allegations of sexual abuse (Brown, Pipe, Lewis; Lamb, & Orbach, 2012; Bruck, Ceci, & Francoeur, 2000; Hungerford, 2005; Poole & Bruck, 2012; Poole & Dickinson, 2011). The boy being interviewed in the Wee Care case inserted his finger into the anus of the doll and told the prosecutor that two other boys at school had also "had their temperatures taken."

The two other boys were then questioned. Neither seemed to know anything about having their temperature taken, but one boy said Kelly Michaels had touched his penis. The mother of the first child told a parent member of the school board what the children had said. He questioned his own son, who told him that Kelly Michaels had touched his penis with a spoon. When Wee Care School was made aware of these allegations, they sent out a letter to all parents "regarding serious allegations made by a child." A social worker who directed a hospital sexual assault unit was invited to make a presentation to parents. At that presentation, she asserted that a third of all children would be victims of an "inappropriate sexual experience" by the time they reached 18. She encouraged parents to look for telltale signs that their children may have been abused: nightmares, genital soreness, masturbation, bedwetting, or noticeable changes in behavior.

Over a period of 6 months, several professionals interviewed children and their families to determine the extent of the sexual abuse. Many of the children were interviewed on several occasions. A psychotherapist who treated 13 of the children held five group therapy sessions during which children discussed how they had been sexually abused. Prosecutors and their experts also interviewed the children on multiple occasions. Kelly Michaels was convicted of 115 counts of child sexual abuse based on the testimony of 19 children. Michaels was sentenced to 47 years in prison but served only five years. She was released after the New Jersey Supreme Court held that she had been denied a fair trial primarily because, "the interviews of the children were highly improper and utilized coercive and unduly suggestive methods" (*State v. Michaels,* 1994).

As the details of the case became public, it became clear that children from Wee Care School had been subjected to highly suggestive and even coercive questioning from adults. Children under the age of 5 are acutely sensitive to such questioning (Principe, et al., 2011). Several varieties of biased questioning were used in the sexual abuse cases described above. The least coercive form was simply repeating the question several times until the child gave the desired response. Here is an excerpt from an interview in the Wee Care case (Ceci & Bruck, 1996, p. 122):

Interviewer: When Kelly kissed you, did she ever put her tongue in your mouth?
Child: No.
Interviewer: Did she ever make you put your tongue in her mouth?
Child: No.
Interviewer: Did you ever have to kiss her vagina?
Child: No.

Interviewer: Which of the kids had to kiss her vagina?
Child: What's this? [child points to audio recorder]
Interviewer: No, that's my toy, my radio box. . . . Which kids had to kiss her vagina?
Child: Me

To explore the effect of asking the same question more than once, researchers repeatedly asked children about events that their parents said had never occurred (e.g., getting their finger caught in a mousetrap). After repeated questioning, 58% of preschool-aged children were able to give detailed descriptions of at least one event they initially said had never happened. Twenty-five percent of the preschoolers managed to create false memories for the majority of fictitious events (Ceci & Bruck, 1996). Information provided by an adult interviewer who asks a question several times is likely to be incorporated into the child's description of an event. Also, by simply repeating the question, the interviewer may signal to the young child that denial of the event is unacceptable to the adult.

A team of researchers at the University of Texas at El Paso analyzed transcripts of interviews with children who had claimed to be sexually molested at the McMartin and Wee Care preschools (Garven, Wood, Malpass, & Shaw, 1998; Schreiber et al., 2006). Transcripts clearly revealed that the interviewers used a variety of techniques designed to elicit the responses desired by interviewers: repeated questioning, questions suggesting that particular events occurred, offering praise or rewards for the desired answers, criticizing or disagreeing with children who gave unwanted answers, and inviting children to speculate or imagine what might have happened. Substantial research now indicates that interviewers in many of the preschool cases began with the strong belief that children had been sexually abused. This belief led investigators to question children in ways that made it likely that their preexisting suspicions would be confirmed (Schreiber et al., 2006).

Based on their analysis of transcripts, the University of Texas researchers designed an experiment that made use of the techniques interviewers employed in the preschool abuse cases. A number of 3- to 6-year-old children were invited to listen to a man who came to their classroom to tell the story of the Hunchback of Notre Dame. After telling the story, the man handed out cupcakes and napkins, said goodbye, and left the room. One week later, the children were asked about things the storyteller had done (taking off his hat, giving out cupcakes, etc.) as well as things the storyteller had not done (putting a sticker on a child's knee, throwing a crayon at a child who was talking). In a control condition where neutral, noncoercive questions were used, 4- to 6-year olds said "yes" to fewer than 10% of the questions about events that never happened. Three-year-olds said "yes" to 31% of such questions. In the conditions that made use of techniques from the McMartin transcripts, 4- to 6-year-olds answered "yes" to 50% of the misleading questions while 3-year-olds answered "yes" to 81% of the misleading questions (Garven, et et al., 1998) (see Figure 11.1).

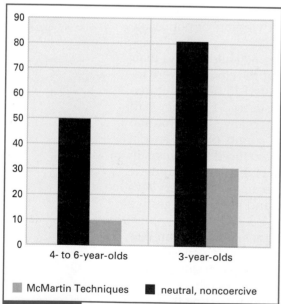

McMartin Techniques ■ neutral, noncoercive

FIGURE 11.1 In a control condition where neutral, noncoercive questions were used, 4- to 6-year olds said "yes" to fewer than 10% of the questions about events that never happened. Three-year-olds said "yes" to 31% of such questions. In the conditions that made use of techniques from the McMartin transcripts, 4- to 6-year-olds answered "yes" to 50% of the misleading questions while 3-year-olds answered "yes" to 81% of the misleading questions (*Garven, Wood, Malpass, & Shaw, 1998*)

The techniques used in the research studies probably underestimate the effects of the techniques used in the actual cases. Keep in mind that the questioning techniques used by interviewers in the real sexual abuse cases were much more forceful and intimidating than those used by researchers. Also, in the real cases, children were questioned several times by different interviewers. In some cases, children shared information in "group therapy" sessions. Interviewers shared information with parents, and parents shared information with one another. These conditions raised the level of anxiety and suspicion, and probably served to make the claims of abuse increasingly extreme. Factors that bias the reports of children can interact to amplify negative effects. Repeated interviews, if done carefully, may increase the number of accurate details disclosed by children. But, if repeated interviews are combined with a biased interview style, and there is a significant delay between the alleged sexual abuse and the interviews, the reports of children are likely to be contaminated and unreliable (Goodman & Quas, 2008).

 ## EFFECTIVE INTERVIEWING OF CHILDREN

Clearly, the interviewing techniques described above lead to biased and distorted reports and recollections. But what techniques should interviewers use? One extensively researched questioning procedure was developed in cooperation with the National Institute of Child Health and Development (NICHD). The procedure is designed to reduce biased and suggestive questioning. Research has shown that use of the **NICHD Investigative Interview Protocol** helps guide interviewers away from biased questions and toward a style of questioning that is more likely to elicit true responses from children (Lamb, Orbach, Hershkowitz, Esplin & Horowitz, 2007). Instead of using closed-ended questions ("Did he touch you on your bottom?") that require a "yes or no" answer, the protocol encourages children to provide as much information as possible in response to open-ended prompts (e.g., "Tell me what happened" or "Tell me more about that" or "What happened next?"). In addition, suggestive questions are carefully avoided. Suggestive questions are those that imply that the interviewer expects or desires a particular response (e.g., "He wanted you to kiss him, didn't he?") or those that include options not volunteered by the child (e.g., asking, "did he put his hand on your privates?") (Lamb, Hershkowitz, Orbach, & Esplin, 2008).

Interviewers using the NICHD Protocol move through a series of phases designed to put the child at ease and to elicit uncontaminated reports of what a child has experienced. During an introductory phase, the interviewer introduces himself or herself; emphasizes that the child should describe events in detail and tell the truth; and explains basic ground rules (e.g., the child can and should say "I don't remember" or "I don't know" when appropriate). Next comes the rapport-building phase. In this portion of the interview, the goal is to create a relaxed, supportive environment for the child and to establish rapport between the child and interviewer. To familiarize the child with the interviewing process, the interviewer may ask the child to describe a recent nonthreatening event in detail (e.g., a birthday or family outing). This gives the child an opportunity to practice giving the interviewer a full narrative of the event. The substantive phase comes next. In this phase, open prompts are used to focus the child on the incident under investigation. For example, the interviewer might say, "Tell me why you came to talk to me" or, "I heard you talked to a policeman. Tell me what you talked about." Such questions are followed up with prompts such as, "Tell me everything about that." If the child makes an allegation of abuse, further information is solicited during the follow-up phase. Once the child offers his or her account of what happened, the interviewer asks the child whether the behavior occurred "one time or more than one time" and then asks incident-specific information based on the child's account. For example, the interviewer may say, "You said that _____ did _____. Tell me everything about that." More directive questions are asked *only after* the child's free recall of the incident has been exhaustively elicited by the interviewer. Examples of these more directive questions include, "When did it happen?" or "What color was the car?" (Lamb, et al., 2007).

Interviews with children using the NICHD procedures are almost always recorded on video. This allows judges, jurors, lawyers, and experts to see exactly how the interview was conducted. It is particularly important to record the initial interview with the child because it is likely to contain the clearest indicators of whether a child is telling the truth (Saykaly, Talwar, Lindsay, Bala, & Lee, 2013). Table 11.1 lists the most common forms of prompts used in the NICHD Protocol.

There is also research demonstrating the usefulness of three other techniques. The first is clear, simplified instructions that emphasize true and full disclosure by the child. For example, in preparing the child, an interviewer might use a "don't know" instruction ("If I ask you a question and you don't know the answer, then just say I don't know"). The second technique is an "oath to tell the truth" ("It's *very important* that you tell me the truth; can you *promise* that you *will* tell me the truth?"); and the third is an explicit statement that the interviewer does not know what happened ("I

TABLE 11.1

Interviewer Prompts Used in the NICHD Protocol

Type of Prompt	Definition	Examples
Facilitator	Nonsuggestive prompt to continue with an ongoing response.	"Ok" "Yes" "Uh-huh" "So he hit you" (immediately after child said "and then he hit me.")
Invitation	An open-ended request that the child recall information about the incident. Can be formulated as a statement, question, or imperative.	"Tell me everything that happened." "Tell me more about that."
Cued invitation	A type of invitation that refocuses the child's attention on details she or he mentioned and uses them as cues to prompt further free-recall of information.	"You mentioned [event, action, object]. Tell me more about that." "You mentioned [action]; then what happened?"
Directive	A cued-recall prompt that focuses the child's attention on information *already mentioned* and requests additional information of a specific sort, typically using wh-questions (who, what, when, where, how).	"What color was that shirt?" (When the shirt had been mentioned). "Where/when did that happen?" "Where did he touch you?" (When the child has described being touched by a male).

Adapted from: *Lamb, M. E., Orbach, Y., Hershkowitz, I., Esplin, P. W., & Horowitz, D. (2007). Structured forensic interview protocols improve the quality and informativeness of investigative interviews with children: A review of research using the NICHD Investigative Interview Protocol. Child Abuse and Neglect, 31, 1201–1231.*

HOT TOPIC

Child Sexual Abuse Accommodation Syndrome

In many areas, the creation of a psychological syndrome has had a major influence on how alleged crime victims or perpetrators are treated by the legal system (see Chapters 8 and 13). Such is the case in the area of child sexual abuse. **Child sexual abuse accommodation syndrome (CSAAS)** was proposed and elaborated on by Ronald Summit (Summit, 1983; 1998). Based on his clinical experience, Summit surmised that child victims of sexual abuse typically experience feelings of helplessness, confusion, and fear. These feelings cause child victims to behave in ways that conceal the abuse. Specifically, children suffering from CSAAS are believed to show three behavioral symptoms—delayed disclosure of the abuse (because of embarrassment, shame, or allegiance to the abuser); denial that any sexual abuse occurred; and recantation of allegations of abuse after initial claims of abuse. Indeed, some proponents of CSAAS believe that a tentative and partial report by a child is more likely to be authentic. For example, here is a quote from a psychotherapist's expert testimony about disclosures of sexual abuse from a young child:

> The majority of children who are sexually abused underreport the extent and severity of the abuse. If I would have heard about lengthy disclosures with a specific beginning, middle and end to the story, I would have been less impressed since that type of recounting is not likely with sexually abused children (*Lillie v. Newcastle City Council*, 2002, p. 42).

A belief in the legitimacy of CSAAS has influenced how investigative interviews are conducted. Because police officers, social workers, and others who interview children about suspected sexual abuse are guided by their belief in CSAAS, they tend to rely on more directive, repetitive, suggestive forms of interviewing (London, Bruck, Wright, & Ceci, 2008; O'Donohue & Benuto, 2012). After all, if victimized children are likely to delay reporting the abuse, deny that the abuse occurred, and then recant even after admitting they had been abused, it makes sense to continue to press a child to make a (presumably true) admission and to push past any attempts by the child to recant an earlier (presumably true) admission. Reviews of research that analyze actual interviews of sexually abused children reveal that, while delayed disclosure of sexual abuse is not unusual, denial of abuse and recantation are unusual (London, Bruck, Ceci & Shuman, 2005; London, et al., 2008). Specifically, researchers have found that, "most children do disclose abuse within the first or second interview [and that] only a small minority of these children recant their abuse reports" (p. 217). One interesting finding is that the minority of children who do recant are more likely to have been abused by a parental figure and to lack support from the parent who did not abuse the child (Malloy, Lyon, & Quas, 2007). Expert testimony describing CSAAC is sometimes permitted at trial to explain the counterintuitive behavior of a child victim of sexual abuse, but generally not as proof that abuse actually occurred (*State v. R.B.*, 2005).

don't know what's happened to you. I won't be able to tell you the answers to my questions") (Lyon, Carrick, & Quas, 2010; Lyon, Malloy, Quas, & Talwar, 2008).

It is not uncommon for sexually abused children to delay disclosing abuse, particularly if they fear negative consequences for themselves or their family (e.g., physical harm, anger from members of their family; Malloy, Brubacher, & Lamb, 2011). However, it is important to emphasize that if interviews with children about suspected sexual abuse are conducted in a careful, unbiased, nonsuggestive manner, children are generally able to provide accurate reports of events (Malloy, La Rooy, Lamb, & Katz, 2011).

TESTIMONY BY CHILDREN AT TRIAL

It appears that jurors tend to believe the testimony of children in sexual abuse cases. Interestingly, younger children who testify that they were abused are somewhat more likely to be believed than adolescents who testify. This is apparently because younger children are seen as too unsophisticated about sexual matters to create false allegations (Bottoms & Goodman, 1994; Goodman, 2006). Of course, this willingness to believe young children probably does not extend to the more fantastic claims of sexual abuse (involving underground tunnels, spaceships, and hot air balloons) that made their way into some of the preschool sexual abuse cases described earlier.

Child testimony poses a difficult dilemma for the legal system. Although defendants are generally entitled to confront their accusers face to face in court, it is usually unrealistic to expect children to speak freely in the presence of someone who

has harmed them. In addition, the sterility, formality, and strangeness of the courtroom make it an especially inhospitable and intimidating setting for a young child. To spare young children the frightening and sometimes traumatizing experience of testifying in court, all but nine states allow an exception to the hearsay rule when a child is the alleged victim in a crime. **Hearsay testimony—** testifying about what someone else said outside of court—is usually inadmissible. The reasoning is that the person who made the remarks cannot be cross-examined, and the jury cannot assess his or her truthfulness. However, when a child is the alleged victim, a teacher or parent or physician or other adult is often permitted to stand in for the child and testify about what the child said. But how do jurors respond to such evidence? In an important study of this issue, researchers questioned 248 jurors from 42 different trials (Myers, Redlich, Goodman, Prizmich, & Imwinderlried, 1999). In each of the trials, there was child testimony as well as adult hearsay testimony on behalf of the child. Findings revealed that the testimony of adult hearsay witnesses was seen as more consistent,

Is it realistic to expect children to testify in court?
(*Glow Images/Getty Images*)

more credible, more complete, and more accurate than the testimony of child witnesses. Perhaps it is not surprising that adult testimony was viewed as more consistent and complete than child testimony. Adults tend to be more confident and to give more thorough, detailed responses to questions. Another clue about why adults were perceived as more accurate has to do with the attentiveness of jurors. Jurors carefully scrutinized the demeanor of the child victims in a search for clues to uncertainty or deception. They looked carefully at the children's facial expressions, eye contact, pauses, hesitations, gestures, speech errors and overall nervousness. They may have interpreted some of these signs of nervousness as uncertainty, or even lying, by children.

An alternative method for presenting the testimony of children is the use of **closed-circuit television (CCTV).** In the case of *Maryland v. Craig* (1990), the U.S. Supreme Court held that if a child victim was likely to experience significant emotional trauma by being in the presence of the defendant, the child's testimony could be presented via CCTV. Using this technique, a large television in the courtroom enables the defendant, judge, and jury to see the testimony, but the child and the defense and prosecuting attorneys are in another room. The *Craig* decision was a significant departure from the Court's prior rulings on this issue. In effect, the Court held that a defendant's right to confront his or her accuser was outweighed by the need to protect child victims from emotional harm. The *Craig* decision was also based on the reasoning that the truth-finding function of the trial was sometimes best served by allowing children to testify by means of CCTV. That is, allowing children to testify outside the courtroom serves the goal of obtaining full and truthful testimony from children (Cordon, Goodman, & Anderson, 2003).

In a carefully conducted study of child testimony and the use of CCTV, Gail Goodman and her colleagues (1998) had 5- to 6-year-olds and 8- to 9-year-olds participate in a play session with a male confederate who either placed stickers on their exposed body parts (e.g., toes, arms, belly buttons) or placed stickers on their clothing. About two weeks later, the children testified about the play session in a real courtroom via live testimony or CCTV. Mock jurors recruited from the community then viewed a simulated trial containing the child testimony. The researchers found that the use of CCTV reduced the amount of emotional distress children experienced and enabled children to give more accurate testimony. These benefits were achieved without any lowering of the conviction rate.

Other techniques have been used in an effort to make the experience of courtroom testimony less aversive for children. For example, some research suggests that children benefit by being allowed to *choose* whether to testify via CCTV or take the witness stand (Quas & Goodman, 2012). In some courts, child witnesses are permitted to bring a support person or, in some cases, to bring a support animal, such as a dog or a hamster, when they testify. Brief "court schools" that familiarize a child with courtroom procedures and personnel show some promise, although further research is needed to test their efficacy (McAuliff, 2010).

RECOVERED MEMORIES OF SEXUAL ABUSE

Although allegations of child sex abuse rings still occasionally arise in the United States and other countries (e.g., see Bensussan, 2011), by the mid-1990s, sensational claims of multiperpetrator sexual abuse at U.S. preschools had dropped sharply. But claims of a different type of child sexual abuse shot up dramatically. This type of claim involved adults who began to remember that they had been sexually abused years, or even decades, earlier. As the 1990s progressed, these reports began to accumulate at an alarming pace.

The controversy over the authenticity of what came to be known as **recovered memories** highlighted important tensions in the field of psychology and law. First, attempts by scientists to evaluate the accuracy of recovered memories took place in a politically charged atmosphere—those who disputed claims of recovered memories were often accused of being on the side of child molesters and of encouraging the denial of sexual abuse. Those who believed in the validity of recovered memories were sometimes accused of supporting witch-hunts that led to the criminal prosecution of innocent people. The controversy also deepened the split between psychological scientists (who tended to be highly skeptical of recovered memories) and psychotherapists (who tended to view recovered memories as credible) (McNally, 2004).

Were the Memories Created or Recovered?
In examining the accumulating cases of recovered memories, several researchers began to discern common patterns. These patterns suggested that some memories of sexual abuse were not recovered but implanted (Beli, 2012; Geraerts et al., 2009).

The typical series of events leading to the discovery of a long-forgotten memory of being sexually abused usually began with an adult woman who sought out psychotherapy for help in dealing with emotional or interpersonal problems. Often, the therapist fixed on the client's childhood experiences and began to strongly suspect sexual abuse. Based on these suspicions, the client was encouraged to be receptive to vague inklings of abuse as the return of repressed memories. Some therapists

ℱOCUS ON ℭAREERS

Social Science Analyst

Carrie Mulford, Ph.D.
Social Science Analyst
National Institute of Justice, Office of
Justice Programs, U.S. Department
of Justice

(COURTESY OF CARRIE MULFORD)

As a social science analyst at the National Institute of Justice (NIJ), my goal, and the goal of my agency, is to use science to improve knowledge and understanding about crime and justice issues. Using my training in community and developmental psychology, I work with researchers and practitioners to identify knowledge gaps, and NIJ provides funding for research projects to fill those gaps.

As part of that work, we are involved in every stage of the research funding process. The first step is to keep abreast of the needs in the field by reading journal articles, attending conferences, participating in interagency working groups, planning topic area meetings, and engaging in informal conversations with stakeholders. Then, NIJ social science analysts are responsible for writing the content of our solicitations for research. When applications are received, the analysts manage the external peer review process and are responsible for ensuring that each application gets a thorough and fair review. We then assist NIJ leader-

ship in making tough decisions about which projects to fund.

Once a project is funded, social science analysts have regular contact with the principal investigators to provide guidance and work through the challenges that inevitably come up in the course of conducting applied research. As projects near completion, we collaborate with the researchers on developing a plan to disseminate the findings to the field. Most of our principal investigators publish their results in academic journals and present at academic conferences, but as social science analysts at NIJ, we strive to reach a broader audience of research consumers. To do this, we develop NIJ publications, post findings on our topical web pages, host webinars, and make presentations at practitioner conferences.

One of the things I love about being a social science analyst at NIJ is the variety that results from being

involved in the full research process. Some activities, like reviewing final reports and applications, require the critical thinking and analytic skills that I developed in graduate school. For example, in assessing an application, it would be difficult to determine whether the proposed statistical analyses were appropriate for answering the proposed research questions without the rigorous statistical training that a Ph.D. in psychology requires. Other activities, like writing products for dissemination or speaking at conferences, use a different set of skills that were also part of my training as a community and developmental psychologist.

The other thing I enjoy about being a social science analyst is the applied nature of the work. It is very rewarding when a tool that you helped validate or an intervention that you helped evaluate is being requested and used by practitioners in the field. Sometimes we get requests from Congress or the White House that need to be answered very quickly. And, sometimes, current events will put a spotlight on topics that have been either neglected or less visible (e.g., gun violence research after the Newtown shootings in 2012). To thrive in a federal research agency, you need to be flexible, able to work under tight deadlines, and willing to cover new topic areas.

encouraged their clients to read books or watch videos suggesting that victims of child sexual abuse experienced symptoms similar to the ones the client herself was experiencing (e.g., depression, unsatisfying relationships). Over the course of weeks or months, the therapist might try hypnosis, guided imagery, or dream interpretation to assist the client in trying to recover her presumably repressed memories. Under hypnosis or a similarly relaxed and suggestible state, episodes of sexual abuse would be vividly imagined. Finally, a client might be encouraged to join therapy groups whose members included others who had recovered memories of being sexually abused.

Some researchers argued that, through the process described above, false memories were implanted during therapy. Over time, as the false memories became more vivid and elaborate, they took on the appearance of authentic memories. But many psychotherapists had a simpler explanation: The memories of abuse had been repressed and later recovered during therapy. The concept of **repression** (popularized by Sigmund Freud) holds that painful, threatening, or traumatic memories can be pushed out of conscious awareness (McNally & Geraerts, 2009). This repression of traumatic memories was thought to occur unconsciously and involuntarily. According to the repression hypothesis, traumatic memories could remain intact, but locked away in the unconscious for years or even decades. To unearth these deeply buried memories, it might be necessary to use relaxation and visualization techniques.

Although research psychologists have carefully documented the processes of remembering and forgetting, they point out that there is little evidence for the concept of repression. David Holmes, a researcher at the University of Kansas put it forcefully:

> **Despite over sixty years of research involving numerous approaches by many thoughtful and clever investigators, at the present time there is no controlled laboratory evidence supporting the concept of repression. It is interesting to note that even most of the proponents of repression agree with that conclusion. However, they attempt to salvage the concept of repression by derogating the laboratory research, arguing that it is contrived, artificial, sterile and irrelevant to the "dynamic processes" that occur in the "real world" (1990, p. 96).**

But even outside the rarified world of the research laboratory, there is little evidence of repression. Indeed, considerable evidence suggests that most people have vivid memories of traumatic events. For example, a study of 5- to 10-year-old children who had witnessed the murder of one or both parents found no evidence that these children repressed their traumatic memories (Malmquist, 1986). Although they tried to keep these terrifying images of violence out of their minds, they could not. Like other victims of traumatic events, their problem was not repression but intrusion—despite their attempts to suppress the memory, the memory intruded into consciousness. Soldiers who have experienced massacres on the battlefield are often tormented by unwelcome flashbacks, rape victims are often haunted by memories of the rape that intrude into their consciousness, and people who have been tortured have great difficulty putting memories of that torture out of their minds (Davis & Loftus, 2009). This is not to say that some disturbing memories cannot be forgotten. However, it is important to note that the most common response to a traumatic experience is not forgetting but uncontrolled remembering. Because of the vividness and persistence of most traumatic memories, it is difficult to accept that some traumatic memories could vanish from conscious awareness for years or even decades.

The Ingram Case

In one extraordinary case, a man recovered memories not of having been abused, but of having been a sexual abuser of children. The strange case of Paul Ingram illustrates some of the processes involved in the creation of a false memory.

Paul Ingram was a pillar of his community. He was a sheriff's deputy in the city of Olympia, Washington, he was deeply religious, and active in his local church. For most of his life, he was also considered a good father. Then, something terrible happened. One of his daughters accused him of sexually abusing her years earlier. Although Ingram strenuously denied these charges, local police were not convinced by his denials. Over the course of 5 months, they repeatedly questioned Ingram about the details of this alleged sexual abuse. They assisted his recall by telling him, over and over again, exactly how he had abused his children. Mr. Ingram prayed and asked the Lord to restore his memories of these horrible crimes. Investigators hypnotized him to dredge up old memories. And, eventually, Ingram confessed to gang-raping his own daughter, repeated violent assaults, animal sacrifices, and being a leader in a satanic cult that had killed 25 babies. If the confessions were true, the police had successfully exposed a prolific child abuser, rapist, and serial killer.

The story began to unravel when Richard Ofshe—a leading researcher of false confessions—joined the investigation. To test Ingram's suggestibility, Ofshe created a false accusation to see if Ingram would construct a memory of the false event. The false event (which was not one of the actual allegations in the case) was that Ingram had forced his daughter and son to have sex with each other while he watched. At first, Ingram had no recollections of this sordid event. But, after thinking and praying for guidance, he started to recall the details of the event. One day later, he confessed to committing the false crime. His account of what happened was strikingly vivid and detailed. He remembered the time of day, the day of the week, the room where the act had occurred, exactly what sex acts he told his children to perform, his thoughts during the event, and the reactions of his son and daughter.

Based on this result and other evidence, Ofshe argued that Ingram was an exceptionally suggestible and imaginative person whose intense praying induced a trancelike state. After imagining acts of sexual abuse while in this state, the imagined events became difficult to distinguish from authentic memories (Ofshe & Watters, 1994). Despite a massive police investigation—which included digging up several sites where bodies were allegedly buried—no physical evidence was ever found to link Ingram to the crimes or even to suggest that the crimes had ever happened. Nevertheless, Ingram was convicted and sent to prison. Paul Ingram served 12 years in prison and remains a registered sex offender.

The Ingram case is unusual because it involves recovered memories of being the *perpetrator* of sexual abuse. Recovered memories of being the *victim* of sexual abuse are far more common. But many elements of the Ingram case—a vulnerable and suggestible person, an interviewer who strongly suspected that sexual abuse occurred, and the use of hypnosis or other trancelike states—are at play in more typical cases of recovered memories.

 ## RESEARCH ON IMPLANTING FALSE MEMORIES

During the peak of the recovered-memory debate, psychologists who believed in repression correctly pointed out that no research showed that false memories could be implanted and mistaken for real memories of actual events. So, in the mid-1990s, Elizabeth Loftus, a leading researcher in the area of memory, set out to test the proposition that false memories could be implanted. Of course, it would be cruel and unethical to implant a traumatic memory of sexual abuse intentionally. As an alternative, Loftus set out to create a memory of being "lost at the mall." Twenty-four people, ranging in age from 18 to 53, were asked to tell what they remembered about four childhood events. Three of the four events had actually happened—they were experiences reported by parents or other close relatives. But the fourth event had never happened. That event involved being lost in a mall (or another public place) around age 5, crying, being rescued by an elderly woman, and then being reunited with the family. Participants were asked about the four events twice. After two interviews conducted over a period of weeks, 25% of the people came to remember most or all of the implanted "lost in the mall" event (Loftus, 1997).

A series of follow-up studies by Ira Hyman and his colleagues attempted to create memories of other, more unusual, false events. Using the same basic procedures as the earlier "lost in the mall" studies, participants in the study were told, "When you were 5, you were at the wedding reception of some friends of the family, and you were running around with some other kids, when you bumped into the table and spilled the punch bowl on the parents of the bride." At first, none of the participants could remember the punch bowl event. However, 27% eventually came to accept

RECOVERED MEMORIES

An Interview with Elizabeth Loftus
by Andrea Krauss

(COURTESY OF ELIZABETH LOFTUS)

How did you become interested in cases of sexual abuse?
Loftus: In the mid-1990s, the repressed memory theory had become very popular among psychologists. Someone would know almost nothing about the fact that they were abused as a child. But the repressed experience, years later, could then cause psychological problems. Through psychotherapy, it was possible—according to those who defended the repression hypothesis—to bring back the repressed memory and treat it. Based on this idea, the craziest stories were soon in circulation. Patients suddenly, and seriously, believed that they had been sexually abused in childhood. But they weren't being cured. And, when all this was happening, therapists could point to no scientific evidence that the repressed memory theory was valid.

How widespread did the theory become?
Debra A. Poole of Central Michigan University carried out a study in 1995 and found that in the United States and the United Kingdom, about a fourth of all therapists were using methods that could be characterized as dangerous:

Among them were hypnosis, dream interpretation, or direct demands on patients to imagine that they had been sexually abused as children. These methods are, in part, still popular today.

Why would psychotherapists want to encourage their patients to believe they had been victims of abuse?
According to this therapeutic system, patients could not remember their traumas anymore. But, as the psychologists and psychiatrists attempted to help bring memories back to life, there was an increasing chance that they would implant false memories in patients. Many therapists traced every mental problem back to sexual abuse. . . .

Do you believe that traumatic events cannot be repressed?
I am not saying that it does not happen. We just don't have any reliable way to determine if it has in a given individual. As long as that is true, we should avoid theories that, so far, have done more harm than good.

Can real and false memories be distinguished later?
Not reliably. Real memories are usually more detailed. But, the more often false memories are explicitly formulated, the livelier they become, and they thus seem more credible.

What would you advise therapists—and patients—to do?
A therapist should not start out with the assumption that repressed sexual abuse is the only possible explanation for psychological problems. He or she should consider other causes. And they should remain aware of the power of suggestion in their own actions. If I were a patient, I would hasten to get a second opinion if my therapist seemed to employ dubious methods.

the event as real. Some of the false recollections were quite vivid. For example, one participant described the father of the bride as:

> **A heavyset man, not like fat, but like tall and big beer belly, and I picture him having a dark gray suit . . . grayish dark hair and balding on top . . . with a wide square face, and I picture him getting up and being kind of irritated or mad (Hyman, Husband, & Billings, 1995, p. 194).**

These studies not only showed that false memories could be implanted with relatively little effort, they also highlighted the crucial importance of visual imagery in creating false memories. In the punch bowl studies, people who scored higher on tests measuring the vividness of visual imagery also tended to develop the most detailed and elaborate false memories. In addition, people who were instructed to relax and imagine an event they could not initially recall were much more likely to develop a false memory of the event. Later research suggested that memories of mildly traumatic events—being attacked by an animal, having a serious outdoor accident, or being hurt by another child—can be implanted in about a third of the people tested (Davis & Loftus, 2009; Porter, Yuille, & Lehman, 1999).

Several conclusions can be drawn from research on implanted memories. First, false memories cannot be successfully implanted in everyone. In the research summarized above, only about a quarter to a third of people came to accept a false memory as real (Meyersburg, Bogdan, Gallo, & McNally, 2009). Second, it appears that some techniques routinely used in therapy to search out childhood memories—hypnosis, dream interpretation, guided imagery—facilitate the production of detailed visual images that can later be mistaken for real memories. Third, expectancies seem to play a crucial role. For example, one study found that people who were told that it is possible to remember whether a colored mobile dangled above their crib the day after their birth are more likely to remember actually seeing one (Spanos, Burgess, Burgess, Samuels, & Blois, 1999). Similarly, people who believe that they have lived before often initially remember events from their "past lives" while under hypnosis (Peters, Horselenberg, Jelicic, & Merckelbach, 2007). Finally, the relative success of experiments designed to implant false memories is surprising because the techniques experimenters used were relatively weak. In real cases, the people who recovered memories of sexual abuse were subjected to much greater pressure over much longer periods.

The controversy over recovered memories has cooled during the past decade, but some residual bitterness remains. Although many claims of recovered memories appear to have been implanted through the use of suggestive therapy techniques, there are also cases where forgotten episodes of actual abuse were suddenly recalled. For example, in one well-documented case, a 30-year-old man became anxious and agitated while watching a movie in which the main character dealt with traumatic recollections of being sexually abused as a child. After the movie ended, the man experienced a flood of vivid memories. The memories involved being sexually abused by a priest during a camping trip 18 years earlier (Schooler, 1994). The reemergence of this traumatic memory occurred without psychotherapy and prior to widespread public awareness of the recovered memory debate. As in other cases where people have recovered memories that appear to be authentic, the memory came back spontaneously and the person was astonished by the sudden, unexpected memory (Geraerts, 2012).

Several explanations for the forgetting and remembering of sexual abuse have been proposed. The simplest explanation is the transience of memory—forgetting

SCIENTIFIC AMERICAN SPOTLIGHT

Traumatic Therapies Can Have Long-Lasting Effects on Mental Health
By Kelly Lambert and Scott O. Lilienfeld

Sheri Storm initially sought psychological treatment because of insomnia and anxiety associated with divorce proceedings and a new career in radio advertising. She had hoped for an antidepressant prescription or a few relaxation techniques. But, after enduring hypnosis sessions, psychotropic medications, and mental ward hospitalizations, Storm had much more to worry about than stress. She had "remembered" being sexually abused by her father at the age of 3 and forced to engage in bestiality and satanic ritual abuse that included the slaughtering and consumption of human babies. According to her psychiatrist, these traumatic experiences had generated alternative personalities, or "alters," within Storm's mind. Storm is now convinced that her multiple personality disorder was *iatrogenic*, the product of her "therapy." She reports that over time, her "memories" were fabricated and consolidated by a multitude of techniques—long hypnotherapy sessions, multiple psychotropic medications, sodium amytal (purportedly a truth serum), isolation from family members and mental-ward hospitalizations. For Storm, this therapy was physically, mentally, and emotionally grueling. Years after the psychiatric sessions have ceased, she is still tormented by vivid memories, nightmares, and physical reactions to cues from her fictitious past.

Storm's case is similar to those of many other patients who underwent recovered-memory therapy that revealed sordid histories of sexual abuse and demonic ceremonies. Although the scientific literature suggests that traumatic events are rarely, if ever, repressed or forgotten, this type of therapy was widespread in the 1990s and is still practiced today. Only after several high-profile lawsuits did the American Medical Association issue warnings to patients about the unreliability of recovered memories. Amid the heated controversy, the American Psychiatric Association discontinued the diagnostic category of multiple personality disorder, replacing it with the slightly different diagnosis of dissociative identity disorder. It seemed that science and the legal system had triumphed over sloppy therapeutic techniques. Some patients received substantial monetary settlements, their therapists were exposed in the media, and scientists produced convincing evidence that false memories could indeed be implanted in the human mind. Case closed. Or was it? For Storm and others like her, bad therapy seems to have altered the brain's emotional circuitry, with lasting effects on memory and mental health.

Research suggests that Storm's case is not unique. According to a report of the Crime Victims Compensation Program in Washington state, recovered-memory therapy may have unwanted negative effects on many patients. In this survey of 183 claims of repressed memories of childhood abuse, 30 cases were randomly selected for further profiling. Interestingly, this sample was almost exclusively Caucasian (97%) and female (97%). The following information was gleaned:

- 100% of the patients reported torture or mutilation, although no medical exams corroborated these claims.
- 97% recovered memories of satanic ritual abuse.
- 76% remembered infant cannibalism.
- 69% remembered being tortured with spiders.
- 100% remained in therapy 3 years after their first memory surfaced in therapy, and more than half were still in therapy 5 years later.
- 10% indicated that they had thoughts of suicide prior to therapy; this level increased to 67% following therapy.
- Hospitalizations increased from 7% prior to memory recovery to 37% following therapy.
- Self-mutilations increased from 3 to 27%.
- 83% of the patients were employed prior to therapy; only 10% were employed 3 years into therapy.
- 77% were married prior to therapy; 48% of those were separated or divorced after 3 years of therapy.
- 23% of patients who had children lost parental custody.
- 100% were estranged from extended families.

Although there is no way to know whether recovered-memory techniques were the sole cause of these negative outcomes, these findings raise profoundly troubling questions about the widespread use of such techniques.

that occurs with the passage of time (Schacter, 2001). But transience is only a small part of the story because most memories of important events deteriorate gradually; they do not simply vanish without a trace. Researchers who have examined authentic (as opposed to fictitious) recovered memories found that the forgotten sexual abuse was often not initially experienced by the child as traumatic. However, the memory did become emotionally distressing when it was recalled by an adult who recognized it as sexual abuse (McNally & Geraerts, 2009). In addition, for authentic recovered memories, there was often a lack of reminders of the abuse. For example, if a child's family moved away from the neighborhood where the abuse occurred or if the abuser left town or died, forgetting became easier. Another potential explanation follows from the finding that people who say they were sexually abused as children are more likely to temporarily forget the abuse if the abuser is a family member or trusted caretaker. Some researchers have suggested that forgetting may occur because the child is physically and emotionally dependent on the abusive family member (Anderson, 2001). Memories of the abuse would damage the essential relationship between caregiver and child by creating fear and distrust. To prevent this damage, and to maintain an adaptive relationship with the caregiver, a child might selectively recall positive memories. By repeatedly and selectively retrieving positive memories, retrieval of negative memories becomes increasingly difficult. The negative memory may only enter awareness when exposure to powerful cues (such as watching a movie about child sexual abuse) allows the victim to retrieve the memory.

Individual differences are also part of the story. Some people may simply be better at keeping unpleasant experiences out of their minds. Lynn Myers and her colleagues have identified people who appear to be especially good at denying their emotional responses. When physiological measures (like blood pressure, heart rate, and muscle tension) indicate that such people are experiencing high levels of stress and anxiety, they claim to feel relaxed and free of stress. People with this repressive coping style are less able to remember negative events from their past and are also less able to remember details of the negative events they do recall (Derakshan, Eysenck, & Myers, 2007; Myers & Brewin, 1998).

In short, there appear to be cases where people have constructed false memories of sexual abuse. There also seem to be cases where memories of sexual abuse have resurfaced after having been forgotten for years. How can we know which memories were created and which were recovered? Based on their careful review of the scientific literature on recovered memories, Stephen Lindsay and Don Read (1994; 2001) conclude that we should consider five criteria when evaluating claims of recovered memories of abuse. Specifically, we should be especially skeptical of allegedly recovered memories that: (1) were recovered over time using suggestive or coercive techniques; (2) began as vague images or feelings instead of clear, detailed recollections; (3) involve repeated abuse that extended into adolescence (abuse after childhood is unlikely to be forgotten); (4) involve abuse that occurred before the age of 3 or in very early childhood (before enduring memories can be formed); and (5) involve extremely rare forms of abuse (e.g., sexual abuse as part of a satanic ritual).

By the year 2000, claims of recovered memories had plummeted. There are good reasons for the sharp decline. Many people who once claimed that they had recovered memories of sexual abuse later retracted those claims (Ost, Costall, & Bull, 2002). Some of those people (and the people they had accused of being abusers) brought successful lawsuits against psychotherapists who had created false memories. As a consequence, many therapists switched to less suggestive approaches.

▶ IN CONCLUSION

Often, the only witness to child sexual abuse is the victim. Eliciting a full and accurate account of a crime from a child victim is a delicate process. Children are more suggestible than adults and their accounts of abuse can be corrupted by suggestive interviewing techniques. Biased questioning can lead to false accusations against innocent people or thwart the successful prosecution of actual sexual abusers. Researchers have revealed how biased questioning can create distorted accounts of abuse. They have also developed unbiased techniques that allow us to elicit fuller, more accurate accounts from child victims. When the alleged victim of child sexual abuse is now an adult who has recovered long-forgotten memories of being abused, it is important to examine whether those memories might have been constructed through highly suggestive psychotherapeutic techniques.

It is critical to treat human memory as carefully as crime scene investigators treat fingerprints and DNA. Just as with physical evidence, great care must be taken to prevent the contamination of psychological evidence. Only then can the legal system do the essential work of convicting the guilty and releasing the innocent.

▶ CRITICAL THINKING QUESTIONS

1. Why would children claim to have been sexually abused if they were not?

2. What types of interview styles might lead to false claims of abuse by children?

3. How do the NICHD Investigative Interview Protocol and other safeguards produce more accurate reports from children?

4. Should *adult* victims of abuse be permitted to testify in court via CCTV?

5. What factors contribute to the creation of false memories?

6. What criteria might we use to distinguish true from false memories of sexual abuse?

7. If you were a juror in a case involving a recovered memory of sexual abuse, what sort of evidence would be necessary to convince you—beyond a reasonable doubt—that the defendant is guilty?

▶ KEY TERMS

anatomically detailed doll (p. 218)

Child sexual abuse accommodation

syndrome (CSAAS) (p. 223)

closed circuit television (CCTV) (p. 224)

hearsay testimony (p. 224)

NICHD Investigative Interview Protocol (p. 221)

recovered memories (p. 225)

repression (p. 227)

12 Child Custody Disputes

▶ **Varieties of Custody Arrangements**
▶ **Research on Children's Responses to Divorce**
▶ **The Psychologist's Contribution to Custody Decisions**
▶ **Custody Mediation as an Alternative to Litigation**

When he was just 5 years old, Mark Painter's mother, Jeanne, was killed in an automobile accident. His father, Harold, was having difficulty raising Mark alone, so he asked his late wife's parents—Dwight and Margaret Bannister—to care for Mark. For nearly 2 years, Mark lived with the Bannisters on their farm in Ames, Iowa. After Mr. Painter remarried, he wanted to take 7-year-old Mark back to live with him and his new wife, Marilyn, in California. The Bannisters refused, and Mr. Painter sued to regain custody of his child. An Iowa court was faced with the task of determining which custody arrangement would be best for Mark.

Mark's two sets of possible parents could not have been more different. Harold Painter had been raised by foster parents. He had flunked out of both high school and trade school. He enlisted in the Navy but soon dropped out. Although he managed to complete his GED and a couple years of college, he quit college to work at a small newspaper. When he married Mark's mother, he had held seven different jobs in the 10 years since he had left college. At the time of the automobile accident that killed his wife, he was being supported by her.

Harold did have a plan for his life after he regained custody of Mark. He would work as a freelance writer and photographer and,

> "settle myself and Mark in Sausalito, California . . .[at] a retreat for wealthy artists, writers, and such aspiring artists and writers as can fork up the rent money. My plan is to do expensive portraits, and sell prints to the tourists who flock in from all over the world." (Painter v. Bannister, 1966, p. 155)

Mr. Painter described himself as "agnostic or atheist" and had no interest in formal religious training for Mark.

In contrast, the Bannisters were college graduates with stable jobs in a middle-class community in rural Iowa. All their children were college graduates and were happily married. They were respected members of their community, with Mr. Bannister having served on the school board and teaching Sunday school at the Congregational Church. The Iowa court was presented with a clear choice: a stable, churchgoing, conventional family in the Midwest or a somewhat unstable nonreligious person and his new wife who planned to sell portraits near San Francisco. In the end, the court awarded custody to the Bannisters. Even though Mr. Painter was Mark's biological father, and even though the Bannisters would be in their 70s by the time Mark graduated from high school, the court felt that the Bannisters could provide Mark with

> a stable, dependable, conventional, middle-class, middle west background and an opportunity for a college education and profession, if he desires it. (Painter v. Bannister, 1966, p. 154).

The custody of Mark Painter had to be decided between his biological father, Harold Painter, and his mother's parents, Dwight and Margaret Bannister. Pictured are Harold Painter and his wife, Marilyn, with a photo of Mark behind them. *(AP Photo)*

Did the Iowa court make the right decision? Would a California court have reached a different result? How should courts make decisions about the custody of children? What factors should the courts consider? In this chapter, we review the legal system's decision making in child custody cases (usually as a result of divorce or a separation, but sometimes as the result of the death of a parent). We also explain the role of psychologists in custody decisions, and we look to the relevant research for guidance about how to improve such decisions. Yet, it is important to note at the outset that there is no "right" way to parent, and notions of appropriate parenting behavior are clearly affected by societal norms, cultural influences, historical practices, and myriad other factors.

Unfortunately, no national data exist on rates of divorce, separation, or cohabitation that involve children. We do know that approximately 40% of children will experience the divorce of their parents and that the rates of separation are even higher among nonmarried, cohabiting couples (Emery, Otto, & O'Donohue, 2005). When parents separate, psychologists are often asked to make predictions about what kind of child custody arrangement will be best for the children of those parents. If one of the parents is incompetent to raise children, the task of deciding custody is greatly simplified—the children go to the fit parent. But far more frequently, courts must try to structure a fair custody arrangement that takes into account the needs of the children, as well as the desires of two parents who may now despise one another but who both love their children. The "best" arrangement for a particular child is often uncertain. Should it be the one that will promote happiness? The one that ensures financial security and material comfort? Physical health? Psychological well-being? Perhaps it should be the arrangement that facilitates academic or eventual career success. Or, maybe it should be the arrangement that creates the least amount of disruption in the child's life. To complicate matters further, keep in mind that the arrangement must not only serve the child's current interests, but must also serve his or her interests many years into the future. ◀

 ## VARIETIES OF CUSTODY ARRANGEMENTS

First, some basic distinctions: Courts distinguish between legal custody and physical custody. **Physical custody** refers to how much time a child spends with each parent. If parents share physical custody, the child lives with each parent some of the time. For example, an 8-year-old may live with his mother most of the time but he may stay with his father every Wednesday and Thursday, every other weekend, and most of the summer. **Legal custody** concerns the rights and responsibilities of parents. For example, a parent with legal custody has the authority to decide which school a child should attend and what religious training (if any) the child will receive. If medical care is needed, that parent will make treatment decisions. Such decisions must be negotiated if parents share legal custody (sometimes referred to as **joint legal custody**), but even with joint legal custody, the parent who is supervising the child will make everyday decisions without consulting the other parent. The basic alternative to joint (or shared) custody is sole custody. In **sole custody,** one parent has legal and physical custody while the other typically has some rights to visit the child at regular intervals. Although there is no universally agreed upon time-sharing distinction between joint and sole physical custody, some scholars have suggested that the child must spend the equivalent of two overnights a week for the custody to be considered shared by the courts (Emery, et al., 2005). Interestingly, surveyed child custody evaluators do not share the courts' broad definition of joint physical custody, with the evaluators generally believing that somewhere between a 40% to a 60% split of time is necessary for an arrangement to be considered joint physical custody (Ackerman & Pritzl, 2011).

A child custody dispute can be resolved by the courts using any combination of these arrangements. One parent can have sole legal and physical custody, one parent can have sole physical custody but shared legal custody, the parents can share physical custody with one parent having sole legal custody (this is the most unusual of the four), or both parents can share physical and legal custody.

In theory, it may seem ideal to have a child spend the same amount of time with each parent, but this arrangement is often difficult from a practical standpoint. It can be hard on a child to spend alternate weeks with each parent, particularly if one parent lives far from the child's current school and friends. Estimates of actual custody arrangements indicate sole physical custody by the mother (68–88%) is far more common than sole custody by the father (8–14%), and both are more common than equal-sharing arrangements (only 2–6%) (Braver, Ellman, Votruba, & Fabricius, 2011). Joint legal custody is also common and has been increasing in recent decades. Its primary advantage is that it ensures that both parents remain closely involved in raising the child, which may be psychologically beneficial to both children and parents (Stahl, 2014). A secondary benefit of joint legal custody is that financial support of the child is more stable. Too often, a custodial parent may have to seek child support payments constantly from an embittered parent who does not have custody rights. Researchers have found that mothers, fathers, and children usually prefer joint legal custody to sole custody, and joint legal custody can improve family adjustment and cohesiveness. However, despite these considerable benefits, joint legal custody is not always the best arrangement. A significant disadvantage is that it requires two feuding parents to engage in regular communication, cooperation, and coordination (Braver et al., 2011; Krauss & Sales, 2000).

As you might expect, sole custody is the preferred arrangement when one parent is clearly incompetent, addicted to drugs, or physically or psychologically abusive toward the child. However, even in cases in which both parents are competent and caring, it is sometimes argued that sole custody is in a child's best interest. A child with a strong need for stability may benefit by continuing to live in the family home with one custodial parent. Also, a sensitive child may be shielded from the conflicts that often arise if two hostile parents who share custody must continue to interact with one another to arrange visits and make decisions about the child. Indeed, there is strong evidence that **high conflict** or hostility-ridden relationships between parents are associated with emotional disruption for the child and poorer long-term adjustment (Cummings & Davies, 2002). Consequently, neither joint legal custody nor sole physical custody is best in all

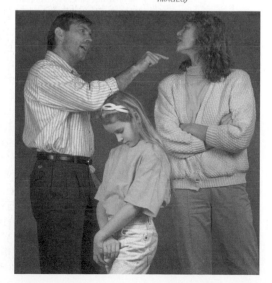

Research suggests that children feeling caught between parents leads to worse outcomes for them. *(LARRY JOUBERT/GETTY IMAGES)*

situations. Unfortunately, there is little long-term research on the effects of different custodial arrangements. The available research simply has not identified large differences in the post-divorce adjustment of children that can be attributed to specific custodial arrangements (Stahl, 2014).

Most custody decisions—about 90%—are made without resorting to litigation (Emery, et al., 2005). If the divorcing parents both agree to a particular custody arrangement (on their own or with the help of a mediator), a judge will almost always endorse that arrangement. Among divorcing parents who turn to the courts to decide child custody, about one-third can be described as engaging in extreme levels of conflict, and about 8% to 15% of families will continue to experience high levels of conflict in the years following the divorce (APA, 2012). The intensity of negative feelings in these cases puts children at acute risk for emotional damage.

The Evolution of the Best Interest of the Child Standard

Determining child custody used to be simple. Under English common law, the legal doctrine of *Pater familias* controlled the disposition of children after divorce, and because women were not permitted to own property, fathers were automatically entitled to custody of their children (Melton et al., 2007). By the 1800s, the idea of children as mere property had been replaced by the idea that childhood was an important stage of life that contributed to the development of the adult person.

Current law in all states now requires that custody arrangements serve the best interests of the child. This has become known as the **best interest of the child standard (BICS).** In some ways, this is a laudable and elegant standard—there is no presumption that either the father or the mother is entitled to custody, and the needs of parents and other interested parties are secondary to what is best for the child. The overriding goal is to place the child in the most favorable environment. Yet, it is important to remember that peoples' views of what constitutes a child's best interest have fluctuated over time.

The Tender Years Doctrine. By the end of the nineteenth century, a precursor of BICS—the **tender years doctrine**—was the prevailing standard for deciding child custody. Under this rule, children of a young age and all female children were supposed to be placed with the mother unless there were extenuating circumstances. The doctrine was articulated in the 1899 case of *People v. Hickey*:

> An infant of tender years will generally be left with the mother, where no objection is shown to exist as to her, even if the father be without blame, because of the father's inability to bestow on it that tender care which nature requires, and which it is the peculiar province of the mother to supply; and this rule will apply with much force in case of female children of a more advanced age. (p. 21)

Though the doctrine now appears outdated and sexist, it seemed perfectly natural and self-evident at the time it was written. It was not until the middle of the twentieth century that fathers began to assert their rights to custody and to challenge the gender stereotyped view of parent–child relations implied by the old doctrine. Although the tender years doctrine has been abandoned, the tendency of courts to award custody to the mother persists (Braver et al., 2011).

Primary Caretaker Rule. After the abolition of the tender years doctrine, many scholars suggested that the **primary caretaker rule** should be used to determine the best interest of the child. The primary caretaker rule instructs that courts should award primary custody to the parent who was primarily responsible for raising the child prior to the divorce. Courts have held that "continuity of care" and that the "warmth, consistency, and continuity of the primary relationship" is critical to the well-being of the child (O'Donohue, Beitz, & Cummings, 2008). To determine who the primary caretaker is, courts consider a number of factors including: (1) which parent buys and washes the child's clothes; (2) who bathes and grooms the child; (3) who disciplines the child and helps with homework; (4) who cares for the child when he or she is ill; and (5) who arranges for the child to spend time with friends. Because women still tend to assume primary responsibility for child rearing more often than do men, those states that favor the primary caretaker standard award physical custody to mothers in more than 80% of cases (Hetherington & Kelley, 2003).

The Uniform Marriage and Divorce Act of 1976. Current formulations of the BICS vary considerably by state, but most use elements of the **Uniform Marriage and Divorce Act (UMDA) of 1976** in their legal decision making. The UMDA proposed five criteria to be used for determining custody: (1) the wishes of the child's parents; (2) the wishes of the child; (3) the relationships between the child and his or her parents, siblings, and any other person who significantly affects the child's best interests; (4) the child's adjustment to home, school, and community; and (5) the physical and mental health of everyone involved with the child. Yet, nothing in the UMDA tells the judge (or the jury in Texas, the only state where juries decide these cases) how to balance and weight these different criteria in reaching a decision. Some states have added idiosyncratic factors to the UMDA criteria. Among these add-ons are the moral fitness of the parents and the economic stability of the parents (Stahl, 2014).

Weaknesses of the BICS. There are at least three central problems with current formulations of the BICS. The first is vagueness. How can each factor be reliably measured? How much weight should be assigned to each factor? At what age should the judge ask a child's preference? Should it matter what underlies that child's preference? What if a child prefers her father because he is less likely to discipline her for bad behavior? How should the child's preference be balanced against that child's adjustment to home, school, or community?

Here, as in other areas of law, vagueness places discretion in the hands of judges. And, if judges strongly favor maternal custody, the current standard may not be a great step forward from the old "tender years" doctrine. Indeed, about 75 percent of children continue to be placed in sole physical and legal custody with their mothers (Emery, et al., 2005). Further, a large body of psychological research suggests that prejudice (e.g., sexism or gender bias) is especially likely to influence decision making when guidelines are vague and when outcomes are difficult to determine (Kahneman, 2011).

There are clear cases in which judges' biases appear to have affected their decisions (as the Iowa's court judge's biases about Midwesterners and Californians likely affected the decision in the chapter's opening vignette). For example, in the case of Palmore v. Sidoti (1984), a judge took custody of a Caucasian girl away from her mother and granted custody to the father because the mother had since married an African-American man. The judge's decision was based on his belief that the girl would suffer from "social stigmatization" as a consequence of living in a mixed-race household. Although the ruling was upheld by a Florida appeals court, the U.S. Supreme Court eventually overturned the decision, holding that, "custody decisions cannot turn on racial considerations" (see also, Legal Spotlight: Same-Sex Unions and Child Custody).

A second problem is that the BICS may unintentionally escalate conflicts and litigation between parents. A divorcing parent who is seeking custody of a child gains an advantage by exaggerating every fault and failing of the other parent. If, for example, the father portrays the mother as irresponsible or immoral, he might

LEGAL SPOTLIGHT

Same-Sex Unions and Child Custody

On December 19, 2000, following passage of Vermont's civil union law, a law that allowed the creation of a legal partnership between same-sex individuals, Janet Jenkins and Lisa Miller traveled from their home in Virginia to Vermont to enter into a civil union, and both changed their last name to Miller-Jenkins. In 2001, Lisa and Janet decided to start a family. Lisa was artificially inseminated, and Isabella Miller-Jenkins was born in April of 2002. A year later, the couple separated and Lisa moved back to Virginia with Isabella. Lisa eventually filed for dissolution of their civil union in Vermont and indicated that, while she would maintain primary custody of Isabella, Janet (who still lived in Vermont) would have visitation rights. Shortly thereafter, Lisa became a fundamentalist Christian, renounced her homosexuality and prior relationship with Janet, and refused to comply with Janet's visitation rights.

In July 2004, Virginia passed the Marriage Affirmation Act (MAA), which prohibited marriages between same-sex partners and refused to recognize same-sex marriages from other states. After the act's passage, Lisa sought both sole custody and sole parentage of Isabella and sought to have the prior Vermont custody agreement declared "null and void" in a Virginia court. A Virginia trial court acceded to Lisa's request, while a Vermont court held Lisa in contempt for failing to abide by the Vermont custody agreement.

In Miller-Jenkins v. Miller-Jenkins, first a Virginia Court of Appeals (2006) and then the Virginia Supreme Court (2008) attempted to determine the appropriate custody

(AP Photo/Rutland Herald, Vyto Starinskas, File)

arrangement between Lisa and Janet and which state had jurisdiction over the visitation dispute. Both Virginia courts held that the federally instituted Parental Kidnapping Prevention Act (PKPA) (928 USC § 1738A) required that Virginia give full faith and credit, which means that they must follow the previous state's ruling, to the custody decision of the Vermont courts. The PKPA act specified that a custody decision or visitation decree must be followed by a subsequent state if the child and the parents had been residing in the first state for the 6 months prior to the dissolution of the civil union (which the couple had). The PKPA was designed to prevent the unlawful removal of children from one jurisdiction to another in order to avoid the custody and visitation decisions that one parent did not feel was fair in the initial jurisdiction.

The appropriateness of the Virginia courts offering full faith and credit to the Vermont custody decision was contested because of Virginia's MAA passage and the federal Defense of Marriage Act (DOMA, 28 U.S.C. § 1738C, 1996), which made clear that same-sex marriages and civil unions did not have to be given "full faith and credit" by states that did not recognize them. DOMA would eventually be determined unconstitutional by the United States Supreme Court in 2013, but Virginia's high-court decisions clarified that, even when DOMA was law, it did not prohibit states from recognizing the full faith and credit of other states' custody decisions under the PKPA act, regardless of whether the parents were involved in a same-sex union or marriage.

be more likely to win custody of the child. The lingering anger and distrust created by such allegations can disrupt the child's post-divorce adjustment. Also, because neither party is likely to be able to predict the outcome of litigation under the vague BICS, there will be fewer settlements before trial, and longer, more conflict-ridden legal proceedings (Krauss & Sales, 2000; Stahl, 2014). In other words, parties are more likely to "roll the dice," even when they do not have a strong case because it is difficult for them to predict what the court will decide.

A third problem with the BICS is that it asks courts to predict the future. Judges must imagine what form of custody will promote healthy development of the child years after the decision is made. Judges as well as psychologists have demonstrated very limited ability to predict the future in a variety of situations (see e.g., Chapter 14 Predicting Violent Behavior). While we know a great deal about the type of parenting and environments that lead to bad outcomes for children, we know far less about the factors that lead to good outcomes.

To circumvent the vagueness of the BICS, many states have adopted what are called **preferred custody arrangements.** This means that a particular type of custody—usually either joint legal custody or sole physical custody—will be ordered by the court *unless* it can be shown that this preferred arrangement is not in the child's best interest. In other words, the preferred arrangement is the de facto rule unless one party can strongly demonstrate that it should not be. Preferred arrangements have the benefit of discouraging litigation because parents and their lawyers know in advance how custody disputes are likely to be resolved.

Approximation Rule. Another more concrete child custody standard, the **approximation rule,** has been advocated by several scholars and the American Law Institute, a nonpartisan organization that provides legal scholarship, commentary, and model rules on a variety of important legal topics (American Law Institute, 2002). According to this rule, courts

> should allocate custodial responsibilities so that the proportion of custodial time the child spends with each parent approximates the proportion of time each parent spent performing caretaking functions for the child before the parent's separation. (ALI, §2.90, 2002)

Under this formulation, the custody arrangement should approximate the caretaking relationships that existed prior to the divorce. The goal of this rule is stability and continuity. Therefore, if most of the child's important decisions were made jointly by both parents prior to the divorce then the court would award shared or joint legal custody after the divorce. Likewise, if the father was primarily responsible for shuttling the kids from activity to activity pre-divorce, he would continue to play this role post-divorce. Applying the approximation rule, it should come as no surprise that judges consistently award mothers sole custody more often—mothers are often responsible for more pre-divorce child care duties, therefore it makes sense for them to continue in that role after divorce. It remains an open question whether the greater frequency of maternal sole custody awards is a result of judges' biases, a result of judges' attempts to maintain continuity and stability in custodial arrangements, or some combination of both.

Many fathers' groups have protested the approximation rule because it increases the likelihood of maternal sole physical custody. They argue that pre-divorce caretaking behavior does not necessarily reflect what arrangement is best for the child post-divorce, and that greater pre-divorce maternal childcare may be the result of men being more economically successful. It is likely that many men would have chosen to spend more time with their children if it had been economically feasible. Additionally, they contend that post-divorce childcare functions are likely to include substantial changes from pre-divorce behavior (e.g., a mother may have to work more hours post-divorce), and that the approximation rule does not take these realities into consideration. Fathers' advocacy groups have proposed an **Equal Custody presumption,** in which children spend equal time living with each parent, unless evidence suggests this is impractical (e.g., if there is a history of domestic violence). Only the District of Columbia currently follows the Equal Custody presumption, but one recent survey of jury pool members in Arizona suggests that approximately 70 percent of participants favor this sharing arrangement, even in cases of high conflict between the parties (Braver et al., 2011).

 ## RESEARCH ON CHILDREN'S RESPONSES TO DIVORCE

It is important to ask whether research can tell us what type of custody will serve the children's best interests. Clearly, the ideal custody arrangement is one in which both parents are strongly committed to their children and in which each parent is also committed to helping the children maintain healthy relationships with the other parent. That ideal is often difficult to achieve, but psychological research offers us some clues about how to avoid harm and how to promote healthy adjustment.

For a variety of reasons, it is difficult to uncover the specific effects of divorce on children. First, a full understanding of the adjustment process requires **longitudinal research**—research that collects data over a long period of time. It is very difficult, expensive, and time-consuming to collect data from parents and children over a period of many years. Second, it is hard to distinguish between psychological problems that predate the divorce and problems that were caused by the divorce. For example, written records may indicate that a child was having disciplinary problems at school prior to the divorce, but it is hard to know whether those problems were caused by conflict in the home or difficulties at school. Finally, the outcome of interest—healthy adjustment—is difficult to measure. The multifaceted concept of **adjustment** may include satisfying social relationships, self-esteem, feelings of contentment, and school achievement, as well as the relative absence of psychological problems such as depression and aggressive behavior. Because no single measure can capture every facet of adjustment, researchers usually try to use batteries of psychological tests as well as in-depth interviews to gather data about the adjustment process. Fortunately, despite the formidable obstacles to research on the effects of divorce, there are now several longitudinal studies and many comparisons of same-age children from divorced and intact families. The positive news from this research is that the great majority of children whose parents divorce manage to adapt and grow into psychologically healthy adults. Of course, this is not to diminish the psychological, social, emotional, and financial disruptions often produced by divorce.

Surprisingly, judicial decisions about appropriate custody arrangements after divorce are often uninformed by psychological research (Krauss & Sales, 2000; Stahl & Martin, 2013). There are many research findings the courts ought to consider. For example, one line of research suggests that maintaining contact with an extended family can help to buffer children against the negative effects of divorce. If a child has strong relationships with grandparents or aunts or uncles or neighbors, that child may be able to turn to those adults for support before, during, and after the divorce. There is even research suggesting that sibling relationships ought to be given some weight in custody decisions. If children feel isolated from friends following a divorce, they often rely on brothers or sisters for emotional support. More generally, siblings help each other develop social and problem-solving skills. Of course, non-relatives who share close relationships with a child also play a role in adjustment. Indeed, children tend to define family in terms of emotional ties rather than biological relationships. It may be that this "**psychological family**" is particularly important to preserve in the wake of divorce (Gindes, 1995; Otto & Martindale, 2007).

The child's personality also plays a role in adaptation after divorce. Our personalities shape our social relationships and our close relationships shape our personalities. Some researchers have identified a cluster of personality traits termed "**resilience**" that are related to adaptation to divorce (Kelly & Emery, 2003). In a large longitudinal study (698 children followed for more than 40 years), researchers tracked the development of children who were identified as being at risk for developing psychological problems because of severe family discord. Despite being at high risk, about a third of these children grew up without significant psychological problems (Werner, 2005). These "resilient" children were able to thrive during and after divorce because of their abilities to elicit positive interactions from others, to maintain or expand relationships with supportive adults, and to find caretakers who nurtured their self-esteem and feelings of competence.

Minimal conflict between parents is also an important factor that is strongly associated with positive adjustment after divorce. Children whose divorced parents are classified as "high-conflict" generally experience the worst post-divorce outcomes (Melton et al., 2007). Bad outcomes are especially likely when children feel caught between warring parents who continue to have contentious contact with each other. When there is minimal conflict between parents, or when the conflict subsides over time, a continuing positive relationship with the noncustodial parent helps to promote successful long-term adjustment (Emery, et al., 2005).

In addition, economic security plays a significant role in a child's post-divorce adjustment. This form of security typically declines after a divorce. The reason appears to be that sole physical and legal custody by a mother is still the most common custodial arrangement, and sole-custody mothers typically experience a significant drop in their income after divorce, even when child support payments are included in the calculation (Krauss & Sales, 2000). It is not surprising that a sudden drop in financial security produces deleterious effects when combined with the emotional strains of divorce. Custodial parents often struggle to provide the same environment for their child using substantially fewer resources. Some burdens placed on the custodial parent (e.g., more child care or psychotherapy for the child) require significant financial resources. Generally, the problems experienced by children of divorced parents appear to be especially intense during the year or two following divorce. This is when feelings of loss, separation, anger, and depression may be exacerbated by financial insecurity, dealing with the logistics of setting up separate households, and transporting the children between parents.

The research findings summarized in this section underscore the importance of making case-by-case determinations of child custody. Judges and evaluators should take into account the individual personality of each child and strive to craft custody arrangements that minimize parental conflict, promote economic security, and preserve supportive relationships with adults (even those relationships beyond the child's nuclear family).

HOT TOPIC

Parental Alienation Syndrome

Parental alienation syndrome (PAS) was first described by Richard Gardner in 1985 and refers to one parent's attempt to make their children unfairly fear the other parent involved in a custodial dispute. Alienation from the targeted parent is hypothesized to occur through a campaign of disparaging remarks and behaviors from the other parent. Gardner suggested that there were three levels of PAS—mild, moderate, and severe—and that PAS only occurs in response to a child custody dispute.

At the severe level, the child becomes brainwashed by the offending parent and is unable to have visitation with the other parent because of the anxiety and fear such a visit would arouse in the child. The child may even act out violently against the targeted parent. The syndrome is characterized by the following behaviors and feelings: (1) a large number of negative statements directed against the targeted parent by the offending parent; (2) claims by the child that his or her negative beliefs about the targeted parent were not prompted by the other parent; (3) imagined or rehearsed scenarios where the other parent has been mean or abusive to the child; (4) the child's extreme loyalty to the offending parent; (5) a lack of remorse for cruel acts against the targeted parent; and (6) a generalized fear reaction to people associated with the targeted parent (Kennedy, 2009). In 2008, parental alienation syndrome received renewed

Alec Baldwin accused his ex-wife, Kim Basinger, of creating parent alienation syndrome in their daughter, Ireland, from their broken marriage. (*John Kopaloff/Getty Images*)

media attention in the acrimonious divorce and custody battle of celebrities Alec Baldwin and Kim Basinger. Baldwin claimed that Basinger turned their daughter Ireland against him and blamed Basinger's alienation of him for a notorious voicemail message he left on his daughter's phone. In 2008, Baldwin authored a book on parental alienation, entitled *A Promise to Ourselves: A Journey through Fatherhood and Divorce*, and intimated that he might leave acting to serve as a spokesman for the syndrome. (Despite the contentious relationship between Ireland and Alec during the custody battle, they currently appear to be on good terms.)

Unfortunately, although courts in many jurisdictions and countries have accepted expert psychological testimony on this syndrome, there are limited scientific data to support it (Kennedy, 2009). Like much syndrome evidence used in courts (see Chapter 10), almost no peer-reviewed studies of this phenomenon have been published. Nearly all the literature on this topic falls into two categories—research conducted by Richard Gardner or anecdotal accounts of a child's behavior. Further, this syndrome bears little resemblance to identified psychological problems, such as depression or anxiety. In the end, the question remains whether PAS is a common pattern of behavior that can be reliably identified and treated or simply an intuitively appealing description of the egregious behavior of a few parents.

 ## THE PSYCHOLOGIST'S CONTRIBUTION TO CUSTODY DECISIONS

The criteria for deciding custody arrangements are inescapably psychological. As discussed above, these criteria involve assessments of the quality of interpersonal relationships, emotional attachments between parent and child, coping ability, and stability of relationships over time. For this reason, courts often call on psychological experts to help them determine the appropriate custodial arrangement after a divorce. Sometimes, a clinical psychologist acts as an adviser to the court, and sometimes psychologists who have different views of what is best for a particular child will offer opposing testimony in support of the father or the mother. Often, judges appoint their own psychological expert to conduct a custody evaluation on behalf of the court. It is also possible for each side to hire its own expert or for both sides to contribute money to hire a shared, independent expert (Bow, 2006).

Sometimes, psychologists who are seeing one or more of the parties pre-divorce may be asked to testify about their clients strengths and weaknesses and what they think is the most appropriate custody arrangement. This question is problematic for psychologists because it involves a **multiple relationship:** a situation in which they are acting as both a treating therapist for a specific client as well as serving as an objective expert for the court. Generally, psychologists are ethically required to refrain from taking on these dual roles because they may lack the objectivity to view the family custodial arrangement in a neutral manner, and also because they may lack adequate knowledge of the other parties involved (i.e., the children or the spouse if they are seeing one of the parents, or the parents and siblings if they are seeing one of the children) (APA, 2010).

The Role of the Psychological Expert

The role of psychologists in custody decision making is one of the most controversial areas of forensic psychological practice. In fact, child custody evaluations are one of the top reasons for ethics board complaints and malpractice suits leveled against psychologists. One survey of 213 psychologists who conduct child custody evaluations found that more than half had received at least one ethics board complaint and 1 in 5 had also faced a malpractice suit (Ackerman & Pritzl, 2011). No matter what conclusions the psychologist reaches, it is likely that at least one parent in the custody dispute will be unhappy. In addition, some scholars have argued that there is precious little scientifically that psychologists can offer to the courts in this area. As one respected scholar noted:

> ... there is probably no forensic question on which overreaching by mental health professionals has been so common and so egregious. Besides lacking scientific validity, such opinions have often been based on clinical data that are, on their face, irrelevant to the legal question in dispute. (Melton et al., 2007, p. 540)

While courts have generally welcomed the participation of clinical psychologists in child custody proceedings, parents and scientists may find the performance of mental health experts deficient. In fact, many scholars are especially perplexed by experts who offer ultimate issue testimony—testimony that directly answers the fundamental question before the court. In custody disputes, that question is "What is the best child custody arrangement post-divorce?" Scholars are critical of ultimate issue testimony because mental health experts lack the true expertise to answer this question and because our legal system specifically leaves the ultimate issue to the trier of fact (the judge or jury). (Other controversies surrounding psychological experts offering ultimate issue testimony are described in Chapters 1, 8, and 9.)

Psychologists who are asked to conduct a child custody assessment should rely on multiple sources of information. The American Psychological Association guidelines (2009) suggest that custody evaluators gather information relevant to a number of issues, including: (1) the psychological best interest of the child, (2) the

---

TABLE 12.1

Summary of APA's Guidelines for Child Custody Evaluations in Family Law Proceedings

I. Orienting Guidelines: Purposes of the Child Custody Evaluation
    a. The purpose of the evaluation is to assist in determining the psychological best interest of the child.
    b. The child's welfare is paramount.
    c. The evaluation focuses upon parenting attributes, the child's psychological needs, and the resulting fit.

II. General Guidelines: Preparing for the Custody Evaluation
    a. Psychologists strive to gain and maintain specialized competence.
    b. Psychologists strive to function as impartial evaluators.
    c. Psychologists strive to engage in culturally informed, nondiscriminatory evaluation practices.
    d. Psychologists strive to avoid conflicts of interest and multiple relationships in conducting evaluations.

III. Procedural Guidelines: Conducting the Child Custody Evaluation
    a. Psychologists strive to establish the scope of the evaluation in a timely fashion, consistent with the nature of the referral question.
    b. Psychologists strive to obtain appropriately informed consent.
    c. Psychologists strive to employ multiple methods of data gathering.
    d. Psychologists strive to interpret assessment data in a manner consistent with the context of the evaluation.
    e. Psychologists strive to complement the evaluation with the appropriate combination of examinations.
    f. Psychologists strive to base their recommendations, if any, upon the psychological best interest of the child.
    g. Psychologists create and maintain professional records in accordance with ethical and legal obligations.

The complete text of the Guidelines can be found at www.apa.org/practice/guidelines-evaluation-child-custody-family-law.pdf. It should be noted that APA Guidelines are aspirational in nature and are not intended to supersede legal decisions or the APA's ethics code.

---

strengths and weaknesses of the parents, (3) the needs of the child, and (4) how well parenting attributes "fit" the needs of the child (APA, 2010; see Table 12.1 for a summary of the APA Guidelines for Child Custody Evaluations in Family Law Proceedings). Other organizations have also promulgated model standards to help mental health practitioners in their assessments of these difficult decisions, including the Association of Family and Conciliation Courts (AFCC, 2005, see http://www.afccnet.org/), and the American Academy of Adolescent and Child Psychiatry (AAACP, 2011).

A well-conducted evaluation might begin with an interview with each parent and each child. To further assess the relationships between parent and child, the evaluator will then usually set up a situation in which each parent can be observed interacting with each child (e.g., a parent and child might be asked to plan a vacation together). To supplement information gathered from interviews and direct observation, written records relevant to the custody decision are then reviewed. Relevant documents might include children's school records (e.g., report cards, attendance records, and disciplinary reports) and records of medical treatment for physical or mental health problems. Sometimes, there are also interviews with people who may have observed or interacted with the family over time: grandparents, aunts and uncles, nannies, teachers, and the family physician. Finally, the psychologist is likely to administer standardized psychological tests designed to assess the mental health of the parents and children. On average, surveys of child custody evaluators indicate that they spend about 45 hours on each evaluation (Ackerman & Pritzl, 2011). Occasionally, after going through the process of assessment, couples may decide to opt out of litigation and resolve the custody dispute themselves.

Psychological Tests and Their Problems

Most psychologists who conduct custody evaluations use general tests of psychological functioning when evaluating parents. The most commonly used instruments include: the Minnesota Multiphasic Personality Inventory second edition (MMPI-2), the Millon Multiaxial Personality Inventory second or third edition (MCMI-II/III), and the Rorschach inkblot test (Stahl, 2014). There is considerable question as to whether these general tests are applicable to custody decision making (Otto, Edens, & Barcus, 2000). The primary problem is that scores on these tests have little relevance for answering the most vexing child custody question: "What is the appropriate placement for the child?" An additional problem is that parents engaged in custody disputes may not respond honestly to these tests. For most types of forensic evaluations (e.g., competence, insanity), the most common form of inappropriate test taking strategy involves trying to appear more psychologically disturbed than one actually is. However, the opposite response style, simply called **faking good,** is more common in custody evaluations. This form of behavior involves trying to hide psychological impairments in order to receive a more favorable custody arrangement.

The child caught up in a custody dispute is also evaluated. For this purpose, an even wider array of general psychological tests has been used, which can be broken down into three categories: (1) **personality tests,** which measure whether the child suffers from a psychological disorder (e.g., Minnesota Multiphasic Personality Inventory-Adolescent Edition [MMPI-A] or the Millon Adolescent Clinical Inventory [MACI]); (2) **intelligence tests,** which measure overall intellectual functioning (e.g., Wechsler Intelligence Scale for Children [WISC]); and (3) **projective tests,** which measure the child's response to ambiguous stimuli (e.g., Rorschach inkblot test, family drawing, or kinetic family drawing). Surveys of child custody evaluators reveal that no one psychological test was used by an evaluator more than 80% of the time, but that the MMPI-A, IQ tests, and projective drawing tests were all given by over 50% of evaluators (Ackerman & Pritzl, 2011). The continued use of projective drawing tests is especially distressing because scholars have repeatedly cautioned against their use for the same reasons they have criticized use of the Rorschach inkblot test: a demonstrated lack of validity and reliability in forensic evaluations (Lilienfeld, Wood, & Garb, 2000) (see Scientific American Spotlight: Rorschach Test: Wasted Ink? for discussion of this controversy).

Some attempts have been made to create more focused forensic assessment instruments (FAIs) for determining the custody arrangement that will be in the best interest of a child (recall that FAIs are designed by psychologists to answer questions specific to a particular legal standard). The two most prominent are the **Bricklin Perceptual Scales (BPS)** and the **Ackerman-Schoendorf Scales for Parent Evaluation of Custody (ASPECT).** These child-custody-specific FAIs are used by about one in five evaluators (Bow, 2006). The BPS has the ambitious but ambiguous goal of evaluating the child's "gut-level, unconscious perceptions of parental

SCIENTIFIC AMERICAN SPOTLIGHT

Rorschach Test: Wasted Ink?
by Scott O. Lilienfeld, James M. Wood, and Howard N. Garb

> "It looks like two dinosaurs with huge heads and tiny bodies. They're moving away from each other but looking back. The black blob in the middle reminds me of a spaceship."

Once deemed an "x-ray of the mind," the Rorschach inkblot test remains the most famous—and infamous—projective psychological technique. An examiner hands 10 symmetrical inkblots one at a time in a set order to a viewer, who says what each blot resembles. Five blots contain color; five are black and gray. Respondents can rotate the images. The one above is a simulation and is an inverted version of an Andy Warhol rendering; the actual Rorschach blots cannot be published.

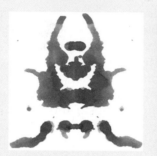

Responses to the inkblots purportedly reveal aspects of a person's personality and mental health. Advocates believe, for instance, that references to moving animals—such as the dinosaurs mentioned above—often indicate impulsiveness, whereas allusions to a blot's "blackness"—as in the spaceship—often indicate depression.

Swiss psychiatrist Hermann Rorschach probably got the idea of showing inkblots from a European parlor game. The test debuted in 1921 and reached high status by 1945. But a critical backlash began taking shape in the 1950s, as researchers found that psychologists often interpreted the same responses differently and that particular responses did not correlate well with specific mental illnesses or personality traits.

Today, the Comprehensive System, meant to remedy those weaknesses, is widely used to score and interpret Rorschach responses. But it has been criticized on similar grounds. Moreover, several recent findings indicate that the Comprehensive System incorrectly labels many normal respondents as pathological.

Human Figure Drawings: Misleading Signs

Psychologists have many projective drawing instruments at their disposal, but the Draw-a-Person Test is among the most popular—especially for assessing children and adolescents. A clinician asks the child to draw someone of the same sex and then someone of the opposite sex in any way that he or she wishes. (A variation involves asking the child to draw a person, house and tree.) Those who employ the test believe that the drawings reveal meaningful information about the child's personality or mental health.

In a sketch of a man, for example, small feet would supposedly indicate insecurity or instability—a small head, inadequacy. Large hands or teeth would be considered signs of aggression; short arms, a sign of shyness. And feminine features—such as long eyelashes or darkly colored lips—would allegedly suggest sex-role confusion.

Yet research consistently shows that such "signs" bear virtually no relation to personality or mental illness. Scientists have denounced these sign interpretations as "phrenology for the 20th century," recalling the 19th-century pseudoscience of inferring people's personalities from the pattern of bumps on their skulls.

Still, the sign approach remains widely used. Some psychologists even claim they can identify sexual abuse from certain key signs. For instance, alleged signs of abuse include a person older than the child, a partially unclothed body, a hand near the genitals, a hand hidden in a pocket, a large nose and a mustache. In reality, the connection between these signs and sexual abuse remains dubious, at best.

(A: Martin/Custom Medical Stock, B: Image Source/Alamy)

behavior" (Bricklin, 1984, p. 40). An additional measure developed by Bricklin—the **Perception-of-Relationships Test (PORT)**—attempts to measure how strongly the child seeks emotional closeness and positive interactions with each parent. Clearly, it is important to assess parenting ability and emotional attachment between parent and child when trying to decide custody arrangements. However, serious questions have been raised about the scientific validity and reliability of both the BPS and the PORT. Until additional data have been collected and analyzed, it is not clear how much confidence should be placed in the Bricklin measures (Otto & Martindale, 2007).

The other prominent set of specialized scales is the Ackerman-Schoendorf Scales for Parent Evaluation of Custody (ASPECT). It incorporates data from several established tests of both adults and children, including: (1) the MMPI-2, (2) the Rorschach inkblot test, (3) an intelligence test, (4) a projective story, and (5) a series of parent questionnaires. Ratings are based on information gathered through interviews, observations, answers on a questionnaire, and a battery of psychological tests. The evaluator combines the ratings to yield an overall index of each parent's effectiveness. Although the structured approach offered by the ASPECT may eventually improve the usefulness of custody recommendations, the validity and reliability of the ASPECT have not yet been convincingly demonstrated.

Several thoughtful reviews of these measures caution psychologists to view results with considerable skepticism (Emery, et al., 2005; Otto, et al., 2000). Despite the heavy criticism of these instruments for their lack of empirical validity, their use has more than doubled over the last 15 years (Ackerman & Pritzl, 2011).

Judges' Views of Experts

When a psychologist writes a child custody evaluation report for the judge, he or she must strive for scientific objectivity and try to remain neutral (APA, 2009; Otto, Buffington-Vollum, & Edens, 2003). Because of perceived bias, most judges prefer court-appointed or neutral experts over those hired by either side in the dispute. The goal of the expert should not be to provide ultimate issue testimony about the best custody arrangement, but to clearly and fully describe the character of the family relationships. This ideal is difficult to achieve. Many judges want psychologists to simply recommend the best custody arrangement. And, most evaluators are all too willing to offer such pronouncements—one study found that experts made recommendations in about 60% of cases (Ackerman & Pritzl, 2011). Moreover, it has been estimated that judges followed the experts' recommendations in about 60% to 90% of the cases (Otto & Martindale, 2007). Perhaps this is not surprising. Judges may realize they do not possess the psychological knowledge to make the custody decision. From their perspective, it may make sense to defer to psychologists.

In a national survey, child custody judges and attorneys were asked about the information provided by psychologists. Both groups reported that expert testimony was not one of the top factors that they relied upon in making their arguments or in reaching their decisions—a claim at odds with the finding that judges follow the recommendations made by those experts in the vast majority of cases (Bow & Quinnell, 2004). The judges and lawyers cited three main criticisms of expert psychological testimony: a lack of objectivity, a tendency to ignore legal criteria, and a lack of data to support conclusions.

CUSTODY MEDIATION AS AN ALTERNATIVE TO LITIGATION

In an effort to contain the damage caused by bitter, protracted court battles, many states have enacted **mandatory mediation laws.** These laws require couples seeking a divorce to first attempt to reach a settlement with the help of a mediator. Mediation has the added benefit of lowering court costs and it usually eliminates the need for a full psychological assessment. In many cases, mediation helps to deescalate family conflict and clear the way for a custody agreement.

A **mediator** is a neutral third party who brings the couple together in a nonadversarial setting. The goal of mediation is to get parents to rise above their differences and to focus on the needs of their children. The hope is that this private, less adversarial, less formal process will enable parents to work through differences. Mediators may be psychologists, social workers, lawyers, or specially trained laypersons. The aim is to construct a divorce settlement and custody arrangement that both parents can endorse. The mediator does not impose an agreement but tries to create an environment in which the parents can craft their own agreement. Compared with a courtroom proceeding, mediation is much less structured and formal. During mediation, any information that might be useful can be considered. Mediation sessions typically include a single mediator and the two parents. What transpires during mediation is confidential, and parents are free to generate a variety of creative custody options. A significant body of research suggests that mediation leads to far fewer cases reaching the courtroom and that mediation usually leads to custodial arrangements that are quite similar to those that would have been reached through litigation (Emery, et al., 2005; Kitzmann, Parra, & Jobe-Shields, 2012).

In a series of well-conducted studies on mediation, Robert Emery and his colleagues arranged to have divorcing couples randomly assigned to either mediation or litigation (Emery, Laumann-Billings, Waldron, Sbarra, & Dillon, 2001). Overall, the researchers found that mediation led to custody agreements more quickly and in fewer sessions; couples who went through mediation were more satisfied with the custody settlement; and mediation as compared to litigation often led to more contact with and a more positive relationship with the noncustodial parent. Yet, some research suggests that mothers are somewhat more satisfied with the outcomes of litigation as compared to mediation. One explanation of this finding, supported by other research, is that women are most likely to "win" child custody disputes in court (because of judges' preference for sole maternal custody). Consequently, mothers may believe that they could have reached a "better" custody arrangement through litigation. On the other hand, even though the outcomes between litigation and mediation are largely the same, men are more satisfied in mediation because they feel like they had more of a voice in the decision-making process (Emery et al., 2001; Emery, Matthews, & Kitzmann, 1994). It is important to note that, so far, there are limited data to support the claim that mediation leads to improved long-term emotional and psychological health in children (Kitzmann, Parra, & Jobe-Shields, 2012).

Sometimes, mediation should be avoided. In cases in which there has been spousal abuse, mediation may lead to harm by providing the abuser with continued access to his victim. Also, in cases in which the wife or the husband is not fully competent—one or the other is severely depressed, mentally ill, developmentally disabled, or under the influence of drugs—it is unlikely that the impaired parent will be able to effectively represent him- or herself during mediation.

Parent Coordination

Even after using the "non-adversarial" option of mediation, some parents continue to experience high conflict over custody disputes and arrangements. These high-conflict relationships tend to cause the most continuing psychological damage and lead to the worst post-divorce adjustment for children. During the past decade, researchers have attempted to develop and test interventions for the 8% to 15% of couples that continue to engage in extreme and intense hostility in the years during and following separation (Stahl & Martin, 2013). Although several names have been used to describe interventions with high conflict parents (e.g., special masters, co-parenting facilitators, etc.), the most common term is **parent coordination** (APA, 2012). Parent coordination interventions usually occur after mediation, settlement conferences, and custody evaluations have failed to achieve the desired results. In 2005, the Association of Family and Conciliation Courts created guidelines for practitioners involved in parent coordination proceedings (AFCC Task Force on Parenting Coordination, 2005). The guidelines were instrumental in the development of the American Psychological Association's guidelines in 2012.

APA characterizes the parent coordination process as

"... a non-adversarial dispute resolution process that is court-ordered or agreed upon by divorced or separated parents who have an ongoing pattern of high conflict and/or litigation about their children." (APA, 2012, p. 65)

The parent coordinator acts as an arbitrator of disagreements between the parties, and the goals of the parent coordination process include the following: (1) to help parents create and comply with court orders and parenting plans; (2) to make decisions concerning custody and visitation that are consistent with the developmental and psychological needs of the child; (3) to reduce the intense conflict between the parents; and (4) to reduce the relitigation of child custody issues. To date, limited research exists on the effectiveness of such programs, but the data that do exist suggest that these interventions may decrease hostility and aid the court in reaching a faster resolution of custody and visitation issues (APA, 2012).

▶ IN CONCLUSION

Although it is impossible to predict the future, the legal system is often required to try. With or without the help of psychologists and other social scientists, the legal system will continue to make predictions about which custody arrangement will promote the well-being of children for years to come. This consequential prediction ought to be based on the best information currently available. The research summarized above will not enable courts to make perfect decisions. However, the knowledge accumulated through research will continue to inform and improve those decisions. This does not, however, absolve psychologists of their ethical duty to offer expertise only in areas in which they possess scientifically based knowledge. Psychologists who play a role in the determination of a child custody arrangement after a divorce should be cautious and only provide information for which there is a solid scientific foundation. Otherwise, they run the risk of letting their personal values shape the lives of those they evaluate.

At present, psychologists do not possess the ability to ascertain which arrangement meets the vague definition of a child's "best interest." As a result, psychologists should refrain from answering this ultimate issue question, and the legal system should refrain from asking them to do so. Both fields need to work more collaboratively so that the legitimate expertise of psychologists is more effectively used by the legal system.

▶ CRITICAL THINKING QUESTIONS

1. What factors should be included in the BICS legal standard?

2. What are the strengths and limitations of the BICS?

3. What role (if any) should a parent's sexual orientation or lifestyle choices play in child custody decision making?

4. Should Parent Alienation Syndrome be admitted into court even though it has little scientific support?

5. Should mediation be required before parents can litigate custody disputes?

6. In what ways can mental health practitioners' best aid legal decision making in child custody cases?

▶ KEY TERMS

Ackerman-Schoendorf Scales for Parent Evaluation of Custody (ASPECT) (p. 247)
adjustment (p. 242)
approximation rule (p. 241)
best interests of the child standard (BICS) (p. 238)
Bricklin Perceptual Scales (BPS) (p. 247)

Equal Custody presumption (p. 242)
faking good (p. 247)
high conflict (p. 237)
intelligence tests (p. 247)
joint legal custody (p. 236)
legal custody (p. 236)
longitudinal research (p. 242)
mandatory mediation laws (p. 249)

mediator (p. 250)
multiple relationship (p. 245)
parent coordination (p. 251)
Perception-of-Relationships Test (PORT) (p. 248)
personality tests (p. 247)
physical custody (p. 236)
preferred custody arrangements (p. 241)

primary caretaker rule (p. 239)
projective tests (p. 247)
psychological family (p. 243)
resilience (p. 243)
sole custody (p. 236)
tender years doctrine (p. 238)
Uniform Marriage and Divorce Act (UMDA) of 1976 (p. 239)

13 Juries and Judges as Decision-Makers

▶ The Process of Jury Decision-Making
▶ The Effects of Biasing Information
▶ The Group Dynamics of Jury Deliberations
▶ Jury Nullification
▶ Jury Reform
▶ Judges Compared to Juries

Late one evening, Trayvon Martin, a 17-year-old African-American high school student, was walking back to the house where he was staying. He was returning from a convenience store after buying a bag of Skittles and a bottle of iced tea. The house where he was staying was in a gated community where George Zimmerman—a 28-year-old White and Hispanic American—served as the volunteer neighborhood-watch coordinator. Zimmerman was sitting in his car when he noticed Martin walking inside the gated community. Zimmerman judged Martin to be suspicious and called the Sanford Police Department. He told the 911 operator that, "This guy looks like he's up to no good, or he's on drugs or something." While still on the phone with the police, Zimmerman got out of his car and began to follow Martin. During the recorded call, Zimmerman expressed his frustration, saying that, "these f-ing punks always get away." At one point in the call, the police dispatcher asked, "Are you following him?" Zimmerman responded, "Yeah," and the dispatcher replied, "Okay; we don't need you to do that." Minutes later, Zimmerman and Martin got into a fight. Screams for help were recorded on 911 calls from neighbors who reported the altercation. During the fight, Zimmerman pulled out a gun he was carrying and shot Martin (who was unarmed) through the heart.

During the summer of 2013, George Zimmerman went on trial for killing Trayvon Martin. The trial was streamed live on television and watched by millions. Zimmerman had told police that he killed the teenager in self-defense, and self-defense was the argument his lawyers made at trial. Prosecutors argued that Zimmerman had profiled and stalked Martin, and that Zimmerman had been emboldened by his possession of a concealed handgun. On July 13, 2013, Zimmerman was found "not guilty" of both second-degree murder and manslaughter by a jury of 6 women (6-person juries are permitted in Florida for all criminal trials except those for which the death penalty is an option). The jury had deliberated for about 16 hours and, according to interviews with jurors, their initial vote was three for "not guilty," two for manslaughter, and one for second-degree murder.

Demonstrators upset with the verdict protested in several cities across the United States. Television and internet pundits spent days dissecting the trial, and they offered many explanations for the puzzling verdict:

- The jury did not include any African Americans. Five of the women were white; one was Hispanic.
- Under Florida's permissive self-defense law, lethal force is not illegal. The instructions to jury stated that: "If George Zimmerman was not engaged in an unlawful

Trayvon Martin (*EPA EUROPEAN PRESSPHOTO AGENCY B.V./ALAMY*)

George Zimmerman (*POOL/GETTY IMAGES*)

activity and was attacked in any place where he had a right to be, he had no duty to retreat and had the right to stand his ground and meet force with force, including deadly force if he reasonably believed that it was necessary to do so to prevent death or great bodily harm to himself or another or to prevent the commission of a forcible felony."

- The definition of manslaughter (which the jury asked the judge to clarify during deliberations) was too complex, and the level of certainty required was too high. The jury instructions stated: "George Zimmerman cannot be guilty of manslaughter by committing a merely negligent act or if the killing was either justifiable or excusable homicide."

- To convict Zimmerman of second-degree murder, the jury would need to reach the conclusion that "there was an unlawful killing of Trayvon Martin by an act imminently dangerous to another and demonstrating a depraved mind without regard for human life" and, "done from ill will, hatred, spite or an evil intent."

- The judge did not allow two "voice analysis" experts to testify in court. Both were willing to testify that the voice crying for help was Trayvon Martin's voice. The judge did not allow the lawyers to use the term "racial profiling" (although she did permit them to use the term "profiling").

- The prosecution didn't really want or expect a "guilty" verdict. They only wanted to placate protesters who were demanding that Zimmerman be put on trial. The trial was used to take the heat off the prosecutor's office and redirect public anger at the jury.

The Zimmerman trial raises several important issues about the role of juries in the justice system. Does the size of the jury matter? Would the verdict have been different if Florida used 12-person juries? Does the racial composition of juries matter? Would a jury with one or more African Americans have interpreted the evidence differently? Would the outcome of the trial have been different if the judge had allowed testimony from the voice-analysis experts? Was the language of the jury instructions too convoluted to be clearly understood by jurors? Are most jurors simply too stupid or bigoted to get it right?

Although the Zimmerman verdict seemed wrong to most Americans as a matter of justice, it may have been reasonable as a matter of law. As one of the jurors said after the trial, "We wanted to find him guilty of something, but couldn't under the law."

This chapter explores how jurors and judges use the information presented at trial to make the consequential decisions assigned to them by the legal system. Those decisions change lives: Large sums of money might be paid, a defendant might be sent to prison, or released from prison, or even sentenced to death. ◄

 ## THE PROCESS OF JURY DECISION-MAKING

It is useful to think of a trial as a decision-making device. A trial is an elaborate, highly structured method of providing a jury (or a judge) with the information necessary to make a considered, impartial decision.

One useful way of describing the decision-making processes of jurors is to use **mathematical models.** In many such models, jurors are assumed to use a sort of mental meter that moves toward either a "guilty" or "not guilty" verdict based on the weight of the evidence. Pieces of evidence presented at trial are represented as numerical weights that shift the mental meter in one direction or the other. Over the course of the trial, jurors continually update their judgments, although a particular piece of evidence—for example, a persuasive eyewitness—may be so heavily weighted that the meter becomes "frozen" and further evidence does little to shift the juror's overall judgment (Hastie, 1993; Vidmar & Hans, 2007).

A prominent alternative to mathematical models is the **story model** of juror decision-making (Pennington & Hastie, 1993). The story model proposes that jurors create stories to make sense of evidence presented at trial. A story is defined as a causal chain of events. That is, initiating events cause characters to have psychological responses and to form goals that motivate actions, and then these actions lead to consequences. For example, in a case used in some studies of the story model, a man named Johnson stabs and kills a man named Caldwell and is put on trial for first-degree murder. The undisputed events are that one afternoon, the two men had an argument in a bar and Caldwell threatened Johnson with a razor blade. Johnson left the bar but returned late in the evening. He and Caldwell got into a fight outside the bar. Johnson pulled a knife and stabbed Caldwell, who died from the wound. Jurors must decide whether Johnson acted in self-defense or whether it was premeditated murder. The researchers found that jurors who reached a self-defense verdict inferred that Johnson was afraid and that he pulled his knife to prevent Caldwell from killing him. Jurors reaching a first-degree murder verdict inferred that Johnson felt angry and humiliated by the afternoon quarrel, that he decided to go home to get his knife, and that he returned to the bar with the intention of killing Caldwell. In this case, and in many real cases, the inferences necessary to complete the story—for example, whether Johnson was motivated by anger or fear—are informed by a juror's past experience and preexisting knowledge of similar events.

According to the story model, jurors construct their stories while hearing the evidence at trial. Next, they learn about possible verdicts (usually at the end of the trial when the judge reads instructions to jurors), and finally, they select the verdict that best fits with the story they have constructed to make sense of the evidence. The story model has proven to be a useful way of describing juror decision processes in several types of trials, including murder, rape, and sexual harassment (Huntley & Costanzo, 2003; Olsen-Fulero & Fulero, 1997; Pennington & Hastie, 1993). However, we do not yet know how the differing stories of individual jurors become reconciled during jury deliberation.

The Impact of Evidence

A substantial body of research indicates that the strength of the relevant evidence is the best predictor of a jury verdict (Taylor & Hosch, 2004). For example, a large-scale analysis of juries in four states found that various measures of the "weight" and "direction" of evidence (as rated by judges, jurors, and attorneys) were the strongest predictors of verdicts (Eisenberg et al., 2005; Hannaford-Agor & Hans, 2003). In one of the most comprehensive studies to date, data was collected from 179 criminal jury trials (Devine, et al., 2009). Jurors, judges, and attorneys rated characteristics of the trials they participated in, and those characteristics were then correlated with trial outcomes. One major finding was that the strength of the evidence relevant to the charge (e.g., murder, rape, robbery) was the strongest predictor of whether the defendant was found "guilty" or "not guilty." Of course, this is how it should be—we want verdicts to be based on the evidence presented at trial.

The reassuring finding that verdict decisions are primarily based on relevant evidence does not mean that *only* evidence matters. In the study just described, some characteristics other than evidence strength—for example, severity of the charge against the defendant, negative pretrial publicity, and trial complexity—were modestly correlated with verdicts. Interestingly, the influence these other variables had on verdicts followed a pattern predicted by what has been called the **liberation hypothesis** (Kalven & Zeisel, 1966). This hypothesis proposes that, in most trials, jury verdicts are usually determined by the strength of the evidence because evidence for conviction or acquittal is compelling. However, in cases where the evidence is ambiguous or close, jurors will be "liberated" from the constraints of evidence. That is, lack of clear evidence favoring the defense or prosecution forces jurors to base their decisions on factors such as prior beliefs, past experience, or even prejudice. We now turn our attention to these and other nonevidentiary factors that sometimes sway jury decisions.

THE EFFECTS OF BIASING INFORMATION

The legal system expects a lot from jurors: to set aside prejudices and preconceptions, to make sense of the copious and often contradictory evidence presented at trial, and to understand how the law applies to the specific case they are hearing. Although jurors may try their best to live up to these expectations, sometimes bias slips into the decision-making process.

Defendant Characteristics

The wealth, social status, and gender of defendants do not appear to influence verdicts in any simple or straightforward way (Vidmar & Hans, 2007). The physical attractiveness of a defendant does not seem to matter much either. Although some evidence suggests that jurors treat good-looking defendants more leniently and treat ugly defendants more harshly, the effect is weak (Mazzella & Feingold, 1994). However, if a very attractive defendant uses his or her attractiveness to commit a crime—for example, if a handsome young man seduces rich, older women to steal their fortunes—jurors do take attractiveness into account and hand down more severe sentences. Characteristics that seem relevant to a defendant's propensity for criminal behavior, like gang membership, also raise the probability of conviction (Eisen, et al., 2013). As discussed more fully in Chapter 6, the defendant's race appears to interact with juror race in racially charged trials (Sommers & Ellsworth, 2009), and there is a small but reliable tendency for people to treat defendants of their own race more leniently (Mitchell, Haw, Pfeifer, & Meissner, 2005).

Jurors also appear to consider the defendant's moral character by comparing his or her character to that of the victim. If the moral character of the victim is significantly superior to that of the defendant, jurors tend to judge the defendant more harshly (Devine, Clayton, Dunford, Seying, & Pryce, 2001). For example, if a drug addict assaults and robs another drug addict outside a house where drugs are sold, he is likely to be treated less harshly than if he assaults and robs a physician outside her home. Interestingly, jurors also seem to evaluate how much the defendant has already suffered for his crimes. If the defendant is badly injured during the commission of a crime, jurors are more lenient (Ellsworth & Mauro, 1998).

In civil trials, individuals who are sued tend to be ordered to pay lower damage awards than corporations that are sued for similar bad acts. Many have attributed this finding to the fact that corporations have more money—"deeper pockets," as it is commonly expressed. But researchers have found that the more important reason is that corporations are expected to behave more responsibly than individuals (Hans, 2000; MacCoun, 1993). An individual may have a lapse in judgment and harm others. But the groups of individuals who make decisions for corporations are expected to be well trained and to have checks and balances in place to guard against bad group judgment. Consequently, jurors hold them more accountable for the consequences of their decisions.

Inadmissible Evidence

Jurors are told to ignore all types of **inadmissible evidence** (e.g., information that might be prejudicial). Inadmissible information may come from witnesses or attorneys. When one attorney calls out "objection" in response to a question or statement made by the opposing counsel or a witness, the judge must either **sustain** or **overrule** the objection. If the judge sustains the objection, he or she will tell the jury to "disregard" the inadmissible statement (e.g., that a criminal defendant has a prior criminal record or that a civil defendant has a large insurance policy). In other words, jurors are supposed to forget they ever heard it and not let it influence them. Most attorneys are skeptical about whether jurors can disregard inadmissible statements made during trial. As many attorneys say, "You can't unring a bell."

Research suggests that attorneys' intuition is usually right—you cannot force jurors to forget what they just heard. Indeed, the judge's admonition may sometimes have the opposite of its intended effect—telling jurors to disregard a statement may actually cause jurors to give that statement extra weight (Lieberman & Arndt, 2000; Pickel, Karam, & Warner, 2009). But why? One explanation is based on what have been called **ironic processes.** When we make an effort not to think about something, that thing often dominates our thoughts, especially when we are under stress and much of our mental capacity is already in use (Wegner, 2004). Anyone who has suffered from obsessive thoughts has experienced this effect. Another explanation is suggested by what is known as **reactance theory.** According to this theory, people are motivated to maintain their freedom (Brehm & Brehm, 1981). Jurors may perceive the judge's admonition as a threat to their freedom to make a decision based on all the available evidence. Jurors may react to that threat by giving the inadmissible evidence greater weight than they would have otherwise. Third (as discussed in Chapter 6), jurors tend to rely on broad commonsense notions of justice. Even though a piece of information is legally inadmissible, if jurors believe that information will help them to reach the right decision, they are likely to use it.

In a study of jurors' ability to disregard inadmissible testimony, mock jurors decided a case in which a man who had been recently fired from his job was accused of stealing $5,000 from his former boss (Pickel, 1995). When questioned by the prosecution, one of the defendant's former coworkers made a hearsay statement: He reported that someone had told him that the defendant said his boss would "be sorry" and that he "could walk in and get the cash without being seen." In another condition, when questioned by the prosecution, the coworker made a statement about the defendant's prior conviction ("he had to serve a few days in jail for a perjury conviction"). The defense attorney objected to these statements, and in response to that objection, the judge either ruled the evidence admissible, ruled the evidence inadmissible, or ruled it inadmissible and explained the legal basis for the ruling. Results showed that the judge's instruction to disregard the inadmissible evidence was effective for hearsay evidence but backfired for prior-conviction evidence. In this and other studies, whether jurors make use of inadmissible evidence seems to depend not on legal considerations, but on whether jurors believe it is fair to consider the evidence. As Pickel notes, if jurors conclude,

> based on their sense of what is just, that it would be unfair to use evidence to determine guilt, then they will disregard the evidence. Alternatively, if they decide that it is not necessarily unfair to consider the evidence, then they probably will be unwilling to ignore it completely, thus producing the backfire effect (p. 422).

The available research clearly indicates that jurors do not simply purge inadmissible evidence from their memories. Indeed, based on a meta-analysis of 48 studies, researchers reached the conclusion that inadmissible evidence has a reliable effect on verdicts. Further, a judge's admonition to ignore the information often accentuates that information and amplifies its impact on jurors (Steblay, Hosch, Culhane, & McWethy, 2006). Looking across studies, it is clear that jurors are reluctant to disregard inadmissible evidence if they consider it useful for reaching a verdict, and judge's instructions do not neutralize the impact of stricken evidence. Jurors are especially likely to make use of such evidence if the judge gives no reason for ignoring the evidence or rejects the evidence due to an unexplained technicality. However, providing a reasonable explanation for ignoring the evidence (e.g., it is described as unreliable or irrelevant to the case), tends to lessen its impact (Daftary-Kapur, Dumas, & Penrod, 2010).

A related problem concerns the use of **impeachment evidence**—evidence meant to damage the credibility of a witness's statements. Here, a defendant may sometimes be asked about prior dishonest conduct for the purpose of establishing the honesty of his or her current testimony. But, instead of using this information in the legally specified manner, research indicates that jurors use it to draw broader conclusions. They are likely to see past dishonest behavior as symptomatic of an enduring predisposition toward dishonest behavior. Here, as in other areas, jurors use a broader conception of justice. In life outside the courtroom, knowledge of a person's past behavior is a key determinant of how we interpret that person's current behavior. It is unrealistic to expect jurors to ignore past convictions, especially if these convictions were for crimes similar to the one being considered at trial (Eisenberg & Hans, 2009; Finkel, 2002).

Complex Evidence

Sometimes jurors are told not to consider evidence, and other times they are simply unable to fully understand the evidence. Jurors are often exposed to complex scientific and technical evidence, and that evidence is usually presented via expert testimony. **Expert witnesses** offer testimony based on specialized knowledge, training, or experience (see Chapter 1). For example, experts may testify about the meaning of DNA evidence based on the chemical analysis of blood, semen, skin, or saliva. There may be fingerprint analysis or ballistics tests, or testimony about sloppy medical procedures, faulty building construction, or the causes of disease. Although most jurors have limited knowledge in these specialized areas, they must strive to understand expert testimony. One study of the impact of complex medical testimony varied both the complexity of the expert testimony and the credentials of the prosecution expert. The case involved a worker who alleged that he had developed liver cancer and an immune system disorder because of exposure to polychlorinated biphenyls in his workplace (Cooper, Bennett, & Sukel, 1996). When the expert (a professor of biochemistry) offered complex testimony full of specialized jargon, he was persuasive only if his credentials were very strong—that is, when his degrees were from prestigious universities, when he taught at a prestigious university, and when he had published widely. When the testimony was less complex, the strength of the expert's credentials was not important. The jurors were able to

(KAREN MOSKOWITZ/GETTY IMAGES)

make sense of the testimony and draw conclusions based on the content of the testimony. These findings suggest that if the expert's message is difficult to comprehend, jurors may weight the testimony based on more peripheral cues like the apparent credibility of the expert.

More generally, research on the impact of expert testimony has found that if an expert is effectively cross-examined, or if an expert's testimony is contradicted by the testimony of another expert, the impact of the testimony is weakened (Costanzo, Krauss, & Pezdek, 2007). In addition, testimony that is clear, specific to the issues in the case, and somewhat repetitive appears to be most persuasive (Kovera, Gresham, Borgida, Gray, & Regan, 1997). However, expert testimony is not accepted uncritically by jurors and does not appear to have an overpowering impact on verdicts. Indeed, in some cases, jurors regard it with special skepticism because they may perceive experts as "hired guns" (Diamond, 2006).

 ## THE GROUP DYNAMICS OF JURY DELIBERATIONS

Juries are unusual groups regulated by unusual rules. First, unlike most decision-making groups, juries are comprised of people who may have little in common and no established relationships. It is likely that the people who serve on a particular

The Effects of Technology in the Courtroom

Like many environments, courtrooms sometimes have difficulty adapting to new technologies. Advances in audiovisual presentation technologies now allow defenders or prosecutors to create computer animations or video simulations of how a litigated event (e.g., a murder, a building collapse, a burglary) *might* have occurred. We don't yet know if such video re-enactments lend more credibility to a particular account of a crime in the eyes of jurors. However, research suggests that even something as basic as a PowerPoint presentation can have an impact on jurors' assessment of evidence. In two studies based on a real case in which a railroad company was sued by African-American employees for racial discrimination, researchers looked at the use of PowerPoint in opening statements. The side that used PowerPoint to illustrate key arguments was rated as being more persuasive and received better verdict outcomes (Park & Feigenson, 2013).

Increasingly, brain-scan images and videos produced using MRIs and fMRIs (see Chapter 3) are being used in court to show brain damage or abnormalities that might render a defendant less culpable for his crimes. In a study of whether a murderer should be sentenced to life in prison or the death penalty, researchers found that the use of neuroimages indicating brain abnormalities made jurors less likely to impose the death penalty (Greene & Cahill, 2012). An overarching concern of courts is that unequal access to sometimes expensive technologies, such as computer animation or brain imaging, may give the side with more money an unfair advantage in court.

A final technology-related concern of the courts is continuous access to the Internet via cellphones and other portable devices. Jurors are instructed to base their verdicts only on evidence presented at trial. But, nearly every juror now has the capacity to research trial-related issues using the Internet. Jurors also have the capacity to communicate with fellow jurors, friends, and relatives about the trial. Although judges can instruct jurors not to use their mobile devices in ways that might undermine the trial process, it is unclear whether such cautions are effective.

jury have never met before the trial. And, after the verdict, they may never see each other again. Second, during the trial, jurors are relatively passive spectators of the courtroom proceedings. They are usually not allowed to question lawyers or witnesses, and they are not permitted to discuss the impending decision with friends or family. Finally, jurors are expected to absorb information, store it up for later use in the deliberation room, and suspend final judgment until after all the evidence has been presented. The hope is that jurors will rely on the evidence, be guided by the law, and that any biases or misunderstandings will be counterbalanced or corrected during group deliberation.

Most of the research summarized in this chapter concerns jurors rather than juries, individuals rather than groups. It makes sense to study jurors because it is individual jurors who must listen to and make sense of the evidence. But the crucial outcome—the verdict—is decided by the jury as a group. How does the group affect the decision-making process?

The most direct way of understanding the dynamics of juries would be to observe a large number of actual juries to see if there are recurring patterns in how groups of jurors pool their collective wisdom to arrive at a final verdict. Unfortunately for researchers, the law (with very few exceptions) precludes this direct approach. It was first tried nearly 60 years ago. As part of the groundbreaking University of Chicago Jury Project of the 1950s, the deliberations of five juries in civil cases in Wichita, Kansas, were tape-recorded. Although presiding judges and lawyers had approved these recordings, jurors were not told that they were being audiotaped. When the media became aware of these tape recordings, a national scandal ensued. Newspaper editorials denounced this violation of the privacy rights of juries, and a U.S. Senate subcommittee held hearings about the scandal. There was even an attempt to portray the research as part of a subversive communist plot. In their defense, the researchers

(Harry Kalven, Hans Zeisel, Rita James Simon, Edward Levi, and Fred Strodtbeck) argued that attempts to improve the jury system should be based on full and accurate data about how juries actually make decisions. Apparently, this argument did little to reassure policymakers. The tape recordings were never analyzed, and the controversy led to the enactment of statutes banning the observation or recording of jury deliberations (Kalven & Zeisel, 1966). Because of this ban, nearly all of the research on jury deliberations comes out of observations of mock juries or from real jurors who are interviewed after their jury service has been completed.

Strong Jurors and the Power of the Majority

Lawyers attempt to predict the group dynamics of a jury during *voir dire*. They talk about some potential jurors as **strong jurors** or key jurors or jury leaders: jurors who seem likely to have a disproportionate influence on the deliberation process. Potential jurors judged to be "strong" are often well educated, articulate, and have high occupational status (relative to other potential jurors). A powerful fictional portrayal of a strong juror can be found in the classic film *Twelve Angry Men*. In that film, a lone juror holds steady in his belief that a defendant should be acquitted. Through logic and heroic perseverance in the face of group pressure, he persuades the other 11 jurors to change their mistaken guilty votes. Unfortunately, research indicates that such jurors are quite rare. In reality, majorities tend to prevail. If a jury begins deliberations with an 8-to-4 majority, there is a strong probability that the majority will persuade or pressure members of the minority to change their votes. In Kalven and Zeisel's classic study, 215 juries began with a clear majority. Of those 215 juries, 209 reached the verdict favored by the initial majority. Their conclusion was that "the deliberation process might well be likened to what the developer does for exposed film; it brings out the picture, but the outcome is predetermined" (p. 488). In addition, majorities can bring strong social pressure to bear on jurors holding the minority opinion, and majorities tend to have more persuasive arguments at their disposal.

In an official sense, the foreperson is the leader of the jury. Although some research suggests the foreperson's vote is more strongly predictive of outcome than the votes of other jury members (Devine et al., 2007), the juror selected as foreperson does not necessarily exert disproportionate influence on the verdict decision. In fact, the foreperson sometimes contributes less to the discussion of the evidence because he or she is preoccupied with procedural issues such as tabulating votes or making sure that all jurors have an opportunity to express their views. The role may be more that of moderator and organizer than leader and controller (Kerr, Niedermeier, & Kaplan, 1999). Any special influence the foreperson does possess is likely to stem from the ability to determine the order in which other jurors speak and the amount of time each juror is allowed to speak. Perhaps because the role of foreperson is temporary and the main job of juries is to reach a verdict, the selection of a foreperson is likely to be quick and informal—80% of actual juries appear to select a foreperson within 5 minutes of beginning deliberation (Diamond, 2006). Research reveals several factors that increase the odds of being chosen as foreperson: speaking first, having task-relevant expertise (e.g., a nurse may be more likely to become foreperson in a medical malpractice case), being an extrovert, having served as a juror on a prior case, having high job status, sitting at the head of the table, and asking the question, "should we elect a foreperson?" (Diamond, 2007).

Although majorities usually prevail, what has been called the **leniency bias** is also at work in criminal trials. That is, in evenly split juries, or almost evenly split juries, where roughly half the jurors favor "guilty" on the initial vote and the other half favor "not guilty," it is much more likely that the final verdict will be "not guilty" (Kerr & MacCoun, 2012; MacCoun & Kerr, 1988). Under such conditions, the process of deliberation and the high standard of reasonable doubt seem to favor acquittal. In the deliberation room, jurors who favor acquittal need only to create reasonable doubt, while jurors favoring conviction must find a way to remove nearly all doubt. Looking across several studies, Dennis Devine and his colleagues came to the following conclusion about 12-person juries in criminal cases:

> **If 7 or fewer jurors favor conviction at the beginning of deliberation, the jury will probably acquit, and if 10 or more jurors believe the defendant is guilty, the jury will probably convict. With 8 or 9 jurors initially favoring conviction, the final verdict is basically a toss-up** (Devine, et al., 2001, p. 722).

Stages in the Deliberation Process

The dynamics of juries differ depending on the characteristics of the case being decided and the people who make up the jury. But, based on observations of mock juries and postverdict interviews with actual jurors, many juries appear to move through a three-stage process (Stasser, 1992). During the first phase—**orientation**—juries elect a foreperson, discuss procedures, and raise general issues. At the outset of deliberation, jurors tend to be confused about how to proceed. Some juries take a vote immediately to get a sense of where people stand, some juries postpone voting and begin by discussing the issues to be decided, and other juries begin by discussing each witness who testified at trial. Observations of the deliberation process suggest that about 30% of juries take a vote shortly after they begin deliberations and then orient their subsequent discussions around the verdict options. This **verdict-driven style** of structuring the deliberation process tends to encourage jurors to sort the evidence into two categories: supporting conviction or supporting acquittal. Other juries adopt an **evidence-driven style,** in which the first vote is postponed until after jurors have had a careful, systematic discussion of the evidence (Levett, Danielsen, Kovera, & Cutler, 2005).

Postponing a vote until after the evidence is discussed appears to produce richer, more probing discussions. Once a vote has been taken, there is a tendency for jurors to focus on defending their position. For example, in a questionnaire study of jurors from 179 juries, taking an early first vote on verdict was negatively correlated with all measures of evidence review (Devine, Buddenbaum, Houp, Stolle, & Studebaker, 2007). That is, juries that focused on verdicts early were significantly less likely to spend time reviewing and discussing evidence in the case. Thus, early voting on verdict appears to produce a deliberation process clearly contrary to the legal ideal of careful, thorough group analysis of the evidence presented at trial.

During the second phase—**open conflict**—differences in opinion among members of the jury become apparent and coalitions may form between members of the group. Often, the tone of the discussion becomes contentious, with each faction challenging how others interpret the evidence. Some jurors may even attack the character or integrity of jurors who disagree with them. The process of reaching a verdict through group deliberation is essentially a process of persuasion. Either all jurors (if the verdict must be unanimous) or a majority of jurors (if only a majority is required) must be persuaded to join with others. Sometimes jurors are swayed through a process of **informational influence:** They change their opinions because other jurors make compelling arguments. At other times, jurors do not really change their private views, but they do change their votes in response to **normative influence.** That is, they give in to group pressure (Mason, Conrey, & Smith, 2007). When a strong majority is trying to persuade one or two "holdouts" to reach a unanimous verdict, group pressure can be intense (Costanzo & Costanzo, 1994). Research on civil trials suggests a difference in the type of influence used during culpability and penalty decisions. Mock juries asked to make a more fact-based decision—whether or not a defendant should be held liable—tended to rely on informational influence in the form of factual arguments. In contrast, mock juries asked to make a more subjective, value-laden decision (the amount of punitive damages) tended to rely on normative influence (Hans, 1992). Morality-based decisions—such as whether to sentence a defendant to life in prison or the death penalty—must rely on appeals to basic fairness and group values, whereas fact-based decisions can follow from logical analysis of evidence (Costanzo & Costanzo, 1992).

Deliberations enter the third and final phase—**reconciliation**—when jurors reach a common understanding and agreement, or when one faction capitulates. During this final phase, attempts may be made to soothe hurt feelings and make everyone feel satisfied with the verdict. Of course, hung juries never make it to the reconciliation phase.

Just as in other groups, a few people tend to dominate discussions during jury deliberations. In 12-person juries, the three people who are most vocal use up about 50% of the deliberation time and the three least vocal people contribute very little. Roughly 70% to 75% of the deliberation time is devoted to discussions of evidence, with about 20% of the time devoted to the law and the judge's instructions (Ellsworth, 1989). Although some attorneys believe that jurors are preoccupied with irrelevant and superficial characteristics of the attorneys or witnesses (e.g., clothes, hairstyle, or speaking style), research suggests that juries spend very little time on irrelevant or trivial details. Jurors appear to take their job very seriously, and they make a sincere effort to follow the rules, as they understand them. Fortunately, group deliberation does create a fuller, more accurate view of the evidence. But, unfortunately, it does not appear to improve understanding of the law (Vidmar & Hans, 2007). This is probably because the law is not entirely clear nor communicated clearly in the judge's instructions.

For a limited time, a team of researchers was permitted to observe the discussions and deliberations of 50 actual civil juries in Arizona (Diamond, Vidmar, Rose, Ellis, & Murphy, 2003). This groundbreaking study is described later in this chapter. However, at this point, it is worth noting the Arizona researchers found it useful to compare jury discussions to another familiar type of group: "Jury discussions are, in effect, committee meetings similar to committee meetings that occur in a wide range of non-trial venues" (p. 47). Like long committee meetings, jury deliberations can be focused and highly structured at times, but meandering and nonlinear at other times. Topics may be introduced without being pursued; brief side conversations may emerge between two or more people. Some issues are raised and then dropped, only to be raised again later. Like all other human decision-making groups, juries are not paragons of efficiency.

One other finding of the Arizona study is worth noting: Juries tend to make a sincere effort to consider the views of every member of the group. Reassuringly, researchers found that "there is a strong overlay of equality displayed in juror interactions, regardless of the socioeconomic status of the members" (Diamond, Vidmar, Rose, Ellis, & Murphy, 2002, p. 49).

Size of the Jury

One of the main determinants of group dynamics is group size. For centuries, English law dictated a 12-person jury. It is not entirely clear why lawmakers settled on 12 people per jury instead of 10 or 15 people, or some other number. Some say that it is due to the influence of Christianity (Christ had 12 apostles); some say it is simply another example of the English affinity for the number 12 (12 inches to a foot, 12 pence to a schilling, 12 of anything equals a dozen). At any rate, the American colonies inherited the 12-person jury. And 12 remained the standard jury size until the mid-1900s. Then, in *Williams v. Florida* (1970), the Supreme Court reviewed the case of a man who had been convicted of armed robbery by a 6-person jury. The Court decided that it was constitutionally permissible to reduce the size of juries to 6 in noncapital cases (any case where there is no possibility of the death penalty). In *Ballew v. Georgia* (1978), the Court clarified the size requirement, ruling that 5-person juries are too small and 6-person juries were the constitutional minimum.

In permitting these radical departures from past practice, the Court appeared to rely on social-scientific evidence. With respect to jury size, the Court cited six "research findings" indicating that there was "no discernible difference" between the verdicts reached by 6-person and 12-person juries. But the Court got the science wrong. In 1977, Michael Saks reviewed the existing research on jury size. He noted that most of the six "experiments" the Court referenced did not qualify as systematic research studies at all: Some were casual observations, one was an account of a case that used a 6-person jury, and one was a description of how smaller juries might save money. The one true experiment cited by the justices was misinterpreted. The justices reached a conclusion opposite from the conclusion reached by researchers.

Based on his own extensive research and the research of other social scientists, Saks reached the conclusion that, compared to smaller juries, large juries deliberate longer, recall evidence more accurately, generate more arguments, agree more on their ratings of jury performance, are more representative of the community, and produce more consistent verdicts (Saks, 1997). Larger juries are more representative in a few ways. There is broader representation of demographic groups (e.g., by gender, race, and ethnicity), there are more people in opinion minorities, and there is a greater range of opinion and expertise (Roper, 1980). Jury size seems to have more influence on process than on outcomes. On average, the verdicts of 6- and 12-person juries do not differ significantly, but 6-person juries are less predictable. Put differently, if 100 juries of 6 and 100 juries of 12 all decide the same case, there will be a more even split on verdict among the 6-person juries. Also, the verdicts of larger juries are more likely to match the opinions of the larger community (Saks, 1996). This is important because juries are intended to represent the conscience of the community.

Decision Rules (Unanimous or Majority Rule)

A second crucial requirement of the jury system—the decision rule requiring a unanimous verdict—was established during the fourteenth century. The American colonies inherited both 12-person juries and unanimous verdicts. But, during the same time that the Court was making changes in jury size, it began to allow for nonunanimous verdicts. In 1972, the Supreme Court (*Apodaca, Cooper, & Madden v. Oregon*, 1972; *Johnson v. Louisiana*, 1972) ruled that nonunanimous decisions (with splits as large as 9 to 3) were constitutional. The 1979 decision in *Burch v. Louisiana* held that if a 6-person jury is used, verdicts must be unanimous. Only 26 states now require unanimity in misdemeanor verdicts, although 44 states require it in criminal felony trials; unanimity is always required in capital murder trials.

Michael Saks also investigated decision rules and found that juries required to reach unanimity deliberated longer than majority-rule juries and were also more likely to hang (Saks & Marti, 1997). Perhaps fewer hung juries and quicker decisions are good news, but there was also a fundamental problem in majority-rule juries: Their deliberations tended to come to a halt as soon as the requisite majority was reached (e.g., 9 out of 12). Further, Saks found that the requirement of unanimity empowers the minority to "effectively alter the course set by the majority" (p. 78).

A later study examined the effects of three decision rules on 69 mock juries (Hastie, Penrod, & Pennington, 1998). After watching a realistic 2.5-hour videotape of a murder trial, the juries were told to deliberate until they reached a unanimous verdict, or until they reached a verdict by either a 10-to-2 or an 8-to-4 majority. The majority-rule juries were dramatically different in process from the unanimous verdict juries. They took votes earlier and spent significantly more time voting, which meant that they spent less time discussing the evidence. These juries were more likely to exert direct (normative) pressure on others to change their votes and, once the requisite number of votes was reached (either 10 or 8), further discussion shut down. Because of this vote-oriented, quicker, more socially intimidating atmosphere, members of majority-rule juries were left feeling less informed, less certain about their verdicts, and with fewer positive feelings about their fellow jurors. Also, jurors holding the minority opinion participated more when unanimity was required, and they were perceived as more influential by other jurors. The evidence seems to indicate that nonunanimous juries do save time, but at the cost of less thorough evaluation of the evidence. Since thorough evaluation of evidence is the primary function of the jury, this is a critical problem. Research findings validate the conclusions of the Supreme Court's minority opinion in *Johnson:*

> **The collective effort to piece together the puzzle . . . is cut short as soon as the requisite majority is reached . . . polite and academic conversation is no substitute for the earnest and robust argument necessary to reach unanimity.**

Many jurists and politicians have argued for nonunanimous juries because of one particular perceived benefit: a reduction in the number of "**hung juries**"—those that cannot reach a unanimous verdict. It is true that unanimous juries "hang" about twice as often as majority-rule juries do. However, as some scholars have noted, hung juries have "traditionally been taken as a sign that the jury system is operating as it should, without majorities prevailing by brute force" (Ellsworth & Mauro, 1998, p. 693). In 1966, Kalven and Zeisel found that only 3.1% of majority-rule juries hung and only 5.6% of unanimous juries hung. Although the frequency of hung juries is somewhat higher in a few large cities with more diverse populations (e.g., New York, Los Angeles, Chicago), the overall rate is only 6.2% nationally (Hannaford–Agor & Hans, 2003). According to some researchers, the process of deliberation affords jurors who are in the minority to persuade the majority, or

> **". . . to hang the jury when the evidence is close enough to undermine agreement on the appropriate verdict. This suggests an active deliberation process that results in verdicts consistent with the majority only when this process convinces the minority jurors." (Salerno & Diamond, 2010)**

Juries tend to hang in cases where the evidence is inconclusive and where differing perspectives are reasonable and therefore difficult to resolve. Hung juries are also more likely in cases where the law is perceived as complex or unfair, and when jurors vote early and adopt a verdict-driven style of deliberation (Mott, Kauder, Ostrom, & Hannaford-Agor, 2003). The strength of the evidence, the effectiveness of the arguments, the clarity of the law, and community sentiment also influence the rate of hung juries.

A final note about hung juries: Sometimes a jury will pass a note to the judge saying that after hours or days of arduous deliberations, jurors still cannot reach a verdict—they are hopelessly deadlocked. If the judge accepts the jury's judgment, a mistrial must be declared. But, in most jurisdictions, the judge has the option of using the **dynamite charge.** This charge to the jury (also called the "Allen charge" or the "shotgun instruction") is an effort to break the deadlock. The judge asks the jury "to reexamine your views and to seriously consider each other's arguments with a disposition to be convinced." We might expect such an instruction to shift the balance toward normative influence and against the minority that is holding out against a strong majority. Research suggests that this instruction causes jurors to feel coerced and may even mislead jurors into thinking that a hung jury is not a viable option (Kassin, Smith, & Tulloch, 1990; Thimsen, Bornstein, & Miller, 2009).

 ## JURY NULLIFICATION

Juries deliberate in private and are not required to justify or explain the reasoning behind their verdicts. They also have the power to reject or "nullify" the law. That is, juries may base their verdicts on reasoning that ignores, disregards, or goes beyond the law. In part, this result is permitted because juries are expected to represent the moral conscience of the community. That moral conscience may lead them to a different conclusion than the law prescribes (I.A. Horowitz, 2008). Even if a defendant is technically guilty in the eyes of the law, he or she may be morally right.

Prior to the American Revolution, **jury nullification** provided a means of resisting oppressive laws put in place by the British Crown. For example, during the Colonial era, a printer named John Peter Zenger was put on trial for seditious libel because he printed articles mocking the royal governor. The trial judge forbade the defense from presenting witnesses to testify that Zenger's claims were true. In an impassioned closing argument, Zenger's defense attorney implored the jury to look past the law to find justice:

> It is not the cause of a poor printer, nor of New York alone, which you are now trying. No! It may in its consequence affect every freeman that lives under a British government on the main of America. It is the best cause. It is the cause of liberty. (King, 2000, p. 104)

The jury was persuaded. They ignored the law and acquitted Zenger. But, jury nullification has become a double-edged sword. Sometimes, it has enabled jurors to find a just verdict in defiance of the law. At other times, it has enabled jurors to ignore just laws in favor of prejudice. Prior to the Civil War, many juries refused to enforce the 1850 Fugitive Slave Law and acquitted defendants who helped slaves escape to freedom in the North. However, following the Civil War, some juries ignored the law and refused to convict whites accused of beating blacks. More modern examples of nullification include Mormon juries in Utah that have refused to convict bigamists or polygamists, and juries that acquitted draft resistors and antiwar activists during the war in Vietnam.

During the 1990s, a Michigan physician named Jack Kevorkian was put on trial four times for breaking the law prohibiting doctors from helping their patients commit suicide. There was no question that Kevorkian was guilty of killing his patients. But, every one of the patients he killed was suffering from a terminal disease, all were in excruciating pain, and all had asked for Dr. Kevorkian's assistance in ending their lives. In the first three trials, juries refused to convict Kevorkian, apparently believing that the law was unjust and that Kevorkian was acting to end the terrible suffering of his patients. In

Jack Kevorkian with one of his patients. *(AP Photo)*

a final effort to push his challenge of the laws against euthanasia, Dr. Kevorkian made a videotape showing him giving a terminally ill man a lethal injection. In his fourth trial, he was found guilty of second-degree murder and sentenced to prison. Despite periodic attempts to restrict or eliminate the power of juries to nullify, nullification remains intact. However, judges almost never tell jurors that they can disregard the law and follow their conscience when deciding on a verdict. This "don't tell" policy may be a reasonable compromise. In one of the few experimental investigations of the effect of informing jurors of their nullification powers, Irwin Horowitz compared juries exposed to several types of cases (I.A. Horowitz, 1988). In some conditions, either the judge or the defense attorney informed the jury that it could ignore the law if following the law would lead to an injustice. When juries were explicitly informed about their nullification powers, they were more lenient toward defendants in a case in which a nurse helped a cancer patient commit suicide and in a case in which a mentally impaired man illegally purchased a handgun. However, these same instructions *increased* the likelihood of conviction in a drunk-driving case where a pedestrian had been killed. The nullification instructions appeared to give jurors permission to treat sympathetic defendants more leniently and to treat unsympathetic defendants more harshly (I.A. Horowitz, Kerr, & Niedermeier, 2001).

One last point about nullification: Sometimes what appears to be disregard for the law may actually be the result of an inability to understand the law. As noted earlier, jurors do an admirable job of assimilating evidence and remembering it during deliberation. However, they do not understand judge's instructions very well, and deliberation with other jurors does not seem to improve their comprehension. The occasional jury decision that seems irrational can often be traced to the inadequacies of lawyers or witnesses and the confusing instructions provided by the court.

 JURY REFORM

As Phoebe Ellsworth and Robert Mauro point out, criticism of juries is not new:

> For centuries the same concerns have been expressed: jurors are ignorant and lazy, governed by passion rather than reason, incapable of understanding the applicable law, their decisions turning on all manner of

> **legally impermissible considerations. The critics claim dangerous trends in the pattern of legal outcomes; the "evidence" however, is typically a short list of highly visible cases (1998, p. 698).**

Two other prominent jury researchers—Neil Vidmar and Valerie Hans—make a similar point in their book on juries:

> **... given the right environment, the proper tools, and the appropriate instructions, juries are reliable, fair, and accurate. (2007, p. 10)**

Although juries have been maligned in the popular press as being lazy or irrational, research indicates not only that jurors rely on the evidence presented at trial to reach a verdict decision, but also that jurors take their jobs seriously and conduct their deliberations in a serious way. For example, in a postverdict survey of 267 actual jurors, 98% reported that they had adequate opportunities to express their views of the case, and more than 90% agreed that the deliberation process was characterized by rigor, listening to others views, equality, and mutual respect (Gastil, Burkhalter, & Black, 2007).

Despite a few well-publicized cases where juries have awarded plaintiffs huge amounts of money, there is no evidence that these sensationalized cases are indicative of a larger trend. Researchers who have analyzed patterns of jury verdicts over time have concluded that, in criminal cases, there has been no increase in verdicts favoring defendants. In civil cases, there is no evidence of a trend favoring plaintiffs or dramatic increases in median compensatory damage awards (Bornstein & Robicheaux, 2008; MacCoun, 1993).

One case that received national media attention and, for many Americans, came to symbolize the irrationality of juries, involved a 79-year-old woman named Stella Liebeck. ABC News (Pearle, 2007) called the case "the poster child of excessive lawsuits." Ms. Liebeck bought a cup of coffee at the drive-through window at a McDonald's restaurant in Albuquerque, New Mexico. As she sat in her parked car, she held the cup of coffee between her thighs and took off the lid to add cream and sugar. The coffee spilled, and Ms. Liebeck was badly burned. When McDonald's agreed to pay only $800 of her $11,000 in medical bills, she sued McDonald's, alleging that the coffee was too hot. A jury agreed and awarded her $2.7 million in damages. Those are the bare facts of the case. However, the jury considered other facts. First, Liebeck had to stay in the hospital for eight days receiving treatment for third-degree burns. She needed several skin grafts. McDonald's coffee was served at a temperature 20 degrees hotter than coffee from other fast-food restaurants. More than 700 previous complaints had been filed about the dangerously hot temperature of the coffee, and McDonald's had settled many of the complaints by paying out about $500,000. Despite hundreds of complaints and the half-million dollar payout, McDonald's had not lowered the temperature of its coffee. Company officials admitted at trial that they knew their coffee was served too hot to drink and that it could cause serious burns. The jury settled on damages of $2.7 million because that was roughly equal to McDonald's coffee sales for a two-day period.

The jury award did not stand for long. The trial judge reduced the award to $480,000, and Ms. Liebeck settled for an even lower amount. As for McDonald's, the corporation responded to the settlement and the publicity by finally lowering the temperature of its coffee. Other fast-food chains took the step of lowering the temperature of their hot chocolate—a favorite drink among young children.

Calls for jury reform come from two very different groups. Moderate reformers seem to believe we have a good system that could be made better. This group tends to focus on ways of helping jurors do their job well. Suggestions include allowing jurors to take notes during trials (some jurisdictions still do not allow note-taking), paying jurors more money for their time, reducing the amount of time jurors spend waiting around, rewriting jury instructions to improve comprehension, making jurors more comfortable while they wait for *voir dire* (e.g., most jurisdictions now provide Internet access in the jury assembly room), and allowing jurors to ask questions of witnesses by handing written questions to the judge (who then decides if the questions are admissible). In contrast, radical reformers seem to believe that jurors are incapable of doing the job well and that the jury system should be overhauled or even abandoned. Those who believe the system is badly broken have called for strict limits on the size of monetary awards, a further move away from unanimous decisions to majority-rule decisions, eliminating the use of juries in complex or technical cases, and simply replacing juries with judges or panels of judges.

Simplifying Instructions to the Jury

After all the evidence has been presented and all the testimony has been heard, attorneys deliver their closing arguments and the trial ends. It is at that time that the judge usually reads instructions to the jury. These instructions contain information about the available verdict categories (e.g., manslaughter versus second-degree murder) and the standard of proof to be used ("reasonable doubt" or a "preponderance of evidence" or "clear and convincing evidence"). Although these instructions are intended to be helpful, research has consistently demonstrated that jurors have great difficulty understanding them. This lack of comprehensibility is due to both the vagueness of the legal concepts and the poor quality of the writing. The instructions are packed with legal terminology and are written in a complex, convoluted style. The quotes from the jury instructions in the Zimmerman case illustrate this point. Indeed, two jurors from the case later described the instructions as "very confusing."

The judge usually reads instructions to the jury without providing examples and without attempting to apply the legal categories to the case at hand. Moreover, judges almost never attempt to clarify instructions because they fear that any such attempt will provide grounds for an appeal (Miles & Cottle, 2011). To illustrate the problem, consider the following instruction used to define negligence in civil cases:

> **One test that is helpful in determining whether or not a person was negligent is to ask and answer whether or not, if a person of ordinary prudence had been in the same situation and possessed of the same knowledge, he would have foreseen or anticipated that someone might have been injured as a result of his action or inaction. If such a result from certain conduct would be foreseeable by a person of ordinary prudence with like knowledge and in like situation, and if the conduct reasonably could be avoided, then not to avoid it would be negligence. (Charrow & Charrow, 1979)**

A linguist and a lawyer rewrote these instructions to improve clarity while preserving the accuracy of legal concepts. They shortened the sentences, cut out unusual or abstract words and phrases ("ordinary prudence"), reduced redundancy ("foreseen or anticipated"), and avoided negatives. Here are the simplified instructions:

In order to decide whether or not the defendant was negligent, there is a test you can use. Consider how a reasonably careful person would have acted in the same situation. Specifically, in order to find the defendant negligent, you would have to answer "yes" to the following two questions:

1. Would a reasonably careful person have realized in advance that someone might be injured as a result of the defendant's conduct? And,
2. Could a reasonably careful person have avoided behaving as the defendant did?

If your answer to both questions is "yes," then the defendant is negligent. (Charrow & Charrow, 1979, p. 1328)

These clearer instructions led to clearer understanding among jurors. In studies comparing conventional legalistic instructions to simpler, rewritten instructions, the clearer instructions lead to significantly better understanding of crucial legal concepts. Similarly, some researchers have improved juror comprehension by creating flow charts that visually illustrate the steps that would lead to a particular verdict decision (Brewer, Harvey, & Semmler, 2004; Brewer & Semmler, 2002). Figure 13.1 illustrates the decision process necessary to find a defendant "not guilty" by reason of self-defense.

Although the simpler, clearer instructions improve juror comprehension and simplify the task of the jury, they do not solve the problem completely. The abstract nature of legal concepts and the inherent ambiguities in those concepts may mean that understanding can never be perfect. As one scholar concluded, "it is the law itself that is incomprehensible" (Tanford, 1990a, p. 110).

It is not only the content of instructions that matters, timing also matters. Typically, jurors are not provided with instructions until the trial is over. One helpful innovation is to read instructions to jurors before the trial begins. The value of this procedure is that it allows jurors to evaluate the legal relevance of the evidence as they hear it. **Preinstructions** (read to jurors before the trial begins) appear to provide a schema that helps jurors to organize information presented at trial. In one study, two groups of mock jurors watched an auto theft trial and reached verdicts based on the evidence (Smith, 1991). But one group did not receive the instruction about presumed innocence until *after* the trial was over. The conviction rate for that group was 59%. The other group of mock jurors received the instruction *before* evidence was presented. For that group, the conviction rate dropped to 37%. It appears that pretrial instructions create a mindset among jurors

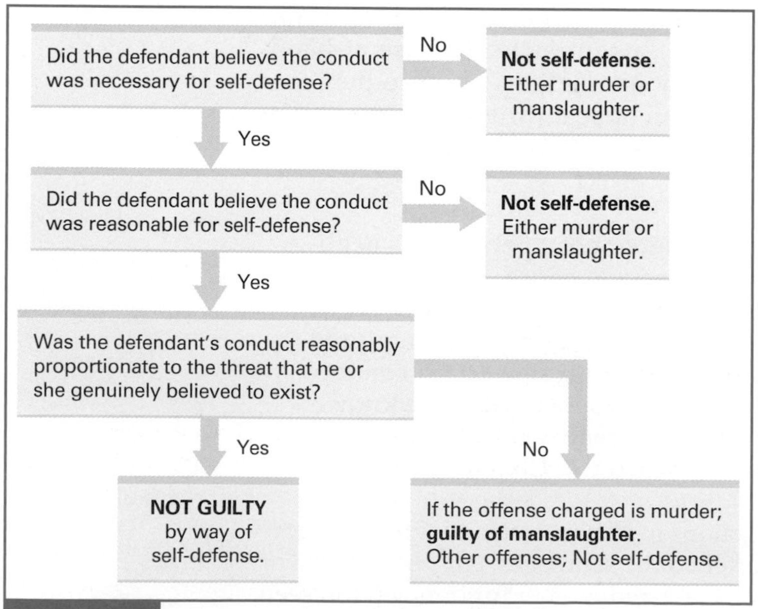

FIGURE 13.1 A flow chart for finding self-defense.

Did the defendant believe the conduct was necessary for self-defense? — No → **Not self-defense.** Either murder or manslaughter.

Yes ↓

Did the defendant believe the conduct was reasonable for self-defense? — No → **Not self-defense.** Either murder or manslaughter.

Yes ↓

Was the defendant's conduct reasonably proportionate to the threat that he or she genuinely believed to exist?

Yes ↓ — No →

NOT GUILTY by way of self-defense.

If the offense charged is murder; **guilty of manslaughter.** Other offenses; Not self-defense.

that causes them to evaluate evidence differently. Waiting to tell jurors to presume innocence until after they have heard all the evidence may simply be "too little, too late." They may have already formed a strong opinion about the defendant's guilt.

In a study of jury trials in Wisconsin, 33 juries were given instructions only after the trial had ended, while another 34 juries received both preinstructions and postinstructions (Heuer & Penrod, 1989). The juries were randomly assigned to the two conditions. As compared to post-instructed-only jurors, the pre- and post-instructed jurors were more satisfied with their trial experience and felt that they had a clearer understanding of how to apply the relevant law to the evidence presented at trial. Unfortunately, only one state (Arizona) requires judges to preinstruct. In many other states, the decision about whether to give preinstructions is left to the discretion of the individual judge.

Allowing Jury Discussion during Trial

One of the more controversial changes proposed by advocates of jury reform is to allow juries to discuss evidence among themselves while the trial is in progress. Advocates of this change have argued that being able to talk about evidence during breaks should help jurors correct misunderstandings prior to formal deliberations,

HOT TOPIC

Should we use professional jurors?

What do you want to do after you graduate from college? Perhaps you should be able to consider a career as a professional juror. For decades, some legal commentators and scholars have advocated for a jury system that relies not on eligible members of the local community, but on people trained to do the job of professional juror. The usual argument is that modern trials are often too complex for ordinary citizens to fully understand. As one commentator put it:

> "With prosecutors now depending on more sophisticated types of evidence—such as deoxyribonucleic acid (DNA), physics-based blood spatter analysis and forensics, computer-based crime scene re-enactments, and other complicated advances in science and biology—to obtain convictions, the need for jurors to be able to separate, analyze, and arrive at accurate conclusions based on the evidence presented at trial is becoming arguably more demanding and difficult for the lay juror" (Maxwell, 2010, p. 18).

Not only that, but jurors are also expected to quickly understand the law. Another commentator notes that

> "it takes law students three years to learn the law—or at least a semester to learn a specific subject like torts—and yet juries are

expected to understand the law after just one brief lecture from the judge." (Solove, 2013)

To prepare for a career as a professional juror, college students might major in something like "juror studies" and receive training in areas such as legal procedure, psychology, forensic science, accounting principles, and ethics. There might even be specialized tracks in criminal or civil trials. After graduation, these specially trained jurors would enter a career of listening to trials, deliberating, and reaching verdicts. Salary would be comparable to that of teachers or police officers, or other public service jobs. Of course, this would require a massive infusion of funds to cover the salaries of a large pool of potential professional jurors in every jurisdiction where trials are held. Although some money could be saved by streamlining the *voir dire* process, that savings would be relatively small compared to the new costs.

There might also be issues of bias. If your job was to show up in court every day, you would likely become friends with some lawyers or judges. You might, perhaps unconsciously, let your personal feelings about a particular lawyer interfere with your judgment. You might agree too easily with your good friend who has served with you as a professional juror on many cases. And, you might become more jaded and conviction-prone after years of watching criminal trials. Perhaps most important, after several years on the job, would you still be able to represent the conscience of the community?

improve later recall of information, and make deliberations more efficient. Opponents of this reform have argued that early discussion of evidence would close off full debate and lead jurors to reach premature verdicts. The state of Arizona tried out this controversial reform and allowed researchers to evaluate it. Specifically, Arizona permitted jurors to discuss the trial evidence and testimony among themselves, but only "in the jury room during trial recesses as long as all jurors are present; the jurors are admonished to reserve judgment about the outcome of the case until they begin deliberations" (Hans et al., 2005, p. 35).

In a multiyear experiment examining the impact of this reform, researchers followed 50 actual civil juries (Diamond, Vidmar, Rose, Ellis, & Murphy, 2002). Discussions during trial as well as verdict deliberations were videotaped and analyzed. Trial materials (transcripts, exhibits, instructions, verdict sheets) were also analyzed, and questionnaires were completed by lawyers, jurors, and judges. The 50 juries were randomly assigned to two groups: One group was permitted to discuss evidence during trial recesses in accordance with the rule quoted above, and the second group was required to forego discussion of evidence until final jury deliberations. The results of the study provide some support for the value of the innovation. Jurors did use recesses to gather information from one another, help each other remember details of testimony, seek clarification, discuss the meaning of the facts presented, and discuss what evidence they would like to hear to help them with their decision. Here is an example of a predeliberation discussion about medical testimony:

juror 3: [Plaintiff] had all of those prior injuries he didn't disclose.
juror 2: I thought that was weird. It wasn't like they had to go to different doctors. It was all in one file.
juror 5: It's not unusual for doctors to disagree.
juror 7: His [treating doctor's] ability to treat patients seems to be just prescribe more drugs.
juror 2: It is just my opinion but [the plaintiff's] doctor wasn't very good, and at least this witness today knew . . .
juror 6: I would like to see [the exhibit about his medication] again. I just want to see what happened after the accident. (Diamond, Vidmar, Rose, Ellis, & Murphy, 2002, p. 53)

Unfortunately, the effects of the rule were not entirely positive. Sometimes jurors in both groups violated the rules given by the court. In the "discuss" group, jurors often discussed the case even though not all jurors were present. And, in the "no-discuss" group, some juries (less than half) made multiple comments about the case before deliberations. While none of the juries in the "discuss" group reached a verdict decision prior to deliberation, several jurors did indicate which verdict they were leaning toward before the trial had ended. Overall, such statements did not tend to disproportionately favor either the plaintiff or the defendant. And, fortunately, these statements did not predict the positions jurors actually took during deliberations—that is, predeliberation statements about verdict did not seem to change the outcome of the trial.

Predeliberation discussions were longer and more numerous when the trial was long and complex than when it was briefer and simpler. The major benefit in the "discuss" group was improved recall and understanding of trial evidence. This benefit was apparently achieved without tilting juries toward one side or the other—plaintiffs were equally likely to win in discuss or no-discuss groups and damage awards did not differ significantly. Both groups of jurors deliberated about the same amount of time, and both groups took about the same amount of time before taking the first vote. However, discuss jurors rated their juries as more thorough and open-minded than no-discuss juries.

Accurate recall of testimony for use during deliberation is essential if juries are to reach verdicts based on the evidence. Allowing jurors to discuss evidence during trial appears to boost such recall, so it may be worth spreading this innovation to other courtrooms. But the negative effects of the innovation—jurors who discuss evidence without all other jurors present, and jurors who prematurely express verdict preferences—need to be weighed against the benefit of improved recall of evidence. The researchers speculate that the negative effects might be reduced or even eliminated by some small changes. Specifically, they suggest that every juror be given a written copy of the rules of discussion, that a written copy be prominently posted in the jury room, and that the judge give a brief verbal reminder of the admonition (no discussion without all jurors present, and no opinions about verdict) before every recess. Finally, the researchers suggest that if judges are given the power to assign a temporary predeliberation presiding juror, that juror might be able to take responsibility for making sure discussion rules are followed.

The Arizona researchers were given unprecedented access to jurors. Their findings provide valuable insights into the functioning of real juries. However, it is unclear whether other researchers will be given such access in the future. That is unfortunate. Controlled access to real juries would give us a deeper understanding of how juries behave in other types of trials (e.g., criminal trials). Every year, juries make tens of thousands of important decisions. If we hope to improve the jury system, any change ought to be based on accurate data about how juries actually make decisions. The best way to collect such data is to try out small changes using controlled experiments and to evaluate the effects of those changes carefully.

JUDGES COMPARED TO JURIES

If juries were eliminated or used much less often, what would we put in their place? We cannot feed the facts of a case into a computer and have the computer spit out a well-considered, impartial verdict. Because the main alternative to trial by jury is trial by judge, it is important to look at how judges make decisions, as well as how often and why their decisions differ from those of juries.

One lofty view of judges emphasizes their impartiality and their immunity to the biases and errors of thinking that supposedly infect the thinking of jurors. One judge put it this way:

> Impartiality is a capacity of mind—a learned ability to recognize and compartmentalize the relevant from the irrelevant and to detach one's emotions from one's rational facilities. Only because we trust judges to be able to satisfy these obligations do we permit them to exercise power and oversight (Peckham, 1985, p. 262).

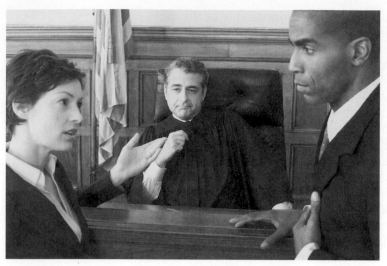

Are judges more or less impartial than jurors? (MASTERFILE)

This flattering assessment of the cognitive abilities of judges does not seem to be supported by the available data. To test the presumed impartiality and emotional detachment of judges, researchers asked 88 judges and 104 jurors to evaluate a product liability case. The plaintiff alleged that because a gasoline container had no "flame arrester," the container exploded, burning him severely over much of his body. The decisions of judges and jurors were compared to see if judges were less affected by biasing information—for example, information that the makers of the gasoline containers had previously issued a warning about a risk of "flame flashbacks" from its gasoline containers. Interestingly, judges were no better at ignoring this inadmissible evidence than were jurors. Yet, even though both groups were equally influenced by biasing information, both judges and jurors believed that judges would be better able to disregard inadmissible evidence (Landsman & Rakos, 1994). In another study, different researchers found that a group of 167 federal judges was vulnerable to most of the cognitive biases that affect lay decision-makers when judging legal materials (Guthrie, Rachlinski, & Wistrich, 2001).

There is even evidence that judges do not have much awareness of their own decision-making processes. In a classic study of sentencing decisions conducted at a time when judges still had considerable discretion, Vladimir Konečni and Ebbe Ebbesen (1982) analyzed more than 400 sentencing hearings. Prior to each hearing, judges received a file containing information about the offender's personal history and prior convictions, as well as a report written by a probation officer. During each sentencing hearing, judges heard sentencing recommendations from prosecutors and defenders and listened to the offender's statement on his own behalf. When asked to describe how they made their sentencing decisions, judges gave lengthy reports of how they carefully weighed multiple, subtle characteristics of the crime and the criminal (e.g., family situation, drug/alcohol addiction, prior record, severity of the crime, mental status of the offender, probability of rehabilitation, expressed remorse of defendant). However, the data contradicted the judges' accounts. Researchers found that judges merely accepted the recommendation of the parole officer in 84% of the cases (in the remaining cases, judges were more lenient 10% of the time and more severe 6% of the time). When the researchers looked at how the parole officers reached their recommendations, they found that those recommendations were almost fully determined by three factors: the severity of the crime, the offender's prior criminal record, and jail/bail status (whether the defendant was held in jail or released on bail between arrest and conviction). The researchers concluded that the sentencing hearings were merely expensive "legal rituals" that "presented a false impression of the functioning of the criminal justice system" (p. 326).

More recent research confirms the basic findings of the sentencing decision research. In a study of decisions by judges about whether a juvenile should be tried as an adult or tried in juvenile court, researchers looked at 17 possible predictors of judges' decisions, including defendant characteristics such as age at time of the crime, receptiveness to rehabilitation, race, substance abuse history, and employ-ment history (Means, Heller, & Janofsky, 2012). About 77% of the time, judges simply accepted the recommendation of a forensic evaluator (a psychologist or psychiatrist) who had evaluated the defendant on level of maturity, amenability to rehabilitation, likelihood of future violence, and the presence of a mental disorder. Also, in a study of bail decisions (whether to grant bail for a defendant), researchers were able to predict judge's decisions about 94% of the time by looking at prior decisions made by police and prosecutors (Dhami, 2003). The research on judge's decision processes seems to indicate that rather than conducting a thorough and sophisticated analy-sis of all potentially relevant legal variables, judges (like most other professionals) generally rely on quick heuristics that are likely to produce desirable outcomes most of the time. Indeed, one influential factor shaping judicial decisions is the need to manage their workload—to move cases through the system quickly and efficiently (Robbennolt, MacCoun, & Darley, 2010).

Judges, like jurors, are biased. Prejudice and partiality based on attitudes, life experiences, and basic values are an inescapable part of human decision-making. However, although safeguards are in place to neutralize juror biases, few compara-ble safeguards exist to deal with judges' biases. The legal system assumes that many jurors are likely to be biased. That is why attorneys are given challenges for cause as well as peremptory challenges during *voir dire*. Although it is possible for a judge to be removed from a case (e.g., if he or she has a direct personal or financial interest in a case), it rarely happens. Another check against juror biases is that every jury con-tains several people who have somewhat different biases. Because juries must reach a group verdict, there is only a slight chance that a lone biased juror will sway the rest of the jury. No comparable safeguard is in place to protect against biased judges. An individual judge who makes a decision in isolation from others does not have his or her biases challenged by others. Finally, judges are systematically exposed to potentially biasing information that jurors never see. Pretrial motions made to the judge usually contain information that will not be presented at trial but that may in-fluence a judge's verdict. In contrast, juries are systematically shielded from biasing pretrial information (Diamond, 2006; Landsman & Rakos, 1994).

It may seem that the general public is more willing to place their trust in judges rather than juries. However, in a large-scale survey of prospective jurors in Texas, re-searchers found a significant preference for using juries rather than judges to decide cases. The jury over judge preference was even stronger among people who had al-ready served on one or more juries, and it was also stronger when respondents imag-ined themselves as a defendant in a criminal trial (Rose, Ellison, & Diamond, 2008).

Agreement between Juries and Judges

As part of their classic study of the American jury, Kalven and Zeisel gathered data from more than 500 judges about the verdicts they would have reached in cases that were actually decided by juries. Analyzing data from approximately 3,500 cases, Kalven and Zeisel found that judges and juries agreed on verdicts in 74% of crimi-nal cases and 78% of civil cases. When juries and judges disagreed, juries tended to be somewhat more lenient—in 16% of those cases, juries acquitted when the judge would have convicted. Other data supports these conclusions. Nearly 30 years later, an analysis of 77 criminal trials found a jury/judge agreement rate of 74% (Heuer & Penrod, 1994). Here again, juries tended to be more lenient—this time, in 20% of the cases. A third study analyzed verdicts in 318 cases and found a jury/judge agreement rate of 75%, with judges being more likely to convict in 19% of cases (Eisenberg et

TABLE 13.1

Jury–Judge Agreement Rates Averaged Across Studies

	Jury acquitted	*Jury convicted*
Judge acquitted	13%	5%
Judge convicted	19%	63%

al., 2005). Table 13.1 summarizes agreement rates across studies.

The high agreement rates are comforting in that both juries and judges appear to be evaluating the evidence in similar ways and reaching similar conclusions. But, what about the disagreement rate? Does it mean that judges reached the wrong decision about 24% of the time? Or, does it mean that juries reached the wrong decision about 24% of the time? Or, does it simply mean that judges and juries sometimes weigh the evidence differently and reach their decisions in different ways? The Kalven and Zeisel study did collect some information on the nature of the cases in which disagreement occurred. They asked judges to rate the evidence in each case as being either easy or difficult, and as clearly favoring one side or being a close call. Rates of disagreement were *not* higher in cases that judges rated as "difficult," but disagreement rates *were* higher in cases judges rated as "close." These findings suggest that jury/judge disparities are likely due to reasonable differences of opinion in cases where the evidence does not clearly favor one side. Further, disagreements cannot be easily attributed to jurors' inability to understand complex evidence (as some radical reformers have suggested). Although judges clearly understand the law better than lay jurors do, no evidence suggests that judges understand specialized technical or expert testimony better than jurors do (Lempert, 1993). And, if 6 or 12 heads are better than one, we might expect a jury to understand complex testimony much better than a judge.

Perhaps another explanation for the disparity between judges and jurors is prior experience. In research comparing more than 200 juries over more than 2 years, juries containing one or more members with prior jury experience were more likely to convict than juries with only first-time jurors (Dillehay & Nietzel, 1999). Put differently, experienced jurors tend to be more conviction prone. Perhaps experience has a similar effect on judges. It could be that because judges see people accused of terrible crimes day after day, they become increasingly jaded and less likely to sympathize with defendants.

Juries tend to be more lenient than judges in less serious cases involving crimes such as possession of a small amount of marijuana or gambling or shoplifting inexpensive items. In serious cases involving crimes such as rape or murder, juries are not more lenient (Diamond, 2003). Judges may give more weight to legal considerations, while juries may focus more on broader conceptions of justice. After all, juries are meant to represent the conscience of the community. It is appropriate for judges and juries to reach decisions differently, and it would not be desirable if they were always in agreement. In civil cases, the rate of juror/judge agreement seems to be even higher than in criminal cases (Vidmar & Hans, 2008). Indeed, judges are more likely than juries are to rule in favor of plaintiffs who have been injured by medical procedures. In experimental studies in which judges and arbitrators evaluate the same civil cases as mock jurors, there is either no significant difference in the amount of damage awards, or judges and arbitrators give somewhat higher awards (Vidmar & Rice, 1993).

One leading scholar on juries and judges—Shari Seidman Diamond—has described several advantages of using juries instead of judges. First, she notes that the jury lends legitimacy to unpopular decisions and "acts as a lightning rod . . . absorbing the criticism and the second-guessing that may follow an unpopular verdict" (2001, p. 7). In contrast, when a judge—a professional representative of the legal system—reaches an unpopular decision, that decision indicts the fairness of the whole system. Second, juries can allow community standards to dictate their verdicts in ways that judges cannot. Judges are more tightly bound by the law. Diamond cites the case of a mentally retarded man who was acquitted by a jury on the charge of possessing a gun. The man wanted to be a police detective and had bought the gun because a magazine article said it was required to train for becoming a detective. If the judge had acquitted the defendant, a precedent would have been established that would weaken the gun possession law. Diamond notes that jurors can "temper the harshness of the law without introducing a change in precedent" (p. 10).

▶ IN CONCLUSION

Jurors do a difficult job under difficult circumstances. Despite having to follow the strange rules of the courtroom, they take their responsibilities seriously and attempt to deliver a fair verdict. The rules and procedures of the courtroom sometimes interfere with jurors' ability to do their jobs, and sometimes jurors' own biases intrude on their impartiality. Judges' decisions are shaped by a different set of biases, and their training and experience render them unable to represent the conscience of the community. We should do all we can to help jurors do their important job well. Although trial by jury is an imperfect system, it is difficult to imagine a more perfect alternative.

▶ CRITICAL THINKING QUESTIONS

1. What can we do to help jurors do their job better? Do any of your suggested reforms harm jurors' ability to follow the law or render an impartial verdict?

2. What is the right policy on jury nullification? Is it "don't tell"? Should we tell every jury that jurors have the right to nullify the law to reach a just verdict? Or, should we abolish jury nullification?

3. Should judges be permitted to use the "dynamite charge" instruction? If so, what should the judge say?

4. Should the legal system actively promote an evidence-driven deliberation style? If so, how?

5. If you were on trial for a serious crime (we realize this would never happen to you), would you rather be tried by a jury, a judge, or a three-judge panel? Why?

6. Should jurors be allowed to discuss evidence with each other while the trial is in progress? If so, what restrictions would you place on these discussions?

7. Can you think of a way to conduct a research project to test whether a particular jury reform is effective?

▶ KEY TERMS

dynamite charge or shotgun instruction (p. 266)
evidence-driven deliberation style (p. 262)
expert witness (p. 259)
impeachment evidence (p. 258)

inadmissible evidence (p. 257)
informational influence (p. 262)
ironic processes (p. 257)
jury nullification (p. 266)
leniency bias (p. 261)
liberation hypothesis (p. 256)

mathematical models (p. 255)
normative influence (p. 263)
open conflict (p. 262)
orientation stage (p. 262)
overrule objection (p. 257)
preinstructions (p. 270)
reactance theory (p. 257)

reconciliation stage (p. 263)
story model (p. 255)
strong jurors (p. 261)
sustain objection (p. 257)
verdict-driven deliberation style (p. 262)

14 Predicting Violent Behavior: The Psychology of Risk Assessment

▶ Sexually Violent Predators and the Law
▶ Risk Assessment and the Law
▶ Methods and Outcomes of Risk Assessment
▶ Clinical versus Actuarial Risk Assessment
▶ Types of Risk Factors
▶ Guided Professional Judgment Instruments
▶ Jurors' Reactions to Risk Assessment Evidence
▶ Treatment to Reduce the Risk of Violence

Leroy Hendricks had a long, sordid history of sexually abusing children. In 1955, at the age of 20, he pled guilty to indecently exposing himself to two young girls. Over the next 30 years, multiple sexual offenses followed. In 1957, he was convicted of playing strip poker with a 11-year old girl. In 1960, he was convicted of molesting two young boys, ages 7 and 8, at a carnival where he was a ride foreman. In 1963, he was convicted of molesting a 7-year-old boy. In 1967, he was convicted of sexually assaulting an 8-year-old boy and an 11-year-old girl. While on parole in 1972, he was convicted of sexually abusing his own step-children, including one who suffered from cerebral palsy. And, in 1984, he was convicted of taking indecent liberties with two 13-year-old boys in an electronics store where he worked. For this last offense, under the habitual offender felon law in Kansas, Hendricks was eligible to receive 45 to180 years in prison. However, the prosecutor dropped one charge and Mr. Hendricks pled guilty to the other charge, eventually receiving a 10-year sentence (Logan, 1998). In 1994, at the age of 59, Leroy Hendricks was set to be released from prison. ◀

SEXUALLY VIOLENT PREDATORS AND THE LAW

In the early 1990s, a number of states—including Kansas—adopted **sexually violent predator civil commitment laws (SVP laws).** As of 2013, 20 states and the federal government had passed such laws (Scurich & Krauss, 2013) (see Figure 14.1).

SVP laws allow for the civil, as opposed to criminal, confinement of individuals who are about to leave prison and who are found likely to commit future acts of sexual violence. Leroy Hendricks became the first person to be subjected to involuntary civil confinement under Kansas's SVP law. The basis of civil commitment laws is twofold: (1) the state's authority to protect its citizens from dangerous individuals (its **police power**) and, (2) the state's duty to protect those citizens who cannot care for themselves, sometimes referred to as the state's *parens patriae* (literally "parent of the country") **power.** Many scholars believe that SVP laws, however, are focused almost exclusively on states' police power and purposively neglect the care and treatment of the mentally ill (Ewing, 2011).

During his commitment trial, Leroy Hendricks admitted: (1) that he was a **pedophile,** an individual who has "recurrent, intense . . . sexual urges or behaviors

Leroy Hendricks shortly after his arrest for his crimes (*Brian Corn/ KRT/Newscom*)

involving sexual activity with a prepubescent child or children (generally age 13 or younger)" (APA, 2013, pp. 697–698); (2) that "when he got stressed out" he could not control his urge to molest children; and (3) "the only way to guarantee it [that he would not molest any more children] is to die" (*Kansas v. Hendricks,* 1997). A Kansas court found Hendricks to be a sexually violent predator, and he was civilly committed to treatment. In 2005, he was supposed to be released from civil confinement. At the time, he was 70-years-old, debilitated by severe diabetes and a stroke, and he spent most of his time in a wheelchair. Yet, because no community would allow him to move in, he remains in a secure treatment facility. Hendricks is not alone. According to one recent report, nearly 4500 sex offenders have been committed under SVP laws since 1990, and only 494 of them had been released by 2007 (Gookin, 2007).

Leroy Hendricks's long history of sexual offenses, his own admissions during trial, and the legal system's failure to change his behavior, all suggest that the Kansas legislature's decision to pass an SVP law was not unfounded. Further, during the 1990s, there were a number of well-publicized cases in which sex offenders were released from prison and almost immediately committed heinous crimes against

FIGURE 14.1 Blue shading indicates states that have SVP laws. Gray shading indicates states that do not have SVP laws.

children (e.g., the 1994 sexual assault and murder of 7-year-old Megan Kanka). In addition, a number of research studies suggest that a very small percentage of criminals are responsible for a high percentage of all crimes, and this relationship also appears to exist for sex offenders (Yang, Wong, & Coid, 2010). States have a strong interest in stopping egregious crimes against some of their most vulnerable citizens—children. SVP laws were viewed as a useful means of preventing future crimes.

One reason states enacted SVP laws was the widespread belief that sex offenders are difficult to treat and that they will continue to commit sex crimes unless they are incapacitated. It turns out, however, that rates of reoffense for sexual crimes are often reported as being quite a bit lower than rates for other offenses. One large analysis of 118 separate studies involving over 28,000 individual cases followed for up to 7 years found an overall sexual reoffense conviction rate of 11.5% (Hanson & Morton-Bourgon, 2009). Other large-scale studies have found similar sexual reoffense rates, with the rates falling between 10% and 20%. In these studies, reoffense rates did increase over time, reaching 24% when offenders were followed for 15 years (Zara & Farrington, 2013).

Although the reoffense rate for sexual offenders appears to be lower than is usually assumed, it is important to remember that it may be impossible to know the actual rate. First, because many sexual crimes go unreported, calculated reoffense rates are likely to be significantly lower than the true rates. Researchers can only examine self-reports of sexual crimes, arrests for sexual crimes, and/or convictions for sexual crimes. Using self-report data leads to higher estimates of reoffense rates than using the number of arrests, and data on arrests suggest higher reoffense rates than data on convictions. This is because many reports do not lead to arrests, and many arrests do not lead to convictions. Sexual reoffense rates may also be affected by: (1) which group of offenders are followed (offenders with different demographic characteristics have different rates of reoffense); (2) how long the offenders are followed (rates tend to increase if offenders are followed for longer periods of time); and (3) whether nonsexual as well as sexual offenses are included in the analysis (sex offenders recommit nonsexual crimes at a much higher rate than they recommit sexual crimes).

States have legitimate interests in identifying repeat offenders and in creating laws to protect citizens from those offenders (see Hot Topic: Sexual Offender Community Notification and Registration Laws). Yet, in order for these laws to work properly, we must be able to identify those sex offenders who are most likely to engage in future criminal conduct. The job of predicting violent behavior has largely fallen to psychologists and psychiatrists, but there is great controversy over whether such predictions are accurate. Because Leroy Hendricks was the first offender to be civilly committed under Kansas's SVP law, the issue of predicting his future behavior was critical to his confinement. Mr. Hendricks's case found its way to the Supreme Court. Along with questions about mental health practitioners' predictive accuracy, the Court was asked to decide if SVP laws violated the Constitution. Specifically, did SVP laws: (1) create double punishment for the same crime (**double jeopardy**)? (2) criminally punish individuals with a penalty that they did not know was a possibility when they committed the act (*ex post facto*)? or (3) arbitrarily or unreasonably deprive individuals of their rights to freedom (**substantive due process**)?

In the 1997 *Kansas v. Hendricks* case, a sharply divided Supreme Court (5 to 4) ruled that SVP laws did not violate double jeopardy and *ex post facto* constitutional concerns because these laws imposed civil confinement rather than criminal punishment and that constitutional restrictions on punishment only applied to criminal matters. The Court also held that the Kansas SVP law did not violate substantive due

HOT TOPIC

Sexual Offender Community Notification and Registration Laws

In July of 1994, Megan Kanka, age 7, was kidnapped, raped, and murdered by her next-door neighbor, Jesse Timmendequas. She was supposedly lured into his house by an invitation to see his new puppy. Megan's body was eventually dumped in a nearby park. Timmendequas was a repeat violent sexual offender who had twice been convicted of molesting children. He was sentenced to death for his horrible crimes. His sentence became life imprisonment without parole when New Jersey abolished capital punishment in 2007.

Megan's parents were outraged that they were never told that their next-door neighbor was a repeat sex offender. They started the Megan Nicole Kanka Foundation, with the goal that "Every parent should have the right to know if a dangerous sexual offender moves into their neighborhood." Megan's parents were also instrumental in changing the law. In 1996, President Clinton signed into effect *Megan's Law,* which requires states to make personal and private information about known sex offenders available to the public (known as *community notification*). However, states have wide discretion in how they implement this law. They can choose what types of sexual crimes lead to mandatory community notification and how notification is to occur (for information on each state's law, see www.klaaskids.org/pg-legmeg.htm).

Maureen Kanka, mother of Megan Kanka (*RAYMOND HOLMAN JR KRT/NEWSCOM*)

Other laws strengthened the community notification requirement. The 1994 Jacob Wetterling Act requires states to record the names of people convicted of certain crimes against children in a national registry. Schools, churches, day care centers, and volunteer youth groups can consult this registry when screening prospective employees. Further, in 2006, the Adam Walsh Child Protection and Safety Act created a U.S. Department of Justice Internet-based national sex offender database (for access see www.nsopw.gov/Core/Conditions). As a result, the public can now search the national sex offender database.

It is an open, empirical question whether these legislative changes will have any effect on the rates of sexual reoffenses. Some research suggests that the changes have had little or no effect (Sandler, Freeman, & Socia, 2008). Proponents argue that because registration and notification laws make it easier to track and protect the public from known sex offenders, such laws should lead to fewer crimes. On the other hand, opponents contend that sex offenders actually have low rates of reoffense and that such laws unfairly impinge on their rights. Moreover, some states impose registration and notification requirements for less severe acts, such as "mooning" or public urination. Opponents also note that the laws may encourage vigilantism against released sex offenders who have reformed and wish to become productive members of society.

process, a point we will return to later in this chapter. This chapter will focus on the specific risk predictions required by the legal system and research on the question of whether or not psychologists and psychiatrists are able to predict future violence.

RISK ASSESSMENT AND THE LAW

The issue of future dangerousness is important in many legal contexts. As a practical matter, parole boards and prison release review boards must decide if an inmate being considered for parole is likely to commit future acts of violence if released back into the community. In the workplace, managers must try to screen out job applicants who show a propensity toward violence. Human resource managers may even be asked to decide whether an employee who is acting strangely is likely to become violent on the job. School psychologists may be held legally accountable if they failed to notice warning signs before a student smuggles a gun into school and opens fire in the cafeteria. Police must decide if a homeless person who is screaming on a public street should be forcibly taken to a mental institution. In some states, jurors in capital cases are asked to consider whether a convicted murderer poses a future danger when they decide between a sentence of life in prison or the death penalty. While there are a number of general concerns regarding risk prediction, psychologists are asked slightly different questions about risk depending on the specific legal context.

In each of these contexts, the challenge is to achieve an optimal balance between the need to protect society and the need to protect the rights of a possibly dangerous individual. Society has a legitimate interest in being protected from violent individuals. But those individuals have a right to be protected from harassment by authorities and from arbitrary arrest and detention based on mere suspicion (See Scientific American Spotlight for discussion of this issue with regard to mental illness). Many scholars have argued that **preventative detention**—holding someone in a jail or hospital because he or she might become violent—is ethically problematic (Hayes et al., 2009). Others have argued that mental health professionals should simply refuse to make predictions about future dangerousness because the accuracy of such predictions has not yet been clearly demonstrated (Edens, Buffington-Vollum, Keilin, Roskamp, & Anthony, 2005; Krauss, McCabe, & Lieberman, 2012). The courts, however, have not expressed these same reservations. Courts have almost uniformly upheld the legitimacy of psychological experts offering testimony on individuals' future dangerousness even when: (1) a substantial portion of their profession has suggested that they are not very good at making these predictions; and (2) the legal decision at issue determines whether a criminal defendant lives or dies.

Future Dangerousness and the Death Penalty

For a defendant to receive the death penalty in Texas or Oregon, a sentencing jury must find beyond a reasonable doubt that, "there is a probability that the defendant would commit criminal acts of violence that would constitute a continuing threat to society" (Texas Criminal Code, 2010). Expert testimony on the so-called **future dangerousness standard** is commonly provided by psychologists or psychiatrists. Four other states (Oklahoma, Virginia, Idaho, and Wyoming) use a defendant's potential future dangerousness as a central consideration in capital sentencing, and a majority of states that permit the death penalty allow expert testimony on this issue. Interestingly, since 1976, just three states— Texas, Oklahoma, and Virginia—have been responsible for over half the total executions in the United States (Dorland & Krauss, 2005). Figure 14.2 details the executions rates since 1976 in these three states and the United States as a whole.

In the early case of *Barefoot v. Estelle* (1983), the Supreme Court considered whether allowing such potentially

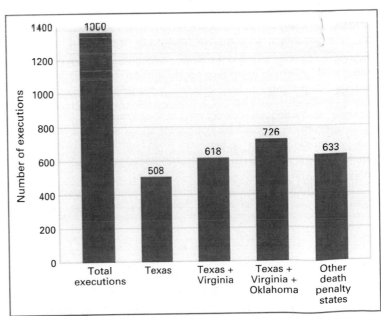

FIGURE 14.2　Executions in the United States, Texas, Virginia, and Oklahoma from 1976-2013. Texas, Oklahoma, and Virginia all use future dangerousness as an integral part of their sentencing decision making.

SCIENTIFIC AMERICAN SPOTLIGHT

Deranged and Dangerous?
By Hal Arkowitz and Scott O. Lilienfeld

In 2011, a 22-year-old college dropout, Jared Lee Loughner, shot Arizona congresswoman Gabrielle Giffords through the head near a Tucson supermarket, causing significant damage to Giffords's brain. In the same shooting spree, Loughner killed or wounded 18 others, including a federal judge and a nine-year-old girl.

Information from Loughner's postings on YouTube and elsewhere online suggest that he is severely mentally ill. Individuals with serious mental illnesses have perpetrated other recent shootings, including the massacre in 2007 at Virginia Tech in which a college senior, Seung-Hui Cho, killed 32 people and wounded 17. These events and the accompanying media coverage have probably fed the public's perception that most profoundly mentally ill people are violent. Surveys show that 60 to 80% of the public believes that those diagnosed with schizophrenia, in particular, are likely to commit violent acts. Although studies have pointed to a slight increase in the risk of violent behaviors among those afflicted with major psychiatric ailments, a closer examination of the research suggests that these disorders are not strong predictors of aggressive behavior. In reality, severely mentally ill people account for only 3 to 5% of violent crimes in the general population. Rather than thinking of people with severe mental illness as generally dangerous, scientists are now pinpointing those other factors that might augur violent behavior more reliably. One strong candidate is drug abuse. Sociologist Henry J. Steadman and his colleagues reported that almost a third of severely mentally ill patients with substance abuse problems engaged in one or more violent acts in the year after they left the hospital. For discharged patients who did not abuse drugs, the corresponding figure was only 18%.

In a 2009 meta-analysis, of 204 studies exploring this connection, psychologist Kevin S. Douglas and his associates found a slightly greater likelihood of aggressive behaviors among those with severe mental illnesses. Yet this connection is much weaker than the public seems to believe it is and does not necessarily mean that these serious disorders cause violence. Douglas's team also flagged drug abuse as one of several factors that contributed to the connection between mental illness and violence. In addition, it found the link was even stronger for patients who suffered from delusions, hallucinations or disorganized thinking. Thus, a mentally ill person is more at risk of committing an act of aggression when that individual is also abusing a drug and shows particular symptoms. Substance abuse greatly boosts the chances of violent behavior in healthy subjects, too, suggesting that drug use may be a much better predictor of violence than mental illness. What is more, proper treatment of mental illness can effectively eliminate the small risk of violent behavior posed by a grave disorder.

The stereotype of the crazed individual killing multiple strangers in public simply does not hold up to scrutiny. Although some noteworthy tragedies fit this description, these instances are quite rare. In fact, given how few mentally ill people become violent, a person with a severe psychological disorder is more likely to be a victim than a perpetrator of violence.

Mentally ill people are victims in their own right. A severe psychiatric condition is a terrible burden, even without being treated with suspicion by the community. A widespread belief that the afflicted are violent contributes to the stigma of mental illness and may interfere with their seeking and obtaining appropriate assistance. Debunking this misconception will likely lead to progress in helping troubled individuals and, by making treatment more broadly accessible, greatly reduce the threat that a small number of these individuals may pose to society.

Jared Lee Loughner (*AP Photo/U.S. Marshal's Office, File*)

inaccurate expert testimony was unconstitutional. In the summer of 1978, Thomas Barefoot was living with four roommates in a trailer in Killeen, Texas. On August 6, 1978, Barefoot told one of his roommates that he was going to commit robbery in Harker Heights, Texas, after he created a diversion by setting a building on fire. The next day, another roommate gave Barefoot (who was wearing a white T-shirt and blue jeans) a ride to Harker Heights. After stopping at a convenience store to fill a milk jug with gasoline, the roommate dropped Barefoot off next to the Silver Spur nightclub. An eyewitness subsequently saw a man matching Barefoot's description running away from the burning nightclub, and that same eyewitness reported the suspicious individual to the police. A short distance from the fire, a Harker Heights police officer spotted a suspicious man close to the highway. Another eyewitness reported that he saw a man in a white T-shirt and blue jeans approach the police officer from the bushes and shoot him in the head at point blank range. Barefoot returned to his trailer the same day in a T-shirt and blue jeans covered with blood spatter and told his roommate that "he had to get out of town because he wasted a cop." Barefoot was later arrested at the bus station carrying a gun that matched the ballistics of the one that killed the police officer.

A Texas jury found Barefoot guilty of capital murder because he had intentionally shot and killed a police officer. As a result, Barefoot was eligible for the death penalty. At his capital sentencing hearing, two psychiatrists who had never interviewed Barefoot, testified that there was a "100% and absolute chance" that he would continue to be a danger. In his appeal, Barefoot argued that his constitutional rights had been violated by allowing such unfounded "expert" pronouncements at trial. He bolstered his claim with empirical research contained in an *amicus curiae* brief filed by the American Psychiatric Association. The brief summarized the five existing studies on expert predictions of future danger, and highlighted the finding that such predictions were incorrect two out of three times (APA, 1982). The Supreme Court was not persuaded by Barefoot's arguments nor the American Psychiatric Association's brief. The Court held that banning expert testimony on future dangerousness was much like asking the courts to "disinvent the wheel" (*Barefoot v. Estelle*, 1983). The Supreme Court also remained convinced that capital jurors were capable of recognizing the weaknesses of experts' predictions and were capable of taking those weaknesses into account.

While the Supreme Court's decision in *Barefoot v. Estelle* made it clear that expert predictions of risk were admissible in capital sentencing despite their potential inaccuracy, one important issue remained unanswered: Texas and many other states had not defined what they meant by "continuing danger to society." Several scholars have argued that the standard must now refer to prison society since any capital defendant not sentenced to death must receive life *without* the possibility of parole (LWOP; Cunningham, Sorensen, & Reidy, 2009; Edens, et al. 2005). This creates a difficult problem for psychologists who perform future risk evaluations because the factors that contribute to violence in prison are different from the factors that contribute to violence in general society. Only a few courts have addressed this issue, and it remains unclear which "society" the expert is making a prediction about in most death penalty cases.

Civil Commitment

The decision to place someone in a psychiatric facility against his or her will is known as **involuntary civil commitment.** Although involuntary treatment of the mentally ill dates back to ancient times, it was not until the nineteenth century that state asylums were built specifically for the care and housing of the mentally ill. Up until the middle of the twentieth century, there were few requirements for an individual to be involuntarily placed in an asylum. As late as the 1970s, a majority of states simply required one physician to find that an individual was mentally ill and in need of treatment. The number of people housed in mental asylums reached its peak in the mid-twentieth century (nearly 550,000 people were in asylums in 1955; Melton et al., 2007).

Several factors led to a steep decline in the population of mental hospitals throughout the last half of the twentieth century. The so-called **deinstitutionalization** of mentally ill patients was partly motivated by a humanitarian urge to help mental patients lead fuller, more satisfying lives beyond the confines of psychiatric hospitals. The hope was that former mental patients would be reintegrated into the community and would learn to function in the world at large. However, deinstitutionalization was also partly motivated by the less than humanitarian desire to cut back on the financial cost of hospitalization for mentally ill patients (Perlin, 2000). Legislative reforms, legal challenges to hospitalization, and the advent of antipsychotic medications all gave strong momentum to the deinstitutionalization movement.

The civil rights movement in the United States also had important implications for which types of mentally ill patients could be committed, and for the procedures used to decide whether civil commitment was appropriate. States moved beyond allowing mentally ill persons to be involuntarily hospitalized based solely on a doctor's belief that they needed treatment. To hospitalize someone against his or her will, most states now require that: (1) the person suffer from a severe mental disorder that substantially affects their functioning; and (2) if future dangerousness is a rationale for their commitment, a mental health professional must predict that the individual will likely cause significant harm to himself or herself or others in the near future. In fact, several Supreme Court cases made clear that mental illness alone or dangerousness alone is not a constitutionally acceptable reason for involuntary civil commitment (*Foucha v. Illinois*, 1992; *O'Connor v. Donaldson*, 1975). Eventually, most jurisdictions began to require that people being considered for involuntary commitment be provided with many (but not all) of the procedural rights guaranteed in a criminal trial. Unfortunately, courts have been slow to stringently apply these rights in actual cases (Winnick, 2001).

Exact requirements for involuntary civil commitment differ widely among states. Some states, such as Florida, require that an individual who is being committed on "dangerousness to others" grounds show a "substantial likelihood in the near future" of inflicting "serious bodily harm as evidenced by recent behavior." Other states simply mandate that the individual exhibit a "real and present" threat of future danger to self or others (Melton et al., 2007). As a result of these differences in definitions, mental health professionals must answer different questions in predicting future risk. In some jurisdictions, the psychologist must show recent evidence and sometimes even a recent specific dangerous act, and this recent behavior must be linked to a future risk of serious injury. Other jurisdictions do not require past dangerous behavior nor do they specify that predicted future acts would result in serious injury.

In some states, psychologists must decide if therapeutic clients pose a serious danger to others and must take reasonable steps to warn people that their client might do harm (see Legal Spotlight: The Tarasoff and Ewing Cases). If an individual is deemed to be **a danger to self or others** as a result of mental illness, every state has provisions for hospitalizing that person against his or her will. In addition, many states allow for involuntary hospitalization of individuals who are **gravely disabled.** Such people are unable to arrange for their basic needs of food, shelter, and safety because of mental illness. It is important to recognize that these forms of civil confinement are based on different interests and operate very differently from criminal confinement. An important underpinning of civil confinement is the state's *parens* *patriae* power. As a result, civil confinements are defined not as punishment but as a means to help people who cannot care for themselves. Therefore, unlike criminal incarcerations where treatment and rehabilitation are considered minor goals, in civil commitment these interests are supposed to dominate.

Involuntary civil commitment differs from criminal confinement in other important respects, including: (1) the burden of proof necessary to confine someone (criminal trials require proof beyond a reasonable doubt while involuntary civil commitments use a lesser burden of proof—the clear and convincing evidence standard); (2) the length of confinement (the length of criminal punishment is specified while civil confinement can continue indefinitely if the individual is deemed to still be a danger to himself or others); and (3) the reason for confinement (in criminal matters the defendant is charged for something he or she has done, while in involuntarily

 LEGAL SPOTLIGHT

The Tarasoff and Ewing Cases

The 1976 case of *Tarasoff v. Regents of the University of California* changed the way mental health professionals deal with clients who might pose a risk of violent behavior.

Prosenjit Poddar, a graduate student at the University of California at Berkeley, killed Tatiana Tarasoff, a student who had repeatedly rejected his romantic advances. Prior to the killing, Poddar had been receiving psychotherapy at the university health center, and during a session he expressed his desire to kill Tatiana.

Tarasoff's parents sued the university, charging that the psychotherapist should have told Tatiana that Poddar had threatened her. The lawsuit was successful, even though the psychotherapist had alerted campus police that Poddar had made a death threat against Tatiana. Campus police had interviewed Poddar, eventually releasing him because they believed that he was not dangerous. Two months after this interview, Poddar stabbed Tatiana to death in her home.

The California Supreme Court held that psychotherapists had a *duty to protect* their client's identifiable potential victims. As a result of this decision, when a patient poses a serious risk of violence, therapists are obliged to take "reasonable care" to protect an identifiable intended victim (e.g., by notifying the police and/or the potential victim). In the years following the Tarasoff case, courts and

Tatiana Tarasoff (left) and Prosenjit Poddar (right) *(AP Photo)*

legislatures in many states enacted some form of "duty to protect" laws.

The decision in the Tarasoff case produced a strong reaction among psychologists. Many felt its requirements would undermine the effectiveness of therapy by breaking the bonds of trust and confidentiality between therapist and client. It also focused attention on the issue of whether mental health professionals were capable of predicting which clients might be violent in the future.

More recently, the California Court of Appeals, in *Ewing v. Goldstein* (2004), appears to have expanded the "duty to protect" requirement. The court decided that the information provided by a family member of an adult client and not the client could also trigger the "duty to protect" requirement. In the Ewing case, the client's father called his son's therapist and indicated that he believed his son might kill his ex-girlfriend's new boyfriend. This did occur, the boyfriend's parents sued, and the court did not dismiss the lawsuit against the psychotherapist. Under the court's reasoning, if a therapist believes information from family members is credible, that belief alone could trigger the duty to protect an identifiable victim. This ruling potentially puts therapists in the unenviable position of trying to determine the credibility of individuals with whom they have had no previous contact.

civil confinement the issue is what the person might do in the future). Over the years, involuntary civil hospitalizations have come to more closely resemble criminal confinement both in purpose and in procedural rights granted during the commitment hearings.

In particular SVP confinements, which are a considered a special form of involuntary civil commitment, clearly focus more on the protection of society than on treatment of the offender. These trials also afford many of the same rights that criminal trials provide to defendants (e.g., the right to trial, the right to an attorney, the right to cross-examine witnesses, etc.).

Sexually Violent Predator Civil Commitment

It is unlikely that Leroy Hendricks (introduced in the vignette at the beginning of this chapter) could have been involuntarily civilly committed under most states' existing laws. Although Hendricks suffered from a mental illness, namely pedophilia, this disorder is generally not considered sufficiently severe to meet most states' civil commitment statutes. For the individual to be involuntarily civilly committed, many states now require that the mental illness be substantial enough to cause impairments in decision making, behavior, memory, and/or the ability to recognize reality (Melton, et al, 2007). Moreover, Hendricks had not engaged in any recent overt act that could have provided evidence for the recent dangerous behavior that some states mandate (he was in prison for the 10 years prior to his commitment trial). SVP laws were enacted, in part, to make sure people like Leroy Hendricks did not return to the community even if they could not be involuntarily committed.

At the time SVP laws were adopted, another point of controversy was whether any real stated interest in providing effective treatment. Unlike other civil commitment laws, SVP laws focused on protection of citizens rather than on treatment for individual offenders. In fact, during Leroy Hendricks's original trial there was very little evidence available that repeat sex offenders could be successfully treated (Ewing, 2011; La Fond, 2005). Another issue was the definition of a sexually violent predator. The broadly written Kansas SVP statute defines a sexual predator as:

> **Any person who has been convicted or charged with a sexually violent offense and who suffers from a mental abnormality or personality disorder which makes the person likely to engage in predatory acts of sexual violence. (Kan. Stat. Ann. 59–29a02(a); 1994, amended in 1996, as cited in Kansas v. Hendricks 117 S. Ct. 2072 (1997), p. 2072.)**

Notice that the statute uses the term "mental abnormality or personality disorder" instead of "serious mental disorder." Use of this broader category was intended to include all those individuals who were not diagnosed with a severe mental disorder. The SVP law's mental illness definition also includes the term "personality disorders"—a wide-reaching category of enduring personality characteristics that affect individuals' ability to interact effectively in a variety of settings. One of the personality disorders, **antisocial personality disorder,** involves "a pervasive pattern of disregard for and violation of the rights of others, occurring since age 15 years" (APA, p. 659). Rates of antisocial personality disorder in the general population are relatively low (.3% to 3.3%) (APA, 2013), but some estimate that the rate for prison inmates may be as high as 70% (Rotter, Way, Steinbacher, & Smith, 2004). (See Table 14.1 for the diagnostic criteria of ASPD.)

TABLE 14.1

DSM-5 Diagnostic Criteria for Antisocial Personality Disorder (301.7)

A. There is a pervasive pattern of disregard for and violation of the rights of others occurring since age 15 years, as indicated by three (or more) of the following:
   1. Failure to conform to social norms with respect to lawful behaviors as indicated by repeatedly performing acts that are grounds for arrest
   2. Deceitfulness, as indicated by repeated lying, use of aliases, or conning others for personal profit or pleasure
   3. Impulsivity or failure to plan ahead
   4. Irritability and aggressiveness, as indicated by repeated physical fights or assaults
   5. Reckless disregard for safety of self or others
   6. Consistent irresponsibility, as indicated by repeated failure to sustain consistent work behavior or honor financial obligations
   7. Lack of remorse, as indicated by being indifferent to or rationalizing having hurt, mistreated, or stolen from another

B. The individual is at least age 18 years.
C. There is evidence of conduct disorder with onset before age 15 years.
D. The occurrence of antisocial behavior is not exclusively during the course of schizophrenia or a manic episode.

Advocates of SVP laws suggested that the expansive definition of mental illness was necessary because sexual offenders rarely seek treatment and often have not been diagnosed with a mental illness. Consequently, it would be difficult to characterize many repeat sex offenders as mentally ill under a more restrictive definition. On the other hand, those opposed to the laws argued that the broad definition of mental illness, which may include about two-thirds of all prisoners, unfairly allows SVP laws to be applied to individuals well beyond those who are high-risk sexual offenders.

This latter argument served as part of the basis for Leroy Hendricks's substantive due process claim in *Kansas v. Hendricks*. The Supreme Court disagreed. The Court held that states have great leeway in defining what constitutes mental illness for civil commitment proceedings, and that states are not bound to require that a serious mental disorder exists for involuntary civil commitment to take place. Hendricks also claimed that the fact that no effective treatment existed for his disorder prevented the state from justifying his commitment. The Supreme Court also found this argument unpersuasive, stating, "we have never held that the Constitution prevents a state from civilly detaining those for whom no treatment is available, but who nevertheless pose a danger to society" (*Kansas v. Hendricks*, 1997). In effect, the Supreme Court determined that the *parens patriae* treatment rationale was largely unnecessary, and that the state could detain a wide range of individuals simply because they pose a risk of future danger.

A later Supreme Court case, *Kansas v. Crane* (2002), clarified the Court's holding in the Hendricks case. Unlike Leroy Hendricks, the defendant in this case, Michael Crane, believed he could control his sexual urges. In its *Kansas v. Crane* decision, the Supreme Court explained that to commit an individual under SVP laws, he or she must: (1) suffer from some form of mental illness (although states would have great latitude in determining how to define mental illness); (2) pose a future danger to society; and (3) have serious difficulty controlling his or her urges. The Court did not specify what "serious difficulty" was or how it could be measured. At present, mental health professionals are called upon as experts to address all three of these issues for the courts (Krauss & Scurich, 2013; Miller, Amenta, & Conroy, 2005). Yet the question that remains most controversial is the manner in which psychologists determine if a sex offender "is likely to engage in predatory acts of sexual violence." This component of the SVP legal standard clearly involves a future prediction of a specific kind of risk—future sexual violence. We now turn to the question of how and how well psychologists predict future risk.

METHODS AND OUTCOMES OF RISK ASSESSMENT

The most important reason for trying to predict future violence is the obvious one: If we can predict who will become violent, perhaps we can prevent him or her from becoming violent. With this important goal in mind, social scientists have set out to develop methods for improving predictions.

The traditional way of discussing and presenting research findings in the area of prediction is by referring to a 2-by-2 contingency table (see Table 14.2). The two rows of the table concern the prediction: Will the patient become violent or not? The two columns of the table concern the actual outcome: Did the person actually commit an act of violence at some later time? Of course, researchers have to wait to find out the answer to this question. If we cross the prediction with the outcome, there are four possibilities, two accurate and two inaccurate. If it was predicted that a person would become violent and then that person does become violent, it is called a **true positive.** A **true negative** occurs when a person who was predicted not to become violent turns out not to be violent. The two forms of error are called either **false positives** (predictions of violence that do not come true) or **false negatives** (people predicted to be nonviolent who later become violent). True predictions are sometimes called hits, and false predictions are sometimes called misses. Most efforts to improve prediction have involved measuring a variety of factors known to be or suspected to be associated with individual violence. These factors are then correlated with actual violence in institutions (usually psychiatric hospitals or prisons) or in the community. The goal is to identify those factors that reliably predict later violence.

Requiring mental health professionals or others to predict who is likely to become violent skips over the more basic question: Are they able to do it well? Based on early research in the area, the answer to that question was a resounding "no." Two major studies published during the 1970s revealed the difficulty of predicting violence, and both of these studies were summarized in the American Psychiatric Association research brief presented in *Barefoot v. Estelle* (1983).

The first study followed 98 inmates for 4 years following their release from a hospital for the criminally insane (the Supreme Court ordered their release because of Constitutional violations). Although all 98 were considered dangerous, only 20 were later arrested and only 7 of those 20 were arrested for a violent crime. That is, despite being considered dangerous, only 7.14% of the total sample later became violent (Steadman & Cocozza, 1974). That is a staggering false positive rate of 92.8%. A few years later, as a result

TABLE 14.2

Outcome: Did the Person Later Become Violent?			
		Actual Outcome	
Prediction		*Violent*	*Non-Violent*
Did we predict that the person would become violent?	Positive	True positive	False positive
	Negative	False negative	True negative

of *Dixon v. Attorney General of the Commonwealth of Pennsylvania* (1971), more than 400 purportedly dangerous mentally ill offenders were released from a prison hospital. Researchers found that 3 years after their release, only 14.5% had been arrested or hospitalized for violent behavior (Thornberry & Jacoby, 1979). The surprising news from these and other studies was that so few people considered dangerous by the criminal justice system actually ended up committing violent crimes when set free in the community. Indeed, in virtually all of the early studies, errors in predicting violence were in the same *false positive* direction: The great majority of people predicted to become violent did not become violent (Monahan, 1981).

 ## CLINICAL VERSUS ACTUARIAL RISK ASSESSMENT

The strategies used by psychologists to predict future violence range from clinical intuition to highly structured scientific approaches. Intuitive approaches are sometimes referred to as **unstructured clinical judgment** because no rules specify how a clinician should collect and combine information. Science-based approaches specify what information should be collected, and even sometimes how much weight to afford to each piece of information when making a prediction. Although research shows that predictions based on more scientific approaches to risk assessment are not infallible, such methods clearly produce more accurate predictions than those based on the subjective judgments of psychotherapists, judges, jurors, and prison administrators (Heilbrun, 1997).

Unstructured Clinical Judgment

One reason for the relative weakness of clinical prediction is the lack of feedback about success or failure. When clinical psychologists make predictions about whether or not a client will later become violent, they seldom find out whether the client actually becomes violent at some later time. It is impossible to improve the accuracy of predictions without knowing which predictions turn out to be correct and which predictions turn out to be wrong. Without clear data on the accuracy of their predictions, clinicians are left to rely on biased thinking: a plausible but untested theory, mere intuition, or even prejudice. For example, a clinician might believe that individuals who commit particularly heinous crimes are more likely to reoffend, although in actuality there may be no relationship between the brutality of a crime and whether an offender will commit future crimes.

Mental health experts also tend to ignore base rate information in making their risk predictions. **Base rate** refers to the overall likelihood of an event or behavior in a given population. In this case, the base rate refers to the number of people in a particular population who actually become violent. If a psychologist (or parole board or judge) is asked to predict how many people out of 100 are likely to become violent, and only 10 later become violent, it will be exceedingly difficult to predict which 10 will actually be violent without misidentifying a significant number of nonviolent people as violent. In other words, if the base rate is low—that is, if the behavior is very infrequent—our ability to predict that behavior will be very limited (Grove & Meehl, 1996). Also, because clinicians were often unaware of how rarely an offender was likely to reoffend—known as the **base rate of reoffense**—they were very prone to overpredicting violent behavior. Unfortunately, research shows that even when clinicians are made aware of base rates, they still tend to ignore them and overpredict the likelihood of violence (Skeem

TABLE 14.3

A 2-by-2 Table of 100 Predictions When the Base Rate Is 10% and the Predictive Accuracy Is 80%*

		Actual Outcomes	
		Violent	Non-violent
Predicted outcomes for violence	Positive	8 true positive	18 false positive
	Negative	2 false negatives	72 true negatives

*It should be noted that a predictive accuracy of 80% is significantly higher than has been demonstrated for even the best risk prediction instruments. Notice that the false positives are more than twice the true hits, creating a false positive error rate of 18/26, or 69%. This high rate means that over two-thirds of those predicted to be violent will not actually be violent.

TABLE 14.4

A 2-by-2 Table of 100 predictions When the Base Rate Becomes 50%*

	Prediction	Actual Outcome	
		Violent	Non-Violent
Did we predict that the person would become violent?	Positive	40 true positive	10 false positive
	Negative	10 false negatives	40 true negatives

*Fifty percent is the rate at which effective prediction is usually best but much higher than is seen in almost every high-risk population, and the predictive accuracy remains 80%. Notice that the rate of false positive error plummets to 10/50, or 20%, leading to far fewer mispredictions of violence as a proportion of the total predicted to be violent. However, decreasing the false positive rate increases the rate at which individuals who are actually violent are predicted not to be (false negative errors). In this case, it is 10/50, or 20%, which is significantly higher than the rate in Table 14.3, where it is 2/74, or approximately 3%. There is always a trade-off between these two types of errors.

& Monahan, 2011). (See Tables 14.3 and 14.4 for examples of how base rates affect accuracy of prediction.)

To some extent, the amazingly poor ability of mental health professionals to predict future violence was also an artifact of the research methods used. In many studies, researchers followed only inmates who had been released. But, for obvious reasons, the most consistently violent people serving time in prisons and hospitals are never released into the community. Consequently, it was the people who were less likely to be violent who were released and then studied by researchers. Put differently, the people whose violence was easiest to predict were usually not included in research. The fact that these more violent inmates were not released or studied lowered the base rate of violence, and a lower base rate makes predictive accuracy harder to achieve. Finally, many of the early studies only focused on individuals' rearrest and/or reconviction for a violent offense. This narrow definition of what constituted a future violent act further lowered the base rates in the studies.

In a series of books and articles, John Monahan and his colleagues proposed a series of methodological and statistical reforms that might improve the accuracy of predictions. A key consideration was the information used to predict violence. Researchers were urged to gather more data and more forms of data (Monahan, 2007; Monahan & Steadman, 1994). They called for researchers to gather information about physiological factors, psychological factors, and personal history, as well as information about the situations the person might face after release from an institution.

Just as predictors needed to be expanded and refined, so did measures of outcome. Measures of violent behavior needed to be more sensitive and inclusive. Researchers were urged to distinguish between types of violence (e.g., shoving or punching or stabbing or shooting), targets of violence (e.g., spouse or child or stranger), and contexts in which violence occurs (e.g., at home or in public). Using only arrest records—as most early studies did—led to an underestimation of violent behavior because much violence is unreported or goes unnoticed by police. Also, because even a violent crime can be prosecuted as a lesser, nonviolent crime through plea-bargaining, some truly violent behavior never even shows up in police reports or court records. Additional data needed to be gathered from interviews with the people being studied and the people with whom they interact. In one study, estimates of violent behavior rose from 4.5% to 27.5% when such additional measures of violent behavior were added to analyses (Steadman et al., 1998). Later studies using more sophisticated methods found that mental health professionals were more accurate than first thought when making long-term predictions of violence, and even more accurate for some short-term predictions of dangerousness (Lieberman, Krauss, Kyger, & Lehoux, 2007; Mossman, 1994). Nevertheless, expert predictions of risk by mental health professionals needed improvement.

Actuarial Techniques

Early research led to a new generation of risk assessment research, and the development of new methods for predicting future risk. One of these methods, **actuarial prediction,** was soon found to outperform clinical predictions of future violence in a number of comparisons (Mossman, 1994). Actuarial methods of prediction require that relevant risk factors be systematically combined (typically using a statistical equation) to calculate an estimate of future violence. The risk factors and their weights in the equations are identified through prior research, which collects large amounts of data on individuals who have been followed for an extended time period (sometimes up to 10 years). Researchers uncover risk characteristics that best predict violent behavior, and factors that are more strongly correlated with future violence are weighted more heavily in the equation. It is a **nomothetic, quantitative approach.** That is, it is based on characteristics identified in research on large *groups* of people, and it relies on *statistics.* In comparison, **clinical prediction** is an **idiographic, qualitative approach** that focuses on a specific *individual,* and relies on *subjective judgments* made by a clinical psychologist. Actuarial predictions are built on the findings of past research and clinical predictions are built on the past professional experience of the clinician.

In 2001, a prominent team of researchers published a book describing a massive study of the relationship between mental disorder and violence. In summarizing the ability of clinicians to make accurate predictions, the researchers reached the following conclusion:

> **It is no longer reasonable to expect clinicians unaided to be able to identify the variables that may be influential for a particular person, integrate that information, and arrive at a valid estimate of the person's risk for violence. . . . At best, predictions will involve approximations of the degree of risk presented by a person, presented as a range rather than a single**

number, with the recognition that not every person thus classified, even one accurately determined to be in a high risk group, will commit a violent act. (Monahan et al., 2001, p. 143)

During the past 20 years, several actuarial risk assessment devices have been constructed to improve predictive accuracy. These instruments were created using specific populations and were designed to predict specific outcomes. For example, the **Violence Risk Appraisal Guide (VRAG)** was created by Vernon Quinsey and his colleagues (1998) by following 618 Canadian men who had committed at least one serious violent offense. Approximately 30% of their sample eventually received a new criminal charge for a violent offense during the follow-up period. Researchers selected the 12 variables that best predicted those who reoffended. The final equation achieved approximately 75% accuracy in classifying the original sample into those who would and would not reoffend. Using similar methods, other researchers created instruments to predict sexual recidivism among sex offenders (e.g., the Static-99; Hanson & Thornton, 2000). New actuarial instruments for assessing the risk of future sexual offending are being developed.

Although few doubt that actuarial instruments outperform clinical predictions of future violence, a number of concerns have been raised about their use by mental health professionals in legal proceedings (Hart & Cooke, 2013; Monahan, 2003; Skeem & Monahan, 2011). First, the generalizability of actuarial instruments has been questioned. **Generalizability** refers to how well these instruments perform outside the original population and outcome on which they were created. For example, since the VRAG was created based on Canadian offenders, it is an open question as to how well it predicts the violent behavior of offenders in the United States. Also, the VRAG was not specifically designed to predict sexual reoffenses. However, because the risk factors differ somewhat for the two types of risk predictions, the creators of the VRAG developed a similar instrument, the **Sexual Offending Risk Appraisal Guide (SORAG)** specifically for predictions of sexual reoffending.

 ## TYPES OF RISK FACTORS

If you think for a few minutes, you can probably generate a long list of factors that might plausibly be related to future violent behavior. During the past few decades, researchers have sifted through mountains of data to find the best predictors of violence. A number of useful predictors have been identified. Several researchers have distinguished among three broad categories of risk factors (or "markers") that are reliably associated with violent behavior: (1) historical or "static" markers, (2) dynamic markers, and (3) risk management markers (Douglas & Skeem, 2005; Douglas & Webster, 1999; Skeem & Monahan, 2011).

Historical Markers

Most actuarial instruments rely almost exclusively on what are called static or historical risk factors. For example, all 12 risk factors used in VRAG are best described as "static" because they do not change over time. They are part of the person's history or they cannot be changed through intervention. Markers in this category include past violent behavior, young age at first offense, early abuse of alcohol and/or other drugs, major mental disorder, psychopathy, early maladjustment at home or school, attempted or actual escapes from psychiatric facilities, and presence of a personality disorder. It is reasonable to focus on such factors because research suggests that the most useful risk predictors are historical. Past behavior is often the strongest predictor of future behavior.

Being young (generally classified as under the age of 30) is associated with violent behavior. Especially at risk are people whose first act of violence was committed at a young age. Consistent conflict or disturbance in personal relationships—for example, being abusive toward a spouse or an inability to maintain lasting relationships—is another solid correlate of later violence. Childhood maladjustment also predicts future violence. It encompasses disturbed family relationships such as being removed from parental care before age 16, being subjected to cruelty or physical abuse from caregivers, and failing at school or being expelled from school because of behavior problems. A history of drug abuse may also be associated with violence because distressed people may use drugs to relieve their suffering and because drug use may lower inhibitions against violence (Heilbrun, Douglas, & Yasuhara, 2009).

The remaining factors in the "historical" category—personality disorder, major mental disorder, and psychopathy—all indicate impaired psychological functioning. Personality disorders include antisocial traits (being manipulative, irresponsible, and exploitive of others), while major mental disorders include schizophrenia, whose sufferers often operate under paranoid delusions that others are conspiring to do them harm (although the research is more mixed on whether schizophrenics are more prone to violent behavior; Monahan, 2003). Finally, **psychopathy** is a distinctive, extreme form of antisocial disorder characterized by a lack of empathy for others and a lack of remorse for cruel or violent behavior. Although psychopaths tend to be glib and superficially charming, they also tend to be dishonest, manipulative, and unwilling to accept responsibility for their antisocial behavior. Historically, psychopaths have been considered especially difficult to treat, but recent research questions this assumption (Skeem, Polaschek, Patrick, & Lilienfeld, 2011).

Dynamic Markers

Dynamic predictors fluctuate over time. Moods, attitudes, and thought processes do not remain fixed over time and can be responsive to treatment. A major dynamic factor is lack of insight into oneself or others. People who become violent tend to have less awareness of their mental disorder and tend to lack awareness into the motives and behaviors of others. They also tend not to recognize their need for treatment. In an interesting series of studies illustrating one aspect of this lack of insight, researchers found that, compared to typical adolescents, violent adolescents were much more likely to attribute hostile intent to others (Dodge, Price, Bachorowski, & Newman, 1990; Fontaine, Yang, Dodge, Pettit, & Bates, 2009). Behaviors (facial expressions, statements, gestures) that most people interpreted as neutral and nonthreatening were viewed as hostile and provocative by violent adolescents. Other researchers have found that to justify their actions, violent youths often report that their victims "brought it on themselves," deserved to be the targets of violence, or did not suffer greatly from being attacked (Henderson & Hewstone, 1984). Not surprisingly, persistent strong feelings of anger and hostility are consistently related to violent behavior. People who are physically aggressive tend to have more intense feelings of anger and hostility and tend to act impulsively on those feelings (Novaco, 2007).

What is called **psychiatric symptomatology** is also a dynamic factor. Sometimes, psychiatric symptoms are "active" in the sense that they are readily apparent in a person's thoughts and behavior. At other times, symptoms may be dormant. Symptoms can sometimes be dampened by medication and some types of symptoms follow a cyclical pattern, waxing and waning over time. Especially important are what have been called **threat/control-override (TCO) symptoms** (Link & Stueve, 1994; Teasdale, Silver, & Monahan, 2006). TCO symptoms refer to beliefs—common in schizophrenics—that other people or forces are controlling one's thoughts or implanting thoughts in one's mind. Paranoid schizophrenics believe that other people want to do them harm. This perceived threat from others overrides self-control. When someone who is already suspicious and fearful of others starts to hear voices commanding him or her to act violently, violent behavior is more likely to follow (Monahan et al., 2001). Other symptoms, such as sadistic fantasies, intrusive homicidal thoughts, self-injury, and suicide attempts are also associated with violence (Bonta, Law, & Hanson, 1998).

Impulsivity and failure to respond to treatment are additional dynamic risk markers for violence. **Impulsivity** is the inability to exert control over one's emotions, thoughts, and behaviors. It can lead directly to violence, particularly when it is expressed as a lack of control over anger (Barratt, 1994). A final marker in this category is **lack of responsiveness to treatment.** Some psychiatric patients may lack the ability to benefit from treatment, others may not be motivated to change, and some may deteriorate after release from an institution. Many people who are released from psychiatric institutions simply stop taking their medication.

Risk Management Markers

Violence is also a function of how well the adjustment of a potentially violent person is managed after that person leaves a treatment facility (Otto & Douglas, 2009). The general finding here is simple and logical: Stable, supportive post-release environments lower the risk of violence. To the degree that the person has adequate housing and is capable of managing basic necessities such as food and finances, the risk of violence is reduced. Post-release treatment is also critical. Those at highest risk for violence require more intensive post-release supervision and treatment. Treatment plans after release must address the specific needs of each person. Release into an environment that includes easy access to guns or drugs lowers the barriers against violence.

A person's social environment can either encourage or discourage violence. Antisocial peers may entice a released patient into violent behavior while a supportive network of friends and relatives may keep violent tendencies in check. What appears to be critical is not the size of the social network but whether the people in that network are kind, sympathetic, and skilled at dealing with the person at risk (Estroff & Zimmer, 1994). The social network can harm as well as help; disappointment with family members or frequent arguments may elevate the risk of violence. The general level of stress created by less than optimal living situations increases the likelihood of violence; so does failure to continue taking medication or failure to continue therapy. Finally, lack of availability of follow-up care in the community contributes strongly to all of these problems.

Taking All Three Types of Markers into Account

Clearly, all three types of risk factors can influence the risk of future violence. Unfortunately, the vast majority of actuarial measures contained few if any dynamic or risk management markers. Reasons for the neglect of dynamic and risk management markers included: (1) they are more difficult to measure than historical risk factors; (2) they generally contribute less to accurate prediction than historical risk factors; (3) they are less well-studied than historical factors; and (4) to be useful, they may require repeated measurements. Despite these difficulties, new instruments are now being developed that attempt to include both dynamic and risk management factors.

A key implication of only using historical factors in risk assessment is that an individual's future risk will not change over time. This is especially significant in SVP or involuntary civil commitment proceedings. If only static markers are assessed, people who are committed will never become less risky—even if they are successfully treated during their confinement. For example, if only static markers are used to assess risk, the fact that Leroy Hendricks was 70-years-old and largely immobilized in a wheelchair would have no bearing on his risk at the time of his release. Clearly, actuarial instruments need to incorporate more dynamic and risk management markers in their calculations (McDermott, Edens, Quanbeck, Busse, & Scott, 2008).

Actuarial risk prediction instruments have one more important failing. Because they are based upon large group (nomothetic) data, they do not often include rare factors that may be especially predictive or protective of risk in a particular case. For example, no actuarial instrument includes physical incapacitation (paraplegia or being the victim of a severe stroke) as a protective factor, even though people who are incapacitated usually cannot commit future acts of violence. Actuarial instruments simply overlook physical incapacitation because it occurs so rarely in the populations that the actuarial instruments were based on.

Whether or not a clinician using an actuarial instrument should adjust his or estimate of risk based on a rare factor is controversial. For example, if the best actuarial methods suggest that a particular person is very unlikely to become violent, but while talking to a clinical psychologist the person threatens to harm someone, should the psychologist not take that information into account (Monahan, 2003)? Scholars disagree. Some believe that actuarial instruments should never be adjusted (Quinsey et al., 2006) because allowing clinical adjustment can infect the decision-making process with biases. Other scholars argue it would be unethical not to adjust a risk estimate under the circumstances mentioned above (Monahan, 2003). Research to date does not appear to support clinicians adjusting their actuarial assessments with other risk factors (Hanson & Morton Bourgon, 2009; Scurich & Krauss, 2013). For the most part, clinicians appear to be injecting more error than accuracy when they adjust their estimates.

Finally, it can be argued that, even though actuarial risk prediction judgments are better than unstructured clinical hunches, they are not sufficiently accurate to enable decisions about whether an individual should be sentenced to death or whether an individual should be confined indefinitely (Krauss et al., 2012). In the end, it will be up to the courts to determine what role actuarial risk assessment instruments will play in these consequential legal decisions.

 ## GUIDED PROFESSIONAL JUDGMENT INSTRUMENTS

Because of concerns about purely actuarial risk prediction instruments, several researchers have created risk assessment tools intended to guide the decision making of clinicians. These instruments were designed to combine the accuracy of actuarial methods with the flexibility of clinical decision making. The HCR-20 (Historical Clinical Risk Management Scheme-20) is a good example of what is often called the guided professional judgment approach. Although a number of guided professional judgment instruments exist, we will focus on the HCR-20 because it is has received the most research attention to date.

ℱocus on ℭareers

Violence Risk Expert
Joel A. Dvoskin, Ph.D., ABPP
University of Arizona College of Medicine

(*Courtesy of Dr. Joel A. Dvoskin, PhD, ABPP*)

Currently, three themes typically dominate my work. First, much of my work revolves around the study and prevention of interpersonal violence and suicide, especially in regard to workplaces, campuses, and mental health and criminal justice settings. Second, I frequently testify about issues related to conditions of confinement in jails, prisons, and psychiatric hospitals, including suicide prevention and mental health services. Third, as a former state mental health administrator, I frequently consult to organized systems of care regarding the provision of mental health services in the public sector.

The services I provide include expert testimony; consultation; education and public speaking; mediation; and workplace and campus violence prevention. My clients have included corporations, law firms, departments of corrections and mental health, federal agencies, professional and collegiate sports leagues and associations, public school systems, colleges, and universities.

As an expert witness, the most important challenge is to strive for objective and evenhanded opinions.

Ideally, an expert's testimony should be the same, no matter which side called them as an expert. However, objectivity is hard to achieve. Each of us is subject to biases, only some of which are within our conscious awareness. The best response to this challenge is not to pretend that I am not biased, but to counteract and correct for my biases through transparency in the manner in which I formed my opinion.

As a consultant, I am frequently asked to advise government agencies about effective and cost-effective ways to provide services to the seriously mentally ill and those suffering from co-occurring substance use disorders.

As a violence prevention consultant, I work with corporations, labor unions, school districts, sports leagues, colleges, and universities. These activities have included training and systems consultation as well as crisis response. The training provided by my colleagues and I has two important goals: (1) creating an environment in which everyone feels safe, respected, and fairly treated; and (2) identifying troubled people and troubling situations as early as possible so that they can be assisted, managed, and resolved in a cost-effective and beneficent manner. For many of our clients, we develop crisis assessment and response teams, to whom we may provide case specific, often emergency consultation.

My somewhat unusual career allows me to combine my diverse interests in research, public policy, clinical assessment and treatment, and the law. I have a very strong belief in "science for practice." At its best, behavioral science results in changes at the system or individual level; and practice that ignores science is often counterproductive, or even harmful. My career allows me to serve as a "bridge" between behavioral science and the very practical worlds in which corporations and government agencies reside.

The **HCR-20** consists of a checklist of 20 items, 10 assessing "historical" risk factors, 5 assessing present "clinical" risk factors, and 5 assessing future "risk" factors. Each item is scored 0 (absent), 1 (possibly or partially present), or 2 (definitely present). Based on the scoring of the 20 items, the practitioner is supposed to offer a statement concerning whether the assessed individual is low, medium, or high risk (Webster, Douglas, Eaves, & Hart, 1997). Unlike an actuarial instrument, the clinician is not bound to weight the factors in any equation. The clinician can choose to give any amount of weight he or she deems appropriate to any item.

The factors included in the HCR-20 were not based on a specific population that was followed for an extended period of time. Instead, all are factors frequently identified in the research literature. This is an advantage. Because the HCR-20 was not

TABLE 14.5			
Strengths and Weaknesses of Different Assessment Methods			
Types of risk assessment	*Based on*	*Strengths*	*Weaknesses*
Unstructured clinical judgment	The experience and intuition of the clinician	Idiographic, related to the specific individual being evaluated	May be biased by clinician's beliefs and perceptions Tend to overpredict violence (false positives) Does not take into account base rate of re-offense Generally, no follow-up to provide feedback to clinician
Actuarial prediction	Empirical research factors shown to be predictive in the population on which it is based	Based on large amounts of data collected over extended periods and statistics, eliminating subjective biases	Nomothetic, may not generalize to the individual being evaluated May rely too heavily on static factors Does not account for rare, dynamic, or risk management factors
Guided professional judgment	A combination of clinical experience and empirically derived factors	Based on empirically derived risk factors Not based on a specific population, so avoids problems of generalizability Can account for rare, dynamic, and risk management factors	Because the clinician assigns weights and combines factors, may still be subject to clinician's biases

constructed on a specific population, it does not face the same generalizability issues as actuarial instruments. Unlike an actuarial instrument, it also allows the clinician to include relevant dynamic, risk management, or rare risk factors in its prediction. Initial research has also suggested that the HCR-20 outperforms clinical predictions of future dangerousness (Douglas & Reeves, 2009; Douglas & Webster, 1999).

However, the HCR-20's greatest strengths—its flexibility and its reliance on clinical decision making—are also its greatest weaknesses. Clinicians using it might combine risk factors in an appealing but inaccurate manner and may be influenced by all the biases associated with clinicians' nonscientific predictions of risk. Yet, research to date suggests that the HCR-20 and other guided professional judgment instruments outperform unstructured clinical judgment and achieve accuracy similar to actuarial instruments.

There is little evidence that one particular risk assessment instrument or type of instrument (actuarial, guided professional judgment) outperforms any of the others on a consistent basis (Tully, Chou, & Browne, 2013; Yang et al., 2010). A brief summary of the advantages and limitations of each of these methods is contained in Table 14.5.

 ## JURORS' REACTIONS TO RISK ASSESSMENT EVIDENCE

Actuarial methods (informed by research and using statistical techniques) and guided professional judgment instruments produce more accurate predictions than clinical judgments based on intuition and professional experience. Unfortunately, the idiographic, individualized nature of a clinical prediction may be more appealing to jurors and judges. One study examined this issue in a simulated death penalty hearing. It used mock jurors to explore the Supreme Court's assumption about the ability of jurors to understand the shortcomings of expert risk testimony. In some conditions, an expert testified about the future dangerousness of a defendant based on clinical methods, and in other conditions, an expert testified about future dangerousness based on actuarial methods. Results indicated that clinical testimony had a significantly greater impact on juror's ratings of dangerousness than did actuarial testimony. Cross-examination or a competing expert did undercut the persuasiveness of both types of testimony. But, clinical testimony withstood such attacks better—jurors' faith in the clinical prediction was less shaken by cross-examination or by competing expert testimony (Krauss & Lee, 2003; Krauss & Sales, 2001).

Although actuarial and guided professional judgment instruments produce better predictions, jurors appear more likely to believe a clinical psychologist who testifies in great detail about a particular defendant and then makes a prediction based on professional experience and judgment. Clinical testimony seems to be easier to understand and more directly relevant to the defendant on trial. Actuarial testimony may seem more abstract, harder to understand, and less directly relevant to the particular defendant jurors are being asked to judge.

Follow-up research has supported the finding that clinical testimony has more impact on jurors. Interestingly, studies have found that when similar expert testimony is presented to college students in a mock SVP hearing, there is no significant difference between jurors' reliance on actuarial and clinical predictions of dangerousness (Guy & Edens, 2003; McCabe, Krauss, & Lieberman, 2010). However, when more representative jurors are presented with the same SVP trial, the expected favoritism for clinical expert testimony over actuarial testimony is clearly apparent (Krauss et al., 2012; McCabe et al., 2010). Further research is needed to determine if this bias in juror decision-making can be corrected.

 ## TREATMENT TO REDUCE THE RISK OF VIOLENCE

Instead of focusing our efforts on trying to predict violence, it might be more productive to focus on preventing and managing the risk of violence in the community (La Fond, 2008). Indeed, the disruptions in care created by releasing offenders into unsupportive, unsupervised environments is consistently associated with higher rates of reoffending (Morgan et al., 2013). Several researchers have investigated what can be done to help mentally disordered criminals adapt successfully to the inevitable stressors of life outside an institution. A review of treatment programs found that effective treatment—treatment that promotes better adjustment and improves public safety—tends to be comprehensive (Harris & Rice, 1997). The best programs strongly emphasize assisting offenders in several domains of life. Some programs provide help with housing and getting a job, and also provide training and advising for family members. Comprehensive programs help to improve the social skills and impulse control of offenders and offer services that help prevent social isolation. Treatment must also be tailored to the legal status of the client. Offenders who are hospitalized because they have been deemed to be incompetent to stand trial should be given shorter hospital stays and more focused treatment designed to restore competence. In contrast, offenders who have been found not guilty by reason of insanity need longer-term treatment that will equip them for eventual release into the community.

Communication is a key component of all post-release treatment programs. People running the programs are obliged to communicate with legal officials about behaviors that may violate conditions of release or threaten public safety (e.g., contact with a former victim). Clear communication with the client is also essential. Indeed, many researchers suggest that there ought to be a specific contract with the client. That contract should list required behaviors and specify the consequences of failing to comply with the contract (Heilbrun & Peters, 2000). Required behaviors might include taking medications, showing up for scheduled sessions with therapists, not taking illegal drugs, and not possessing a weapon. An offender might also be required to find employment and housing. Once offenders demonstrate that they can function well under restrictive conditions after release, they can gradually be given more freedom. For example, they may first be held in a restrictive hospital, later in a hospital that allows occasional travel from the institution, still later in a supervised community home or halfway house, and, finally, they would be permitted to live in the community but still be required to visit local treatment centers regularly.

If the goal is effective risk management, ongoing monitoring of the client is essential. The client must be frequently reassessed to determine if the risk of violence has changed. Further, the focus must be on dynamic risk factors that might be changed through treatment, and there must be interventions available for lowering one's risk if it becomes elevated (Hodgins et al., 2007; Morgan et al., 2013).

► IN CONCLUSION

Although it is impossible to predict future behavior perfectly, predictions are a crucial component of legal decision making. Expert predictions about future dangerousness may determine whether an individual is confined for the rest of his or her life. Such predictions may even determine whether a defendant is sentenced to life or death. The psychologists involved in these consequential predictions are ethically obliged to understand the strengths and limitations of their expertise. They should base their conclusions on the best research currently available and consider whether the courts are asking them to provide expertise beyond what is appropriate. The knowledge accumulated through research will continue to inform and improve risk predictions and may also help the legal system reconsider its use of future risk in legal determinations.

► CRITICAL THINKING QUESTIONS

1. What are the strengths and weaknesses of the present legal standard for civil commitment?

2. Should clinicians' have a Tarasoff duty? What are the advantages and disadvantages of this potential legal liability?

3. What should be the trade-off between false positives and false negatives? Should it depend on the legal context (e.g., death penalty versus civil commitment)?

4. What are the strengths and weaknesses of the present legal standard for sexual predator civil commitment?

5. Should sex offenders be treated differently from other types of offenders?

6. If community notification laws have no effect on recidivism rates, should they be abandoned?

7. Are SVP laws morally and ethically appropriate? Should it matter whether effective treatment exists for dangerous individuals, or should protection of society be a sufficient goal to incapacitate individuals?

8. When (if ever) should clinical judgment be used to overrule actuarial predictions of future risk?

▶ KEY TERMS

a danger to self or others (p. 286)

actuarial prediction (p. 293)

antisocial personality disorder (p. 288)

base rate (p. 291)

base rate of reoffense (p. 291)

clinical prediction (p. 293)

community notification (p. 282)

deinstitutionalization (p. 286)

double jeopardy (p. 281)

duty to protect laws (p. 287)

ex post facto (p. 281)

false negative (p. 290)

false positive (p. 290)

future dangerousness standard (p. 283)

generalizability (p. 294)

gravely disabled (p. 286)

HCR-20 (p. 298)

idiographic, qualitative approach (p. 293)

impulsivity (p. 296)

involuntary civil commitment (p. 285)

lack of responsiveness to treatment (p. 296)

Megan's law (p. 282)

nomothetic, quantative approach (p. 293)

parens patriae power (p. 279)

pedophile (p. 279)

police power (p. 279)

preventative detention (p. 283)

psychiatric symptomatology (p. 295)

psychopathy (p. 295)

Sexual Offending Risk Appraisal Guide (SORAG) (p. 294)

sexually violent predator civil commitment laws (SVP laws) (p. 279)

substantive due process (p. 281)

Tarasoff v. Regents of the University of California (1976) (p. 287)

threat/control override (TCO) symptoms (p. 296)

true negative (p. 290)

true positive (p. 290)

unstructured clinical judgment (p. 291)

Violence Risk Appraisal Guide (VRAG) (p. 294)

15 Workplace Law: Harassment, Discrimination, and Fairness

- ▶ The Evolution of Sexual Discrimination Law
- ▶ Sexual Harassment: Prevalence and Perceptions
- ▶ The Legal Boundaries of Sexual Harassment
- ▶ The Psychology of Sexual Harassment
- ▶ A Broader Look at Workplace Discrimination
- ▶ Racial Discrimination in the Workplace
- ▶ The Psychology of Perceived Fairness

It was a type of love letter, though less romantic and gushy than most. The man, an executive at a large company, sent the letter to his beloved—a junior vice president at the same company. He wrote:

> I know this may seem silly or unnecessary to you, but I really want you to give very serious consideration to the matter as it is very important to me. I want to assure you that under no circumstances will I allow our relationship or, should it happen, the end of our relationship, to impact on your job or our working relationship.

Attached to the letter was a copy of the company's sexual harassment policy. The woman's response was similar in tone:

> My relationship with you has been (and is) voluntary, consensual, and welcome. I also understand that I am free to end this relationship at any time and, in doing so, it will not adversely impact on my job (Merrill & Knox, 2010).

The letters—which were suggested by the company's lawyer—were written as part of a "consensual relationship agreement." The hope is that such agreements will help shield companies from sexual harassment lawsuits when a love affair at work ends badly. Their use reflects a growing awareness of the legal risks associated with sexually charged interactions at work. This chapter explores how the law attempts to regulate decision-making and social interaction in the workplace. ◀

THE EVOLUTION OF SEXUAL DISCRIMINATION LAW

Sexual discrimination law was created by a political miscalculation. During congressional debate over the **Civil Rights Act of 1964** (known as **Title VII**), a conservative U.S. representative named Howard Smith attached an amendment. His amendment added a ban on gender discrimination to Title VII's ban on racial discrimination in employment. Smith hoped that adding sexual discrimination to Title VII would cause the entire bill to go down in defeat. During debate, he mockingly suggested that his amendment would "protect our spinster friends." To Smith's surprise, the Civil Rights Act, and his amendment to it, passed. Discrimination based on race and gender became illegal.

In 1979, Yale Law Professor Catharine MacKinnon published her influential book *Sexual Harassment of Working Women*. Her argument—radical at the time—was that sexual harassment was a form of discrimination. She defined two types of sexual harassment: quid pro quo and hostile environment. **Quid pro quo harassment** involves a "more or less explicit exchange: the woman must comply sexually or forfeit an employment benefit" (p. 48). For example, a woman might be told that if she fails to submit to a sexual request, she will not be given a coveted job or promotion. The second form of harassment—**hostile environment**—describes a situation where life is made so difficult for the victim that she cannot carry out her job responsibilities. MacKinnon described it this way: "Less clear, and undoubtedly more pervasive, is the situation in which sexual harassment simply makes the work environment unbearable" (p. 49). The two basic forms of sexual harassment identified by MacKinnon are now enshrined in law.

By 1980, the **Equal Employment Opportunity Commission (EEOC)**—the government agency created to enforce Title VII—issued the first federal guidelines on gender discrimination. Sexual harassment was defined as "unwelcome sexual advances, requests for sexual favors, and other verbal or physical conduct of a sexual nature." A hostile environment exists where an employee is subjected to unwelcome sexual conduct that interferes with the performance of work activities or creates an intimidating, hostile, abusive, or offensive work environment. Quid pro quo is a stronger form of harassment because it involves direct sexual barter or coercion. An employee is told that in exchange for sexual favors, she will receive a benefit—for example, a bonus, a salary increase, a promotion, a desirable job assignment, or a favorable performance evaluation. Alternatively, an employee might be told that she will experience negative consequences if she refuses to submit sexually. These sorts of crude attempts at sexual bargaining are quite rare compared to hostile-environment harassment.

EEOC guidelines state that employers have an obligation (an "affirmative duty" in the words of the guidelines) to maintain a workplace free from harassment, intimidation, or insult. Further, employers must act to eliminate harassing practices and correct the damaging effects of such practices (*EEOC v. Murphy Motor Freight Lines*, 1980). Plaintiffs in harassment cases must show that unwelcome verbal and physical behaviors created an intimidating or offensive environment that unreasonably interfered with job performance or restricted employment opportunities. In addition, they must usually show that the employer knew, or should have known, about the harassing conduct but failed to take prompt and appropriate action to remedy the situation (*Burlington Industries v. Ellerth*, 1998; *Faragher v. Boca Raton*, 1998).

SEXUAL HARASSMENT: PREVALENCE AND PERCEPTIONS

A precise accounting of how much sexual harassment occurs on the job is difficult to obtain for several reasons: not all studies have asked about the same types of harassment or used the same checklists of harassing behaviors. Also, people are often asked about events dating back several years. Such retrospective reports of harassment may be biased because of distorted memories. Finally, rates of harassment vary across work settings. Some settings are relatively free of harassing behavior, while others are rife with harassment. Despite these difficulties, several clear patterns emerge from the available data. First, virtually every study has found that females are far more likely than males to be the victims of sexual harassment. Overall, women experience harassment at a rate three to four times the rate for men. In a series of four large-scale surveys of federal employees in 1987, 1994, and 2007, about 42% of women and 15% of men claimed to have experienced sexual harassment at work during the previous two years (U.S. Merit Systems Protection Board, 2007). Similarly, 43% of women lawyers working in large law firms reported being pinched, touched, or cornered in a sexually harassing way by a partner in their firm (Slade, 1994), and 41% of female medical students reported that they had experienced sexual harassment (Frank, Carrera, Stratton, Bickel, & Nora, 2006). Surveys found even higher rates of reported harassment among military personnel—60% for females and 27% for males (Bergman & Henning, 2008; Langhout et al., 2006; Street, Kimerling, Bell, & Pavao, 2011). Looking across several studies, Barbara Gutek (1993; 2007a) has estimated that approximately 53% of working women had been sexually harassed by men at some time during their careers and about 16% of working men had been sexually harassed by women at some time during their careers. The most likely targets of harassment are young, unmarried women.

A second interesting finding concerns the ratio of men to women in the work setting. Women working in jobs dominated by men (e.g., engineering, trucking, surgery, construction) are more likely to experience sexual harassment (Leskinen, Cortina, & Kabat, 2011). Work settings where women are a distinct minority tend to be more sexualized than settings where males and females are roughly equal in number. The more sexualized culture of workplaces where men greatly outnumber women is sometimes manifested in the display of posters and calendars depicting women in suggestive dress or poses, sexual jokes, sexual terms and metaphors, and obscene language. Also, men appear to over-infer sexual behavior. Compared to women, men are more likely to interpret touch by a co-worker in a sexual way, and men are more likely to mistake friendly behavior for sexual seduction (Gutek, 2007a; O'Connor, 2007).

A third conclusion is that when males are victims of harassment, the harassment is slightly more likely to come from another male than from a female. That is, slightly more than half the time, males are harassed by other males. In contrast, when women are the victims, their harassers are other women only about 2% of the time (Waldo, Berdahl, & Fitzgerald, 1998). Male–male harassment appears to have a different character than cross-gender harassment. Male perpetrators tend to harass other men through the use of lewd and obscene comments and through "enforcement of the male gender role" that is, by suggesting that another male performs unmanly activities or behaves in an effeminate way (Foote & Goodman-Delahunty, 1999). For example, in a field study of workplace harassment, fathers who spent a significant amount of time caring for their children experienced more harassment and mistreatment than traditional fathers who were less involved with childcare or than men without children

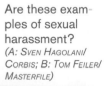

Are these examples of sexual harassment?
(*A: Sven Hagolani/ Corbis; B: Tom Feiler/ Masterfile*)

(Berdahl & Moon, 2013). When men are harassed by women, the harassment generally involves either unwanted sexual attention or disparaging gender-related comments such as "men only have one thing on their mind" or "men are too clueless and insensitive to make good managers" (Waldo et al., 1998).

But which behaviors do people label as sexual harassment? At the extremes, there is widespread agreement. Less than 10% of males and females classify staring, flirting, occasional use of coarse language, or nonsexual touching as harassment; but 99% of males and females view sexual bribery (requiring sexual favors in exchange for job benefits) as harassment (Frazier, Cochran, & Olson, 1995). If the harasser is the victim's boss or someone else who has power over her pay, promotion, or work assignments, men and women view the harassment as more serious. There is also widespread agreement that aggressive, unwelcome physical contact—grabbing, groping, sexual touching—should be defined as illegal harassment. But even though there is near consensus between men and women about mild and extreme behaviors, there is considerable disagreement about more ambiguous behaviors: repeated requests for dates, sexual jokes, public displays of calendars depicting swimsuit models, or frequent crude language. Women tend to perceive such behaviors as more offensive and potentially harassing. Based on meta-analyses of hundreds of studies, we can say that the greater tendency for women to classify behaviors as potentially harassing is modest, but it emerges most strongly when jurors consider the ambiguous mid-range of harassing behaviors (Blumenthal, 1998; Rotundo, Nguyen, & Sackett, 2001). If the harassment is severe, both men and women will condemn the behavior and if the harassment is mild, men and women will generally agree that it does not rise to the level of harassment.

 ## THE LEGAL BOUNDARIES OF SEXUAL HARASSMENT

The courts have had difficulty providing a clear, precise definition of hostile environment harassment. When does boorish, crude, or inappropriate behavior cross a legal line and become illegal sexual harassment? Does telling dirty jokes or repeatedly asking a woman at work for a date constitute harassment? What if a man asks a woman for a date a third time after she has politely declined twice?

Because there is no precise list of sexually harassing behaviors, most courts have relied on a **reasonable person standard.** And because concepts such as "offensive" are inherently subjective, a judgment must be made about whether other similar people would have experienced a particular work environment as hostile. Consequently, a woman alleging sexual harassment must establish that a reasonable person would have found the behavior in question severe enough and pervasive enough to create an abusive working environment (*Harris v. Forklift Systems,* 1993; *Oncale v. Sundowner Offshore Services, Inc.,* 1998). By focusing on the reasonable similar person, the law attempts to prevent claims based on trivial or mildly offensive conduct and claims by unusually sensitive employees. Some courts have instructed jurors to interpret evidence from the perspective of a **reasonable woman.** This reasonable woman standard was first proposed in 1991, in the case of *Ellison v. Brady.* In that case, the Ninth Circuit Court of Appeals adopted that standard, partly in response to research suggesting that males and females have different views of sexual conduct in the workplace. In that case, Kerry Ellison had been harassed by a coworker who wrote her a series of sexually suggestive love letters. The court reasoned that women would be more likely than men to view the letters as menacing and disturbing. Indeed, some research has found that people define a broader range of behaviors as harassing if they are told to use a reasonable woman standard (Wiener & Hurt, 2001).

Social scientists have raised several concerns about the creation of a reasonable woman standard (Gutek & O'Connor, 1995; Winter & Vallano, 2012). First, research finds only small differences in how males and females define harassment. Those differences are usually only evident when the incidents are much less severe than those that typically end up in court. Second, the reasonable woman standard is inconsistent with legal standards in other areas of law. For example, courts would be unlikely to consider analogous separate standards for reasonable religious persons or reasonable nonreligious persons. Third, instead of creating a separate standard, it would be more productive to create a consensus about what constitutes sexual harassment. Fourth, distinguishing a reasonable woman from a reasonable person may contribute to sexist attitudes by suggesting that we need to treat women as weak, fragile, oversensitive, and in need of special protection.

At least for now, the Supreme Court has held that a reasonable person would need to find the environment hostile and that the environment must be "both objectively and subjectively offensive" (*Faragher v. Boca Raton*, 1998; *Harris v. Forklift Systems*, 1993).

Current Status of Harassment Law

Sexual harassment is still a relatively new and unsettled area of law, but several court decisions have drawn clearer boundaries. The case of *Harris v. Forklift Systems, Inc.* (1993) marked a turning point in sexual harassment law. Theresa Harris had been the rentals manager at Forklift Systems in Nashville, Tennessee. The company president had made several sexually suggestive and demeaning remarks to her over the course of nearly two years (e.g., asking her in public whether she had had sex with clients to get their accounts). For a while, she simply tried to ignore his comments. Eventually, she confronted him, and he promised to stop. When he continued to make sexually suggestive comments, she quit. She appealed her case all the way to the U.S. Supreme Court.

The Supreme Court agreed to hear Harris's case because lower courts seemed to be using different standards in deciding such cases. One point of disagreement concerned impact. Some courts seemed to require that the victim experience psychological injury, while other courts seemed to require only that the harassment interfere with the performance of job duties. A second point of disagreement concerned perspective. Some courts had used a more subjective perspective—the impact of the alleged harassment on the plaintiff in the particular case. Other courts used a more objective perspective—they asked whether a reasonable person would have judged the work environment as hostile and offensive. In a unanimous decision, the Court ruled in favor of Theresa Harris. The decision held that it was not necessary to demonstrate psychological injury and that a reasonable person standard should be applied.

In *Oncale v. Sundowner Offshore Services, Inc.* (1998), the Court made clear that sexual harassment law is gender-blind. The *Oncale* ruling reinstated the case of Joseph Oncale, a man who had suffered harassment while working on an oil rig in the Gulf of Mexico. He claimed that, while in the shower room, his male co-workers attacked him and shoved a bar of soap between his buttocks. Also, three co-workers held him down and threatened to rape him. A lower court had held that male-on-male harassment did not qualify as discrimination unless the harasser was gay and choosing his victim *because of* his gender. The U.S. Supreme Court rejected that reasoning and ruled that same-sex harassment could be grounds for a lawsuit.

The Supreme Court has declared that gender-related jokes, teasing, and occasional use of abusive language do not qualify as illegal conduct. The Court ruled that "innocuous differences in ways men and women routinely interact with members of the same sex and of the opposite sex" do not constitute harassment and that harassment law should not be viewed as a "general civility code" (*Faragher v. Boca Raton,* 1998). Lower courts have been instructed to apply a **totality of circumstances test** to gauge whether the conduct in question created an unlawful hostile environment. That is, courts must evaluate the context of the objectionable conduct, as well as its frequency and severity. Courts have emphasized two responsibilities of employers: (1) to prevent harassment by establishing clear policies and training procedures, and (2) to correct harassment by thoroughly investigating complaints and taking disciplinary actions against harassers. Victims are responsible for reporting harassment and taking advantage of complaint procedures (*Burlington Industries, Inc. v. Ellerth,* 1998; *Faragher v. Boca Raton,* 1998).

Sexual Harassment Lawsuits

It is important to note that legal, permissible sexual behavior at work is far more common than illegal sexual harassment. The law does not attempt to regulate behavior that is merely inappropriate, crude, or offensive. Usually, only severe cases of harassment that result in significant injuries end up in court.

For a case to go to trial, several elements usually need to be in place: clearly harassing conduct, a plaintiff who is willing to endure the strains of litigation, a lawyer who is willing to take the case (usually on a contingency basis), witnesses who are willing to testify that harassment occurred, and an organization that failed to prevent or correct illegal conduct. At trial, a jury often must weigh conflicting stories about what really happened to decide if the alleged behavior rises (or sinks) to the level of unlawful sexual harassment. For example, if a victim experiences harassment over a significant period and fails to report the incidents, it may later be argued in court that the victim welcomed the attention or did not really find the behavior offensive or serious. The counterargument would be that the victim delayed reporting the incidents because she feared retaliation from the harasser or because she wanted to avoid conflict or potential loss of privacy. It might also be argued that the upper-level management of the organization either actively or passively created an atmosphere that tolerated harassment. Generally, only egregious cases make it to court, and, even among those that are litigated, only about 35% are decided in favor of the plaintiff (Terpstra & Baker, 1992). The three cases described below led to litigation.

Case 1: In a lawsuit against Boeing Aerospace Corporation, the plaintiff was a woman who delivered tools to several production buildings. She was fired after claiming that she could not return to her job because of the stress caused by the persistent harassment she experienced at work (Gutek, 2007b). According to testimony presented at trial, the environment at Boeing included publicly displayed posters showing women in suggestive poses (e.g., a poster showing a dog licking a woman's genitals and a magazine advertisement for an inflatable female sex partner). There was routine use of sexual slang (e.g., referring to the women's restroom as the "beaver pond") and several incidents of hostility against women. The plaintiff found a condom filled with hand lotion in her coat pocket and found feces smeared on her car. A male supervisor had sexually propositioned several female employees. At trial, attorneys for Boeing argued that the plaintiff encouraged sexually suggestive behavior. She was a bodybuilder who had recently had breast implants. These facts came up at trial. For example, a photograph of herself displayed on her desk at work showed her flexing her muscles in a bikini. The plaintiff lost her case at trial.

Case 2: A very different kind of sexual harassment case involved the large accounting firm of Price Waterhouse. Here, the problem was not sexual hostility but discrimination based on violations of gender stereotypes. Ann Hopkins was not promoted to partner despite her popularity with clients, despite having brought in millions of dollars in new accounts, and despite having worked more billable hours than anyone else who was being considered for partner. Traits that were considered desirable in her male colleagues—being ambitious, aggressive, competitive, and driven—were, in her case, viewed as indicative of an "interpersonal skills problem." She was advised, in part, to be more "ladylike," to walk and talk in a more feminine way, to "wear make-up, have her hair styled, and wear jewelry," and to "take a course at charm school." Hopkins eventually won her case, even though Price Waterhouse appealed all the way to the Supreme Court (Fiske & Stevens, 1993).

Case 3: Evidence of sexual harassment was clear and pervasive at Mitsubishi's massive automotive assembly plant in Normal, Illinois. Some men at the plant simulated masturbation in front of women, and others exposed themselves to female co-workers. The harassment was frequently physical. Several male workers grabbed women's breasts, and some men used air guns to deliver painful blasts to women's breasts and crotches. Supervisors ignored or retaliated against women who complained. One supervisor warned a woman who complained that if she pursued the complaint, the harassers would fabricate stories about her wild sexual exploits to redirect attention toward her. Another supervisor took no action when one man threatened to rape and kill a female co-worker. In 1997, Mitsubishi Company agreed to pay $9.5 million to settle a lawsuit brought by 27 women workers. Then, in 1998, Mitsubishi abandoned a three-year fight against federal charges of sexual harassment at the plant and agreed to pay $34 million to more than 300 female employees (Braun, 1998).

Only a few studies have explored how jurors make sense of evidence presented during sexual harassment trials. For example, one study asked people who had reported for jury duty to read a summary of a sexual harassment trial. Both the severity of the harassment and the response of the company being sued varied across conditions. Mock jurors awarded more in compensatory damages when the harassment was severe rather than mild, and jurors awarded less in punitive damages when the company had enforced its own harassment policy (Cass, Levett, & Kovera, 2010). Other studies have found that the mock juror verdicts against a woman bringing a sexual harassment lawsuit were predicted by low perceived credibility of the woman, hostility toward women in the workplace, and jurors' inability to imagine themselves in the woman's position (this is sometimes called "self-referencing"); (O'Connor, Gutek, Stockdale, Geer, & Melançon, 2004).

One large study looked at juror decision-making across eight realistic simulated trials conducted by a trial-consulting firm (Huntley & Costanzo, 2003). All eight simulations involved real cases that were about to go to trial, and all involved male harassers and female victims. Jurors were drawn from the actual trial venues, and real attorneys presented arguments and evidence in abbreviated form. The researchers discovered clear differences between jurors who found the employer liable and jurors who did not. Jurors who found the employer liable believed that the victim was a good employee of good character, that the company knew about the harassment and failed to respond, that the harassment was systemic (i.e., the harasser victimized others or other people in the company were also harassers), that the company retaliated against the victim for complaining about the harassment, that the victim feared she would lose her job if she reported the harassment, and that the victim suffered (psychologically and in her job) because of the harassment.

In contrast, jurors who found the company not liable believed that the victim was oversensitive and exaggerating her claims, that the victim may have encouraged or contributed to the harassment, that the company acted to stop the harassment once it became aware of it, that the company had anti-harassment policies in place, that the victim brought the lawsuit to retaliate against the company, and that the victim failed to follow proper reporting procedures. Although the two sets of jurors diverged sharply in their interpretations of evidence, all jurors focused on the victim's character, the consequences suffered by the victim, and the company's response (or lack of response).

In a study of female professionals who worked at a large financial services firm, researchers analyzed more than a dozen potential predictors of women's decisions to join or opt out of a sexual harassment class-action lawsuit against the company. Those women who decided to join the lawsuit were significantly more likely to perceive that the company did not take harassment seriously, to believe that it was risky to complain about harassment, to have already left the company, to have experienced offensive and disturbing forms of harassment, and to report suffering psychological distress as a result of harassment (Wright & Fitzgerald, 2009).

Careful analyses of hundreds of sexual harassment cases have revealed the characteristics that make lawsuits successful (Pierce, Muslin, Dudley, & Aguinis, 2008; Terpstra & Baker, 1992). The two factors that best predict a decision for the plaintiff are severe harassment and witnesses who corroborate the plaintiff's charges. The probability of winning a case is also increased if documents support the harassment claim, if the victim had told management about the harassment before filing charges, and if the company then failed to take action against the harasser. Averaging across studies, plaintiffs won only about 36% of the cases. Unfortunately, the outcomes of sexual harassment cases do not depend on legally relevant criteria alone. The judge's personal characteristics—specifically, age and political orientation—also played a role. In federal cases, older judges tended to favor the defendant, while younger judges tended to favor the plaintiff. Similarly, judges appointed by a Republican president tended to favor the defendant, while judges appointed by a Democratic president tended to favor plaintiffs. Indeed, the judge's personal characteristics shifted the probability of a particular decision by about 28% (Kulik, Perry, & Pepper, 2003).

THE PSYCHOLOGY OF SEXUAL HARASSMENT

Some Causes

Sexually harassing behaviors may arise from different motives. Some problematic behavior is motivated by a man's genuine romantic interest in a female coworker. Because of a lack of social skills or insensitivity to social cues, the man may persistently proposition the woman, despite her expressions of disinterest. Unable to accept the woman's disinterest, the frustrated man may then escalate his overtures, or the experience of being rebuffed may trigger hostility toward the woman. Alternatively, the underlying motive may begin as hostility. In such cases, harassment may be manifested as attempts to intimidate, dominate, or humiliate (Pryor, 2009).

Motive may interact with job type in ways that promote different forms of sexual harassment (Glick & Fiske, 2007). Traditionally female "pink collar" jobs, such as nurse, teacher, secretary, or flight attendant, may encourage forms of harassment rooted in men's earnest desire for intimacy with women. Because such jobs tend to emphasize the traditional female roles of nurturing and sexual attractiveness, they may elicit protectiveness and sexual attention. In contrast, jobs that have been historically held by men may encourage different forms of harassment. Because occupational status and achievement is a significant component of male identity, the job success of women in traditionally male occupations may threaten the self-esteem of some men. Those men may then engage in harassment to undermine women's job performance. "Blue collar" jobs such as mechanic, laborer, dockworker, or construction worker emphasize traditionally masculine traits such as strength and toughness. In these work settings, women are more likely to face competitive and hostile forms of harassment in which the perpetrator seeks to dominate women and show that women do not belong. "White collar" jobs such as physician, lawyer, professor, or business executive have tended to be dominated by males and may be seen as embodying traits such as intelligence, confidence, and ambition. Women in these occupational roles have often been subject to hostile harassment in an effort to "put women in their place" and maintain male dominance (Berdahl, 2007; Rudman, Moss-Racusin, Phelan, & Nauts, 2012).

As noted earlier, sexual harassment of women is far more likely to occur in workplaces where men significantly outnumber women. Of course, this is often the situation when women first enter occupations traditionally held by men. The entry of women into such workplaces may disrupt the masculine work culture and lead to discomfort, tension, and resentment among some men. A comfortable camaraderie may be disrupted. Because the men in such settings may have no experience dealing with a female co-worker, there may be a tendency to relate to female co-workers based on gender stereotypes (e.g., women should be warm, nurturing, and concerned with their physical appearance). Violations of these stereotypes (e.g., a tough, strong woman working on a loading dock) may lead to a hostile response (Foote & Goodman-Delahunty, 2005). When small numbers of women begin to enter supervisory roles in a particular profession, sexual harassment may be motivated by a desire to control or dominate such women, rather than a desire for sexual contact (McLaughlin, Uggen, & Blackstone, 2012).

Some Effects

The targets of harassment experience a variety of complex negative effects. For example, an analysis of the reactions of 72 plaintiffs in sexual harassment lawsuits revealed four distinct emotional consequences: demoralization, anxious arousal, fear, and self-blame (Wright & Fitzgerald, 2007). Some researchers have attempted to link the coping strategies of victims of sexual harassment to the coping strategies people typically use to cope with stressful events. One large-scale study of victims of sexual harassment identified two basic forms of coping: internal and external (Fitzgerald, Swan, & Fischer, 1995). **Internally focused coping** involves attempts to manage cognitive and emotional reactions to the harassment. For example, a victim may ignore the behavior and do nothing, tell herself that the behavior is not having an effect on her, or tell herself that she simply does not care that much. She might also blame herself for misleading the harasser, or she might attribute his behavior to benign causes such as loneliness or a lack of social skills. **Externally focused coping** involves practical efforts to manage or modify the harassing environment. Examples of this type of coping include attempts to avoid contact with the harasser, appease the harasser, or avoid direct confrontation through the use of humor or excuses. The victim might also tell friends and co-workers about the harassment, tell the harasser to stop, notify a supervisor, bring an internal complaint, or file a formal complaint with EEOC.

The type of coping a particular victim uses depends on how she interprets the event and how she perceives the consequences of a particular course of action. Specifically, the victim will evaluate the likely impact of a particular response (Greathouse et al., 2009). For example, she might consider how reporting the harassment to a supervisor might damage her personal and professional well-being. She will also look at the potential costs and benefits of other options realistically available to her. Research indicates that milder, less-confrontational responses are far more common than formal complaints or lawsuits. As might be expected, researchers have found that severe (i.e., obvious and repeated) harassment is more likely to elicit formal complaints, while less explicit or transitory harassment is likely to be met with avoidance or appeasement (Wiener & Winter, 2007). Among the most common reasons women gave for not filing a complaint are: "I didn't think the problem was serious enough," "I had no faith in the complaint process," "I feared that complaining would have a negative impact on me," and "I took care of the problem myself." One woman put it this way,

> It absolutely still is an issue and people have a fear of making a complaint because it is a career killer. You try to deal with it informally or you just get out (McDonald, Charlesworth, & Cerise, 2011, p. 285).

A meta-analysis of more than 40 studies that collected data from nearly 70,000 people shows that being the target of harassment is associated with a variety of harms including negative physical symptoms, emotional distress, withdrawal from work, and even some aspects of posttraumatic stress disorder (Willness, Steel, & Lee, 2007). Yet, despite such findings, under current law, plaintiffs must not only prove that sexual harassment occurred but also that the harassment produced harm. This "proof" can be established by the plaintiff's own testimony combined with the circumstances of the case (*Turic v. Holland Hospitality, Inc.*, 1996), but it is more commonly established by having the plaintiff submit to a psychological evaluation (Fitzgerald, Collinsworth, & Lawson, 2013). Often, the plaintiff is evaluated by a psychological expert recruited by the plaintiff's attorney, as well as an expert recruited by the defendant's attorney. As an alternative to this double-proof approach, Louise Fitzgerald (2004) has proposed that *if* it is proven that harassment occurred, there ought to be a presumption of harm. This presumption already exists in some areas of the law (e.g., defamation).

Prevention

When psychologists analyze and try to predict behavior, they focus on the interaction between the person and the situation. Whether and how strongly a personality trait is expressed depends on whether the situation encourages or discourages expression of the trait. For example, even if you are a boisterous, outgoing person, it is unlikely that you will be loud and loquacious at a funeral or at the library. The situation will inhibit your natural tendencies. Similarly, even if a man is inclined to harass co-workers, his inclination is unlikely to be expressed if the workplace environment strongly discourages harassment.

To assess whether someone is predisposed to harass others, John Pryor and his colleagues developed the **Likelihood to Sexually Harass (LSH) scale** (Pryor & Whalen, 1997; Pryor, 2009). Men with high scores on the LSH scale tend to describe themselves in stereotypically masculine terms, have a strong need to dominate women, endorse traditional sex roles, endorse myths about rape (e.g., that women want to be sexually overpowered), and are more likely to have sexual fantasies involving themes of coercion. However, the actual behavior of these "high LSH" men is powerfully controlled by the workplace environment. In research using the LSH scale, Pryor and his colleagues found that local norms had a dramatic impact on whether women were harassed. Specifically, if managers were perceived as tolerant or dismissive of harassing behaviors, incidents of harassment were more frequent. In other words, if a workplace is perceived as soft on harassment, men who are predisposed to harass are likely to express their predispositions (Krings & Facchin, 2009). From a legal perspective, a work environment in which sexual harassment seems to be tolerated puts a company at great risk.

Based on their analysis of the psychological dynamics of sexual harassment, Susan Fiske and Peter Glick (1995; Glick & Fiske, 2007) make several recommendations for reducing the incidence of harassment. These recommendations include making clear that sexual informality and sexual joking are inappropriate in a professional environment, eliminating sexually explicit materials in the workplace, and taking steps to make sure that recruiting and promotion are gender neutral. To the extent that victims perceive a risk of punishment for complaining, a lack of punishment for offenders, and a likelihood that complaints will not be taken seriously, the probability of harassment increases (Willness, Steel, & Lee, 2007). Other researchers emphasize that increasing the number of the underrepresented gender (males in nursing, females in engineering) to a critical mass of 20% or more of employees changes the climate of the workplace and removes the pernicious perception that people have been hired merely because of their gender (Pettigrew & Martin, 1987). Other ways of reducing harassing and discriminatory behavior are discussed more fully later in this chapter.

 ## A BROADER LOOK AT WORKPLACE DISCRIMINATION

During the late 1800s and early 1900s, the distinctively American idea of **employment at will** was created. For employers, this principle meant that employees may be fired "at will" without cause and without notice, for good reasons or bad reasons, for moral or immoral reasons, or for no reason at all. Conversely, it meant that people could quit their jobs at any time, without cause or notice. The presumption of "at will" employment persists in the law. Most employees can still be terminated for any reason *unless* that reason is prohibited by law. Title VII and subsequent laws have put limits on the ability of employers to hire or fire at will.

Title VII prohibits discrimination based on race, color, national origin, religion, and gender. What is termed "discriminatory adverse action" may include discriminatory firing of an employee, failure to promote, or unfair restriction of employment opportunities. The **Age Discrimination in Employment Act (ADEA)** was passed in 1967, extending protection to people over the age of 40, and the **Americans with Disabilities Act (ADA),** which became law in 1990, prohibits discrimination based on physical and mental disabilities. The overriding purpose of these laws is to provide clear legal protection for the free expression of political and religious beliefs (as guaranteed by the Constitution and the Bill of Rights) and to prevent disparate treatment of employees on the basis of immutable personal characteristics such as race, national origin, gender, age, and disability. In the eyes of the law, these employee characteristics are legally **protected categories.** (See the Scientific American Spotlight box in this section to learn how researchers can detect someone's biases toward different groups of people.)

Employers can be held liable for four broad categories of discrimination: (1) hostile workplace environment, (2) disparate treatment, (3) adverse impact, and (4) failure to provide "reasonable accommodation" for someone with a disability (Goodman-Delahunty, 1999a). The first category—hostile workplace environment—has already been discussed.

Disparate treatment occurs when an employer treats some workers less favorably because of some personal characteristic, such as race, gender, or religion. A successful claim of disparate treatment requires the employee to prove (by a preponderance of the evidence) that the employer *intended* to discriminate. Intent is difficult to prove and generally requires evidence that management made comments which show intent to discriminate, as well as statistical evidence that management systematically excluded certain groups (e.g., females) from benefits such as promotions. Even where such comments exist, an employer will try to prove that apparent intent did not influence actual practices in hiring, firing, promotion, salary increases, or other benefits. And, even if it appears that the plaintiff has been denied some employment benefit, the employer will claim that the reason behind the denial was legitimate—some

SCIENTIFIC AMERICAN SPOTLIGHT

Detecting Implicit Bias
By Siri Carpenter

The most prominent method for measuring implicit bias is the Implicit Association Test (IAT), introduced in 1998 by Anthony G. Greenwald of the University of Washington and his colleagues. Since then, researchers have used the IAT in more than 500 studies of implicit bias. The test measures how quickly people sort stimuli into particular categories. For example, on an IAT examining implicit attitudes toward young versus old people, a test taker uses one key to respond to young faces and positive words such as "joy" and "peace" and another to respond to old faces and negative words such as "agony" and "terrible." Then the test taker does the reverse, pairing young faces with negative words and old faces with positive words. (Researchers vary the order of the pairings for different test takers.) The difference in response times for the two conditions suggests how strongly that person associates these social groups with positive versus negative concepts. To take the IAT, visit https:// implicit.harvard.edu /implicit

(A: TOM CHANCE/AGE FOOTSTOCK; B: TOM CHANGE/AGE FOOTSTOCK; C: COMSTOCK IMAGES/AGE FOTOSTOCK)

deficit in the worker's skills or job performance. Frequently, claims of discriminatory treatment on the job are accompanied by other claims, such as defamation (saying or writing something that damages the reputation of an employee), intentional infliction of emotional distress, or retaliation for whistle-blowing (e.g., a company firing a worker who exposes test results indicating that a product is dangerous).

Adverse impact occurs when employment practices that may not look discriminatory on the surface have the clear effect of discriminating against a particular group. Put differently, if the result of treating all employees the same is that some groups are systematically prevented from receiving some job benefit, adverse impact has occurred. In the case of *Griggs v. Duke Power Co.* (1971), African-American employees successfully challenged Duke Power's practice of requiring a high school diploma and a particular score on a scholastic aptitude test to decide who was hired or promoted. Although that practice was not intended to discriminate, it resulted in fewer African Americans being hired and promoted. The Court held that the use of such tests had to be abandoned unless it could be demonstrated that test scores were clearly related to the ability to perform the job for which they were required. Some adverse impact is tolerated if the practice can be justified by "business necessity." If there had been clear evidence that a high school diploma or a particular score on the test predicted actual job performance, then the company might have been permitted to continue the practice. Adverse impact extends beyond the issue of employment testing. For example, if recruiting for job candidates is done informally through word of mouth, and this practice effectively excludes members of particular groups, an adverse impact claim can be made.

One more example: In the past, some police departments had a height requirement. People who wanted to become police officers had to be at least 5 feet, 9 inches tall. The argument was that taller officers would be better able to defend themselves in dangerous situations (e.g., apprehending a criminal) and that taller (presumably more physically intimidating) officers would not need to defend themselves. That is, taller people would be less likely to be challenged by criminal suspects trying to escape. Because women are, on average, shorter than men, the policy resulted in far fewer women being qualified to serve as police officers. While the courts ruled that such height requirements were illegal because of their adverse impact on female applicants, other physical characteristics such as strength, stamina, and agility are legal and justifiable because they are clearly related to job requirements. Police officers can be required to demonstrate lifting strength, endurance, and running speed (Simmons, 1997).

In a series of cases refining the doctrine of adverse impact, courts have held that, not only must there be disparate treatment between groups, but those differences in treatment must be caused by specific employment practices (*Lopez v. Laborers International Union 18*, 1993). In 2009, the Supreme Court decided a case brought by a group of 17 white firefighters and one Latino firefighter who had been denied promotions even though they had earned the requisite scores on a written test (*Ricci v. DeStefano*, 2009). After the tests had been scored, the New Haven Fire Department decided to throw out the exam results, ostensibly because they were afraid of a possible lawsuit by a group of African-American firefighters who had not scored high enough to be promoted. The Court ruled that the fire department could not use good intentions about promoting racial diversity to discriminate against white employees. In the majority opinion, the Court held that because the testing process was "open and fair" and there was "no strong basis" for believing the test was unfair, there was no legal justification for setting aside the test results.

The fourth type of claim only refers to cases involving religion or disabilities. Employees may claim that employers failed to make sufficient adjustments to allow them to participate in religious rituals or observe religious holidays. A legal claim can also be made if an employer fails to make adequate adjustments to permit employees to work effectively despite the limitations of their disabilities. Such **reasonable accommodations** are required unless they create an "undue hardship or burden" on the employer's business. In *Trans World Airlines Inc. v. Hardison* (1977), the airline operated seven days a week, 24 hours per day. Mr. Hardison observed a Saturday Sabbath and refused to work Saturdays. However, because of lack of seniority, he was required to work Saturdays. His supervisors tried unsuccessfully to find someone who would voluntarily switch schedules with him, but no one with greater seniority was willing to switch. The employer refused to force another worker to switch schedules and refused to offer extra pay to entice others to work on Saturdays. The Court ruled against the employee and held that Trans World Airlines had attempted to accommodate Hardison but was not required, "to carve out a special exception to its seniority system."

For a claim of discrimination based on religion, several elements have to be in place: There must be a sincerely held, bona fide religious belief that interferes with a job requirement, the employer must be made aware of the conflict, and the employee must suffer some adverse effects because the employer refused to reasonably accommodate the religious practices (*Anderson v. General Dynamics*, 1978).

The 1991 Civil Rights Act made compensatory damages available in cases of unlawful employment discrimination. If an organization is found guilty of discrimination, a variety of legal remedies are possible. If someone has been fired, they can be reinstated. Lost wages can be paid, retroactive promotions can be made, and retroactive pay raises can be ordered. However, to receive damages for emotional distress, the plaintiff must present evidence of actual emotional or psychological harm caused by discrimination. The range of psychological harms might include anxiety-related problems—such as depression, insomnia, extreme fatigue, mental anguish—or damage to one's professional reputation and social standing. Punitive damages are also possible but only when an employer is shown to have acted with "malice or reckless indifference to the federally protected rights of an aggrieved person." This more extreme form of damages is intended to punish the employer, deter future discrimination by that employer, and send a message to other employers that malicious discrimination will result in severe consequences.

To initiate a lawsuit, an employee must have suffered some form of injury because of the company's conduct. And, to prevail at trial, the employee/plaintiff must prove that the company/defendant's action or failure to act caused the injuries the plaintiff sustained (Kane & Dvoskin, 2011). If a jury finds the defendant liable, plaintiffs can be compensated for both economic damages (e.g., lost salary and medical bills) and noneconomic damages. Noneconomic losses are less easily translated into money, and include loss of enjoyment of life, pain and suffering, and psychological injury. Assessing psychological injury is a complex, multistep process that takes into account the plaintiff's activities, social relationships, and psychological functioning before, during, and after the acts of discrimination. When assessing cognitive, emotional, and interpersonal changes in the plaintiff, efforts are made to rule out other possible causes of distress, such as changes in family circumstances or psychological problems that predate the experience of workplace discrimination (Foote & Goodman-Delahunty, 2013). However, research indicates that courts are very skeptical about psychological injuries and often make it difficult for plaintiffs to claim or recover psychological damages (Vallano, 2013).

Although psychological injuries are difficult to prove in court, there is a large body of research showing that perceived discrimination and injustice can produce negative emotional reactions (anger, resentment, depression, reduced self-esteem) and unhealthy behaviors (drinking, smoking, and inactivity associated with depression) (Greenberg, 2010; Major, Mendes, & Dovidio, 2013).

It is important to recognize that bringing a discrimination lawsuit is usually difficult and traumatic for plaintiffs. They often feel that the legal system is stacked against them, and they are seldom prepared for the time, expense, and emotional upheaval a lawsuit produces. Although defendants may also feel that the system is unfair to them, large companies have at their disposal far more financial resources, as well as larger and more skilled legal teams. And, because the responsibility is spread across the company, there is less personal hardship for the representatives of the company. Here is the "advice" one human resources officer gives to workers who threaten to sue his company:

> You know what? If you want to sue me, sue me. Lots of people have sued me. . . . But there's some things you need to understand. You need to understand that I have a job and I get paid every day. And your lawsuit is just a job to me. If I don't win, my world doesn't stop. And I still get paid. But it's going to become your single focus in life and it's going to keep you from getting a job because future employers are going to see this seething pot and they're not going to want to have anything to do with you. So before you sue me, you ought to think about that (Berrey, Hoffman, & Nielsen, 2012, p. 20).

▶ RACIAL DISCRIMINATION IN THE WORKPLACE

During much of the twentieth century, racism against African Americans was blatant, routine, and supported by law. The law permitted segregation of whites from blacks at work and at school. The first black Americans to integrate schools and businesses faced open hostility expressed in verbal abuse, racial slurs, physical assaults, and even death threats.

But the law and public opinion have both changed dramatically since then. Now, the law expressly prohibits intentional workplace discrimination based on race. It is illegal to hire, promote, or fire someone because of his or her race. This is a clear step forward from the times when employment decisions were made in an unapologetically racist manner. But, is this prohibition sufficient to prevent racism in the workplace? It is usually very difficult to prove that an employment decision was racially motivated because it is rare for employers to admit that they were motivated by racism. Employers can usually claim that a particular decision was not based on race, but rather on some aspect of merit.

(CHRISTINA MICEK)

Public opinion surveys spanning more than 40 years indicate a steady decline in reported prejudice toward blacks. Only a tiny percentage of white Americans now say that they would object to having a black friend or co-worker (Gallup, 2013). Part of the explanation for this decline is that racism is much less prevalent than it used to be. But, another part of the explanation may be that it is simply no longer acceptable to admit to feeling racial prejudice. Both explanations appear to have validity. Many researchers and many lines of evidence suggest a decisive shift away from blatant forms of racism toward more subtle forms of racism. Modern racism differs from traditional racism in that it is less extreme, less conscious, and less overt. And, whereas it used to be acceptable to claim that members of a particular racial group were simply inferior, modern discriminatory conduct tends to be attributed to nonracial factors. Most people want to see themselves as fair-minded and free of racial prejudice, but they still feel some discomfort and suspicion in the presence of racially different people. This discomfort generally reveals itself in subtle but consequential behaviors that favor similar people (Dovidio & Gaertner, 2004; Dovidio & Hebl, 2005).

In an experiment that illustrates the subtlety of prejudice, white people were shown several photographs of white and black people and asked to imagine interacting with the people in the photos. They were also asked to rate how much they would probably like the person. Overall, they reported liking the black people slightly more than they liked the white people. But, a more direct measure of liking—movements of facial muscles associated with positive or negative emotions—indicated more positive reactions to white people and more negative reactions to black people (Vanman, Paul, Kaplan, & Miller, 1990). Were the people lying about who they liked best? Not necessarily. Not wanting to feel prejudice, they may not have been fully aware of their feelings of discomfort. Some studies that further underscore the automatic nature of responses to race have used reaction time measures (Gaertner, Dovidio, Nier, Hodson, & Houlette, 2005). Researchers have reasoned that it takes longer to react to stimuli that are inconsistent with attitudes than it does to process information that fits with existing attitudes. In a series of experiments, white participants pressed a button in response to word pairs that appeared on a screen. Racially charged words like "blacks" and "whites" were paired with positive words (e.g., smart) or negative words (e.g., stupid). Participants quickly rejected the negative terms for both blacks and whites, but they more quickly associated positive terms with whites than with blacks. These differences were evident in people who were not classified as racist according to standard paper-and-pencil tests (Nosek & Hansen, 2008).

Studies in both the laboratory and the field have looked at racial bias in hiring decisions. In a classic study of subtle differences in cross-racial interactions, researchers asked people to conduct job interviews with several equally qualified black or white job candidates. There was no evidence of overt prejudice against black candidates. However, there were subtle measurable differences: When interviewing a black candidate, white interviewers sat farther away, made more speech errors (i.e., used more pauses and more fillers like "um" or "ah"), and held shorter interviews. In response, the black job candidates behaved in a more anxious, awkward manner (Word, Zanna, & Cooper, 1974). In another experiment, researchers looked at how white evaluators rated black and white job applicants. There was no evidence of discrimination in cases where black and white applicants were either highly qualified or poorly qualified for the position. However, when applicants had acceptable but ambiguous qualifications, the evaluators were nearly 70% more likely to recommend white job applicants rather than black job applicants (Dovidio & Gaertner, 2000). When the "right" decision was ambiguous, race was used to tip the scales in favor of the white candidate to the detriment of the black candidate. Finally, in a field experiment, white, Latino, and black males between the ages of 20 and 24 visited 340 potential employers in New York City. The men were matched on physical appearance (height, weight, attractiveness), as well as social skill (e.g., talkativeness, eye contact). They were also trained and given scripts to ensure that their behavior was similar during job interviews. Most important, their resumes presented identical educational backgrounds and work experience. Results indicated that white applicants received callbacks or job offers 31% of the time, compared to 25% for Latinos and 15% for blacks (Pager & Western, 2012).

People who know they are prejudiced are reluctant to admit it. And even people who sincerely believe they are not prejudiced may behave differently around people of another race than they behave around people of their own race. Subtle forms of racism are likely to leak out via subtle nonverbal cues and, consequently, create colder, more strained social interactions. These more awkward interactions are likely to lead to more negative impressions and attributions about other people's intentions and abilities. In the workplace, the effects of subtle "modern" racism may have especially strong effects when very few members of a minority group are on the job. When only a few "token" minorities are on the job, they tend to receive disproportionate praise for their achievements and disproportionate criticism for their failures (Pettigrew & Martin, 1987). In addition, members of the majority group often doubt the competence of the first minorities to enter a work environment, believing that they were hired for the sake of minority representation, not because of their abilities (Crosby, 2004).

Some researchers have observed that prejudice is similar to a bad habit. Like most habits, prejudice resists change and cannot be tamed by logic alone. Even when people make sincere efforts to be unbiased when dealing with people of different races, automatic, irrational, emotional reactions still assert themselves. Reducing prejudice is possible, but it happens slowly over time and through repeated positive contact with people from disfavored groups (Devine, Rhodewalt, & Sieminko, 2008). Ironically, direct, overt racism is easier to deal with than indirect, covert, modern racism. Antidiscrimination laws are powerful tools for correcting blatant discrimination. But subtle, nonconscious racism may be harder to change. Some legal scholars have argued that there is a fundamental mismatch between the forms of racial bias condemned by law and racism as it is actually practiced in organizations (Krieger & Fiske, 2006). For example, racial biases and preferences in hiring decisions are not likely to be expressed as outright rejection of minority job candidates. If the employer does not *intend* to exclude minority candidates, but simply pays more attention to or gives more weight to information that favors white candidates, it is far more difficult to prove unlawful discrimination (Pager & Western, 2012).

Reducing Racial Bias

Fortunately, there is research suggesting that even subtly discriminatory behavior can be effectively reduced. Some clear lessons can be drawn from the American experience of desegregation of the public schools. Much social-psychological research was prompted by the landmark Supreme Court decision *Brown v. Board of Education* in 1954 (see Chapter 1). In that decision, the Court ruled that separate schools for blacks and whites were inherently unequal and therefore unconstitutional. This ruling led to massive desegregation of the public schools. It came as a great surprise to many that the effects of this desegregation were not entirely positive. In fact, a comprehensive review of the research on desegregation revealed that 53% of the studies found that desegregation led to an increase in prejudice of whites toward blacks, 34% reported no change in prejudice, and only 13% found a decrease in prejudice (Stephan, 1986). The discouraging findings of that review prompted researchers to try to identify the conditions under which interracial contact decreases prejudice.

Research conducted over the past several decades has revealed that four conditions are essential to reducing stereotypes and prejudice. First, there must be **equal-status contact** between groups. Bringing in members of a disfavored group and placing them in low-status jobs may only reinforce stereotypes that such people are undeserving of, and unsuited for, higher-status positions. Second, the organization (e.g., the school or business) must promote one-on-one interactions instead of permitting members of the two groups to avoid each other. Third, the environment must be structured to foster cooperation. Specifically, members of the two groups must be induced to work together in an effort to achieve so-called **superordinate goals**— goals that are important to both groups. For example, members of the two groups could be assembled into mixed, interdependent work teams in which each member of the team plays an important role. This approach ensures that people must rely on and attempt to help each other. Fourth, local social norms must favor intergroup contact and equal treatment—it must be viewed as desirable to try to work well with members of the other group. Such norms are generally created and supported by people who have authority in the work environment (Forsyth, 2006).

In addition to the four conditions described above, it is also important to highlight the job qualifications of members of the new group, to increase the number of people from the underrepresented group in supervisory positions, to require clear accountability for behavior, and to monitor employee relations over time (Fiske & Glick, 1995). When these conditions are in place, racial (or gender) integration is likely to reduce prejudice and enhance the functioning of the organization.

THE PSYCHOLOGY OF PERCEIVED FAIRNESS

To understand the concept of unfair discrimination, it is necessary to consider the opposite, more fundamental concept of fairness. Fairness almost always serves as the official justification for decisions about hiring, promotion, benefits, salaries, bonuses, and firing. Claims of harassment or discrimination and lawsuits against employers are motivated by a perceived lack of fairness. (See the Scientific American Spotlight box in this section to read about how psychology and technology can be used together to create fair hiring practices.)

The lofty ideal of just treatment was neatly expressed by the philosopher Aristotle in the fourth century BC: "All virtue is summed up in dealing justly." In 1670, Blaise Pascal noted that what we view as just depends on prevailing circumstances: "We see neither justice nor injustice which does not change its nature with change in climate." But my favorite quote about justice came from one of my daughters, who discovered the concept of justice when she was about 3 years old. Whenever she was told that she had to go to bed, or take a bath, or leave a playground, she would loudly protest, "Not fair! Not fair!" After a week or two of this, I asked her to clarify what she meant by "not fair." Her answer was direct and succinct: "Not fair is when I don't get what I want." My daughter's brilliant insight has now been buttressed by psychological research. We are not dispassionate arbiters of fairness—our judgment that some decision or action is unfair is most often triggered by not getting what we want. And, as you probably suspect, we are far less likely to view a decision as unfair if it results in us getting more than we actually deserve.

Unlike philosophers, psychologists are more concerned with how people *actually* think and behave than with how people *ought* to think and behave. When psychologists have examined how people think about fairness, three interrelated dimensions have emerged: distributive, procedural, and interactional (Colquitt, Zapata-Phelan,

& Roberson, 2005). **Distributive justice** refers to how available rewards are distributed or divided up among members of a group. More specifically, it concerns the relationship (or lack of relationship) between contributions and outcome. The second dimension—**procedural justice**—concerns the perceived fairness of the procedures and rules used to allocate the available benefits. That is, the way outcomes are decided. If people feel that they have an opportunity to "state their case" and voice their concerns during the decision-making process, they are much more likely to view the procedure as fair (Finkel, 2000; Tyler, 2006). Although there is a strong relationship between fair procedures and fair outcomes, fair procedures sometimes lead to unjust outcomes, and unfair procedures sometimes lead to just outcomes. The third dimension people use when deciding whether someone has been treated fairly is called **interactional justice.** Here the concern is style: Were people treated courteously and with respect? Interactional justice refers to the consideration and care shown by the people who have the power to allocate rewards. So, in sum, what matters is who gets what, how it is decided who gets what, and how people are treated during and after those decisions are made.

Three Models for Allocating Rewards

In his analysis of distributive justice, Edward Sampson identified three basic schemes for dividing up resources (Sampson, 1975). The principle of need dictates that each person gives to the group based on his or her ability and each person gets from the group according to what he or she needs. This standard of distributive justice tends only to be used in small, intimate groups. For example, if one child in a three-child family suffers from a serious chronic illness, a family may devote most of its financial resources to medical treatment for the child. The parents, and perhaps even the siblings, will spend a disproportionate amount of time and energy caring for the sick child. Brothers and sisters will receive less—less attention, less money, less time from their parents. The sick child simply needs more, so that child gets more.

The second and simplest norm of justice is **equality.** Using this principle, everybody gets the same rewards. Let us say a small but successful software company of 10 people has managed to budget $1 million to distribute as salary. How much does each person get as salary? Maybe the company should just divide the money equally and give everybody a salary of $100,000. Of course, some might argue that not everyone *deserves* the same salary. That may be true. But the advantage of using equality is that in groups where everyone makes a different but important contribution and the value of each contribution is difficult to calculate, equality promotes social harmony (Lerner & Lerner, 1981; Tyler, 2006a). At least temporarily, the small software company might want to reward all 10 workers equally to encourage everyone to work together as equal members of a team. Because the social functioning of the group is essential to its continued success, it might be best to postpone the potentially divisive, emotionally charged discussion of who deserves more.

The third norm of distributive justice—**equity**—is the most widely used. The idea is that rewards ought to be distributed in proportion to each person's contributions to the group. That is, people who contribute more ought to receive more benefits. Although equity may harm group cohesiveness and social harmony, it tends to encourage people to work harder on those tasks that are well compensated. At least in the abstract, the principle of equity seems eminently reasonable.

The problem is that it is usually difficult to quantify contributions, to decide on what constitutes merit. Put differently, *which* contributions should be defined as worthy of lesser or greater rewards? Take lawyers. In a big law firm, money is usually generated by billing clients for the time of attorneys. So, perhaps lawyers' salaries

SCIENTIFIC AMERICAN SPOTLIGHT

Technology, Psychology, and the Search for the Best Employees

By Tomas Chamorro-Premuzic and Christopher Steinmetz

The goal of a recruiter is to find the person who best fits the requirements and culture of a given job. Typically, a recruiter crafts an advertisement for the position, posts it to the company website and some job boards, collects applications—résumés, cover letters, and references—then selects a few candidates for interviews. This process is rather flawed. It ignores some of the core findings of industrial and organizational psychology on how to screen candidates. Take IQ, for example. IQ has been shown to be a consistent predictor of performance across a variety of jobs because it reflects how quickly a person can be trained. Yet it remains an unpopular selection tool. Administering IQ tests may be too onerous for most companies, but scores on standardized exams (such as the SAT and the GRE) are highly correlated with IQ scores and can be regarded as a proxy for learning potential.

Another powerful predictor of career success, the personality test, has gained a somewhat stronger foothold in employee selection. Hundreds of independent research studies have demonstrated that these tests are better indicators of future career success than letters of recommendation, interviews, and educational credentials. The personality tests that have been shown to forecast performance are based on the "five-factor model," a well-supported and thoroughly researched framework for understanding how our personalities differ. According to it, we can be analyzed along five continuous, nonoverlapping dimensions: openness, conscientiousness, extroversion, agreeableness, and emotional stability. Conscientiousness and, to a lesser extent, high emotional stability are the most consistent predictors of success across jobs and criteria.

Yet neither of these psychometric tests fits seamlessly into the recruiting process. One reason is that evaluators tend to focus on the everyday behaviors of candidates because this information is easily accessible in an in-person interview. Another explanation, derived from numerous studies across several cultures, is that applicants tend to view such tests as less fair than face-to-face interviews and work samples. Perceptions of fairness matter; they can affect applicants' self-esteem, along with their motivation to continue pursuing employment and ultimately accept the job.

Help from Social Networks

Recent findings suggest that aspects of personality can be gleaned from our digital footprints. In a study by psychologists Simine Vazire and Samuel D. Gosling of the University

(PHOTO COURTESY OF MARK COSTANZO)

Paula Fellini

Entrepreneur; Artist; Jogger
Four years of sales experience

I live in the great state of Colorado.
I am 24 years old and loving life.
I am a creative thinker who enjoys a challenging, high-energy work environment.
My hobbies are painting, fishing, mountain climbing, and snow boarding.
Favorite Book: Consider the Lobster by David Foster Wallace
Favorite Movie: Annie Hall

ought to be based on who bills the most hours per year. While it is true that nearly every law firm values billable hours, it cannot be the only consideration. Let us say one of the attorneys bills relatively few hours but brings in several clients—that is, because she is smart and charming and gregarious, several people hire her firm to do legal work. Bringing in clients (which may involve playing golf and going to social events) is an important contribution, even though it may cut into billable hours. Perhaps another attorney raises the profile of the firm by serving as president of the of Texas at Austin, for example, people who perused 89 personal websites were equally good at detecting the conscientiousness and openness of the site owner as a long-time acquaintance. A study by Tal Yarkoni of the University of Colorado at Boulder analyzed the words used in 695 blogs and their owners' responses on a personality test. He found that neurotic bloggers commonly used words such as "awful" and "lazy," whereas agreeable writers were more likely to describe something as "wonderful" and conscientious word-slingers often used "completed."

A 2011 study by psychologists Ralf Caers and Vanessa Castelyns of the University College Brussels found that of 353 HR professionals polled, 43% admitted to drawing conclusions about applicants' personalities based on their Facebook profiles, such as extroversion and maturity. Recruiters encounter some risk here: As they casually peruse an applicant's data trail, they may become biased at an earlier stage in the process by traits such as attractiveness, facial maturity, a handicap, or obesity than if they had observed these details for the first time only in person. Recruiters may unconsciously decide against inviting someone in for an interview based on features that have nothing to do with job performance.

More useful metrics might emerge from software capable of categorizing Web data into personality dimensions. This field is in its infancy, but there are a few simple, free online apps. *TweetPsych* scores the emotional and intellectual content of a person's Twitter activity on a range of topics—such as learning, money, emotions, and anxiety—as compared with others in its database. *YouAreWhatYouLike* compiles personality profiles in line with the five-factor model based solely on what a person purports to "Like" on Facebook. It can generate labels along several dimensions, such as "liberal and artistic," "calm and relaxed," and "well organized."

Videos and Games

Typically, the bedrock of any talent search, in-person interviews tend to be conducted in a free-form manner that can easily feed false perceptions. Studies have shown, for example, that interviews are often systematically biased against ethnic minorities, women, and elderly individuals. Even an applicant's perfume can introduce bias. A better, more predictive approach is to conduct structured interviews, in which every applicant answers the same list of questions. Using this method, different evaluators are more likely to reach similar judgments on a candidate than when the interviews are more conversational. Yet free-form interviews predominate, in part because of ignorance among hirers and in part because managers view the format as impinging on their autonomy.

Another major area of innovation is "gamification," the use of video games in the hunt for talent. By applying behavioral theories to a player's actions during the game, the software can generate a complex personality profile for that user. Games are a type of situational judgment test—another metric, in addition to IQ and personality tests, that researchers have found can predict performance on the job. *Insanely Driven* helps employers assess candidates' "fit" with the company's culture. Players of *Insanely Driven* must handle numerous tough situations as they race to an important meeting. The test is based on four measures of personality—adjustment, ambition, sensitivity, and prudence—taken from the Hogan Personality Inventory, a widely accepted assessment that is based on the five-factor model.

Bigger and Bigger Data

The latest breed of web-crawling, digital-recruiting tools uses algorithms that attempt to synthesize all existing information about a candidate. Beyond the inevitable scouring of every social media platform, companies seeking talent will also want to comb through news articles, blog posts, shopping histories, e-mails, comment sections, forums, and anything else that becomes available online.

Merging today's fragmented services could conceivably construct the most accurate psychological profiles yet. Companies could find their dream candidates before they even submit an application and target only the people who possess the right skills and style to perform well on the job—and who will enjoy it, too. These new tools will not only refine our talent-identification methods, they will also help more people find the perfect job.

local bar association and writing a legal column for the local newspaper. Perhaps another attends to the firm's internal functioning by mediating disputes between co-workers, setting the agenda for meetings, or developing a vision for the long-term development of the firm. Maybe another attorney is not much good at bringing in new clients, but her thorough knowledge of the law enables her to write winning briefs. The point is that there is no single, unassailable method for determining the value of different contributions, no precise calculus for deciding the relative merit of different work activities. Fair allocation of rewards is substantially subjective. In the abstract, virtually everyone supports the appealing concepts of performance-based rewards, accountability, and merit. But, in practice, it is often extremely difficult to translate these vague, value-laden—but appealing concepts into clear measures that everyone agrees are fair.

Research on Perceptions of Fairness

For decades, psychologists have studied how individuals and groups distribute rewards. Several laboratory studies have involved bringing people together in small or large groups to perform a task or solve a problem. Sometimes the tasks are mathematical or verbal, and other times, the tasks involve simulated business decisions (e.g., deciding how to allocate a hypothetical budget). Once the task is complete, participants (and often outside observers) are asked to distribute the available rewards (usually money). Other types of studies have used interviews and surveys of working people (Choi, 2011; Smith, Thomas, & Tyler, 2006). Typically, people are asked about fairness of the salary structure at work and other job benefits.

We can draw several conclusions from this body of research. First, judgments of fairness tend to be self-serving. Although we tend to feel distressed about not

HOT TOPIC

The Gender Gap in Salaries

One persistent inequality is the salary discrepancy between men and women. Overall, women earn about 77% of what men earn, and college-educated men earn an average of $14,508 more annually than college-educated women earn (AAUW, 2014). The gender pay gap persists, although it has narrowed significantly over the past two decades. This narrowing is likely due to women entering higher-paying career categories and gaining job seniority (Lewis & Oh, 2009).

One prominent partial explanation for the lingering pay gap involves the larger role still played by women in childrearing. To the extent that some professional women work fewer hours or take family leave, their salaries are likely to suffer. Indeed, statistical studies that control for a wide range of variables find that both men and women who take a career break, reduce their hours, or are out of the labor force for family reasons, sharply reduce their salaries over time (Coltrane, Miller, DeHaan, & Stewart, 2013). There appears to be a "flexibility stigma" or "caregiver bias" in the sense that workers who reduce

their work hours to care for children (or even to care for ailing parents) are judged to be insufficiently devoted to their careers. Although many companies allow for work flexibility to keep talented workers and to accommodate childrearing responsibilities, few workers take advantage of options to work part-time, or to share a job, or to work a compressed work week (Williams, Blair-Loy, & Berdahl, 2013).

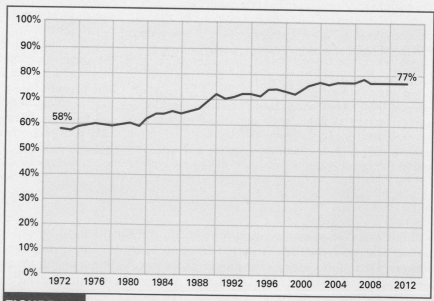

FIGURE 15.1 (*The American Association of University Women, The Simple Truth about the Gender Pay Gap, Fall 2013 edition*)

getting as much as we feel we deserve, we tend not to be as bothered by getting more than we deserve (Moliner, Martínez-Tur, Peiró, Ramos, & Cropanzano, 2012). (For example, college students tend to complain to professors when they receive a course grade that is lower than they expected, but they tend not to complain when they are given a grade higher than they expected.) Another aspect of this self-serving tendency is that people tend to rate their own contributions somewhat higher than outside observers rate their contributions. A second conclusion is that males and females seem to differ in how they apply principles of fairness. As compared to men, women tend to undervalue their contributions. For example, in laboratory studies where both men and women are asked to work as long as they think is fair for a specific sum of money, women tend to work about 20% to 25% longer. Also, when asked to divide rewards fairly between themselves and a co-worker, men take more of the reward and give correspondingly less to a co-worker. Women tend to divide the money more equally (Kaiser & Major, 2006; Major, 1993). Also, in surveys of workers, women tend to value salary somewhat less than men do. As compared to men, female workers seem to place more value on good co-workers, control over schedules, sense of accomplishment, and good working conditions (Jackson, 1989). (See the Hot Topic box in this section for more information on gender and salary.)

Bias against mothers who work reduced hours to care for children may help to explain the pay gap, but it is only a small part of the explanation. The gap remains even when comparing males and females who work the same number of hours. One study found that even after controlling for college major, occupation, number of hours worked per week, and economic sector, American women earn less than men just one year after college graduation (Corbett & Hill, 2012). In a study of physician/researchers working at universities, women earned 83 cents for every dollar earned by men even after adjusting for differences in specialty, institutional characteristics, academic productivity, academic rank, work hours, and other factors (Jagsi et al., 2012).

Interestingly, factors that used to account for much of the gap, like education and experience, no longer do, because the differences between men and women on such factors have shrunk significantly (Bolitzer & Godtland, 2012). Gender pay gaps exist at career entry and tend to expand over time even after taking into account specialization, working hours, and other relevant factors (Lips, 2013).

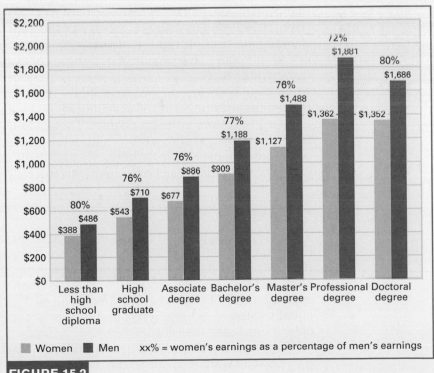

Women ■ Men   xx% = women's earnings as a percentage of men's earnings

FIGURE 15.2

A third conclusion is that, in deciding whether they are fairly rewarded, people compare their inputs and outcomes to the inputs and outcomes of similar others. People try to assess whether they are being treated the same as similar co-workers doing similar jobs (Latham, 2006). Although these comparisons may be influenced by self-serving biases, they help anchor judgments to the reality of the workplace. A final conclusion is that because no distribution of rewards is entirely equitable for everyone, people's satisfaction with their outcomes often depends heavily on procedural and interactional considerations. If employees feel that the procedures used to decide outcomes are reasonable and are communicated clearly and courteously, they are more likely to accept the outcomes. Mysterious, biased, or poorly communicated procedures can create dissatisfaction—even when they result in equitable allocations. Fair, clearly communicated procedures can dampen dissatisfaction even when allocations are inequitable.

People often feel that their employer has treated them unfairly. Perceived inequities have consequences for employers. For example, one study tracked employee behavior at three manufacturing plants owned by the same parent company. To reduce expenses, salaries were temporarily cut. The researchers arranged to vary conditions so that, at the first plant, no salary cuts were made. At the second plant, workers were told that, to cut expenses, 15% salary cuts would be made for 10 weeks. At the third plant, workers were given the same salary cut but with an explanation of why the cuts were necessary and an expression of regret from management. As predicted, company inventories of supplies revealed that a dramatic rise in employee theft occurred at the second plant, the plant where management provided no reasonable explanation for the salary cut (Greenberg & Alge, 1998).

Over the past few decades, there has been considerable research on workplace justice. A recent meta-analysis of 66 studies found a strong positive relationship between perceived justice in the workplace and organizational effectiveness (Whitman, Caleo, Carpenter, Horner, & Bernerth, 2012). Distributive justice was most strongly linked to measures of worker productivity and customer satisfaction, while interactional and procedural justice were more strongly linked to worker feelings of commitment to the organization, group cohesion, and lack of negative behaviors (e.g., withdrawal).

A large body of evidence now shows that if employees feel that they have been treated unfairly (in terms of distributive, procedural, or interactional justice), they often act to restore a sense of equity. They may try to "get even." They may spend fewer hours at work, not work as hard while on the job, spread rumors about or form coalitions against the people who treated them unfairly, steal from the employer, sabotage the initiatives of management, or quit. They may even file lawsuits.

▶ IN CONCLUSION

Virtually all employment litigation is an attempt to punish perceived injustice and restore perceived fairness in the workplace. Employment law has done a lot to reduce harassment and discrimination. However, current law is a weak tool for creating full justice in the workplace. There is often a wide gap between what people expect on the job and what the law requires. The law does not guarantee fair and equal treatment of employees, and it does not require employers to make reasonable, merit-based decisions.

Employment law lays down boundaries employers cannot cross, but for employers who want to create a truly fair workplace, following the law is only a start.

► CRITICAL THINKING QUESTIONS

1. Should there be a separate standard for sexual harassment depending on whether the victim is a male or a female?

2. What are the causes of sexual harassment?

3. How much should the behavior of the victim matter in determining whether sexual harassment occurred?

4. What accommodations are reasonable for religious employees?

5. What principles and standards would you use in deciding salaries for professors at a university or attorneys at a law firm?

6. What would be on your list of "protected categories"? Why?

7. Are there circumstances in which men and women should receive different salaries for doing the same job?

► KEY TERMS

adverse impact (p. 315)
Age Discrimination in Employment Act (ADEA) (p. 314)
Americans with Disabilities Act (ADA) (p. 314)
Civil Rights Act of 1964 (Title VII) (p. 303)
disparate treatment (p. 314)
distributive justice (p. 321)

employment at will (p. 313)
Equal Employment Opportunity Commission (EEOC) (p. 304)
equality (p. 321)
equal-status contact (p. 320)
equity (p. 321)
externally focused coping (p. 312)
hostile environment harassment (p. 304)

interactional justice (p. 321)
internally focused coping (p. 311)
Likelihood to Sexually Harass (LSH) scale (p. 313)
procedural justice (p. 321)
protected categories (p. 314)
quid pro quo harassment (p. 304)

reasonable accommodations (p. 316)
reasonable person standard (p. 306)
reasonable woman standard (p. 306)
superordinate goals (p. 320)
totality of circumstances test (p. 308)

16 Corrections: Sentencing, Imprisonment, and Alternatives

▶ Sentencing Decisions
▶ Types of Imprisonment
▶ The Goals of Imprisonment
▶ The Evolution of Prisons in the United States
▶ Prisoner Rights and the Role of the Courts
▶ Basic Statistics on Prisons and Prisoners
▶ The Distinctive Culture of Prison
▶ Does Prison Work?
▶ Alternatives to Prison

Prison is the centerpiece of our system of punishment. Beginning in 1972 and continuing for nearly four decades, the prison system in the United States expanded whether the crime rate rose or fell. The rate of imprisonment (usually expressed as the number of people in prison for every 100,000 people in the U.S. population) climbed from 93 per 100,000 in 1972 to 502 per 100,000 in 2009 (Carson & Sabol, 2012). It was not until about 2010 that the prison population began to slowly decline. The circular rationale for our heavy reliance on prison was neatly summed up by the former head of the National Criminal Justice Commission:

> If crime is going up, then we need to build more prisons to hold more criminals; and if crime is going down, it's because we built more prisons—and building even more prisons will therefore drive down crime even lower (Okafo, 2009, P. 20).

Most prisons no longer look like the huge stone fortresses featured in Hollywood movies. Though many still have gun towers and high walls or fences topped with coils of razor wire, new features have been added to improve security. For example, Folsom prison in California is encircled by a "death wire" fence that can send a lethal jolt of electricity into anyone who touches it. The federal super maximum security prison in Florence, Colorado, uses 168 video cameras to continuously monitor the activities of inmates. Inside the cells, there is no moveable furniture, and there are no detachable objects (such as toilet handles or soap dishes) that might be converted into weapons. Every prisoner experiences something close to perpetual solitary confinement—the cells are built at angles so that prisoners are not able to see or talk to one another.

At some points in our history, prisons have been optimistically viewed as giant laboratories for reforming the lives and habits of people who have gone astray. At other times, they have been pessimistically viewed as little more than vast warehouses for vile criminals who can never be reformed. This chapter examines what happens after a defendant is found guilty: how the legal system decides on appropriate sentences for convicted criminals, the role of prisons, the psychological effects of imprisonment, and alternatives to prison. ◀

SENTENCING DECISIONS

After conviction and before punishment, the criminal must be sentenced. How judges, jurors, and the public decide on the appropriate punishment for a particular crime depends not only on the seriousness of the crime, but also on attributions about the criminal. When people attempt to explain the behavior of others, they distinguish between **internal causes** (such as personality or free choice) and **external causes** (such as powerful situational forces). Psychologists who study attributions also refer to two other dimensions of perceived cause: controllability and stability. **Controllability** refers to whether or not a person could have controlled their behavior, and **stability** refers to whether the cause appears to be temporary or permanent. Criminal behaviors that are attributed to internal, controllable, stable causes evoke more anger and stronger punitive responses (Georges, Wiener, & Keller, 2013). Crimes attributed to external, less controllable, unstable causes may elicit sympathy, more lenient sentences, and an interest in rehabilitation (Templeton & Hartnagel, 2012; Weiner, Graham, & Reyna, 1997). Consider the case of a man who robs a convenience store. We would be more inclined to lean toward minimal punishment or rehabilitation if he has no criminal record (his criminal behavior does not appear to be stable), if he was mentally deficient (his behavior was less controllable), and his friends persuaded him to do it (his actions were the result of external causes). In contrast, an armed robber who has a prior criminal record, is of normal intelligence, and who acted on his own is likely to provoke feelings of anger rather than compassion or mercy.

Disparities and Guidelines

Two people who commit the same crime do not necessarily receive the same punishment. Sentencing disparities are sometimes the logical result of differences in the details of seemingly similar crimes. But, too often, disparities arise from the biased discretion of judges. In an early study of judicial discretion, researchers asked 50 federal judges to evaluate 20 case files and recommend sentences for each defendant. There were dramatic differences across judges. For example, in a tax evasion and credit fraud case, the sentences ranged from a 3-year prison term with no fine, to a 20-year prison term combined with a $65,000 fine (Partridge & Eldridge, 1974).

The race and gender of defendants and the political leanings of judges all appear to play a role in sentencing decisions. A large-scale study of federal courts found that Hispanics and blacks, males, and younger defendants received harsher sentences than whites, females, and older defendants. After controlling for characteristics of the crimes, researchers found that young Hispanic males have the highest odds of incarceration and young black males received the longest sentences (Doerner & Demuth, 2010). An analysis of more than 10,000 felony cases found that although men and women were convicted at the same rates for similar crimes, male judges gave women significantly lighter sentences (Associated Press, 1984). Another large-scale study revealed that, for drug and property crimes, females were less likely to be sentenced to prison than males. When females were sentenced to prison, they received lighter sentences than males convicted of similar crimes. For violent crimes, women and men were equally likely to be sent to prison, although women received substantially shorter sentences (Rodriguez, Curry, & Lee, 2006). Finally, a multi-year, 50-state study of juveniles who were sentenced to life in prison (the harshest punishment available for juveniles) found that life sentences were most likely when the juvenile was African American, when the sentencing judge was elected (rather than appointed), and when the jurisdiction was politically conservative (Carmichael & Burgos, 2012).

Partly in an effort to reduce such troubling inequities in sentencing, several states and the federal government have constructed elaborate **sentencing guidelines** to restrain the discretion of judges. Guidelines generally list factors that ought to be considered when determining a sentence—for example, type of crime, viciousness of crime, defendant's prior criminal record, circumstances of the current offense, and the average sentence given for similar crimes. However, in many jurisdictions, although judges must consult the guidelines, they are not required to hand down the recommended sentence. In these jurisdictions, judges must usually declare that they considered the guidelines and must provide some written justification for deviating from the guidelines (Miller, 2006).

A more radical approach involves **determinate sentencing** (sometimes called mandatory sentencing), which requires judges to hand down a sentence that falls within a pre-specified range if a defendant is found guilty of a particular crime. Concern over sentencing disparity, a widespread public perception that judges were too lenient, and the desire of elected officials to appear "tough on crime" led to passage of the Sentencing Reform Act of 1984. As a result, a commission of judges, lawyers, and legislators was established to develop sentencing guidelines. The federal guidelines devised by the commission may be the most elaborate sentencing system ever developed (Figure 16.1 shows a section of the sentencing guidelines).

The guidelines required judges to refer to a "grid" (a table with rows and columns). The 43 rows of the grid are intended to indicate the severity of the offense, and the six columns of the grid represent six levels of prior criminal history. The rows are further subdivided into four "zones" and the columns are further subdivided by "criminal history points" that range from "0" to "13 or more." The body of the table lists specific sentence ranges expressed in months. The lowest sentence range for a level-1 offense with no prior criminal history is 0 to 6 months, and the highest range is 360 months to life. At roughly the midpoint of the grid (level 21, category 4), the range is 57 to 71 months in prison. Robbery is a level-20 offense, but that level can be adjusted upward if there are aggravating circumstances (e.g., a gun was used, the victim was seriously injured), or adjusted downward if there are mitigating circumstances (e.g., the defendant accepts personal responsibility for his crime, his accomplice was more responsible for the crime). Aside from the personal characteristic of prior criminal history, characteristics of the defendant such as age, intelligence, education, family relationships, drug addiction, and employment stability are usually not part of the sentencing calculation at the federal level (Ruback & Wroblewski, 2001). The inability of judges to take defendant characteristics into account required one federal judge to sentence a quadraplegic man to 10 years in prison for selling LSD (*United States v. Goff*, 1993).

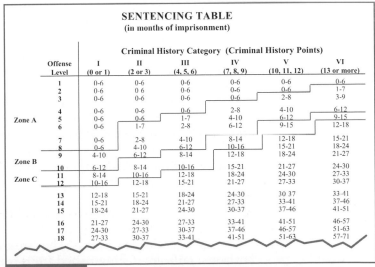

SENTENCING TABLE
(in months of imprisonment)

	Offense Level	Criminal History Category (Criminal History Points)					
		I (0 or 1)	II (2 or 3)	III (4, 5, 6)	IV (7, 8, 9)	V (10, 11, 12)	VI (13 or more)
Zone A	1	0-6	0-6	0-6	0-6	0-6	0-6
	2	0-6	0-6	0-6	0-6	0-6	1-7
	3	0-6	0-6	0-6	0-6	2-8	3-9
	4	0-6	0-6	0-6	2-8	4-10	6-12
	5	0-6	0-6	1-7	4-10	6-12	9-15
	6	0-6	1-7	2-8	6-12	9-15	12-18
Zone B	7	0-6	2-8	4-10	8-14	12-18	15-21
	8	0-6	4-10	6-12	10-16	15-21	18-24
	9	4-10	6-12	8-14	12-18	18-24	21-27
Zone C	10	6-12	8-14	10-16	15-21	21-27	24-30
	11	8-14	10-16	12-18	18-24	24-30	27-33
	12	10-16	12-18	15-21	21-27	27-33	30-37
	13	12-18	15-21	18-24	24-30	30-37	33-41
	14	15-21	18-24	21-27	27-33	33-41	37-46
	15	18-24	21-27	24-30	30-37	37-46	41-51
	16	21-27	24-30	27-33	33-41	41-51	46-57
	17	24-30	27-33	30-37	37-46	46-57	51-63
	18	27-33	30-37	33-41	41-51	51-63	57-71

FIGURE 16.1 Sentencing table (in months of imprisonment)

Critics viewed these guidelines as unnecessarily complex and undesirably rigid. Some social scientists argued that the guidelines created a mere "facade of precision" and needlessly required "judges to consider and give specific weight to an ever-growing number of inappropriately detailed sentencing factors" (Ruback & Wroblewski, 2001, p. 742). In 2005, the U.S. Supreme Court reached a decision that made use of the federal guidelines less rigid. In the case of *United States v. Booker,* the Court abandoned the mandatory component of the guidelines. The jury in Mr. Booker's case had found him guilty of charges that—based on the sentencing guidelines—would authorize the judge to sentence him to a maximum of 262 months in prison for "possession with intent to distribute" 92 grams of crack cocaine. However, based on facts of the case not heard by the jury, the judge gave Mr. Booker 360 months in prison. The Supreme Court decided that the sentencing guidelines should become advisory instead of mandatory. Judges must now rely on the facts found by the jury and must *consult* (but are not bound by) the guidelines when deciding on a sentence.

The "three strikes and you're out" laws passed by voters and legislatures in many states are interesting variants of mandatory sentencing. The state of Washington passed the first three-strikes law in 1993, and now more than 25 states have such laws (McCarthy, 2009). Generally, **three-strikes laws** require that criminals receive a long sentence or a life sentence when they are convicted of a third felony. Some states have narrow three-strikes laws that target only violent or sexual offenders, while other states have more broadly written laws. If the felonies involve violence like rape or murder, these laws seem reasonable and popular with the public. But many controversial cases have involved nonviolent "strikes" such as stealing a few slices of pizza, forging a check for a few hundred dollars, or possession of marijuana for personal use (Currie, 2013). Many criminologists have argued that the more broadly written versions of such laws are inefficient and needlessly expensive. Prison is far more expensive than any sentencing option, except the death penalty. And, often, people are sentenced to a long prison term for a third strike at a time when they are "aging out" of violent crime. Because 65% to 70% of violent crimes are committed by males under the age of 30, three-strikes laws usually incarcerate offenders near the end of their criminal careers (Chen, 2007; Greenwood et al., 1994). In addition, three-strikes laws appear to have a direct effect on making sentences harsher for Black men who commit felonies (Sutton, 2013).

Decisions about sentencing continue to be made and modified even after a criminal has served time behind prison bars. **Parole** refers to releasing inmates from prison—under the supervision of a parole officer—before their entire sentence has been served. Parole decisions are usually made by panels called parole boards. In many states, guidelines have been crafted to constrain the discretion of these boards. Research on parole decisions indicates that at least six characteristics raise the risk that parole will be denied: bad behavior while in prison, an initial sentence that is perceived by the parole board as too lenient for the crime, being in prison for a violent crime, a long criminal history, evidence of mental illness, and input from victims or families urging denial of parole (Caplan, 2007).

 ## TYPES OF IMPRISONMENT

First, a few basic distinctions. The criminal justice system can hold people in jails or prisons. **Jails** are distinguished from prisons by their function. Jails are short-term holding cells operated by cities or counties and administered by local authorities (usually county sheriffs or city police). Sometimes, people convicted of misdemeanors (relatively minor crimes usually punishable by less than a year in prison) serve out short sentences in the local jail. Jails are also places where potentially dangerous defendants charged with serious violent crimes can be held before and during trial. Nonviolent criminals (e.g., embezzlers or thieves) might be held in jail before and during trial to prevent them from fleeing to escape justice. Later, if a defendant is convicted, he or she is held in jail between conviction and sentencing, and between sentencing and transport to a prison. Jails (like prisons) are overcrowded. Several detainees might be held in a large cell and many scandals have involved assaults on nonserious offenders by violent offenders held in the same cell (Quinn, 2007).

Prisons hold convicted criminals for long periods of time—sometimes years, sometimes decades. Most prisoners will eventually be released into free society, but a small minority will live out the remainder of their natural lives behind prison walls. A tiny minority of prisoners (a fraction of 1%) will be held until they are killed in an execution chamber. Every state has its own prison system where it houses people convicted of felonies. There are also **federal prisons** for people who break federal law. Federal laws attempt to target crimes that reach beyond the borders of individual states or crimes that involve multistate conspiracies. At present, drug offenders are the single largest group of inmates in federal prisons, constituting about 48% of the total (Bureau of Justice Statistics, 2012).

State and federal prisons range from minimum security to maximum security. At one end of the continuum are the open-security federal prisons for offenders convicted of nonviolent drug offenses or white-collar crimes such as insider trading, fraud, or embezzlement. These "Club Feds" as they are sometimes facetiously called, often have no fences or guards or cellblocks. Prisoners are held in cottages or dormitories; they interact with few restrictions and spend much of their time doing light prison labor. These institutions usually have exercise equipment and sometimes they even have tennis courts and softball leagues. Some medium-security "campus style" prisons feature small, scattered buildings enclosed by a tall fence (Clear, Cole, & Reisig, 2010).

At the other end of the continuum are **supermax prisons** (super maximum-security prisons). These prisons are reserved for people deemed to be especially serious criminals, or for inmates who have been transferred from other prisons because of significant behavior problems. Inmates are held in small cells, interaction is tightly controlled, and educational and recreational opportunities are scarce or entirely absent. An early version of a supermax prison was built on the small island of Alcatraz in San Francisco Bay. In 1934, the escape-proof island prison became home to about 300 prisoners judged to be of "the vicious and irredeemable type" (Rotman, 1995). It is now a state park and major tourist attraction. Farther up the California coast, just below the Oregon border, stands Pelican Bay Prison, a modern supermax prison that holds prisoners considered to be the worst, most incorrigible criminals. Inmates in Pelican Bay's Secure Housing Unit (known as the "SHU") spend nearly 23 hours a day alone in their cells without counseling, vocational training, or prison jobs. During the remaining hour, prisoners are permitted to exercise (often in shackles) in the prison "yard." According to the federal judge who heard a class-action suit alleging inhumane conditions at Pelican Bay, these conditions of extreme isolation and sensory deprivation "press the outer bounds of what most humans can psychologically tolerate" (*Madrid v. Gomez*, 1995, p. 1267). Indeed, over time, many of the inmates exposed to such conditions develop serious mental illness, including profound depression and psychosis (Mears, 2008).

HOT TOPIC

Modern Solitary Confinement in Supermax Prisons

The practice of solitary confinement (sometimes called "punitive segregation") involves removing an inmate from the general prison population and placing him or her in a special isolated cell away from most human contact. Historically, putting a prisoner in solitary was used as a punishment for breaking prison rules—for example, fighting with prison guards or disrupting the operations of the prison.

The negative mental health consequences of solitary confinement have been recognized for well over a century. In 1890, a U.S. Supreme court decision observed that,

> A considerable number of the prisoners fell, after even a short confinement, into a semi-fatuous condition, from which it was next to impossible to arouse them, and others became violently insane; others still, committed suicide; although those who stood the ordeal better were not generally reformed, and in most cases did not recover sufficient mental activity to be of any subsequent service to the community. (In re Medley, 134 U.S. 160 (1890) p. 167)

A full century later, a U.S. district judge made the following observation about the effect of isolation at a supermax prison in Texas:

> As the pain and suffering caused by a cat-o-nine-tails lashing an inmate's back are cruel and unusual punishment by today's standards of humanity and decency, the pain and suffering caused by extreme levels of psychological deprivation are equally, if not more, cruel and unusual. The wounds and resulting scars, while less tangible, are no less painful and permanent when they are inflicted on the human psyche. (*Ruiz v. Johnson, 1999,* p. 914).

The practice of placing prisoners in solitary for days or even weeks at a time is a continuing concern, but the nature of confinement in "supermax" prisons has given rise to concerns about the effects of holding inmates in near total isolation for a sentence that may span years or even decades. Supermax inmates spend 23 hours a day in a windowless cell. During their one hour of out-of-cell time, they are permitted to exercise alone in a small walled-off area. Their meals are delivered through a slot in their cell door and they eat alone in their cell. Group activities (e.g., dining in the cafeteria with other inmates, attending group religious services) and educational or therapeutic programs are typically forbidden. Visits are often conducted via closed circuit television. This enforced isolation is combined with enforced idleness due to restrictions on personal property and access to the prison library. Heavy reliance on video monitoring in modern supermax prisons means that even face-to-face contact with prison guards is rare. An inmate's only physical contact with another human may occur when a guard handcuffs and shackles the inmate so that he can be transported to the exercise area (Shalev, 2009). In supermax prisons, solitary confinement

THE GOALS OF IMPRISONMENT

Even the terms used to describe prisons reveal ambivalence. "Penal institution" implies a place of punishment; the term "penitentiary" is religious in origin and refers to a place where one can repent and atone for one's sins; and the term "correctional institution" suggests a place where the behavior of the criminal can be improved or corrected.

Prisons serve many ends. The simplest goal is **incapacitation** through containment. If a criminal is securely contained inside prison walls, he or she is unable to harm people outside the prison. Society is spared the crimes that may have been committed if the prisoner were still free. Successful incapacitation requires only that prisons hold criminals securely—that they cannot escape. A second goal of prison is **deterrence.** For a particular criminal, it is hoped that the experience of suffering in prison will dissuade him from committing further crimes after he is released from prison (this is called **specific deterrence**). We also hope for **general deterrence**—that other people will choose not is not a brief punishment; it is a perpetual state of being.

The psychologically damaging effects of prolonged isolation in supermax prisons have been documented by many researchers (Haney, 2006). These effects range in severity depending on the vulnerability of the inmate and the length of confinement, but include reactions such as insomnia, chronic anxiety, violent fantasies, confused thought processes, uncontrollable anger, hallucinations, emotional breakdowns, chronic depression, and suicidal thoughts, and self-mutilation. These symptoms may be amplified if the inmate already suffers from some form of mental illness before he enters a supermax cell (Metzner & Fellner, 2010).

Eventually, a majority of prisoners held in supermax conditions will be released into free society. Although researchers have recommended several reforms to blunt the destructive effects of isolation, these reforms have not been widely adopted. They include providing special training for and supervision of correctional staff who work in supermax prisons; prohibiting mentally ill convicts from being housed in long-term supermax conditions; allowing prisoners to meet with mental health professionals; allowing inmates to interact with other inmates in dining halls, during religious services, and through educational programs; and limiting the duration of supermax confinement (Arrigo & Bullock, 2009).

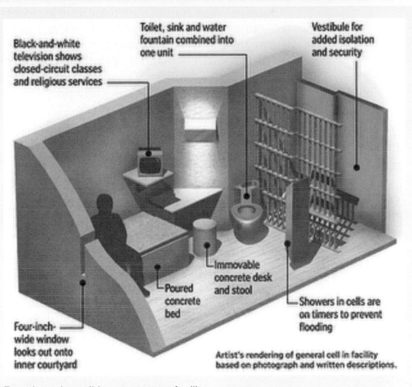

Black-and-white television shows closed-circuit classes and religious services

Toilet, sink and water fountain combined into one unit

Vestibule for added isolation and security

Four-inch-wide window looks out onto inner courtyard

Poured concrete bed

Immovable concrete desk and stool

Showers in cells are on timers to prevent flooding

Artist's rendering of general cell in facility based on photograph and written descriptions.

Drawing of a cell in a supermax facility

to commit crimes because they fear going to prison. Deterrence theory implies that we should make prisons as unpleasant as possible to boost their deterrent power.

The third goal, **retribution,** is less practical and more emotional. Most of us feel a sense of rage and revulsion when we hear about an especially hideous crime (e.g., the murder of a child). We want to see the murderer punished. Prison is a punishing environment where the convict will suffer. Because societies are held together, in part, by a shared consensus of what constitutes immoral behavior, law-abiding members of society feel a justified sense of moral outrage when someone commits a terrible crime. The criminal who violates the moral order must be punished to restore moral balance. Retribution, it is argued, promotes moral solidarity among law-abiding citizens and educates potential criminals about which behaviors are strongly condemned (Berns, 1979). The problem with retribution is that there is no precise formula for deciding how much suffering to inflict. And there is also the question of how much pain can be ethically inflicted on criminals. Retribution is largely backward looking in that it focuses on the crime.

The final, most forward-looking goal of prisons is **rehabilitation.** Nearly all prisoners will eventually be released back into free society, so it makes sense to try to "improve" criminals during their time in prison. Although, for decades, punishment took priority over rehabilitation, prisons in the United States were developed for the explicit purpose of transforming criminals into productive members of society. A core problem is that the optimistic goal of rehabilitation is in conflict with other goals of imprisonment. Painful, unpleasant prisons are likely to make prisoners angrier and more aggressive while providing few of the skills necessary to become law-abiding citizens.

THE EVOLUTION OF PRISONS IN THE UNITED STATES

In the American colonies, lists of crimes included not only theft, assault, rape, and murder, but also moral transgressions such as witchcraft, adultery, idolatry, and blasphemy. A range of punishments was available. Vagabonds who wandered into town and committed a crime could simply be banished and threatened with severe punishment if they ever returned. But locals who were judged guilty of crimes were usually subjected to **public shaming.** The offender might be locked into the stocks (typically a wood structure that holds the wrists and neck) or a public cage. Townspeople would be able to taunt and spit on them to show their disapproval of the crime. Some offenders were chained or tied to a post and publicly whipped. Justice was not equal. Those who were wealthy or well-connected were often permitted to pay a fine as a way of avoiding the stocks or the lash. One innovation in the colonies was a graduated series of punishments for repeat offenders. The first conviction of a thief could lead to a fine or a whipping. For the second theft, the fine would be tripled, the offender would sit for an hour on the gallows with a noose around his neck, and he would then be tied to the whipping post for 30 lashes. For the third offense, the criminal was hanged (Rotman, 1995). This may have been the first "three-strikes" law.

Men in stocks
(BETTMANN/CORBIS)

Following the Revolutionary War, Americans were eager to develop a system of criminal punishment distinct from the laws inherited from England. Reformers sought to abandon the "corrupt, barbarous, and unjust" punishments of the monarchy (Drapkin, 1989). The death penalty was greatly restricted in nearly every state and, instead of beating and killing, the new country decided to rely on incarceration. Criminals would be kept apart from the rest of society and the cruel punishments of the past would be set aside. Between 1790 and 1800, eight states built prisons (Clear, et al., 2010).

The 1800s

The American optimism that fueled the construction of prisons slowly eroded from 1800 through 1820. Two decades of experience with prisons led many to conclude that prisons created as many problems as they solved. Escapes, small-scale disturbances, and even large-scale riots were frequent. During their time in prison, inmates freely shared their knowledge of the criminal trades and used their time to refine their criminal skills. By 1820, most public officials had come to believe that prisons spawned crime instead of suppressing it.

Disillusionment with prisons and changes in society prompted a deeper analysis of the causes and consequences of crime. Earlier attitudes toward criminals were rooted in religious beliefs and so no real theory of crime was necessary. If humans were born sinful, some evil deeds were simply inevitable. But as American society became more distinctive and more secular, religious explanations lost some of their resonance. During the first half of the nineteenth century, a new theory of criminal behavior began to gain prominence. Dorothea Dix, a leading social reformer of the period, neatly summed up the emerging perspective: "It is to the defects of our social organization, to the multiplied and multiplying temptations to crime that we chiefly owe the increase in evil doers" (cited in Rothman, 1995, p. 105).

This was a fundamental shift in thinking about crime. The cause for criminal behavior was no longer located only within the individual criminal. Societal disorganization was also to blame. Reformers cited several trends that encouraged criminality: the decline of the influence of the church, the increased mobility of citizens that led to unstable communities where neighbors no longer cared about one another, schools that failed to discipline children and teach them the difference between right and wrong, and uninvolved fathers who spent too much time at work and allowed their children to leave home at too young an age (Friedman, 1993). These new, more social-psychological theories of crime seemed to demand a fresh approach to dealing with criminals. Prisons were reconceived and redesigned. Rehabilitation became the new ideal. To reform criminals, prisons would have to reeducate and reshape prisoners. If families, churches, schools, and neighborhoods had failed to instill proper values and habits, prisons would do the job.

During the 1820s, prisons were established in New York and Pennsylvania with the goal of putting the new rehabilitative model into practice. In Pennsylvania, inmates remained in their cells for virtually their entire sentence. They ate alone in their cells, worked alone in their cells (spinning wool was the usual work), and slept alone in their cells. To enforce lack of contact between inmates, new prisoners were escorted to their cells with hoods over their heads so that they would not see or be seen by other inmates. Prisoners were not permitted to correspond with friends or family and visitors were rare. After all, outsiders were part of the unwholesome social environment that had produced criminal behavior. The Bible was the only reading material permitted (Friedman, 1993). The New York system was a bit more relaxed: Though prisoners spent most of their time in individual cells, they were allowed to eat and work in groups. The groups, however, were silent and noninteractive—talking was forbidden and even the exchange of glances was prohibited.

News of prisons in the United States reached the countries of Europe and representatives were dispatched to examine these great laboratories for human reform. In 1842, Charles Dickens, the great English novelist and journalist toured Philadelphia prison. He was not impressed:

> **Those who devised this system and those benevolent gentlemen who carry it into execution, do not know what they are doing. I believe that very few men are capable of estimating the immense amount of torture and agony that this dreadful punishment, prolonged for years, inflicts upon the sufferers. . . . Those who have undergone this punishment must pass into society again morally unhealthy and diseased. (Dickens, 1850, p. 128)**

Most observers seemed to agree with Dickens's assessment of the Pennsylvania system. Critics pointed out fundamental problems: It was impractical and expensive, and the extreme isolation drove many prisoners insane. Mental breakdowns, self-mutilations, and suicides were common (Friedman, 1993).

Around this time, overcrowding was emerging as a major problem. By 1866, roughly a third of all prisoners were being housed two to a cell (McKelvey, 1977). This meant that silence and isolation—the foundation of earlier rehabilitative models—were no longer possible. Although rehabilitation was still the official goal of prisons, the sheer size of the inmate population and the increase in the number of serious offenders frustrated efforts at reform. And, to preserve their precarious authority in overcrowded prisons, officials often resorted to brutal forms of discipline. Prisoners were subjected to "bucking"—tying or cuffing the wrists together, forcing the arms over the bent knees, and inserting a bar under the knees and over the elbows. A ball and chain could be cuffed to an inmate's ankle for months at a stretch. Solitary confinement in an isolated cell, a concrete box, or even a tall, narrow cage was widely used. Prisoners could be "thrown in the hole" for days, or even weeks, with a daily food ration of as little as 4 ounces of bread and a quart of water (Cockrell, 2013).

Bigotry also contributed to the abandonment of reform. Prisons were holding a disproportionate number of new immigrants (especially Irish), and there was less sympathy for inmates. Many felt that the new immigrants were morally and intellectually inferior. When rehabilitation failed, it was usually blamed on the incorrigible nature of the inmates rather than on the failures of the prison system (Friedman, 1993). By the beginning of the twentieth century, most reforms had been abandoned. Advocates of rehabilitation were often derided as naive and idealistic. Security and maintenance of minimal order began to seem like the only achievable goals.

The 1900s

For the first half of the twentieth century, prisons felt the growing influence of medical and social science. Some criminals began to be seen as suffering from psychological dysfunctions that could benefit from therapeutic treatment. This "medical model" bolstered the commitment to indeterminate sentencing: Just as it made no sense for a physician to decide on the length of a hospital stay immediately after diagnosis, it made no sense to sentence convicts to an immutable prison term immediately after conviction. Just as patients were to be released from the hospital whenever they were cured, inmates were to be released from prison whenever they were rehabilitated. There would be periodic reviews of an inmate's progress. And, if there was clear evidence that an inmate was participating in constructive prison activities and showing signs of improvement, his or her sentence could be reduced.

Use of the medical model had other implications. In medical practice, curing an ailment requires accurate diagnosis and individualized treatment. For prisons, this meant that officials needed to develop classification schemes for differentiating one inmate from another on the basis of his or her problems. In theory, classification would dictate therapeutic approach (McKelvey, 1977). Unfortunately, given the vagueness of prisoner classification schemes of the time, there was considerable disagreement about which inmates belonged in which category. And, of course, many prisoners belonged in more than one category. In addition, well-behaved, more treatable prisoners usually failed to receive treatment or retraining, but inmates classified as incorrigible or unresponsive to treatment could be treated more harshly.

By the late 1960s, there was growing concern about the brutality and ineffectiveness of prisons. Based on a multiyear study, the President's Commission on Law Enforcement and the Administration of Justice issued a report in 1966. That report painted a bleak picture of prison conditions:

Life in many institutions is at best barren and futile, at worst unspeakably brutal and degrading. To be sure, the offenders in such institutions are incapacitated from committing further crimes while serving their sentences, but the conditions in which they live are the poorest possible preparation for their successful reentry into society, and often merely reinforce in them a pattern of manipulation and destructiveness. (cited in Rothman, 1995, p. 173)

Public dissatisfaction with prisons and a series of prison riots in California, Pennsylvania, Kansas, and New York helped to fuel a sort of anti-prison movement, emphasizing rehabilitation, reintegration into the community, and alternatives to incarceration (Smith & Schweitzer, 2012). But this tentative commitment to reform faded fast. In 1975, an influential analysis of 231 prison rehabilitation programs reached the following conclusion: "With few and isolated exceptions, the rehabilitative efforts that have been reported so far have had no appreciable effect on recidivism" (Lipton, Wilks, & Martinson, 1975, p. 22). This "nothing works" conclusion combined with state budget cuts produced devastating effects on prisons beginning in the late 1970s. In addition to the perceived ineffectiveness of rehabilitation, the victim's rights movement shifted the focus away from offenders. An increasing emphasis on crime victims made the public less interested in reforming criminals and more interested in making criminals "pay" for their crimes (Phelps, 2012). By the 1980s, many prison educational and vocational programs were dramatically scaled back or even eliminated. Sports and recreational programs were curtailed in many prisons. Indeed, nearly all programs came under attack as examples of coddling criminals and being soft on crime. During the late 1980s and early 1990s, state and national politicians began to compete for the label of "tough on crime." Candidates pledged to imprison more criminals for longer periods of time and to impose the death penalty more often (Ellsworth & Gross, 1994).

 ## PRISONER RIGHTS AND THE ROLE OF THE COURTS

Until the middle of the twentieth century, federal and state courts did not exert much control over the internal management of prisons. There were several reasons for this hands-off doctrine: It was felt that judges lacked the expertise to intervene in prison administration, that tinkering by the courts would undermine prison discipline, that complaints from prisoners usually involved privileges rather the rights, and that societal standards favored (or at least accepted) the harshness of prisons (National Advisory Commission on Criminal Justice Standards and Goals, 1973).

Especially during the years when Earl Warren served as chief justice of the Supreme Court, there was a broad expansion of civil liberties for many of society's least powerful groups, including racial minorities, women, children, and prison inmates. An early victory for prisoners came in 1964, when Muslim inmates were permitted to receive copies of the Koran, eat meals free of pork, and hold religious meetings (*Cooper v. Pate*, 1964). In *Procunier v. Martinez* (1974), the Supreme Court approved the rights of prisoners to receive mail and to make use of law students and paralegals to investigate their cases. Through the 1960s and 1970s, the courts responded to prisoner class-action lawsuits by defining minimum health care standards and raising due-process standards for disciplinary actions against prison inmates. Courts also imposed limits on prison overcrowding.

HOT TOPIC

Free Will and the Purpose of Prisons

Is criminal behavior the result of free will? Do criminals *choose* to commit horrible crimes? Our legal system assumes free choice *unless* evidence can be presented to prove that the criminal did not act freely (e.g., a murderer may be judged "insane," or a driver who runs over a pedestrian might be acquitted if he lost control of his car because of a heart attack). In legal jargon, to be held culpable or blameworthy, the guilty deed must be accompanied by a guilty mind.

Recently, several prominent neuroscientists (Gazzaniga, 2011; S. Harris, 2012) and some social psychologists (Wegner, 2003) have argued that free will may be an illusion or that, even if free will exists, it is highly constrained. The basic argument is that a particular combination of genetics and environment determines each person's behavior and that no one is able to choose their genetic endowment or their environment (at least during their formative childhood years). In addition, there appears to be no "ghost in the machine" that directs our behavior, no decision maker separate from our biological, neural machinery (which is a product of our genetics and environment). Further, several experiments suggest that the electrical activity in the brain indicating that a decision has been made precedes conscious awareness of that decision. As some researchers have put it, "The brain acts before the mind decides" (Koch, 2012, p. 26).

Another set of findings is especially relevant to the legal system: A variety of disruptions in brain chemistry—resulting from neurotransmitter imbalances, brain tumors, hormonal imbalances, or frontal lobe dementia—can

(AARON GOODMAN)

produce behaviors ranging from murder to pedophilia to compulsive gambling (Eagleman, 2011). Put differently, changes in brain functioning, rather than conscious choice, can cause people to commit criminal acts. Of particular relevance are disruptions in the brain regions associated with fear and aggression (e.g., the amygdala) or regions associated with impulse control (e.g., the prefrontal cortex). Changes in brain chemistry change our emotions, our cravings, our reactions to stimuli, our decision-making processes, and our capacity for self-restraint. Because people's brains differ substantially (as the result of genetic and environmental influences they do not choose), not every adult possesses the same ability to act wisely or in accordance with the law.

If one of the foundational principles of our legal system—that people freely choose their criminal behavior—is mistaken, it has profound implications for criminal justice. It is the judgment of culpability that dictates how a criminal will be treated after conviction (Greene & Cohen, 2004). If free will is largely or entirely an illusion, it would mean that criminals may not have been able to act differently than they did act. And, if we do *not* assume that criminals freely choose to act in cruel or irresponsible ways, it no longer makes sense to punish or seek retribution. It would, however, still make sense to keep society safe by taking dangerous criminals off the streets, and it would still makes sense to try to reform criminals. In a "no free will" justice system, the goals of sentencing would be limited to incapacitating criminals and rehabilitating them so that they could eventually reenter society.

But the Court's willingness to act on behalf of inmates did not continue into the 1980s. In 1981, the Supreme Court signaled its intention to retreat from its commitment to easing inhumane conditions in prisons. In *Rhodes v. Chapman,* the Court suggested that as long as conditions were not "grossly disproportionate to the severity of the crime" and not "totally without penological justification," they would no longer be viewed as "cruel and unusual." Double-celling (holding two people in a 6- by 10-foot cell), for example, was judged to be acceptable. In the Court's view, "To the extent that such conditions are restrictive and even harsh, they are part of the penalty that criminal offenders pay for their offenses against society" (p. 337). A decade later, in *Wilson v. Seiter* (1991), the Court went even further: To be judged cruel and unusual, conditions would not only have to be inhumane, but officials would need to show "deliberate indifference" to those inhumane conditions. Extending this new standard in 1994 in a case in which an inmate had been raped by other inmates, the Court held that inmates would be required to prove "subjective recklessness" on the part of prison officials (*Farmer v. Brennan*, 1994). Some changes in prison policy came from Congress rather than the courts. In a rare recent victory for prisoners, Congress passed the Prison Rape Elimination Act (PREA) in 2003. PREA established a commission to conduct research and develop a strategy for solving the crime of rape against prisoners.

Prisons hold a large number of mentally ill inmates, and prison administrators are obliged to provide treatment for serious mental illness. But to qualify as "serious," the condition must "result in further significant injury, not routine discomfort that is part of the penalty that criminal offenders pay for their offenses against society" (*McGuckin v. Smith*, 1992). Whether or not a prisoner receives treatment is typically left to the discretion of prison wardens. If a prisoner is perceived as faking to get sympathy or time away from his or her cell, requests for help may be denied. A prisoner cannot be forced to take psychoactive medications until it has been determined that the drug is medically warranted or necessary to prevent that prisoner from doing harm to him- or herself or others (*Washington v. Harper*, 1990). Based on several

studies, it is estimated that about 14% of inmates suffer from a serious mental illness, such as schizophrenia, bipolar disorder, or major depression (Skeem, Manchak, & Peterson, 2011).

In *Brown v. Plata* (2011), the U.S. Supreme Court found egregious violations of prisoners' constitutional right to receive medical and mental health treatment in California prisons. These violations were due to severe overcrowding. At the time of the case, California's prison system had grown to about 156,000 inmates, although the system was only designed to house approximately 85,000 inmates. The court ordered the release of more than 46,000 prisoners. In the majority opinion, Justice Kennedy wrote, "After years of litigation, it became apparent that a remedy for the constitutional violations would not be effective absent a reduction in the prison system population" (p. 1922).

Prison crowding in California (*JUSTIN SULLIVAN/GETTY IMAGES*)

 ## BASIC STATISTICS ON PRISONS AND PRISONERS

The U.S. prison population reached a historic peak in 2008–2009 when 2.3 million people were housed in America's jails and prisons (Currie, 2013). Although the prison population has been slowly declining for the past few years, the United States still imprisons a larger percentage of its citizens for longer periods of time than any other industrialized democracy in the world. Since the 1980s, the rate of incarceration in the United States has averaged about five times higher than that of any other industrialized democracy (see Table 16.1). The five U.S. states with the highest rates of incarceration are, in order, Louisiana, Mississippi, Alabama, Texas,

TABLE 16.1

Estimated Number of Inmates Held in State or Federal Prison, or in Local Jails, by Gender, Race, and Hispanic Origin, 2000–2008

Year	Males				Females			
	Total	*White*	*Black*	*Hispanic*	*Total*	*White*	*Black*	*Hispanic*
2000	1,775,700	663,700	791,600	290,900	156,200	63,700	69,500	19,500
2001	1,800,300	684,800	803,400	283,000	161,200	67,700	69,500	19,900
2002	1,848,700	630,700	818,900	342,500	165,800	68,800	65,600	25,400
2003	1,902,300	665,100	832,400	363,900	176,300	76,100	66,800	28,300
2004	1,947,800	695,800	842,500	366,800	183,400	81,700	67,700	28,600
2005	1,992,600	688,700	806,200	403,500	193,600	88,600	65,700	29,300
2006	2,042,100	718,100	836,800	426,900	203,100	95,300	68,800	32,400
2007	2,090,800	755,500	814,700	410,900	208,300	96,600	67,600	32,100
2008	2,103,500	712,500	846,000	427,000	207,700	94,500	67,800	33,400

Note: *Table excludes American Indians, Alaska Natives, Asians, Native Hawaiians, and other Pacific Islanders, and persons identifying two or more races.*

Source: *U.S. Bureau of Justice Statistics.*

and Oklahoma. There are more people living behind bars in Alabama than in all of the prisons in Canada, and more prisoners in Louisiana than in all of the prisons in Japan. Our high rate of incarceration persists despite a dramatic drop in both violent and nonviolent crimes over the past 15 years. Crime rates have now fallen back to where they were in the 1970s, when the rate of imprisonment was only 110 per 100,000 in population (Innes, 2010). At the beginning of 2013, the rate was 480 per 100,000 in population (Carson & Sabol, 2012).

The total prison population is a function of two numbers: the number of people sent to prison, and the length of time they stay in prison. This means that reducing the prison population could be accomplished by preventing crime, by decreasing the number of people sent to prison (e.g., by using probation or other alternatives), by reducing the length of prison sentences, or by reducing recidivism. Conversely, longer sentences, mandatory sentencing, three-strikes laws, reductions in the use of parole, and the increased imprisonment of juveniles have all contributed to the stunning rise in the rate of imprisonment (Quinn, 2007). The prison population explosion has also been fueled by the rising number of people imprisoned for drug offenses. As part of the so-called "war on drugs" federal sentencing guidelines and those of many states were modified to encourage or require long prison terms for many drug offenses.

People who go to prison tend not to come from privileged or stable circumstances. About 40% of prisoners have at least one other family member who has been incarcerated. About 62% are regular drug users before incarceration, and less than one-third have completed high school. Only 18% are married, and just over half earned less than $16,000 in the year preceding incarceration. Though our prisons have experienced a population boom, they are not exploding with only rapists, murderers, and other violent criminals. Approximately 53% of people sentenced to state prisons were convicted of violent crimes. The remaining 47% were convicted of drug, property, or "other" crimes. As shown in Figure 16.2, in federal prisons, only 7.6% have been convicted of violent crimes, while 48% were convicted of drug offenses (Carson & Sabol, 2012).

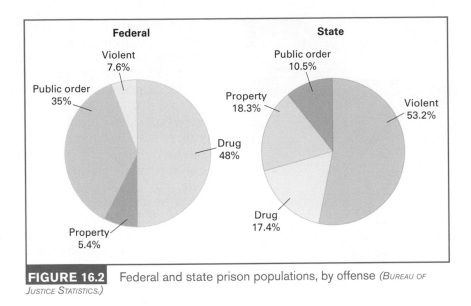

FIGURE 16.2 Federal and state prison populations, by offense (*Bureau of Justice Statistics.*)

Another startling feature of prisoners in the United States is the color of their skin. Black men are incarcerated at a rate about six times higher than white men, and black males between the ages of 20 and 34 have the highest incarceration rate of any racial or gender group (Sabol & Coutoure, 2008). Black males have a 29% chance of serving at least 1 year in prison during their lifetimes, whereas Hispanic males have a 16% chance, and White males have a 5% chance (Lutze, Johnson, Clear, Latessa, & Slate, 2012). Once convicted, blacks are more likely to receive a prison sentence and less likely to receive alternative sentences such as electronic monitoring, intensive supervision, or drug- and alcohol-treatment programs (B.D. Johnson & Dipietro, 2012). (See Figure 16.3 to see the racial composition of U.S. prison population compared with U.S. population as a whole.)

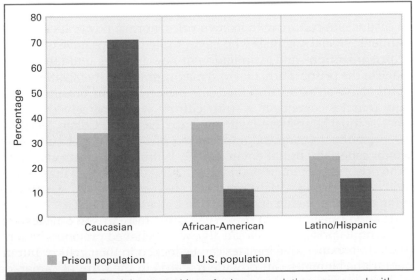

FIGURE 16.3 Racial composition of prison population compared with U.S. population as a whole (*Source: Bureau of Justice Statistics, 2013*)

The male-to-female ratio of the prison population is wildly disproportionate to the general population. About 93% of the prisoners in state and federal prisons are male (Sentencing Project, 2014). Psychologists have devoted considerable attention to identifying reliable differences between the behavior of men and women. Many of the differences identified are small or subtle. But the largest gender difference is in the propensity for aggression and violent behavior. Males are far more likely to be violent, more likely to come into contact with the criminal justice system, and more likely to end up behind prison walls for violent crimes (and even for high-risk, nonviolent crimes such as burglary and car theft).

Probably because women represent only about 7% of the adult prison population, there has been relatively little research on life inside women's prisons. Females are far more likely to be held in minimum-security prisons and dormlike rooms instead of cells. Only about 36% of female inmates were sent to prison for violent offenses (Carson & Golinelli, 2013). Violence is much less prevalent in women's prisons. Female prisoners appear to attempt self-mutilation and suicide at higher rates than male prisoners and are more likely than men to be given psychoactive, mood-altering drugs (Wright, Van Voorhis, Salisbury, & Bauman, 2012). About half the women in prison are white (49%) and about 28% are black. Sixty-two percent have children under the age of 18 (as compared with 51% of male prisoners; Sabol & Couture, 2011).

THE DISTINCTIVE CULTURE OF PRISON

Prison is a distinct subculture with its own rules, norms, power hierarchy, rewards, and punishments. Social scientists who have studied prisons have written about the process of **prisonization**—the assimilation of new inmates into the values, norms, and language of the prison. Particularly in maximum-security facilities, the values of criminal gangs have also been imported into prison from the outside world (Jacobs, 1983). Many inmates come from a street culture where perceived disrespect and threats to honor must be answered with violence (Nisbett & Cohen, 1996). These two processes—prisonization and the importation of violent street culture—combine to produce an especially brutal environment. Within the self-contained culture of prison, some prisoners are interested in staying out of trouble so that they can finish their sentences and get out. Others see themselves as "convicts" who have no hope of ever living a productive life on the outside (Silberman, 1995).

Rewards and punishments in prison can come from prison officials or other inmates. For example, prison officials can give well-behaved prisoners better work assignments, and uncooperative inmates can be locked in their cells or put in solitary confinement. Other inmates can provide rewards in the form of camaraderie and protection, or punishment in the form of intimidation and violence.

The Power of the Prison Situation

One of the great lessons of social psychology is that powerful situations can sometimes overwhelm individual differences. That is, at times, personality characteristics have much less influence on behavior than the characteristics of the situations that people find themselves in. One of the earliest and most compelling demonstrations of the power of situations was a prison simulation study conducted at Stanford University in 1971.

Each potential participant in the Stanford prison study was given an extensive battery of psychological tests, and the 20 most psychologically healthy young men were accepted for inclusion in the study. Then came the crucial event: ten of the men were randomly assigned to the role of prison guard, and ten were randomly assigned to the role of prisoner. A few days later, police cars pulled up to the homes of the "prisoners" with red lights flashing. The young men were handcuffed and taken into custody. Next, they were arrested, booked, fingerprinted, and escorted to a simulated prison in the basement of the Stanford University psychology building. They were stripped, searched, and given a prison uniform—a loose-fitting white smock with an identification number and a pair of sandals. The "guards" wore khaki uniforms and carried handcuffs, nightsticks, keys, and whistles. Other prisonlike conditions were put in place. There were routine headcounts of the prisoners, supervised trips to the toilet, meals at preset times, and prisoners remained in the mock prison 24 hours a day. With these basic conditions in place, the participants were simply allowed to interact (Drury, Hutchens, Shuttlesworth, & White, 2012).

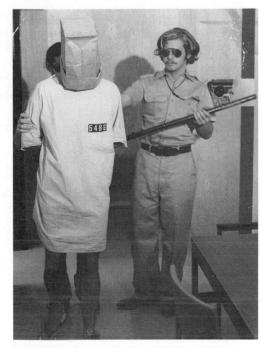

"Prisoners" and "guards" in the Stanford Prison Study *(Duke Downey/ San Francisco Chronicle/Corbis)*

After 2 weeks, the researchers were going to retest the participants to see if there had been subtle shifts in attitudes or self-concepts. But something unexpected and disturbing happened—the guards seemed intoxicated with their new power and became increasingly abusive. Physical abuse was not permitted, so the guards resorted to verbal harassment. They also employed more direct forms of abuse such as solitary confinement, waking up prisoners in the middle of the night for surprise headcounts, withholding toilet privileges, and making the prisoners do pushups while a guard rested a heavy foot on the prisoner's back. Initially, some prisoners resisted. But after only a few days, even the rebellious prisoners became passive and demoralized. The experimenters released the first prisoner after only 36 hours because he was showing signs of severe depression and the entire experiment had to be abruptly terminated after only 6 days. In the words of the researchers,

> Our planned two-week experiment had to be aborted after only six days because the experience dramatically and painfully transformed most of the participants in ways we did not anticipate, prepare for, or predict. (Haney, Banks, & Zimbardo, 1973, p. 91)

So, what should be made of this famous study? Many have criticized the Stanford study as unrealistic. Perhaps the mock guards were merely reenacting roles they had seen in movies and, clearly, 6 days in a simulated prison cannot possibly recreate the realities experienced by actual guards and prisoners. But there are a couple of important implications of the experiment. First, if a relatively tame simulation can produce such striking effects in so little time, then the vastly more potent realities of an actual prison might be expected to produce far more extreme effects. Second, because all participants were psychologically healthy and randomly assigned to conditions, we cannot attribute the changes in the behavior of the participants to personality differences. Something intrinsic to the situation—for example, the gross disparity in power between prisoners and guards—at least temporarily transformed the attitudes and behaviors of the participants.

The Harshness of Prison Life

Because it is impossible to fully simulate the realities of prison life in the laboratory, and because it would be unethical to expose research participants to the punishing conditions of prison life, social scientists have relied on other methods to investigate prisons. Researchers have relied on observational methods, in-depth interviews with prisoners and prison officials, and analysis of prison records over time (e.g., number of violent incidents). Based on these data, several scholars have described the ways in which life inside prison is strikingly different from life on the outside (Haney, 2006; Toch & Adams, 2002). First, the prisoner is banished from the outside world—separated from the people and surroundings he or she cares about. Over time, most inmates lose contact with all but the most devoted friends and family members. Inmates are assigned to prisons based primarily on their crimes and the availability of space. Family members (who tend not to be rich) must often travel great distances to visit prisoners. Mail (except from the inmate's attorney) can be censored or even destroyed. Second, prisoners have no decision-making power over important aspects of their lives. Where they can go, how they spend their time, what they eat, and who they associate with, are all largely decided by prison officials. Third, the physical environment is stark and oppressive. In most large maximum-security prisons, inmates spend nearly all their time in a windowless, 6-foot by 10-foot cell. They often share this cell with one other person. Fourth, there is an extreme lack of privacy, particularly for double-celled inmates. Prisoners can be observed by prison officials at all times. Fifth, there is the threat or reality of violence—from other prisoners, from groups of prisoners, and from guards. Sixth, there is enforced idleness and routine. Life in the modern American prison is characterized by relentless, deadening routine. These conditions and their psychological effects have been described by prisoners in the following ways:

> **The major problem is monotony. It is the dull sameness of prison life, its idleness and boredom that grinds me down. Nothing matters; everything is inconsequential other than when you will be free and how to make time pass until then. But boredom, interrupted by occasional bursts of fear and anger, is the governing reality of life in prison. (Morris, 1995, p. 205)**

> **Prison not only robs you of your freedom, it attempts to take away your identity. Everyone wears a uniform, eats the same food, follows the same schedule. It is by definition a purely authoritarian state that tolerates no independence and individuality . . . . It is dehumanizing, for it forces you to adapt by becoming more self-contained and insulated. (Mandela, 1994, p. 376)**

A core feature of prison life is violence and the threat of violence. Many of the cultural norms inside prison concern enforcement of rules through violence. One prominent prison scholar points out that prisons "have a climate of violence which has no free-world counterpart. Inmates are terrorized by other inmates and spend years in fear of harm" (Toch, 1997, p. 53). This chronic state of fear and vigilance takes a heavy psychological toll. What has been called the "convict code" emphasizes that inmates who "snitch" on other inmates should be beaten, stabbed, or even killed, and that each prisoner should show loyalty only to himself and members of his group or gang. Violence is often the most effective means of reaching goals in prison, and any attack on a member of a gang must be avenged by that gang (Silberman, 1995). Two prisoners describe it similarly:

> You have to protect your manhood and live by a different code where a lot of things that you could let go when you are out you can't let go when you are in a penitentiary because if you do, people take that as a sign of weakness; they will then mistreat you until you stand up for yourself; but on the street you can pretty much pass that because, you know, who cares? (Mbuba, 2012, p. 237)

> It is no accident that convicts speak of penal institutions as gladiator schools. . . . If you are a man, you must either kill or turn the tables on anyone who propositions you with threats of force. It is the custom among prisoners. Here in prison the most respected and honored men among us are those who have killed other men, particularly other prisoners. (Abbott, 1991, p. 126)

Homosexual rape is used to demean and dominate other inmates. And, if the victim fails to fight off the rapist or to retaliate against him, he is likely to become the target of further sexual assaults (Jones & Pratt, 2008). An inmate can be placed in protective custody (away from the general prison population), but because a request to be placed in protective custody may be seen as a form of "snitching," it can put the victim in further danger. Many inmates are presented with a simple choice: either fight or submit sexually. Younger, more vulnerable inmates are especially likely to be raped and some are even treated as sexual slaves who can be sold or traded to other inmates (Rideau & Wikberg, 1992). One inmate put it this way:

> If you are weak or don't want to bring violence into your life and don't hang with anybody, a big dude will probably approach and befriend you and begin to share his stuff with you, hang with you and then, when nobody is around, he will suddenly turn against you and strike. (Mbuba, 2012, p. 238)

Criminal behavior continues inside prison, and much of that behavior is facilitated by prison gangs. One reason gangs flourish in many prisons is that inmates vastly outnumber guards. As one prison scholar put it, "It is not always appreciated by the general public that immediate power within the prison belongs to the prisoners" (Morris, 1995, p. 221). Prison guards are often acutely aware

Prison gang members (*Andrew Lichtenstein/Corbis*)

of the precariousness of their authority. Here are a few quotes from interviews with prison guards (Martin, Lichtenstein, Jenkot, & Forde, 2012):

> Inmates allow us to be in this institution every day, and they allow us to leave. I think that anytime they want to take over, then they can. (p. 97)

> This is a hostile and dangerous environment. We are spread thin. Sometimes we have to monitor several hundred inmates by ourselves. We have become prey. (p. 99)

> They are breathing down our neck, and they know we are outnumbered. There could be a hostage situation at any time. (p. 99)

An ironic effect of legal rulings limiting the ability of prison officials to physically punish prisoners has been an increase in the power of prison gangs. In response to such rulings, prison officials began to take a more passive approach toward prisoners. That is, officials became less likely to respond to complaints of prisoners who were physically or sexually abused by other prisoners. In effect, prisoners were left to "fend for themselves" (R. Johnson, 1996). Some scholars have characterized prison gangs as a form of "self-governance" that emerges to increase order and predictability for those living inside prison walls (Skarbek, 2012).

Gangs with names like the Aryan Brotherhood, the Gangsta Killer Bloods, the Mexican Mafia, and the Nazi Lowriders have a powerful influence on prison culture. Prison gangs are often subsidiaries of street gangs and the norms and leadership structures sometimes transfer from one setting to the other. New prisoners are motivated to join a gang because of fear of other inmates, or to gain a sense of belonging, or to increase their status, or to gain access to drugs and other contraband (Winterdyk & Ruddell, 2010). Within prisons, gang members can bribe correctional officers to facilitate crimes such as extortion, homosexual prostitution, gambling, drug sales, and robbery (Worrall & Morris, 2012). According to some studies, about half of all prison violence is the result of gang activities. The oath taken by members of the Nuestra Familia gang makes expectations of violence very clear: "If I go forward, follow me. If I hesitate, push me. If they kill me, avenge me. If I am a traitor, kill me" (Siegel, 2012, p. 547). In many large prisons, inmates have little choice but to join a gang. One prisoner puts it this way:

> If you show up to prison and don't join the gang of your race, you'll be a target for the other gangs within days . . . . When there's a war, you're a target just because of the color of your skin, so you might as well. You're going to have to defend yourself, you've gotta take sides. (Sullivan, 2006, p. 4)

𝓕OCUS ON 𝓒AREERS

Correctional Psychologist
Edward "Rhett" Landis, Ph.D., ABPP
Chief Psychologist
Federal Correctional Complex—
Butner, NC

I have spent my entire career in the public sector, and am currently an administrator, overseeing mental health programs at a complex of five correctional institutions housing over 5000 federal inmates and detainees. My department includes psychologists, Master's-level therapists, psychology interns, a social worker, and support staff. Together, we provide varied prison and hospital-based programs, including forensic evaluations for the federal courts, in-patient mental health treatment, psychology services for medically ill inmates, an internship, and programs such as residential and nonresidential substance-abuse treatment and suicide prevention. I am responsible for organizing, staffing, and implementing these services in the context of a complex web of legal and ethical considerations.

The inmate population we serve is extraordinarily diverse and includes the full adult age range, individuals from around the United States and many other countries, and varied personal backgrounds. In my agency, psychologists are the primary pro-

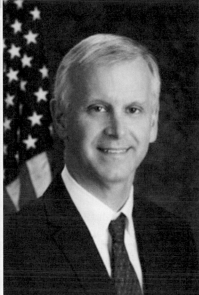

(Edward "Rhett" Landis)

viders of mental health services. Nationally, persons with serious mental illness are more often found in jails and prisons than in hospitals. As a consequence, our staff are at the forefront in treating an extremely needy, but often disadvantaged and disenfranchised population. Knowing that our programs reduce recidivism and help reintegrate mentally ill offenders into the community is extremely rewarding. Earlier in my career, I served as Training Director and remain involved in the implementation of our

internship program. I am very proud to have played a role in the training of over 100 psychologists who have made significant contributions in various government agencies, universities, and the private sector. Several are now members of my department.

My background is in forensic applications of clinical psychology, specifically to criminal matters. My mentor in graduate school served as President of the American Academy of Forensic Psychology during its early years, and ensured that students appreciated the interface of law and psychology. I took courses in the university's law school and served as a research assistant to the Dean. I subsequently completed an internship with a strong focus on forensic work. That background was essential preparation for my current duties. My colleagues and I deal with courts and attorneys every day, and understanding how correctional treatment and related issues will be viewed in a legal context allows us to advocate for meaningful rehabilitation and reentry programs and to effectively assist the federal courts. During graduate school, I received practicum training in two major medical centers. That background has been invaluable in our work with inmate-patients, particularly those with terminal illnesses.

DOES PRISON WORK?

Imprisonment is a public program paid for by taxpayers. The effectiveness of that program can be evaluated by researchers. Of course, prisons may achieve some goals but not others. And, in deciding whether prisons work, there needs to be a cost-benefit analysis—we need to consider whether prisons are worth the cost and whether less expensive alternatives might work as well or better.

Of all possible responses to crime except for the death penalty, prison is by far the most expensive, costing on average over $31,000 per prisoner per year, with some prisons spending more than $60,000 per inmate (Henrichson & Delaney, 2012). Prison is so costly because it is so encompassing. When we put someone behind bars, we pay for their basic needs 24 hours per day, 365 days per year, year after year. Sometimes, it makes sense to pay this steep price. It is imperative to take murderers out of circulation, even if it is costly. Moreover, even from a crassly financial perspective, a justification can be made for imprisoning murderers. According to some estimates, a single murder costs society more than $1 million because of lost wages and productivity and increased public services to families of victims (Currie, 2013). However, for nonviolent offenders, it is difficult to justify imprisonment from a financial perspective. Money spent on prisons is money not spent on other pressing public needs (e.g., education, health care, crime prevention). Large-scale economic analyses of prison costs have concluded that, "whatever the other reasons put forward for or against the use of prison, it is reasonable to conclude that using it for anyone but those convicted of serious offenses is a waste of public resources" (Marsh, Fox, & Hedderman, 2009, p. 144).

As prisoners age and develop health problems, it costs even more to keep them behind bars. Some states have established special geriatric prisons to house elderly, ailing inmates. The average cost of imprisonment for prisoners over the age of 55 is more than $80,000 per year (Thompson, 2008; Vestal, 2013). Medical care for elderly prisoners is especially costly, in part, because prisoners often arrive with serious health problems such as chronic substance abuse, brain injury, mental illness, or nutritional deficiencies (Stahl, 2012). In addition, prison is not an environment that promotes physical or mental health. Poor nutrition, lack of exercise, physical injuries, inadequate medical care, fear, high levels of stress, and a lack of intellectual and recreational opportunities combine with the normal aging process to produce prisoners with increasingly serious health problems. Prisoners serving long sentences suffer from what has been called "accelerated aging"—a hastening of the aging process that causes prisoners to develop health problems associated with old age about 15 years earlier than people outside prison (Maschi, Kwak, Ko, & Morrissey, 2012). Because of the large number of prisoners now over 50 years old and the accelerated aging of inmates, the rate of dementia among prisoners is projected to increase by more than 60% by 2030. In the general population, the increase is predicted to be about 2% over the same period (Wilson & Barboza, 2010).

Moreover, infectious diseases (e.g., HIV, tuberculosis, gonorrhea, chlamydia, and hepatitis B and C) spread quickly among prisoners. The rate of HIV/AIDS among state and federal prisoners is about 12 times higher than the rate in the general population (Hammett, 2006; Pew, 2013). Prisons also spawn new strains of infectious disease. For example, in the 1990s, the emergence of a virulent, drug-resistant form of tuberculosis was traced to prisons in the state of New York (Ross & Harzke, 2012). Diseases are often spread through sexual activity, fighting, drug use, and tattooing. Although sex is prohibited in nearly all U.S. prisons, it is impossible to prevent. As one prison official put it, "some prisoners are bisexual or homosexual. Others are simply bored, lonely, curious, and experimenting" (Okie, 2007, p.105). Tattooing is also forbidden. But many prisoners have contracted hepatitis when getting tattoos from other prisoners.

Another way of assessing the effectiveness of prisons is to ask how well they achieve their stated goals. Prisons do an extraordinarily good job of incapacitating criminals. Once a criminal is admitted into a maximum-security prison, the chance of escape is near zero. The individual prisoner is prevented from committing crimes in free society (though not in prison) for as long as he or she is inside prison walls. Unfortunately, just because a particular criminal is kept away from society does not always mean that the crime rate will fall. This is because of what criminologists call the problem of "new recruits." For chronically violent offenders—for example, some rapists, child molesters, and murderers—further crimes are probably prevented by holding the violent offender in prison. But financially motivated crimes, such as selling drugs, stealing cars, and fencing stolen property, seem to be organized like a labor market. If a criminal is taken off the streets, a sort of job vacancy is created which tends to be quickly filled with a new recruit (Petersilia, 1994).

If measured against the goal of retribution, prison is also a great success. Few doubt that any period of confinement in a maximum-security prison is a frightening, numbing experience marked by anxiety, frustration, unrelenting monotony, and loss of control. Even though minimum-security prisons are vastly more pleasant than maximum-security prisons, even minimum security inflicts the essential pains of imprisonment: loss of autonomy, loss of power, loss of privacy, banishment from loved ones, and removal from the opportunities of free society.

When measured against the goal of rehabilitation, prisons are a failure. As noted earlier, the obvious problem with abandoning the goal of rehabilitation is that nearly all prisoners will eventually return to free society. Roughly 700,000 inmates are released from state and federal prisons each year (Sabol & Couture, 2008). If no attempt has been made to give those released convicts the skills and resources necessary to mend their ways, they will be likely to return to a life of crime. There is ample evidence that prison does little to improve the behavior of criminals. Indeed, the experience of serving time in prison appears to have a **criminogenic** effect—it increases the likelihood of subsequent criminal behavior.

One influential early study compared two groups of convicts. The groups were matched on a variety of variables including age, crime committed, and prior criminal record. The researchers attempted to create two groups that differed only in the sentence they received: One group was sent to prison, while the other group received probation. After tracking the offenders for more than 3 years, the researchers found that the prison group did worse than the probation group. Compared with the probation group, drug offenders who had been to prison were 11% more likely to be charged with another crime, violent offenders sent to prison were 3% more likely to be charged again, and property offenders were 17% more likely to reoffend (Petersilia, Turner, & Peterson, 1986). In this study, prison time increased the risk of future crime. Similarly, more recent research has found that prisoners who serve their entire sentences are more likely to be reconvicted and re-incarcerated compared with similar prisoners who are released early to relieve prison crowding (Schlager & Robbins, 2008).

Careful, large-scale reviews of hundreds of studies show a similar pattern: Locking up people behind prison walls either does nothing to stop their criminal behavior or makes it more likely (Nagin, Cullen, & Johnson, 2009; Villetaz, Killias, & Zoder, 2006). Furthermore, the overall rate of **recidivism** is not encouraging. Following their release from prison, about 67% of former inmates will eventually be rearrested and sent back to prison. Just over half the people released are back in prison within 3 years (Sentencing Project, 2014). Clearly, the harmful aspects of prison seem to work against rehabilitation. One prominent criminologist summed it up this way:

> Any gains we get from incapacitation may be undercut by the tendency of imprisonment to produce crime. We get some "payoff" in crime reduction while offenders are actually behind bars. But what happens when they get out, as nearly all of them do? . . . the experience of prison may, in any of several ways, make prisoners worse—make them more rather than less likely to commit further crimes after they are released. (Currie, 2013, p. 198)

Rehabilitation programs take many forms, but all aim to change the criminal so that he or she will be less likely to continue breaking the law after release. Some programs involve group therapy intended to change the thinking and behavior of criminals.

Educational and training programs are also rehabilitative in that they attempt to provide prisoners with marketable skills that lead to productive employment after release (Visher, Debus, & Yahner, 2008). Finding a job after release from prison—a difficult challenge for most ex-convicts—has a strong rehabilitative effect (Duwe, 2012). One psychological factor that appears to facilitate successful reentry into society is inmate optimism about the reentry process. Two of the most important factors that create such optimism are the rehabilitative treatment received while in prison and the belief that family support will be available after release (Visher & O'Connell, 2012).

There have now been several large-scale analyses of what makes rehabilitation programs successful. Based on their extensive analyses of programs, Lawrence Sherman and his colleagues found that the most effective programs attempt to (1) correct educational and job skill deficits, (2) change attitudes and thinking patterns that promote criminal behavior, (3) improve self-awareness and self-esteem, (4) enhance interpersonal relationship skills, (5) reduce drug abuse, and (6) reduce contact with criminal peers (Sherman, Farrington, Welsh, & MacKenzie, 2002). In addition, a meta-analysis of 58 studies examining the effectiveness of **cognitive-behavioral therapy (CBT)** in prisons found that, on average, such therapy reduced recidivism by more than a third (Lipsey, Landenberger, & Wilson, 2007). The components of CBT varied across prisons, but usually the therapy targeted the behaviors listed in Table 16.2. Especially effective are those programs that provide ongoing support and treatment *after* the offender leaves prison.

TABLE 16.2

Skills Targeted in Prison-Based Cognitive-Behavioral Therapy

Cognitive skills—Development of thinking and decision-making skills such as stopping to think before acting, generating alternative solutions to problems, evaluating consequences of actions, and making deliberate decisions about appropriate behavior.

Cognitive restructuring—Use of activities and exercises aimed at recognizing and modifying the distortions and errors that characterize criminogenic thinking.

Interpersonal problem solving—Training to deal with interpersonal conflict and peer pressure.

Social skills—Prosocial behavior, interpreting social cues, taking other persons' feelings into account, empathy.

Anger control—Techniques for identifying anger triggers and cues that arouse anger, learning self-control and how to maintain self-control under stress.

Moral reasoning—Improving the ability to reason about right and wrong behavior, raising the level of moral development, and getting offenders to consider the impact of their behavior on their victims.

Substance abuse—Application of any cognitive or behavioral technique to the specific issue of drug or alcohol abuse.

Behavior modification—Behavioral contracts and/or reward and penalty schemes designed to reinforce appropriate behavior.

Relapse prevention—Strategies to recognize and cope with high-risk situations and halt the relapse cycle before lapses turn into full relapses.

Individual attention—Use of individualized, one-on-one treatment to supplement group therapy.

Adapted from: *Lipsey, M. W., Landenberger, N. A., & Wilson, S. J. (2007). Effects of Cognitive-Behavioral Programs for Criminal Offenders. Center for Evaluation Research and Methodology, Vanderbilt Institute for Public Policy Studies. Reprinted with kind permission from* Springer Science+Business Media: Journal of Experimental Criminology.

ALTERNATIVES TO PRISON

At the far end of the sentencing spectrum is the death penalty. The next most severe option is life in prison without the possibility of parole, followed by a long prison term. But alternatives to prison are available. Perhaps the least serious sentence is to pay a fine (e.g., for a speeding ticket or other traffic violation). Forfeiture of "goods and instrumentalities" used to commit crimes is a more severe type of financial penalty. Federal law allows law enforcement to seize the property of drug traffickers including cars and boats used to transport drugs, buildings used to store drugs, and houses paid for with profits from drug deals. Paying **restitution** with money (e.g., a petty thief paying for stolen property) or through labor (e.g., a teenager may be required to repaint a wall he spray-painted or to pay for items she shoplifted) is a possibility for some types of crimes. Community service is a more general form of restitution. People convicted of nonviolent crimes can be sentenced to community service and placed in a variety of settings including hospitals, homeless shelters, schools, and nursing homes. Restitution is often used in combination with probation and has increasingly been used as a means of compensating victims, helping the community, and repairing the damage caused by minor crimes (O'Hear, 2013).

Probation involves suspending a jail or prison sentence and releasing the criminal into the community under the supervision of a probation officer. The conditions of probation can be fairly strict, requiring the convict to meet weekly with a probation officer, to find and keep a job, to submit to random drug tests, and to attend therapy groups. If the offender violates the conditions of probation, he or she can be sent to prison. Each year, about 1.5 million Americans are placed on probation and about 1.3 million complete their probationary sentence (Siegel, 2012). Unfortunately, probation has a relatively high failure rate. In a massive study of nearly 79,000 probationers in 17 states, 43% of people on probation were rearrested within 3 years (Langan & Cuniff, 1992). Although this recidivism rate is discouraging, it is substantially better than the recidivism rate for inmates released from prison. The cost of probation is less than one fifth of the cost of prison (uscourts.gov, 2011).

A relatively recent variation on probation is **house arrest** (also called home confinement) enforced through some form of electronic monitoring. House arrest is likely to involve many of the same conditions of parole, with the additional requirement that the offender not leave his or her home or yard except to go to school or work. Electronic bracelets locked on to the ankle or wrist alert authorities when the offender leaves the house. A somewhat less high-tech version involves random, frequent, computer-generated phone calls to the offender's home. These phone calls must be answered quickly by the offender (e.g., picked up before the fourth ring). Home arrest is often a last chance—if the offender leaves the designated areas, he or she can be sent to prison.

Residential community corrections centers (better known as halfway houses) are also used as a sentencing option for some offenders. These are places (sometimes large houses or small apartment buildings) where groups of offenders live in a communal environment and attend some form of group therapy. Offenders are usually required to find jobs and to perform household chores. Originally, these facilities were designed to ease the shock of reentry into free society. The final months of a prison sentence could be spent in a halfway house so that the ex-convict could find a job, find an apartment, build up cash reserves, and reestablish family relationships. Currently, if a judge believes that a particular offender should not be sentenced to prison but needs a more structured environment than probation, that offender can be sentenced to a residential community corrections center (Mackenzie, 2006).

Alternatives to prisons are essential for several reasons. First, all alternatives to prison are much cheaper than prison. Second, prison is much too severe a punishment for many crimes and may make offenders more likely to commit crimes. Third, there is simply not enough public money to build and maintain prisons to hold every criminal. Fourth, alternatives allow first-time offenders and people convicted of less serious crimes to avoid the trauma and stigma of imprisonment.

▶ IN CONCLUSION

Prisons are an essential component of our criminal justice system, but they are expensive, frequently harmful, and other less severe sanctions often produce better results. More than a century and a half ago, de Tocqueville and Beaumont wrote that the United States had been swept up into a "monomania of the penitentiary system." They criticized the American belief that prisons could be "a remedy for all the evils of society." The monomania of the prison is still with us today and seems to drive public policy more now than it did in de Tocqueville's time. Although much crime and suffering can be prevented by sending the worst criminals to prison, social scientists have argued for a more differentiated approach that makes greater use of the full spectrum of sanctions: probation, treatment, rehabilitation, and parole. In most cases, lower cost penalties that achieve better results ought to be preferred. Our overreliance on prisons diverts resources from other public priorities such as education, health care, and programs that help to prevent crime and promote public safety.

▶ CRITICAL THINKING QUESTIONS

1. Which factors should and should not be taken into account when sentencing someone convicted of a crime? Why those factors and not other factors?

2. Who should go to prison and for how long? Murderers? Rapists? Drug addicts? People convicted of financial crimes? All of them?

3. Do supermax prisons need to be humane?

4. Should prison conditions and programs be allowed to vary substantially from state to state?

5. What should be the dominant goal of prisons? Should the goal be the same for every prisoner?

▶ KEY TERMS

cognitive-behavioral
   therapy (CBT) (p. 352)
controllability (p. 330)
criminogenic (p. 351)
determinate sentencing
   (p. 331)
deterrence (p. 334)
external causes (p. 330)
federal prisons (p. 333)

general deterrence
   (p. 334)
house arrest (p. 353)
incapacitation (p. 334)
internal causes (p. 330)
jail (p. 332)
parole (p. 332)
prisonization (p. 344)
prisons (p. 333)

probation (p. 353)
public shaming (p. 336)
recidivism (p. 351)
rehabilitation (p. 336)
residential community
   corrections centers
   (p. 353)
restitution (p. 353)
retribution (p. 335)

sentencing guidelines
   (p. 331)
specific deterrence
   (p. 334)
stability (p. 330)
supermax prisons (p. 333)
three-strikes laws (p. 332)

17 The Death Penalty

▶ **Capital Punishment in Context**
▶ **Supreme Court Decisions**
▶ **Research on Capital Murder Trials**
▶ **Racial Disparities and the Death Penalty**
▶ **The Death Penalty as a Deterrent to Murder**
▶ **Errors and Mistakes in Death Penalty Cases**

In 2011, Troy Davis was executed by the state of Georgia for the murder of a police officer. The officer—Mark MacPhail—was moonlighting as a security guard when he attempted to break up a fight between two men in the parking lot of a Burger King. MacPhail was shot and killed by a man with a .38-caliber handgun.

The evidence the prosecution presented at trial was compelling. Nine eyewitnesses identified Davis as the man who had fought with a homeless man in the parking lot and then shot MacPhail. Two other prosecution witnesses—a neighbor of the Davis family and a prisoner at the local jail where Davis was being held—testified that Davis had admitted to them that he was the killer. Although the gun used to commit the murder was never recovered, a ballistics expert testified at trial that the bullet casings found at the crime scene matched casings from a gun used at a different crime scene. Davis had allegedly fired the same gun at the other crime scene.

After Davis was convicted and sentenced to die, new evidence came to light and several of the witnesses for the prosecution began to change their stories. Three people who had not testified at trial came forward with affidavits stating that Sylvester Coles—the eyewitness who first identified Troy Davis as the shooter confessed to them that he (Coles) was actually the shooter. In addition, the two men who had testified at trial that Davis had confessed to them recanted their testimony in post-trial affidavits. They claimed that they had implicated Davis for personal reasons (revenge) and because of pressure from the police. An acquaintance of both Davis and Coles came forward to claim that while eating at the Burger King, he saw Sylvester Coles standing over Officer MacPhail's body just after the shooting. Seven of the nine eyewitnesses who had identified Davis as the killer later recanted their testimony, saying that police pressured them into identifying Davis. Finally, the Georgia Bureau of Investigations conceded that the ballistics evidence used against Davis was not reliable and accurate (Maxwell, Findley, & Hardiman, 2011). In his last words before being executed, Davis declared his innocence:

> Well, first of all I'd like to address the MacPhail family. I'd like to let you all know that despite the situation—I know all of you still are convinced that I'm the person that killed your father, your son, and your brother, but I am innocent. The incidents that happened that night was not my fault. I did not have a gun that night. I did not shoot your family member. But I am so sorry for your loss. I really am—sincerely.
>
> All that I can ask is that each of you look deeper into this case, so that you really will finally see the truth. ◀

Troy Davis (left)
and Officer Mark
MacPhail (right)
(A: AP PHOTO/GEORGIA
DEPARTMENT OF COR-
RECTIONS; B: AP PHOTO
SAVANNAH POLICE
DEPARTMENT)

CAPITAL PUNISHMENT IN CONTEXT

In most democratic countries, the death penalty is viewed as a violation of basic human rights. It has been abolished in Canada and Mexico, Australia, New Zealand, and all the countries of Western Europe. South Africa made the death penalty unconstitutional in 1995, and most of the countries of Central and South America have abandoned it or reserve it only for extraordinary crimes such as treason. Many countries refuse to extradite criminals to the United States if they might be eligible for the death penalty, and some countries donate money and legal aid to their citizens who face execution in the United States. The existence of the death penalty is far more common in countries ruled by authoritarian regimes (Johnson & Zimring, 2009). In those parts of the world where the death penalty is still used, hanging and shooting are the most widely used forms of legal execution. Beheading is also widely used (Amnesty International, 2013).

The modern, technological forms of execution familiar to Americans—the electric chair, the gas chamber, and lethal injection—are only used in the United States. All 32 states with the death penalty now list lethal injection as the sole or preferred method of execution. Many states use a "three-drug protocol" that combines an anesthetic, a paralytic agent, and a drug that stops the heart. An increasing number of states are turning to a "one-drug protocol" that delivers a lethal dose of an anesthetic. In a few states, an alternative method (such as electrocution) may be used at an inmate's request or if lethal injection is eventually halted by the courts. Four states—Texas, Virginia, Oklahoma, and Florida—have been responsible for 59% of all U.S. executions since 1976. Texas alone accounts for about 38% of all executions in the United States (Bureau of Justice Statistics, 2014).

Although 32 states, the federal government, and the U.S. military authorize use of the death penalty, executions are rare. Even in years when executions are relatively frequent, less than 1% of murderers are executed. From 2000 to the beginning of 2013, 722 people were killed in execution chambers in the United States. During that same period, approximately 1,725 defendants were sentenced to death. Unless the pace of executions increases dramatically, most of the more than 3,000 prisoners currently on death row will die of natural causes before they are escorted to the execution chamber.

For those states that retain the death penalty, aggravated murder is the only crime punishable by death. The definition of aggravated murder varies across jurisdictions, but it generally includes murder for hire, murder of more than one person, murder of a police officer, murder of a child, and murder during the commission of another felony (e.g., robbery, rape, drug dealing). Under federal law, capital crimes include treason and espionage, murdering a government official, using a weapon of mass destruction, and sending bombs or other lethal weapons (e.g., anthrax) through the U.S. mail.

Politicians and media pundits often note that Americans support the death penalty. When asked the simple question, "Are you in favor of the death penalty for a person convicted of murder?" just over 60% of Americans typically say "yes" (see Figure 17.1, Jones, 2013). So it is fair to say that, generally, Americans favor the death penalty. However, when asked about alternative punishments (e.g., life without the possibility of parole), American's support for capital punishment drops sharply. For example, in a national poll of registered voters, a clear majority of respondents (61%) preferred a punishment *other* than the death penalty for murderers. Although 33% favored the death penalty over all other options, 39% favored a sentence of life with no possibility of parole that included restitution to the victim's family, 13% favored life with no possibility of parole, and 9% favored life with the possibility of parole (Death Penalty Information Center, 2010). The perception of strong public support for the death penalty is important because it influences the decision-making of politicians, and because it is occasionally used by the Supreme Court as an indicator of prevailing "standards of decency" among the American public (Bessler, 2012).

Another politically potent issue is the financial cost of the death penalty. Particularly during the past two decades, the price of capital punishment has been a prominent topic of discussion in state governments (Bienen, 2010). Analyses of costs in several states all reach the same conclusion: Maintaining the death penalty is far more expensive than abandoning it. For example, California (the state

TABLE 17.1
States without the Death Penalty (year of abolition in parentheses).
Alaska (1957)
Connecticut (2012)
Hawaii (1957)
Illinois (2011)
Iowa (1965)
Maine (1887)
Maryland (2013)
Massachusetts (1984)
Michigan (1846)
Minnesota (1911)
New Jersey (2007)
New Mexico (2009)
New York (2007)
North Dakota (1973)
Rhode Island (1984)
Vermont (1964)
West Virginia (1965)
Wisconsin (1853)

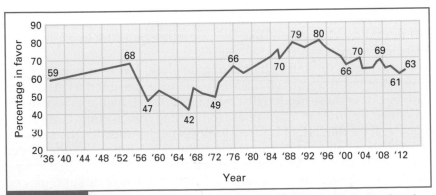

FIGURE 17.1 Are you in favor of the death penalty for a person convicted of murder? *(Copyright © 2013 Gallup Inc. All rights reserved. This content is used by permission; however, Gallup retains all rights of republication.)*

with the most people on death row) spends an estimated $137 million per year to maintain the death penalty, but would only need $11.5 million for a system having life imprisonment without parole as the maximum punishment (California Commission on Administration of Justice, 2008). In Maryland, the cost of prosecuting a capital case is $1.9 million more than the cost of prosecuting a comparable murder case where the death penalty is not sought. In North Carolina, $10.9 million could be saved each year if the death penalty were abolished (Dieter, 2009). Death penalty cases are more expensive at pretrial, during trial, and after conviction. More pretrial preparation and investigation is necessary. Jury selection takes longer. More attorney time and court time is needed. Capital murder trials have unique attributes (e.g., death qualification and a penalty phase, described in the next section) that make them longer and more complicated. And, all of these costs are incurred even if the defendant is eventually sentenced to life in prison. The minority of capital defendants who are sentenced to death then begin the long, slow, expensive process of appeals. Finally, there are the costs of maintaining separate, high-security death rows and the costs of maintaining execution chambers and the machinery that causes death.

SUPREME COURT DECISIONS

Constitutional challenges to the death penalty have been based on the Eighth Amendment's prohibition against "cruel and unusual punishment" or the Fourteenth Amendment's guarantee of "equal protection" under the law. In 1972, in the case of *Furman v. Georgia,* the Supreme Court ruled in a 5 to 4 decision that capital punishment—as then administered—was unconstitutional. However, the majority was deeply divided about *why* the death penalty should be considered unconstitutional. Each of the five justices in the majority wrote a separate opinion based on somewhat different reasoning. The points on which all five justices seemed to agree were that the penalty was "wantonly and freakishly applied," that there was "no meaningful basis for distinguishing the few cases in which it is imposed from the many cases in which it is not," and that these problems were probably due to "the uncontrolled discretion of judges or juries." The *Furman* decision did not rule out use of the death penalty in principle; it only prohibited the way it was being carried out at the time.

Following the *Furman* decision, many state legislatures redesigned their death penalty sentencing procedures to address the concerns of the Court. Specifically, they tried to find ways of controlling the discretion of jurors in capital murder trials. In 1976, in *Gregg v. Georgia* and its companion cases, the Supreme Court rejected the idea of erasing all discretion by making death sentences mandatory for certain types of murder, but it approved a series of reforms designed to guide the discretion of jurors. Under these **guided discretion** statutes, defendants accused of capital murder are tried by juries in a two-phase (bifurcated) proceeding. Guilt is decided in the first phase. If the defendant is found guilty of capital murder, the sentence (either death by execution or life in prison without the possibility of parole) is decided in the second **penalty phase.** As a further check against the "unbridled discretion" of jurors, all death sentences are supposed to be reviewed by state supreme courts. Executions resumed in 1977 when Gary Gilmore abandoned his appeals and was killed by a firing squad in Utah.

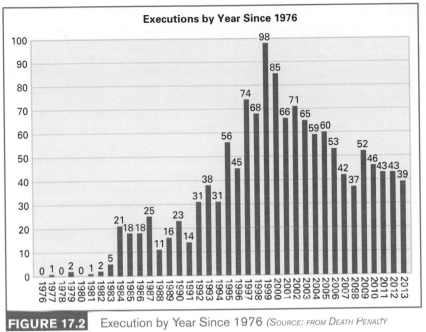

FIGURE 17.2   Execution by Year Since 1976 (SOURCE: FROM DEATH PENALTY
INFORMATION CENTER)

During the penalty phase of a capital trial, jurors are typically instructed to "weigh" those characteristics of the murder and the murderer that support a death sentence (these are called **aggravating factors**) against those characteristics that support a sentence of life imprisonment (these are called **mitigating factors**). Aggravating factors increase the wrongfulness of the defendant's actions or the harmful impact of the crime. In contrast, mitigating factors reduce the defendant's blameworthiness and make execution less appropriate as a punishment (even though such factors do not justify or excuse the crime). Several cases decided by the Supreme Court since *Gregg* have focused on what jurors can and cannot consider as they attempt to weigh aggravating against mitigating factors. The Court has held that jurors must be allowed to consider "any aspect of a defendant's character or record and any of the circumstances of the offense" that are offered as mitigation; and that jurors "may determine the weight to be given to relevant mitigating evidence." However, jurors "may not give it no weight by excluding such evidence from consideration" (*Lockett v. Ohio*, 1978). Jurors may also consider predictions about the defendant's future behavior and potential adjustment to prison (see Chapter 14), as well as how the death of the victim harmed his or her survivors (see Table 17.2 for a sample list of aggravating and mitigating factors).

Since 2000, other decisions have placed further limits on death sentences. In 2002, in a 6 to 3 decision, the Court put an end to the execution of mentally retarded prisoners (*Atkins v. Virginia*). Writing for the majority, John Paul Stevens argued that "a national consensus has developed" against executing mentally retarded prisoners and that "because of their disabilities in areas of reasoning, judgment, and control of their impulses . . . they do not act with the level of moral culpability that characterizes the most serious adult criminal conduct." Less than a week later, in a 7 to 2 decision (*Ring v. Arizona*), the Court held that only juries (not judges) can decide whether a convicted murderer should be sentenced to death or life imprisonment.

TABLE 17.2
List of Aggravating and Mitigating Factors given to Jurors in California **(The factors are given as a single list, not separated into two lists.)**
(a) The circumstances of the crime[s] of which the defendant was convicted in this case and any special circumstances that were found true.
(b) Whether or not the defendant has engaged in violent criminal activity other than the crime[s] of which the defendant was convicted in this case. *Violent criminal activity* is criminal activity involving the unlawful use, attempt to use, or direct or implied threat to use force or violence against a person.
(c) Whether or not the defendant has been convicted of any prior felony other than the crime[s] of which (he/she) was convicted in this case.
(d) Whether the defendant was under the influence of extreme mental or emotional disturbance when (he/she) committed the crime[s] of which (he/she) was convicted in this case.
(e) Whether the victim participated in the defendant's homicidal conduct or consented to the homicidal act.
(f) Whether the defendant reasonably believed that circumstances morally justified or extenuated (his/her) conduct in committing the crime[s] of which (he/she) was convicted in this case.
(g) Whether at the time of the murder the defendant acted under extreme duress or under the substantial domination of another person.
(h) Whether, at the time of the offense, the defendant's capacity to appreciate the criminality of (his/her) conduct or to follow the requirements of the law was impaired as a result of mental disease, defect, or intoxication.
(i) The defendant's age at the time of the crime[s] of which (he/she) was convicted in this case.
(j) Whether the defendant was an accomplice to the murder and (his/her) participation in the murder was relatively minor.
(k) Any other circumstance, whether related to these charges or not, that lessens the gravity of the crime[s], even though the circumstance is not a legal excuse or justification.

Other decisions narrowed those eligible for executions and the type of crimes for which executions could be sought. In *Roper v. Simmons* (2005), the Court abolished the death penalty for all juvenile offenders. The justices based their ruling, in part, on psychological research indicating that key psychological capacities—such as impulse control, rational decision-making, and long-term foresight—are not yet fully developed in juveniles. The Court reasoned that juvenile murderers should not be executed because they are inherently less culpable for their crimes.

In 2008, the Supreme Court revisited the relationship between rape and the penalty of death. Although the high court had prohibited capital punishment for the crime of rape more than 30 years earlier (*Coker v. Georgia*, 1977), it did not explicitly prohibit the death penalty for rapists of children. In 2008, six states still permitted execution as a penalty for child rape (although none had imposed it). In response to an attempt by the state of Louisiana to execute a man who had raped a child, the Court ruled that, unless the victim dies, the death penalty is not constitutional for rapists (*Kennedy v. Louisiana*). Finally, in *Baze v. Rees* (2008), the Court held that the method of lethal injection does not "inflict unnecessary or wanton pain" and therefore it does not violate the Eighth Amendment's ban on cruel and unusual punishment.

HOT TOPIC

Should We Execute the Elderly?

In 2004, 74-year-old James Hubbard was killed in Alabama's execution chamber for a murder he had committed 27 years earlier. He became the oldest person to be executed in more than 60 years. He suffered from prostate cancer, colon cancer, and dementia. His memory impairment was so severe that he sometimes did not know who he was. He was so weak and frail that other inmates would help him walk to the shower and comb his hair.

Several other inmates over the age of 70 have been executed over the past decade. However, most elderly inmates die of natural causes on death row before they are sent to the execution chamber (as did Viva Nash, the man pictured here).

On average, people sentenced to death spend 14.83 years on death row between conviction and execution. As the table below shows, the amount of time on death row has been slowly but steadily increasing. Although the average stay on death row is about 15 years, many inmates wait much longer—the record for the longest wait is held by Michael Selsor, who lived on death row for more than 36 years before he was executed in 2012.

The long delays between conviction and execution are largely due to the process of appeals in capital cases. This methodical, deliberate process was established to prevent the execution of a wrongfully convicted person. Budget cuts and a lack of qualified defense attorneys willing to handle capital appeals further elongate this already lengthy process.

According to the Bureau of Justice Statistics, in 2000, only 2.3% of death row inmates were age 60 or over. By the beginning of 2012, 10.2% were age 60 or older.

This "graying of death row" has raised legal and ethical questions that will grow more urgent in the coming decades (see Rapaport, 2012). For example:

- Does it violate the Eighth Amendment's prohibition against "cruel and unusual punishment" to confine someone under the harsh conditions of death row for more than a decade?
- Is it cruel to keep someone *under the threat of death* for 15 or 20 years?
- Is it especially cruel for someone who is already suffering from the afflictions of old age?
- Should we commute the death sentences of death row inmates over the age of 70 to life sentences?
- Are age and disability even relevant considerations in determining whether a condemned prisoner should be executed?
- Is the dignity and legitimacy of the legal system undermined when it uses its power to execute an aged, ailing prisoner?

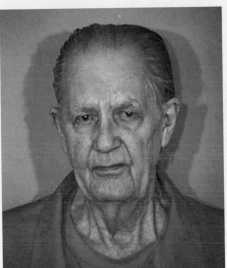

Viva Nash (*AP Photo/Arizona Department of Correction*)

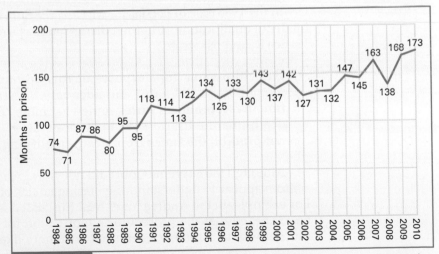

FIGURE 17.3 Average Time between Sentencing and Execution (Months)
(*Source: Death Penalty Information Center*)

RESEARCH ON CAPITAL MURDER TRIALS

In addition to the bifurcated structure of death penalty trials, there is another unique aspect of capital trials—the process of **death qualification.** During *voir dire*, before the guilt phase begins, potential jurors in capital murder cases are asked about their willingness to vote for the death penalty *if* the defendant is found guilty. In 1985, in the case of *Wainwright v. Witt*, the Supreme Court ruled that potential jurors whose beliefs "substantially impair" their ability to consider or impose a death sentence must be excused from serving on a capital jury. If a potential juror expresses a lack of willingness to seriously consider execution as a punishment, he or she is not permitted to serve on a capital jury. This typically means that about a quarter to a third of potential jurors are excluded from serving on capital juries (Rozelle, 2006; W.C. Thompson, 1989). Those excluded potential jurors are more likely to be female, African American, and politically liberal. Those remaining on the jury are more likely to be male, white, and to believe that "murderers deserve to die" (Summers, Hayward, and Miller, 2010).

Research shows that death qualification affects both who gets on the jury and the attitudes of jurors toward the defendant. Compared to jurors who are screened out by the process, death-qualified jurors are more likely to vote to convict the defendant. Death-qualified jurors are not only more conviction-prone when deciding guilt, they also tend to be more receptive to aggravating factors and less receptive to mitigating factors during the penalty phase (Bowers, Sandys, & Steiner, 1998; Butler, 2008). A second, more subtle effect occurs because jurors try to make sense of the odd process of death qualification. Jurors who answer a series of questions about their willingness to vote for a death sentence during *voir dire* often infer that both defense attorneys and prosecutors anticipate a conviction and a death sentence (Butler, 2007b; Luginbuhl & Burkhead, 1994). Why else would they be asking about a death sentence before the trial even begins? This effect works against the defendant.

In the 1986 case of *Lockhart v. McCree*, the Supreme Court reviewed the research on death qualification, and then dismissed it as irrelevant. In the majority decision, Justice Rehnquist wrote:

> **We will assume for purposes of this opinion that the studies are both methodologically valid and adequate to establish that death-qualification in fact produces juries somewhat more "conviction-prone" than non-death-qualified juries. We hold, nonetheless, that the Constitution does not prohibit the states from death-qualifying juries in capital cases.**

Although the Supreme Court did not view the research as important, many prosecutors appear to understand the biasing effects of the death-qualification process. For example, in the Andrea Yates trial (discussed in Chapter 9) some legal scholars have argued that the prosecutor's motivation for charging Ms. Yates with *capital* murder was to assemble a jury that was more likely to convict her on the murder charges. In fact, once Yates was convicted, prosecutors did not vigorously pursue a death sentence during the penalty phase. In his penalty phase summation, the prosecutor appeared to argue against execution: "If you want to sentence her to life rather than a death sentence, you will have done the right thing" (Stack, 2002, p. A14). Apparently, the goal was to use the death-qualification process to, "get a pro-prosecution jury, one more likely to reject the insanity defense and return a verdict of guilt" (Dershowitz, 2002, p. A18).

The penalty phase of a capital murder trial is qualitatively different from other criminal proceedings. The question posed to jurors is not, "did the defendant commit the crime?" but, "should the defendant be killed in the execution chamber?" That question cannot be answered by examining the facts of the case or by applying rules of logic. To help jurors make this life-or-death decision, judges instruct jurors to *weigh* aggravating factors against mitigating factors. Unfortunately, those instructions appear to provide little help. Research using both trial simulations and post-verdict interviews with actual jurors demonstrate that jurors misunderstand the penalty-phase instructions. For example, many jurors wrongly believe that they cannot consider the full range of mitigating factors, or that if they find any aggravating factors to be present, they *must* vote for death. Many jurors also mistakenly believe that unless they vote for death, the murderer will be eligible for parole (Fleury-Steiner, 2004; Wiener et al., 1998).

The meanings of the key terms "aggravating" and "mitigating" are unclear to jurors, and jurors are unclear about how to "weigh" the two sets of factors. Here is a quote from a juror who was interviewed after serving on a capital murder trial:

> The different verdicts that we could come up with depended on if mitigating outweighed aggravating or if aggravating outweighed mitigating, or all of that. So we wanted to make sure. I said "I don't know that I exactly understand what it means." And then everybody else said, "No, neither do I," or "I can't give you a definition." So we decided to ask the judge. Well, the judge wrote back and said, "You have to glean it from the instructions." (Haney, Sontag, & Costanzo, 1994, p. 157)

If jurors are not able to rely on the court to clarify the nature of their task, they must rely on their own rough translations of the meaning of penalty-phase instructions. Here is how a different juror put it:

> All that becomes very foggy and gray and just sort of burns off in the sun . . . Did he do it? Yeah. Did he mean it? Yeah. That's what the people on the jury broke it down to. (Costanzo & Costanzo, 1994, p. 161)

Indeed, even a defendant's history of being abused as a child—a factor that should clearly be considered as mitigating—can be easily discounted. One juror explained away severe abuse of the defendant this way:

> You can't blame that on his childhood. He's an adult now. He knows what he's doing. He knows it's wrong. All of us had some outstanding circumstances as a child. But there's a point where you stop crying over spilt milk. Maybe your dad was cruel to you, or maybe your mother made you work so hard. But how often can you use that as a rubber crutch. In other words, there's a point in your life when you have to get up on your own two feet and look straight ahead (Stevenson, Bottoms, & Diamond, 2010, p. 25).

The lack of clear guidance on how to decide between life and death may increase the influence of emotion and prejudice. Listening to the details of a horrible murder naturally arouses feelings of anger in jurors. That anger is likely to shape the interpretation of aggravating and mitigating factors. For example, in a study that tracked juror emotions over the course of a capital sentencing trial, researchers found that the more intense a juror's anger, the more likely that juror was to vote for death.

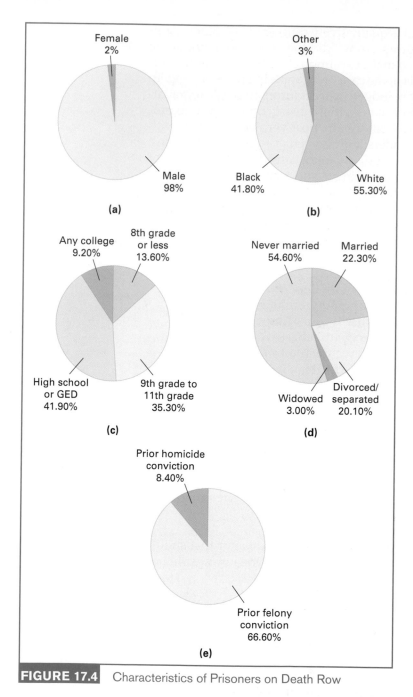

Female
2%

Male
98%

(a)

Other
3%

Black
41.80%

White
55.30%

(b)

Any college
9.20%

8th grade
or less
13.60%

High school
or GED
41.90%

9th grade to
11th grade
35.30%

(c)

Never married
54.60%

Married
22.30%

Widowed
3.00%

Divorced/
separated
20.10%

(d)

Prior homicide
conviction
8.40%

Prior felony
conviction
66.60%

(e)

FIGURE 17.4 Characteristics of Prisoners on Death Row

Furthermore, as the intensity of jurors' anger increased, jurors became less objective and assigned less weight to the mitigating factors presented by the defense (Georges, Wiener, & Keller, 2013). If instructions to jurors are difficult to understand, jurors may fall back on their own preconceptions or prejudices. In an experimental test of this proposition, 397 mock jurors watched a realistic videotaped simulation of a capital penalty trial for a defendant who had been found guilty of robbery and murder (Lynch & Haney, 2000). The content of the videotape and the jury instructions were held constant for all mock jurors, but the race of the defendant and the race of the victim were varied. There were four conditions: white defendant/black victim, white defendant/white victim, black defendant/black victim, and black defendant/white victim. The findings revealed that both race and comprehension of instructions had an impact on sentencing. In the condition where the defendant was white and the victim was black, 40% of mock jurors handed down a death sentence. But, in the condition where the defendant was black and the victim was white, 54% of mock jurors recommended a sentence of death. Perhaps more important, the researchers found an interaction between comprehension of instructions and race of defendant. Among jurors who understood the instructions well, the rate of death sentences did not differ as a function of race. However, among jurors with poor comprehension of instructions, the rate of death sentences for white defendants was 41%, while the rate for black defendants was 60%.

To test the effects of instructions on death sentencing, other researchers looked at the interaction between defendant race (black or white) and type of jury instructions (standard or simplified). The clearer, simplified instructions led to better comprehension and significantly reduced the bias against black defendants (Shaked-Schroer, Costanzo, & Marcus-Newhall, 2008). These findings suggest that if the instructions given to jurors fail to provide jurors with clear, comprehensible guidance about how to make the life-or-death decision, racial bias may creep into the decision-making process. Unfortunately, the process of jury deliberation—which is intended to correct misunderstandings and increase the rationality of decisions—may increase the tendency for white jurors to sentence black defendants to death (Lynch & Haney, 2009).

As in other areas of the law (see Chapter 13), revised jury instructions that take into account basic principles of cognitive psychology and psycholinguistics can help capital jurors choose between life and death. For example, by simplifying sentence structure, using concrete language, removing double negatives, using the defendant's actual name, and listing only those aggravating and mitigating factors that are relevant in the case being considered, a juror's understanding of penalty phase instructions can be significantly improved (Smith & Haney, 2011). We should do all we can to assist the jurors who are called upon to make this consequential and often agonizing decision. However, because the decision about whether a particular defendant deserves to die for his crimes is inherently moral and subjective, it is impossible to wring out all the ambiguity in penalty-phase instructions.

 ## RACIAL DISPARITIES AND THE DEATH PENALTY

Prior to the Civil War, the behavior of blacks in the south was regulated by a set of laws called "The Black Codes." Blacks could be executed for theft, but whites could pay a fine. The rape of a black woman was not considered a crime, but many black men were executed for allegedly raping white women. Although blacks and whites later became equal under the law, discrimination persisted. Racial discrimination in the application of the death penalty continued and was especially conspicuous in cases of rape. Between 1930 and 1967, 455 men were executed for the crime of rape. Of those men, 89% were black. In 1973, researchers analyzed 361 rape convictions. After statistically controlling for many other variables, the researchers found that the best predictor of a death sentence was the race of the offender combined with the race of the victim (Wolfgang & Riedel, 1973). Black men convicted of raping white women were 18 times more likely to be sentenced to death than any other racial combination (white/black, black/black, or white/white). Use of the death penalty for the crime of rape was examined in the 1977 case of *Coker v. Georgia*. In that case, the Supreme Court held that the death penalty was disproportionately severe for the crime of rape. Surprisingly, the shocking racial disparities in the imposition of the death penalty for rape were not an explicit factor in the Court's decision. However, it may have been that research on racial disparity had an influence behind the scenes (Ellsworth & Mauro, 1998).

Although evidence of racial discrimination is clearest for cases involving rape, discrimination has not been limited to the crime of rape. Several analyses of death penalty cases indicate that race has an impact at several stages in the legal process. Following arrest, black defendants are more likely than white defendants to be charged with capital murder, and, once charged, they are more likely to be convicted. Following conviction, blacks are more likely to be sentenced to death and, once sentenced, they are more likely to be executed (Baldus, Woodworth, Zuckerman, Weiner, & Broffitt, 1998; Bowers, 1984). The race of the *victim* is especially important. If the victim is white, prosecutors are more than twice as likely to seek a death sentence than if the victim is black, and blacks who kill whites are about four times more likely to be charged with capital murder than blacks who kill blacks (Baldus et al., 1998; Paternoster & Kazyaka, 1988). In a sophisticated analysis of race and the death penalty, David Baldus, George Woodworth, and Charles

HOT TOPIC

Competency for Execution (CFE)

Long ago, the U.S. Supreme Court held that it was unconstitutional to execute an inmate sentenced to die *while* he or she was mentally incompetent (*Ford v. Wainright*, 1986). More than 20 years later (in *Panetti v. Quarterman*, 2007), the Court held that a condemned prisoner must have, "a rational understanding of the reason for the execution." (See Chapter 8 for a full discussion of the issues surrounding the legal concept of competence). What is sometimes called "the last competence" refers to a prisoner's ability to rationally understand the connection between his crime and his approaching execution.

The involvement of mental health professionals in assessing CFE raises significant ethical issues. Commentators who defend the assessment of CFE argue that psychologists are merely conducting an honest, objective evaluation on the specific issue of competence; they are not deciding the fate of the condemned inmate. That is a decision for the courts. Alternatively, those who oppose CFE assessments argue that psychologists cannot separate themselves from the consequences of their evaluations (Shapiro, 2005; DeMatteo, Murrie, Anumba, & Keesler, 2011). After all, a finding that an inmate is competent might clear away the only obstacle preventing an execution. Alternatively, finding that an inmate is "not competent" might halt an impending execution. A few psychologists have decided to perform CFE evaluations only for the defense as a means of avoiding violating their ethical obligation to "do no harm" (Weinstock, Leong, & Silva, 2010).

Three psychologists who perform CFE evaluations have offered the decision tree shown to assist others in deciding whether to agree to conduct a CFE evaluation. Note that the decision tree emphasizes both moral values and a commitment to objectivity.

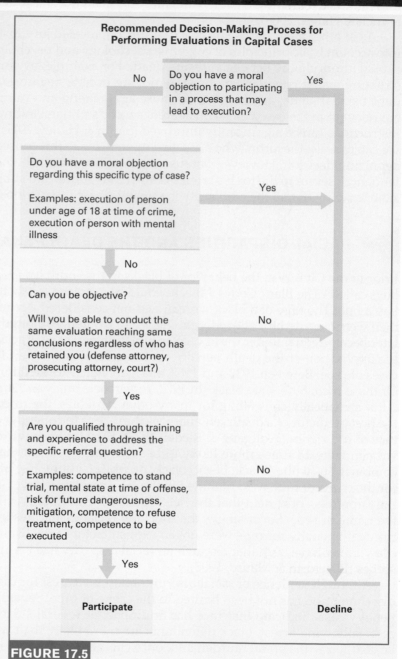

FIGURE 17.5

Recommended Decision-Making Process for Performing Evaluations in Capital Cases

Do you have a moral objection to participating in a process that may lead to execution?
— No / Yes

Do you have a moral objection regarding this specific type of case?

Examples: execution of person under age of 18 at time of crime, execution of person with mental illness
— Yes / No

Can you be objective?

Will you be able to conduct the same evaluation reaching same conclusions regardless of who has retained you (defense attorney, prosecuting attorney, court?)
— No / Yes

Are you qualified through training and experience to address the specific referral question?

Examples: competence to stand trial, mental state at time of offense, risk for future dangerousness, mitigation, competence to refuse treatment, competence to be executed
— No / Yes

Participate   **Decline**

Pulaski (1990) found that, even after taking over 20 relevant variables into account, prosecutors decided to seek the death penalty five times more often against killers of whites than against killers of blacks. In addition, Baldus and his colleagues analyzed 594 homicides in Georgia. They found that blacks convicted of killing whites were sentenced to death in 22% of capital cases, while whites convicted of killing blacks received a death sentence only 3% of the time. Looking more deeply at their data, the researchers took into account more than 250 characteristics of the murder, the offender, and the victim. Even after removing the influence of all these variables, the odds of receiving a death sentence were 4.3 times higher for murderers of whites than for murderers of blacks.

These findings were presented to the Supreme Court in the case of *McCleskey v. Kemp* (1987). In the view of many social scientists, the majority of the Court (it was a 5 to 4 decision) was frustratingly unreceptive to this evidence. Although the justices were unable to offer any explanation for the striking racial disparities, they were unwilling to accept the research findings. The majority decision in *McCleskey* (written by Justice Powell) held that some unfairness is tolerable and inevitable because discretion is an inescapable aspect of capital sentencing. In addition, the Court held that any discrimination in McCleskey's case was not intentional and the defendant's attorney had failed to present, "evidence specific to his own case that would support an inference that racial consideration played a part in his sentence." Put differently, to overturn a death sentence because of racial bias, there would need to be strong evidence that jurors acted with "discriminatory purpose." Some scholars have pointed out that this standard of proof is higher than the legal standard needed to demonstrate discrimination in housing or employment. Consequently, "a person denied housing or employment has more protection from racial discrimination than a person whose life is at stake" (Ellsworth & Mauro, 1998, p. 720).

More recent analyses of both state and federal court decisions indicate that discrimination in death sentences—particularly by race of victim—persists. Blacks and whites are about equally likely to become the victims of aggravated murder (the kind punishable by death). However, a black murderer whose victim is white is six times more likely to receive a death sentence than a white murderer whose victim is black (Baldus et al., 1998; Radelet & Pierce, 2006). Race makes a difference even after a defendant has been sentenced to death. Most inmates on death row die before being sent to the execution chamber. But black death row inmates convicted of killing white victims have the highest probability of actually being executed (Jacobs, Qian, Carmichael, & Kent, 2007). At present, 41% of the prisoners on death row are African American.

 ## THE DEATH PENALTY AS A DETERRENT TO MURDER •

Largely because of a belief in deterrence, early forms of execution were gruesome, slow, and public. More terrifying executions were thought to be more powerful deterrents. And, if more people watched, more potential criminals would be deterred. Executions were festive public events. In Germany, prior to the 1700s, huge crowds gathered to watch criminals be broken at the wheel. On a raised stage, criminals would be tied to a large wagon wheel. The executioner would methodically smash the bones of the legs and arms with a steel bar before bringing death by a blow to the throat (M. Costanzo, 1997). To deter crime in England, criminals were disemboweled and decapitated after being strangled in a public ceremony. The heads of executed criminals were displayed at crossroads and on London Bridge to serve as visible warnings to potential wrongdoers (Laurence, 1932).

The proposition that capital punishment deters homicide can be tested. If the death penalty does deter murder, states with the death penalty should have relatively low murder rates. To test this hypothesis, researchers have compared the murder rates in no-death-penalty states to murder rates in similar, geographically adjacent death-penalty states (e.g., Michigan is compared to Ohio, Rhode Island to Connecticut, North Dakota to South Dakota). Findings indicate that, overall, states with the death penalty have significantly *higher* murder rates than states without it (Donohue & Wolfers, 2006; Sellin, 1980).

A second hypothesis derived from deterrence theory is that murder rates should rise or fall when death penalty laws change. We can test this hypothesis by closely examining murder rates over time. Specifically, deterrence theory predicts that, if a state abolishes the death penalty (or suspends it for a time), the murder rate will rise because the deterrent is no longer in effect. Conversely, if a state establishes the death penalty (or reinstates it after a period of absence), murder rates should fall because the deterrent is now in effect. Like the first hypothesis, this second hypothesis has not been supported by the data (Bailey & Peterson, 1997; Zimring, 2008). Multiple studies conducted in the United States and 12 other countries provide no evidence that capital punishment suppresses the murder rate (Archer & Gartner, 1984).

When comparing adjacent states or measuring changes in murder rates over time, most studies have used statistical procedures that remove the influence of other factors known to affect rates of violence (e.g., unemployment, number of young men in the population, size of police force). In addition, some studies have looked only at the specific types of murder punishable by death, for example, killing of a police officer (Bailey & Peterson, 1994). Finally, many studies have looked at the effects of each actual execution rather than the effect of simply having the death penalty on the books. Despite many decades of research by a variety of researchers using a variety of methods, there is still no credible evidence that the death penalty deters murderers (Nagin & Pepper, 2012). Indeed, a few researchers have come to the opposite conclusion: that executions increase murder rates. An analysis of data from nearly 70 studies found that executions usually *stimulate* a small increase in murders (one to four murders) in the weeks following an execution (Bowers, 1988). Careful examinations of more than 60 years of data on the death penalty and murder rates have revealed this same effect (Donohue & Wolfers, 2006, 2007). This **brutalization effect** is stronger for highly publicized executions. Like other forms of violence in the media, executions may weaken inhibitions against violent behavior, desensitize people to killing, and communicate the message that killing is a justifiable response to provocation.

Deterrence is a theory about psychological processes in the mind of the murderer. It posits that potential murderers will be restrained by the knowledge that they might be executed if they act on their desire to kill—that is, their fear of execution will stop them from killing. There are several problems with this theory. First, there is no evidence that people engage in a rational weighing of costs and benefits before committing a murder. In fact, most murders are crimes of passion—the product of rage, jealousy, hatred, or fear (Costanzo, 1997). In addition, murderers are often under the influence of drugs or alcohol. Second, most murderers believe that they will not be put to death. And, they are right. As noted earlier, the probability that they will be executed is very low. Of course, many murderers believe they will not even be caught or that, if they are caught, they will not be convicted or sentenced to death. Third, it is not clear whether the prospect of being executed elicits more or less fear than the prospect of life in prison without parole. Life in prison without hope of release may be no less frightening than the remote possibility of being executed sometime in the distant future.

ERRORS AND MISTAKES IN DEATH PENALTY CASES

One way of gauging the effectiveness of our system of capital punishment is to analyze how many death verdicts are overturned and why they are overturned. In a massive study of how cases move through the legal system, researchers examined every capital case in the United States over a 22-year period (Liebman, Fagan, & West, 2000). They found that 68% of death sentences were reversed because of serious errors at trial. When these reversed cases were retried, 82% of the defendants were given a punishment less than death and 7% of the defendants were found "not guilty" of the crime that had sent them to death row. The most frequent causes of error included incompetent defense lawyers (37% of cases), faulty or misleading jury instructions (20% of cases), and various forms of prosecutorial misconduct, such as suppression of evidence or intimidation of witnesses (19% of cases). Although 7% of death row inmates were later found to be "not guilty," this study does not tell us if any innocent people were actually executed. Once an inmate is executed, all appeals cease.

The most troubling form of error in capital cases is the wrongful conviction, imprisonment, and execution of an innocent person. In their landmark study of wrongful convictions since 1900, Hugo Bedau and Michael Radelet identified 416 people who were wrongfully convicted of murder and sentenced to death (Radelet, Bedau, & Putnam, 1992). In 23 of those cases, their analysis suggests that the innocent person was executed. What makes these wrongful convictions especially disturbing is that most were caused by factors that are difficult for the legal system to detect. The main causes for these miscarriages of justice were police error (coerced or false confessions, sloppy or corrupt investigation), prosecutorial error (suppression of exculpatory evidence, overzealousness), witness error (mistaken eyewitness identification, perjured testimony), as well as various other errors, such as misleading circumstantial evidence, forensic science errors, incompetent defense lawyers, exculpatory evidence that is ruled inadmissible, insufficient attention to alibis, and

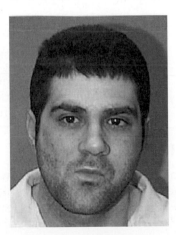

Were these three men executed for crimes they didn't commit? *Research their cases and draw your own conclusions.* From left to right: Larry Griffin, executed 1995; Ruben Cantu, executed 1993; Todd Willingham, executed 2004. (A: *AP PHOTO/ MISSOURI DEPARTMENT OF CORRECTIONS, FILE;* B: *AP PHOTO/TEXAS DEPARTMENT OF CRIMINAL JUSTICE;* C: *AP PHOTO/TEXAS DEPARTMENT OF CRIMINAL JUSTICE, FILE*)

pressure created by community outrage. Between 1989 and 2013, 105 prisoners were released from death row because of exonerating evidence (National Registry of Exonerations, 2013).

Perhaps the most important recent development in the death penalty debate has been the use of DNA evidence to prove the innocence of people on death row. In 18 cases so far, some form of biological trace evidence (e.g., skin under the fingernails of a victim that fought against her killer, a semen stain on the panties of a victim of rape and murder) was used to identify the real murderer and to exclude the wrongly convicted person (innocence project, 2014). Although it is essential for prisoners on death row to have access to DNA testing that may exonerate them, DNA is only useful in a small minority of murder cases. To make use of DNA testing to prove guilt or innocence, biological evidence (e.g., blood, semen, saliva, skin) must be available. In most murder cases, biological evidence does not exist—either none was left at the scene or none was properly collected at the scene, or if it was collected, it was not preserved by police. As recently as 2002, the Los Angeles Police Department destroyed biological evidence in more than 1,100 cases involving rape (Daunt & Berry, 2002). Some of these cases involved prisoners on death row who had been convicted of murder during the commission of a rape.

In a case that probably ended in the execution of an innocent man, no biological evidence was available. Gary Graham was convicted of shooting a man in a grocery store parking lot during a holdup. The sole evidence against him was the eyewitness testimony of a woman who claimed to have seen Graham through her windshield from across a parking lot. Two other eyewitnesses who were willing to testify that Graham was *not* the killer were never called to testify at trial. Later, after viewing videotaped testimony from these two uncalled witnesses, three jurors in the case signed affidavits saying that they would have acquitted Graham if they had been allowed to hear from these other two witnesses at trial. The Texas Board of Pardons found this evidence unpersuasive. In June 2000, a team of prison guards escorted Gary Graham to the execution chamber and strapped him to the lethal injection gurney. He proclaimed his innocence to the very end.

▶ IN CONCLUSION

Social science can often provide answers to the question, "What works?" If we are interested in finding out which forms of punishment or rehabilitation are effective for which types of criminals, researchers can usually tell us. But, arguments about punishment often turn on political and moral considerations. Although questions of morality are largely beyond the reach of social science, data are essential to inform moral decisions. Whether the death penalty is morally justified depends, in part, on whether it is imposed fairly and consistently, without discrimination or error. We must assess the morality of the death penalty and other punishments not by imagining how they might work in a perfect world, but by looking at how and how well they actually work in the real world.

▶ CRITICAL THINKING QUESTIONS

1. Because no legal system is perfect, there will always be some number of errors in capital cases. What level of error is acceptable in death penalty cases?

2. Should people who oppose the use of the death penalty be allowed to serve as jurors in capital trials?

3. Why do you think the United States is different from other advanced democracies in its continued use of the death penalty?

4. Does the empirical research on capital punishment influence your support for, or opposition to, the death penalty? Can you think of any empirical research that would affect your support or opposition to the death penalty?

5. Does it matter how many years a condemned prisoner spends on death row before he or she is executed?

6. What are the best arguments in support of the death penalty? What are the best arguments against the death penalty?

► KEY TERMS

aggravating factors
   (p. 359)
brutalization effect
   (p. 368)

competency for execution
   (CFE) (p. 366)
death qualification
   (p. 362)

deterrence (p. 368)
guided discretion
   (p. 358)

mitigating factors
   (p. 359)
penalty phase (p. 358)

Glossary

Ackerman-Schoendorf Scales for Parent Evaluation of Custody (ASPECT) A specific type of forensic evaluation of the parents in a child custody case that incorporates data based on standardized guidelines from the results of several psychological tests administered to both parents and children.

actuarial prediction A method of prediction that uses relevant risk factors which are systematically combined (typically using a statistical equation) to calculate an estimate of the probability of future violence.

actus reus Meaning "guilty act." The physical act of committing a crime.

acute battering phase In a violent relationship, the second phase in the cycle of abuse. It is characterized by multiple incidents of battering, such as hitting, slapping, kicking, choking, and using objects or weapons, as well as sexual abuse and verbal threats and abuse.

acute crisis phase The first stage of rape trauma syndrome (RTS), it usually lasts a few weeks and includes severe physical symptoms (e.g., sleeplessness, loss of appetite, trembling, numbness, or pain), as well as severe emotional disturbance manifested in symptoms such as extreme fear, shame, persistent nightmares, depression, or even suicide attempts. The victim's intellectual functioning is also likely to be impaired.

a danger to self or others When a person has threatened to inflict severe bodily harm on himself or herself or on other people, and the threat is a real possibility. If a person meets this standard, then he or she may be involuntarily committed.

adjudicative competence The various types of abilities needed to participate effectively in all stages of the legal process. It consists of two components: (1) foundational competence—a basic understanding of the trial process as well as the capacity to provide a lawyer with information relevant to the trial; and (2) decisional competence—the capacity to make informed, independent decisions.

adjustment The psychological process of children coming to terms with the divorce of their parents. Adjustment can be either positive or negative.

adversarial system A system of justice in which opposing parties present competing versions of the evidence in an effort to win a favorable judgment. In the United States, a trial is an adversarial proceeding because lawyers (adversaries) compete to win a verdict in their favor. The American legal system assumes that truth will emerge through a contest between adversaries who present opposing interpretations of the evidence to a neutral fact finder (a jury or judge).

adverse impact Employment practices that may not look intentionally discriminatory on the surface, but that have the clear effect of discriminating against a particular group in practice.

affirmative defense An aspect of a case in which a defendant bears the burden of proof in a trial, such as for proving insanity.

Age Discrimination in Employment Act (ADEA) Law enacted in 1967 extending protection to people over the age of 40. Prohibits discriminatory adverse actions by the employer because of the age of the employee.

aggravating factors Circumstances of the crime or aspects of the defendant that increase the seriousness of the crime or the culpability of the defendant. These factors are most commonly used in criminal sentencing or death penalty decision-making.

ALI standard A definition of insanity proposed by the American Law Institute (ALI), which states, "A person is not responsible for criminal conduct if at the time of such conduct, as a result of mental disease or defect, he lacks substantial capacity either to appreciate the criminality [wrongfulness] of his conduct or to conform his conduct to the requirements of the law."

allele Genetic characteristics; variations of a DNA sequence at a given locus. Various forms of a gene located at the same locus in each pair of chromosomes.

Americans with Disabilities Act (ADA) Enacted into law in 1990, this law prohibits employment discrimination based on physical and mental disabilities.

amicus curiae **brief** "Friend of the court" brief. A written document submitted to the court by parties with no direct involvement, but a strong interest in the case. The American Psychological Association has submitted such briefs to summarize relevant research and to clarify the overall meaning of a set of findings.

anatomically detailed doll Dolls with realistic male or female genitalia. Used to help reluctant children show investigators the type of sexual abuse that may have been perpetrated against them.

anchor point In geographic profiling, the location from which the offender leaves to commit a crime. Usually the anchor point is the criminal's home, but it could also be a workplace or other location.

anthropometry The first scientific forensic identification technique. It required taking 11 measurements, including left foot length, cranium size, height, length of arm, and length of the middle finger.

antipsychotic medication Treatment drugs used to reduce the severity and frequency of psychotic symptoms (e.g., hallucinations and delusions) experienced by severely mentally ill patients. Side effects may include muscle tremors or rigidity, and a risk of developing tardive dyskinesia.

antisocial personality disorder A personality disorder involving a pattern of disregard for the rights of others and the ability to commit violent acts without any subsequent feelings of guilt.

approximation rule A child custody standard whereby the post-divorce custody arrangement should approximate the caretaking relationships that existed prior to the divorce.

auditory hallucinations A psychotic symptom in which a sufferer hears voices that are not actually present.

authentic-coerced false confession A result of a long or intense interrogation during which a suspect becomes convinced, even temporarily, that she or he may have actually committed the crime.

authentic-voluntary false confession Occurs when someone suffering from delusions confesses to a crime with little or no pressure from interrogators.

authoritarianism A personality trait with the following characteristics: conventional values, rigid beliefs, intolerance of weakness, identification with and submission to authority figures, and suspicion of and punitive attitude toward people who violate established norms and rules.

base rate The frequency with which an event occurs in a given population.

base rate of re-offence The rate at which offenders in general reoffend. It is substantially lower than what most lay people and mental health professionals think.

battered woman syndrome (BWS) A group of symptoms that are often caused by severe domestic violence, physical abuse, and depression. Used by the legal system to explain why a battered woman does not escape her abuser or seek assistance or to explain why a battered woman might injure or kill her abuser.

behavioral investigative advice (BIA) Advice offered to investigators by social scientists. For example, advice on how to use the media, what questions to ask during police interviews with suspects, and whether a crime might be part of a series of crimes.

belief in a just world The tendency for people to believe that "people get what they deserve and deserve what they get."

best interests of the child standard (BICS) In child custody cases, the legal standard in which there is no presumption that either of the parents is entitled to custody, and parental needs and other interested parties are secondary to what is best for the child. The overriding goal is to place the child in the most favorable environment.

beyond a reasonable doubt Standard of proof used in criminal trials. To convict a criminal defendant, the jury or judge must be strongly persuaded (to have no reasonable doubt) that the defendant is guilty of the crime. The prosecution bears the burden of convincing the jury or judge of guilt beyond a reasonable doubt.

beyond the ken Outside of people's common knowledge and understanding. In the courtroom, expert testimony must provide new and relevant information that is beyond the ken of jurors.

bias-reducing instructions Specific instructions given to eyewitnesses during a lineup identification procedure. They remove the presumption that the witness is obliged to identify someone from the available options and they also discourage the witness from looking to others in the room for clues about who is the "right" person to identify.

biometrics The identification of an individual person based on measurable anatomical traits or distinctive patterns in a person's fingerprints, voice, iris, retina, or face.

black rage syndrome A dubious and highly publicized psychological disorder argued in court to excuse irresponsible behavior. It claims that a black person's criminal actions may be due to the experience of racial oppression.

blind Most experiments are "blind" in the sense that the people serving as subjects are unaware of the hypotheses of the experimenter and unaware of whether they are serving in the experimental or the control group. Similarly, when the accuracy of forensic identification examiners is tested, it is essential that the examiners not be given information about what others believe is the correct identification.

blind lineup administrators The person directing the lineup or photo spread has no knowledge of which person in the lineup or photo spread is the actual suspect.

bona fide doubt Meaning "good faith" doubt, it refers to any reasonable doubt.

borderline personality disorder A severe personality disorder characterized by unstable relationships, dramatic mood swings, manipulativeness, intense fear of abandonment, and impulsive outbursts.

Brandeis brief A legal, argumentative document submitted by Louis Brandeis to the 1908 U.S. Supreme Court in *Muller v. Oregon*. The brief incorporated medical, scientific, and government reports that favored a particular party in the litigation. This document set a precedent for the courts to consider research in their decisions.

Bricklin perceptual scales (BPS) A forensic evaluation used in a child custody case to assess the child's perception of each parent in the areas of supportiveness, competence, consistency, and other desirable traits.

brief Written documents submitted by parties to a judge or panel of judges. Typically, a brief offers interpretations of relevant law and summarizes facts and arguments for a party to the dispute.

brutalization effect The increase in the rate of murders in the weeks following an execution, in which the execution itself is believed to be the cause.

buffer zone In geographic profiling, the area in which the criminal is less likely to commit crimes.

burden of proof In a court of law, the duty of one party to prove affirmatively the facts of its side.

case linkage The process of determining whether two or more crimes were committed by the same person.

certainty of guilt The interrogation tactic of persistently confronting the suspect with accusations of guilt and using evidence ploys to bolster the accusations.

challenge for cause A reason for a lawyer to dismiss a potential juror during *voir dire*. A lawyer claims that a certain juror will be unable to render an impartial verdict because of bias or prejudice.

change of venue Moving the trial to a community that has not been exposed to pretrial publicity and its potentially biasing effects.

child sexual abuse accommodation syndrome (CSAAS) A cluster of behavioral and emotional manifestations (e.g., helplessness, confusion, and fear) hypothesized to occur in children who have been victims of sexual abuse.

chronic late syndrome A dubious psychological disorder used in court to excuse irresponsible behavior. The syndrome presumably causes the afflicted to be chronically late to meetings, work, and other activities.

Civil Rights Act of 1964 (Title VII) The first comprehensive law aimed at discriminatory employment practices. Title VII made it illegal to discriminate on the basis of race, color, religion, sex, or national origin.

civil trial A hearing in which a plaintiff sues a defendant for an alleged harm. If the defendant is found liable, monetary damages are typically awarded.

Civil Trial Bias Scale A scale consisting of 16 items designed to measure attitudes about the appropriate role of government in regulating businesses, appropriate standards for workplace and product safety, and whether or not most civil suits are justified.

clear and convincing evidence A standard of proof between the less demanding standard of "preponderance of evidence" (used in most civil cases) and the more demanding standard of "beyond a reasonable doubt" (used in criminal cases). It requires that the truth of issue be highly probable and is used only in a minority of civil cases.

clinical prediction An idiographic, qualitative approach that focuses on a specific individual and relies on the subjective judgment and intuition of clinicians.

clinical psychologist Experts in the study and treatment of various forms of psychological dysfunction and mental illness.

closed-circuit television A technique for allowing a victim to testify without being physically present in the courtroom. A large television in the courtroom enables the defendant, judge, and jury to see the testimony, but the victim and attorneys are in another room. It is sometimes permitted so that a child victim can avoid testifying in the presence of the person who may have abused him or her.

closing argument A speech made by both sides' attorneys after all the evidence in a case has been presented. Its purpose is to persuade jurors that one side's interpretation of the evidence is correct.

Code of Professional Responsibility A set of ethical rules, developed by the American Bar Association (ABA), governing the conduct of lawyers. It requires lawyers to "represent their clients zealously within the bounds of the law." It focuses on the legal efficacy of an argument as opposed to its veracity.

cognitive-behavioral therapy (CBT) A form of treatment that focuses on helping the client learn and use new thinking skills and behaviors to modify negative behaviors.

cognitive dissonance A psychological theory that holds that once a person has committed to a particular belief or course of action, he or she will be motivated to justify that belief or behavior.

cognitive interview A subtle, step-by-step procedure designed to relax the witness and to reinstate mentally the context surrounding the crime. The goal is to improve the retrieval of accurate information while avoiding the increased suggestibility of hypnosis.

cognitive privacy The legal problem of how to determine at what point lie detection devices invade people's right to privacy or violate their right not to incriminate themselves.

cognitive test An insanity test based on a person's ability to distinguish right from wrong in committing acts.

cognizable group A group of jurors that share a characteristic that distinguishes them from other potential jurors. Gender and race are cognizable groups.

collateral sources of information Information from a third party.

community notification Making personal and private information of a known sex offender readily available to the public and to the community in which the offender resides.

comparison question test (CQT) A questioning procedure for use with the polygraph—formerly called the "control question test"—designed to correct some problems associated with the older RIT.

comparison questions During a polygraph test, these questions involve behaviors that are uncomfortable for suspects but not directly related to the crime under investigation. They are deliberately broad so that anyone who answers "no" is assumed to be lying. Comparison questions are sometimes referred to as "known lie" questions.

compensatory damages A sum of money awarded to a plaintiff in a civil case for the purpose of compensating him or her for losses caused by the defendant.

competence Whether an individual has sufficient present ability to perform necessary legal functions.

Competence Assessment for Standing Trial for Defendants with Mental Retardation (CAST-MR) A measure of a mentally ill person's competency to stand trial. The test uses both open response and multiple-choice questions to assess basic legal requirements like the ability to assist defense counsel and understand courtroom proceedings.

competency for execution Sometimes called "the last competence," this term refers to a prisoner's ability to rationally understand the connection between his crime and his approaching execution.

Competency Screening Test A test to measure a person's competency to stand trial. The participant completes 22 sentence fragments to test their knowledge of legal proceedings.

competency to plead guilty A person can plead guilty if that plea is "knowing, voluntary, and intelligent."

competency to stand trial (CST) The ability to participate adequately in criminal proceedings and to aid in one's own defense.

competency to waive an attorney Whether a defendant has the ability to understand the legal consequences of self-representation and to carry out the responsibilities of self-representation. The Supreme Court held that a competency to waive an attorney has a higher standard than competency to stand trial for a mentally ill defendant.

Computer-Assisted Determination of Competence to Proceed (CADCOMP) An assessment of a defendant's psychological functioning and competency to stand trial. A defendant answers 272 questions, which are scored and distilled by a computer program into a narrative report on competence.

confidence ratings Rating of how confident a witness is that he or she correctly identified the true criminal. Confidence tends to increase in the period between the initial identification and testimony in court, therefore confidence ratings are recorded immediately after identification.

confirmation bias An inclination to search out evidence that confirms our beliefs and to ignore evidence that contradicts our beliefs.

consensual relationship agreement An agreement signed by employer and employees confirming that a romantic or sexual relationship between co-workers is voluntary and consensual.

contextual bias A tendency for extraneous influences (emotions, expectations, and motivations) in the immediate environment to taint our judgments.

contextual or functional approach An interpretation of forensic assessments in light of specific demands of the particular legal case or issue.

contrition phase In a violent relationship, the third, calm stage in the cycle of abuse. It is characterized by the batterer being overcome with remorse and treating the victim with kindness, expressing regret for hurting the victim, and promising to never repeat such violence.

controllability A criminal's ability to control his or her behavior.

control question test (CQT) The questioning procedure most frequently used during polygraph exams. It measures relative arousal as the indicator of innocence or guilt.

countermeasures Techniques used to influence physiological responses during polygraph tests. These techniques reduce detection of guilty suspects by 50%.

credibility assessment An evaluation of whether a person is lying.

criminogenic The increased likelihood of subsequent criminal behavior resulting from incarceration. A term used to describe environments that tend to produce criminal behavior.

criteria-based content analysis (CBCA) A lie detection technique that uses systematic analysis of written statements to assess the truthfulness of a description of an event.

cross-examine The questioning conducted by an attorney of the opposing side's witness.

cross-race effect A phenomenon in which people have more difficulty recognizing the faces of people outside their racial group than the faces of those within their racial group. Also known as *own-race bias*.

CSI effect The modern phenomenon of forensic science television shows causing people to have heightened expectations of the capabilities of real-life forensic identification technology.

culture A set of shared basic assumptions about the relative importance of competing goals, how disputes should be resolved, and what procedures to follow in striving for goals.

cycle of abuse Recurring phases in a violent relationship, which include tension building, acute battering, and contrition.

danger to self or others *See* a danger to self or others

Daubert **trilogy** Three specific court cases—*Daubert v. Merrell Dow Pharmaceuticals, Inc.* (1993); *General Electric Co. v. Joiner* (1997); and *Kumho Tire Ltd. v. Carmichael* (1999)—that expanded the role of the judge as gatekeeper. Together, their precedents delegated authority to the trial judge for evaluating the validity and relevance of proposed expert testimony and determining its admissibility in court.

death qualification During *voir dire* in capital cases, the process during which jurors answer a series of questions about their willingness to vote for a death sentence if the defendant is found guilty.

deinstitutionalization movement A movement beginning in the twentieth century calling for reintegrating mentally ill patients into the mainstream. The idea was to transition away from isolating the mentally ill in hospitals and to release them into the community where mental health services would be provided.

delusion A fixed, false belief held even when contradicted by evidence.

determinate sentencing Requirements for judges to hand down a sentence that falls within a prespecified range if a defendant is found guilty of a particular crime.

deterrence The theory that instilling fear of punishment in people will prevent future criminal acts.

diminished capacity Impaired mental functions that prevent the afflicted person from having the required *mens rea*, or mental state, for certain crimes.

direct examination The questioning conducted by an attorney of his or her own witness.

disorganized killers People who kill impulsively by picking their victims at random, acting out of sudden rage or because they hear voices telling them to kill. They are more likely to use any weapon that happens to be available, to leave the weapon at the crime scene, and to engage in acts of necrophilia.

disparate treatment When an employer treats some employees less favorably because of some personal characteristic such as race, gender, or religion.

distance decay In geographic profiling, the principle that the probability of an attack decreases as distance from past crime locations increases.

distributive justice Perception of the fairness of the distribution of available rewards among members of a group. A rational, fair relationship between employee contributions and rewards.

DNA (deoxyribonucleic acid) Miniscule, tightly coiled strands of molecules that carry the genetic instructions for all living cells.

double blind A technique for reducing bias in experiments. In double-blind research, neither the people serving as subjects nor the people conducting the experiment know which subjects are in the control group and which subjects are in the experimental group. Similarly, when the accuracy of forensic identification examiners is tested, the examiners should not be given information about what others believe is the correct identification and they should not even be aware that they are being tested (e.g., a fingerprint should arrive during the course of his or her normal work with no indication that it is part of a proficiency test).

double jeopardy The prosecution of a defendant for a crime for which he or she has already been tried.

Durham standard or **product test** An insanity standard under which the defendant is not held criminally liable if the crime was caused by a mental illness.

Dusky v. United States **(1960)** A U.S. Supreme Court case that defined the qualifications for being competent to stand trial. A competent defendant must have "sufficient present ability to consult with his attorney with a reasonable degree of rational understanding and whether he has a rational as well as factual understanding of the proceedings against him."

duty to protect laws Laws that mandate psychotherapists to take "reasonable care" to protect their clients' identifiable potential victims, such as by notifying the police and/or the potential victim.

dynamite charge (also called the *shotgun instruction*) In an effort to break a deadlock that might result in a hung jury, the judge asks the jurors to go back, reexamine the evidence, review each other's arguments, and try to reach a verdict.

electroencephalogram (EEG) The tracing of neural impulses of the brain.

employment at will A principle of law which holds that, in the absence of a contract to the contrary, an employment relationship can be terminated at any time by the employer or employee, for any reason or for no reason whatever.

encoding The first stage of memory processing. Information is gathered and placed in a form that can be held in memory.

Equal Employment Opportunity Commission (EEOC) Government agency created to enforce Title VII of the Civil Rights Act of 1964.

equal-focus camera perspective A neutral point of view in a video recording showing both the suspect and the interrogator. This positioning of the camera best enables jurors to assess the voluntariness of the confession and the coerciveness of the interrogation.

equality A principle of allocating rewards which dictates that each person gets the same reward regardless of contribution.

equal-status contact A condition of group contact necessary to break down stereotypes and reduce prejudice.

equity A principle of allocating rewards which dictates that people should receive rewards proportionate to their contributions to the group.

equivocal death The death of a person when the cause is unknown.

estimator variables Factors that are outside the control of the legal system and that are related to the accuracy of an eyewitness identification (e.g., weapon focus, lighting conditions, etc.).

Evaluation of Competency to Stand Trial Instrument-Revised (ECST-R) A measure of a person's competency to stand trial. This 18-item assessment uses a semi-structured interview to specifically assess a defendant's factual and rational understanding of courtroom proceedings as well as the ability to consult with counsel.

evaluation research An empirical assessment of a program's effectiveness in achieving its intended goals. For example, research designed to determine if a specific legal practice should be continued, abandoned, or modified.

evidence-driven deliberation style During the deliberation process, when juries vote on the verdict only after engaging in a careful, systematic discussion of the evidence.

evidence ploys A technique used to strengthen the "certainty of guilt" strategy in interrogation. Police cite real or fabricated evidence that clearly establishes guilt.

excluded No longer considering a person as a suspect as a result of forensic analyses, showing that the features between two samples (e.g., DNA, fingerprints) are substantially inconsistent.

exculpatory scenarios The interrogation strategy of offering justifications or excuses for committing the crime. Works by redefining the act as less serious, or by shifting blame onto someone else, or by blaming the circumstances surrounding the act.

experts People who have acquired specialized knowledge through significant education or relevant experience. Expert witnesses are usually allowed to provide an opinion in court pertaining to their specialized field.

expert witness Witnesses appearing in a trial where their testimony is based on specialized knowledge, training, or experience.

ex post facto Literally means "after the fact." Refers to laws adopted after the crime was committed making the offense illegal or changing the penalty for the offense. Such laws are prohibited from being applied to crimes committed before the law was enacted.

external causes Criminal behavior attributed to the situation or environment of the criminal.

external locus of control The tendency of people to see their outcomes in life as due to forces outside them.

externally focused coping When a victim of sexual harassment engages in practical efforts to manage or modify the harassing environment.

eye movement memory assessment A lie detection method that tracks visual attention to a scene based on eye movement, scanning path, pupil dilation, and gaze fixation to help assess guilty knowledge.

faking good In a psychological evaluation, individuals may attempt to hide psychological impairments in order to appear more psychologically healthy.

false negative An inaccurate prediction that something will not occur when indeed it will, such as when a person is predicted to be nonviolent but later is violent.

false positive An inaccurate prediction that something will occur when it does not, such as when a person is predicted to become violent but never does become violent.

federal prisons Prisons for offenses against federal laws.

fillers or **foils** The alternative suspects in a lineup or photo spread. They should resemble each other and match the witness's verbal description of the offender. Also known as *distractors*.

first-degree murder The highest charge of homicide, requiring that the perpetrator engaged knowingly in the premeditated killing of another human being.

Fitness Interview Test-Revised (FIT-R) A measure of a person's competency to stand trial. It assesses both legal knowledge and psychopathology.

five-level model of expert testimony A guide for what type of expert testimony should be allowed to link mental illness to a particular legal outcome. It has been used in discussions of expert testimony on rape trauma syndrome and battered woman syndrome.

flexible standard A standard of competency to stand trial that may be raised or lowered depending on the complexity of the trial and the abilities a defendant will need to navigate a particular legal proceeding.

forensic assessment instrument (FAI) Mental health instruments designed by psychologists to answer questions specific to a particular legal standard.

forensic identification The process of linking a piece of physical trace evidence to an individual, usually a criminal suspect.

forensic psychology The use of psychological knowledge or research methods to advise, evaluate, or reform the legal system.

foreseeable future The time period in which an action or event is predicted to occur.

friction ridges The tiny swirling lines on humans' fingertips and the palms of their hands.

functional magnetic resonance imaging (fMRI) A specialized MRI that maps activity in the brain. The scans are strung together to produce a moving image of brain activity, even as the person under study performs different kinds of tasks.

fundamental attribution error The tendency to attribute other people's behavior to dispositional causes (e.g., traits or personality) and to dismiss the situational pressures acting on the person.

future dangerousness standard The determination of whether the defendant is likely to commit criminal acts of violence that would constitute a continuing threat to society. Used in some states for death penalty decision-making.

gatekeepers Judges must use certain criteria to assess the scientific validity of potential testimony before allowing the purportedly scientific evidence to be heard at trial.

gatekeeping role As determined in the U.S. Supreme Court case *Daubert v. Merrell Dow Pharmaceuticals, Inc.* (1993), judges must assess the scientific validity of potential testimony before allowing it to be heard at trial.

general deterrence The theory that punishing an offender will prevent other similarly situated individuals from committing future illegal acts because they have learned that crime leads to punishment.

generally violent antisocial batterer This type of batterer is less selectively violent and generally predisposed to violent behavior toward the people around him. He tends to be antisocial, prone to impulsive behavior, and dependent on alcohol or other drugs. This type of batterer shows the highest recidivism rate.

generalizability The extent to which assessment instruments perform outside the original population and outcome on which they were created. In other words, how well the results of a test can be applied to the larger population.

geographic profiling The process of estimating the general vicinity of the criminal's home, place of work, or the potential location of the next crime. The estimate is based on the pattern of past crimes and the geographic features of a particular place. Also known as "criminal spatial mapping."

gold standard The best possible test or procedure available.

good cop–bad cop approach Psychological interrogation technique used by the police for extracting confessions. Two interrogators work as a team, one playing the "bad" (angry and intimidating) cop, and the other playing the "good" (sympathetic) cop.

gravely disabled The inability of a person to meet his or her basic needs (like food or shelter) and to provide self-care.

guided discretion The use of special instructions and procedures to control the discretion of jurors in capital murder trials.

Guilty Knowledge Test (GKT) A test used to detect whether or not someone knows facts that only the true perpetrator would know. Scenes and events from a crime, otherwise unfamiliar to an innocent person, are presented to the suspect. A guilty person's recognition of those stimuli should be reflected in elevated physiological arousal.

guilty but mentally ill (GBMI) An alternative verdict in which the defendant is found guilty of the crime and sentenced to prison with treatment for his or her mental health problems.

HCR-20 (Historical Clinical Risk Management Scheme-20) A risk assessment tool which is a guided professional judgment instrument that helps mental health clinicians estimate a person's probability of being violent based upon 20 historical, clinical, and risk factors.

hearsay testimony The testimony provided by the witness based on what others have said to him or her. The witness does not have direct knowledge of the evidence.

hedonistic type A type of serial killer who kills for thrills and takes sadistic sexual pleasure in the torture of the victims.

heightened arousal or hypervigilance A criteria of PTSD. A state of extreme sensitivity and attentiveness to potential threats, causing insomnia and fear.

high conflict Hostility-ridden relationships between parents involved in a custody dispute, which is associated with emotional disruption for the child and poorer long-term adjustment.

high-definition infrared thermal imaging A technology that monitors miniscule shifts in the heat of the human face as a means of detecting deception.

Hinckley case The 1983 trial of John Hinckley for the attempted murder of President Ronald Reagan. The court used the ALI standard for determining whether the defendant should be found not guilty by reason of insanity (NGRI). Because the burden of proof for showing insanity rested on the prosecution instead of the defense, Hinckley was found NGRI. Public outcry for this verdict led to the 1984 Insanity Defense Reform Act (IDRA).

hostile environment harassment A form of sexual harassment by which life is made so difficult for the victim that she cannot carry out her job responsibilities.

house arrest A measure by which a person is confined by the authorities to his or her residence.

hung jury A jury that cannot reach a unanimous verdict because jurors are unable to agree.

hypervigilance A state of heightened sensitivity to the environment and intensified behaviors to detect danger.

hypnosis A technique for inducing a relaxed, focused state in which the subject is highly receptive and responsive to suggestions made by the hypnotist.

hypnotic hypernesia Improved ability to recall events during hypnosis.

idiographic qualitative approach A form of data collection that focuses on specific individual characteristics rather than group attributes, and relies on intuitive, descriptive, and nonmathematical information to form an opinion.

imminent bodily harm Severe harm likely to be inflicted in the immediate future.

impeachment evidence Evidence intended to damage the credibility of a witness's statements.

impulsivity The inability to exert control over one's emotions, thoughts, and behaviors.

inadmissible evidence Testimony or other material that cannot be received into evidence at a trial for consideration by the jury or judge.

incapacitation Securely containing people inside prison walls during their sentence to prevent them from engaging in criminal activity outside prison.

inconclusive Incomplete, contaminated, or impossible to analyze trace evidence.

Indiana v. Edwards **(2008)** A U.S. Supreme Court case which held that the dignity and fairness of the trial process required that a judge appoint an attorney for a competent but mentally ill defendant if necessary. The case also called for a higher level of competence than competence to stand trial.

individuation The conclusion that a trace (e.g., fingerprint) found at the crime scene came from one source (e.g., the defendant) to the exclusion of all other sources in the world.

informational influence During the deliberation process, when a member of the jury changes his or her opinion because of the compelling arguments made by other jury members.

insanity The legal concept referring to the criminal's state of mind at the time the crime was committed. It requires that, due to a mental illness, a defendant lacks moral responsibility and culpability for the crime, and therefore should not be punished.

Insanity Defense Attitudes-Revised Scale (IDA-R) A psychological instrument that assesses the attitudes of potential jurors and the general public toward the insanity defense.

Insanity Defense Reform Act (IDRA) Federal law passed after the Hinckley trial that required that there be a presumption of sanity and that defendants prove "by clear and convincing evidence" that they were insane at the time of the crime.

instrumental-coerced false confession As a result of a long or intense interrogation, a suspect falsely confesses to a crime to end the interrogation or because he or she becomes convinced that confession is his or her best option.

instrumental-voluntary false confession Occurs when the suspect voluntarily admits to a crime he or she did not commit. The goal might be to achieve notoriety or to protect a friend or family member.

intelligence tests Psychological tests administered to measure the overall intellectual functioning of an individual.

internal causes Behavior attributed to personality or individual choice.

internal locus of control Locus of control refers to how people tend to explain what happens to them. People with an internal locus of control tend to see their outcomes in life as due to their own abilities or effort. People with an external locus of control tend to see their outcomes as due to forces outside them, such as luck or other people with more power.

internally focused coping An attempt by a victim to manage her cognitive and emotional reactions to sexual harassment.

interrater reliability The degree to which two or more observers or analysts independently arrive at the same measurement.

invade the province of the jury To "usurp the role of the jury," or interfere with the jury's role as a fact-finder.

Inventory of Legal Knowledge An instrument specifically designed to detect feigning/malingering in the CST context. This 61-item true/false test is designed for English-speaking defendants who have some knowledge of the American criminal justice system.

involuntary civil commitment To place someone in a psychiatric facility for treatment against his or her will.

involuntary manslaughter A charge of homicide that requires a lesser intent to kill. Also known as *second-degree murder.*

ironic processes The process of making an effort not to think about something, but that leads to thinking about it more.

irresistible impulse An insanity defense in which the defendant's mental condition inhibited the ability to control his or her actions at the time of the offense, even though the defendant may have known the act was wrong.

jail Short-term holding cells operated by cities or counties and administered by local authorities.

joint legal custody In a child custody case, the parents share custody and neither parent is the noncustodial parent.

judicial nullification instruction An instruction given to the jury by a judge informing jurors that they can disregard a strict interpretation of the law if such an interpretation would result in an unjust verdict.

Juror Bias Scale A scale developed to measure jurors' beliefs about how likely it is that someone who is on trial for a crime actually committed that crime, and how certain a juror needs to be before convicting a defendant. The scale also measures general cynicism about the legal system and has been shown to predict how a juror will eventually vote.

jury nullification In a criminal case, the process whereby the jury disregards the relevant law and renders a verdict based on what they believe is fair and just.

Jury Selection and Service Act of 1968 Litigation mandating federal and state courts to assemble juries that constitute a "fair cross-section of the community."

knowing, voluntary, and intelligent guilty plea A defendant must admit guilt with the understanding of the charges against him or her and the potential consequences of conviction.

lack of responsiveness to treatment Nonreaction to intervention to assist mentally ill individuals with their psychological problems,

laser doppler vibrometry A lie detection technique that monitors physiological stress (e.g., respiration, heart rate, muscle tremors) via a near-infrared light beam aimed at the neck of a subject a few hundred feet away. It is currently under development.

latent prints Fingerprints that are found on a surface at the scene of a crime.

learned helplessness Behavior characterized by resignation to unpleasant conditions due to not being able to control or escape the situation for an extended period of time. Even when the opportunity to escape arises, the person will not attempt to leave because of the belief that resistance is futile.

legal custody In child custody cases, concerns which parent makes important decisions about the welfare of the child (e.g., medical treatment).

legal realism An early twentieth-century movement that attempted to redefine the purpose of law. It was based on the idea that social policy goals and research evidence should play a major role in judicial decisions.

leniency bias In evenly split juries, where roughly half the jurors favor "guilty" on the initial vote and the other half favor "not guilty," the process of deliberation will favor acquittal.

liar's stereotype False behavioral indicators of lying. They include crossed legs, shifting and fidgeting, grooming gestures, and avoiding eye contact.

liberation hypothesis A prediction that in cases in which the evidence is ambiguous or close, jurors will base their decisions on factors such as prior beliefs, assumptions, pretrial publicity, or even prejudice.

Likelihood to Sexually Harass (LSH) scale A questionnaire developed to assess whether someone is predisposed to sexually harass women.

Likert scale A multipoint scale that measures a person's level of agreement to a question. It typically ranges from "strongly disagree" to "strongly agree."

loci Sites of alleles on a strand of DNA.

locus of control How people tend to explain what happens to them by locating the cause of behavior either internally or externally.

longitudinal research Research that collects data at several points over a long period of time.

loss of control During an interrogation, the interrogator controls the environment and removes the psychological comfort of familiar surroundings. This causes the suspect to feel vulnerable, anxious, and off-balance.

MacArthur Competence Assessment Tool-Criminal Adjudication (MacCAT-CA) A shorter, 22-item version of the MacSAC-CD measuring a person's competency to stand trial. This test takes about 30 minutes to administer and is designed to be used by clinicians who are performing competence evaluations for the courts.

MacArthur Judgment Evaluation (MacJEN) tool A test designed to evaluate immaturity of judgment in adolescents and how this immaturity affects adolescent decision-making in a variety of legal contexts. It consists of three vignettes followed by a series of structured interview questions and objective responses corresponding to psychosocial risk factors (risk appraisal, future orientation, and resistance to peer pressure).

MacArthur Structured Assessment of the Competencies of Criminal Defendants (MacSAC-CD) A measure of a defendant's adjudicative competence. It uses a vignette followed by open-ended and true/false questions to assess the defendant's understanding of the legal system, reasoning skills, and appreciation of his or her own circumstances.

malingering The deliberate feigning or gross exaggeration of physical or psychological symptoms in order to gain a positive outcome or to avoid punishment.

mandatory mediation laws Laws requiring couples seeking a divorce to first attempt to reach a settlement with the help of a mediator.

***Manson* criteria** Five factors, as set forth in *Manson v. Braithwaite* (1977), that should be taken into account when evaluating the accuracy of an eyewitness's identification: (1) the witness's opportunity to view the perpetrator, (2) the witness's level of attention, (3) the accuracy of the witness's previous description of the offender, (4) the degree of certainty displayed by the witness, and (5) the amount of time between witnessing the crime and making the identification.

match plus statistics A statistical, detailed statement that gives information about how rare or common a particular matching characteristic is in the relevant population.

mathematical models The use of mathematical equations to describe the relationships between variables and to predict outcomes.

measurement validity Whether a technique measures what it is supposed to measure.

mediator A neutral third party who works with a couple contemplating divorce in a nonadversarial setting. The goal is to deescalate family conflicts and reach a divorce agreement and child custody arrangement.

Megan's law Signed into law in 1996, requires states to make personal and private information about known sex offenders available to the public.

memory trace A biochemical change in the brain that represents memory.

mens rea Meaning "guilty mind." Different crimes require different levels of mental awareness and understanding.

mense rea The modern form of "mastery of mind," or the "guilty mind" that must accompany wrongful behavior.

mens rea **defense** A case presented by the defense that concedes the defendant committed the crime (*actus reus*), but argues that the defendant lacked the requisite mental awareness and intent.

Mental State at the Time of Offense Screening Evaluation (MSE) A test that attempts to assess whether a defendant's crimes were influenced by a significant mental disorder.

meta-analysis A statistical procedure that compiles the overall findings from a large group of related research studies.

Minnesota Multiphasic Personality Inventory **second edition (MMPI-2)** A widely used psychological test. It is a general measure of psychopathology based on a participant's responses to 567 true/false questions. It offers information on the participant's psychological distress, symptoms, and possible diagnosis.

minutiae The measurable features of a fingerprint.

Miranda rights Constitutional guarantees that must be read to all suspects in police custody. They consist of four parts: (1) the right to remain silent, (2) the right to an attorney during police questioning, (3) the right to a court-appointed attorney, and (4) clarification of previously listed rights if necessary.

mission-oriented types A type of serial killer who is less likely to be psychotic and is motivated by a desire to kill people he or she regards as evil or unworthy.

mitigating factors Circumstances surrounding a crime or characteristics of a criminal that lessen the degree of guilt or the severity of the crime. These are relevant in criminal sentencing and death penalty decision-making.

M'Naghten rule The most common insanity standard in the United States. It consists of three components: (1) a presumption that defendants are sane and responsible for their crime; (2) a requirement that, at the moment of the crime, the accused must have been laboring "under a defect of reason" or "from disease of the mind"; and (3) a requirement that the defendant "did not know the nature and quality of the act he was doing, or if he did know it, that he did not know what he was doing was wrong."

mock crimes In lie detection research, some people commit prearranged "mock crimes" (such as stealing money from an office) so that researchers can determine if a polygraph examiner can detect which people committed mock crimes and which did not.

multiple regression A statistical technique that combines a large group of variables to predict an outcome variable. For example, multiple regression might be used to try to predict the verdicts of juries by using the characteristics of jurors as predictor variables.

multiple relationships The APA ethics codes dictates that psychologists refrain from engaging in multiple relationships if they are unethical. An example of an unethical multiple relationship occurs when a psychologist acts as both a treating therapist for a specific client as well as an objective expert for the court.

NASH system A classification system for types of deaths. There are four categories: natural, accidental, suicide, and homicide.

neurolaw Legal approach intending to show a link between brain abnormalities and an individual's illegal behavior.

NICHD Investigative Interview Protocol An interviewing technique designed for investigating child sexual abuse cases, where the child is encouraged to provide as much information as possible to open-ended questions. Suggestive questions are carefully avoided to reduce bias.

nomothetic quantitative approach A form of data collection that focuses on group characteristics rather than on the characteristics of a specific individual. It is a systematic, statistical approach to forming an opinion about an individual in which conclusions are based on characteristics identified in research on large groups of people and then applied to the specific individual.

no reasonable avenue of escape A situation in which there is no easy way to avoid confrontation or to leave the situation. A requirement for some states' self-defense claims.

normative influence Interpersonal, group pressure that impacts jurors during the deliberation process, causing them to change their votes but not their views.

not guilty by reason of insanity (NGRI) An affirmative defense that suggests that the defendant, because of his or her insanity, should not be held criminally responsible.

one day or **one trial system** A method to make jury service less burdensome. Potential jurors who are selected to serve fulfill their jury duty after the trial is over. Those who are not selected fulfill their jury duty at the end of the day.

one dissimilarity doctrine The idea that no identification will be made if a single unexplained dissimilarity in two fingerprints is discovered.

open conflict The second phase of a deliberation process, in which differences in opinion among members of the jury become apparent and coalitions may form among members of the group.

opening statement Speeches presented by attorneys for both sides at the beginning of trials. These statements highlight the issues at stake and provide jurors with an overview of evidence that will be heard.

organized killers People who kill by carefully selecting and stalking their victims and planning out what they will do to their victims. They show patience and self-control by waiting for the right opportunity and cleaning up evidence after the murder.

orientation stage The first phase of the deliberation processes during which juries elect a foreperson, discuss procedures, and raise general issues.

overrule objection A judge's negation in response to an objection to testimony or evidence presented at trial by one of the attorneys.

paranoid schizophrenia A serious mental illness in which an individual loses touch with reality.

parens patriae **power** Literally means "parent of the country," refers to the state's duty to protect those citizens who cannot care for themselves.

parent coordination Intervention with high-conflict parents. Parent coordination interventions usually occur after mediation, settlement conferences, and custody evaluations have failed to achieve the desired results.

parental alienation syndrome Refers to one parent's attempt to make their children unfairly fear the other parent involved in a custody dispute.

parole Releasing inmates from prison, under the supervision of a parole officer, before their entire sentence has been served.

pedophile A psychological disorder in which an individual has sexual urges toward or engages in sexual behaviors with prepubescent children.

penalty phase The second phase of a capital murder trial. During the penalty phase, jurors are asked to decide whether the defendant should be sentenced to life in prison or death by execution. Also called the *sentencing phase.*

Perception of Relationships test (PORT) In child custody cases, test used to measure how strongly the child seeks emotional closeness and positive interactions with each parent.

peremptory challenge The privilege for lawyers to dismiss potential jurors without giving a reason for removal and without approval from the judge. They are limited.

persistent symptoms A criteria of PTSD in which effects of the disorder last more than a month.

personality tests Psychological tests designed to assess personality traits or to assess whether someone suffers from a psychological disorder.

physical custody In a child custody case, refers to how much time each child spends with each parent.

Police and Criminal Evidence Act (PACE) Litigation passed in England in 1986 to regulate interrogation tactics. It prohibited the police from lying to, bullying, threatening, and intimidating the suspect as a means of inducing a confession. In addition, all interviews with suspects conducted at police stations must be recorded and vulnerable suspects must be accompanied by an "appropriate adult."

policeman at the elbow test A volitional insanity test requiring that the defendant's impulse had to be so overwhelming that he or she would have committed the act even if a police officer stood beside the defendant at the time of the crime.

police power The state's authority to protect its citizens from dangerous individuals.

polygraph A machine that records a person's physiological responses to questions asked by an examiner. It measures physiological arousal, such as a rapid heart rate, quickened breathing, rising blood pressure, and increased skin moisture.

postidentification feedback effect The tendency for biased feedback after identification to distort the memory of eyewitnesses. Such feedback inflates eyewitnesses' confidence in their identification.

postpartum depression A condition occurring after childbirth. Its symptoms are identical to those of clinical depression and can include: loss of pleasure in most activities, depressed mood, sleep difficulties, weight gain or loss, loss of energy, fatigue, extreme guilt, and suicidal thoughts.

postpartum psychosis A severe mental disorder in which a mother displays psychopathic symptoms exacerbated or caused by childbirth. It is characterized by auditory hallucinations, delusions, clinical depression, and thought disorder.

posttraumatic stress disorder (PTSD) A severe anxiety disorder following a traumatic event. It is diagnosed in people who have "experienced, witnessed, or were confronted with an event or events that involved actual or threatened death or serious injury, or a threat to the physical integrity of self or others," and who have responded with "intense fear, helplessness, or horror." There are four criteria: reexperiencing of the event, avoidance of stimuli associated with the event, heightened arousal or hypervigilance, and persistent symptoms that last more than a month.

power-oriented type A type of serial killer who enjoys capturing and controlling the victim before killing.

precedent A past judicial decision that guides judges in making future decisions about similar legal issues.

preferred custody arrangements In child custody cases, the de facto type of custody ordered by the court unless one party can demonstrate it is not in the best interest of the child.

preinstructions Instructions read to the jurors by the judge before a trial begins.

preponderance of the evidence Standard of proof common in civil trials. Requires that a judge or jury find that the plaintiff's version of the facts is more probable than not. The weight of the evidence is greater for one side than for the other (51% or more of the weight of the evidence).

presumption of CST Defendants are presumed to be competent unless proven otherwise. The defense bears the burden to prove incompetence.

Pretrial Juror Attitude Questionnaire (PJAQ) builds on the items in the Juror Bias Scale. Like the other scales described above, the PJAQ uses a Likert format. It consists of 29 items divided into six subscales.

pretrial publicity The coverage of a high-profile case, in the newspapers, on Web sites, on television, and in other forms of media before the trial even begins.

preventative detention Holding someone in detention or in a hospital because he or she might become violent.

primary caretaker rule In child custody cases, proposes that courts should award primary custody to the parent who was primarily responsible for raising the child prior to the divorce.

prisonization The process of assimilating new inmates into the values, norms, and language of a prison.

prisons Institutions designed to hold people convicted of serious crimes for long periods of time.

probation Sentence imposed in lieu of incarceration whereby the person is released into the community under the supervision of a probation officer.

probative evidence Information that attempts to prove a proposition at issue in a case or to allow triers of fact to infer an important fact. To be admissible in court, the probative value of a piece of evidence must not be substantially outweighed by its prejudicial value.

pro bono Free legal services provided by attorneys or trial consultants generally for clients who otherwise cannot afford legal assistance.

procedural justice Perceived fairness of the procedures and rules used to allocate available benefits or rewards.

profiling The process of drawing inferences about a criminal's personality, behavior, motivation, and demographic characteristics based on crime scenes and other evidence.

projective tests Psychological tests that assess a person's psychological characteristics based on his or her responses to ambiguous stimuli.

protected categories Employee characteristics legally protected to ensure the free expression of political and religious beliefs, and to prevent disparate treatment of employees on the basis of immutable personal characteristics such as race, national origin, gender, age, and disability.

psychiatric symptomatology A dynamic risk factor in predicting violent behavior. Sometimes it is active (i.e., readily apparent in a person's thoughts and behavior) and other times it is dormant.

psychological autopsy When a death is equivocal (that is, it is uncertain whether the death was accidental, natural, suicide, or homicide), a psychological autopsy is an effort to reconstruct the psychological state of a person prior to his or her death.

psychological family "Family" defined in terms of emotional ties rather than biological relationships.

psychometrics The measurement of psychological characteristics.

psychopathy A distinctive, extreme form of antisocial disorder characterized by a lack of empathy for others and a lack of remorse for cruel or violent behavior.

public shaming The practice of making a person convicted of a crime to appear in a public arena where he or she is subjected to humiliation and taunting.

punitive damages In a civil case, damages (monetary fines) awarded to the plaintiff for the purpose of punishing the defendant for willful, wanton, or reckless behavior.

qualitative statement A subjective, nonstatistical statement indicating the strength of a match (weak, moderate, or strong).

quid pro quo harassment Sexual harassment by which an employee must comply with some sort of sexual request or face a career detriment.

racial profiling Using a person's race or ethnicity for determining whether he or she is likely to commit a crime.

random match probabilities (RMPs) Calculated estimates of the frequency of each allele in an appropriate reference population.

rape myths Common misconceptions about rape. One is that when a man initiates sexual activity and the woman says she does not want to have sex, she does not really mean it.

rape shield laws Laws passed to prevent lawyers from delving into the sexual histories of alleged rape victims at trial.

rape trauma syndrome (RTS) A group of symptoms that represent how women might respond to the trauma of being raped. RTS hypothesizes that recovery from rape follows two stages: an acute crisis phase and a longer-term reorganization phase.

reactance theory Proposes that people are motivated to maintain their sense of freedom. For example, judicial admonitions can be perceived as a threat to jurors' freedom to make a decision based on all the available evidence. Therefore, such admonitions may lead jurors to give greater weight to the information they were told to ignore.

reasonable accommodation Reasonable adjustments made by the employer to permit employees to work effectively despite the limitations of their disabilities.

reasonable and proportional to the danger that existed A response not excessive in relationship to the harm in question.

reasonable person standard A standard used by some courts to help determine if harassing behavior was illegal. The behavior must be offensive to a reasonable person.

reasonable woman standard First proposed in 1991 by the Ninth Circuit Court, where, in the case of *Ellison v. Brady,* the jurors were instructed to interpret the evidence from the perspective of a reasonable woman who might find the evidence more menacing than a man.

recidivism Committing new offenses after having been released after completing a prison sentence.

reconciliation stage The final phase of a jury deliberation process when attempts may be made to soothe hurt feelings and make everyone feel satisfied with the verdict.

recovered memories Refers to cases in which adults "recover" memories of having been sexually abused years or even decades earlier.

recross Questioning of a witness conducted by the opposing attorney after direct examination, cross-examination, and redirect.

redirect Questioning conducted by the directing attorney of his or her own witness after cross-examination.

reexperiencing of the event A criteria of PTSD in which the afflicted individual replays the traumatic event, such as through recurrent nightmares or memories.

rehabilitation The attempt to improve criminals during their prison sentence so that they will become productive members of society once released from prison.

Relationship/family-only (FO) batterer About 50 percent of batters fall into this type. They are characterized by limited marital violence, almost no violence outside the family, lack of a personality disorder, and relatively low rates of alcohol/drug abuse and depression.

Reid technique A method of interrogation consisting of nine steps, which focus on how to facilitate the interrogation process, how to communicate with the suspect, and what to say to the suspect.

relevant–irrelevant test (RIT) The first systematic questioning procedure developed for use with the polygraph machine. It used three types of questions: (1) nonarousing questions that are not relevant to the behavior being investigated, (2) arousing questions that are not relevant to the behavior being investigated, and (3) relevant questions that are especially arousing for the person who actually committed the crime.

reliability The consistency or repeatability of a measure or observation.

relief hypothesis Proposes that in some divorce cases, children are relieved from serious interpersonal conflict and emotional turbulence by the divorce of their parents.

reorganization phase The second stage of rape trauma syndrome (RTS) involves the long process of recovery from rape.

repression In psychotherapy, a hypothesis that holds that painful, threatening, or traumatic memories can be pushed out of conscious awareness and locked away in the unconscious for years or even decades.

residential community corrections center An alternative to a prison sentence where the offender lives in communal environments and attends therapy sessions.

resilience A cluster of personality traits that help a child adapt to emotional or physical turmoil in their environment.

restitution Paying for damages, either in money or labor, in compensation for a loss or injury that occurred as a result of a minor offense.

restoration of CST Raising the defendant's competency level to meet the requirements to be able to stand trial. Typically involves treatment with antipsychotic medication.

retribution A perspective on punishment that suggests punishment for a crime should be proportionate to the harm caused. It is intended to make the harmed party feel that justice has been served by punishing the perpetrator.

retrieval One phase of memory processing. Involves locating and pulling out stored information from the brain.

retrieval inhibition The phenomenon of selectively retrieving only some aspects of a memory while inhibiting recall of other aspects.

Revised Legal Attitudes Questionnaire (RLAQ) A scale developed to assess attitudes that might be related to verdicts in criminal trials. Using a Likert scale, it measures responses to 30 statements about the legal process.

ridgeologists Examiners who use a holistic approach to compare prints, looking at all available detail.

right to refuse treatment Medical treatment may not be forced upon a person, even if involuntarily committed, unless that person is also incompetent to make treatment decisions and a number of other factors are found.

Rogers Criminal Responsibility Assessment Scales (R-CRAS) A psychological evaluative instrument that attempts to translate the legal standards of insanity into components such as the ability to control one's thoughts and the ability to control one's behavior.

schizophrenia A serious mental illness whose sufferers lose touch with reality exhibiting a wide range of psychotic symptoms, including auditory hallucinations, thought disorder or disorganized thinking, and delusions.

scientific jury selection Selecting people to serve on a jury through the systematic application of social scientific expertise.

scripts Widely held beliefs about sequences of actions that typically occur in particular situations.

second-degree murder A charge of homicide that requires a lesser intent to kill. Also known as *involuntary manslaughter*.

self-defense A justifiable response to an imminent threat of bodily harm, using reasonable and proportional force to stop that threat.

Sell v. United States **(2003)** The Supreme Court ruled that an incompetent criminal defendant who was not a danger to himself or others could be forcibly medicated if and only if: (1) such treatment was medically appropriate; (2) the treatment was unlikely to have side effects that would undermine the trial fairness; and (3) such treatment was necessary to further a significant government interest, such as the prosecution of a serious crime.

sentencing guidelines A structured system for imposing punishment in which specific factors are weighted in determining a sentence—for example, type of crime, viciousness of crime, defendant's prior criminal record, circumstances of the current offense, and the average sentence given in the past for similar crimes.

sequential lineup An eyewitness identification process in which the eyewitness sees one person (or photograph) at a time, decides whether that was the perpetrator, and then continues to the next person.

serial killers Murderers who kill three or more people in separate events with a cooling-off period between murders.

Sexual Offending Risk Appraisal Guide (SORAG) A risk assessment instrument designed to predict sexual reoffenses.

sexually violent predator civil commitment laws (SVP laws) Laws allowing for the civil confinement of individuals who are found likely to commit future acts of sexual violence after incarceration.

shadow jury In high-stakes trials, a group of people who are selected to match the demographics of the actual jury and sit in the courtroom during the real trial. This surrogate jury provides feedback to the attorneys about their reactions to the evidence.

shock incarceration An alternative to prison in which young offenders are briefly incarcerated in a maximum security setting under difficult conditions.

signature The distinctive, personal aspect of the crime that presumably reveals the personality of the killer.

similarity–leniency hypothesis A prediction that jurors who are similar to the defendant will empathize and identify with the defendant, and thus be less likely to convict.

simple match A nonstatistical statement indicating that the trace and source share certain class characteristics.

simultaneous lineup A common eyewitness identification process in which several people stand side by side (or several facial photographs are laid out next to one another) and the eyewitness selects the person believed to be the perpetrator.

social agency framework In battered woman cases, testimony that offers a detailed explanation of the victim's behavior by stressing the difficulties she faced in everyday life that prevented her from leaving the relationship or seeking assistance.

social isolation During interrogation, the suspect is held alone to deprive him or her of emotional support and to reduce contradictory information.

social media analysis The process of scouring the Internet—focusing on Facebook, Google, Twitter, and public records websites—to gather personal information and create a fuller profile of each potential juror's attitudes, interests, and experiences.

sole custody In a child custody case, one parent has legal and physical custody while the other typically has some rights to visit the child at regular intervals.

source attribution When samples of trace evidence match samples taken from a suspect or from a tool used by the suspect, indicating that the two samples came from a common source.

specific deterrence The theory that punishing an individual offender dissuades that person from committing future illegal acts because he or she has learned that crime will leads to punishment.

specific intent crime Crimes that require a specific *mens rea* for successful criminal prosecution. The specific intent can be: premeditation, intent, knowledge, gross negligence, or negligence.

stability One dimension of attribution theory. Whether criminal behavior is attributed to temporary or permanent causes.

stare decisis "Let the decision stand." The principle that future judicial decisions should be based on precedent.

statutory exclusions A state transfer policy preventing certain categories of cases from being tried in juvenile court.

storage One phase of memory processing which involves holding the encoded information in the brain over time.

story model A psychological theory on how jurors decide cases. Proposes that jurors create stories to explain evidence as a causal chain of events.

striations Groove markings on a bullet.

strong jurors Jurors who seem likely to have a disproportionate influence on the deliberation process. Also referred to as *key jurors* or *jury leaders*.

suborning perjury The criminal act of persuading or purposefully allowing another person to lie about a material issue while under oath.

substantive due process Prohibits arbitrary or unreasonable deprivation of the freedom of individuals and ensures that fundamental constitutional rights are not violated.

supermax prisons Maximum security prisons for serious or violent inmates.

superordinate goals Overarching goals common to members of diverse groups. Part of the method for inducing members of opposing groups to work together productively.

supplemental juror questionnaire Questionnaires that prospective jurors fill out before *voir dire* (these questionnaires are submitted by attorneys and approved by the judge). Questions might include information about personal experiences.

sustain objection The affirmation and approval of a judge in response to an objection to testimony or evidence presented at trial by one of the attorneys.

syndromes Patterns of behaviors or traits that tend to describe groups of similar people. In the medical and psychiatric fields, "syndrome" refers to a cluster of related symptoms that lead to a significant dysfunction in the performance of normal activities.

system variables Factors that can be controlled by the legal system. Most commonly used in eyewitness identification research (e.g., lineup procedures).

Tarasoff v. Regents of the University of California **(1976)** The California Supreme Court held that psychotherapists had a duty to take "reasonable care" to protect their client's identifiable potential victims when the client poses a serious risk of violence.

tender years doctrine A standard in child custody cases, prevalent in the nineteenth century, where young children and all female children were placed under the care of the mother unless there were extenuating circumstances.

tension-building phase In a violent relationship, the first phase in the cycle of abuse. It is characterized by rising emotional tension, anger, blaming, and arguing, and there are some relatively small incidents of abuse.

test–retest reliability The consistency of results over time. Also known as *temporal consistency*.

thought disorder Difficulty thinking and speaking in a coherent manner. Also known as *disorganized thinking*.

threat/control-override (TCO) symptoms A type of dynamic risk factor used in predicting a person's future violent behavior. These symptoms refer to beliefs—common in schizophrenics—that other people or forces are controlling one's thoughts or implanting thoughts in one's mind.

three-strikes laws Requirement that criminals receive a long sentence or a life sentence when they are convicted of a third felony.

totality of circumstances A standard by which a decision is based on all the surrounding facts that give context to the case. This standard is used to evaluate the "voluntariness" of a defendant's confession.

totality of circumstances test A standard used to determine if the objectionable conduct constitutes sexual harassment by taking into account the context of the behavior, as well as its frequency and severity.

trace evidence Physical evidence left at the scene of the crime (e.g., fingerprints, hair, skin cells, fibers from clothes) or physical evidence transported from the crime scene (e.g., carpet fibers, hair or blood from a victim).

trial by ordeal A method of testing the innocence or guilt of a person by subjecting them to painful experiences believed to communicate divine intervention.

trial consultants Advisors hired to provide expertise in the service of litigants. They use psychological knowledge to influence trial processes such that they produce favorable outcomes for the client. Psychologists hired as trial consultants help attorneys with jury selection, witness preparation, and/or trial strategy.

trier of fact The person(s) given responsibility for evaluating the evidence presented at trial and rendering a verdict. In a jury trial, the jury acts as the fact finder while the judge determines which evidence is admissible and the relevant law to be applied.

true negative An accurate prediction that something will not occur, such as when a person is predicted to not become violent and the person indeed does not become violent.

true positive An accurate prediction that something will occur, such as when a person is predicted to become violent and then does become violent.

tunnel vision A biased tendency to seek out evidence that fits a profile or stereotype while ignoring contrary evidence.

Twinkie defense The 1978 defense of Dan White against two charges of murder. His defense argued that his mental state was badly impaired by a deep depression exacerbated by his heavy intake of junk food.

ultimate issue testimony Expert testimony that specifically answers the legal question in a particular case. It answers the question that the trier of fact (a judge or jury) must decide.

unbiased lineups Lineups and photo spreads constructed such that the actual suspect does not stand out from the fillers. Nothing about the procedure draws extra attention to the actual suspect.

unconscious transference The unintentional act of misidentifying one person for another as a result of remembering a familiar face of a person near the scene of the crime.

Uniform Marriage and Divorce Act (UMDA) of 1976 A child custody standard that was created by a panel of legal scholars and is followed in many jurisdictions. The standard proposes five criteria to be used for determining custody: 1) the wishes of the child's parents; 2) the wishes of the child; 3) the relationships between the child and his parents, his siblings, and any other person who significantly affects the child's best interests; 4) the child's adjustment to home, school, and community; and 5) the physical and mental health of everyone involved with the child.

unscored buffer In a Guilty Knowledge Test (GKT), the first question asked. It is not scored and discarded because people tend to react more strongly to the first item in a series.

unstructured clinical judgment Strategy for psychologists to predict future violence without the guidance of any rules on how to collect and combine information. Also referred to as *intuitive approaches.*

venire A group or panel of prospective jurors that is questioned by judges and attorneys to determine who will serve on a jury for a particular case.

verdict-driven deliberation style During the deliberation process, some juries vote shortly after they begin and conduct subsequent discussions around the verdict votes.

Violence Risk Appraisal Guide (VRAG) An actuarial risk assessment instrument constructed to improve predictive accuracy. It was developed on a mentally ill Canadian criminal population to predict recidivism.

visionary types Serial killers who are usually psychotic. They have visions or believe they hear voices from God or spirits instructing them to kill certain types of people.

voir dire The final stage of the jury selection process during which lawyers and judges question potential jurors to uncover juror biases and to determine who will be chosen to serve on a particular jury.

volitional capacity Part of the ALI insanity standard in which the defendant's ability to control his or her actions at the time of the offense are examined.

waterboarding An abusive interrogation method that involves binding a suspect and forcibly submerging his or her head underwater or pouring water into his or her nose and mouth without allowing the suspect to breathe, causing him or her to experience the sensation of drowning.

weapon focus effect The distracting influence of the presence of something unexpected or posing a great danger. Occurs when an eyewitness sees a perpetrator holding a weapon and focuses his or her attention on that weapon. Consequently, the eyewitness's shifted attention impairs the ability to recognize the assailant.

wild beast test A test used historically to determine whether a person is insane. It defines insanity as a mental deficiency in "understanding and memory" and asks whether a defendant acted like a "wild beast."

wizards People who can detect lies at a much higher rate than average using only their powers of observation. Wizards seem to notice more verbal and nonverbal cues than the average person.

References

AAUW. (2014). *The simple truth about the gender pay gap.* Retrieved from http://www.aauw.org/research/the-simple-truth-about-the-gender-pay-gap/

Abramson, J. (1995). *We, the jury.* New York, NY: Basic Books.

Abbott, J. H. (1991). *In the belly of the beast.* New York: Vintage Books.

Ackerman, M. J., & Pritzl, T. B. (2011). Child custody evaluation practices: A 20-year follow-up. *Family Court Review, 49,* 618–628. doi:10.1111/j.1744-1617.2011.01397.x

Adler, S. (1994). *The jury: Trial and error in the American courtroom.* New York, NY: Times Books.

Alicke, M. D. (2000). Culpable control and the psychology of blame. *Psychological Bulletin, 126,* 556–574. doi:10.1037/0033-2909.126.4.556

Alison, L. (2005). From trait-based profiling to psychological contributions to apprehension methods. In L. Alison (Ed.), *The forensic psychologist's casebook: Psychological profiling and criminal investigation* (pp. 3–22). Devon, UK: Willan.

Alison, L., McLean, C., & Almond, L. (2007). Profiling suspects. In T. Newburn, T. Williamson, & A. Wright (Eds.), *Handbook of criminal investigation* (pp. 493–516). Devon, UK: Willan.

Alison, L., & Rainbow, L. (Eds.) (2011). *Professionalizing offender profiling: Forensic and investigative psychology in practice.* London, England: Routledge.

Alison, L., Smith, M., Eastman, O., & Rainbow, L. (2003). Toulmin's philosophy of argument and its relevance to offender profiling. *Psychology, Crime & Law, 9,* 173–183. doi:10.1080/1068316031000116265

Allison, J. A., & Wrightsman, L. S. (1993). *Rape: The misunderstood crime.* Thousand Oaks, CA: Sage.

Almirall, J. R., & Furton, K. G. (2003). Trends in forensic science education: Expansion and increased accountability. *Annals of Bioanalytic Chemistry, 376,* 1156–1159. doi:10.1007/s00216-003-1891-4

American Academy of Child and Adolescent Psychiatry. (2011). Practice parameter for child and adolescent forensic evaluations. *Journal of the American Academy of Child & Adolescent Psychiatry, 50,* 1299–1312. doi:10.1016/j.jaac.2011.09.020

American Law Institute. (2002). *Principles of the law of family dissolution: Analysis and recommendations.* Philadelphia, PA: Author.

American Psychiatric Association. (1982). *Brief for Amicus Curiae in support of appellee, Barefoot v. Estelle. No. 82-6080, 463 U.S. 880.* Washington, DC: American Psychiatric Association. Retrieved from http://www.psychiatry.org/learn/library--archives/amicus-briefs

American Psychiatric Association. (1983). Statement on the insanity defense. *American Journal of Psychiatry, 140,* 681–688. Retrieved from http://ajp.psychiatryonline.org/journal.aspx?journalid=13

American Psychiatric Association. (2013). *Diagnostic and statistical manual of mental disorders* (5th ed.). Arlington, VA: American Psychiatric Publishing.

American Psychological Association. (2010). *Ethical principles of psychologists and code of conduct.* Retrieved from http://www.apa.org/ethics/code2002.html

American Psychological Association. (2010). *Guidelines for child custody evaluations in family law proceedings.* Retrieved from http://www.apa.org/practice/guidelines/child-custody.pdf

American Psychological Association. (2012). *Guidelines for the practice of parenting coordination.* Retrieved from http://www.apa.org/practice/guidelines/parenting-coordination.aspx?item=1

American Psychological Association. (2013). Specialty guidelines for forensic psychology. *American Psychologist, 68,* 7–19. doi:10.1037/a0029889

Amnesty International. (2013). *Annual report 2012: The state of the world's human rights.* London, England: Author. Retrieved from http://www.amnesty.org/en/annual-report/2012

Anderson, I., & Lyons, A. (2005). The effect of victims' social support on attributions of blame in female and male rape. *Journal of Applied Social Psychology, 35,* 1400–1417. doi:10.1111/j.1559-1816.2005.tb02176.x

Anderson, M. C. (2001). Active forgetting: Evidence for functional inhibition as a source of memory failure. In J. J. Freyd & A. P. DePrince (Eds.), *Trauma and cognitive science: A meeting of minds, science, and human experience* (pp. 48–64). New York, NY: Haworth Press.

Aosved, A. C., & Long, P. J. (2006). Co-occurrence of rape myth acceptance, sexism, racism, homophobia, ageism, classism, and religious intolerance. *Sex Roles, 55,* 481–492. doi:10.1007/s11199-006-9101-4

Archer, D., Costanzo, M., & Akert, R. (2001). The Interpersonal Perception Task (IPT): Alternative approaches to problems of theory and design. In J. Hall & F. Bernieri (Eds.), *Interpersonal sensitivity: Theory and measurement* (pp. 161–182). Mahwah, NJ: Erlbaum.

Archer, D., & Gartner, R. (1984). *Violence and crime in cross-national perspective.* New Haven, CT: Yale University Press.

Aronson, E. (2007). The evolution of cognitive dissonance theory: A personal appraisal. In A. R. Pratkanis (Ed.), *The science of social influence: Advances and future progress* (pp. 115–135). New York, NY: Psychology Press.

Arrigo, B. A., & Bullock, J. A. (2008). The psychological effects of solitary confinement on prisoners in supermax units: Reviewing what we know and recommending what should change. *International Journal of Offender Therapy and Comparative Criminology, 52,* 622–640. doi:10.1177/0306624X07309720

Associated Press. (1984, November 24). Judicial leniency toward women found. *San Diego Tribune,* p. A12.

Associated Press. (2002, February 19). *Attorney cites Yates' mental ills: Testimony begins in children's death trial.* Retrieved from http://lubbockonline.com/stories/021902/nat_0219020045.shtml

Association of Family and Conciliation Courts. (2005). *Guidelines for parenting coordination.* Retrieved from http://www.afccnet.org/Portals/0/AFCCGuidelinesforParentingcoordinationnew.pdf

Atkinson, R. C., & Shiffrin, R. M. (1968). Human memory: A proposed system and its control processes. In K. W. Spence & J. T. Spence (Eds.), *Psychology of learning and motivation* (Vol. 2, 89–195). New York, NY: Academic Press.

Bailey, W. C., & Peterson, R. D. (1994). Murder, capital punishment, and deterrence: A review of the evidence and an examination of police killings. *Journal of Social Issues, 50,* 53–74. doi:10.1111/j.1540-4560.1994.tb02410.x

Bailey, W. C., & Peterson, R. D. (1997). Murder, capital punishment, and deterrence: A review of the literature. In H. A. Bedau (Ed.), *The death penalty in America: Current controversies* (pp. 135–161). New York, NY: Oxford University Press.

Baldus, D. C., Woodworth, G. G., & Pulaski, C. A. (1990). *Equal justice and the death penalty: A legal and empirical analysis.* Boston, MA: Northeastern University Press.

Baldus, D. C., Woodworth, G., Zuckerman, D., Weiner, N. A., & Broffitt, B. (1998). Racial discrimination and the death penalty in the post-*Furman* era: An empirical and legal overview with recent findings from Philadelphia. *Cornell Law Review, 83,* 1638–1770.

Baldwin, A. (2008). *A promise to ourselves: A journey through fatherhood and divorce.* New York, NY: St. Martin's Press.

Barnard, G. W., Thompson, J. W., Jr., Freeman, W. C., Robbins, L., Gies, D., & Hankins, G. C. (1991). Competency to stand trial: Description and initial evaluation of a new computer-assisted assessment tool (CADCOMP). *Bulletin of the American Academy of Psychiatry and Law, 19,* 367–381. Retrieved from http://www.jaapl.org

Barratt, E. S. (1994). Impulsiveness and aggression. In J. Monahan & H. J. Steadman (Eds.), *Violence and mental disorder: Developments in risk assessment* (pp. 61–79). Chicago, IL: University of Chicago Press.

Barthel, J. (1976). *A death in Canaan.* New York, NY: E. P. Dutton.

Baskin, D. R., & Sommers, I. B. (2010). Crime-show-viewing habits and public attitudes toward forensic evidence: The "CSI Effect" revisited. *The Justice System Journal, 31,* 97–113. Retrieved from http://www.ncsc.org/Publications-and-Library/Justice-System-Journal.aspx

Ben-Shakhar, G., Bar-Hillel, M., & Kremnitzer, M. (2002). Trial by polygraph: Reconsidering the use of the guilty knowledge technique in court. *Law and Human Behavior, 26,* 527–541. doi:10.1023/A:1020204005730

Ben-Shakhar, G., & Furedy, J. (1990). *Theories and applications in the detection of deception.* New York, NY: Springer-Verlag.

Bennell, C., Bloomfield, S., Emeno, K., & Musolino, E. (2013). Classifying serial sexual murder/murderers: An attempt to validate Keppel and Walter's (1999) model. *Criminal Justice and Behavior, 40,* 5–25. doi:10.1177/0093854812460489

Bennell, C., Jones, N., Taylor, P. J., & Snook, B. (2006). Validities and abilities in criminal profiling: A critique of the studies conducted by Richard Kocsis and his colleagues. *International Journal of Offender Therapy and Comparative Criminology, 50,* 344–360. doi:10.1177/0306624X05277660

Bennell, C., Snook, B., MacDonald, S., House, J. C., & Taylor, P. J. (2012). Computerized crime linkage systems: A critical review and research agenda. *Criminal Justice and Behavior, 39,* 620–637. doi:10.1177/0093854811435210

Bensussan, P. (2011). Forensic psychiatry in France: The Outreau case and false allegations of child sexual abuse. *Child and Adolescent Psychiatric Clinics of North America, 20,* 519–532. doi:10.1016/j.chc.2011.03.002

Berdahl, J. L. (2007). The sexual harassment of uppity women. *Journal of Applied Psychology, 92,* 425–437. doi:10.1037/0021-9010.92.2.425

Berdahl, J. L., & Moon, S. H. (2013). Workplace mistreatment of middle class workers based on sex, parenthood, and caregiving. *Journal of Social Issues, 69,* 341–366. doi:10.1111/josi.12018

Bergman, M. E., & Henning, J. B. (2008). Sex and ethnicity as moderators in the sexual harassment phenomenon: A revision and test of Fitzgerald et al. (1994). *Journal of Occupational Health Psychology, 13,* 152–167. doi:10.1037/1076-8998.13.2.152

Berns, W. (1979). *For capital punishment: Crime and the morality of the death penalty.* New York, NY: Basic Books.

Berrey, E., Hoffman, S. G., & Nielsen, L. B. (2012). Situated justice: A contextual analysis of fairness and inequality in employment discrimination litigation. *Law & Society Review, 46,* 1–36. doi:10.1111/j.1540-5893.2012.00471.x

Bersoff, D. N. (1999). Preparing for two cultures. In R. Roesch, S. D. Hart, & J. R. P. Ogloff (Eds.), *Psychology and law: The state of the discipline* (pp. 375–401). New York, NY: Kluwer/Plenum.

Bersoff, D. N., Goodman-Delahunty, J., Grisso, J. T., Hans, V., Poythress, N. G., & Roesch, R. G. (1997). Training in law and psychology: Models from the Villanova conference. *American Psychologist, 52,* 1301–1310. doi:10.1037/0003-066X.52.12.1301

Bessler, J. D. (2012). *Cruel and unusual: The American death penalty and the founders' Eighth Amendment.* Boston, MA: Northeastern University Press.

Bienen, L. B. (2010). Capital punishment in Illinois in the aftermath of the Ryan commutations: Reforms, economic realities, and a new saliency for issues of cost. *Journal of Criminal Law & Criminology, 100,* 1301–1402. Retrieved from http://scholarlycommons.law.northwestern.edu/jclc/

Black, M. C., Basile, K. C., Breiding, M. J., Smith, S. G., Walters, M. L., Merrick, M. T., . . . Stevens, M. R. (2011). *The National Intimate Partner and Sexual Violence Survey (NISVS): 2010 summary report.* Atlanta, GA: National Center for Injury Prevention and Control, Centers for Disease Control and Prevention.

Blandon-Gitlin, I., Pezdek, K., Rogers, M., & Brodie, L. (2005). Detecting deception in children: An experimental study of the effect of event familiarity on CBCA ratings. *Law and Human Behavior, 29,* 187–197. doi:10.1007/s10979-005-2417-8

Blandon-Gitlin, I., Sperry, K., and Leo, R. (2011). Jurors believe interrogation tactics are not likely to elicit false confessions: Will expert witness testimony inform them otherwise? *Psychology, Crime & Law, 17,* 239–260. doi:10.1080/10683160903113699

Blume, J., & Paalova, E. (2011). Life, death, and neuroimaging: The advantages and disadvantages of the defense's use of neuroimages in capital cases—Lessons from the front. *Mercer Law Review, 62,* 909–931. Retrieved from http://www.law.mercer.edu/academics/lawreview/

Blumenthal, J. A. (1998). The reasonable woman standard: A meta-analytic review of gender differences in perceptions of sexual harassment. *Law and Human Behavior, 22,* 33–57. doi:10.1023/A:1025724721559

Boeschen, L. E., Sales, B. D., & Koss, M. P. (1998). Rape trauma experts in the courtroom. *Psychology, Public Policy, and Law, 4,* 414–432. doi:10.1037/1076-8971.4.1-2.414

Bolitzer, B., & Godtland, E. M. (2012). Understanding the gender–pay gap in the federal workforce over the past 20 years. *American Review of Public Administration, 42,* 730–746. doi:10.1177/0275074011434801

Bond, C. F., & DePaulo, B. M. (2006). Accuracy of deception judgments. *Personality and Social Psychology Review, 10,* 214–234. doi:10.1207/s15327957pspr1003_2

Bond, C. F., & DePaulo, B. M. (2008). Individual differences in judging deception: Accuracy and bias. *Psychological Bulletin, 134,* 477–492. doi:10.1037/0033-2909.134.4.477

Bond, G. D. (2009). *Deception detection expertise. Law and Human Behavior, 32,* 339–351. doi:10.1007/s10979-007-9110-z

Bonnie, R. J., & Grisso, T. (2000). Adjudicative competence and youthful offenders. In T. Grisso & R. Schwartz (Eds.), *Youth on trial: A developmental perspective on juvenile justice* (pp. 70–103). Chicago, IL: University of Chicago Press.

Bonta, J., Law, M., & Hanson, R. K. (1998). The prediction of criminal and violent recidivism among mentally disordered offenders: A meta-analysis. *Psychological Bulletin, 123,* 124–143. doi:10.1037/0033-2909.123.2.123

Bornstein, B. H., & Robicheaux, T. R. (2008). Crisis, what crisis? Perception and reality in civil justice. In B. H. Bornstein, R. L. Weiner, R. Schopp, & S. L. Winborn (Eds.), *Civil juries and civil justice: Psychological and legal perspectives* (pp. 1–19). doi:10.1007/978-0-387-74490-2_1

Botello, T., Noguchi, T., Sathyavagiswaran, L., Weinberger, L. E., & Gross, B. H. (2013). Evolution of the psychological autopsy: Fifty years of experience at the Los Angeles County Chief Medical Examiner-Coroner's Office. *Journal of Forensic Sciences, 58,* 924–926. doi:10.1111/1556-4029.12138

Bottoms, B. L., & Goodman, G. S. (1994). Perceptions of children's credibility in sexual assault cases. *Journal of Applied Social Psychology, 24,* 702–732. doi:10.1111/j.1559-1816.1994.tb00608.x

Bottoms, B. L., Najdowski, C. J., & Goodman, G. S. (2009). *Children as victims, witnesses, and offenders: Psychological science and the law.* New York, NY: Guilford Press.

Bow, J. N. (2006). Review of empirical research on child custody practice. *Journal of Child Custody, 3,* 23–50. doi:10.1300/J190v03n01_02

Bow, J. N., & Quinnell, F. A. (2004). Critique of child custody evaluations by the legal profession. *Family Court Review, 42,* 115–127. doi:10.1111/j.174-1617.2004.tb00637.x

Bowers, C. M. (2002). Identification from bitemarks: Scientific issues. In D. L. Faigman, D. H. Kaye, M. J. Saks, & J. Sanders (Eds.), *Science in the law: Forensic science issues* (pp. 244–293). St. Paul, MN: West.

Bowers, W. J. (1988). The effect of executions is brutalization, not deterrence. In K. C. Haas & J. A. Inciardi (Eds.), *Challenging capital punishment: Legal and social science approaches* (pp. 49–89). Newbury Park, CA: Sage.

Bowers, W. J. (with Pierce, G. L., & McDevitt, J. F.). (1984). *Legal homicide: Death as punishment in America, 1864–1982.* Boston, MA: Northeastern University Press.

Bowers, W. J., Sandys, M., & Steiner, B. D. (1998). Foreclosed impartiality in capital sentencing: Jurors' predispositions, guilt-trial experience, and premature decision-making. *Cornell Law Review, 83,* 1476–1556.

Braun, S. (1998, June 12). Mitsubishi to pay $34 million in sexual harassment case. *Los Angeles Times,* pp. A1, A20.

Braver, S. L., Ellman, I. M., Votruba, A. M., & Fabricius, W. V. (2011). Lay judgments about child custody after divorce. *Psychology, Public Policy, and Law, 17,* 212–240. doi:10.1037/a0023194

Brehm, S. S., & Brehm, J. W. (1981). Psychological reactance: A theory of freedom and control. New York, NY: Academic Press.

Brennan, S (2011). Self-reported spousal violence, 2009. In *Family violence in Canada: A statistical profile* (pp. 8–19). Ottawa, Ontario, Canada: Statistics Canada. Retrieved from http://www.statcan.gc.ca/pub/85-224-x/85-224-x2010000-eng.pdf

Brewer, N. (2006). Uses and abuses of eyewitness identification confidence. *Legal and Criminological Psychology, 11,* 3–24. doi:10.1348/135532505X79672

Brewer, N., Harvey, S., & Semmler, C. (2004). Improving comprehension of jury instructions with audio-visual presentation. *Applied Cognitive Psychology, 18,* 765–776. doi:10.1002/acp.1036

Brewer, N., & Semmler, C. (2002). Using a flow-chart to improve comprehension of jury instructions. *Psychiatry, Psychology, and Law, 9,* 262–270. doi:10.1375/13218710260612136

Bricklin, B. (1984). *The Bricklin perceptual scales: Child-perception-of-parent series* [Test]. Furlong, PA: Village.

Broda-Bahm, K. (2011, February 28). *Conduct a social media analysis on your potential jurors* [Web log post]. Retrieved from http://www.persuasivelitigator.com/2011/02/social-media-analysis.html

Brodsky, S. L. (2009). *Principles and practice of trial consultation.* New York, NY: Guilford Press.

Brodsky, S. L. (2013). *Testifying in court: Guidelines and maxims for the expert witness.* Washington, DC: American Psychological Association.

Brown, D., Pipe, M.-E., Lewis, C., Lamb, M. E., & Orbach, Y. (2012). How do body diagrams affect the accuracy and consistency of children's reports of bodily touch across repeated interviews? *Applied Cognitive Psychology, 26,* 174–181. doi:10.1002/acp.1828

Browne, A. (1987). *When battered women kill*. New York, NY: Free Press.

Bruck, M., Ceci, S. J., & Francoeur, E. (2000). Children's use of anatomically detailed dolls to report genital touching in a medical examination: Developmental and gender comparisons. *Journal of Experimental Psychology: Applied, 6*, 74–83. doi:10.1037/1076-898X.6.1.74

Brussel, J. A. (1968). *Casebook of a crime psychiatrist*. New York, NY: Bernard Geis.

Buckhout, R. (1974, December). Eyewitness testimony. *Scientific American, 231*, 23–31.

Bugliosi, V. (1996). *Outrage: Five reasons why O. J. Simpson got away with murder*. New York, NY: Island Books.

Bull, R., & Soukara, S. (2010). What really happens in police interviews. In G. D. Lassiter & C. A. Meissner (Eds.), *Police interrogations and false confessions: Current research, practice, and policy recommendations* (pp. 81–95). Washington, DC: American Psychological Association.

Bureau of Justice Statistics. (2008, December 17). *Criminal victimization, 2007* (NCJ 224390). Washington, DC: U.S. Department of Justice. Retrieved from http://www.bjs.gov/content/pub/pdf/cv07.pdf

Bureau of Justice Statistics. (2011, September). *Criminal victimization, 2010* (NCJ 235508). Washington, DC: U.S. Department of Justice. Retrieved from http://www.bjs.gov/content/pub/pdf/cv10.pdf

Bureau of Justice Statistics. (2012). *Sourcebook of criminal justice statistics online: Criminal defendants disposed of in U.S. district courts* (Table 5.22.2009). Retrieved from http://www.albany.edu/sourcebook/pdf/t5222009.pdf.

Bureau of Justice Statistics. (2014). *Capital punishment, 2013—Statistical tables* (NCJ 245789). Washington, DC: Author. Retrieved from http://www.bjs.gov/index.cfm?ty=pbdetail&iid=4991

Burgess, A. W., & Holmstrom, L. L. (1974). Rape trauma syndrome. *American Journal of Psychiatry, 131*, 981–999. Retrieved from http://ajp.psychiatryonline.org/journal.aspx?journalid=13

Burgess, A. W., & Holmstrom, L. L. (1979). Adaptive strategies and recovery from rape. *American Journal of Psychiatry, 136*, 1277–1282. Retrieved from http://ajp.psychiatryonline.org/journal.aspx?journalid=13

Burl, J., Shah, S., Filone, S., Foster, E. and DeMatteo, D. (2012). A survey of graduate training programs and coursework in forensic psychology. *Teaching of Psychology, 39*, 48–53. doi:10.1177/0098628311430313

Butler, B. (2007). The role of death qualification in jurors' susceptibility to pretrial publicity. *Journal of Applied Social Psychology, 37*, 115–123. doi:10.1111/j.0021-9029.2007.00150.x

Butler, B. (2008). The role of death qualification in venirepersons' susceptibility to victim impact statements. *Psychology, Crime & Law, 14*, 133–141. doi:10.1080/10683160701483534

Butler, B. (2010). My client is guilty of "this," but not guilty of "that": The impact of defense-attorney concessions on juror decisions. *American Journal of Forensic Psychology, 28*, 5–19.

Caers, R., & Castelyns, V. (2011). LinkedIn and Facebook in Belgium: The influences and biases of social network sites in recruitment and selection procedures. *Social Science Computer Review, 29*, 437–448. doi:10.1177/0894439310386567

California Commission on the Fair Administration of Justice. (2008). *Official recommendations on the fair administration of the death penalty in California*. Retrieved from http://www.ccfaj.org/rr-dp-official.html

Campbell, D. T. (1969). Reforms as experiments. *American Psychologist, 24*, 409–429.

Campbell, R., & Wasco, S. (2005). Understanding rape and sexual assault: 20 years of progress and future directions. *Journal of Interpersonal Violence, 20*, 127–131. doi:10.1177/0886260504268604

Campos, P. F. (1998). *Jurismania: The madness of American law*. New York, NY: Oxford University Press.

Cantor, N. (1930). Law and the social sciences. *American Bar Association Journal, 16*, 385–392.

Caplan, J. M. (2007). What factors affect parole? A review of empirical research. *Federal Probation, 71*, 16–21. Retrieved from http://www.uscourts.gov/FederalCourts/ProbationPretrialServices/FederalProbationJournal.aspx

Caplan, L. (1984). *The insanity defense and the trial of John W. Hinckley, Jr*. New York, NY: Godine.

Carmichael, J. T., & Burgos, G. (2012). Sentencing juvenile offenders to life in prison: The political sociology of juvenile punishment. *American Journal of Criminal Justice, 37*, 602–629. doi:10.1007/s12103-011-9135-1

Carroll, J. S. (1980). An appetizing look at law and psychology. *Contemporary Psychology, 25*, 362–364.

Carson, E. A., & Golinelli, D. (2013). *Prisoners in 2012: Trends in admissions and releases, 1991–2012* (NCJ 243920). Washington, DC: Bureau of Justice Statistics. Retrieved from http://www.bjs.gov/content/pub/pdf/p12tar9112.pdf

Carson, E. A., & Sabol, W. J. (2012). *Prisoners in 2011* (NCJ 239808). Washington, DC: Bureau of Justice Statistics. Retrieved from http://bjs.gov/content/pub/pdf/p11.pdf

Cass, S. A., Levett, L. M., & Kovera, M. B. (2010). The effects of harassment severity and organizational behavior on damage awards in a hostile work environment sexual harassment case. *Behavioral Science and the Law, 28*, 303–321.

Cassell, P. G., & Hayman, B. S. (1996). Police interrogation in the 1990s: An empirical study of the effects of Miranda. *UCLA Law Review, 43*, 839–931.

Catalano, S. (2012). *Intimate partner violence, 1993–2010* (NCJ 239203). Washington, DC: Bureau of Justice Statistics. Retrieved from http://www.bjs.gov/index.cfm?ty=pbdetail&iid=4536

Cauffman, E., & Steinberg, L. (2000). (Im)maturity of judgment in adolescence: Why adolescents may be less culpable than adults. *Behavioral Sciences & the Law, 18*, 741–760. doi:10.1002/bsl.416

Cavoukian, A. (1979, June). *The effect of polygraph evidence on people's judgments of guilt*. Paper presented at the meeting of the Canadian Psychological Association, Quebec City, Canada.

Ceci, S. J., & Bruck, M. (1996). *Jeopardy in the courtroom: A scientific analysis of children's testimony*. Washington, DC: American Psychological Association.

Chainey, S., & Tompson, L. (2008). *Crime mapping case studies: Practice and research*. New York, NY: Wiley.

Champod, C., & Evett, I. W. (2001). A probabilistic approach to fingerprint evidence. *Journal of Forensic Identification, 51*, 101–122.

Charrow, R. P., & Charrow, V. R. (1979). Making legal language understandable: A psycholinguistic study of jury instructions. *Columbia Law Review, 79,* 1306–1374.

Chen, E. (2007, November). Impacts of "three strikes and you're out" on crime trends in California and throughout the United States. Paper presented at the annual meeting of the American Society of Criminology, Atlanta, GA.

Choi, S. (2011). Organizational justice and employee work attitudes: The federal case. *The American Review of Public Administration, 41,* 185–204. doi:10.1177/0275074010373275

Cialdini, R. (2008). *Influence: Science and applications* (5th ed.). Boston, MA: Allyn & Bacon.

Cimerman, A. (1981). They'll let me go tomorrow: The Fay case. *Criminal Defense, 8,* 7–10.

Clark, S. E. (2012). Costs and benefits of eyewitness identification reform: Psychological science and public policy. *Perspectives on Psychological Science, 7,* 238–259. doi:10.1177/1745691612439584

Clear, T. R., Cole, G. F., & Reisig, M. D. (2010). *American corrections* (9th ed.). Belmont, CA: Wadsworth/Cengage Learning.

CNN. (2002, March 1). *Psychiatrist: Yates thought she was defeating Satan.* Retrieved from http://edition.cnn.com/2002/LAW/03/01/yates.trial/index.html

Cockrell, J. F. (2013). Solitary confinement: The law today and the way forward. *Law and Psychology Review, 37,* 211–227.

Cole, S. A. (2001). *Suspect identities: A history of fingerprinting and criminal identification.* Cambridge, MA: Harvard University Press.

Cole, S. A. (2005). More than zero: Accounting for error in latent fingerprint identification. *Journal of Criminal Law and Criminology, 95,* 985–1078. Retrieved from http://scholarlycommons.law.northwestern.edu/jclc/

Cole, S. A. (2006). Is fingerprint identification valid? Rhetoric of reliability in fingerprint proponents' discourse. *Law & Policy, 28,* 109–135. doi:10.1111/j.1467-9930.2005.00219.x

Cole, S. A. (2009). Forensics without uniqueness, conclusions without individualization: The new epistemology of forensic identification. Law, Probability & Risk, 8, 233–255. doi:10.1093/lpr/mgp016

Colquitt, J. A., Zapata-Phelan, C. P., & Roberson, Q. M. (2005). Justice in teams: A review of fairness effects in collective contexts. In J. J. Martocchio (Ed.), *Research in personnel and human resources management* (Vol. 24, pp. 53–94). Bingley, UK: Emerald Group.

Coltrane, S., Miller, E. C., DeHaan, T., & Stewart, L. (2013). Fathers and the flexibility stigma. *Journal of Social Issues, 69,* 279–302. doi:10.1111/josi.12015

Conner, K. R., Beautrais, A. L., Brent, D. A., Conwell, Y., Phillips, M. R., & Schneider, B. (2011). The next generation of psychological autopsy studies. *Suicide and Life-Threatening Behavior, 41,* 594–613. doi:10.1111/j.1943-278X.2011.00057.x

Cook, A. E., Hacker, D. J., Webb, A. K., Osher, D., Kristjansson, S. D., Woltz, D. J., & Kircher, J. C. (2012). Lyin' eyes: Ocular-motor measures of reading reveal deception. *Journal of Experimental Psychology: Applied, 18,* 301–313. doi:2012-10769-001

Cooper, J., Bennett, E. A., & Sukel, H. L. (1996). Complex scientific testimony: How do jurors make decisions? *Law and Human Behavior, 20,* 379–394. doi:10.1007/BF01498976

Copson, G. (1995). *Coals to Newcastle: A study of offender profiling.* London, England: Home Office.

Corbett, C., & Hill, C. (2012). *Graduating to a pay gap: The earnings of women and men one year after college graduation.* Washington, DC: American Association of University Women. Retrieved from http://www.aauw.org/resource/graduating-to-a-pay-gap-the-earnings-of-women-and-men-one-year-after-college-graduation/

Cordon, I. M., Goodman, G. S., & Anderson, S. J. (2003). Children in court. In P. J. van Koppen & S. D. Penrod (Eds.), *Adversarial versus inquisitorial justice* (pp. 167–189). New York, NY: Springer Science + Business Media.

Corey, D., Malpass, R. S., & McQuiston, D. E. (1999). Parallelism in eyewitness and mock witness identification. *Applied Cognitive Psychology, 13,* 541–558. doi:10.1002/(SICI)1099-0720(199911)13:1+<S41::AID-ACP632>3.0.CO;2-A

Costanzo, M. (1997). *Just revenge: Costs and consequences of the death penalty.* New York, NY: St. Martin's Press.

Costanzo, M., & Costanzo, S. (1992). Jury decision making in the capital penalty phase: Legal assumptions, empirical findings, and a research agenda. *Law and Human Behavior, 16,* 185–201. doi:10.1007/BF01044797

Costanzo, M., & Gerrity, E. (2009). The effects and effectiveness of using torture as an interrogation device: Using research to inform the policy debate. *Social Issues and Policy Review, 3,* 179–210. doi:10.1111/j.1751-2409.2009.01014.x

Costanzo, M., Krauss, D., & Pezdek, K. (Eds.). (2007). *Expert psychological testimony for the courts.* Mahwah, NJ: Erlbaum.

Costanzo, M., & Leo, R. A. (2007). Research findings and expert testimony on police interrogations and confessions to crimes. In M. Costanzo, D. Krauss, & K. Pezdek (Eds.), *Expert psychological testimony for the courts* (pp. 69–98). Mahwah, NJ: Erlbaum.

Costanzo, M., Shaked-Schroer, N., & Vinson, K. (2010). Juror beliefs about police interrogations, false confessions, and expert testimony. *Journal of Empirical Legal Studies, 7,* 231–247. doi:10.1111/j.1740-1461.2010.01177.x

Costanzo, S., & Costanzo, M. (1994). Life or death decisions: An analysis of capital jury decision making under the special issues sentencing framework. *Law and Human Behavior, 18,* 151–170. doi:10.1007/BF01499013

Cox, J. M., Goldstein, N. E. S., Dolores, J., Zelechoski, A. D., & Messenheimer, S. (2012). The impact of juveniles' ages and levels of psychosocial maturity on judges' opinions about adjudicative competence. *Law and Human Behavior, 36,* 21–27. doi:10.1037/h0093953

Crano, W. D., & Seyranian, V. (2009). How minorities prevail: The context-comparison and leniency contract model. *Journal of Social Issues, 65,* 335–363. doi:10.1111/j.1540-4560.2009.01603.x

Crosby, F. J. (2004). *Affirmative action is dead; long live affirmative action.* New Haven, CT: Yale University Press.

Cummings, E. M., & Davies, P. T. (2002). Effects of marital conflict on children: Recent advances and emerging themes in process-oriented research. *Journal of*

Child Psychology and Psychiatry, 43, 31–63. doi:10.1111/1469-7610.00003

Cunningham, M. D., Sorensen, J. R., & Reidy, T. J. (2009). Capital jury decision-making: The limitations of predictions of future violence. *Psychology, Public Policy, and Law, 15,* 223–256. doi:10.1037/a0017296

Currie, E. (2013). *Crime and punishment in America* (Rev. and updated ed.). New York, NY: Picador.

Cutler, B. L. (2013). *Reform of eyewitness identification procedures.* doi:10.1037/14094-000

Cutler, B. L., Penrod, S. D., & Dexter, H. R. (1990). Juror sensitivity to eyewitness identification evidence. *Law and Human Behavior, 14,* 185–191. doi:10.1007/BF01062972

Daftary-Kapur, T., Dumas, R., & Penrod, S. D. (2010). Jury decision-making biases and methods to counter them. *Legal and Criminological Psychology, 15,* 133–154. doi:10.1348/135532509X465624

Daftary-Kapur, T., Groscup, J. L., O'Connor, M., Coffaro, F., & Galietta, M. (2011). Measuring knowledge of the insanity defense: Scale construction and validation. *Behavioral Sciences & The Law, 29,* 40–63. doi:10.1002/bsl.938

Dahir, V. B., Richardson, J., Ginsburg, P., Gatowski, S., Dobbin, S. A., & Merlino, M. (2005). Judicial application of Daubert to psychological syndrome and profile evidence: A research note. *Psychology, Public Policy, and Law, 11,* 62–82. doi:10.1037/1076-8971.11.1.62

Dando, C., Wilcock, R., & Milne, R. (2009). Novice police officers' application of the cognitive interview procedure. *Psychology, Crime & Law, 15,* 679–696. doi:10.1080/10683160802203963

Daunt, T., & Berry, S. (2002, July 30). LAPD says evidence destroyed. *Los Angeles Times,* pp. B1, B4.

Davidson, J. R. T., & Foa, E. B. (1991). Refining criteria for posttraumatic stress disorder. *Hospital and Community Psychiatry, 42,* 259–261. Retrieved from http://ps.psychiatryonline.org/journal.aspx?journalid=18

Davis, D., & Follette, W. (2002). Rethinking the probative value of evidence: Base rates, intuitive profiling, and the "post diction" of behavior. *Law and Human Behavior, 26,* 133–158. doi:10.1023/A:1014693024962

Davis, D., & Leo, R. A. (2006). Psychological weapons of influence: Applications in the interrogation room. *Nevada Lawyer, 14,* 14–18.

Davis, D., & Leo, R. A. (2010). Overcoming judicial preferences for person- versus situation-based analyses of interrogation-induced confessions. *Journal of the American Academy of Psychiatry and the Law, 38,* 187–94. Retrieved from http://www.jaapl.org

Davis, D., & Leo, R. A. (2012). Interrogation-related regulatory decline: Ego depletion, failures of self-regulation, and the decision to confess. *Psychology, Public Policy, and Law, 18,* 673–704. doi:10.1037/a0027367

Davis, D., & Loftus, E. (2009). The scientific status of "repressed and recovered" memories of sexual abuse. In J. L. Skeem, K. S. Douglas, & S. O. Lilienfeld (Eds.), *Psychological science in the courtroom: Controversies and consensus* (pp. 55–79). New York, NY: Guilford Press.

Davis, D., & O'Donahue, W. (2003). The road to perdition: Extreme influence tactics in the interrogation room. In W. O'Donahue (Ed.), *The handbook of forensic psychology* (pp. 897–996). New York, NY: Basic Books.

Davis, T. E., III. (2012). Where to from here for ASD and anxiety? Lessons learned from child anxiety and the issue of DSM-5. *Clinical Psychology: Science and Practice, 19,* (362). doi:10.1111/cpsp.12014

Death Penalty Information Center. (2010). *Innocence and the death penalty.* Retrieved from http://www.deathpenalty-info.org/innocence-and-death-penalty

Deffenbacher, K. A., Bornstein, B. H., & Penrod, S. D. (2006). Mugshot exposure effects: Retroactive interference, mugshot commitment, source confusion, and unconscious transference. *Law and Human Behavior, 30,* 287–307. doi:10.1007/s10979-006-9008-1

Deffenbacher, K. A., Bornstein, B. H., Penrod. S. D., & McGorty, E. K. (2004). A meta-analytic review of the effects of high stress on eyewitness memory. *Law and Human Behavior, 28,* 687–706. doi:10.1007/s10979-004-0565-x

DeMatteo, D., Marczyk, G., Krauss, D. A., & Burl, J. (2009). Educational and training models in forensic psychology. *Training and Education in Professional Psychology, 3,* 184–201. doi:10.1037/a0014582

DeMatteo, D., Murrie, D. C., Anumba, N. M., & Keesler, M. E. (2011). *Forensic mental health assessments in death penalty cases.* New York, NY: Oxford University Press.

Department of Justice. (1999). *Eyewitness evidence: A guide for law enforcement.* Washington, DC: National Institute of Justice.

DePaulo, B. M., Lindsay, J. J., Malone, B. E., Muhlenbruck, L., Charlton, K., & Cooper, H. (2003). Cues to deception. *Psychological Bulletin, 129,* 74–118. doi:10.1037/0033-2909.129.1.74

Derakshan, N., Eysenck, M. W., & Myers, L. B. (2007). Emotional information processing in repressors: The vigilance-avoidance theory. *Cognition and Emotion, 21,* 1585–1614. doi:10.1080/02699930701499857

Dershowitz, A. M. (2002, March 17). Andrea Yates' prosecutors used the death penalty as a trial tactic [Commentary]. *Los Angeles Times.* Retrieved from http://articles.latimes.com/2002/mar/17/opinion/oe-dersh17

Devery, C. (2010). Criminal profiling and criminal investigation. *Journal of Contemporary Criminal Justice, 26,* 393–409. doi:10.1177/1043986210377108

Devine, D. J., Buddenbaum, J., Houp, S., Stolle, D. P., & Studebaker, N. (2007). Deliberation quality: A preliminary examination in criminal juries. *Journal of Empirical Legal Studies, 4,* 273–303. doi:10.1111/j.1740-1461.2007.00089.x

Devine, D. J., Buddenbaum, J., Houp, S., Studebaker, N., & Stolle, D. P. (2009). Strength of evidence, extraevidentiary influence, and the liberation hypothesis: Data from the field. *Law and Human Behavior, 33,* 136–148. doi:10.1007/s10979-008-9144-x

Devine, D. J., Clayton, L. D., Dunford, B. B., Seying, R., & Pryce, J. (2001). Jury decision making: 45 years of empirical research on deliberating groups. *Psychology, Public Policy, and Law, 7,* 622–727. doi:10.1037/1076-8971.7.3.622

Devine, P. G., Rhodewalt, F., & Siemionko, M. (2008). Personality and prejudice in interracial interactions. In F. Rhodewalt (Ed.), *Personality and social behavior* (pp. 223–249). New York, NY: Taylor & Francis.

Dewey, J. (1929). *The quest for certainty.* New York, NY: Putnam's.

Dhami, M. K. (2003). Psychological models of professional decision making. *Psychological Science, 14,* 175–180. doi:10.1111/1467-9280.01438

Diamond, S. S. (2003). Convergence and complementarity between professional judges and lay adjudicators. In P. J. van Koppen & S. D. Penrod (Eds.), *Adversarial versus inquisitorial justice: Psychological perspectives on criminal justice systems* (pp. 321–332). New York, NY: Plenum.

Diamond, S. S. (2006). Beyond fantasy and nightmare: A portrait of the jury. *Buffalo Law Review, 54,* 717–763.

Diamond, S. S. (2007, July-August). Dispensing with deception, curing with care: A response to Judge Dann on nullification. *Judicature, 91,* 20–26.

Diamond, S. S., Vidmar, N., Rose, M., Ellis, L., & Murphy, B. (2003). Juror discussions during civil trials: Studying an Arizona innovation. *Arizona Law Review, 45,* 1–81.

Dickens, C. (1850). *American notes for general circulation.* London, England: MacDonald and Sons.

Dieter, R. C. (2009). *Smart on crime: Reconsidering the death penalty in a time of economic crisis.* Washington, DC: Death Penalty Information Center. Retrieved from http://www.deathpenaltyinfo.org/documents/CostsRptFinal.pdf

Dillehay, R. C., & Nietzel, M. T. (1999). Prior jury experience. In W. Abbott & J. Batt (Eds.), *A handbook of jury research* (pp. 101–117). Philadelphia, PA: American Law Institute—American Bar Association.

Divaa. (n.d.) *Guilt and shame* [Website comment]. Retrieved from http://www.pandys.org/escapinghades/guilt-shame.html

Dixon, L., & Gill, B. (2002). Changes in the standards for admitting expert evidence in federal civil cases since the *Daubert* decision. *Psychology, Public Policy, and Law, 8,* 251–308. doi:10.1037/1076-8971.8.3.251

Dodge, K. A., Price, J. M., Bachorowski, J.-A., & Newman, J. P. (1990). Hostile attributional biases in severely aggressive adolescents. *Journal of Abnormal Psychology, 99,* 385–392. doi:10.1037/0021-843X.99.4.385

Doerner, J. K., & Demuth, S. (2010). The independent and joint effects of race/ethnicity, gender, and age on sentencing outcomes in U.S. federal courts. *Justice Quarterly, 27,* 1–27. doi:10.1080/07418820902926197

Domanico, A. J., Cicchini, M. D., & White, L. T. (2012). Overcoming Miranda: A content analysis of the Miranda portion of police interrogations, *Idaho Law Review, 49,* 1–22. Retrieved from http://www.uidaho.edu/law/law-review

Donaldson, S. I., & Scriven, M. (Eds.). (2003). *Evaluating social programs and problems.* Mahwah, NJ: Erlbaum.

Donohue, J. J., & Wolfers, J. (2006). Uses and abuses of empirical evidence in the death penalty debate. *Stanford Law Review, 58,* 791–846. Retrieved from http://www.stanfordlawreview.org

Donohue, J. J., & Wolfers, J. (2007). The death penalty: No evidence for deterrence. *The Economists' Voice, 3*(5). doi:10.2202/1553-3832.1170

Dorland, M., & Krauss, D. (2005). The danger of dangerousness in capital sentencing: Exacerbating the problem of arbitrary and capricious decision-making. *Law and Psychology Review, 29,* 63–104.

Douglas, J. E., Burgess, A. W., Burgess, A. G., & Ressler, R. K. (1992). *Crime classification manual: A standard system for investigating and classifying violent crime.* New York, NY: Simon & Schuster.

Douglas, J., & Dodd, J. (2007). *Inside the mind of BTK.* San Francisco, CA: Jossey-Bass.

Douglas, J., & Olshaker, M. (1997). *Journey into darkness.* New York, NY: Pocket Books.

Douglas, K. S., Guy, L. S., & Hart, S. D. (2009). Psychosis as a risk factor for violence to others: A meta-analysis. *Psychological Bulletin, 135,* 679–706. doi:10.1037/a0016311

Douglas, K. S., & Reeves, K. A. (2009). Historical-clinical-risk management-20 (HCR-20) violence risk assessment scheme: Rationale, application, and empirical overview. In R. Otto & K. S. Douglas (Eds.), *Handbook of violence risk assessment* (pp. 147–186). Oxford, England: Routledge.

Douglas, K. S., & Skeem, J. L. (2005). Violence risk assessment: Getting specific about being dynamic. *Psychology, Public Policy, and Law, 11,* 347–383. doi:10.1037/1076-8971.11.3.347

Douglas, K. S., & Webster, C. D. (1999a). The HCR-20 violence risk assessment scheme: Concurrent validity in a sample of incarcerated offenders. *Criminal Justice and Behavior, 26,* 3–19. doi:10.1177/0093854899026001001

Douglas, K. S., & Webster, C. D. (1999b). Predicting violence in mentally and personality disordered individuals. In R. Roesch, S. D. Hart, & J. R. P. Ogloff (Eds.), *Psychology and law: The state of the discipline* (pp. 175–239). New York, NY: Kluwer/Plenum.

Douglass, A. B., & McQuiston-Surrett, D. M. (2006). Post-identification feedback: Exploring the effects of sequential photospreads and eyewitnesses awareness of the identification task. *Applied Cognitive Psychology, 20,* 991–1007. doi:10.1002/acp.1253

Douglass, A. B., Neuschatz, J. S., Imrich, J., & Wilkinson, M. (2010). Does post-identification feedback affect evaluations of eyewitness testimony and identification procedures? *Law and Human Behavior, 34,* 282–294. doi:10.1007/s10979-009-9189-5

Douglass, A. B., & Steblay, N. M. (2006). Memory distortion in eyewitnesses: A meta-analysis of the post-identification feedback effect. *Applied Cognitive Psychology, 20,* 859–869. doi:10.1002/acp.1237

Dovidio, J. F., & Gaertner, S. L. (2000). Aversive racism and selection decisions: 1989 and 1999. *Psychological Science, 11,* 315–319. doi:10.1111/1467-9280.00262

Dovidio, J. F., & Gaertner, S. L. (2004). Aversive racism. In M. P. Zanna (Ed.), *Advances in experimental social psychology* (Vol. 36, pp. 1–52). San Diego, CA: Elsevier Academic Press.

Dovidio, J. F., & Hebl, M. R. (2005). Discrimination at the level of the individual: Cognitive and affective factors. In R. L. Dipboye & A. Colella (Eds.), *Discrimination at work: The psychological and organizational bases* (pp. 11–35). Mahwah, NJ: Erlbaum.

Dowden, C., Bennell, C., & Bloomfield, S. (2007). Advances in offender profiling: A systematic review of the profiling literature published over the past three decades. *Journal of Police Criminal Psychology, 22,* 44–56. doi:10.1007/s11896-007-9000-9

Drapkin, I. (1989). *Crime and punishment in the ancient world.* Lexington, MA: Lexington Books.

Drizin, S. A., & Leo, R. A. (2004). The problem of false confessions in the post-DNA world. *North Carolina Law Review, 82,* 891–1007.

Drizin, S., & Reich, M. (2004). Heeding the lessons of history: The need for mandatory recording of police interrogations to accurately assess the reliability and voluntariness of confessions. *Drake Law Review, 52,* 619–646. Retrieved from http://students.law.drake.edu/lawReview/

Dror, I. E., & Charlton, D. (2006). Why experts make errors. *Journal of Forensic Identification, 56,* 600–616.

Dror, I. E., Charlton, D., & Péron, A. (2006). Contextual information renders experts vulnerable to making erroneous identifications. *Forensic Science International, 156,* 74–78. doi:10.1016/j.forsciint.2005.10.017

Dror, I. E., & Hampikian, G. (2012). Subjectivity and bias in forensic DNA mixture interpretation. *Science & Justice, 51,* 204–208. doi:10.1016/j.scijus.2011.08.004

Dror, I. E., Péron, A., Hind, S., & Charlton, D. (2006). When emotions get the better of us: The effect of contextual top-down processing on matching fingerprints. *Applied Cognitive Psychology, 19,* 799–809. doi:10.1002/acp.1130

Drury, S., Hutchens, S. A., Shuttlesworth, D. E., & White, C. L. (2012). Philip G. Zimbardo on his career and the Stanford Prison Experiment's 40th anniversary. *History of Psychology, 15,* 161–170. doi:10.1037/a0025884

Dunbar, R. I., & Shultz, S. (2007, September 7). Evolution in the social brain. *Science, 317,* 1344–1347. doi:10.1126/science.1145463

Dutton, D. G. (2000). *The domestic assault of women.* Vancouver, Canada: University of British Columbia Press.

Dutton, D. G. (2007). *The abusive personality* (2nd ed.). New York, NY: Guilford Press.

Dutton, D. G. (2008). My back pages: Reflections on thirty years of domestic violence research. *Trauma, Violence and Abuse, 9,* 131–143. doi:10.1177/1524838008319146

Duwe, G. (2012). Evaluating the Minnesota Comprehensive Reentry Plan (MCORP): Results from a randomized experiment. *Justice Quarterly, 29,* 347–383. doi:10.1080/07418825.2011.555414

Eagleman, D. (2011). *Incognito: The secret lives of the brain.* New York, NY: Pantheon.

Edens, J. F., Buffington-Vollum, J. K., Keilin, A., Roskamp, P., & Anthony, C. (2005). Predictions of future dangerousness in capital murder trials: Is it time to "disinvent the wheel?" *Law and Human Behavior, 29,* 55–86. doi:10.1007/s10979-005-1399-x

Edens, J. F., Smith, S., Magyar, M. S., Mullen, K., Pitta, A., & Petrila, J. (2012). "Hired guns," "charlatans," and their "voodoo psychobabble": Case law references to various forms of perceived bias among mental health expert witnesses. *Psychological Services, 9,* 259–271. doi:10.1037/a0028264

Eggen, D., & Vedantam, S. (2006, May 1). Polygraph results often in question. *The Washington Post,* p. B1.

Eisen, M. L., Gomes, D. M., Wandry, L., Drachman, D., Clemente, A., & Groskopf, C. (2013). Examining the

prejudicial effects of gang evidence on jurors. *Journal of Forensic Psychology Practice, 13,* 1–13. doi:10.1080/15228932.2012.713831

Eisen, M. L., Oustinovskaya, M., Kistorian, R., Morgan, D. Y., & Mickes, L. (2008). The effect of question format on resistance to misleading postevent information and self-reports of events occurring during hypnosis. *International Journal of Clinical and Experimental Hypnosis, 56,* 198–213. doi:10.1080/00207140701672946

Eisenberg, T., & Hans, V. P. (2009). Taking a stand on taking a stand: The effect of a prior criminal record on the decision to testify and on trial outcomes. *Cornell Law Review, 94,* 1353–1390. Retrieved from http://scholarship.law.cornell.edu/lsrp_papers/

Eisenberg, T., Hannaford-Agor, P. L., Hans, V. P., Waters, N. L., Munsterman, G. T., Schwab, S. J., & Wells, M. T. (2005). Judge-jury agreement in criminal cases: A partial replication of Kalven and Zeisel's *The American Jury. Journal of Empirical Legal Studies, 2,* 171–206.

Ekman, P. (1985). *Telling lies.* New York, NY: W. W. Norton.

Elaad, E. (2009). Effects of context and state of guilt on the detection of concealed crime information. *International Journal of Psychophysiology, 71,* 225–234. doi:10.1016/j.ijpsycho.2008.10.001

Elaad, E., & Ben-Shakhar, G. (2009). Countering countermeasures in the concealed information test using covert respiration measures. *Applied Psychophysiology and Biofeedback, 34,* 197–208. doi:10.1007/s10484-009-9090-5

Elaad, E., Ginton, A., & Jungman, N. (1992). Detection measures in real-life guilty knowledge tests. *Journal of Applied Psychology, 77,* 757–767. doi:10.1037/0021-9010.77.5.757

Ellsworth, P. C. (1989). Are twelve heads better than one? *Law and Contemporary Problems, 52,* 205–224. Retrieved from http://scholarship.law.duke.edu/lcp/

Ellsworth, P. C., & Gross, S. R. (1994). Hardening of the attitudes: Americans' views on the death penalty. *Journal of Social Issues, 50,* 19–52. doi:10.1111/j.1540-4560.1994.tb02409.x

Ellsworth, P. C., & Mauro, R. (1998). Psychology and law. In D. T. Gilbert, S. T. Fiske, & G. Lindzey (Eds.). *The handbook of social psychology* (Vol. 2, pp. 684–732). Boston, MA: McGraw-Hill.

Emery, R. E., Laumann-Billings, L., Waldron, M. C., Sbarra, D. A., & Dillon, P. (2001). Child custody mediation and litigation: Custody, contact, and coparenting 12 years after initial dispute resolution. *Journal of Consulting and Clinical Psychology, 69,* 323–332. doi:10.1037/0022-006X.69.2.323

Emery, R. E., Matthews, S. G., & Kitzmann, K. M. (1994). Child custody mediation and litigation: Parents' satisfaction and functioning one year after settlement. *Journal of Consulting and Clinical Psychology, 62,* 124–129. doi:10.1037/0022-006X.62.1.124

Emery, R. E., Otto, R. K., & O'Donohue, W. T. (2005). A critical assessment of child custody evaluations: Limited science and a flawed system. *Psychological Science in the Public Interest, 6,* 1–29. doi:10.1111/j.1529-1006.2005.00020.x

Estroff, S. E., & Zimmer, C. (1994). Social networks, social support, and violence among persons with severe, persistent mental illness. In J. Monahan & H. J. Steadman (Eds.), *Violence and mental disorder: Developments in risk assessment* (pp. 259–295). Chicago, IL: University of Chicago Press.

Eule, J. (1978). The presumption of sanity: Bursting the bubble. *UCLA Law Review, 25,* 637–699.

Everington, C. T. (1990). The competence assessment for standing trial for defendants with mental retardation (CAST-MR): A validation study. *Criminal Justice and Behavior, 17,* 147–162. doi:10.1177/0093854890017002001

Evett, I. W., & Williams, R. L. (1996). A review of the sixteen points fingerprint standard in England and Wales. *Journal of Forensic Identification, 46,* 49–73.

Ewing, C. P. (1987). *Battered women who kill: Psychological self-defense as legal justification.* Lexington, MA: D. C. Heath.

Ewing, C. P. (2011). *Justice perverted: Sex offense law, psychology, and public policy.* New York, NY: Oxford University Press.

Ewing, C. P., & McCann, J. T. (2006). *Minds on trial: Great cases in law and psychology.* New York, NY: Oxford University Press.

Faigman, D. L. (1999). *Legal alchemy: The use and misuse of science in the law.* New York, NY: Freeman.

Faigman, D. L. (2004). *Laboratory of justice: The Supreme Court's 200-year struggle to integrate science and law.* New York: Henry Holt & Company.

Faigman, D. L. (2013). The Daubert revolution and the birth of modernity: Managing scientific evidence in the age of science. *UC Davis Law Review, 46,* 893–930. Retrieved from http://lawreview.law.ucdavis.edu

Faigman, D. L., & Monahan, J. (2009). Standards of legal admissibility and their implications for psychological science. In J. L. Skeem, K. S. Douglas, & S. O. Lilienfeld (Eds.), *Psychological science in the courtroom: Controversies and consensus.* New York, NY: Guilford Press.

Feldman, R. S., Forrest, J. A., & Happ, B. R. (2002). Self-presentation and verbal deception: Do self-presenters lie more? *Basic and Applied Social Psychology, 24,* 163–170. doi:10.1207/S15324834BASP2402_8

Finkel, N. J. (1995). *Commonsense justice: Jurors' notions of the law.* Cambridge, MA: Harvard University Press.

Finkel, N. J. (2000). But it's not fair! Commonsense notions of unfairness. *Psychology, Public Policy, and Law, 6,* 898–952. doi:10.1037/1076-8971.6.4.898

Finkel, N. J. (2002). *Not fair! The typology of commonsense unfairness.* Washington, DC: American Psychological Association.

Finkel, N. J. (2007). Insanity's disconnect, the law's madness, and the irresistible impulses of experts. In M. Costanzo, M. Krauss, & K. Pezdek (Eds.), *Expert psychological testimony for the courts* (pp. 177–201). Mahwah, NJ: Erlbaum.

Fisher, G. (1997). The rise of the jury as lie detector. *Yale Law Journal, 103,* 575–713.

Fisher, R. P., & Geiselman, R. E. (2010). The Cognitive Interview method of conducting police interviews: Eliciting extensive information and promoting Therapeutic Jurisprudence. *International Journal of Law and Psychiatry, 33,* 321–328. doi:10.1016/j.ijlp.2010.09.004

Fisher, R. P., & Schreiber, N. (2007). Interviewing protocols to improve eyewitness memory. In M. Toglia, R. Lindsay, D. Ross, & J. Reed (Eds.), *The handbook of eyewitness psychology: Vol. 1. Memory for events* (pp. 53–80). Mahwah, NJ: Erlbaum.

Fiske, S. T., & Glick, P. (1995). Ambivalence and stereotypes cause sexual harassment: A theory with implications for organizational change. *Journal of Social Issues, 51,* 97–115. doi:10.1111/j.1540-4560.1995.tb01311.x

Fiske, S. T., & Stevens, L. E. (1993). What's so special about sex? Gender stereotyping and discrimination. In S. Oskamp & M. Costanzo (Eds.), *Gender issues in contemporary society* (pp. 173–196). Newbury Park, CA: Sage.

Fiske, S. T., & Taylor, S. E. (2008). *Social cognition: From brains to culture.* Boston, MA: McGraw-Hill.

Fiske, S. T., & Taylor, S. E. (2013). *Social cognition: From brains to culture.* Thousand Oaks, CA: Sage.

Fitzgerald, L. F. (2004). Who says? Legal and psychological constructions of women's resistance to sexual harassment. In C. A. MacKinnon & R. B. Siegel (Eds.), *Directions in sexual harassment law* (pp. 94–110). New Haven, CT: Yale University Press.

Fitzgerald, L. F., Collinsworth, L. L., & Lawson, A. K. (2013). Sexual harassment, PTSD, and criterion A: If it walks like a duck . . . . *Psychological Injury and Law, 6,* 81–91. doi:10.1007/s12207-013-9149-8

Fitzgerald, L. F., Swan, S., & Fischer, K. (1995). Why didn't she just report him? The psychological and legal implications of women's responses to sexual harassment. *Journal of Social Issues, 51,* 117–138. doi:10.1111/j.1540-4560.1995.tb01312.x

Fitzgerald, R. J., Price, H. L., Oriet, C., & Charman, S. D. (2013). The effect of suspect-filler similarity on eyewitness identification decisions: A meta-analysis. *Psychology, Public Policy, and Law, 19,* 151–164. doi:10.1037/a0030618

Fleury-Steiner, B. (2004). *Jurors' stories of death: How America's death penalty invests in inequality.* Ann Arbor: University of Michigan Press.

Flin, R., Boone, J., Knox, A., & Bull, R. (1992). The effect of a five-month delay on children's and adults' eyewitness memory. *British Journal of Psychology, 83,* 323–336. doi:10.1111/j.2044-8295.1992.tb02444.x

Fontaine, R. G., Yang, C., Dodge, K. A., Pettit, G. A., & Bates, J. E. (2009). Development of response evaluation and decision (RED) and antisocial behavior in childhood and adolescence. *Developmental Psychology, 45,* 447–459.

Foote, W. E., & Goodman-Delahunty, J. (1999). Same-sex harassment: Implications of the Oncale decision for forensic evaluation of plaintiffs. *Behavioral Sciences & the Law, 17,* 123–139. doi:10.1002/(SICI)1099-0798(199901/03)17:1<123::AID-BSL334>3.0.CO;2-V

Foote, W. E., & Goodman-Delahunty, J. (2005). *Evaluating sexual harassment: Psychological, social, and legal considerations in forensic examinations.* Washington, DC: American Psychological Association.

Forsyth, D. R. (2006). *Group dynamics* (4th ed.). Pacific Grove, CA: Brooks/Cole.

Foster, J. K. (2008). *Memory: A very short introduction.* New York, NY: Oxford University Press.

Fox, J. A., & Levin, J. A. (2011). *Extreme killing: Understanding serial and mass murder* (2nd ed.). Thousand Oaks, CA: Sage.

Fradella, H. F., O'Neill, L., & Fogarty, A. (2004). The impact of Daubert on forensic science. *Pepperdine Law Review,*

31, 323–361. Retrieved from http://digitalcommons. pepperdine.edu/plr/

Frank, E., Carrera, J. S., Stratton, T., Bickel, J., & Nora, L. M. (2006). Experiences of belittlement and harassment and their correlates among medical students in the United States: Longitudinal survey. *BMJ, 333,* 682–684. doi:10.1136/bmj.38924.722037.7C

Frazier, P. (2003). Perceived control and distress following sexual assault: A longitudinal test of a new model. *Journal of Personality and Social Psychology, 84,* 1257–1269. doi:10.1037/0022-3514.84.6.1257

Frazier, P. A., Cochran, C. C., & Olson, A. M. (1995). Social science research on lay definitions of sexual harassment. *Journal of Social Issues, 51,* 21–39. doi:10.1111/j.1540-4560.1995.tb01306.x

Freud, S. (1959). Psychoanalysis and the ascertaining of truth in courts of law. In E. Jones (Ed.), *Collected papers of Sigmund Freud* (Vol. 2, pp. 13–24). New York, NY: Basic Books. (Original work published 1906)

Friedman, L. M. (1993). *Crime and punishment in American history.* New York, NY: Basic Books.

Fulero, S. (2004). Expert psychological testimony on the psychology of interrogations and confessions. In G. D. Lassiter (Ed.), *Interrogations, confessions, and entrapment* (pp. 247–263). New York, NY: Kluwer.

Fulero, S. M., & Finkel, N. J. (1991). Barring ultimate issue testimony: An insane rule? *Law and Human Behavior, 15,* 495–507. doi:10.1007/BF01650291

Funder, D. C. (2004). *The personality puzzle.* New York, NY: W. W. Norton.

Gaertner, S. L., Dovidio, J. D., Nier, J., Hodson, G., & Houlette, M. A. (2005). Aversive racism: Bias without intention. In L. B. Nielsen & R. L. Nelson (Eds.), *Handbook of employment discrimination research: Rights and realities* (pp. 377–393). doi:10.1007/1-4020-3455-5_19

Gallup. (2013). *Race relations.* Retrieved from http://www. gallup.com/poll/1687/race-relations.aspx

Ganis, G., Kosslyn, S., Stose, S., Thompson, W. L., & Yurgelun-Todd, D. (2003). Neural correlates of different types of deception: An fMRI investigation. *Cerebral Cortex, 13,* 830–836. doi:10.1093/cercor/13.8.830

García-Bajos, E., Migueles, M., & Aizpurua, A. (2012). Bias of script-driven processing on eyewitness memory in young and older adults. *Applied Cognitive Psychology, 26,* 737–745. doi:10.1002/acp.2854

Gardner, R. (1985). Recent trends in divorce and custody litigation. *Academy Forum, 29,* 3–7.

Garven, S., Wood, J. M., Malpass, R. S., & Shaw, J. S., III (1998). More than suggestion: The effect of interviewing techniques from the McMartin Preschool case. *Journal of Applied Psychology, 83,* 347–359. doi:10.1037/0021-9010.83.3.347

Gastil, J., Burkhalter, S., & Black, L. W. (2007). Do juries deliberate? A study of deliberation, individual difference, and group member satisfaction at a municipal courthouse. *Small Group Research, 38,* 337–359. doi:10.1177/1046496407301967

Gatowski, S. I., Dobbin, S. A., Richardson, J. T., Ginsburg, G. P., Merlino, M. L., & Dahir, V. (2001). Asking the gatekeepers: A national survey of judges on judging expert

evidence in a post-*Daubert* world. *Law and Human Behavior, 25,* 433–458. doi:10.1023/A:1012899030937

Gauld, A. (1992). *A history of hypnotism.* Cambridge, England: Cambridge University Press.

Gazzaniga, M. S. (2011). *Who's in charge? Free will and the science of the brain.* New York, NY: HarperCollins.

Georges, L. C., Wiener, R. L., & Keller, S. R. (2013). The angry juror: Sentencing decisions in first-degree murder. *Applied Cognitive Psychology, 27,* 156–166. doi:10.1002/acp.2880

Geraerts, E. (2012). Cognitive underpinnings of recovered memories of childhood abuse. In R. F. Belli (Ed.), *True and false recovered memories: Toward a reconciliation of the debate* (pp. 175–191). New York, NY: Springer Science + Business Media.

Geraerts, E., Lindsay, D. S., Merckelbach, H., Jelicic, M., Raymaekers, L., Arnold, M. M., & Schooler, J. W. (2009). Cognitive mechanisms underlying recovered memory experiences of childhood sexual abuse. *Psychological Science, 20,* 92–98. doi:10.1111/j.1467-9280.2008.02247.x

Gindes, M. (1995). Guidelines for child custody evaluations for psychologists: An overview and commentary. *Family Law Quarterly, 29,* 39–50.

Gladwell, M. (2007, November 12). Dangerous minds. *The New Yorker, 2007,* 36–46.

Glick, P., & Fiske, S. T. (2007). Sex discrimination: The psychological approach. In F. J. Crosby, M. S. Stockdale, & S. A. Ropp (Eds.), *Sex discrimination in the workplace: Multidisciplinary perspectives* (pp. 155–187). Malden, MA: Blackwell.

Goldberg, S. (1994). *Culture clash: Law and science in America.* New York, NY: NYU Press.

Golding, S. L., & Roesch, R. (1988). Competency for adjudication: An international analysis. In D. N. Weisstub (Ed.), *Law and mental health: International perspectives* (Vol. 4, pp. 73–109). Elmsford, NY: Pergamon.

Goodman-Delahunty, J. (1999). Civil law: Employment and discrimination. In R. Roesch, S. D. Hart, & J. R. P. Ogloff (Eds.), *Psychology and law: The state of the discipline* (pp. 277–337). doi:10.1007/978-1-4615-4891-1_8

Goodman-Delahunty, J., & Foote, W. (2013). Using a five-stage model to evaluate workplace discrimination injuries. *Psychological Injury and Law, 6,* 92–98. doi:10.1007/s12207-013-9154-y

Goodman, G. S. (2006). Children's eyewitness memory: A modern history and contemporary commentary. *Journal of Social Issues, 62,* 811–832. doi:10.1111/j.1540-4560.2006.00488.x

Goodman, G. S., & Melinder, A. (2007). Child witness research and forensic interviews of young children: A review. *Legal and Criminological Psychology, 12,* 1–19. doi:10.1348/135532506X156620

Goodman, G. S., & Quas, J. A. (2008). Repeated interviews and children's memory: It's more than just how many. *Current Directions in Psychological Science, 17,* 386–390. doi:10.1111/j.1467-8721.2008.00611.x

Goodman, G. S., Tobey, A., Batterman-Faunce, J., Orcutt, H., Thomas, S., Shapiro, C., & Sachsenmaier, T. (1998). Face-to-face confrontation effects of closed-circuit technology on children's eyewitness testimony and jurors' decisions. *Law and Human Behavior, 22,* 165–203. doi:10.1023/A:1025742119977

Goodrum, S., Umberson, D., & Anderson, K. (2001). The batterer's view of the self and others in domestic violence. *Sociological Inquiry, 71,* 221–240. doi:10.1111/j.1475-682X.2001.tb01109.x

Goodwin, K. A., Kukucka, J. P., & Hawks, I. M. (2013). Co-witness confidence, conformity, and eyewitness memory: An examination of normative and informational social influences. *Applied Cognitive Psychology, 27,* 91–100. doi:10.1002/acp.2877

Gookin, K. (2007, August). *Comparison of state laws authorizing involuntary commitment of sexually violent predators: 2006 update, revised* (Report ID 07-08-1101). Olympia: Washington State Institute for Public Policy. Retrieved from http://www.wsipp.wa.gov/rptfiles/07-08-1101.pdf

Gowensmith, W. N., Murrie, D. C., & Boccaccini, M. T. (2012). Field reliability of competence to stand trial opinions: How often do evaluators agree, and what do judges decide when evaluators disagree? *Law and Human Behavior, 36,* 130–139. doi:10.1037/h0093958

Gowensmith, W. N., Murrie, D. C., & Boccaccini, M. T. (2013). How reliable are forensic evaluations of legal sanity? *Law and Human Behavior, 37,* 98–106. doi:10.1037/lhb0000001

Greathouse, S. M., Levett, L. M., & Kovera, M. (2009). Sexual harassment: Antecedents, consequences, and juror decisions. In D. Krauss & J. Lieberman (Eds.), *Psychological expertise in court* (pp. 151–174). London, England: Ashgate.

Greenberg, J. (2010). Organizational injustice as a health risk. *Academy of Management Annals, 4,* 205–243. doi:10.1080/19416520.2010.481174

Greenberg, J., & Alge, B. J. (1998). Aggressive reactions to workplace injustice. In R. W. Griffin, A. O'Leary-Kelly, & J. M. Collins (Eds.), *Dysfunctional behavior in organizations: Pt. A. Violent and deviant behavior* (pp. 83–117). Greenwich, CT: JAI Press.

Greene, E., & Cahill, B. S. (2012). Effects of neuroimaging evidence on mock juror decision making. *Behavioral Sciences & the Law, 30,* 280–296. doi:10.1002/bsl.1993

Greene, J., & Cohen, J. (2004). For the law, neuroscience changes nothing and everything. *Philosophical Transactions of the Royal Society of London B, 359,* 1775–1785. doi:10.1098/rstb.2004.1546

Greenwood, P. W., Rydell, C. P., Abrahamse, A. F., Caulkins, J. P., Chiesa, J., Model, K. E., & Klein, S. P. (1994). *Three strikes and you're out: Estimated benefits and costs of California's new mandatory-sentencing law.* Santa Monica, CA: Rand.

Gregoriou, C. (2011). *Language, ideology and identity in serial killer narratives.* New York, NY: Taylor & Francis.

Grier, W. H., & Cobbs, P. M. (1968). *Black rage.* New York, NY: Basic Books.

Griffin, P., Addie, S., Adams, B., & Firestine, K. (2011). *Trying juveniles as adults: An analysis of state transfer laws and reporting. National Report Series Bulletin* (NCJ 232434). Washington, DC: Bureau of Justice Statistics. Retrieved from: https://www.ncjrs.gov/pdffiles1/ojjdp/232434.pdf

Grisso, T. (1991). A developmental history of the American Psychology-Law Society. *Law and Human Behavior, 15,* 213–232.

Grisso, T., & Saks, M. J. (1991). Psychology's influence on constitutional interpretation: A comment on how to succeed. *Law and Human Behavior, 15,* 371–398. doi:10.1007/BF01044618

Grisso, T., Steinberg, L., Woolard, J., Cauffman, E., Scott, E., Graham, S., . . . Schwartz, R. (2003). Juveniles' competence to stand trial: A comparison of adolescents' and adults' capacities as trial defendants. *Law and Human Behavior, 27,* 333–363. doi:10.1023/A:1024065015717

Gross, S. (1996). The risks of death: Why erroneous convictions are common in capital cases. *Buffalo Law Review, 44,* 469–500.

Grove, W. M., & Meehl, P. E. (1996). Comparative efficiency of informal (subjective, impressionistic) and formal (mechanical, algorithmic) prediction procedures: The clinical-statistical controversy. *Psychology, Public Policy, and Law, 2,* 293–323. doi:10.1037/1076-8971.2.2.293

Grubb, A., & Turner, E. (2012). Attribution of blame in rape cases: A review of the impact of rape myth acceptance, gender role conformity and substance use on victim blaming. *Aggression and Violent Behavior, 17,* 443–452. doi:10.1016/j.avb.2012.06.002

Gudjonsson, G. H. (2003). *The psychology of interrogations, confessions, and testimony.* Chichester, West Sussex, England: Wiley.

Gudjonsson, G. H., Sigurdsson, J. F., & Einarsson, E. (2004). The role of personality in relation to confessions and denials. *Psychology, Crime & Law, 10,* 125–135. doi:10.1080/10683160310001634296

Gutek, B. A. (1993). Responses to sexual harassment. In M. Costanzo & S. Oskamp (Eds.), *Gender issues in contemporary society* (pp. 197–216). Newbury Park, CA: Sage.

Gutek, B. A. (2007a). Commentary on research relevant to sex discrimination and sexual harassment. In E. Borgida & S. Fiske (Eds.), *Beyond common sense: Psychological science in the courtroom* (pp. 327–339). doi:10.1002/9780470696422.ch17

Gutek, B. A. (2007b). My experience as an expert witness in sex discrimination and sexual harassment litigation. In F. J. Crosby, M. S. Stockdale, & S. A. Ropp (Eds.), *Sex discrimination in the workplace: Multidisciplinary perspectives* (pp. 131–142). Oxford, UK: Blackwell.

Gutek, B. A., & O'Connor, M. (1995). The empirical basis for the reasonable woman standard. *Journal of Social Issues, 51,* 151–166. doi:10.1111/j.1540-4560.1995.tb01314.x

Guthrie, C., Rachlinski, J. J., & Wistrich, A. J. (2001). Inside the judicial mind. *Cornell Law Review, 86,* 777–830.

Guy, L. S., & Edens, J. F. (2003). Juror decision-making in a mock sexually violent predator trial: Gender differences in the impact of divergent types of expert testimony. *Behavioral Science and the Law, 21,* 215–237. doi:10.1002/bsl.529

Haber, L., & Haber, R. N. (2008). Scientific validation of fingerprint evidence under *Daubert. Law, Probability & Risk, 7,* 87–109. doi:10.1093/lpr/mgm020

Haber, R. N., & Haber, L. (2013). The culture of science: Bias and forensic evidence. *Journal of Applied Research in Memory and Cognition, 2,* 50–52. doi:10.1016/j.jarmac.2013.01.005

Hafemeister, T. L., & Melton, G. B. (1987). The impact of social science research on the judiciary. In G. B. Melton

(Ed.), *Reforming the law: Impact of child development research* (pp. 27–59). New York, NY: Guilford Press.

Hafer, C. L. (2000). Do innocent victims threaten the belief in a just world? Evidence from a modified Stroop task. *Journal of Personality and Social Psychology, 79,* 165–173. doi:10.1037/0022-3514.79.2.165

Hagen, M. (1997). *Whores of the court.* New York, NY: Harper-Collins.

Hall, T. A., Cook, N. E., & Berman, G. L. (2010). Navigating the expanding field of law and psychology: A comprehensive guide to graduate education. *Journal of Forensic Psychology Practice, 10,* 69–90. doi:10.1080/15228930903446690

Hammett, T. M. (2006). HIV/AIDS and other infectious diseases among correctional inmates: Transmission, burden, and an appropriate response. *American Journal of Public Health, 96,* 974–998. doi:10.2105/AJPH.2005.066993

Hammond, L., & Youngs, D. (2011). Decay functions and criminal spatial processes: Geographical offender profiling of volume crime. *Journal of Investigative Psychology and Offender Profiling, 8,* 90–102. doi:10.1002/jip.132

Haney, C. (1981). Psychology and legal change: On the limits of a factual jurisprudence. *Law and Human Behavior, 4,* 147–199. doi:10.1007/BF01040317

Haney, C. (2006). *Reforming punishment: Psychological limits to the pains of imprisonment.* Washington, DC: American Psychological Association.

Haney, C., Banks, W., & Zimbardo, P. (1973). Interpersonal dynamics in a simulated prison. *International Journal of Criminology and Penology, 1,* 69–97.

Haney, C., Sontag, L., & Costanzo, S. (1994). Deciding to take a life: Capital juries, sentencing instructions and the jurisprudence of death. *Journal of Social Issues, 50,* 149–176. doi:10.1111/j.1540-4560.1994.tb02414.x

Hannaford-Agor, P., & Hans, V. P. (2003). Nullification at work? A glimpse from the National Center for State Courts study of hung juries. *Chicago-Kent Law Review, 78,* 1249–1277. Retrieved from http://scholarship.kentlaw.iit.edu/cklawreview/

Hans, V. P. (1992). Jury decision making. In D. K. Kagehiro & W. S. Laufer (Eds.), *Handbook of psychology and law* (pp. 56–76). New York, NY: Springer.

Hans, V. P. (2000). *Business on trial: The civil jury and corporate responsibility.* New Haven, CT: Yale University Press.

Hans, V. P., Dann, B. M., Kaye, D. H., Farley, E. J., & Albertson, S. (2005). Testing jury reforms. *Delaware Lawyer, 23,* 34–36. Retrieved from http://www.delawarebarfoundation.org/delaware-lawyer-publication/

Hans, V. P., & Jehle, A. (2003) Avoid bald men and people with green socks—Other ways to improve the voir dire process in jury selection. *Chicago-Kent Law Review, 78,* 1179–1201. Retrieved from http://scholarship.kentlaw.iit.edu/cklawreview/

Hans, V. P., Kaye, D. H., Dann, B., Farley, E. J., & Albertson, S. (2011). Science in the jury box: Jurors' comprehension of mitochondrial DNA evidence. *Law and Human Behavior, 35,* 60–71. doi:10.1007/s10979-010-9222-8

Hans, V. P., & Lofquist, W. S. (1994). Perceptions of civil justice: The litigation crisis attitudes of civil jurors. *Behavioral Sciences & the Law, 12,* 181–196. doi:10.1002/bsl.2370120207

Hans, V. P., & Vidmar, N. (1986). *Judging the jury.* New York, NY: Plenum.

Hanson, R. K., & Morton-Bourgon, K. (2009). The accuracy of recidivism risk assessments for sex offenders: A meta-analysis of 118 prediction studies. *Psychological Assessment, 21,* 1–21. doi:10.1037/a0014421

Hanson, R. K., & Thornton, D. (2000). Improving risk assessment for sex offenders: A comparison of three actuarial scales. *Law and Human Behavior, 24,* 119–136. doi:10.1023/A:1005482921333

Harris, G. T., & Rice, M. E. (1997). Mentally disordered offenders: What research says about effective service. In C. D. Webster & M. A. Jackson (Eds.), *Impulsivity: Theory, assessment, and treatment* (pp. 361–393). New York, NY: Guilford Press.

Harris, S. (2012). *Free will.* New York, NY: Simon & Schuster.

Hart, S. D., & Cooke, D. J. (2013). Another look at the (Im-) precision of individual risk estimates made using actuarial risk assessment instruments. *Behavioral Sciences & the Law, 31,* 81–102. doi:10.1002/bsl.2049

Hartfield, L. C. (2002, November). Daubert/Kumho challenges to handwriting analysis. *The Champion, 2002,* 24–36. Retrieved from http://www.nacdl.org/Champion IssuesList.aspx

Hastie, R. (1993). Algebraic models of juror decision processes. In R. Hastie (Ed.), *Inside the juror: The psychology of juror decision making* (pp. 84–115). Cambridge, MA: Cambridge University Press.

Hastie, R., Penrod, S. D., & Pennington, N. (1983). *Inside the jury.* Cambridge, MA: Harvard University Press.

Hayes, R., Barnett, M., Sullivan, D. H., Nielssen, O., Large, M., & Brown, C. (2009). Justifications and rationalizations for the civil commitment of sex offenders. *Psychiatry, Psychology and Law, 16,* 141–149. doi:10.1080/13218710802227020

Heilbrun, K. (1997). Prediction versus management models relevant to risk assessment: The importance of legal decision-making context. *Law and Human Behavior, 21,* 347–359. doi:10.1023/A:1024851017947

Heilbrun, K., Douglas, K. S., & Yasuhara, K. (2009). Violence risk assessments: Core controversies. In J. L. Skeem, K. S. Douglas, & S. O. Lilienfeld (Eds.), *Psychological science in the courtroom: Controversies and consensus* (pp. 333–357). New York, NY: Guilford Press.

Heilbrun, K., & Peters, L. (2000). Community-based treatment programmes. In S. Hodgins & R. Müller-Isberner (Eds.), *Violence, crime and mentally disordered offenders: Concepts and methods for effective treatment and prevention* (pp. 193–215). Chichester, UK: Wiley.

Henderson, M., & Hewstone, M. (1984). Prison inmates' explanations for interpersonal violence: Accounts and attributions. *Journal of Consulting and Clinical Psychology, 52,* 789–794. doi:10.1037/0022-006X.52.5.789

Henig, R. (2006, February 5). The new science of lying. *The New York Times Magazine,* pp. 1–12.

Henrichson, C., & Delaney, R. (2012). *The price of prisons: What incarceration costs taxpayers.* New York, NY: Vera Institute of Justice. Retrieved from http://www.vera.org/pubs/special/price-prisons-what-incarceration-costs-taxpayers

Hetherington, E. M., & Kelley, J. (2003). *For better or for worse: Divorce reconsidered.* New York, NY: W. W. Norton.

Heuer, L., & Penrod, S. (1989). Instructing jurors: A field experiment with written and preliminary instructions. *Law and Human Behavior, 13,* 409–430. doi:10.1007/BF01056412

Heuer, L., & Penrod, S. D. (1994). Trial complexity: A field investigation of its meaning and effects. *Law and Human Behavior, 18,* 29–51. doi:10.1007/BF01499142

Hickey, E. W., & Harris, B. R. (2013). Serial killing. In J. A. Siegel & P. J. Saukko (Eds.), *Encyclopedia of forensic sciences* (2nd ed., Vol. 3, pp. 197–201). London, England: Elsevier.

Hicks, S. J., & Sales, B. D. (2006). *Criminal profiling: Developing an effective science and practice.* Washington, DC: American Psychological Association.

Hodell, E. C., Dunlap, E. E., Wasarhaley, N. E., & Golding, J. M. (2012). Factors impacting juror perceptions of battered women who kill their abusers: Delay and sleeping status. *Psychology, Public Policy, and Law, 18,* 338–359. doi:10.1037/a0025145

Hodgins, S., Tengström, A., Eriksson, A., Österman, R., Kronstrand, R., Eaves, D., . . . Vartiainen, H. (2007). A multisite study of community treatment programs for mentally ill offenders with major mental disorders: Design, measures, and the forensic sample. *Criminal Justice and Behavior, 34,* 211–228. doi:10.1177/0093854806291248

Hofstede, G. (1991). *Culture and organizations.* London, England: McGraw-Hill.

Hoge, S. K., Bonnie, R. J., Poythress, N., Monahan, J., Eisenberg, M., & Feucht-Haviar, T. (1997). The MacArthur adjudicative competence study: Development and validation of a research instrument. *Law and Human Behavior, 21,* 141–179. doi:10.1023/A:1024826312495

Holmes, D. S. (1990). The evidence for repression: An examination of sixty years of research. In J. L. Singer (Ed.), *Repression and dissociation: Implications for personality theory, psychopathology, and health* (pp. 85–102). Chicago, IL: University of Chicago Press.

Holmes, O. W. (1881). *The common law.* Boston, MA: Little, Brown.

Holmes, O. W. (1897). The path of law. *Harvard Law Review, 10,* 457–471.

Holmes, R. M., & Holmes, S. T. (2010). *Serial murder* (4th ed.). Thousand Oaks, CA: Sage.

Holst, V. F., & Pezdek, K. (1992). Scripts for typical crimes and their effects on memory for eyewitness testimony. *Applied Cognitive Psychology, 6,* 573–587. doi:10.1002/acp.2350060702

Holtzworth-Munroe, A., Meehan, J. C., Herron, K., Rehman, U., & Stuart, G. L. (2000). Testing the Holtzworth-Munroe and Stuart (1994) batterer typology. *Journal of Consulting and Clinical Psychology, 68,* 1000–1019. doi:10.1037/0022-006X.68.6.1000

Holtzworth-Munroe, A., & Stuart, G. L. (1994). Typologies of male batterers: Three subtypes and the differences among them. *Psychological Bulletin, 116,* 476–497. doi:10.1037/0033-2909.116.3.476

Honts, C. R. (1995). The polygraph in 1995: Progress in science and the law. *North Dakota Law Review, 17,* 987–1020.

Honts, C. R., Raskin, D., & Kircher, J. (1994). Mental and physical countermeasures reduce the accuracy of polygraph tests. *Journal of Applied Psychology, 79,* 252–259. doi:10.1037/0021-9010.79.2.252

Horowitz, I. A. (1988). Jury nullification: The impact of judicial instructions, arguments, and challenges on jury decision making. *Law and Human Behavior, 12,* 439–453. doi:10.1007/BF01044627

Horowitz, I. A. (2008). Jury nullification: An empirical perspective. *Northern Illinois University Law Review, 28,* 425–452. Retrieved from http://www.niu.edu/law/organizations/law_review/index.shtml

Horowitz, I. A., Kerr, N. L., & Niedermeier, K. E. (2001). Jury nullification: Legal and psychological perspectives. *Brooklyn Law Review, 66,* 1207–1249.

Horowitz, S. W., Kircher, J. C., Honts, C. R., & Raskin, D. C. (1997). The role of comparison questions in physiological detection of deception. *Psychophysiology, 34,* 108–115. doi:10.1111/j.1469-8986.1997.tb02421.x

Horwitz, S., & Ruane, M. E. (2003). *Sniper: Inside the hunt for the killers who terrorized the nation.* New York, NY: Random House.

Houck, M. M., & Budowle, B. (2002). Correlation of microscopic and mitochondrial DNA hair comparisons. *Journal of Forensic Sciences, 47,* 1–4. doi:10.1520/JFS15515J

Houck, M. M., & Siegel, J. A. (2010). *Fundamentals of forensic science.* Burlington, MA: Elsevier.

Hubler, S. (1998, November 19). When a justice system stumbles. *Los Angeles Times,* p. E1.

Human Rights Watch (2005). *CIA whitewashing torture: Statements by Goss contradict U.S. law and practice.* Retrieved from http://www.hrw.org/news/2005/11/20/cia-whitewashing-torture

Hungerford, A. (2005). The use of anatomically detailed dolls in forensic investigations: Developmental considerations. *Journal of Forensic Psychology Practice, 5,* 75–87. doi:10.1300/J158v05n01_05

Huntley, J. E., & Costanzo, M. (2003). Sexual harassment stories. Testing a story-mediated model of juror decision-making in civil litigation. *Law and Human Behavior, 27,* 29–51. doi:10.1023/A:1021674811225

Huss, M. T., & Ralston, A. (2008). Do batterer subtypes actually matter? Treatment completion, treatment response, and recidivism across a batterer typology. *Criminal Justice and Behavior, 35,* 710–724. doi:10.1177/0093854808316218

Hyman, I. E., Jr., Husband, T. H., & Billings, F. J. (1995). False memories of childhood experiences. *Applied Cognitive Psychology, 9,* 181–197. doi:10.1002/acp.2350090302

Iacono, W. G. (2008). Effective policing: Understanding how polygraph tests work and are used. *Criminal Justice and Behavior, 35,* 1295–1308. doi:10.1177/0093854808321529

Iacono, W. G., & Patrick, C. J. (1999). Polygraph (lie detector) testing: The state of the art. In I. B. Weiner & A. K. Hess (Eds.), *The handbook of forensic psychology* (2nd ed., pp. 440–473). New York, NY: Wiley.

Inbau, F. E., Reid, J. E., Buckley, J. P., & Jayne, B. C. (2013). *Criminal interrogation and confessions.* Burlington, MA: Jones and Bartlett.

Innes, C. A. (2010). The simple solution for reducing correctional costs. *Corrections Today, 72,* 31–35. Retrieved from https://www.aca.org/publications/ctmagazine.asp

Innocence Project (2013). Retrieved from http://www.innocenceproject.org

Innocence Project. (n.d.). *The innocent and the death penalty.* http://www.innocenceproject.org/Content/The_Innocent_and_the_Death_Penalty.php

International Association for Identification (IAI). (1999). Resolution vii. *Identification News, 29,* 2–3.

International Committee of the Red Cross. (1995). *The Geneva Conventions of 1949 and their additional protocols.* Geneva, Switzerland: Author. Retrieved from http://www.icrc.org/eng/resources/documents/publication/p0173.htm

Irving, B., & McKenzie, I. K. (1989). *Police interrogation: The effects of the Police and Criminal Evidence Act, 1984.* London, England: Police Foundation.

Jackson, L. A. (1989). Relative deprivation and the gender wage gap. *Journal of Social Issues, 45,* 117–133. doi:10.1111/j.1540-4560.1989.tb02363.x

Jackson, R. L., Rogers, R., & Sewell, K. W. (2005). Forensic applications of the Miller Forensic Assessment of Symptoms Test (MFAST): Screening for feigned disorders in competency to stand trial evaluations. *Law and Human Behavior, 2,* 199–210. doi:10.1007/s10979-005-2193-5

Jacob Wetterling Crimes Against Children and Sexually Violent Offender Registration Act, Pub. L. 103-322, title XVII, subtitle A, § 170101 et seq., 108 Stat. 2038, 42 U.S.C. § 14071 et seq. (1994.)

Jacobs, D., Qian, Z., Carmichael, J. T., & Kent, S. L. (2007). Who survives on death row? An individual and contextual analysis. *American Sociological Review, 72,* 610–632. doi:10.1177/000312240707200406

Jacobs, J. B. (1983). *New perspectives on prisons and imprisonment.* Ithaca, NY: Cornell University Press.

Jagsi, R., Griffith, K., Stewart, A., Sambuco, D., DeCastro, R., & Ubel, P. A. (2012). Gender differences in the salaries of physician researchers. *Journal of the American Medical Association, 307,* 2410–2417. doi:10.1001/jama.2012.6183

James, W. (1907). *Pragmatism.* New York, NY: Longmans, Green.

Janofsky, M. (1998, June 5). Maryland troopers stop drivers by race, suit says. *The New York Times,* p. A10.

Jeffreys, A. J. (1993). Hypervariable minisatellite regions in human DNA. *American Journal of Human Genetics, 53,* 1–5. doi:10.1038/314067a0

Jobes, D. A., Casey, J. O., Berman, A. L., & Wright, M. (1991). Empirical criteria for the determination of suicide and manner of death. *Journal of Forensic Sciences, 36,* 244–256. doi:10.1520/JFS13025J

Johnson, B. D., & Dipietro, S. M. (2012). The power of diversion: Intermediate sanctions and sentencing disparity under presumptive guidelines. *Criminology, 50,* 811–850. doi:10.1111/j.1745-9125.2012.00279.x

Johnson, C., & Haney, C. (1994). Felony voir dire: An exploratory study of its content and effects. *Law and Human Behavior, 18,* 487–507. doi:10.1007/BF01499170

Johnson, D. T., & Zimring, F. E. (2009). *The next frontier: National development, political change, and the death penalty in Asia.* Oxford, UK: Oxford University Press.

Johnson, R. (1996). *Hard time: Understanding and reforming the prison.* Belmont, CA: Wadsworth.

Joint Resolution Regarding the Implementation of the Policy of the United States Government in Opposition to the Practice of Torture by any Foreign Government. 98 Stat. 1721 (1984).

Jones, E., Williams, K., & Brewer, N. (2008). "I had a confidence epiphany!" Obstacles to combating post-identification confidence inflation. *Law and Human Behavior, 32,* 164–176. doi:10.1007/s10979-007-9101-0

Jones, J. M. (2013, October 29). *U.S. death penalty support lowest in more than 40 years.* Retrieved from http://www.gallup.com/poll/165626/death-penalty-support-lowest-years.aspx

Judicial Committee on Model Jury Instructions for the Eighth Circuit. (2013). *Manual of model criminal jury instructions.* Retrieved from http://juryinstructions.ca8.uscourts.gov/crim_manual_2013_redo.pdf

Kahneman, D. (2011). *Thinking, fast and slow.* New York, NY: Farrar, Straus and Giroux.

Kaiser, C. R., & Major, B. (2006). A social psychological perspective on perceiving and reporting discrimination. *Law & Social Inquiry, 31,* 801–830. doi:10.1111/j.1747-4469.2006.00036.x

Kalven, H., & Zeisel, H. (1966). *The American jury.* Boston, MA: Little, Brown.

Kane, A. W., & Dvoskin, J. A. (2011). *Evaluation for personal injury claims.* New York, NY: Oxford University Press.

Karlinsky, N., & Burke, M. (2006, August 30). *Does Karr believe he did it? The truth in John Mark Karr's false confession.* Retrieved from http://abcnews.go.com/US/Legal Center/story?id=2372612&page=1

Kassin, S. M. (1998). Eyewitness identification procedures: The fifth rule. *Law and Human Behavior, 22,* 649–653. doi:10.1023/A:1025702722645

Kassin, S. M. (2008). False confessions: Causes, consequences, and implications for reform. *Current Directions in Psychological Science, 17,* 24–43. doi:10.1111/j.1467-8721.2008.00584.x

Kassin, S. M. (2012). Why confessions trump innocence. *American Psychologist, 67,* 431–445. doi:10.1037/a0028212

Kassin, S. M., Drizin, S. A., Grisso, T., Gudjonsson, G. H., Leo, R. A., & Redlich, A. D. (2010). Police-induced confessions: Risk factors and recommendations. *Law and Human Behavior, 34,* 49–52. doi:10.1007/s10979-009-9188-6

Kassin, S. M., & Fong, C. T. (1999). "I'm innocent!" Effects of training on judgments of truth and deception in the interrogation room. *Law and Human Behavior, 23,* 499–516. doi:10.1023/A:1022330011811

Kassin, S. M., & Gudjonsson, G. H. (2004). The psychology of confessions: A review of the literature and issues. *Psychological Science in the Public Interest, 5,* 33–67. doi:10.1111/j.1529-1006.2004.00016.x

Kassin, S. M., Leo, R. A., Meissner, C. A., Richman, K. D., Colwell, L. H., Leach, A.-M., & La Fon, D. (2007). Police interviewing and interrogation: A self-report survey of police practices and beliefs. *Law and Human Behavior, 31,* 381–400. doi:10.1007/s10979-006-9073-5

Kassin, S. M., Meissner, C., & Norwick, R. J. (2005). "I'd know a false confession if I saw one": A comparative study of college students and police investigators. *Law and Human Behavior, 29,* 211–228. doi:10.1007/s10979-005-2416-9

Kassin, S. M., & Neumann, K. (1997). On the power of confession evidence: An experimental test of the fundamental difference hypothesis. *Law and Human Behavior, 21,* 469–484. doi:10.1023/A:1024871622490

Kassin, S. M., & Norwick, R. J. (2004). Why people waive their Miranda rights. *Law and Human Behavior, 28,* 211–221. doi:10.1023/B:LAHU.0000022323.74584.f5

Kassin, S. M., & Sukel, H. (1997). Coerced confessions and the jury: An experimental test of the harmless error rule. *Law and Human Behavior, 21,* 27–46. doi:10.1023/A:1024814009769

Kassin, S. M., Smith, V. L., & Tulloch, W. F. (1990). The dynamite charge: Effects on the perception and deliberation behavior of mock jurors. *Law and Human Behavior, 14,* 537–550. doi:10.1007/BF01044880

Kebbell, M. R., & Wagstaff, G. F. (1998). Hypnotic interviewing: The best way to interview witnesses? *Behavioral Sciences & the Law, 16,* 115–129. doi:10.1002/(SICI)1099-0798(199824)16:1<115::AID-BSL296>3.0.CO;2-I

Kelly, D. J., Quinn, P. C., Slater, A. M., Lee, K., Ge, L., & Pascalis, O. (2007). The other-race effect develops during infancy. *Psychological Science, 18,* 1084–1090. doi:10.1111/j.1467-9280.2007.02029.x

Kelly, J. B., & Emery, R. E. (2003). Children's adjustment following divorce: Risk and resilience perspectives. *Family Relations: An Interdisciplinary Journal of Applied Family Studies, 52,* 352–362. doi:10.1111/j.1741-3729.2003.00352.x

Kennedy, M. A. (2009). Psychological syndrome evidence. In D. Canter (Series Ed.) & D. Krauss & J. Lieberman (Vol. Eds.), *Psychology, crime, & law: Vol. 2. Psychological expertise in court* (pp. 103–121). Burlington, VT: Ashgate.

Kerr, N. L., Hymes, R. W., Anderson, A. B., & Weathers, J. E. (1995). Defendant-juror similarity and mock juror judgments. *Law and Human Behavior, 19,* 545–568. doi:10.1007/BF01499374

Kerr, N. L., & MacCoun, R. J. (2012). Is the leniency asymmetry really dead? Misinterpreting asymmetry effects in criminal jury deliberation. *Group Processes & Intergroup Relations, 15,* 585–602. doi:10.1177/1368430212441639

Kerr, N. L., Niedermeier, K. E., & Kaplan, M. F. (1999). Bias in jurors versus bias in juries: New evidence from the SDS perspective. *Organizational Behavior and Human Decision Processes, 80,* 70–86. doi:10.1006/obhd.1999.2855

Kersten, A. W., Earles, J. L., & Upshaw, C. (2013). False recollection of the role played by an actor in an event. *Memory & Cognition, 41,* 1144–1158. doi:10.3758/s13421-013-0334-5

Kim, Y. S., Barak, G., & Shelton, D. E. (2009). Examining the "CSI-effect" in the cases of circumstantial evidence and eyewitness testimony: Multivariate and path analyses. *Journal of Criminal Justice, 37,* 452–460. doi:10.1016/j.jcrimjus.2009.07.005

King, N. J. (2000). The American criminal jury. In N. Vidmar (Ed.), *World jury systems* (pp. 93–124). Oxford, England: Oxford University Press.

Kircher, J. C., Horowitz, S. W., & Raskin, D. C. (1988). Meta-analysis of mock crime studies of the control question polygraph technique. *Law and Human Behavior, 12,* 79–90. doi:10.1007/BF01064275

Kirk, P. L. (1953). *Crime investigation: Physical evidence and the police laboratory.* New York, NY: Interscience.

Kitzmann, K. M., Parra, G. R., & Jobe-Shields, L. (2012). A review of programs designed to prepare parents for custody and visitation mediation. *Family Court Review, 50,* 128–136. doi:10.1111/j.1744-1617.2011.01434.x

Knapp, M., & Hall, J. (2007). *Nonverbal communication in human interaction.* New York, NY: Wadsworth.

Koch, C. (2012). Finding free will. *Scientific American Mind, 23,* 22–27. doi:10.1038/scientificamericanmind0512-22

Kocsis, R. N. (2004). Psychological profiling of serial arson offenses: An assessment of skills and accuracy. *Criminal Justice and Behavior, 31,* 341–361. doi:10.1177/0093854803262586

Kocsis, R. N. (2005). An empirical assessment of content in criminal psychological profiles. *International Journal of Offender Therapy and Comparative Criminology, 47,* 38–47. doi:10.1177/0306624X02239273

Kocsis, R. N. (2013). The criminal profiling reality: What is actually behind the smoke and mirrors? *Journal of Forensic Psychology Practice, 13,* 79–91. doi:10.1080/15228932.2013.765733

Kocsis, R. N., Hayes, A. F., & Irwin, H. J. (2002). Investigative experience and accuracy in psychological profiling of a violent crime. *Journal of Interpersonal Crime, 17,* 811–823. doi:10.1177/0886260502017008001

Kocsis, R. N., Irwin, H. J., Hayes, A. F., & Nunn, R. (2000). Expertise in psychological profiling: A comparative assessment. *Journal of Interpersonal Violence, 15,* 311–331. doi:10.1177/088626000015003006

Koehler, J. J. (2001). When are people persuaded by DNA match statistics? *Law and Human Behavior, 25,* 493–513. doi:10.1023/A:1012892815916

Koehler, J. J., & Macchi, L. (2004). Thinking about low-probability events. *Psychological Science, 15,* 540–546. doi:10.1111/j.0956-7976.2004.00716.x

Koehler, J. J., & Saks, M. J. (2010). Individualization claims in forensic science: Still unwarranted. *Brooklyn Law Review, 75,* 1187–1208. Retrieved from http://www.brooklaw.edu/intellectuallife/lawjournals/brooklynlawreview/generalinformation.aspx?

Kolata, G., & Peterson, I. (2001, July 21). New way to insure eyewitnesses can ID the right bad guy. *The New York Times,* p. A1.

Konečni, V. J., & Ebbesen, E. B. (1982). An analysis of the sentencing system. In V. J. Konečni & E. B. Ebbesen (Eds.), *The criminal justice system: A social-psychological approach* (pp. 293–332). San Francisco, CA: Freeman.

Koss, M. P., & Harvey, M. R. (1991). *The rape victim: Clinical and community interventions.* Thousand Oaks, CA: Sage.

Koss, M. P., & White, J. W. (2008). National and global agendas on violence against women: Historical perspective and consensus. *American Journal of Orthopsychiatry, 78,* 386–394. doi:10.1037/a0014347

Koutstaal, W., Schacter, D. L., Johnson, M. K., & Gallucio, L. (1999). Facilitation and impairment of event memory produced by photograph review. *Memory and Cognition, 27,* 478–493. doi:10.3758/BF03211542

Kovera, M. B. (2002). The effects of pretrial publicity on juror decisions: An examination of moderators and mediating mechanisms. *Law and Human Behavior, 26,* 43–72. doi:10.1023/A:1013829224920

Kovera, M. B., Gresham, A. W., Borgida, E., Gray, E., & Regan, P. C. (1997). Does expert psychological testimony inform or influence juror decision making? A social cognitive analysis. *Journal of Applied Psychology, 82,* 178–192. doi:10.1037/0021-9010.82.1.178

Kovera, M. B., & McAuliff, B. D. (2000). The effects of peer review and evidence quality on judge evaluations of psychological science: Are judges effective gatekeepers? *Journal of Applied Psychology, 85,* 574–586. doi:10.1037/0021-9010.85.4.574

Kozel, F., Padget, T., & George, M. (2004). A replication study of the neural correlates of deception. *Behavioral Neuroscience, 118,* 852–856. doi:10.1037/0735-7044.118.4.852

Kramer, G. P., Kerr, N. L., & Carroll, J. S. (1990). Pretrial publicity, judicial remedies, and jury bias. *Law and Human Behavior, 14,* 409–438. doi:10.1007/BF01044220

Krauss, D. A., & Lee, D. H. (2003). Deliberating on dangerousness and death: Jurors' ability to differentiate between expert actuarial and clinical predictions of dangerousness. *International Journal of Law and Psychiatry, 26,* 113–137. doi:10.1016/S0160-2527(02)00211-X

Krauss, D. A., McCabe, J. G., & Lieberman, J. D. (2012). Dangerously misunderstood: Representative jurors' reactions to expert testimony on future dangerousness in a sexually violent predator trial. *Psychology, Public Policy, and Law, 18,* 18–49. doi:10.1037/a0024550

Krauss, D. A., & Sales, B. D. (2000). Legal standards, expertise, and experts in the resolution of contested child custody cases. *Psychology, Public Policy, and Law, 6,* 843–879. doi:10.1037/1076-8971.6.4.843

Krauss, D. A., & Sales, B. D. (2001). The effects of clinical and scientific expert testimony on juror decision making in capital sentencing. *Psychology, Public Policy, and Law, 7,* 267–310. doi:10.1037/1076-8971.7.2.267

Krauss, D. A., & Scurich, N. (2013). Risk assessment in the law: Legal admissibility, scientific validity, and some disparities between research and practice. *Behavioral Sciences & The Law, 31,* 215–229. doi:10.1002/bsl.2065

Kravitz, D. A., Cutler, B. L., & Brock, P. (1993). Reliability and validity of the original and revised Legal Attitudes Questionnaire. *Law and Human Behavior, 17,* 661–677. doi:10.1007/BF01044688

Kressel, N. J., & Kressel, D. F. (2002). *Stack and sway: The new science of jury consulting.* Boulder, CO: Westview Press.

Krieger, L. H., & Fiske, S. T. (2006). Behavioral realism in employment discrimination law: Implicit bias and disparate treatment. *California Law Review, 94,* 997–1031. Retrieved from http://scholarship.law.berkeley.edu/californialawreview

Krings, F., & Facchin, S. (2009). Organization justice and men's likelihood to sexually harass: The moderating role of sexism and personality. *Journal of Applied Psychology, 94,* 501–510. doi:10.1037/a0013391

Krug, K. (2007). The relationship between confidence and accuracy: Current thoughts on the literature and a new area of research. *Applied Psychology in Criminal Justice, 3,* 6–35. Retrieved from http://www.apcj.org/journal/

Kruh, I., & Grisso, T. (2009). *Evaluation of juveniles' competence to stand trial.* New York, NY: Oxford University Press.

Kulik, C. T., Perry, E. L., & Pepper, M. B. (2003). Here comes the judge: The influence of judge personal characteristics on federal sexual harassment case outcomes. *Law and Human Behavior, 27,* 69–86. doi:10.1023/A:1021678912133

La Fond, J. Q. (1998). The costs of enacting sexually violent predator laws. *Psychology, Public Policy, and Law, 4,* 468–503. doi:10.1037/1076-8971.4.1-2.468

La Fond, J. Q. (2005). *Preventing sexual violence: How society should cope with sex offenders.* Washington, DC: American Psychological Association.

La Fond, J. Q. (2008). Sexually violent predator laws and the liberal state: An ominous threat to individual liberty. *International Journal of Law and Psychiatry, 31,* 158–171. doi:10.1016/j.ijlp.2008.02.005

Lally, S. J. (2003). What tests are acceptable for use in forensic evaluations? A survey of experts. *Professional Psychology: Research and Practice, 34,* 491–498. doi:10.1037/0735-7028.34.5.491

Lamb, M. E., Hershkowitz, I., Orbach, Y., & Esplin, P. (2008). *Tell me what happened: Structured investigative interviews of child victims and witnesses.* Hoboken, NJ: Wiley.

Lamb, M. E., Orbach, Y., Hershkowitz, I., Esplin, P. W., & Horowitz, D. (2007). A structured forensic interview protocol improves the quality and informativeness of investigative interviews with children: A review of research using the NICHD Investigative Interview Protocol. *Child Abuse & Neglect, 31,* 1201–1231. doi:10.1016/j.chiabu.2007.03.021

Landis, R., Krauss, D., & O'Connor, M. (2003, Spring/Summer). Legal update: Involuntary treatment to restore competency to stand trial is constitutionally permissible in limited circumstances. *American Psychology-Law Society News, 23,* 8–10.

Landsman, S., & Rakos, R. F. (1994). A preliminary inquiry into the effect of potentially biasing information on judges and jurors in civil litigation. *Behavioral Sciences & the Law, 12,* 113–126. doi:10.1002/bsl.2370120203

Langan, P. A., & Cuniff, M. A. (1992). *Recidivism of felons on probation, 1986–89* (NCJ 134177). Washington, DC: Bureau of Justice Statistics. Retrieved from http://www.bjs.gov/index.cfm?ty=pbdetail&iid=3994

Langhout, R. D., Bergman, M. E., Cortina, L. M., Fitzgerald, L. F., Drasgow, F., & Williams, J. H. (2006). Sexual harassment severity: Assessing situational and personal determinants and outcomes. *Journal of Applied Social Psychology, 35,* 975–1007. doi:10.1111/j.1559-1816.2005.tb02156.x

Langleben, D. (2008). Detection of deception with fMRI: Are we there yet? *Legal and Criminological Psychology, 13,* 1–9. doi:10.1348/135532507X251641

Langleben, D. D., & Moriarty, J. C. (2013). Using brain imaging for lie detection: Where science, law, and policy collide. *Psychology, Public Policy, and Law, 19,* 222–234. doi:10.1037/a0028841

Langleben, D. D., Willard, D., & Moriarty, J. C. (2012). Detecting deception. In J. R. Simpson (Ed.), *Neuroimaging in forensic psychiatry: From the clinic to the courtroom* (pp. 217–236). Chichester, England: Wiley.

Lassiter, G. D. (Ed.). (2004). *Interrogations, confessions, and entrapment.* New York, NY: Kluwer.

Lassiter, G. D., Diamond, S. S., Schmidt, H. C., & Elek, J. K. (2007). Evaluating videotaped confessions: Expertise provides no defense against the camera-perspective effect. *Psychological Science, 18,* 224–226. doi:10.1111/j.1467-9280.2007.01879.x

Lassiter, G. D., & Geers, A. L. (2004). Evaluation of confession evidence: Effects of presentation format. In G. D. Lassiter (Ed.), *Interrogations, confessions, and entrapment* (pp. 197–214). New York, NY: Kluwer.

Latham, G. P. (2006). *Work motivation: History, theory, research, and practice.* Thousand Oaks, CA: Sage.

Laurence, J. (1932). *A history of capital punishment: With special reference to capital punishment in Great Britain.* London, England: Sampson, Low, Marston & Company.

Lecci, L., & Myers, B. (2008). Individual differences in attitudes relevant to juror decision making: Development and validation of the Pretrial Juror Attitude Questionnaire (PJAQ). *Journal of Applied Social Psychology, 38,* 2010–2038. doi:10.1111/j.1559-1816.2008.00378.x

Lecci, L. B., & Myers, B. (2009). Predicting guilt judgments and verdict change using a measure of pretrial bias in a videotaped mock trial with deliberating jurors. *Psychology, Crime & Law, 15,* 619–634. doi:10.1080/10683160802477757

Lee, H. Y., Park, E., & Lightfoot, E. (2010). When does a battered woman seek help from the police? The role of battered women's functionality. *Journal of Family Violence, 25,* 195–204. doi:10.1007/s10896-009-9283-y

Leippe, M. R., & Eisenstadt, D. (2007). Eyewitness confidence and the confidence-accuracy relationship in memory for people. In R. C. L. Lindsay, D. F. Ross, J. D. Read, & M. P. Toglia (Eds.), *The handbook of eyewitness psychology: Vol. 2. Memory for people* (pp. 377–425). Mahwah, NJ: Erlbaum.

Lempert, R. O. (1993). Civil juries and complex cases: Taking stock after twelve years. In R. E. Litan (Ed.), *Verdict: Assessing the civil jury system* (pp. 181–247). Washington, DC: Brookings Institution.

Leo, R. A. (1992). From coercion to deception: The changing nature of police interrogation in America. *Crime, Law and Social Change, 18,* 35–59. doi:10.1007/BF00230624

Leo, R. A. (1996). Miranda's revenge: Police interrogation as a confidence game. *Law and Society Review, 30,* 259–288. doi:10.2307/3053960

Leo, R. A. (2008). *Police interrogation and American justice.* Cambridge, MA: Harvard University Press.

Leo, R. A., Costanzo, M., & Shaked-Schroer, N. (2009). Psychological and cultural aspects of interrogation and false confessions: Using research to inform legal decision making. In D. Krauss and J. Lieberman (Eds.), *Psychological expertise in court: Vol. 2. Psychology in the courtroom* (pp. 25–56). London, England: Ashgate.

Lerner, M. J. (1980). *The belief in a just world.* New York, NY: Plenum.

Lerner, M. J., & Lerner, S. C. (Eds.). (1981). *The justice motive in social behavior: Adapting to times of scarcity and change.* New York, NY: Plenum.

Leskinen, E. A., Cortina, L. M. & Kabat, D. B. (2011). Gender harassment: Broadening our understanding of sex-based harassment at work. *Law and Human Behavior, 35,* 25–39. doi:10.1007/s10979-010-9241-5

Levett, L. M., Danielsen, E. M., Kovera, M. B., & Cutler, B. (2005). The psychology of jury and juror decision making. In D. Kipling & N. Brewer (Eds.), *Psychology and law: An empirical perspective* (pp. 365–406). New York, NY: Guilford Press.

Levine, J. A., Pavlidis, I., & Everhardt, N. L. (2002). Seeing through the face of deception. *Nature, 415,* 35. doi:10.1038/415035a

Lewis, G. B., & Oh, S. S. (2009). A major difference? Fields of study and male–female pay differences in federal employment. *American Review of Public Administration, 39,* 107–124. doi:10.1177/0275074008317158

Lieberman, J. D. (2011). The utility of scientific jury selection: Still murky after 30 years. *Current Directions in Psychological Science, 20,* 48–52. doi:10.1177/0963721410396628

Lieberman, J. D., & Arndt, J. (2000). Understanding the limits of limiting instructions: Social psychological explanations for the failures of instructions to disregard pretrial publicity and other inadmissible evidence. *Psychology, Public Policy, and Law, 6,* 677–711. doi:10.1037/1076-8971.6.3.677

Lieberman, J. D., Arndt, J., & Vess, M. (2009). Inadmissible evidence and pretrial publicity: The effects (and ineffectiveness) of admonitions to disregard. In J. D. Lieberman & D. Krauss (Eds.), *Psychology in the courtroom* (pp. 67–96). Hampshire, England: Ashgate.

Lieberman, J. D., Krauss, D. A., Kyger, M., & Lehoux, M. (2007). Determining dangerousness in sexually violent predator evaluations: Cognitive-experiential self-theory and juror judgments of expert testimony. *Behavioral Sciences & the Law, 25,* 507–526. doi:10.1002/bsl.771

Lieberman, J. D., & Sales, B. D. (2007). *Scientific jury selection.* Washington, DC: American Psychological Association.

Liebman, J. S., Fagan, J., & West, V. (2000). Capital attrition: Error rates in capital cases, 1973–1995. *Texas Law Review, 78,* 1839–1861.

Lilienfeld, S. O., & Arkowitz, H. (2011, September/October). Can people have multiple personalities? *Scientific American Mind, 22,* 64–65. doi:10.1038/scientificamericanmind0911-64

Lilienfeld, S. O., Wood, J. M., & Garb, H. N. (2000). The scientific status of projective techniques. *Psychological Science in the Public Interest, 1,* 27–66. doi:10.1111/1529-1006.002

Lindsay, D. S., & Read, J. D. (1994). Psychotherapy and memories of childhood sexual abuse: A cognitive perspective. *Applied Cognitive Psychology, 8,* 281–338. doi:10.1002/acp.2350080403

Lindsay, D. S., & Read, J. D. (2001). The recovered memories controversy: Where do we go from here? In G. Davies & T. Dalgleish (Eds.), *Recovered memories: Seeking the middle ground* (pp. 71–94). New York, NY: Wiley.

Link, B. G., & Stueve, A. (1994). Psychotic symptoms and the violent/illegal behavior of mental patients compared to community controls. In J. Monahan & H. J. Steadman (Eds.), *Violence and mental disorder: Developments in risk assessment* (pp. 137–159). Chicago, IL: University of Chicago Press.

Lips, H. M. (2012). The gender pay gap: Challenging the rationalizations, perceived equity, discrimination, and the limits of human capital models. *Sex Roles, 68,* 169–185. doi:10.1007/s11199-012-0165-z

Lipsey, M. W., Landenberger, N. A., & Wilson, S. J. (2007). Effects of cognitive-behavioral programs for criminal offenders. *Campbell Systematic Reviews, 3*(6), 1–27. doi:10.4073/csr.2007.6

Lipsitt, P. D., Lelos, D., & McGarry, A. (1971). Competency for trial: A screening instrument. *American Journal of Psychiatry, 128,* 105–109. Retrieved from http://ajp.psychiatry online.org/journal.aspx?journalid=13

Lipton, D. S., Martinson, R., & Wilks, J. (1975). *The effectiveness of correctional treatment: A survey of treatment evaluation studies.* New York, NY: Praeger.

Llewellyn, K. N. (1931). *The bramble bush.* Dobbs Ferry, NY: Oceana Press.

Loftus, E. F. (1984). Expert testimony on the eyewitness. In G. L. Wells & E. F. Loftus (Eds.), *Eyewitness testimony: Psychological perspectives* (pp. 273–283). New York, NY: Cambridge University Press.

Loftus, E. F. (1997). Memory for a past that never was. *Current Directions in Psychological Science, 6,* 60–65. doi:10.1111/1467-8721.ep11512654

Loftus, E. F., & Palmer, J. C. (1974). Reconstruction of automobile destruction: An example of the interaction between language and memory. *Journal of Verbal Learning and Verbal Behavior, 13,* 585–589. doi:10.1016/S0022-5371(74)80011-3

Logan, W. A. (1998). The ex post facto clause and the jurisprudence of punishment. *American Criminal Law Review, 35,* 1261–1318.

London, K., Bruck, M., Ceci, S. J., & Shuman, D. W. (2005). Disclosure of child sexual abuse: What does the research tell us about the ways that children tell? *Psychology, Public Policy, and Law, 11,* 194–226. doi:10.1037/1076-8971.11.1.194

London, K., Bruck, M., Wright, D. B., & Ceci, S. J. (2008). Review of the contemporary literature on how children report sexual abuse to others: Findings, methodological issues, and implications for forensic interviewers. *Memory, 16,* 29–47. doi:10.1080/09658210701725732

Luginbuhl, J., & Burkhead, M. (1994). Sources of bias and arbitrariness in the capital trial. *Journal of Social Issues, 50,* 103–124. doi:10.1111/j.1540-4560.1994.tb02412.x

Lutze, F. E., Johnson, W. W., Clear, T. R., Latessa, E. J., & Slate, R. N. (2012). The future of community corrections is now: Stop dreaming and take action. *Journal of Contemporary Criminal Justice, 28,* 42–59. doi:10.1177/1043986211432193

Lykken, D. T. (1998). *A tremor in the blood: Uses and abuses of the lie detector.* New York, NY: Plenum Trade.

Lynch, M., & Haney, C. (2000). Discrimination and instructional comprehension: Guided discretion, racial bias, and the death penalty. *Law and Human Behavior, 24,* 337–358. doi:10.1023/A:1005588221761

Lynch, M., & Haney, C. (2009). Capital jury deliberation: Effects on death sentencing, comprehension, and discrimination. *Law and Human Behavior, 33,* 481–496. doi:10.1007/s10979-008-9168-2

Lynn, S. J., Boycheva, E., Deming, A., Lilienfeld, S. O., & Hallquist, M. N. (2009). Forensic hypnosis: The state of the science. In J. L. Skeem, K. S. Douglas, & S. O. Lilienfeld (Eds.), *Psychological science in the courtroom: Controversies and consensus* (pp. 80–99). New York, NY: Guilford Press.

Lyon, T. D., Carrick, N., & Quas, J. A. (2010). Young children's competency to take the oath: Effects of task, maltreatment, and age. *Law and Human Behavior, 34,* 141–149. doi:10.1007/s10979-009-9177-9

Lyon, T. D., Malloy, L. C., Quas, J. A., & Talwar, V. A. (2008). Coaching, truth induction, and young maltreated children's false allegations and false denials. *Child Development, 79,* 914–929. doi:10.1111/j.1467-8624.2008.01167.x

MacCoun, R. J. (1993). Inside the black box: What empirical research tells us about decision-making by civil juries. In R. E. Litan (Ed.), *Verdict: Assessing the civil jury system* (pp. 137–180). Washington, DC: Brookings Institution.

MacCoun, R. J., & Kerr, N. L. (1988). Asymmetric influence in mock jury deliberation: Jurors' bias for leniency. *Journal of Personality and Social Psychology, 54,* 21–33. doi:10.1037/0022-3514.54.1.21

MacKenzie, D. L. (2006). *What works in corrections? Reducing the criminal activities of offenders and delinquents.* Cambridge, UK: Cambridge University Press.

MacKinnon, C. (1979). *Sexual harassment of working women.* New Haven, CT: Yale University Press.

MacLeod, M. D., & Saunders, J. (2008). Retrieval inhibition and memory distortion: Negative consequences of an adaptive process. *Current Directions in Psychological Science, 17,* 26–30. doi:10.1111/j.1467-8721.2008.00542.x

Madon, S., Guyll, M., Scherr, K., Greathouse, S., & Wells, G. (2012). Temporal discounting: The differential effect of proximal and distal consequences on confession decisions. *Law and Human Behavior, 36,* 13–20. doi:10.1037/h0093962

Madon, S., Yang, Y., Smalarz, L., Guyll, M., & Scherr, K. C. (2013). How factors present during the immediate interrogation situation produce short-sighted confession decisions. *Law and Human Behavior, 37,* 60–74. doi:10.1037/lhb0000011

Major, B. (1993). Gender, entitlement, and the distribution of family labor. *Journal of Social Issues, 49,* 141–159. doi:10.1111/j.1540-4560.1993.tb01173.x

Major, B., Mendes, W. B., & Dovidio, J. F. (2013). Intergroup relations and health disparities: A social psychological perspective. *Health Psychology, 32,* 514–524. doi:10.1037/a0030358

Malloy, L. C., Brubacher, S. P., & Lamb, M. E. (2011). Expected consequences of disclosure revealed in investigative interviews with suspected victims of child sexual abuse. *Applied Developmental Science, 15,* 8–19. doi:10.1080/10888691.2011.538616

Malloy, L. C., La Rooy, D. J., Lamb, M. E., & Katz, C. (2011). Developmentally sensitive interviewing for legal purposes. In M. E. Lamb, D. J. La Rooy, L. C. Malloy, & C. Katz (Eds.), *Children's testimony: A handbook of psychological research and forensic practice* (2nd ed., pp. 1–13). Chichester, England: Wiley.

Malloy, L. C., Lyon, T. D., & Quas, J. A. (2007). Filial dependency and recantation of child sexual abuse allegations. *Journal of the American Academy of Child and Adolescent Psychiatry, 46,* 162–170. doi:10.1097/01.chi.0000246067.77953.f7

Malmquist, C. P. (1986). Children who witness parental murder: Posttraumatic aspects. *Journal of the American*

Academy of Child Psychiatry, 25, 320–325. doi:10.1016/S0002-7138(09)60253-3

Mancini, D. E. (2012). The "CSI effect" in an actual juror sample: Why crime show genre may matter. *North American Journal of Psychology, 15,* 543–564.

Mandela, N. (1994). *Long walk to freedom: The autobiography of Nelson Mandela.* London, England: Little, Brown.

Mann, S., Vrij, A., & Bull, R. (2004). Detecting true lies: Police officers' ability to detect suspects' lies. *Journal of Applied Psychology, 89,* 137–149. doi:10.1037/0021-9010.89.1.137

Marcon, J. L., Meissner, C. A., Frueh, M., Susa, K. J., & MacLin, O. H. (2010). Perceptual identification and the cross-race effect. *Visual Cognition, 18,* 767–779. doi:10.1080/13506280903178622

Marsh, K., Fox, C., & Hedderman, C. (2009). Do you get what you pay for? Assessing the use of prison from an economic perspective. *The Howard Journal, 48,* 144–157. doi:10.1111/j.1468-2311.2008.00556.x

Marston, W. M. (1938). *The lie detector test.* New York, NY: Smith.

Martin, J. L., Lichtenstein, B., Jenkot, R. B., & Forde, D. R. (2012). "They can take us over any time they want": Correctional officers' responses to prison crowding. *The Prison Journal, 92,* 88–105. doi:10.1177/0032885511429256

Maschi, T., Kwak, J., Ko, E. J., & Morrissey, M. (2012). Forget me not: Dementia in prisons. *The Gerontologist, 52,* 441–451. doi:10.1093/geront/gnr131

Mason, W. A., Conrey, F. R., & Smith, E. R. (2007). Situating social influence processes: Dynamic, multidirectional flows of influence within social networks. *Personality and Social Psychology Review, 11,* 279–300. doi:10.1177/1088868307301032

Matsumoto, D., & Juang, L. (2007). *Culture and psychology* (4th ed.). Belmont, CA: Wadsworth.

Maxwell, A., Findley, K. & Hardiman, J. L. (2011). *State of Georgia v. Troy Anthony Davis: Brief of the Georgia Innocence Project as Amicus Curiae in support of appellant.* Retrieved from http://www.innocenceproject.org/docs/Davis_Troy_Innocence_Network_Brief.pdf

Maxwell, L. (2010). The future of the American petit jury system: A look at the problems in the American jury system and the use of professional juries. *The Stevenson University Forensics Journal, 1,* 18–21.

Mazzella, R., & Feingold, A. (1994). The effects of physical attractiveness, race, socioeconomic status, and gender of defendant and victims on judgments of mock jurors: A meta-analysis. *Journal of Applied Social Psychology, 24,* 1315–1344. doi:10.1111/j.1559-1816.1994.tb01552.x

Mazzetti, M. (2013). *The way of the knife: The CIA, a secret army, and a war at the ends of the earth.* New York, NY: Penguin Press.

Mbuba, J. M. (2012). Lethal rejection: Recounting offenders' experience in prison and societal reaction post release. *The Prison Journal, 92,* 231–252. doi:10.1177/0032885512439009

McAuliff, B. (2010). Child victim and witness research comes of age: Implications for social scientists, practitioners, and law. In B. L. Bottoms, C. Najdowski, & G. S. Goodman (Eds.), *Children as victims, witnesses, and offenders* (pp. 233–254). New York, NY: Guilford Press.

McAuliff, B. D., & Groscup, J. (2009). Daubert and psychological science in court: Judging validity from the bench, bar, and jury box. In J. L. Skeem, K. S. Douglas, & S. O. Lilienfeld (Eds.), *Psychological science in the courtroom: Controversies and consensus* (pp. 26–52). New York, NY: Guilford Press.

McAuliff, B. D., & Kovera, M. B. (2007). Estimating the effects of misleading information on witness accuracy: Can experts tell jurors something they don't already know? *Applied Cognitive Psychology, 21,* 849–870. doi:10.1002/acp.1301

McCabe, J. G., Krauss, D. A., & Lieberman, J. D. (2010). Reality check: A comparison of college students and a community sample of mock jurors in a simulated sexual violent predator civil commitment. *Behavioral Sciences & the Law, 28,* 730–750. doi:10.1002/bsl.902

McCarthy, K. E. (2009). *Recent developments on Washington State's "three strikes" law* (2009-R-0006). Hartford, CT: Office of Legislative Research. Retrieved from http://www.cga.ct.gov/2009/rpt/2009-R-0006.htm

McConville, M. (1992). Videotaping interrogations. *New Law Journal, 10,* 960–962.

McCoy, A. (2005). *A question of torture: CIA interrogation, from the cold war to the war on terror.* New York, NY: Metropolitan Books/Henry Holt.

McDermott, B. E., Edens, J. F., Quanbeck, C. D., Busse, D., & Scott, C. L. (2008). Examining the role of static and dynamic risk factors in the prediction of inpatient violence: Variable- and person-focused analyses. *Law and Human Behavior, 32,* 325–338. doi:10.1007/s10979-007-9094-8

McDonald, P., Charlesworth, S., & Cerise, S. (2011). Below the "tip of the iceberg": Extra-legal responses to workplace sexual harassment. *Women's Studies International Forum, 34,* 278–289. doi:10.1016/j.wsif.2011.03.002

McGarry, A. L. (1971). The fate of psychiatric offenders returned for trial. *American Journal of Psychiatry, 127,* 1181–1184. Retrieved from http://ajp.psychiatryonline.org/journal.aspx?journalid=13

McGrath, M. (2004). *Academy of Behavioral Profiling: A letter from the president.* Retrieved from http://www.profiling.org/abp_president.html

McKelvey, B. (1977). *American prisons: A history of good intentions.* Montclair, NJ: Patterson Smith.

McLaughlin, H., Uggen, C., & Blackstone, A. (2012). Sexual harassment, workplace authority, and the paradox of power. *American Sociological Review, 77,* 625–647. doi:10.1177/0003122412451728

McMahon, M. (1999). Battered women and bad science: The limited validity and utility of battered woman syndrome. *Psychiatry, Psychology and Law, 6,* 23–49. doi:10.1080/13218719909524946

McNally, R. J. (2004). *Remembering trauma.* Cambridge, MA: Harvard University Press

McNally, R. J., & Geraerts, E. (2009). A new solution to the recovered memory debate. *Perspectives in Psychological Science, 4,* 126–134. doi:10.1111/j.1745-6924.2009.01112.x

Means, R. F., Heller, L. D., & Janofsky, J. (2012). Transferring juvenile defendants from adult to juvenile court: How Maryland forensic evaluators and judges reach their decisions. *Journal of the American Academy of Psychiatry and Law, 40,* 333–340. Retrieved from http://www.jaapl.org

Mears, D. P. (2008). An assessment of supermax prisons using an evaluation research framework. *The Prison Journal, 88,* 43–68. doi:10.1177/0032885507310964

Meijer, E. H., & Verschuere, B. (2010). The polygraph and the detection of deception. *Journal of Forensic Psychology Practice, 10,* 325-338. doi:10.1080/15228932.2010.481237

Meili, T. (2003). *I am the Central Park jogger.* New York, NY: Scribner.

Meissner, C. A., & Brigham, J. C. (2001). Thirty years of investigating the own-race bias in memory for faces: A meta-analytic review. *Psychology, Public Policy, and Law, 7,* 3–35. doi:10.1037/1076-8971.7.1.3

Meissner, C. A., & Kassin, S. M. (2004). "You're guilty, so just confess!" Cognitive and confirmation biases in the interrogation room. In G. D. Lassiter (Ed.), *Interrogations, confessions, and entrapment* (pp. 85–106). New York, NY: Kluwer.

Melnyk, L., Crossman, A. M., & Scullin, M. H. (2009). The suggestibility of children's memory. In M. P. Toglia, J. D. Read, D. F. Ross, & R. C. L. Lindsay (Eds.), *The handbook of eyewitness psychology: Vol. 1. Memory for events* (pp. 401–427). Mahwah, NJ: Erlbaum.

Melton, G. B. (1987). Bringing psychology to the legal system: Opportunities, obstacles, and efficacy. *American Psychologist, 42,* 488–495. doi:10.1037/0003-066X.42.5.488

Melton, G. B., Petrila, J., Poythress, N. G., Slobogin, C., Lyons, P. M., Jr., & Otto, R. K. (2007). *Psychological evaluations for the courts: A handbook for mental health professionals and lawyers* (3rd ed.). New York, NY: Guilford Press.

Melton, G. B., & Saks, M. J. (1990). AP-LS's pro bono *amicus* brief project. *American Psychology-Law Society News, 10,* 5.

Menninger, K. (1966). *The crime of punishment.* New York, NY: Viking.

Merlino, M. L., Murray, C. I., & Richardson, J. T. (2008). Judicial gatekeeping and the social construction of the admissibility of expert testimony. *Behavioral Sciences & the Law, 26,* 187–206. doi:10.1002/bsl.806

Merrill, J., & Knox, D. (2010). *Finding love from 9 to 5: Trade secrets of office romance.* Santa Barbara, CA: Greenwood Press.

Metzner, J. L., & Fellner, J. (2010). Solitary confinement and mental illness in U.S. prisons: A challenge for medical ethics. *Journal of the American Academy of Psychiatry and the Law, 38,* 104–108. Retrieved from http://www.jaapl.org

Meyer, A., Wagner, B., & Dutton, M. A. (2010). The relationship between battered women's causal attributions for violence and coping efforts. *Journal of Interpersonal Violence, 25,* 900–918. doi:10.1177/0886260509336965

Meyersburg, C. A., Bogdan, R., Gallo, D. A., & McNally, R. J. (2009). False memory propensity in people reporting recovered memories of past lives. *Journal of Abnormal Psychology, 118,* 399–404. doi:10.1037/a0015371

Miles, K. S., & Cottle, J. L. (2011). Beyond plain language: A learner-centered approach to pattern jury instructions. *Technical Communication Quarterly, 20,* 92–112. doi:10.1080/10572252.2011.528345

Miller, G. A. (1969). Psychology as a means of promoting human welfare. *American Psychologist, 24,* 1063–1075.

Miller, H. A., Amenta, A. E., & Conroy, M. A. (2005). Sexually violent predator evaluations: Empirical evidence, strategies for professionals, and research directions. *Law and Human Behavior, 29,* 29–54. doi:10.1007/s10979-005-1398-y

Miller, M. (2006). Sentencing guidelines are not enough: The need for written sentencing opinions. *Behavioral Sciences & the Law, 7,* 3–24. doi:10.1002/bsl.2370070103

Miller, N. (2004). *Domestic violence: A review of state legislation defining police and prosecution duties and powers.* Alexandria, VA: Institute for Law and Justice. Retrieved from http://www.ilj.org/publications/docs/Domestic_Violence_Legislation.pdf

Mitchell, T. L., Haw, R. M., Pfeifer, J. E., & Meissner, C. A. (2005). Racial bias in mock juror decision-making: A meta-analytic review of defendant treatment. *Law and Human Behavior, 29,* 621–637. doi:10.1007/s10979-005-8122-9

Mize, G. E., Hannaford-Agor, P., & Waters, N. L. (2007). *The state-of-the-states survey of jury improvement efforts: A compendium report.* Williamsburg, VA: National Center for State Courts. Retrieved from http://www.ncsc-jurystudies.org/State-of-the-States-Survey.aspx

Mnookin, J. L. (2004). Fingerprint evidence in an age of DNA profiling. *Brooklyn Law Review, 67,* 13–70. doi:10.2139/ssrn.292087

Mnookin, J. L., Cole, S. A., Dror, I. E., Fisher, B. A. J., Houck, M. M., Inman, K., . . . Stoney, D. A. (2011). The need for a research culture in the forensic sciences. *UCLA Law Review, 58,* 725–779. Retrieved from http://www.uclalawreview.org

Mokros, A., & Alison, L. (2002). Is profiling possible? Testing the predicted homology of crime scene actions and background characteristics in a sample of rapists. *Legal and Criminological Psychology, 7,* 25–43. doi:10.1348/135532502168360

Moliner, C., Martínez-Tur, V., Peiró, J. M., Ramos, J., & Cropanzano, R. (2012). Perceived reciprocity and well-being at work in non-professional employees: Fairness or self-interest? *Stress and Health, 29,* 31–39. doi:10.1002/smi.2421

Monahan, J. (1981). *Predicting violent behavior: An assessment of clinical techniques.* Beverly Hills, CA: Sage.

Monahan, J. (2003). Violence risk assessment. In I. B. Weiner (Series Ed.) & A. M. Goldstein (Vol. Ed.), *The handbook of psychology: Vol. 11. Forensic psychology* (pp. 527–542). doi:10.1002/0471264385.wei1126

Monahan, J. (2007). Clinical and actuarial predictions of violence. In D. Faigman, D. Kaye, M. Saks, J. Sanders, & E. Cheng (Eds.), *Modern scientific evidence: The law and science of expert testimony* (pp. 122–147). St. Paul, MN: West.

Monahan, J., & Steadman, H. J. (1994. Toward a rejuvenation of risk assessment research. In J. Monahan & H. J. Steadman (Eds.), *Violence and mental disorder: Developments in risk assessment* (pp. 1–17). Chicago: University of Chicago Press.

Monahan, J., Steadman, H. J., Silver, E., Appelbaum, P. S., Robbins, P. C., Mulvey, E. P., . . . Banks, S. (2001). *Rethinking risk assessment: The MacArthur study of mental disorder and violence*. New York, NY: Oxford University Press.

Monahan, J., & Walker, L. (2009). *Social science in law: Cases and materials* (7th ed.). New York, NY: Foundation Press.

Monahan, J., & Walker, L. (2014). *Social science in law: Cases and materials* (8th ed.). Westbury, NY: Foundation Press.

Montoya, R., & Horton, R. S. (2013). A meta-analytic investigation of the processes underlying the similarity-attraction effect. *Journal of Social and Personal Relationships, 30*, 64–94. doi:10.1177/0265407512452989

Morgan, C. A., III, Hazlett, G., Doran, A., Garrett, S., Hoyt, G., Thomas, P., . . . Southwick, S. M. (2004). Accuracy of eyewitness memory for persons encountered during exposure to highly intense stress. *International Journal of Law and Psychiatry, 27*, 265–279. doi:10.1016/j.ijlp.2004.03.004

Morgan, C. A., III, Southwick, S., Steffian, G., Hazlett, G. A., & Loftus, E. F. (2013). Misinformation can influence memory for recently experienced, highly stressful events. *International Journal of Law and Psychiatry, 36*, 11–17. doi:10.1016/j.ijlp.2012.11.002

Morris, N. (1995). The contemporary prison: 1965-present. In N. Morris & D. J. Rothman (Eds.), *The Oxford history of the prison: The practice of punishment in western society* (pp. 202–231). New York, NY: Oxford University Press.

Mossman, D. (1994). Assessing predictions of violence: Being accurate about accuracy. *Journal of Consulting and Clinical Psychology, 62*, 783–792. doi:10.1037/0022-006X.62.4.783

Moston, S., Stephenson, G., & Williamson, T. M. (1992). The effects of case characteristics on suspect behavior during police questioning. *British Journal of Criminology, 32*, 23–40. Retrieved from http://bjc.oxfordjournals.org

Mott, N. L., Kauder, N. B., Ostrom, B. J., & Hannaford-Agor, P. L. (2003). A profile of hung juries. *Caseload Highlights, 9*. Retrieved from http://cdm16501.contentdm.oclc.org/cdm/ref/collection/juries/id/62

Munsterberg, H. (1908). *On the witness stand: Essays on psychology and crime*. New York, NY: Clark Boardman.

Musick, J., & Otto, R. K. (2006). *Inventory of legal knowledge*. Columbia, SC: Authors.

Myers, B., Latter, R., & Abdollahi-Arena, M. K. (2006). The court of public opinion. *Law and Human Behavior, 30*, 509–523. doi:10.1007/s10979-006-9041-0

Myers, B., & Lecci, L. (2002). Revising the factor structure of the Juror Bias Scale. *Law and Human Behavior, 22*, 239–256. doi:10.1023/A:1025798204956

Myers, J. E. B., Redlich, A. D., Goodman, G. S., Prizmich, L. P., & Imwinkelried, E. (1999). Jurors' perceptions of hearsay in child sexual cases. *Psychology, Public Policy, and Law, 4*, 1025–1051. doi:10.1037/1076-8971.5.2.388

Myers, L. B., & Brewin, C. R. (1998). Recall of early experience and the repressive coping style. *Journal of Abnormal Psychology, 103*, 288–292. doi:10.1037/0021-843X.103.2.288

Nagin, D. S., Cullen, F. T., & Johnson, C. L. (2009). Imprisonment and reoffending. *Crime and Justice, 38*, 115–200. doi:10.1086/599202

Nagin, D. S., & Pepper, J. V. (Eds.). (2012). *Deterrence and the death penalty*. Washington, DC: National Academies Press.

Nahari, G., Vrij, A., & Fisher, R. P. (2012). Does the truth come out in the writing? Scan as a lie detection tool. *Law and Human Behavior, 36*, 68–76. doi:10.1037/h0093965

Najdowski, C. J., & Bottoms, B. L. (2012). Understanding jurors' judgments in cases involving juvenile defendants: Effects of confession evidence and intellectual disability. *Psychology, Public Policy, and Law, 18*, 297–337. doi:10.1037/a0025786

Nance, D. A., & Morris, S. B. (2002). An empirical assessment of presentation formats for trace evidence with a relatively large and quantifiable random match probability. *Jurimetrics, 42*, 403–448.

Narby, D. J., Cutler, B. L., & Moran, G. (1993). A meta-analysis of the association between authoritarianism and juror's perceptions of defendants culpability. *Journal of Applied Psychology, 78*, 34–42. doi:10.1037/0021-9010.78.1.34

National Advisory Commission on Criminal Justice Standards and Goals. (1973). *A national strategy to reduce crime*. Washington, DC: U.S. Government Printing Office.

National Registry of Exonerations. (2012). *Exonerations in the United States, 1989–2012: Report by the National Registry of Exonerations*. Retrieved from https://www.law.umich.edu/special/exoneration/Documents/exonerations_us_1989_2012_full_report.pdf

National Research Council. (2003). *The polygraph and lie detection*. Washington, DC: National Academies Press.

National Research Council. (2004). *Forensic analysis: Weighing bullet lead evidence*. Washington, DC: National Academies Press.

National Research Council, Committee on Identifying the Needs of the Forensic Science Community. (2009). *Strengthening forensic science in the United States: A path forward* (Document No. 228091). Washington, DC: The National Academies Press. Retrieved from https://www.ncjrs.gov/pdffiles1/nij/grants/228091.pdf

Neumann, C. (2012). Fingerprints at the crime-scene: Statistically certain, or probable? *Significance, 9*, 21–25. doi:10.1111/j.1740-9713.2012.00539.x

Nicholson, R. A. (1999). Forensic assessment. In R. Roesch, S. D. Hart, & J. R. P. Ogloff (Eds.), *Psychology and law: The state of the discipline* (pp. 121–173). New York, NY: Kluwer/Plenum.

Nisbett, R. E., & Cohen, D. (1996). *Culture of honor: The psychology of violence in the south*. Boulder, CO: Westview.

Nisbett, R. E., & Ross, L. (1991). *The person and the situation*. New York, NY: McGraw-Hill.

Nosek, B. A., & Hansen, J. J. (2008). The associations in our heads belong to us: Searching for attitudes and knowledge in implicit evaluation. *Cognition and Emotion, 22*, 553–594. doi:10.1080/02699930701438186

Novaco, R. W. (2007). Anger dysregulation. In T. A. Cavell & K. T. Malcolm (Eds.), *Anger, aggression, and interventions for interpersonal violence* (pp. 3–54). Mahwah, NJ: Erlbaum.

Nudelman, G. (2013). The belief in a just world and personality: A meta-analysis. *Social Justice Research, 26*, 105–119. doi:10.1007/s11211-013-0178-y

O'Brien, D. (1985). *Two of a kind: The hillside stranglers*. New York, NY: New American Library Books.

O'Connor, M. (2007). Expert testimony in sexual harassment cases: Its scope, limits, and effectiveness. In M. Costanzo, D. Krauss, & K. Pezdek (Eds.). *Expert psychological testimony for the courts* (pp. 119–148). Mahwah, NJ: Erlbaum.

O'Connor, M., Gutek, B. A., Stockdale, M., Geer, T. M., & Melançon, R. (2004). Explaining sexual harassment judgments: Looking beyond gender of the rater. *Law and Human Behavior, 28,* 69–96. doi:10.1023/B:LAHU.0000015004.39462.6e

O'Donohue, W. T., Beitz, K., & Cummings, N. (2008). A model for constructs relevant to child custody evaluations. *Journal of Forensic Psychology Practice, 7,* 125–139. doi:10.1300/J158v07n04_05

O'Donohue, W., & Benuto, L. (2012). Problems with child sexual abuse accommodation syndrome. *The Scientific Review of Mental Health Practice, 9,* 20–28.

O'Hear, M. M. (2013). Restitution as a penal aim. In G. Bruinsma & D. Weisburd (Eds.), *Encyclopedia of criminology and criminal justice* (pp. 4410–4421). New York, NY: Springer.

O'Sullivan, M. (2007). Unicorns or Tiger Woods: Are lie detection experts myths or rarities? *Law and Human Behavior, 31,* 117–125. doi:10.1007/s10979-006-9058-4

Ofshe, R. (1989). Coerced confessions: The logic of seemingly irrational action. *Cultic Studies Journal, 6,* 1–15. Retrieved from http://www.icsahome.com/articles

Ofshe, R., & Leo, R. (1997a). The decision to confess falsely: Rational choice and irrational action. *Denver University Law Review, 74,* 979–1122.

Ofshe, R., & Leo, R. (1997b). The social psychology of police interrogation: The theory and classification of true and false confessions. *Studies in Law, Politics, and Society, 16,* 189–251.

Ofshe, R., & Watters, E. (1994). *Making monsters.* Berkeley: University of California Press.

Ogloff, J. R. P., & Vidmar, N. (1994). The impact of pretrial publicity on jurors: A study to compare the relative effects of television and print media. *Law and Human Behavior, 18,* 507–525. doi:10.1007/BF01499171

Ogloff, J. R. P., Roberts, C. F., & Roesch, R. (1993). The insanity defense: Legal standards and clinical assessment. *Applied and Preventative Psychology, 2,* 163–178. doi:10.1016/S0962-1849(05)80122-2

Okafo, N. (2009). *Reconstructing law and justice in a postcolony.* Burlington, VT: Ashgate.

Okie, S. (2007). Sex, drugs, prisons, and HIV. *New England Journal of Medicine, 356,* 105–108. doi:10.1056/NEJMp068277

Olczak, P. V., Kaplan, M. F., & Penrod, S. (1991). Attorneys' lay psychology and its effectiveness in selecting jurors: Three empirical studies. *Journal of Social Behavior and Personality, 6,* 431–452.

Olsen-Fulero, L., & Fulero, S. M. (1997). Commonsense rape judgments: An empathy-complexity theory of rape juror story making. *Psychology, Public Policy, and Law, 3,* 402–427. doi:10.1037/1076-8971.3.2-3.402

Oltmanns, T. F., & Emery, R. E. (2007). *Abnormal psychology* (5th ed.). Upper Saddle River, NJ: Prentice-Hall.

Oltmanns, T. F., & Emery, R. E. (2011) *Abnormal psychology* (7th ed.). Upper Saddle River, NJ: Pearson.

Ost, J., Costall, A., & Bull, R. (2002). A perfect symmetry? A study of retractors' experiences of making and then repudiating claims of early sexual abuse. *Psychology, Crime & Law, 8,* 155–181. doi:10.1080/10683160208415004

Otto, A. L., Penrod, S. D., & Dexter, H. D. (1994). The biasing impact of pretrial publicity on juror judgments. *Law and Human Behavior, 18,* 453–469. doi:10.1007/BF01499050

Otto, R. K., Buffington-Vollum, J. K., & Edens, J. F. (2003). Child custody evaluation. In I. B. Weiner (Series Ed.) & A. M. Goldstein (Vol. Ed.), *The handbook of psychology: Vol. 11. Forensic psychology* (pp. 177–208). Hoboken, NJ: Wiley.

Otto, R. K., & Douglas, K. S. (Eds.). (2009). *Handbook of violence risk assessment.* New York, NY: Routledge.

Otto, R. K., Edens, J. F., & Barcus, E. H. (2000). The use of psychological testing in child custody evaluations. *Family & Conciliation Courts Review, 38,* 312–340. doi:10.1111/j.174-1617.2000.tb00578.x

Otto, R. K., & Martindale, D. A. (2007). The law, process, and science of child custody evaluation. In M. Costanzo, D. Krauss, & K. Pezdek (Eds.), *Expert psychological testimony for the courts* (pp. 251–275). Mahwah, NJ: Erlbaum.

Otto, R. K., Musick, J. E., & Sherrod, C. (2010). *Professional manual for the Inventory of Legal Knowledge.* Lutz, FL: Psychological Assessment Resources.

Otto, R. K., Musick, J. E., & Sherrod, C. (2011). Convergent validity of a screening measure designed to identify defendants feigning knowledge deficits related to competence to stand trial. *Assessment, 18,* 60–62. doi:10.1177/1073191110377162

Packer, I. K., & Borum, R. (2013). Forensic training and practice. In R. K. Otto & I. B. Weiner (Eds.), *Handbook of psychology: Vol. 11. Forensic psychology* (2nd ed., pp. 16–36). Hoboken, NJ: Wiley.

Page, M., Taylor, J., & Blenkin, M. (2011). Uniqueness in the forensic identification sciences—Fact or fiction? *Forensic Science International, 206,* 12–18. doi:10.1016/j.forsciint.2010.08.004

Page, M., Taylor, J., & Blenkin, M. (2013). Expert interpretation of bitemark injuries—A contemporary qualitative study. *Journal of Forensic Sciences, 58,* 664–672. doi:10.1111/1556-4029.12108

Pager, D., & Western, B. (2012). Identifying discrimination at work: The use of field experiments. *Journal of Social Issues, 68,* 221–237. doi:10.1111/j.1540-4560.2012.01746.x

Pahlavan, F. (2013). Third parties belief in a just world and secondary victimization. *Behavioral and Brain Sciences, 36,* 30–31. doi:10.1017/S0140525X1200043X

Park, J., & Feigenson, N. (2013). Effects of a visual technology on mock juror decision making. *Applied Cognitive Psychology, 27,* 235–246. doi:10.1002/acp.2900

Partridge, A., & Eldridge, W. (1974). *The Second Circuit sentencing study* (FJC No. 74-4). Washington, DC: Federal Judicial Center. Retrieved from http://www.fjc.gov/public/pdf.nsf/lookup/2dcrstdy.pdf/$file/2dcrstdy.pdf

Paternoster, R., & Kazyaka, A. (1988). The administration of the death penalty in South Carolina: Experiences over the first few years. *South Carolina Law Review, 39,* 245–414.

Pearle, L. (2007, May 2). *I'm being sued for WHAT?* Retrieved from http://abcnews.go.com/TheLaw/story?id=3121086&page=1

Peckham, R. F. (1985). A judicial response to the cost of litigation. *Rutgers Law Review, 37,* 253–271.

Pennington, N., & Hastie, R. (1993). The story model for juror decision-making. In R. Hastie (Ed.), *Inside the juror: The psychology of juror decision making* (pp. 192–222). Cambridge, MA: Cambridge University Press.

Penrod, S. D. (1990). Predictors of jury decision making in criminal and civil cases: A field experiment. *Forensic Reports, 3,* 261–277.

Penrod, S. D. (2003, Spring). Eyewitness identification evidence: How well are witnesses and police performing? *Criminal Justice, 18,* 36–47, 54.

Penrod, S. D., & Cutler, B. (1999). Preventing mistaken convictions in eyewitness identification trials. In R. Roesch, S. D. Hart, & J. R. P. Ogloff (Eds.), *Psychology and law: The state of the discipline* (pp. 89–118). New York, NY: Kluwer/Plenum.

Pérez-Fuentes, G., Olfson, M., Villegas, L., Morcillo, C., Wang, S., & Blanco, C. (2013). Prevalence and correlates of child sexual abuse: A national study. *Comprehensive Psychiatry, 54,* 16–27. doi:10.1016/j.comppsych.2012.05.010

Perlin, M. L. (1994). *The jurisprudence of the insanity defense.* Durham: University of North Carolina Press.

Perlin, M. L. (2000). *The hidden prejudice: Mental disability on trial.* Washington, DC: American Psychological Association.

Perry, R., Sibley, C. G., & Duckitt, J. (2013). Dangerous and competitive worldviews: A meta-analysis of their associations with social dominance orientation and right-wing authoritarianism. *Journal of Research in Personality, 47,* 116–127. doi:10.1016/j.jrp.2012.10.004

Peters, M. J. V., Horselenberg, R., Jelicic, M., & Merckelbach, H. (2007). The false fame illusion in people with memories about a previous life. *Consciousness and Cognition, 16,* 162–169. doi:10.1016/j.concog.2006.02.002

Petersilia, J. (1994). Violent crime and violent criminals: The response of the justice system. In M. Costanzo & S. Oskamp (Eds.), *Violence and the law* (pp. 226–245). Thousand Oaks, CA: Sage.

Petersilia, J. R., Turner, S., & Peterson, J. E. (1986). *Prison versus probation in California: Implications for crime and offender recidivism* (R-3323-NIJ). Santa Monica, CA: Rand. Retrieved from http://www.rand.org/pubs/reports/R3323.html

Peterson, C., Maier, S. F., & Seligman, M. P. (1993). *Learned helplessness: A theory for the age of personal control.* New York, NY: Oxford University Press.

Pettigrew, T. F., & Martin, J. (1987). Shaping the organizational context for Black American inclusion. *Journal of Social Issues, 43,* 41–78. doi:10.1111/j.1540-4560.1987.tb02330.x

Pezdek, K. (2007). Expert testimony on eyewitness memory and identification. In M. Costanzo, D. Krauss, & K. Pezdek (Eds.), *Expert psychological testimony for the courts* (pp. 99–117). Mahwah, NJ: Erlbaum.

Pezdek, K., Blandon-Gitlin, I., & Moore, C. (2003). Children's face recognition memory: More evidence for the cross-race effect. *Journal of Applied Psychology, 88,* 760–763. doi:10.1037/0021-9010.88.4.760

Phares, E. J. (1976). *Locus of control in personality.* Morristown, NJ: Learning Press.

Phelps, M. S. (2012). The place of punishment: Variation in the provision of inmate services staff across the punitive turn. *Journal of Criminal Justice, 40,* 348–357. doi:10.1016/j.jcrimjus.2012.06.012

Pickel, K. L. (1995). Inducing jurors to disregard inadmissible evidence: A legal explanation does not help. *Law and Human Behavior, 19,* 407–424. doi:10.1007/BF01499140

Pickel, K. L., Karam, T. J., & Warner, T. C. (2009). Jurors' responses to unusual inadmissible evidence. *Criminal Justice and Behavior, 36,* 466–480. doi:10.1177/0093854809332364

Pickel, K. L., Ross, S. J., & Truelove, R. S. (2006). Do weapons automatically capture attention? *Applied Cognitive Psychology, 20,* 871–893. doi:10.1002/acp.1235

Pierce, C. A., Muslin, I. S., Dudley, C. M., & Aguinis, H. (2008). From charm to harm: A content-analytic review of sexual harassment court cases involving workplace romance. *Management Research, 6,* 27–45. doi:10.2753/JMR1536-5433060102

Pinizzotto, A. J., & Finkel, N. J. (1990). Criminal personality profiling: An outcome and process study. *Law and Human Behavior, 14,* 215–233. doi:10.1007/BF01352750

Pintar, J., & Lynn, S. J. (2007). *Hypnosis: A brief history.* New York, NY: Wiley-Blackwell.

Pirelli, G., Gottdiener, W. H., & Zapf, P. A. (2011). A meta-analytic review of competency to stand trial research. *Psychology, Public Policy, and Law, 17,* 1–53. doi:10.1037/a0021713

Platt, A., & Diamond, B. (1966). The origins of the "right and wrong" test of criminal responsibility and its subsequent development in the United States. *California Law Review, 54,* 1227–1260. Retrieved from http://scholarship.law.berkeley.edu/californialawreview

Plumm, K., & Terrance, C. (2009). Battered women who kill: The impact of expert testimony and empathy induction in the courtroom. *Violence Against Women, 15,* 186–205. doi:10.1177/1077801208329145

Podlas, K. (2006). The CSI effect: Exposing the media myth. *Fordham Intellectual Property, Media and Entertainment Law Journal, 16,* 429–466. Retrieved from http://ir.lawnet.fordham.edu/iplj/

Podlesny, J. A. (2003) A paucity of operable case facts restricts applicability of the guilty knowledge technique in FBI criminal polygraph examinations. *Forensic Science Communications, 5*(3). Retrieved from http://www.fbi.gov/about-us/lab/forensic-science-communications

Poole, D. A., & Bruck, M. (2012). Divining testimony? The impact of interviewing props on children's reports of touching. *Developmental Review, 32,* 165–180. doi:10.1016/j.dr.2012.06.007

Poole, D. A., & Dickinson, J. J. (2011). Evidence supporting restrictions on uses of body diagrams in forensic interviews. *Child Abuse & Neglect, 35,* 659–669. doi:10.1016/j.chiabu.2011.05.004

Porter, S., Yuille, J. C., & Lehman, D. R. (1999). The nature of real, implanted, and fabricated memories of emotional childhood events. *Law and Human Behavior, 23,* 517–537. doi:10.1023/A:1022344128649

Posey, A. J., & Wrightsman, L. S. (2005). *Trial consulting.* New York, NY: Oxford University Press.

Principe, G. F., Ceci, S. J., & Bruck, M. (2011). *Children's memory: Psychology and the law.* New York, NY: Wiley-Blackwell.

Pryor, J. B. (2009). Sexual harassment. In H. T. Reis & S. Sprecher (Eds.), *Encyclopedia of human relationships* (pp. 1461–1463). Thousand Oaks, CA: Sage. Retrieved from http://www.sage-ereference.com/view/humanrelationships/n480.xml

Pryor, J. B., & Whalen, N. J. (1997). A typology of sexual harassment: Characteristics of harassers and social circumstances under which sexual harassment occurs. In W. O'Donohue (Ed.), *Sexual harassment: Theory, research, and treatment* (pp. 129–151). Needham Heights, MA: Allyn & Bacon.

Quas, J. A., & Goodman, G. S. (2012). Consequences of criminal court involvement for child victims. *Psychology, Public Policy, and Law, 18,* 392–414. doi:10.1037/a0026146

Quas, J. A., & Lench, H. C. (2007). Arousal at encoding, arousal at retrieval, interviewer support, and children's memory for a mild stressor. *Applied Cognitive Psychology, 21,* 289–305. doi:10.1002/acp.1279

Quinlivan, D. S., Neuschatz, J. S., Cutler, B. L., Wells, G. L., McClung, J., & Harker, D. L. (2012). Do pre-admonition suggestions moderate the effect of unbiased lineup instructions? *Legal and Criminological Psychology, 17,* 165–176. doi:10.1348/135532510X533554

Quinn, J. F. (2007). *Corrections: A concise introduction.* Long Grove, IL: Waveland Press.

Quinsey, V. L., Harris, G. T., Rice, M. E., & Cormier, C. A. (1998). *Violent offenders: Appraising and managing risk.* Washington, DC: American Psychological Association.

Quinsey, V. L., Jones, G. B., Book, A. S., & Barr, K. N. (2006). The dynamic prediction of antisocial behavior among forensic psychiatric patients: A prospective field study. *Journal of Interpersonal Violence, 21,* 1539–1565. doi:10.1177/0886260506294238

Radelet, M. L., Bedau, H. A., & Putnam, C. E. (1992). *In spite of innocence: Erroneous convictions in capital cases.* Boston, MA: Northeastern University Press.

Radelet, M. L., & Pierce, G. L. (2006). The role of victim's race and geography on death sentencing in Illinois: Some recent data from Illinois. In C. J. Ogletree, Jr. & A. Sarat (Eds.), *From lynch mobs to the killing state: Race and the death penalty in America* (pp. 117–149). New York, NY: New York University Press.

Ramsland, K. M. (2013). *The human predator: A historical chronicle of serial murder and forensic investigation.* New York, NY: Penguin.

Rapaport, E. (2012). A modest proposal: The aged of death row should be deemed too old to execute. *Brooklyn Law Review, 77,* 1089–1132. Retrieved from http://www.brooklaw.edu/intellectuallife/lawjournals/brooklynlawreview/generalinformation.aspx?

Ratcliff, R., & Van Dongen, H. P. A. (2009). Sleep deprivation affects multiple distinct cognitive processes. *Psychonomic Bulletin & Review, 16,* 742–751. doi:10.3758/PBR.16.4.742

Reardon, M., Danielsen, E., & Meissner, C. A. (2005, March). *Investigating juror perceptions of fingerprint evidence in criminal cases.* Paper presented at the American Psychology-Law Society Conference, La Jolla, CA.

Redlich, A. D. (2004). Mental illness, police interrogations, and the potential for false confession. *Psychiatric Services, 55,* 19–21. doi:10.1176/appi.ps.55.1.19

Redlich, A. D. (2010). The susceptibility of juveniles to false confessions and false guilty pleas. *Rutgers Law Review, 62,* 943–957. Retrieved from http://www.rutgerslawreview.com

Redlich, A. D., & Meissner, C. (2009). Techniques and controversies in the interrogation of suspects. In J. L. Skeem, K. S. Douglas, & S. O. Lilienfeld (Eds.), *Psychological science in the courtroom: Controversies and consensus* (pp. 124–148). New York, NY: Guilford Press.

Reppucci, N., Meyer, J., & Kostelnik, J. (2009). Police interrogation of juveniles: Results from a national survey of police. In K. D. Lassiter & C. Meissner (Eds.), *Interrogations and confessions: Research, practice, and policy* (pp. 98–117). Washington, DC: American Psychological Association.

Ressler, R. K., Burgess, A. W., & Douglas, J. E. (1988). *Sexual homicide: Patterns and motives.* Lexington, MA: Lexington Books.

Ressler, R. K., Burgess, A. W., Douglas, J. E., Hartman, C. R., & D'Agostino, R. B. (1986). Sexual killers and their victims: Identifying patterns through crime scene analysis. *Journal of Interpersonal Violence, 1,* 288–308. doi:10.1177/088626086001003003

Ressler, R. K., & Shachtman, T. (1992). *Whoever fights monsters.* New York, NY: St. Martin's Press.

Rideau, W., & Wikberg, R. (1992). *Life sentences: Rage and survival behind bars.* New York, NY: Times Books.

Risinger, D. M. (2002). Handwriting identification. In D. L. Faigman, D. H. Kaye, M. J. Saks, & J. Sanders (Eds.), *Science in the law: Forensic science issues* (pp. 113–193). St. Paul, MN: West.

Risinger, D. M., & Loop, J. L. (2002). Three card monte, Monty Hall, modus operandi and "offender profiling": Some lessons of modern cognitive science for the law of evidence. *Cardozo Law Review, 24,* 193–286.

Risinger, D. M., & Saks, M. J. (2003, Fall). A house with no foundation. *Issues in Science and Technology, 20,* 35–39. Retrieved from http://issues.org

Risinger, D. M., Saks, M. J., Thompson, W. C., & Rosenthal, R. (2002). The *Daubert/Kumho* implications of observer effects in forensic science: Hidden problems of expectation and suggestion. *California Law Review, 90,* 1–56. Retrieved from http://scholarship.law.berkeley.edu/californialawreview/

Roane, K. R. (2007, April 25). The CSI effect. *U.S. News & World Report, 2007,* p. 48.

Robbennolt, J. K., MacCoun, R. J., & Darley, J. M. (2010). Multiple constraint satisfaction in judging. In D. E. Klein & G. Mitchell (Eds.), *The psychology of judicial decision making* (pp. 27–39). New York, NY: Oxford University Press.

Roche, T. (2006, July 26). The Yates odyssey. *Time.* Retrieved from http://content.time.com/time/magazine/article/0,9171,1001706,00.html

Rodriguez, S. F., Curry, T. R., & Lee, G. (2006). Gender differences in criminal sentencing: Do effects vary across violent, property, and drug offenses? *Social Science Quarterly, 87,* 318–339. doi:10.1111/j.1540-6237.2006.00383.x

Roesch, R., Golding, S. L., Hans, V. P., & Reppucci, N. D. (1991). Social science and the courts: The role of *amicus curiae* briefs. *Law and Human Behavior, 15*, 1–14. Retrieved from http://scholarship.law.cornell.edu/facpub/413

Roesch, R., Zapf, P. A., Eaves, D., & Webster, C. D. (1998). *The fitness interview test* (Rev. ed.). Burnaby, British Columbia, Canada: Simon Fraser University Mental Health, Law, and Policy Institute.

Rogers, R., & Ewing, C. P. (1992). The measurement of insanity: Debating the merits of the R-CRAS and its alternatives. *International Journal of Law & Psychiatry, 15*, 113–123. doi:10.1016/0160-2527(92)90031-U

Rogers, R., Tillbrook, C. E., & Sewell, K. W. (2004). *Evaluation of Competency to Stand Trial-Revised (ECST-R).* Lutz, FL: Psychological Assessment Resources.

Roper, R. T. (1980). Jury size and verdict consistency: "A line has to be drawn somewhere?" *Law and Society Review, 14*, 977–995.

Rose, M. R., Ellison, C., & Diamond, S. S. (2008). Preferences for juries over judges across racial and ethnic groups. *Social Science Quarterly, 89*, 372–391. doi:10.1111/j.1540-6237.2008.00537.x

Rose, M. R. (2009). Access to juries: Some puzzles regarding race and jury participation. *Sociology of Crime, Law, and Deviance, 12*, 119–44. doi:10.1108/S1521-6136(2009)0000012009

Rosenfeld, J. P. (2011). P300 in detecting concealed information. In B. Verschuere, G. Ben-Shakhar, & E. H. Meijer (Eds.), *Memory detection: Theory and application of the concealed information test* (pp. 63–89). Cambridge, MA: Cambridge University Press.

Rosenthal, R., & Jacobson, L. F. (1968). *Pygmalion in the classroom.* New York, NY: Holt, Rinehart, & Winston.

Ross, D. R., Ceci, S. J., Dunning, D., & Toglia, M. P. (1994). Unconscious transference and mistake identity: When a witness misidentifies a familiar but innocent person. *Journal of Applied Psychology, 79*, 918–930. doi:10.1037/0021-9010.79.6.918

Ross, J. M. (2011). Personality and situational correlates of self-reported reasons for intimate partner violence among women versus men referred for batterers' intervention. *Behavioral Sciences & the Law, 29*, 711–727. doi:10.1002/bsl.1004

Ross, M. W., & Harzke, A. J. (2012). Toward healthy prisons: The TECH model and its applications. *International Journal of Prisoner Health, 8*, 16–26. doi:10.1108/17449201211268255

Ross, S. J., & Malpass, R. S. (2008). Moving forward: Response to "Studying eyewitness investigations in the field." *Law and Human Behavior, 32*, 16–21. doi:10.1007/s10979-007-9104-x

Rossmo, D. K., & Velarde, L. (2008). Geographic profiling analysis: Principles, methods and applications. In S. Chainey & L. Tompson (Eds.), *Crime mapping case studies* (pp. 33–43). New York, NY: Wiley.

Rothman, D. J. (1995). Perfecting the prison: United States, 1789–1865. In N. Morris & D. J. Rothman (Eds.), *The Oxford history of the prison: The practice of punishment in western society* (pp. 100–116). New York, NY: Oxford University Press.

Rotman, E. (1995). The failure of reform: United States, 1865–1965. In N. Morris & D. J. Rothman (Eds.), *The Oxford history of the prison: The practice of punishment in western society* (pp. 151–177). New York, NY: Oxford University Press.

Rotter, M., Way, B., Steinbacher, M., Sawyer, D., & Smith, H. (2004). Personality disorders in prison: Aren't they all antisocial? *Psychiatric Quarterly, 73*, 337–349. doi:10.1023/A:1020468117930

Rotundo, M., Nguyen, D. H., & Sackett, P. R. (2001). A meta-analytic review of gender differences in perceptions of sexual harassment. *Journal of Applied Psychology, 86*, 914–922. doi:10.1037/0021-9010.86.5.914

Rozelle, S. D. (2006). The principled executioner: Capital juries' bias and the benefits of true bifurcation. *Arizona State Law Journal, 38*, 769.

Ruback, R. B., & Wroblewski, J. (2001). The federal sentencing guidelines: Psychological and policy reasons for simplification. *Psychology, Public Policy, and Law, 7*, 739–775. doi:10.1037/1076-8971.7.4.739

Rudman, L., Moss-Racusin, C., Phelan, J. E., & Nauts, S. (2012). Status incongruity and backlash effects: Defending the gender hierarchy motivates prejudice against female leaders. *Journal of Experimental Social Psychology, 48*, 165–179. doi:10.1016/j.jesp.2011.10.008

Rumbelow, D. (1975). *The complete Jack the Ripper.* New York, NY: Little, Brown.

Ruva, C. L., & LeVasseur, M. A. (2012). Behind closed doors: The effects of pretrial publicity on jury deliberations. *Psychology, Crime & Law, 18*, 431–452. doi:10.1080/1068316X.2010.502120

Ruva, C., McEvoy, C., & Bryant, J. B. (2007). Effects of pretrial publicity and jury deliberation on juror bias and source memory errors. *Applied Cognitive Psychology, 21*, 45–67. doi:10.1002/acp.1254

Sabol, W. J., & Couture, H. (2008). *Prison inmates at midyear 2007* (NCJ 221944). Washington, DC: Bureau of Justice Statistics. Retrieved from http://www.bjs.gov/content/pub/pdf/pim07.pdf

Sack, K. (1998, October 4). Fugitive in bombing of clinic may be charged with 3 more. *The New York Times*, p. 18.

Saferstein, R. (2010). *Criminalistics: An introduction to forensic science* (10th ed.). Boston, MA: Prentice Hall.

Saks, M. J. (1990). Expert witnesses, nonexpert witnesses, and nonwitness experts. *Law and Human Behavior, 14*, 291–313. doi:10.1007/BF01068158

Saks, M. J. (1996, March-April). The smaller the jury, the greater the unpredictability. *Judicature, 79*, 263–265.

Saks, M. J. (2010). Forensic identification: From a faith-based "Science" to a scientific science. *Forensic Science International, 201*, 14–17. doi:10.1016/j.forsciint.2010.03.014

Saks, M. J., & Kidd, R. (1986). *Social psychology in the courtroom.* New York, NY: Van Nostrand Reinhold.

Saks, M. J., & Koehler, J. J. (2005, August 5). The coming paradigm shift in forensic identification science. *Science, 309*, 892–895. doi:10.1126/science.1111565

Saks, M. J., & Lanyon, R. I. (2007). Pitfalls and ethics of expert testimony. In M. Costanzo, D. Krauss, & K. Pezdek (Eds.), *Expert psychological testimony for the courts* (pp. 277–284). Mahwah, NJ: Erlbaum.

Saks, M. J., & Marti, M. W. (1997). A meta-analysis of the effects of jury size. *Law and Human Behavior, 21,* 451–467. doi:10.1023/A:1024819605652

Salerno, J. M., & Diamond, S. S. (2010). The promise of a cognitive perspective on jury deliberation. *Psychonomic Bulletin & Review, 17,* 174–179. doi:10.3758/PBR.17.2.174

Sales, B. D., & Shuman, D. W. (2007). Science, experts, and law: Reflections on the past and the future. In M. Costanzo, D. Krauss, & K. Pezdek (Eds.), *Expert psychological testimony for the courts* (pp. 9–30). Mahwah, NJ: Erlbaum.

Sampson, E. E. (1975). On justice as equality. *Journal of Social Issues, 31,* 45–64. doi:10.1111/j.1540-4560.1975.tb00996.x

Sanders, J., Faigman, D., Cheng, E., Mnookin, J., Murphy, E., & Blumenthal, J. (2013). *Modern scientific evidence: The law and science of expert testimony.* Eagan, MN: Thomson West.

Sandler, J. C., Freeman, N. J., & Socia, K. M. (2008). Does a watched pot boil? A time-series analysis of New York State's sex offender and notification law. *Psychology, Public Policy, and Law, 14,* 284–302. doi:10.1037/a0013881

Saykaly, C., Talwar, V., Lindsay, R. L., Bala, N. C., & Lee, K. (2013). The influence of multiple interviews on the verbal markers of children's deception. *Law and Human Behavior, 37,* 187–196. doi:10.1037/lhb0000023

Schacter, D. L. (1996). *Searching for memory.* New York, NY: Basic Books.

Schacter, D. L. (2001). *The seven sins of memory.* Boston, MA: Houghton-Mifflin.

Schklar, J., & Diamond, S. S. (1999). Juror reactions to DNA evidence: Errors and expectancies. *Law and Human Behavior, 23,* 159–184. doi:10.1023/A:1022368801333

Schlager, M. D., & Robbins, K. (2008). Does parole work? Revisited: Reframing the discussion of the impact of postprison supervision on offender outcome. *The Prison Journal, 88,* 234–251. doi:10.1177/0032885508319164

Schlegel, J. (1979). American legal realism and empirical social science: From the Yale experience. *Buffalo Law Review, 28,* 459–586.

Schooler, J. W. (1994). Seeking the core: The issues and evidence surrounding recovered accounts of sexual trauma. *Consciousness and Cognition, 3,* 452–469. doi:10.1006/ccog.1994.1026

Schreiber, N., Bellah, L. D., Martinez, Y., McLaurin, K. A., Strok, R., Garven, S., & Wood, J. M. (2006). Suggestive interviewing in the McMartin Preschool and Kelly Michaels daycare abuse cases: A case study. *Social Influence, 1,* 16–47. doi:10.1080/15534510500361739

Schuller, R. A. (1994). Applications of battered woman syndrome evidence in the courtroom. In M. Costanzo & S. Oskamp (Eds.), *Violence and the law* (pp. 113–134). Thousand Oaks, CA: Sage.

Schuller, R. A., & Hastings, P. A. (1996). Trials of battered women who kill: The impact of alternative forms of expert testimony. *Law and Human Behavior, 2,* 167–188. doi:10.1007/BF01499353

Schuller, R. A., & Jenkins, G. (2007). Expert evidence pertaining to battered women: Limitations and reconceptualizations. In M. Costanzo, D. Krauss, & K. Pezdek (Eds.), *Expert psychological testimony for the courts* (pp. 203–225). Mahwah, NJ: Erlbaum.

Schuller, R. A., & Rzepa, S. (2002). Expert testimony pertaining to battered woman syndrome: Its impact on jurors' decisions. *Law and Human Behavior, 26,* 655–673. doi:10.1023/A:1020933618221

Schuller, R. A., Smith, V. L., & Olson, J. M. (1994). Jurors' decisions in trials of battered women who kill: The role of prior beliefs and expert testimony. *Journal of Applied Social Psychology, 24,* 316–337. doi:10.1111/j.1559-1816.1994.tb00585.x

Schulman, J., Shaver, P., Colman, R., Emrick, B., & Christie, R. (1973, May). Recipe for a jury. *Psychology Today, 77,* 37–44.

Schwartz, A. (2005). A systemic challenge to the reliability and admissibility of firearms and toolmark identification. *Columbia Science and Technology Law Review, 6,* 1–42. Retrieved from http://www.stlr.org

Schweitzer, N. J., & Saks, M. J. (2007). The CSI effect: Popular fiction about forensic science affects the public's expectations about real forensic science. *Jurimetrics, 47,* 357–364.

Scientific Working Group on Friction Ridge Analysis, Study and Technology (SWGFAST). (2012). *Standard for reporting friction ridge examinations* (Document #5). Retrieved from http://www.swgfast.org/Documents.html

Scientific Working Group on Friction Ridge Analysis, Study and Technology (SWGFAST). (2013). *Individualization/identification position statement (latent/tenprint)* (Document #103). Retrieved from http://www.swgfast.org/Comments-Positions/130106-Individualization-ID-Position-Statement.pdf

Scurich, N., & Krauss, D. A. (2013). The effect of adjusted actuarial risk assessment on mock-jurors' decisions in a sexual predator commitment proceeding. *Jurimetrics, 53,* 395–413.

Seligman, M. E. P., & Maier, S. F. (1967). Failure to escape traumatic shock. *Journal of Experimental Psychology, 74,* 1–9. doi:10.1037/h0024514

Sellin, J. T. (1980). *The penalty of death.* Beverly Hills, CA: Sage.

Semmler, C., Brewer, N., & Douglass, A. (2012). Jurors believe eyewitnesses. In B. L. Cutler (Ed.), *Conviction of the innocent: Lessons from psychological research* (pp. 185–209). Washington, DC: American Psychological Association.

Senese, L. (2005). *Anatomy of interrogation themes.* Chicago, IL: John E. Reid and Associates.

Sentencing Project. (2014). *Trends in U.S. corrections.* Washington, DC: Author. Retrieved from http://sentencingproject.org/doc/publications/inc_Trends_in_Corrections_Fact_sheet.pdf

Shaked-Schroer, N., Costanzo, M., & Berger, D. E. (2013). Overlooking coerciveness: The impact of interrogation techniques and guilt corroboration on jurors' judgments of coerciveness. *Legal and Criminological Psychology.* Advance online publication. doi:10.1111/lcrp.12011

Shaked-Schroer, N., Costanzo, M., & Marcus-Newhall, A. (2008). Reducing racial bias in the penalty phase of capital trials. *Behavioral Sciences & the Law, 26,* 603–617. doi:10.1002/bsl.829

Shalev, S. (2009). *Supermax: Controlling risk through solitary confinement.* Cullompton, UK: Willan.

Shapiro, D. L. (2005). Ethical dilemmas in competency for execution evaluations. *Journal of Forensic Psychology Practice, 5,* 75–82. doi:10.1300/J158v05n04_05

Sheehy, E., Stubbs, J., & Tolmie, J. (2012). Battered women charged with homicide in Australia, Canada and New Zealand: How do they fare? *Australian & New Zealand Journal Of Criminology, 45,* 383–399. doi:10.1177/0004865812456855

Shelton, D. E., Kim, Y. S., & Barak, G. (2007). A study of juror expectations and demands concerning scientific evidence: Does the "CSI effect" exist? *Vanderbilt Journal of Entertainment & Technology Law, 9,* 331–368. Retrieved from http://www.jetlaw.org

Sherman, L. W., Farrington, D. P., Welsh, B. C., & MacKenzie, D. L. (Eds.). (2002). *Evidence-based crime prevention.* London, England: Routledge.

Siegel, A., & Elwork, A. (1990). Treating incompetence to stand trial. *Law and Human Behavior, 14,* 57–65. doi:10.1007/BF01055789

Siegel, L. J. (2012). *Criminology* (11th ed.). Belmont, CA: Cengage Learning/Wadsworth.

Silberman, M. (1995). *A world of violence: Corrections in America.* Belmont, CA: Wadsworth.

Simmons, R. J. (1997). *Employment discrimination and EEO practice manual.* Van Nuys, CA: Castle.

Simon, R. I. (2006). Imminent suicide: The illusion of short-term prediction. *Suicide and Life-Threatening Behavior, 36,* 296–301. doi:10.1521/suli.2006.36.3.296

Simon, R. J. (1967). *The jury and the defense of insanity.* Boston, MA: Little, Brown.

Skarbek, D. (2012). Prison gangs, norms, and organizations. *Journal of Economic Behavior & Organization, 82,* 96–109. doi:10.1016/j.jebo.2012.01.002

Skeem, J. L., Golding, S. L., Cohn, N., & Berge, G. (1998). The logic and reliability of expert opinion on competence to stand trial. *Law and Human Behavior, 22,* 519–547. doi:10.1023/A:1025787429972

Skeem, J. L., Manchak, S., & Peterson, J. K. (2011). Correctional policy for offenders with mental illness: Creating a new paradigm for recidivism reduction. *Law and Human Behavior, 35,* 110–126. doi:10.1007/s10979-010-9223-7

Skeem, J. L., & Monahan, J. (2011). Current directions in violence risk assessment. *Current Directions in Psychological Science, 20,* 38–42. doi:10.1177/0963721410397271

Skeem, J. L., Polaschek, D. L. L., Patrick, C. J., & Lilienfeld, S. O. (2011). Psychopathic personality: Bridging the gap between scientific evidence and public policy. *Psychological Science in the Public Interest, 12,* 95–162. doi:10.1177/1529100611426706

Skolnick, J. H. (1961). Scientific theory and scientific evidence: An analysis of lie detection. *Yale Law Journal, 70,* 694–728. Retrieved from http://digitalcommons.law.yale.edu

Skolnick, J. H., & Fyfe, J. J. (1993). *Above the law.* New York, NY: Free Press.

Slade, M. (1994, February 25). Law firms begin reining in sex-harassing partners. *The New York Times,* p. B12.

Slobogin, C. (2003). Toward taping. *Ohio State Journal of Criminal Law, 1,* 309–322. Retrieved from http://moritzlaw.osu.edu/students/groups/osjcl/

Slobogin, C., Melton, G. B., & Showalter, C. R. (1984). The feasibility of a brief evaluation of mental state at the time of the offense. *Law and Human Behavior, 8,* 305–321. doi:10.1007/BF01044698

Smith, A. E., & Haney, C. (2011). Getting to the point: Attempting to improve juror comprehension of capital penalty phase instructions. *Law and Human Behavior, 35,* 339–350. doi:10.1007/s10979-010-9246-0

Smith, H. J., Thomas, T. R., & Tyler, T. R. (2006). Concrete construction employees: When does procedural fairness shape self-evaluations? *Journal of Applied Social Psychology, 36,* 644–663. doi:10.1111/j.0021-9029.2006.00030.x

Smith, P., & Schweitzer, M. (2012). The therapeutic prison. *Journal of Contemporary Criminal Justice, 28,* 7–22. doi:10.1177/104398621143220

Smith, V. L. (1991). Impact of pretrial instruction on jurors' information processing and decision making. *Journal of Applied Psychology, 76,* 220–228. doi:10.1037/0021-9010.76.2.220

Snook, B., Eastwood, J., Gendreau, P., Goggin, C., & Cullen, R. M. (2007). Taking stock of criminal profiling: A narrative review and meta-analysis. *Criminal Justice and Behavior, 34,* 437–453. doi:10.1177/0093854806296925

Snyder, H. (2006, December). *Juvenile arrests 2004* (NCJ 214563). Washington, DC: Office of Juvenile Justice and Delinquency Prevention. Retrieved from https://www.ncjrs.gov/pdffiles1/ojjdp/214563.pdf

Softley, P. (1980). *Police interrogation: An observational study in four police stations.* London, England: Her Majesty's Stationery Office.

Solove, D. (2009, March 20). *Should we have professional juries?* [Blog post]. Retrieved from http://www.concurringopinions.com/archives/2009/03/should_we_have.html

Sommers, S. R. (2006). On racial diversity and group decision making: Identifying multiple effects of racial composition on jury deliberations. *Journal of Personality and Social Psychology, 90,* 597–612. doi:10.1037/0022-3514.90.4.597

Sommers, S. R. (2008). Determinants and consequences of jury racial diversity: Empirical findings, implications, and directions for future research. *Social Issues and Policy Review, 2,* 65–102. doi:10.1111/j.1751-2409.2008.00011.x

Sommers, S. (2011). *Situations matter: Understanding how context transforms your world.* New York, NY: Riverhead Books.

Sommers, S. R., & Ellsworth, P. C. (2009). "Race salience" in juror decision-making: Misconceptions, clarifications, and unanswered questions. *Behavioral Sciences & the Law, 27,* 599–609. doi:10.1002/bsl.877

Spanos, N. P., Burgess, C. A., Burgess, M. F., Samuels, C., & Blois, W. O. (1999). Creating false memories of infancy with hypnotic and nonhypnotic procedures. *Applied Cognitive Psychology, 13,* 201–218. doi:10.1002/(SICI)1099-0720(199906)13:3<201::AID-ACP565>3.0.CO;2-X

Spence, S. A., Hunter, M. D., Farrow, T. F., Green, R. D., Leung, D. H., Hughes, C. J., & Ganesan, V. (2004). A cognitive neurobiological account of deception: Evidence from functional neuroimaging. *Philosophical Transactions of the Royal Society of London: Biological Sciences, 359,* 1755–1762. doi:10.1098/rstb.2004.1555

Springer, J. (2002, January 9). *Kids drowned: Mother faces execution.* Retrieved from http://www.unsolvedmysteries.com/usm221002.html?t=News

Stack, M. K. (2002, March 16). Yates draws life sentence. *Los Angeles Times,* p. A14.

Stafford, K. P. (2003). Assessment of competence to stand trial. In I. B. Weiner (Series Ed.) & A. Goldstein (Vol. Ed.), *The handbook of psychology: Vol. 11. Forensic psychology* (pp. 359–380). Hoboken, NJ: Wiley.

Stahl, P. M. (2014). Conducting child custody and parenting evaluations. In I. B. Weiner & R. K. Otto (Eds.), *Handbook of forensic psychology* (4th ed., pp. 137–169). Hoboken, NJ: Wiley.

Stahl, P. M., & Martin, L. (2013). An historical look at child custody evaluations and the influence of AFCC. *Family Court Review, 51,* 42–47. doi:10.1111/fcre.12006

Stal, M. (2012). Treatment of older and elderly inmates within prisons. *Journal of Correctional Health Care, 19,* 69–73. doi:10.1177/1078345812458245

Stasser, G. (1992). Pooling of unshared information during group discussion. In S. Worchel, W. Wood, & J. Simpson (Eds.), *Group process and productivity* (pp. 48–67). Newbury Park, CA: Sage.

Steadman, H. J., & Cocozza, J. J. (1974). *Careers of the criminally insane: Excessive social control of deviance.* Lexington, MA: Lexington Books.

Steadman, H. J., Mulvey, E., Monahan, J., Robbins, P. C., Appelbaum, P. S., Grisso, T., . . . Silver, E. (1998). Violence by people discharged from acute psychiatric inpatient facilities and by others in the same neighborhoods. *Archives of General Psychiatry, 55,* 393–401. doi:10.1001/archpsyc.55.5.393

Steblay, N. M. (1992). A meta-analytic review of the weapon-focus effect. *Law and Human Behavior, 16,* 413–424. doi:10.1007/BF02352267

Steblay, N. M., Besirevic, J., Fulero, S. M., & Jimenez-Lorente, B. (1999). The effects of pretrial publicity on juror verdicts: A meta-analytic review. *Law and Human Behavior, 23,* 219–235. doi:10.1023/A:1022325019080

Steblay, N. M., & Bothwell, R. K. (1994). Evidence for hypnotically refreshed testimony: The view from the laboratory. *Law and Human Behavior, 18,* 635–652. doi:10.1007/BF01499329

Steblay, N. K., Dysart, J. E., & Wells, G. L. (2011). Seventy-two tests of the sequential lineup superiority effect: A meta-analysis and policy discussion. *Psychology, Public Policy, and Law, 17,* 99–139. doi:10.1037/a0021650

Steblay, N., Hosch, H. M., Culhane, S. E., & McWethy, A. (2006). The impact on juror verdicts of judicial instruction to disregard inadmissible evidence: A meta-analysis. *Law and Human Behavior, 30,* 469–492. doi:10.1007/s10979-006-9039-7

Steblay, N. M., & Loftus, E. F. (2008). Eyewitness memory and the legal system. In E. Shafir (Ed.), *The behavioral foundations of policy* (pp. 145–162). New York, NY: Russell Sage.

Steinberg, L. (2003). Is decision making the right framework for the study of adolescent risk taking? In D. Romer (Ed.), *Reducing adolescent risk: Toward an integrated approach* (pp. 18–24). Thousand Oaks, CA: Sage.

Steinberg, L. (2007). Risk taking in adolescence: New perspectives from brain and behavioral science. *Current Directions in Psychological Science, 16,* 55–59. doi:10.1111/j.1467-8721.2007.00475.x

Stephan, W. G. (1986). The effects of school desegregation: An evaluation 30 years after Brown. In M. J. Saks & L. Saxe (Eds.), *Advances in applied social psychology* (Vol. 3, pp. 181–206). Mahwah, NJ: Erlbaum.

Stevenson, M. C., Bottoms, B. L., & Diamond, S. S. (2010). Jurors' discussions of a defendant's history of child abuse and alcohol abuse in capital sentencing deliberations. *Psychology, Public Policy, and Law, 16,* 1–38. doi:10.1037/a0018404

Stoltenborgh, M., van IJzendoorn, M. H., Euser, E. M., & Bakermans-Kranenburg, M. J. (2011). A global perspective on child sexual abuse: Meta-analysis of prevalence around the world. *Child Maltreatment, 16,* 79–101. doi:10.1177/1077559511403920

Street, A. E., Kimerling, R., Bell, M. E., & Pavao, J. (2011). Sexual harassment and sexual assault during military service. In J. I. Ruzek, P. P. Schnurr, J. J. Vasterling, & M. J. Friedman (Eds.), *Caring for veterans with deployment-related stress disorders* (pp. 131–150). doi:10.1037/12323-006

Strodtbeck, F., & Lipinski, R. (1985). Becoming first among equals: Moral considerations in jury foreman selection. *Journal of Personality and Social Psychology, 49,* 927–936. doi:10.1037/0022-3514.49.4.927

Sullivan, L. (2006). *At Pelican Bay Prison, a life in solitary* [Radio broadcast]. Washington, DC: NPR. Retrieved from http://www.npr.org/templates/story/story.php?storyId=5584254

Sullivan, T. (1992). *Unequal verdicts: The Central Park jogger trials.* New York, NY: Simon & Schuster.

Sullivan, T. P. (2004). *Police experiences with recording custodial interrogations.* Chicago, IL: Northwestern University School of Law, Center on Wrongful Convictions.

Sullivan, T. P. (2006). The time has come for law enforcement recordings of custodial interviews, start to finish. *Golden Gate University Law Review, 37,* 175–190. Retrieved from http://digitalcommons.law.ggu.edu/ggulrev/

Summers, A., Hayward, R. D., & Miller, M. K. (2010). Death qualification as systematic exclusion of jurors with certain religious and other characteristics. *Journal of Applied Social Psychology, 40,* 3218–3234. doi:10.1111/j.1559-1816.2010.00698.x

Summit, R. C. (1983). The child sexual abuse accommodation syndrome. *Child Abuse & Neglect, 7,* 177–193. doi:10.1016/0145-2134(83)90070-4

Summit, R. C. (1998). Hidden victims, hidden pain: Societal avoidance of child sexual abuse. In G. E. Wyatt & G. J. Powell (Eds.), *Lasting effects of child sexual abuse* (pp. 39–60). Newbury Park, CA: Sage.

Surprenant, A., & Neath, I. (2009). *Principles of memory: Models and perspectives.* New York, NY: Psychology Press.

Sutton, J. R. (2013). Symbol and substance: Effects of California's three strikes law on felony sentencing. *Law & Society Review, 47,* 37–72. doi:10.1111/lasr.12001

Tanford, J. A. (1990a). The law and psychology of jury instructions. *Nebraska Law Review, 69,* 71–111.

Tanford, J. A. (1990b). The limits of a scientific jurisprudence: The Supreme Court and psychology. *Indiana Law Journal, 66,* 137–173. Retrieved from http://www.repository.law.indiana.edu/ilj/

Tangen, J. M., Thompson, M. B., & McCarthy, D. J. (2011). Identifying fingerprint expertise. *Psychological Science, 22,* 995–997. doi:10.1177/0956797611414729

Taylor-Butts, A., & Porter, L. (2011). Family related homicides, 2000 to 2009. In *Family violence in Canada: A statistical profile* (pp. 32–41). Ottawa, Ontario, Canada: Statistics Canada. Retrieved from http://www.statcan.gc.ca/pub/85-224-x/85-224-x2010000-eng.pdf

Taylor, S., Lambeth, D., Green, G., Bone, R., & Cahillane, M. A. (2012). Cluster analysis examination of serial killer profiling categories: A bottom-up approach. *Journal of Investigative Psychology and Offender Profiling, 9,* 30–51. doi:10.1002/jip.149

Taylor, T. S., & Hosch, H. M. (2004). An examination of jury verdicts for evidence of a similarity-leniency effect, an out-group punitiveness effect or a black sheep effect. *Law and Human Behavior, 28,* 587–598. doi:10.1023/B:LAHU.0000046436.36228.71

Teasdale, B., Silver, E., & Monahan, J. (2006). Gender, threat/control-override delusions and violence. *Law and Human Behavior, 30,* 649–658. doi:10.1007/s10979-006-9044-x

Templeton, L. J., & Hartnagel, T. F. (2012). Causal attributions of crime and the public's sentencing goals. *Canadian Journal of Criminology and Criminal Justice/La Revue canadienne de criminologie et de justice pénale, 54,* 45–65. doi:10.3138/cjccj.2010.E.29

Terpstra, D. E., & Baker, D. D. (1992). Outcomes of federal court decisions on sexual harassment. *Academy of Management Journal, 35,* 181–190.

Thimsen, S., Bornstein, B. H., & Miller, M. K. (2009). The dynamite charge: Too explosive for its own good? *Valparaiso University Law Review, 44,* 93–124. Retrieved from http://scholar.valpo.edu/vulr/

Thompson-Cannino, J., Cotton, R., & Torneo, E. (2009). *Picking Cotton: Our memoir of injustice and redemption.* New York, NY: St. Martin's Press.

Thompson, D. (2008, July 5). Aging inmates add to prison strain in California. *San Jose Mercury News.*

Thompson, J. (1999). *What Jennifer saw* [Transcript of television interview]. Retrieved from http://www.pbs.org/wgbh/pages/frontline/shows/dna/

Thompson, W. C. (1989). Death qualification after *Wainwright v. Witt* and *Lockhart v. McCree. Law and Human Behavior, 13,* 185–215. doi:10.1007/BF01055923

Thompson, W. C. (1997). The National Research Council's second report on forensic DNA evidence: A critique. *Jurimetrics, 37,* 405–424.

Thompson, W. C., & Cole, S. A. (2007). Psychological aspects of forensic identification evidence. In M. Costanzo, D. Krauss, & K. Pezdek (Eds.), *Expert psychological testimony for the courts* (pp. 31–68). Mahwah, NJ: Erlbaum.

Thompson, W. C., Ford, S., Doom, T., Raymer, M., & Krane, D. (2003). Evaluating forensic DNA evidence: Essential elements of a competent defense review: Part 1. *The Champion, 27,* 16–25. Retrieved from http://www.bioforensics.com/articles/index.html

Thompson, W. C., & Schumann, E. L. (1997). Interpretation of statistical evidence in criminal trials: The prosecutor's fallacy and the defense attorney's fallacy. *Law and Human Behavior, 11,* 167–187. doi:10.1007/BF01044641

Thornberry, T. P., & Jacoby, J. E. (1979). *The criminally insane: A community follow-up of mentally ill offenders.* Chicago, IL: University of Chicago Press.

Thornton, J. I., & Peterson, J. L. (2013). The general assumptions and rationale of forensic identification. In D. L. Faigman, J. A. Blumenthal, E. K. Cheng, J. L. Mnookin, E. E. Murphy, & J. Sanders (Eds.), *Modern scientific evidence: The law and science of expert testimony: Vol. 4. Forensics.* Eagan, MN: Thomson West.

Tjaden, P., & Thoennes, N. (2000). *Full report of the prevalence, incidence, and consequences of violence against women: Findings from the National Violence Against Women survey* (NCJ 183781). Washington, DC: National Institute of Justice and the Centers for Disease Control and Prevention. Retrieved from https://www.ncjrs.gov/pdffiles1/nij/183781.pdf

Toch, H. (1997). *Corrections: A humanistic approach.* Monsey, NY: Criminal Justice Press.

Toch, H., & Adams, K. (2002). *Acting out: Maladaptive behavior in confinement.* Washington, DC: American Psychological Association.

Toobin, J. (1996, September 9). The Marcia Clark verdict. *The New Yorker, 1996,* 58–71.

Tremper, C. R. (1987). Organized psychology's efforts to influence judicial policymaking. *American Psychologist, 42,* 496–501. doi:10.1037/0003-066X.42.5.496

Triandis, H. C. (1996). The psychological measurement of cultural syndromes. *American Psychologist, 51,* 407–415. doi:10.1037/0003-066X.51.4.407

Tully, R. J., Chou, S., & Browne, K. D. (2013). A systematic review on the effectiveness of sex offender risk assessment tools in predicting sexual recidivism of adult male sex offenders. *Clinical Psychology Review, 33,* 287–316. doi:10.1016/j.cpr.2012.12.002

Tyler, T. R. (2006). Restorative justice and procedural justice: Dealing with rule breaking. *Journal of Social Issues, 62,* 307–326. doi:10.1111/j.1540-4560.2006.00452.x

United Nations. (1987). Convention against torture and other cruel, inhuman or degrading treatment or punishment. *Treaty Series, 1465,* 85.

United Nations General Assembly. (1948). *Universal Declaration of Human Rights.* New York, NY: Author. Retrieved from http://www.un.org/en/documents/udhr/index.shtml

United States Courts. (2011, June 23). *Newly available: Costs of incarceration and supervision in FY 2010.* Retrieved from http://www.uscourts.gov/news/newsview/11-06-23/Newly_Available_Costs_of_Incarceration_and_Supervision_in_FY_2010.aspx

United States Merit Systems Protection Board. (2007). FY 2007 case processing statistics. In *U.S. Merit Systems Protection Board annual report: Fiscal year 2007* (pp. 23–33). Washington, DC: Author. Retrieved from http://www.mspb.gov/

Vallano, J. P. (2013). Psychological injuries and legal decision making in civil cases: What we know and what we do not know. *Psychological Injury and Law, 6,* 99–112. doi:10.1007/s12207-013-9153-z

Vanman, E. J., Paul, B. Y., Kaplan, D. L., & Miller, N. (1990). Facial electromyography differentiates racial bias in imagined cooperative settings. *Psychophysiology, 27*(Suppl. s4a), S71.

Vendemia, J. M., Buzan, R. F., Green, E. P., & Schillaci, M. J. (2006). Effects of preparedness to deceive on ERP waveforms in a two-stimulus paradigm. *Journal of Neurotherapy, 9,* 45–70. doi:10.1300/J184v09n03_04

Vestal, C. (2013, October 29). *Study finds aging inmates pushing up prison health care costs.* Retrieved from http://www.pewstates.org/projects/stateline/headlines/study-finds-aging-inmates-pushing-up-prison-health-care-costs-85899516112

Vickers, A. L. (2005). *Daubert* critique and interpretation: What existing studies tell us about the application of *Daubert. University of San Francisco Law Review, 43,* 109–147.

Vidmar, N., & Hans, V. P. (2007). *American juries: The verdict.* New Haven, CT: Yale University Press.

Vidmar, N., & Hans, V. P. (2008, March-April). The verdict on juries. *Judicature, 91,* 226–230.

Vidmar, N., Lempert, R. O., Diamond, S. S., Hans, V. P., Landsman, S., MacCoun, R., . . . Horowitz, I. (2000). Amicus brief: Kumho Tire v. Carmichael. *Law and Human Behavior, 24,* 387–400. doi:10.1023/A:1005588112385

Vidmar, N., & Rice, J. J. (1993). Assessments of noneconomic damage awards in medical negligence: A comparison of jurors with legal professionals. *Iowa Law Review, 78,* 883–911.

Viljoen, J. L., & Wingrove, T. (2007). Adjudicative competence in adolescent defendants: Judges' and defense attorney's views of legal standards for adolescents in juvenile and criminal court. *Psychology, Public Policy, and Law, 13,* 204–229. doi:10.1037/1076-8971.13.3.204

Villettaz, P., Killias, M., & Zoder, I. (2006). The effects of custodial versus non-custodial sentences on reoffending: A systematic review of the state of knowledge. *Campbell Systematic Reviews, 2*(13), 1–69. doi:10.4073/csr.2006.13

Visher, C. A. (1987). Juror decision making: The importance of evidence. *Law and Human Behavior, 11,* 1–17. doi:10.1007/BF01044835

Visher, C., Debus, S., & Yahner, J. (2008, October). *Employment after prison: A longitudinal study of releases in three states.* Washington, DC: Urban Institute. Retrieved from http://www.urban.org/UploadedPDF/411778_employment_after_prison.pdf

Visher, C. A., & O'Connell, D. J. (2012). Incarceration and inmates' self perceptions about returning home. *Journal of Criminal Justice, 40,* 386–393. doi:10.1016/j.jcrimjus.2012.06.007

Vlahos, J. (2012). The department of pre-crime. *Scientific American Mind, 306,* 62–67. doi:10.1038/scientificamerican0112-62

Vrij, A. (2004). Why professionals fail to catch liars and how they can improve. *Legal and Criminological Psychology, 9,* 159–181. doi:10.1348/1355325041719356

Vrij, A., Granhag, P. A., Mann, S., & Leal, S. (2011). Outsmarting the liars: Toward a cognitive lie detection approach. *Current Directions in Psychological Science, 20,* 28–32. doi:10.1177/0963721410391245

Vrij, A., Mann, S., & Fisher, R. P. (2006). An empirical test of the behaviour analysis interview. *Law and Human Behavior, 30,* 329–345. doi:10.1007/s10979-006-9014-3

Waldo, C. R., Berdahl, J. L., & Fitzgerald, L. F. (1998). Are men sexually harassed? If so, by whom? *Law and Human Behavior, 22,* 59–79. doi:10.1023/A:1025776705629

Walker, L. (1979). *The battered woman.* New York, NY: Harper & Row.

Walker, L. E. A. (2000). *The battered woman syndrome* (2nd ed.). New York, NY: Springer.

Walker, L. E. A. (2009). *The battered woman syndrome* (3rd ed.). New York, NY: Springer.

Walker, L., & Shapiro, D. (2003). *Introduction to forensic psychology: Clinical and social psychological perspectives.* New York, NY: Kluwer.

Warden, R. (2003). The role of false confessions in Illinois wrongful murder convictions since 1970. Chicago, IL: Northwestern Law School, Bluhm Legal Clinic, Center on Wrongful Convictions.

Warmelink, L., Vrij, A., Mann, S., Leal, S., Forrester, D., & Fisher, R. P. (2011). Thermal imaging as a lie detection tool at airports. *Law and Human Behavior, 35,* 40–48. doi:10.1007/s10979-010-9251-3

Warren, J. I., Murrie, D., Chauhan, P., Dietz, P. E., & Morris, J. (2004). Opinion formation in evaluating sanity at the time of the offense: An examination of 5175 pre-trial evaluations. *Behavioral Sciences & the Law, 22,* 171–186. doi:10.1002/bsl.559

Warren, J. I., Murrie, D., Stejskal, W., Colwell, L., Morris, J., Chauhan, P., & Dietz, P. (2006). Opinion formation in the evaluating the adjudicative competence and restorability of criminal defendant: A review of 8000 evaluations. *Behavioral Sciences & the Law, 24,* 113–132. doi:10.1002/bsl.699

Webb, T. L., & Sheeran, P. (2006). Does changing behavioral intentions engender behavior change? A meta-analysis of the experimental evidence. *Psychological Bulletin, 132,* 249–268. doi:10.1037/0033-2909.132.2.249

Webster, C., Douglas, K., Eaves, D., & Hart, S. (1997). *HCR-20: Assessing risk for violence, version 2.* Burnaby, British Columbia, Canada: Simon Fraser University, Mental Health, Law, and Policy Institute.

Wegner, D. M. (2003). *The illusion of conscious will.* Boston, MA: MIT Press.

Wegner, D. M. (2004). Thought suppression and mental control. In L. Nadel (Ed.), *Encyclopedia of cognitive science* (pp. 395–397). London, England: Macmillan.

Weiner, B., Graham, S., & Reyna, C. (1997). An attributional examination of retributive versus utilitarian philosophies of punishment. *Social Justice Research, 10,* 431–452. doi:10.1007/BF02683293

Weinstock, R., Leong, G. B., & Silva, J. A. (2010). Competence to be executed: An ethical analysis post *Panetti. Behavioral Sciences & the Law, 28,* 690–706. doi:10.1002/bsl.951

Wells, G. L. (1978). Applied eyewitness testimony research: System variables and estimator variables. *Journal of Personality and Social Psychology, 36,* 1546–1557. doi:10.1037/0022-3514.36.12.1546

Wells, G. L. (2006). Eyewitness identification: Systemic reforms. *Wisconsin Law Review, 2006,* 615–643.

Wells, G. L., & Bradfield, A. L. (1998). "Good, you identified the suspect": Feedback to eyewitnesses distorts their reports of the witnessing experience. *Journal of Applied Psychology, 83,* 360–376. doi:10.1037/0021-9010.83.3.360

Wells, G. L., Memon, A., & Penrod, S. D. (2006). Eyewitness evidence: Improving its probative value. *Psychological Science in the Public Interest, 7,* 45–75. doi:10.1111/j.1529-1006.2006.00027.x

Wells, G. L., & Quinlivan, D. S. (2009). Suggestive eyewitness identification procedures and the Supreme Court's reliability test in light of eyewitness science: 30 years later. *Law and Human Behavior, 33,* 1–24. doi:10.1007/s10979-008-9130-3

Wells, G. L., Small, M., Penrod, S., Malpass, R. S., Fulero, S. M., & Brimacombe, C. A. E. (1998). Eyewitness identification procedures: Recommendations for lineups and photospreads. *Law and Human Behavior, 22,* 603–647. doi:10.1023/A:1025750605807

Wells, G. L., Steblay, N. K., & Dysart, J. E. (2012). *A test of the simultaneous vs. sequential lineup methods: An initial report of the AJS National Eyewitness Identification Field Studies.* Des Moines, IA: American Judicature Society. Retrieved from http://216.36.221.170/wc/pdfs/EWID_PrintFriendly.pdf

Werner, E. E. (2005). Resilience research: Past, present, and future. In R. DeV. Peters, B. Leadbeater, & R. J. McMahon (Eds.), *Resilience in children, families, and communities: Linking context to practice and policy* (pp. 3–11). doi:10.1007/0-387-23824-7_1

Westling, W. (2001). Something is rotten in the interrogation room: Let's try video oversight. *John Marshall Law Review, 34,* 537–555. Retrieved from http://repository.jmls.edu/lawreview/

Wheatmann, S. R., & Shaffer, D. R. (2001). On finding for defendants who plead insanity: The crucial impact of dispositional instructions and opportunity to deliberate. *Law and Human Behavior, 25,* 167–183. doi:10.1023/A:1005645414992

White, W. (2003). Confessions in capital cases. *University of Illinois Law Review, 203,* 979–1036. Retrieved from http://illinoislawreview.org

Whitman, D. S., Caleo, S., Carpenter, N. C., Horner, M. T., & Bernerth, J. B. (2012). Fairness at the collective level: A meta-analytic examination of the consequences and boundary conditions of organizational justice climate. *Journal of Applied Psychology, 97,* 776–791. doi:10.1037/a0028021

Wiener, R. L., & Hurt, L. E. (2001). How do people evaluate social sexual conduct at work?: A psycholegal model. *Journal of Applied Psychology, 85,* 75–85. doi:10.1037/0021-9010.85.1.75

Wiener, R. L., Hurt, L. E., Thomas, S. L., Sadler, M. S., Bauer, C. A., & Sargent, T. M. (1998). The role of declarative and procedural knowledge in capital murder sentencing. *Journal of Applied Social Psychology, 28,* 124–144.

Wiener, R. L., & Winter, R. J. (2007). Totality of circumstances in sexual harassment decisions: A decision-making model. In R. L. Wiener, B. H. Bornstein, R. Schopp, & S. L. Willborn (Eds.), *Social consciousness in legal decision making: Psychological perspectives* (pp. 171–196). doi:10.1007/978-0-387-46218-9_9

Wigmore, J. (1909). Professor Munsterberg and the psychology of testimony: Being a report of the case of *Cokestone v. Munsterberg. Illinois Law Review, 3,* 399–445.

Williams, J. C., Blair-Loy, M., & Berdahl, J. L. (2013). Cultural schemas, social class, and the flexibility stigma. *Journal of Social Issues, 69,* 209–234. doi:10.1111/josi.12012

Willness, C. R., Steel, P., & Lee, K. (2007). A meta-analysis of the antecedents and consequences of workplace sexual harassment. *Personnel Psychology, 60,* 127–162. doi:10.1111/j.1744-6570.2007.00067.x

Wilson, J., & Barboza, S. (2010, Summer). The looming challenge of dementia in prisons. *CorrectCare, 24,* 12–14. Retrieved from http://www.ncchc.org/correctcare

Winnick, B. J. (2001). The civil commitment hearing: Applying the law therapeutically. In L. E. Frost & R. J. Bonnie (Eds.), *The evolution of mental health law* (pp. 291–308). Washington, DC: American Psychological Association.

Winick, B. J. (2008). Determining when severe mental illness should disqualify a defendant from capital punishment. In R. Schopp, R. Wiener, B. Bornstein, & S. Willborn (Eds.), *Mental disorder and criminal law: Responsibility, punishment, and competence* (pp. 45–78). doi:10.1007/978-0-387-84845-7_2

Winter, R. J., & Vallano, J. P. (2012). The impact of psychological injuries on sexual harassment determinations. *Psychological Injury and Law, 5,* 208–220. doi:10.1007/s12207-012-9135-6

Winterdyk, J., & Ruddell, R. (2010). Managing prison gangs: Results from a survey of U.S. prison systems. *Journal of Criminal Justice, 38,* 730–736. doi:10.1016/j.jcrimjus.2010.04.047

Wise, R. A., Safer, M. A., & Maro, C. M. (2011). What U.S. law enforcement officers know and believe about eyewitness factors, eyewitness interviews and identification procedures. *Applied Cognitive Psychology, 25,* 488–500. doi:10.1002/acp.1717

Wolfgang, M. E., & Riedel, M. (1973). Race, judicial discretion, and the death penalty. *Annals of the American Academy of Political and Social Science, 407,* 119–133. doi:10.1177/000271627340700110

Wolpe, P. R., Foster, K. R., & Langleben, D. D. (2005). Emerging neurotechnologies for lie-detection: Promises and perils. *The American Journal of Bioethics, 5,* 39–49. Retrieved from http://www.bioethics.net

Woodhams, J., Grant, T., & Price, A. R. (2007). From marine ecology to crime analysis: Improving the detection of serial sexual offences using a taxonomic similarity measure. *Journal of Investigative Psychology and Offender Profiling, 4,* 17–27. doi:10.1002/jip.55

Word, C. O., Zanna, M. P., & Cooper, J. (1974). The nonverbal mediation of self-fulfilling prophecies in interracial interaction. *Journal of Experimental Social Psychology, 10,* 109–121. doi:10.1016/0022-1031(74)90059-6

Worrall, J. L., & Morris, R. G. (2012). Prison gang integration and inmate violence. *Journal of Criminal Justice, 40,* 373–381. doi:10.1016/j.jcrimjus.2012.06.002

Wright, C. V., & Fitzgerald, L. F. (2007). Angry and afraid: Women's appraisal of sexual harassment during litigation. *Psychology of Women Quarterly, 31,* 73–84. doi:10.1111/j.1471-6402.2007.00332.x

Wright, C. V., & Fitzgerald, L. F. (2009). Correlates of joining a sexual harassment class action. *Law and Human Behavior, 33,* 265–282. doi:10.1007/s10979-008-9156-6

Wright, E. M., Van Voorhis, P., Salisbury, E. J., & Bauman, A. (2012). Gender-responsive lessons learned and policy implications for women in prison: A review. *Criminal Justice and Behavior, 39,* 1612–1632. doi:10.1177/0093854812451088

Wright, L. (1994). *Remembering Satan*. New York, NY: Knopf.

Yang, M., Wong, S. C. P., & Coid, J. (2010). The efficacy of violence prediction: A meta-analytic comparison of nine risk assessment tools. *Psychological Bulletin, 136,* 740–767. doi:10.1037/a0020473

Yoshihama, M. (2002). Breaking the web of abuse and silence: Voices of battered women in Japan. *Social Work, 47,* 389–400. doi:10.1093/sw/47.4.389

Zabell, S. L. (2005). Fingerprint evidence. *Journal of Law and Policy, 13,* 143–170. Retrieved from http://www.brooklaw.edu/en/intellectuallife/lawjournals/journaloflawandpolicy/generalinformation.aspx?

Zapf, P. A., Golding, S. L., & Roesch, R. (2006). Criminal responsibility and the insanity defense. In I. B. Weiner & A. K. Hess (Eds.), *The handbook of forensic psychology* (3rd ed., 332–363). Hoboken, NJ: Wiley.

Zapf, P. A., Golding, S. L., Roesch, R., & Pirelli, G. (2014). Assessing criminal responsibility. In I. B. Weiner & R. K. Otto (Eds.), *Handbook of forensic psychology* (4th ed., pp. 315–352). New York, NY: Wiley.

Zapf, P. A., & Roesch, R. (2006). Competency to stand trial: A guide for evaluators. In I. B. Weiner & A. K. Hess (Eds.), *The handbook of forensic psychology* (3rd ed., pp. 305–331). Hoboken, NJ: Wiley.

Zapf, P. A., & Roesch, R. (2011). Future directions in the restoration of competency to stand trial. *Current Directions in Psychological Science, 20,* 43–47. doi:10.1177/0963721410396798

Zapf, P. A., Roesch, R., & Pirelli, G. (2014). Assessing competency to stand trial. In I. B. Weiner & R. K. Otto (Eds.), *Handbook of forensic psychology* (4th ed., pp. 281–314). New York, NY: Wiley.

Zapf, P., Zottoli, T., & Pirelli, G. (2009). Insanity in the courtroom: Issues of criminal responsibility and competency to stand trial. In D. Canter (Series Ed.) & D. Krauss & J. Lieberman (Vol. Eds.), *Psychology in the courtroom: Vol. 2. Psychological expertise in court* (pp. 79–102). Burlington, VT: Ashgate.

Zara, G., & Farrington, D. P. (2013). Assessment of risk for juvenile compared with adult criminal onset implications for policy, prevention, and intervention. *Psychology, Public Policy, and Law, 19,* 235–249. doi:10.1037/a0029050

Zeisel, H., & Diamond, S. S. (1978). The effect of peremptory challenges on jury and verdict: An experiment in a federal district court. *Stanford Law Review, 30,* 491–529.

Zimring, F. E. (2008). *The great American crime decline* (Paperback ed.). New York, NY: Oxford University Press.

Name Index

Note: Page numbers followed by *f* indicate figures; those followed by *t* indicate tables.

Padget, T., 66
Page, M., 76
Pager, D., 319
Pahlavan, F., 126
Painter, H., 235, 236
Painter, J., 235, 236
Painter, M., 235, 236
Palmer, J. C., 141
Pan, W., 12
Panetti, S., 162
Park, E., 200
Park, J., 260
Parra, G. R., 250
Partridge, A., 330
Pascal, B., 320
Paternoster, R., 365
Patrick, C. J., 295
Paul, B. Y., 318
Pavao, J., 305
Pavlidis, I., 68
Pearle, L., 268
Peckham, R. F., 273
Peel, R., 179
Peiró, J. M., 325
Pennington, N., 255, 265
Penrod, S., 121, 271
Penrod, S. D., 125, 130, 136, 140, 141, 148, 149, 258, 265, 275
Pepper, J. V., 368
Pepper, M. B., 310
Perlin, M. L., 184, 286
Péron, A., 84–85
Perry, E. L., 310
Perry, R., 126
Peters, L., 301
Peters, M. J. V., 230
Petersilia, J., 351
Petersilia, J. R., 351
Peterson, C., 198
Peterson, I., 24
Peterson, J. E., 351
Peterson, J. K., 341
Peterson, J. L., 84, 85, 89
Peterson, R. D., 368
Pettigrew, T. F., 313, 319
Pettit, G. A., 295
Pezdek, K., 62, 139, 140, 142, 259
Pfeifer, J. E., 257
Phares, E. J., 126
Phelan, J. E., 311
Phelps, M. S., 339
Phillips, C., 81
Pickel, K. L., 140, 257, 258
Pierce, C. A., 310
Pierce, G. L., 367
Pinizzotto, A. J., 94, 100
Pintar, J., 150
Pipe, M.-E., 219
Pirelli, G., 158, 160, 163, 172, 176, 185
Platt, A., 178
Plumm, K., 200, 201, 205
Poddar, P., 287
Podini, D., 81
Podlas, K., 86

Podlesny, J. A., 61
Polaschek, D. L. L., 295
Poole, B., 134, 141
Poole, D. A., 219, 229
Porter, L., 198
Porter, S., 230
Posey, A. J., 122, 124
Powell, L. F., Jr., 367
Price, A. R., 102
Price, H. L., 146
Price, J. M., 295
Principe, G. F., 218, 219
Pritzl, T. B., 116, 237, 245, 247, 249
Prizmich, L. P., 224
Pryce, J., 257
Pryor, J. B., 311, 313
Pryor, R., 146
Pulaski, C. A., 365, 367
Putnam, C. E., 369

Q
Qian, Z., 367
Quanbeck, C. D., 297
Quas, J. A., 144, 221, 223, 225
Quinlivan, D. S., 136, 145
Quinn, J. F., 333, 342
Quinnell, F. A., 249
Quinsey, V. L., 294, 297

R
Rachlinski, J. J., 274
Radelet, M. L., 367, 369
Rainbow, L., 103, 106
Rakos, R. F., 274
Ralston, A., 200
Ramos, J., 325
Ramsey, J. B., 41
Ramsland, K. M., 97
Rapaport, E., 361
Raskin, D., 55
Raskin, D. C., 53, 56
Ratcliff, R., 31
Raymer, M., 79
Read, J. D., 232
Reagan, R., 181, 184
Reardon, M., 91
Redlich, A. D., 38, 224
Reeves, K. A., 299
Regan, P. C., 259
Rehman, U., 201
Reich, M., 32, 43, 44
Reid, J. E., 32, 44
Reidy, T. J., 285
Reisig, M. D., 333
Reppucci, N., 38
Reppucci, N. D., 22
Ressler, R. K., 98, 99
Reyes, M., 28
Reyna, C., 330
Rhodewalt, F., 319
Rice, J. J., 276
Rice, M. E., 300
Richardson, C., 41–42
Richardson, J. T., 16

Rideau, W., 347
Riedel, M., 365
Riggins, D., 165
Risinger, D. M., 75, 80, 90, 95
Roane, K. R., 86
Robbennolt, J. K., 275
Robbins, K., 351
Roberson, Q. M., 320–321
Roberts, C. F., 185
Robicheaux, T. R., 268
Roche, T., 177
Rodriguez, S. F., 330
Roesch, R., 22, 159, 160, 162, 169, 170t, 171, 176, 185
Rogers, M., 62
Rogers, R., 170t, 172, 192
Roper, R. T., 264
Rorschach, H., 248
Rose, M., 263, 272
Rose, M. R., 116, 275
Rosen, R., 134
Rosenfeld, J. P., 67
Rosenthal, R., 80, 145
Roskamp, P., 283
Ross, D. R., 141
Ross, L., 30
Ross, M. W., 350
Ross, S. J., 140, 148
Rossmo, D. K., 105
Rothman, D. J., 337, 339
Rotman, E., 333, 336
Rotter, M., 288
Rotundo, M., 306
Rozelle, S. D., 362
Ruane, M. E., 106
Ruback, R. B., 331, 332
Ruddell, R., 348
Rudman, L., 311
Rudolph, E., 96, 96f
Rumbelow, D., 95
Ruva, C., 130
Ruva, C. L., 130
Rzepa, S., 203

S
Sabol, W. J., 329, 342, 343, 344, 351
Sack, K., 96
Sackett, P. R., 306
Sadler, M. S., 363
Safer, M. A., 148
Saferstein, R., 73
Saks, M. J., 17, 18, 22, 24, 77, 78, 79, 80, 86, 88, 90, 125, 264, 265
Salerno, J. M., 265
Sales, B. D., 23, 93, 124, 214, 215, 237, 241, 242, 243, 300
Salisbury, E. J., 344
Sampson, E. E., 321
Samuels, K., 230
Sanders, J., 21
Sandler, J. C., 282
Sandys, M., 362
Sargent, T. M., 363
Sathyavagiswaran, L., 110

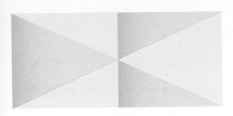

Subject Index

Note: Page numbers followed by *f* indicate figures; those followed by *t* indicate tables.

Case Index